Sounds of Innate Freedom

Sounds of Innate Freedom: The Indian Texts of Mahāmudrā

Sounds of Innate Freedom: The Indian Texts of Mahāmudrā are historic volumes containing many of the first English translations of classic mahāmudrā literature. The texts and songs in these volumes constitute the large compendium called *The Indian Texts of the Mahāmudrā of Definitive Meaning*, compiled by the Seventh Karmapa, Chötra Gyatso (1456–1539). The collection offers a brilliant window into the richness of the vast ocean of Indian mahāmudrā texts cherished in all Tibetan lineages, particularly in the Kagyü tradition, giving us a clear view of the sources of one of the world's great contemplative traditions. In its modern Tibetan edition, there are six volumes containing seven kinds of texts: the *Anāvilatantra* (as a tantric source of mahāmudrā attributed to the Buddha himself) and its commentary, songs of realization, commentaries on songs of realization and other texts, independent tantric treatises, nontantric treatises, edifying stories, and doxographies (presenting hierarchies of different Buddhist and non-Buddhist philosophical systems). This volume contains the majority of songs of realization, consisting of *dohās* (couplets), *vajragītis* (vajra songs), and *caryāgītis* (conduct songs), all lucidly expressing the inexpressible.

Sounds *of* Innate Freedom

The Indian Texts of Mahāmudrā

Volume Five

Translated and Introduced
by Karl Brunnhölzl

Wisdom

Wisdom Publications
199 Elm Street
Somerville, MA 02144 USA
wisdomexperience.org

Library of Congress Cataloging-in-Publication Data is available.
LCCN 2020021301

ISBN 978-1-61429-635-5 ebook ISBN 978-1-61429-636-2

24 23 22 21 20
5 4 3 2 1

Cover design by Gopa & Ted 2. Interior design by Tony Lulek.

Printed on acid-free paper that meets the guidelines for permanence and durability of the Production Guidelines for Book Longevity of the Council on Library Resources.

Printed in the United States of America.

Publisher's Acknowledgment

The publisher gratefully acknowledges the generous help of the Hershey Family Foundation and the Tsadra Foundation in sponsoring the production of this book.

Contents

Foreword by Dzogchen Ponlop Rinpoche xiii
Preface xv
Abbreviations xxi
Introduction 1

(91) A Commentary on "Four and a Half Stanzas" 15
(92) A Pith Instruction on the Four Mudrās 27
(93)–(94) Two Vajra Songs by Nāropa 35
(95)–(96) Two Vajra Songs by Kṛṣṇa 37
(97) A Song on the Connate 39
(98) A Song on Abandoning Thoughts 41
(99) A Dohā Treasure Song on Karmacaṇḍālikā 43
(100) A Dohā Treasure Song on the Ornament of Spring 45
(101) An Instruction on the Connate 47
(102) The Stages of Unsurpassable Universal Purity 49
(103) Familiarizing with the True Reality of View and Conduct Being Unborn 53
(104) The Stages of Familiarizing with the Nāḍī of Nonduality 55
(105) The Subtle Yoga 57
(106) A Dohā Treasure Song on the View of the Nature of True Reality 59

(107) A Dohā Song on View, Meditation, Conduct, and Fruition 61

(108) A Song on True Reality That Is a Dohā Treasure 65

(109) A Dohā Treasure Song on Conduct 67

(110) The View in a Dohā Treasure Song of Connate Ecstasy 69

(111) A Song on the View of the Sugatas 71

(112) A Dohā Song on the True Reality of the Vāyus 73

(113) A Song on the Four Vajras 75

(114) A Song by Guru Maitrīpa 77

(115)–(116) Two Songs by Saraha 79

(117) A Vajra Song by Virūkara 81

(118) A Song by Kāṇhapa 83

(119)–(121) Songs of Guru Dhiṣṭijñāna 85

(122) A Song by Karṇari 89

(123) A Song by Mātṛceṭa 91

(124)–(125) Two Songs of Bada 93

(126) A Song by Ācārya Vīravairocana 95

(127) A Song by Paṇḍita Nāropa 97

(128) A Song by Lūhipa 99

(129) A Song by Ḍombipa 101

(130) A Song by Virūpa 103

(131) A Song by Lavapa 105

(132) A Song by Mahāsukhatā 107

(133) A Song by the Yogī Prasara 109

(134) A Song by Nāgārjuna 111

(135)–(136) Two Dharma Songs by Dīpaṃkaraśrījñāna 113

(137) The View in a Conduct Song Dohā 117

(138) The View of Emptiness 119

(139) The View of Being Free of the Duality of Happiness and Suffering 121

(140) The View of Nonconnection 123
(141) The View of Being Unbound and Letting Go 145
(142) The View of Emptiness and Compassion 147
(143) The View of the Jewel of Mind 149
(144) The View of True Reality in Eight Stanzas 151
(145) The View of Overcoming Mind's Thoughts 153
(146) The View of Driving Away Misery 157
(147) The View of Mere Mind 161
(148) The View of the Skull of Compassionate Conduct 163
(149) The View of Being Unbound 165
(150) The View of Suchness 167
(151) A Conduct Song 169
(152) A Commentary on "A Conduct Song" 175
(153) A Song on Beholding the Dharmadhātu 181
(154) A Vajra Song on the Vajra Seat 205
(155) A Commentary on "A Vajra Song on the Vajra Seat" 211
(156) A Dhyāna Song 225
(157) A Meditation on the Sixteen Bindus 229
(158) A Pith Instruction on Binding Inner and Outer Bodhicitta 231
(159) A Pith Instruction on Familiarizing with the True Reality of the Vāyus 233
(160) Cultivating the Four Yogas 235
(161) Familiarizing with the True Reality of the Vāyus 237
(162) The Perfection Process of the Vajraḍākinī 241
(163) A Synopsis of Ascertaining Prajñā and Means 243
(164) A Pith Instruction Called "Nonestablishment of a Nature" 247
(165) The Jewel Garland 249
(166) The Blessing of Cultivating Compassion 251
(167) Ascertaining the Basic Nature of the Mahāyāna 253

(168) Offering a Piece of Advice for the Mind 255

(169) A Mahāmudrā Practice of Familiarizing with the Guru of Ground, Path, and Fruition 259

(170) Yoginī Conduct by Way of Nāḍī and Bindu 261

(171) A Pith Instruction in Two Syllables 263

(172) A Pith Instruction on Cultivating the Yoga That Accords with Cultivating the Bliss of True Reality 265

(173) The Means to Calm Mind and Thinking 269

(174) The Path of the Perfection Process of All Deities 271

(175) Cultivating the Inconceivable 275

(176) A Pith Instruction on the View of Self-Aware Wisdom 279

(177) The Heart of the Realizations of the Eighty-Four Mahāsiddhas 281

(178) Dohās of the Secret of Mind 301

(179) Vajra Songs by Forty Siddhas, Called "A Garland of Gold" 319

(180) The Expressions of Realization of Thirty-Five Wisdom Ḍākinīs 331

(181) The All-Encompassing Song of the Ḍākinīs 339

(182) The Vajra Songs of All Siddhas, Called "The Light of the True Reality of All Yogīs" 347

(183) A Golden Garland of Mahāmudrā 431

(184) A Letter to Prajñā 465

(185) Dispelling the Obstacles of the Thoughts of Yogīs 481

(186) The Inconceivable and Supremely Secret Hidden Path of the Five Poisons 487

(187) The Reality of the Characteristics of Yoga 495

(188) A Timely Discourse on Making Effort in Prajñā 501

(189) A Chapter on Samādhi Equipment 505

(190) The Supramundane Ritual of the Seven Branches 509

(191) The Ship of the Precious Teachings of the Sugata 511

(192) A Treatise on the Glorious Liberation from Bondage 521

(193) A Pith Instruction on Pure View and Conduct 531

(194) The Path and Fruition of Purifying the Jewel of the Mind 533

(195) A Pith Instruction on the Liberation of Bondage 535

(196) Certainty about the Genuine Path to Accomplishment 537

(197) A Pith Instruction on Untying the Knots in the Yogī's Own Mind 541

(198) The Empowerment of Samādhi 543

(199) A Commentary on "Namo Buddhāya" 545

(200) The Accomplishment of Glorious Great Bliss 547

(201) Twenty-Five Stanzas of Pith Instructions on Letting Your Own Mind Take a Rest 551

(202) An Expression of Realization in Thirty Stanzas 557

Appendix: Jamyang Kyentsé Wangpo's and Jamyang Kyentsé Wangchug's Commentaries on Mitrayogī's *Letting Your Own Mind Take a Rest* (Text 201) and *Pith Instructions on Threefold Essential Reality* 563

Notes 603

Selected Bibliography 729

About the Translator 737

Foreword

A greatly renowned South Indian Buddhist scholar-monk by the name of Rāhulabhadra was once passing through a town. As he maneuvered through the fair, he became mesmerized by a young woman who was straightening a piece of bamboo with three segments. Noticing her exceptional powers of concentration, he asked: "Young lady, what are you doing? Are you an arrow-maker?" Moving in closer, he saw that she had one eye closed and the other looking directly at the piece of bamboo. She was one-pointedly focused on her task, not distracted or disturbed by all the hustle and bustle of the marketplace.

Nevertheless, she answered Rāhulabhadra, saying: "The intention of the Buddha can only be known through signs and skillful means, not through words and concepts." In that moment, the three-kāya nature of buddha-mind became apparent to him through the signs and symbols the young woman, secretly a wisdom ḍākinī, had displayed.[1] A classical text relates the insights that arose in his mind:

> Her one eye closed and the other open is the symbol of closing the eyes of consciousness and opening the eyes of wisdom; the bamboo is the symbol of the nature of mind; the three segments symbolize the three-kāya nature; straightening is the direct path; cutting the bamboo from the root is cutting the root of samsara; cutting the top of the bamboo is cutting ego-clinging; making four slots [for feathers] is the four unborn seals of mindfulness; adding the arrowhead at the end is the need for sharp prajñā; . . .[2]

Sudden awakening took place in his heart and he fully realized mahāmudrā. Recognizing that a wisdom ḍākinī was in front of him, he proclaimed, "You are not an arrow-maker but a symbol-maker!" From that time onward he followed her, abandoning scholarship and adopting the tantric path. He became known as Saraha or Sarahapāda, the "arrow shooter," referring metaphorically to "he who has shot the arrow of nonduality into the heart of duality." Saraha became the foremost mahāsiddha of the tantric tradition of Buddhism.

The dohā lineage in tantric Buddhism began when Saraha, also known as "the Great Brahman," started singing spontaneous songs of realization to his disciples: the king, the queen, and the people of the kingdom. Since then, the great siddhas of the Mahāmudrā lineage have continued to express their realization and instructions to their disciples in pithy and spontaneous songs known as *dohās*. The most renowned of these many songs of realization is Milarepa's *Ocean of Songs*, commonly known as the *Hundred Thousand Songs*. The dohā tradition continues today with numerous songs from my own guru, Dechen Rangdrol, a contemporary mahāsiddha.

I am genuinely excited to have this opportunity to work with Mitra Karl Brunnhölzl to translate the large compendium of texts called *The Indian Texts of the Mahāmudrā of Definitive Meaning*, compiled by the Seventh Karmapa Chötra Gyatso (1456–1539). Making this classic mahāmudrā literature available in English for the first time is a historic and noteworthy project.

As many readers may already be aware, Mitra Karl not only is well versed in Buddhist philosophy and the Tibetan and Sanskrit languages but has also practiced these teachings for many years under the guidance of my guru, Dechen Rangdrol. Mitra Karl has also been studying with me, and I have full confidence and trust that his translation work here will be true to the original.

I want to thank Wisdom Publication for their openness and support in bringing these treasures of the East to the West.

May this book help all to discover the treasure within our ordinary mind of neurosis.

Dzogchen Ponlop Rinpoche
Nalanda West, Seattle, WA

Preface

The large anthology that is called *The Indian Texts of the Mahāmudrā of Definitive Meaning*[3] was compiled by the Seventh Karmapa, Chötra Gyatso.[4] The vast majority of the 217 works that are included in the anthology stems from the Tengyur,[5] and they range from a single sentence to almost two hundred pages. Roughly categorized, they fall under seven genres:

1. the *Anāvilatantra* (selected as a tantric source of mahāmudrā attributed to the Buddha himself) and its commentary[6]
2. songs of realization (dohā, caryāgīti, and vajragīti)
3. commentaries on songs of realization and other texts
4. independent tantric treatises
5. nontantric treatises
6. edifying stories
7. doxographies (presenting hierarchies of different Buddhist and non-Buddhist tenet systems)

In its modern Tibetan book edition, the anthology consists of six volumes (with the modest number of 2,600 pages).

Volume 1 opens with the catalogue of the collection by Karma Dashi Chöpel Lodrö Gyatsö Drayang[7] (a student of Jamgön Kongtrul Lodrö Tayé).[8] The eleven Indian mahāmudrā texts in this volume consist of the *Anāvilatantra* and its commentary, followed by "The Seven Siddhi Texts,"[9] tantric treatises based on the *Guhyasamājatantra*: (1) Padmavajra's *Guhyasiddhi*, (2) Anaṅgavajra's *Prajñopāyaviniścayasiddhi*, (3) Indrabhūti's

Jñānasiddhi, (4) Lakṣmīṃkarā's *Advayasiddhi*, (5) Dārikapa's *Mahāguhyatattvopadeśa*, (6) Vilāsavajrā's *Vyaktabhāvānugatatattvasiddhi*, and (7) Ḍombi Heruka's *Śrīsahajasiddhi*. The final two texts are Indrabhūti's *Sahajasiddhi* and his sister Lakṣmīṃkarā's commentary *Sahajasiddhipaddhati*.[10]

Volume 2 (thirty-four texts) begins with Kerali's *Tattvasiddhi*, followed by "The Sixfold Pith Cycle":[11] (1) Saraha's *Dohakoṣa* (popularly known as "People Dohā"), (2) Nāgārjuna's *Caturmudrānvaya*, (3) Āryadeva's *Cittaviśuddhiprakaraṇa*, (4) Devākaracandra's *Prajñājñānaprakāśa*, (5) Sahajavajra's *Sthitisamāsa*, and (6) Kuddālī's *Acintyakramopadeśa*.[12] Next are the mostly short texts of Maitrīpa's "Cycle of Twenty-Five Dharmas of Mental Nonengagement,"[13] which present a blend of Madhyamaka, Mahāmudrā, and certain tantric principles. This volume concludes with two commentaries by students of Maitrīpa: Karopa's *Mudrācaturaṭīkāratnahṛdaya* on the *Caturmudrānvaya* and Rāmapāla's *Sekanirdeśapañjikā* on Maitrīpa's *Sekanirdeśa*.

Volume 3 (twenty-four texts) starts with Sahajavajra's *Tattvadaśakaṭīkā* (a commentary on Maitrīpa's *Tattvadaśaka*), followed by a number of brief instructional works by Maitrīpa's student Vajrapāṇi, and by Nāropa and Śākyaśrībhadra. The bulk of the volume consists of dohās by Saraha, one autocommentary on them, two commentaries on his "People Dohā" by Advayavajra and Mokṣākaragupta, and an anonymous commentary on his *Twelve Stanzas*.[14] Also included is Kṛṣṇapāda's *Dohakoṣa* and its commentary by paṇḍita Amṛtavajra. This volume ends with the *Karṇatantravajrapāda*, transmitted by Tilopa and Nāropa.

The first text in volume 4 (twenty-one texts) is Advayavajra's extensive commentary on Saraha's "People Dohā." This is followed by a number of dohās and instructional texts by Virūpa, Tilopa, Nāropa, Maitrīpa, Saraha, Kṛṣṇa, and others. The volume ends with a famous collection of fifty songs by twenty different authors (originally in Eastern Apabhraṃśa), including a commentary by Munidatta called *Caryāgītikoṣavṛtti* (half of the songs in this collection are by the three mahāsiddhas Kṛṣṇa, Bhusuku, and Saraha).

Volume 5 contains by far the most texts (112). With only five prose works, the bulk consists of versified songs of realization. The opening *Commentary on "Four and a Half Stanzas"* consists of edifying stories, including summarizing songs. Next, Advayavajra's *Caturmudropadeśa* discusses the four mudrās (karmamudrā, dharmamudrā, samayamudrā, and mahāmudrā). Almost all remaining texts in this volume consist of usually brief tantric songs composed by various mahāsiddhas and others, many of them by Atiśa, the mahāsiddha Jaganmitrānanda,[15] Saraha, Kṛṣṇa, Kambala, Ḍombipa, Nāgārjuna, Lūhipa, and Maitrīpa. There are also seven anthologies of tantric songs by a wide variety of male and female siddhas, yogīs, yoginīs, and ḍākinīs, the longest one among them containing almost four hundred songs. In addition, this volume contains two autocommentaries by Atiśa on two of his songs as well as Āryadeva's *Hidden Path of the Five Poisons* on how to work with our main mental afflictions.

Volume 6 (fifteen texts) consists mainly of tantric treatises. Virūpa's *Sunisprapañcatattvopadeśanāma*, Āryadeva's *Pratipattisāraśataka*, and Lūhipa's *Buddhodaya* are related to the perfection processes of the *Raktayamāritantra*, *Hevajratantra*, and *Cakrasaṃvaratantra*, respectively. Vajrapāṇi's *Guruparamparākramopadeśa* (a commentary on Maitrīpa's *Tattvaratnāvalī*), Jñānakīrti's *Tattvāvatāra*, and Śāntarakṣita's *Tattvasiddhi* (as well as the *Bodhicittavivaraṇa*) are all considered important general source texts of Mahāmudrā in the Kagyü school of Tibetan Buddhism. Furthermore, there are Udbhaṭṭa *Tripiṭakamalla's often-quoted *Nayatrayapradīpa*, Dharmendra's **Tattvasārasaṃgraha*, Udbhaṭṭa *Coyaka's *Mantranayāloka*, and Jñānavajra's **Cittamārgaśodha*, all on general Vajrayāna principles. In addition, this volume contains two short songs by Mahāśabara, Nāgārjuna's *Cittavajrastava*, and the *Bodhicittavivaraṇa* (also attributed to Nāgārjuna).

As this series overview shows, most of the authors of these works are well-known figures among the eighty-four male and female mahāsiddhas or otherwise highly accomplished tantric adepts. That the greatest number of texts is attributed to Maitrīpa and Saraha[16] highlights their being considered as the most significant forebears of the Mahāmudrā lineage in the Kagyü school. In sum, it is no overstatement to consider this collection as "the corpus of Indian Buddhist mahāsiddha literature."

These practitioners were a very mixed crowd, and many lived and taught outside the framework of institutionalized Buddhism in their time. We find kings and queens, princes and princesses, top-notch Buddhist scholars, dropouts, philosophers, housewives, shoemakers, courtesans, monks, male and female lovers, farmers, weavers, prostitutes, cowherds, fishermen, gamblers, musicians, thieves, hermits, hunters, alchemists, rich merchants, barmaids, outcastes, brahmans, gluttons, fools, pearl divers, and many more varieties of practitioners.[17] Besides the officially recognized mahāsiddhas, there were many other male and female yogic practitioners, as well as ḍākinīs, who composed texts and uttered songs of realization. This shows that the teachings and the path of mahāmudrā are accessible to and can be practiced by anyone from any walk of life—whether a king, a servant in a brothel, or a housewife—often even without having to renounce their day jobs.

As for the language of the texts and the songs in this collection, it is the specific context that dictates the meaning of certain expressions. Also, many terms and phrases can have a range of different meanings (in both the common Mahāyāna context and the uncommon contexts of tantra and mahāmudrā). Several layers of meaning often exist simultaneously, some of them only understandable through additional comments, instructions, or certain experiences, many of them restricted to the initiated. Another notable feature is that the antinomian tantric approach often labels the highest and purest spiritual principles with the most despicable and impure names possible in the context of ancient Indian society.

For example, the term "Caṇḍāla" ordinarily refers to a class of people in India who are generally considered to be untouchable outcastes.[18] Figuratively speaking, Caṇḍāla also refers to any vile, filthy, loathsome, criminal, ferocious, or lascivious persons or deeds; the same goes for other outcaste names, such as Ḍombi (wandering troubadours and dancers). On the other hand, in both Hindu and Buddhist tantric practices, outcaste Caṇḍāla or Ḍomba women play a significant role in the worship of the female sexual organ and the subsequent production of a fluid, powerful substance through sexual intercourse with them. The related term "caṇḍālī" either designates a woman in the first day of her menses, the female subtle energy located in the lower abdomen, or the tantric practices related to that energy. In the latter context, "caṇḍālī" sometimes also serves as a name for the central channel (avadhūtī). In addition, among the "divine herbs" that are said to grow in places where Śiva and his wife once made love, the *cāṇḍālī* plant is obviously named for those outcaste women whose menstrual blood has perennially been prized by tantric practitioners for its transformative powers, and the root of this plant exudes a red milk that is used for the alchemistic fixing of mercury.

For reasons of space, it is beyond the purview of this six-volume publication to give detailed explanations for all such terms or provide commentaries on its songs and texts. Another reason for this is that traditionally the practices behind certain texts and terms with multilayered meanings are not explained publicly but only within an established teacher-student relationship after certain prerequisites have been fulfilled.[19]

I would like to offer my heartfelt gratitude and appreciation to Khenchen Tsültrim Gyamtso Rinpoche and Dzogchen Ponlop Rinpoche for having introduced me to the tradition of Indian and Tibetan Buddhist songs of realization. Both of these masters also inspired me as accomplished composers of their own spontaneous poems and songs of insight and realization, in both Tibetan and English. Furthermore, Dzogchen Ponlop Rinpoche is to be thanked for starting me on the project of translating the collection of Indian mahāmudrā texts compiled by the Seventh Karmapa, as well as for his ongoing support during this project in many ways. Without these two masters of both ancient and contemporary expressions of realization, this volume would never have been possible, and on a personal note, I probably would never have started to enjoy singing Buddhist songs.

On the practical side of things, I am deeply grateful for the funding received from *Causa* that enables me to work on this collection of mahāmudrā songs. Heartfelt thanks go to Daniel Aitken at Wisdom Publications for his willingness to publish these texts and for all his ongoing support. I also thank Mary Petrusewicz as my skillful, friendly, and enthusiastic editor at Wisdom Publications. Last but not least, a big thanks to Stephanie Johnston for being my sounding board (both literally and metaphorically) for these songs and her willingness to listen to, participate in, and improve both their words and musical arrangements as these were evolving over time.

Whatever in this volume sounds good, makes sense, inspires, and serves as an antidote to ignorance, confusion, and suffering may be relished as originating from realized masters and scholars truly vast in learning. Everything else, including all mistakes, can safely be said to be mine.

Sarva maṅgalam

Abbreviations

AIBS	The Buddhist Canons Research Database (http://databases.aibs.columbia.edu/)
BA	Gö Lotsāwa's *Blue Annals* ('Gos lo tsā ba gzhon nu dpal, 1996)
BGTC	*Bod rgya tshig mdzod chen mo* (Krang dbyi sun et al., 1985)
C	Cone Tibetan Tripiṭaka
D	Derge Tibetan Tripiṭaka
DPR	Dzogchen Ponlop Rinpoche
GZ	"The Indian Mahāmudrā Texts" (*Phyag chen rgya gzhung*)
GZ1	Dpal spung edition of GZ (Phun tshogs rgyal mtshan, n.d.), 3 vols.
GZ3	Ludrub Gyatso's edition of GZ (Khro ru klu sgrub rgya mtsho, 2009), 6 vols.
H	Lhasa Tibetan Tripiṭaka
Kg	Kangyur (Tib. *bka' 'gyur*)
N	Narthang Tibetan Tripiṭaka
NG	Catalogue of GZ (Bkra shis chos 'phel, 2009)
P	Peking Tibetan Tripiṭaka
PDMT	Dpe bsdur ma edition of Tengyur (Dpe bsdur ma, 1994–2008)
Tg	Tengyur (Tib. *bstan 'gyur*)
TRP	La dvags khrid dpon 'khrul zhig padma chos rgyal, ed., 1978–1985

Introduction

Among the six volumes of the Seventh Karmapa's compilation of Indian Mahāmudrā texts, the fifth contains by far the most individual works (112). With only five prose texts, the bulk of this volume consists of versified songs of realization. Thus, among the six volumes, the fifth represents the primary one with such songs, consisting of dohās, vajragītis ("vajra songs"), as well as caryāgītis ("conduct songs"). Most of these songs are quite short, sometimes just a single stanza. Furthermore, besides individually listed songs by distinct authors, many more are found in the seven song collections in this volume, which were uttered by numerous male and female siddhas, yogīs, yoginīs, and ḍākinīs and later arranged into anthologies of different sizes by others. Thus the overall number of songs in this volume amounts to about 950, the vast majority of which is translated here for the first time into a language other than Tibetan.

The opening work of this volume, *A Commentary on "Four and a Half Stanzas"* (text 91), consists of sixteen edifying stories or fables with a number of intermediate and concluding stanzas or songs that summarize the moral of each.

Next, *A Pith Instruction on the Four Mudrās* (text 92) by Advayavajra (Maitrīpa) begins by combining the three Sutrayānas (Śrāvakayāna, Pratyekabuddhayāna, and Mahāyāna) with the views of the four Buddhist tenet systems (Vaibhāṣika, Sautrāntika, Vijñaptivāda, and Madhyamaka), discussing highest, middling, and lower śrāvakas, pratyekabuddhas, Sautrāntikas, Aspectarians, Nonaspectarians, Mādhyamikas of illusion-like nonduality, and Mādhyamikas of all phenomena being utterly nonabiding. The Mantrayāna is then explained through the four mudrās. Among these, the karmamudrā as "the essence of all four empowerments" (vase, secret, prajñā-jñāna, and fourth empowerment) receives the most attention. The dharmamudrā is what appears as the variety of all perceptible thoughts and phenomena. Mahāmudrā refers to perfect buddhahood in a single instant, the omnipresent essence of all phenomena free from extremes that is nondual and devoid of all obscurations. The samayamudrā represents the fruitional deity maṇḍala that signifies true reality.[20]

Texts 93–176 consist of mostly tantric songs (as well as some nontantric ones) composed by various mahāsiddhas and other masters (except for texts 152 and 155, which are Atiśa's autocommentaries on his own songs 151 and 154, respectively). The authors include a number of famous mahāsiddhas, such as Saraha, Lūhipa, Kṛṣṇa (alias Kāṇhapa), Virūpa, Tilopa, Nāropa, and Maitrīpa, but also many otherwise unknown figures. The only two women among them are the female mahāsiddhas princess Lakṣmīṃkarā (text 145) and Ḍombiyoginī (text 170).[21] Many of these songs have no title and they are often quite short.

Texts 177–183 are all collections of tantric songs by a wide variety of male and female siddhas, yogīs, yoginīs, and ḍākinīs. The introductions or colophons of anthologies 179–183 state that all the songs in them were originally sung in the context of gaṇacakras. The four collections 178–180 and 182 are said to have been compiled by the Indian mahāsiddha Patampa Sangyé (born eleventh century) after he received them from the ḍākinīs, who had initially kept them in their secret treasury.

The Heart of the Realizations of the Eighty-Four Mahāsiddhas (text 177) contains four-line songs (occasionally eight lines) by each one of the famous eighty-four Indian mahāsiddhas (consisting of four women and eighty men). Translations of the corresponding sections of the anonymous commentary **Dohāvṛttisahitacaturaśītisiddhāvadāna*[22] (which is not contained in the Karmapa's collection) are included in the notes on each song.

Dohās of the Secret of Mind (text 178) is an anthology of seventy-nine songs by male and female siddhas and ḍākinīs that were written down by the ḍākinīs and then remained in their secret treasury of preserved songs and teachings until they were later passed on to Patampa Sangyé.

A Garland of Gold (text 179) is a collection of forty-five vajra songs by male and female masters that they sang at the occasion of a gaṇacakra in Uḍḍiyāna.

The Expressions of Realization of Thirty-Five Wisdom Ḍākinīs (text 180) contains the spontaneous songs of the wisdom ḍākinīs upon being requested by the ḍākinī Sukhakauṇapā to sing about their realization during a gaṇacakra held at the charnel ground Śītavana.

The All-Encompassing Song of the Ḍākinīs (text 181) consists of about forty songs by a group of unidentified ḍākinīs that contain their heart advice in answer to a spontaneous song of realization raised by the yogī Kamalaśrī during a gaṇacakra with these ḍākinīs at an unspecified charnel ground in Uḍḍiyāna.

Compiled by Patampa Sangyé, *The Light of the True Reality of All Yogīs* (text 182) is the most extensive anthology in this volume, including 381 vajra songs of realization in nine chapters that were sung by many different male and female siddhas as well as ḍākinīs (some appear more than once), most of whom are otherwise unknown.

Maitrīpa's *Golden Garland* (text 183) is his compilation of about 170 songs in three chapters, uttered by male and female siddhas (some appear more than once) during different gaṇacakras.

Interestingly, texts 177, 179, and 183 (as well as text 90) show some overlaps in that they contain a significant number of the same or very similar songs, though these are often ascribed to different authors in those texts.

There follow further songs by a number of different siddhas and paṇḍitas (texts 184–185, 187–190, 192–194, and 198–200). *The Hidden Path of the Five Poisons* (text 186) is a prose text by Āryadeva on how to work with our main mental afflictions.

Texts 191, 195–197, and 201–202 (as well as, most likely, 192 and 198) are all songs composed by the mahāsiddha Jaganmitrānanda (alias Ajitamitragupta and Mitrayogī; twelfth century), who also visited Tibet and taught there extensively. Though he is hardly known in the later Tibetan tradition, he undoubtedly was one of the most realized masters to ever visit the land of snows. As an emanation of Avalokiteśvara,

Mitrayogī was born a prince in Orissa, and his dharma lineage runs from Avalokiteśvara through Ratnamati, Tilopa, and Lalitavajra. After Mitrayogī had meditated on Avalokiteśvara as his main practice for twelve years, Avalokiteśvara appeared before him and asked about his wishes. Mitrayogī answered, "Please teach me a method so that I can let my mind, which has been tiring itself out in this ocean of saṃsāric suffering since beginningless time, take a rest!" In response, Avalokiteśvara uttered the twenty-five stanzas of text 201, upon which Mitrayogī is said to have attained the supreme siddhi of mahāmudrā.

BA describes Mitrayogī's twenty miraculous deeds in detail, as well as all the cycles of instructions and empowerments that he taught, which are known in brief as "Mitra's One Hundred." In Tibet, besides his many instructions for his close disciple and translator Tropu Lotsāwa Jampa Bal,[23] Mitrayogī also taught the cycle "The Mahāmudrā That Severs Saṃsāra's Stream" (taught to him by Saraha, who received it from five ḍākinīs) to Machig Sangyé Réma,[24] as well as his own version of Six Dharmas.[25] All in all, the Tengyur contains about 130 texts attributed to Mitrayogī under his various aliases.

Later, his teachings were mainly preserved in the Tropu Kagyü, the Shalu[26] tradition of Butön Rinchen Drub,[27] and the Jonang school. According to the great Sakya master Jamyang Kyentsé Wangpo,[28] one of the major figures in the nonsectarian Rimé movement in nineteenth-century Tibet, great scholars say that among the mahāsiddhas who came to Tibet and were able to display the signs of their siddhis in a manifest manner, it was Padmasambhava and Mitrayogī who were completely unrivaled during the earlier and the later disseminations of the teachings, respectively.[29]

Finally, the appendix presents Tibetan commentaries by Jamyang Kyentsé Wangpo and Jamyang Kyentsé Wangchug[30] (1524–1568) on Mitrayogī's *Twenty-Five Stanzas of Pith Instructions on Letting Your Own Mind Take a Rest* (text 201), as well as his short *Pith Instructions on Threefold Essential Reality*.

Among all the authors in this volume, the one with the most individually listed works attributed to him is Atiśa Dīpaṃkaraśrījñāna with ten (texts 135, 136, 151–156, 189, and 190), followed by Mitrayogī with eight (191, 192, 195–198, 201, and 202), Maitrīpa (alias Advayavajra, Avadhūtipa)[31] with six (92, 113, 114, 147, 183, and 188), Saraha (100, 107, 115, and 116) and Kṛṣṇa (alias Kāṇhapa; 95, 96, 118, and 149) with four each, and Nāropa (93, 94, and 127), Ḍombipa (129, 170, and 171), and Kambala (131, 140, and 141) with three each.

Besides these individual texts, many of these and other persons appear several times in a number of the above-mentioned anthologies of songs (though in some cases there could be two or more persons of the same name). For example, this volume contains a total number of twelve songs that are attributed to Kṛṣṇa (alias Kāṇhapa), eleven to Kambala, ten to Ḍombipa, nine to Saraha, and seven each to Nāgārjuna and Lūhipa.

As these songs of awakening display a vast range of themes, styles, metaphors, and lengths, they are a veritable feast offering of profound utterances of realization and instructions. However, notwithstanding their variety, they all point to the single true nature of the mind—mahāmudrā—in many inspiring ways and from a number of different angles, using a dazzling array of skillful means to penetrate the sole vital point of buddhahood being found nowhere but within our own mind.

A Note on Dohā, Vajragīti, and Caryāgīti

Nowadays, both Indian and Tibetan Buddhist songs of realization are often popularly called *dohās* or "vajra songs." However, not all songs of realization are dohās. In fact, there are three genres of Indian songs of realization: (1) dohā ("couplet"), (2) caryāgīti ("conduct song"), and (3) vajragīti ("vajra song"). The Tibetan word *mgur* (often loosely rendered as "dohā" or "vajra song") simply means "song," but over time came to refer specifically to spiritual songs of realization.

The Sanskrit word *dohā* (Apabhraṃśa *doha*, lit. "two-say") has two meanings. Originally, it indicated a distinct meter in poetry with four feet in which the second and fourth feet rhyme, similar to couplets in Western poetry. Since many poems of realization were composed in that meter, *dohā* also came to be a general designation for a genre of rhapsodies, emotionally charged stanzas, and spiritual aphorisms. Such stanzas could also contain or be entirely composed in other meters but would still generically be referred to as dohāṣ. As with our songs here, such poems were often spontaneous expressions of spiritual experiences and realizations. However, it is not certain that all dohās were actually sung, at least not from the outset; they could simply have been recited as poetry. As will be shown below, the transmission of these poems of realization was very fluid and involved constant adaptation, so sometimes melodies for certain stanzas may have been composed or changed by people other than the original composer.

In his commentary on Saraha's famous *Dohakoṣagīti* (popularly known as "People Dohā"), the Kagyü master Karma Trinlépa[32] provides a detailed explanation of the meaning of the common title *Dohakoṣagīti* (*Dohā Treasure Song*), being a profound description of mind's native state—mahāmudrā—and how it is revealed through the path.[33]

First, *doha* (or *dvaha*) means the lack of the two extremes, nonduality, and union; thus, it refers to overcoming dualistic thoughts by letting them dissolve within nonduality. At the time of the ground, mind's native state is not recognized and thus falsely appears as the duality of perceiver and perceived. This duality and the clinging to it are overcome by making path mahāmudrā a living experience, which leads to the fruition (the unity of the two *kāya*s) promoting the welfare of beings.

Second, since Sanskrit *dohā* means "being filled up" or "milking," it is similar to a container being filled by milking. Thus, since the masters are filled with the wisdom of the ultimate nature, they sing songs of such wisdom. Or, being filled through milking refers to being inexhaustible. Or, *dohā* indicates the overflowing of meditative experiences. In addition, the word *dohā* refers to being natural, uncontrived, and loose, the ultimate, true reality, freshness, and so on.

Just as a "treasure" (*koṣa*) is a place where many precious items are stored so that they do not disappear, mind's native state is the locus of all awakened qualities such as connate wisdom. "Song" (*gīti*) means that the instantaneous revelation of this wisdom is spontaneously set to melody from within one's experience, without hiding anything. For the sake of being easily understood by all people high and low, such songs are not constrained by prosody but sung in an ad hoc manner. Hence, they are songs that point out the treasure of the inexhaustible qualities of connate wisdom. Vajra songs (*vajragīti*), the second genre of songs of realization, are either recognizable by the fact that their titles contain the word *vajragīti* or by being identified as sung in the context of a gaṇacakra (originally, vajragītis were only recited or sung at such tantric ritual feasts). Vajra songs often exhibit more ornate poetic refinement than dohās, are usually short (most of them consist of just a single stanza), and are rich in metaphors. They often evoke particular feelings, experiences, or realizations rather than just giving certain instructions.

Finally, conduct songs (*caryāgīti*) speak about the way of life ("conduct") of tantric yogic practitioners.[34] Originally, such songs were probably sung spontaneously at different occasions, but eventually they came to be stand-alone performance songs (often with music and dance). Usually these songs are rather short, many consisting of about five stanzas. However, they are often incorporated in a collection of such songs and accompanied by musical instruments as well as one or more dancers in richly adorned attire, symbolizing Buddhist tantric deities. Thus a tantric performance of such a cycle can last several hours or even an entire day. In this way, following their ad-hoc origins, over time these songs tended to become more elaborate through such musical arrangements and choreographies.[35] The best-known historical example of this genre is a collection of fifty songs called *Caryāgītikoṣa*, which also contains the names of the *rāgas* (melodies) in which each song is to be sung. However, these kinds of songs are still regularly performed to this day during certain ceremonies in the Newari Vajrayāna Buddhist community in Nepal.

However, just as the songs themselves do not follow any strict pattern, the distinctions between these three genres are far from being hard and fast. For example, dohās can also be sung at a gaṇacakra, and vajragītis outside of a gaṇacakra. Also, any of them can be in the dohā meter or other meters, can include more sophisticated prosodic elements, and may or may not be accompanied by music and dancing.

Who Composed These Texts and How?

It can be quite safely assumed that all the treatises and commentaries in this collection were written in Buddhist Sanskrit. However, when it comes to the songs, matters are more complicated. A few of them were probably composed in Sanskrit, such as those by Atiśa, but for most we do not know in which languages they were uttered originally. The majority was definitely not composed in Sanskrit, since many of the authors did not even know Sanskrit, which was the language of the educated elite in India. For the same reason, Sanskrit would not have been a suitable medium to reach a general audience. Thus they were usually presented in local middle-Indic languages or dialects, which are generically referred to as Apabhraṃśas. Used from approximately 300 to 1200 CE, these tongues are distant predecessors of modern North Indian languages such as Bihari and Bengali, and to some extent also Assamese, Oriya, Maithili, and certain forms of Hindi. However, the fact that some dohās, caryāgītis, and vajragītis exist in old Apabhraṃśa manuscripts does not mean that Apabhraṃśa is their actual original language, close as it may be, because Apabhraṃśa refers to literary languages and not vernaculars. At present, apart from the songs in the Newari Vajrayāna tradition (which according to this tradition have always been in Newari), the vast majority of ancient Indian Buddhist dohās, caryāgītis, and vajragītis are only extant in Tibetan translations.

As for the authorship of our texts, while there seems to be greater certainty for most of the treatises and commentaries, when it comes to the songs, it is hard to say who actually composed them. First, these songs were originally spontaneous expressions of spiritual experiences and realizations as a part of the enlightened activity of great masters and, in virtually all cases, were only written down later by others. Thus it is not surprising that for many of them, especially some of Saraha's songs, there exist several versions in different languages (such as Sanskrit, Apabhraṃśa, and Tibetan) that greatly differ in their contents, the order of the stanzas, and the overall length of the text—it can be somewhat difficult to even consider them as different versions of one and the same text. This is mainly due to many rounds of later editing and rearranging, either by commentators or popular usage. It seems safe to assume that some of the songs as they are preserved now may not be by a single author, let alone the one to whom they are attributed at present. All of this is further evidenced by some of the anthologies of such songs in the Tengyur in that many of the songs that these collections share show more or less significant variant readings and are attributed to completely different persons.

Thus the transmission and shaping of these songs always has been fluid, similar to the way in which the songs of the medieval troubadours in Europe were passed on. That is, single lines of a stanza, entire stanzas, or blocks of stanzas may be shifted around in a given text, exchanged between different works (some songs attributed to different authors share common lines or stanzas), or removed from or inserted into preexisting songs. It is clear that almost all these songs have been rewritten and resung many times. Therefore, there often seems to be no fixed wording, as the wording primarily depends on the meaning to be conveyed and thus may be shifted in different contexts and for different audiences. This is nothing unusual in an Indian context; the same approach is shown with medieval and contemporary non-Buddhist devotional songs. They can be sung with different rāgas, stanzas moved around, vocabulary changed, and dialects transposed. As Roger Jackson says,

> Indeed, we only can assert with confidence that when we examine the *Treasury* of Saraha, Kāṇha, or Tilopa, what we have before us is a later compilation by an editor who, for purposes of his own, brought together dohās or groups of dohās that had come to be associated with one or another of those names, names that might or might not once have denoted an actual person. In this sense, there is probably a considerable arbitrariness built in to the compilation of any single *Treasury*, and though commentators on the texts find order and meaning in their arrangement (sometimes, in fact, it is they who have arranged them!), it is quite imaginable that the texts could have been ordered in many different ways and still been found meaningful by readers.[36]

This fluid approach is also explicitly acknowledged by Advaya Avadhūtīpa (Maitrīpa) in the introduction to his commentary on Saraha's "People Dohā":

Others give explanations by commenting in accordance with the root of a text
The tradition of people like me writes the root in accordance with the explanation
This also entails not quoting the words of the scriptures of any of the piṭakas:
there is no end to writing down the words of the scriptures of mantras and tantras

Relying solely on the awakened mind of Śrīmat Śabarapāda,
I shall write this memorandum that is a nectar drop of his speech
for the welfare of myself and those with faith just like myself
by summarizing nothing but the instructions on true actuality[37]

Kurtis Schaeffer says this about Saraha's *Dohakoṣa* and Avadhūtīpa's approach, which applies equally to all other songs of realization:

> The reader must know the words of Saraha despite the fact that his subject is ineffable. In an ironic twist, the power of Saraha's words is precisely their message of ineffability. This seems ultimately to debase the power of the word, and yet the final lines suggest something more; it is not the written word of the tantras that holds the power to express the inexpressible, but song itself. Much as the tales of his life tell us, the realization of the enlightened state encourages Saraha not to write another treatise, another commentary, but to inspire others through the medium of song, which stands above the ordinary language of treatises and tantras.
>
> It is perhaps this claim that gave the commentators on the *Treasury of Dohā Verses* license to write according to the meaning of the dohās as taught by the masters and not according to the letter. . . . This gives Advaya Avadhūti himself, and other commentators after him, the license to change, rearrange, and trans-

> form Saraha's words. In short, Advaya Avadhūti gives himself permission to "author" the words of Saraha by claiming that the real message of Saraha is not in any text of the *Treasury of the Dohā Verses* but rather in the meaning that lives in the hearts of the masters who have realized the message of the dohā.[38]

Thus this tradition explicitly permits changing and rearranging the words of Saraha and other masters, since what they convey is not found in words but only in the awakened minds of those who have already realized the nature of this mind. How this realization is conveyed to others must always depend on the unique circumstances of a living interactive situation—a teacher guiding a particular student in a particular way in accordance with the individual propensities, capacities, and obstacles of that student. Thus it can never be exactly the same for any two people and must be adapted to the situation at hand. This is clearly shown in the greatly differing stories of how certain mahāsiddhas gained realization through the verbal and nonverbal instructions of their gurus. For example, Nāropa awakened by being smacked on the forehead with Tilopa's sandal, Vīṇāpa by playing music, Tantipa by weaving, Lūhipa by eating the entrails of fish, and Kaṅkaripa by being taught to visualize his deceased wife as a ḍākinī, with the nature of bliss and emptiness being inseparable, without any substance or self.

From an ordinary or literary point of view, all this may sound like an arbitrary copy-and-paste approach of plagiarism where anything goes and things are just made up. But from the point of view of the mahāsiddhas and their commentators and editors, this approach is a clear example of what Buddhists call "skillful means." These masters obviously had a different sense of authorship and copyright; they simply used the words of the songs of realization as tools to make the points that they deemed meaningful in a given context, for a given audience, and at a given time. Thus the singing of these songs should not be understood as just a poetry reading or a musical performance but as always situated within an interactive mind-to-mind transmission between teacher and student (or an exchange between realized persons), where the songs are the vehicles through which that transmission takes place.

In that way, these songs of realization (and to some extent the other texts in this collection too) were considered more like a huge, common pool of awakened wisdom, as well as the methods to realize this wisdom, from which the entire community of commentators, editors, and practitioners felt free to pick and choose to suit their particular settings, audiences, and purposes. Thus the transmission of dohās, caryāgītis, and vajragītis is more about using individually adapted tools and methods to convey certain messages and not about preserving original literary documents. In that way, transmission is always fresh and immediate, in tune with real-life interactions between teachers and students. This means that mahāsiddhas such as Saraha are not just historical persons to be emulated; working with and singing their songs can evoke the essence of the realization of such masters—the unmediated presence of the awakened state itself—within ourselves.

The concept of transmission or lineage here is like teaching someone to bake fresh bread. It is not about preserving the specific loaf of bread that someone like Saraha baked many hundreds of years ago by handing it down wrapped up in ornate brocades through the generations, because after a few days nobody could eat such bread. Rather, it is like a hands-on transmission of Saraha's recipe that enables us to bake our own fresh bread with our own ingredients today. Just as there are different kinds of bread (and even the same kinds of bread taste differently in different bakeries), the basic recipe can and needs to be adapted to different circumstances, resources, and tastes. In this way, the fluid transmission of the songs of realization is also a vehicle for creative innovation in Buddhism, which is otherwise officially deemed inappropriate or frowned upon in the traditional framework of strictly adhering to the words of the lineage and one's own guru.

In brief, in the end it is our own true heart—our buddha nature—that expresses itself through these songs and with which we connect through singing. Besides contemplating their meaning, the purpose of singing songs of realization is to gain inspiration, receive blessings, and evoke experiences and realizations from within. Thus we go beyond a merely rational or intellectual approach, activate the element of devotion, and allow our inspiration and openness to become a vehicle for transcending our dualistic mindset.

May this book be considered a small and humble contribution to the living tradition of Mahāmudrā in general and Buddhist songs of realization in particular. May the texts here inspire and be of benefit to countless beings. May these beings realize what those songs sing about—mind's true nature of great bliss beyond any clinging and suffering.

Sarva maṅgalaṃ—May everything be auspicious!

(91) A Commentary on "Four and a Half Stanzas"

Master Nāgārjunagarbha said:

The example of hope is similar to Piṅgalā
Fear is related to the prince full of youth
Clinging to others refers to a mirage's water
Self-clinging refers to ruinous sun-ray images

Dualistic appearances refer to the parrot bird
Rejection means images due to delusion about spoons[39]
Pride based on the view refers to the dyed[40] fox
Clinging to meditation as such refers to Yaśuha[41]

Pride based on conduct refers to Jinapa[42]
A conceited mind due to hardships refers to Bhadrapāla's daughter
Desire for freedom through empowerment refers to Kosala[43]
Expressing contentment through realization refers to the glorious one's son

Guru, lack of the guru, and unsurpassable refer to Gaṅgā
Depreciating the Buddha's words refers to Kṛṣṇapa
Desiring siddhi through bliss refers to Excellent Plain Song[44]
The same through emptiness refers to Caṇḍālaja[45]

The knowledge that is free of these
resembles obtaining a precious jewel[46]

(1) Once, in the area of Vārānasī, the householder Pramoha and Piṅgalā *Siddhidattā [had arranged to] spend some time at the banks of the river Nairañjanā on a fragrant grassy area. She waited for five days and nights but he did not come. Then, becoming disappointed, she went [home] to her mother. The mother said, "Hey, daughter, why do you look so crestfallen?" {2}[47] The girl answered, "Oh, since I waited for the young householder for two nights and three days,[48] I became despaired as my mind was tormented. [Also,] I am hungry, because I went without food." Her mother gave her a panali full of cooked rice. Since she was eating it in a hurry, [some of it] went down into her lungs and caused disturbance there. Upon that, she saw[49] a great friend who was a physician. He looked at her and asked, "What is the matter with this?" She related the above situation to him. The physician said:

Those who hope for anything at all
will neither be at peace nor happy
and all kinds of sufferings increase
To be without hope is happiness supreme

This teaches that you will be ruined by hope. It is the pith instruction to not entertain any hope, which is the first one.

(2) Once upon a time, a prince named *Sārthabhadra received the empowerment of the royal caste on the crown of his head from his father Prabhāva. [The father] said, "Oh prince, dedicate yourself to guarding our gates! Make every effort so that they do not become lost to another throne!" and then passed away. At the time of making the fire offering, the head brahman appeared at the king's palace. Out of fear of being robbed of his throne, [the king] stood up and went for his duties at the gates. Upon that, his younger brother *Jagatsevana[50] came and robbed him of his throne. Then Piṅgalā asked, "Why would you make all this effort?" The fallen king {3} answered:

As my father had instructed me,
when I feared to lose my throne,
I went for my duties at the gates,
so my younger brother robbed my happiness

The brahman said:

A mind with fear does not find any happiness
Those full of anxiety will never be happy
Since those with fear are full of dread,
the wise should relinquish their fear

This is the pith instruction to free yourself from fear, which is the second one.

(3) Once, the bhikṣu Apalāla went to Mount Bird Foot and became tormented by great thirst. Mistaking a mirage for water, he went there to drink but became very exhausted, so he sat down and ate some green plants. The seer Akṣapāda said:

On the hard-to-travel great plain of saṃsāra,
people who desire to search somewhere else
are struck with the hammer of the afflictions,
like the thirsty searching for a mirage's water

This is the pith instruction to give up something to meditate on, which is the third one.

(4) Once, king Ūruja had one thousand sons with five hundred queens. His son Namgaru took the seer Śrī as his darling. Since she had no one but him alone, she cherished him very much. The prince thought, "There is nobody to be cherished but me. Since I lack even the slightest pain of suffering befalling me, if I pass away, my entire retinue will be ruined." Then, one morning, when he took a bath, {4} he sat there while looking eastward at the top of the palace, slightly closing his eyes at the sun rays. In the flickering sun rays, [he thought] he saw a charnel ground arising. Thinking, "I will be tainted by stains," he fled, fell off the top of the palace, and passed away. Then, the upasaka Sumatibhadra said:

Through excessive self-clinging, suffering comes forth
By desiring happiness for oneself, harm for others arises
Through completely casting out the clinging to a self,
you should treat all sentient beings just like a physician

This is the pith instruction to free yourself from self-clinging, which is the fourth one.

(5) Once, in the Jeta grove, prince Sarvārthasiddhi[51] and the black māra Devadatta were born as a parrot with two heads sprouting from a single body. Then, when Devadatta's head had fallen asleep, Siddhārtha dug[52] at the roots of a tree and found medicinal mango and Hāla poison.[53] Saying, "Their quintessence is equally beneficial; I taste it myself," he ate the medicine [and digested it], while the māra Devadatta threw it up [after having eaten it]. Upon that, becoming very angry, Devadatta ate the poison, which destroyed them both. Then the mighty lord of the gods, Śakra,[54] said:

The wise ones who are seeing true reality
should neither adopt medicine-like merit
nor reject what is unfavorable like poison
By adopting and rejecting, they will be ruined

{5} This is the pith instruction to free yourself from adopting and rejecting, which is the fifth one.

(6) Once, in the town Kapilam, a brahman named Sūryadatta had a big, precious stone called "musāragalva"[55] that was able to dispel infectious diseases. This householder had two wives, but both were without a son. Eventually, he set a time for passion with a female householder named Samantā in the town Sukhāvatī and left. When his two former wives followed him, he hid inside a rotten tree trunk. After his two wives returned [to Kapilam], he met his [new] wife Samantā and they had intercourse. Due to an optical illusion, she mistook two golden spoons sticking up from the householder's crown ornament for two people. She said to the brahman, "Hey, handsome, there are two people very close by to subdue us!" The brahman answered, "These are my two wives. If they tell the king about our behavior, he will certainly punish us. So let's

go and escape to another region!" They went to a nasé[56] grove and she recognized that [what she had seen] were [just] spoons. Samantā related [this to the brahman], since she regretted having been deluded. Then the mistress Samantā[57] sang a song:

We have escaped due to our fear of people
If you wish to cast off saṃsāra, do practice![58]
Suffering arises from the original ground, emptiness, {6}
so we are tormented by imagining the nondual as dual

This is the pith instruction to free yourself from adopting and rejecting, which is the sixth one.

(7) Once, in a grass hut at the outskirts of a city in the human realm of Magadha, a dyer named Kaurīmā had poured saffron-colored dye into a vat. After she had covered its opening with tree leaves, she went to pick flowers. A vixen from the charnel ground stepped onto [the leaves covering the vat with] the dye and fell into it, so her body became soaked with the dye. She went to the charnel ground and met a wolf there, [who asked], "Hey, excellent elder sister, who are you?" She answered, "I am the divine herbivore named Śaraṇa whose body is endowed with [the most beautiful] fragrance and color." Then, the wolf reported this to the bears, the tigers, the monkeys, and the lions, so they all encircled her. Thereafter, at the time of the full moon, [the vixen] went to her mother, [saying,] "I am supreme. I am unsurpassable. I am wonderful. I am the foremost lady among the herbivores." Her mother said:

Hey, daughter!
Having bathed in the waters of truthfulness,
you are happy if you live in lower stations
If you're proud due to the fur of bad character
for a long time, it is certain you will be ruined

Still, [the vixen] was unable to let go of her pride about her fur. Then she returned [to the charnel ground] and went to the assembly of the carnivores. Uttering her own yelp, it was [of course simply] that of a vixen, and when the lions uttered their roar, she fainted [out of fear].

Upon that, all herbivores and carnivores {7} each ripped out a bundle of her hairs and mixed them with excrements. At that point, the devaputras spoke these verses:

Those who do not course through mind's power
but course through pride about their fur
will continually miss out on happiness
Since the vixen lost her hairs, she is ruined

Those who do not course due to not wishing
to accomplish the fruition of[59] happiness
but pridefully course due to their doctrines
will be reduced to dust, just like this vixen

This is [the pith instruction] to free your own view from pride, {8} which is the seventh one.

(8) Once, in the country of Kosala, a bhikṣu named Yaśuha practiced the dhyāna of stopping the six collections [of consciousness]. By virtue of that, his breath lacked any shift of inhalation and exhalation. Therefore, he remained [in that state] for five hundred years. Then, the cakravartin king Radiance of Joyful Training[60] said to him:

Oh bhikṣu, let mind[61] look at mind!
Don't just dwell in the sixth pāramitā
of prajñā, but familiarize with this!
Drop the meditative absorption of cessation![62]

Having once again depreciated[63] the meaning [of this], [Yaśuha] was born as a long-lived god due to his clinging to previous [meditative states] without discrimination.[64] Thereafter, he was born as a king in the barbarian borderlands. Then, remembering his [previous] births, he [again] depreciated the teachings and was born as a long-lived god due to his clinging to previous [meditative states] without discrimination. Upon that, remembering his [previous] births, he [yet again] depreciated the teachings, upon which a hole in the earth[65] opened up and he went directly to the Avīci hell. This is [the pith instruction] to free meditation from any focal points, {8} which is the eighth one.

(9) Once, while a brahman named Jinapa was sleeping in his cool pavilion, in his dream [he heard the following]: "Oh son of noble family, adopt pure conduct!" Due to that,[66] he gave rise to [the mindset] for supreme awakening[67] and gathered the accumulations of the five pāramitās devoid of prajñā. All humans and gods venerated him and paid their respect and services to him. Then the bodhisattva Anantamati said to him, "Hey, brahman Jinapa, the five pāramitās lacking prajñā are not supreme. They do not even deserve the names of the five pāramitās. Why is that? Because all phenomena are inexpressible." Nevertheless, [Jinapa] did not become free of clinging [to his conduct]. Being blessed by the māra *Prahaiśvara, he attained the bliss of the Peak of Existence[68] but then plunged down again into the miserable realms. This is [the pith instruction] to free conduct from clinging, which is the ninth one.

(10) Once, the daughter of a king named Bhadrapāla paid her respect and services by way of the riches of the triad of body, speech, and mind to the bhikṣuṇī named Prajāpatī[69] for six years. She performed twenty [forms of] conduct with the thirteen signs of the path for this sovereign lady of the assembly [of nuns].[70] For an equally long time, she also trained in studying [the dharma]. Then, the bhikṣuṇī named Lakṣmī said, "Hey, I give you the quintessence of the entirety of saṃsāra—the true reality of nirvāṇa—and you will become completely free of all fears of saṃsāra." {9} The daughter [of the king] said, "Oh bhikṣuṇī, the result of [my] former virtues[71] is supreme. Since no result more supreme than this will arise, I have no desire [for what you offer]." Lakṣmī answered:

> Not knowing the dharma's very secret,[72]
> the hardships by which you desire results,[73]
> similar to the messengers of a king,
> will entail lots of trouble but little meaning

This is [the pith instruction] to free yourself from being stubbornly content with[74] having performed a lot of difficult things, which is the tenth one.

(11) The *Śrīparamādyatantra* says:

The glorious supreme original one arises from empowerment
If the obstinacies of body, speech, and mind
have been matured through the empowerment,
the glorious supreme original one will be attained[75]

After king Kosala had seen this, he requested empowerment from king Indrabhūti seventeen times.[76] Eventually, king Indrabhūti declared, "Oh king, to familiarize with[77] what is genuine is like a seed. To continually become familiar with it is like a sprout growing through manure. Conduct is similar to making the harvest worthwhile. Therefore, great king, it is appropriate to cultivate such familiarization." Nevertheless, due to the above scriptural passage, [king Kosala] was not able to change his mind for sure.[78] A ḍākinī spoke the following stanza to him:

Wisdom may be pointed out by empowerments
and you may desire to do what is worthwhile,
but to lack familiarity is like the banana tree's fruit:
after it has grown once, it will become extinct

Therefore, you should familiarize [with what is genuine]. This is [the pith instruction] to free yourself from being stubbornly content with nothing but empowerments, {10} which is the eleventh one.

(12) At a time when ḍākinīs and male and female yogic practitioners were assembled at a gaṇacakra, a disciple of Śrī Ḍombi Heruka, named Śrī Siṃha, said:

By realizing[79] phenomena to be empty,
there is nothing to meditate at its end
If you meditate, you become inferior,
as in the example of a king not having
any desire to become a king once again
If all buddhas are realized to be the same
as emptiness, meditation is not needed
Meditation and such are like a fire offering's ashes

All the vajraḍākinīs said, "Hey, you with misplaced desire[80] who rob the secret of the buddhas, listen! Is seeing the moon on the first day [of the lunar month seeing] the full moon? Is the strength of a baby complete right after it has been born? Is the fruit consummate after the seed has been planted? Do the jewels in the ocean come into your hand by [merely] seeing them? Are you able to promote the welfare of sentient beings merely by giving rise to the mindset [for buddhahood]? Is hunger dispelled[81] merely by seeing food? Since [all of this] is unreasonable,[82] the wisdom of unity will be attained if the principal of realization has become pleased by the retinue of being familiar with resting [in it]. Those who are stubbornly content with [nothing but] realization are fools.[83] They are outsiders.[84] They are directly blessed by the māras. They cause their own ruin." With that, the ḍākinīs killed [Śrī Siṃha] and enjoyed him [as their food]. {11} This is [the pith instruction] to free yourself from being stubbornly content with [nothing but] realization, which is the twelfth one.

(13) A daughter of king Dharmapāla named Gaṅgā had looked at all the sūtras and tantras of the Tathāgata. Due to that, she meditated on them in the manner in which her realization [of them] had arisen. Then, on the night when the rākṣasas[85] venerate great awakening, Gaṅgā went to a place where all yogīs assembled and held a gaṇacakra. Being blessed by the ḍākinīs, all yogīs [magically] lifted her body up in the air. In her speech [in answer to this], [Gaṅgā pretended to] be delighted, [but] in her mind, she became very angry. Upon that, Gaṅgā's previous realization disappeared, and she asked the yogīs, "Hey, please explain to me what I did wrong!" The yogīs answered with one voice:

Siddhis are obtained from the guru
Bliss arises from the awareness lady
While lacking the guru, the siddhis
are not attained even with thousandfold effort

Creating siddhis through anything else
resembles food that contains poison
All kinds of harm and obstacles
will then arise through the ḍākinīs

Through those [words], [Gaṅgā] developed devotion. This is [the pith instruction] to give up not relying on the guru, which is the thirteenth one.

(14) Taking Madhyamaka to be supreme, the son of the king of Karṇāta,[86] named Kṛṣṇa,[87] depreciated the entirety of the words of the Buddha and the treatises [on them]. Being seized by the northern yakṣas,[88] he became crazy. {12} Then his father, the king, queried some mantra experts and thereupon made the [according] efforts to expel the obstructors. Śrī Nārotapa[89] said:

The words of the Buddha's awakened mind that is like a wish-fulfilling tree
are turned into all kinds of yānas by the minds of sentient beings
The great māra of clinging to what is unbiased as being biased
will be deceiving us during both this and future [lifetimes]

For the minds of beings, everything is a reality
Ultimately, nothing at all exists as an object
True reality is inseparable from the yogī's mind
Who puts down the Buddha's words goes to the hell realms

Therefore, this is [the pith instruction] to not depreciate any among the Buddha's words, which is the fourteenth one.

(15) A king named Excellent Plain Song had received empowerment from Śrī Kambala. Due to his staying at charnel grounds in Uḍḍiyāna to cultivate bliss, all the hungry ghosts of the charnel grounds created obstacles and greatly distracted his mind. He asked the yoginī Lakṣmīṃkarā,[90] who said:

Karmamudrā is what constitutes the ship of bliss
With the dry shore of emptiness found, what's there to do?
If the contrived mind clings to contrived bliss,
the great ocean of saṃsāra cannot be crossed

Due to this, all yogīs reported [their experiences] to the princess. This is [the pith instruction] to relinquish clinging to bliss, which is the fifteenth one.

(16) Someone named Caṇḍālaja who relied on the great master Kukkuripa {13} focused on the ultimate mind. Due to having cultivated the perfection process in a one-sided manner, he was clinging to the utter nonexistence[91] of all phenomena. Then, most people in the country Jālandhara died from a contagious disease and the entire harvest was destroyed by hail. After no rain had fallen for five years, a brahman who was an expert in secret utterances was asked [about all this]. He replied, "In this region, there lives an insider Buddhist person who has turned to secretly propounding a doctrine of the outsiders. Since he lives here, all kinds of misfortunes have occurred. In this world, he will ruin others, and in the future, he will ruin himself." Śrī Kukkuripa heard this and went to Caṇḍālaja, saying:

First, the phenomena that are entities
should be put to an end by emptiness
But if there is great clinging to emptiness,
that is even more ruinous than clinging to entities

If a poisonous snake has died, it becomes nectar
Applying a mantra to poison, it is supreme medicine
Since that which is sealed turns into bliss,
let go of clinging and familiarize with nonduality!

With this, [Kukkuripa] gave [Caṇḍālaja] the third empowerment.

Thus, through discussing ten examples from the past, master Nāgārjunapāda is in accord with the sūtras and tantras. Therefore, he is to be understood as being a buddha. Through discussing six examples from the future, he is in accord with the siddhas.[92] Therefore, he is to be understood as being an omniscient one. The knowledge that is free of the sixteen flaws[93] is the awakened mind of the Buddha. {14} Therefore, it resembles a precious jewel.

This concludes "A Commentary on[94] *'Four and a Half Stanzas'" spoken by master Nāgārjunagarbha. This great and mighty adept gave it to*[95] *venerable Śavaripāda at Śrī Parvata. The latter transmitted it to venerable *Karopa, who in turn passed it on to venerable Nāropa. There is also a translation of it by Gayādhara and Gö [Lhedsé], which differs greatly from this one.*[96] {15}

(92) A Pith Instruction on the Four Mudrās

In the language of India: *Caturmudropadeśanāma*[97]
In the language of Tibet: *Phyag rgya bzhi'i man ngag zhes bya ba*

I pay homage to Śrī Vajrasattva

> It is emptiness and compassion inseparable,
> profound, and its nature is hard to examine—
> this constitutes the essence of mahāmudrā
> Having paid homage, I shall explain this true reality

Yogīs who wish to enter the pith instructions first need to understand the tenets. There are three kinds of yānas: the Śrāvakayāna, the Pratyekabuddhayāna, and the Mahāyāna. They have four positions: the position of the Vaibhāṣikas, the position of the Sautrāntikas, the position of the Vijñapti[vādins], and the position of the Mādhyamikas. These consist of nine yogas: highest, middling, and lower śrāvakas, pratyekabuddhas, Sautrāntikas, Aspectarians, Nonaspectarians, the Mādhyamikas who proclaim illusion-like nonduality, and the Mādhyamikas who proclaim all phenomena to be utterly nonabiding.

Each one of these has a fourfold [classification] in terms of (1) the approach of analysis, {16} (2) dhyāna, (3) the stains of dhyāna, and (4) the view. Here, analysis refers to their specific discriminating prajñās that are based on study and reflection. Dhyāna refers to their specific prajñās of meditation. The stains of dhyāna refer to the factors that are directly antagonistic to those [prajñās]. The view refers to the distinctive features of their specific prajñās embracing their specific analyses,[98] as well as mentally taking their specific fruitions as objects.

(1) The analysis[99] of the lower śrāvakas is to assert an inexpressible person, which is preceded by claiming [the real existence of external] referents such as blue. [The analysis of] the middling [śrāvakas] accords with that. [The analysis of] the highest [śrāvakas] is to view the person as empty by completely understanding the four realities of the noble ones. [The analysis of] the pratyekabuddhas is that the perceived is empty, while they claim [the real existence of] the perceiver. The Sautrāntikas assert that the perceived is a conglomeration [of particles], while the perceiver consists of the six collections [of consciousness]. The Aspectarians assert that everything is an aspect of cognition, which is the assertion of nondual variety. The Nonaspectarians assert that all these [phenomena of perceiver and perceived] are nothing but mind, having the essence of awareness without any aspect. [The Mādhyamikas of] illusion-like [nonduality] assert that just like illusions, all phenomena are empty of any actual being, with true reality being nonduality. [The Mādhyamikas of] utter nonabiding analyze all that is conventional as being mere designation—in its ultimate essence, it does not abide as anything whatsoever.[100]

(2) As for their dhyānas, [in due order,] they meditate on repulsiveness, rest in counting prāṇa and apāna, {17} rest the mind in the reality of emptiness (that is, in nothing whatsoever appearing, similar to an oil lamp that has been extinguished), rest [the mind] on the tip of their nose, rest the mind by withdrawing the maṇḍala [of phenomena], rest the mind in the aspects of mind, rest in the absence of aspects, rest in reflections, and rest in the essence of not being established as anything whatsoever.

Among these, [Aspectarians] need to rest in the aspects of mind as follows. First, they direct their cognition toward anything that is suitable and then rest by knowing this to be mere mind. As for [Nonaspectarians] resting in the absence of aspects, first, after having worshipped and so on, the students are placed on a seat and made to breathe between their teeth. To begin, they are encouraged to direct their cognition toward something like a flower. Then, a hand is placed on the crown of their head and the following mantra is uttered:

OM ĀḤ[101] RA RA HŪṂ HŪṂ OṂ VAJRAYOGINĪ
ADHITIṢṬHA[102] HŪṂ PHAṬ

Thus, the mantra of their own oath [deity[103] residing] on their head is uttered. Then, once they have made the flower disappear as well, [the specific dhyāna of resting in the absence of aspects] arises swiftly.

(3)–(4) Since their stains of dhyāna and their views are elucidated elsewhere,[104] I do not describe them here.

Thus there are those who are not learned [in these four points] who have blurred vision, those who are learned [in them] who have blurred vision,[105] and those who are learned [in them] who are without blurred vision.[106] [Accordingly,] their [kinds of] compassion focus on sentient beings, focus on the dharma, and are without any focus, respectively.[107]

From among the three yānas, the yāna of secret mantra belongs to the Mahāyāna. Its positions are the latter two [Vijñaptivāda and Madhyamaka]. Its yogas {18} consist of the last four.[108] The texts of the master himself match [this yāna of secret mantra] with the [view of the Madhyamaka of] utter nonabiding.

Nevertheless, it is not the case that this [yāna of secret mantra] is without difference from the [Mahāyāna] in all respects. As [the *Nayatrayapradīpa*] says:

> Though of the same purport, since it is not ignorant,
> since it is abundant in means, since it lacks difficulty,
> and since those with sharp faculties are entitled to it,
> the Mantrayāna is much more distinguished[109]

Therefore, this shall be discussed as follows. [The Mantrayāna consists of] the outer creation process, the profound creation process, the perfection process, the full-perfection process, and the essence process.[110] There is also the tathāgata relief and the Vajradhara relief. Furthermore, the imaginary [nature] is sealed by the dependent [nature], the dependent [nature] is sealed by the perfect [nature], the perfect [nature is sealed] by Vajrasattva, and he is sealed by great bliss.

This is also to be understood by virtue of the four mudrās. The **karmamudrā** consists of the profound creation process and the perfection process. The **dharmamudrā** consists of the full perfection process. **Mahāmudrā** consists of the essence process. The **samayamudrā** consists of the outer creation process.

The seal of the dependent [nature] in the imaginary [nature] consists of the outer creation process. The seal of the perfect [nature] means that even all deities are mere cognizance. The seal of Vajrasattva consists of understanding cognizance to be emptiness. The seal of great bliss consists of rendering this very [emptiness] a living experience [through] the pith instructions. {19}

The **karmamudrā** is the essence of the [four] empowerments: (a) the vase [empowerment], (b) the secret [empowerment], (c) the prajñā-jñāna [empowerment], and (d) the fourth [empowerment].

(a) The vase [empowerment] consists of the [empowerments] up through the empowerment of the master, which purify the body.

(b) The secret [empowerment] consists of granting the bodhicitta arising from the pair of means and prajñā, which purifies speech.

(c) The prajñā-jñāna [empowerment] is threefold: (1) forceful, (2) poor, and (3) excellent.[111] (c1) As for the forceful [prajñā-jñāna empowerment, the following is held]. (i) The external activities, beginning with kissing and embracing, represent ecstasy—that is, [the moment of] variety. (ii) The yoga of the churned and the churning represents [the moment of] maturation—that is, supreme ecstasy. (iii) Experiencing [bodhicitta] in the jewel represents [the moment of] the lack of characteristics—that is, cessational ecstasy. (iv) [Bodhicitta] falling into the lotus represents [the moment of] consummation—that is, connate [ecstasy]. This assertion contradicts the scriptures. For the scriptures teach this with statements such as these:

> In the middle between supreme and cessational ecstasy,
> stabilize it by understanding what is to be pointed out[112]

And:

> the one at cessation's beginning and the supreme's end[113]

Furthermore, this is said:

The four ecstasies are ecstasy, supreme ecstasy, connate
ecstasy, and cessational ecstasy.[114]

"However, [most other] scriptures have connate ecstasy as the last one." That is certainly true, but such is explained by mixing up [the order of the ecstasies] for the sake of persons who fail to rely on a guru and [just] become learned through tomes of scriptures. In such [scriptures], [connate ecstasy] is the fourth in number, {20} but in terms of the meaning it corresponds to the third [moment]. Therefore,[115] [the followers of] the forceful yoga here lack expertise in terms of both the sequence and the meaning.[116]

(c2) Now, the poor bestowing of the [prajñā-jñāna] empowerment shall be discussed. (i) The external activities such as kissing and embracing represent [the moment of] variety—that is, ecstasy. (ii) The yoga of the churned and the churning represents [the moment of] maturation—that is, supreme ecstasy. (iii) Experiencing [bodhicitta] in the jewel represents [the moment of] the lack of characteristics—that is, connate ecstasy. (iv) [Bodhicitta] falling into the lotus represents [the moment of] consummation—that is, cessational ecstasy. This is what is asserted [here], and thus it is not different from [the assertion of] the tīrthikas. Why is that? Because they grasp at the experience [of ecstasy] as being something real. They have expertise in the [correct] sequence but lack expertise in the [correct] meaning.

(c3) Now, the excellent bestowing of the [prajñā-jñāna] empowerment shall be discussed. The four ecstasies of this system are to be understood as follows. (i) [Everything] from the external activities up through the final friction represents the ecstasy of [the moment of] variety. (ii) Experiencing [bodhicitta] reaching the tip of the jewel represents [the moment of] maturation—that is, supreme ecstasy. (iii) The Bhagavān said:

Holder of the sixteen bindus twice halved[117]

Therefore, from among what abides in the form of four bindus, two are located in the part that is the tip of the vajra and two are located in the part that is the anthers of the lotus. This represents [the moment of] the lack of characteristics, that is, connate ecstasy. (iv) All four bindus being located in the part that is the lotus represents [the moment of] consummation,[118] that is, cessational ecstasy. This is stated as follows:

> Having embraced with his two arms
> a prajñā who has reached sixteen, {21}
> with vajra and bell joining in union,
> it is said to be the master's empowerment[119]

And:

> By way of the number of the four empowerments,
> the sequence of ecstasy and so on is to be known[120]

The *Sarvarahasyatantra* says:

> Two are emitted, two equally in the middle
> From the vajra, they touch the lotus
> The cause is sealed by the result—
> this represents the king of great bliss[121]

Thus, the forceful yoga lacks the seal of Akṣobhya, while the poor empowerment lacks the seal of Vajrasattva and also lacks the Vajradhara relief. Here, Vajrasattva sealing Akṣobhya is the middle path. In the scriptures, this is taught briefly, taught in detail, and also taught in great detail. Since these [teachings] are clear in *A Commentary on Empowerment*,[122] I do not write them down here. This is the prajñā-jñāna empowerment, which delights the mind.[123]

(d) As for the fourth [empowerment], the fourth one is the unity as the essence of dependent origination that is not different from the three ecstasies that have the nature of the prajñā-jñāna empowerment. Those two [empowerments] represent the karmamudrā, giving rise to the result of concordant outflow. This is what Master Nāgārjunapāda explains [in his *Caturmudrānvaya*].[124]

The **dharmamudrā** is what appears as the variety of phenomena that are sights and sounds,[125] which is fourfold: (a) the arising of thoughts of variety free of the connate of the karmamudrā, {22} (b) thoughts of variety having ceased and abiding in the form of the connate, (c) [thoughts of] variety and the connate being nondual,[126] and (d) thoughts of both variety and the connate not being observable. [In due order, these four] represent the ecstasy, supreme ecstasy, connate ecstasy, and cessational ecstasy of the dharmamudrā. Therefore, the dharmamudrā is expressed as "the result of maturation," because uncontrived mahāmudrā arises from the nature of the uncontrived true state.[127]

Mahāmudrā is the unity that is the essence of all phenomena, being unborn, free of thoughts of perceiver and perceived, devoid of the obscurations that are afflictive, cognitive, and so on, and experiencing its own specific characteristic just as it is. This is expressed as the result that is stainlessness. Its essence is that it does not have the form of any phenomena of extremes or a middle, is all-pervading, immutable, and [present] at all times. Therefore, mahāmudrā refers to fully perfect[128] buddhahood in a single instant, which lacks any division into the four moments or the four ecstasies.[129]

Nevertheless, the four ecstasies may be presented in relation to the four mudrās: (a) the karmamudrā represents ecstasy, (b) the dharmamudrā represents supreme ecstasy, (c) mahāmudrā represents connate ecstasy, and (d) the samayamudrā represents cessational ecstasy. As for how this is [to be understood], {23} you need to rely on the mouth of the guru at the time of [turning] the wheel of dharma.

The **samayamudrā** is the fruitional deity maṇḍala that signifies true reality. It is samaya, because the venerable lord signifies means, the venerable lady signifies prajñā, and their embrace signifies their being nondual. In due order, in the creation process,[130] (a) after having performed the sevenfold purification, giving rise to the causal Heruka,[131] (b) emanating the circle of female deities, (c) [the causal Heruka] melting into the form of bindus on sun and moon [discs], and (d) the female deities exhorting [the causal Heruka] with melodies and he thus becoming the fruitional vajra holder constitute the four ecstasies of the samayamudrā.[132] Since this fruitional circle of deities is in charge of the welfare of beings, it is expressed as the result produced by persons.[133]

In this way, each of the four mudrās is to be understood as consisting of four ecstasies—that is, sixteen [altogether].[134]

This concludes "A Pith Instruction on the Four Mudrās" composed by master Advayavajra. It was translated by the Indian upādhyāya Vajrapāṇi and the Tibetan lotsāwa bhikṣu Tsültrim Gyalwa. {24}

(93)–(94) Two Vajra Songs by Nāropa

In the language of India: *Vajragīti*[135]
In the language of Tibet: *Rdo rje'i glu*

I pay homage to the Bhagavān Mañjuśrī

The crazy ones who are seized
by the great evil spirit of thoughts[136]
see stones, wood, and so on as gold
There is no precious gold in them [1]

By following the evil spirit of thoughts,
they are fettered moment by moment
By[137] possessing prajñā and compassion,
they should make efforts in overcoming it [2]

This concludes a vajra song by the great master Nāropa.

In the language of India: *Vajragīti*[138]
In the language of Tibet: *Rdo rje'i glu*

I pay homage to the Bhagavān Mañjuvajra

Seized by the beguiling poisonous snake
of these thoughts, your own mind
becomes fettered in just the same ways
in which it keeps entertaining thoughts,
experiencing much meaningless suffering [1]

Through following delusion,
delusion will not be abandoned
The courageous with compassion
need to familiarize with suchness [2]

The [mind] will become free[139]
according to its ways of analyzing
The many-headed poisonous snake
of prajñā continues to devour me [3] {25}

The many-headed, poisonous snake of prajñā
is always nourished by the milk of samādhi
but killed by the mongoose of thoughts [4]

Prajñā's snake with its hundred heads
is constantly devouring Nāropa
Nobody can understand this[140]
Only Nāropa himself gets it,
So ask Nāropa in person! [5]

This concludes a vajra song by the mahāyogī[141] *Nāropa.* {26}

(95)–(96) Two Vajra Songs by Kṛṣṇa

In the language of India: *Vajragīti*[142]
In the language of Tibet: *Rdo rje'i glu*

I pay homage to great compassion

Just as I am,
so are you
What makes us different are thoughts
Snakes come from the ocean of nectar
Overcome your thoughts!

This concludes a vajra song.

In the language of India: *Vajragīti*[143]
In the language of Tibet: *Rdo rje'i glu*

I pay homage to the glorious vajra seat

I say: Without abiding anywhere, Kṛṣṇa's mind appears everywhere topsy-turvy[144]

This concludes a vajra song by master Kṛṣṇapāda. {27}

(97) A Song on the Connate

In the language of India: *Sahajagīti*[145]
In the language of Tibet: *Lhan cig skyes pa'i glu*

I pay homage to the true guru

In the empty forest, a flower bursts into bloom
This single flower possesses all kinds of colors
If this incomparable flower grows, it conquers all directions
Please, just pluck this flower that is so priceless! [1]

It has no root and lacks any branches or leaves
Friends, behold this supreme bud conquering all directions!
If this incomparable flower grows, it conquers all directions
Please, just pluck this flower that is so priceless! [2]

Through picking up its anthers, the illusionist
offers them to Kuliśeśvara,[146] the dharmadhātu
If this incomparable flower grows, it conquers all directions
Please, just pluck this flower that is so priceless! [3]

Examining supreme and cessational ecstasy, seize them!
Offer them with respect at the feet of the true guru!
If this incomparable flower grows, it conquers all directions
Please, just pluck this flower that is so priceless! [4]

This concludes ["A Song on the Connate"] composed by the lord of yogīs, Śāntadeva. It was translated by guru Dhiriśrījñānapāda and lotsāwa Mapen Chöbar.[147] {28}

(98) A Song on Abandoning Thoughts

In the language of India: *Vikalpaparihāragītikānāma*[148]
In the language of Tibet: *Rnam rtog spang ba'i glu zhes bya ba*

I pay homage to Śrī Heruka

The nature of the mind condensed
within the vola,[149] the secret vajra,
follows the nāḍī[150] of the secret bindu
In its union with the kakkola,[151]
hey, how fine[152] it is blazing! [1]

Through the kṛpīṭa's[153] resounding,
the six nāḍī cakras are bound by HŪṂ
The three kāyas are realized as no-self in the dhūtī
Possessing a self-arising flower,
karpūra[154] is fused with the vola
Drink the nectar of kāruṇika! [2]

Those with the fortune of Kāliñjara[155]
should blend with the assembly of yogīs
Dundura[156] means being unfortunate—
abandon it! This is the yogī's samaya [3]

Anointing the body with catuḥsama and musk,[157]
thinking needs to be relinquished
In the assemblies of vīras and vīrās,
assume the pride of Heruka! [4]

Come on![158] The yogīs who take up the load
of the great realm of śava[159] and hand it over
to brahmans sprung from noble families[160]
should not think but remain in their body [5]

Hey, you fortunate ones, worship!
Līla, who is the lion of no-self {29}
and realizes the actuality of emptiness,
is a yogī due to abandoning thoughts, hey! [6]

I am lying there supine on my back,
joining my folded hands at my chest,
focusing on the sky of self-awareness[161] [7]

Having been born, Līla realized nonduality,
attaining the siddhi of a thoughtfree yogī[162]
By having realized this, Līlapa is free [8]

This concludes "A Song on Abandoning Thoughts" composed by master Līlapa. {30}

(99) A Dohā Treasure Song on Karmacaṇḍālikā

In the language of India: *Karmacaṇḍālikādohakoṣagītināma*[163]
In the language of Tibet: *Las kyi gtum mo'i do ha mdzod kyi glu zhes bya ba*

I pay homage to Sarvārthasiddhi[164]

The blazing of the fire of caṇḍālī within
lets the nectar drip down the center,
arriving and remaining at the tip mound
of the lotus that is self-arising [1]

Letting the nectar of the protector drip down,
the longstanding suffering of saṃsāra is overcome
and the fear of approaching Yama is abandoned,
while the garland of buddha qualities emerges [2]

The spreading of great bliss
will be pervading everything
The longstanding suffering of saṃsāra is overcome,
and the fear of approaching Yama is abandoned [3]

In the vajra's tilling and dispersing,[165]
the pair of sun and moon is fused
and dissolves into the expanse of space,
gone to the city of great bliss [4]

Through the buddha qualities in the center of all,
I have arrived at the abode of Ratnasambhava
The longstanding suffering of saṃsāra is overcome,
and the fear of approaching Yama is abandoned [5] {31}

By stopping the vāyus that cause arising,
I went to the abode of Ratnaprakāśa[166]
Examining, examining, and analyzing,
I, Virū,[167] will become accomplished
The longstanding suffering of saṃsāra is overcome,
and the fear of approaching Yama is abandoned [6]

This concludes "A Dohā Treasure Song on Karmacaṇḍālikā" composed by master Virūpa.[168] {32}

(100) A Dohā Treasure Song on the Ornament of Spring

In the language of India: *Vasantatilakadohakoṣagītikānāma*[169]
In the language of Tibet: *Dpyid kyi thig le'i do ha mdzod kyi glu zhes bya ba*

I pay homage to Śrī Heruka

Sebhu,[170] the three kāyas and such,
seeing their spring flowers,
I, this youth, am intoxicated [1]

By having passion for Heruka,
at this first beginning of spring,
may you please protect me!
Don't let me die through torment! [2]

You are delighted by ambhakaruṇa[171]
flowers with their delicious fragrance
The śaripa keeps the drum beat[172]
Carrying a lamp, this is caṇḍālī [3]

"The drawing[173] falls down on me"
I hope that Kanapa arrives
At the time of the first spring,
may you please protect me!
Don't let me die through torment! [4]

If I look into the ten directions,
I do not see anyone else but you
By virtue of the tormenting fire,[174]
I don't even think of my own body [5]

By virtue of my supplicating
four among the eight yoginīs,
Bhagavān, {33} please rise! [6]

This concludes "A Dohā Treasure Song on the Ornament of Spring" transmitted by master Kṛṣṇa and composed by master Saraha. {34}

(101) An Instruction on the Connate

In the language of India: *Sahajāmnāyanāma*[175]
In the language of Tibet: *Lhan cig skyes pa'i gdams pa zhes bya ba*

I pay homage to the bodhisattvas

In the center of the union at the heart
is the nondual bindu, a mustard seed in size
Similar to an entire ocean of milk,
think of it as gradually expanding [1]

Your own and the bodies of others
are filled with stainless nectar, like curd,
Wind diseases dispelled, mind as such bound
This is what I, Medhi, proclaim [2]

Directing mind toward being, nonbeing is realized
Hey, seize your own mind without distraction
The sign of a yogī's accomplishment is without being
Cut through the mutual connection of the two! [3]

Within the nature of being and nonbeing,
the two extremes are absent—the connate is accomplished
The entirety of being is without birth
I did not realize this by having practiced[176] [4]

The essence of all appearances is the mind
Mind as such is not established; this mind's
character is all-pervasive compassion,
which is immutable just like space
Not dwelling in duality is mind as such
This is what I, Medhi, proclaim [5] {35}

Don't contrive self-awareness, let go of doing!
With mind as such, clinging-free and nonminding,[177]
not becoming extinct, it is realized by self-awareness
With it not becoming permanent, doubts are cut through
Its empty nature lacks any permanence or extinction
This is what I, Medhi, proclaim [6]

There is no view or meditation, nor any fruition
Appearing yet being without nature or being
Like the knots of a snake, what thoughts are
is the convention-free unity of being free on their own [7]

Meditating like this, emptiness is realized
This is what I, Medhi, proclaim
I, the yogī, have indeed realized
the emptiness of connate unity [8]

This concludes "An Instruction on Connate Unity"[178] *composed by master Medhini.* {36}

(102) The Stages of Unsurpassable Universal Purity

In the language of India: *Anuttarasarvaśuddhikramanāma*[179]
In the language of Tibet: *Bla med sbyor ba'i rim pa zhes bya ba*[180]

I pay homage to Śrī Heruka

Just as a lotus is growing out of the mud,
in the same way, nondual awareness will
grow out of the darkness of unawareness
Having paid homage to his self-awareness,
through the stages of the unsurpassable yoga,
I shall explain the stainless genuine dharma [1]

With being empty, very empty,
and greatly empty as the third,
fourth, causes and results are all[-empty][181]
Through joining means and prajñā,
you're absorbed in the perfection process [2]

By perceiving the perfection,
this is all-empty luminosity
Through the yoga of threefold self-awareness,
the three causes will be completely pure [3]

By realizing the actuality of emptiness,
the unsurpassable state will be attained
Empty luminosity, prajñā, as well as
mind as such follow[182] what is other [4]

I shall explain this in such a way
here through elaborating on it
The same applies for passion,
utter passion, and great passion [5] {37}

Through the three poisons such as ignorance,
this mind as such of the mobile and immobile
is endowed with peace, passion, and thoughts
during the triad of past, present, and future[183] [6]

Abiding inside just as outside,
be it past, present, or future,
I abide in the past of the past [7]

Always possessing great craving,
utter craving, hunger, thirst,
feeling, the feeling of lying down,
the single instant of utter feeling,
discrimination, and compassion, [8]

in yogīs who possess shame,
experiences and envy accumulate
In this way, the thirty-three
obscure self-aware wisdom[184] [9]

In the practice of yogīs,
in the center of the lotus of great bliss in the sky,
a syllable HAṂ rests on a moon seat
The conventional is lucid and stainless
To seize the coming-and-going vāyus is wisdom [10]

The red crescent moon is prajñā,
the first of the vowels that is a bindu,
to be cultivated so as to seize the vāyus
Similar to a great luminous star,
it's the means to [realize] empty mind as such [11]

Free of form, without any color,
with a peaceful expression, free of unity,[185]
without any conventions of stable or moving [12]

Thus, thanks to the guru's kindness,
through the samādhi of vajra recitation,
the past, the present, and the future
will not be seen as anything at all, no doubt [13]

Just as the cause of fire[186] is present
within dry firewood but not yet blazing,
so bodhicitta is present within symbols
and the effortless[187] but not yet accomplished [14] {38}

Therefore, relinquish your pride and so on,
give rise to vigor, pay service to the guru,
and practice once you obtain empowerment! [15]

Through training in the first yoga,
the eighth bhūmi will be attained
Through perfection with threefold luminosity,[188]
the bhūmi of full perfection is attained [16]

Those who obtained empowerment but denigrate,
who have little vigor, cling to wrong views,
and discuss the guru's flaws but not the qualities
will not attain the path of the victors [17]

Those who lack respectful service but expect to receive it,
who approach with soft words but exhibit an angry way of being,

and who do not pay homage and so on despite seeing the guru
in places where large crowds of people are present
are not proper vessels, who are not given the instructions [18]

Those who attained excellent qualities and possess vigor
are endowed with a joy[189] equaling that of the buddhas
in paying respectful service to the gurus, their retinues, and so on,
and have great yearning for the dharma spoken by the victor [19]

Vajrasattva, the tantras' support who embodies many tantras,
is the one who constitutes the path of the bodhisattvas
The roots of virtue attained by me that serve as causes
are what I dedicate to the six realms—may this be auspicious! [20]

This concludes "The Stages of the Unsurpassable Yoga" composed by master Paṅkaja. {39}

(103) Familiarizing with the True Reality of View and Conduct Being Unborn

In the language of India: *Caryādṛṣṭyanutpannatattvabhāvanānāma*[190]
In the language of Tibet: *Lta spyod skye med kyi sgom pa zhes bya ba*

I pay homage to the gurus

Mind as such is empty and unborn
Uncontrived true reality is dharmatā
Their inseparability is the realization of the view
Meditation does not go beyond that, I declare[191]
Clinging-free yogīs behave in their own ground
To lack any hope in the ten directions is the fruition [1]

Give rise[192] to passion without hoping for it!
Experiences arising naturally—very amazing!
This is what Panaha declares [2]

This is the realization of nondual wisdom
I am imbibing the nectar of great bliss,
adorning my neck with kuñjana[193] garlands
and tightly tying my garment of leaves [3]

Drunk, I roam in the middle of the forest
I, Panaha, am seeing what is amazing

I am not separated from a single one
of the five lords in Pullīramalaya[194]—amazing! [4]

In the abode of nirvāṇa,
I let a flower garden bloom
There, I sip from their anthers
I, the king of the yoga of vola
and kakkola, attained siddhi [5]

This concludes "Familiarizing with View and Conduct Being Unborn" composed by master Panaha. {40}

(104) The Stages of Familiarizing with the Nāḍī of Nonduality

In the language of India: *Advayanāḍikābhāvanākrama*[195]
In the language of Tibet: *Gnyis med kyi rtsa bsgom pa'i rim pa*

I pay homage to nondual great bliss

In the center of the spaciousness of equality,
intoxicated, I scatter jewels in the expanse
Hey, being of a degenerated family is amazing!
In the state of equality, [all] becomes nonduality [1]

Since I do not realize this,
at times, Nilakhandha[196] destroys it
Since I do not realize this,
at times, this mendicant destroys it [2]

Nondual mind becomes dual
The sky embraces my neck[197]
Through the feature of exchanging myself with others,
I annihilated all my relatives [3]

Since I do not realize this,
at times, Nilakhandha destroys it
Since I do not realize this,
at times, this mendicant destroys it [4]

About a girl with a twelve-year-old's youth,
I do not entertain any thoughts at all[198]
Being the abode of activity of all yogīs,
she does her job similar to a harlot [5]

Since I do not realize this, {41}
at times, Nilakhandha destroys it
Since I do not realize this,
at times, this mendicant destroys it [6]

Conch shells, gold, and silver
are totally useless to me[199]
I hang out with agreeable friends
Through[200] embracing Heruka,
my kingdom is very amazing [7]

Even in the very middle of the day,
nobody at all sees it—how amazing!
The eight yoginīs are ecstatic and embrace,
remaining in their embrace with Heruka [8]

This concludes "The Stages of Familiarizing with the Nāḍī of Nonduality" transmitted by master Kṛṣṇa and composed by the great master Nilakhandha. {42}

(105) The Subtle Yoga

In the language of India: *Sūkṣmayoganāma*[201]
In the language of Tibet: *Phra ba'i rnal 'byor gyi nyams len zhes bya ba*

I pay homage to Śrī Yamāntaka

At their homes, householder yogīs
should cultivate the nondual secret embrace
These thoughts of being fearful—
you should hide them all away [1]

In what cannot be measured or grasped,[202]
their caste cannot be understood either
The mendicant Samudra's renown
will be pervading the three worlds[203] [2]

I, in the attire of being intoxicated,
wash and cleanse the five poisons
Kill these thoughts of being fearful
through subduing them inside! [3]

Having cast off the pride of caste,
this is what I, the mendicant, say
Though my senses see all kinds of things,

reminded by the messenger of time,
why should I be coming or going? [4]

Free of the two extremes, goals are accomplished
Abandon these thoughts of being fearful
through subduing this mind! [5]

With this yogī cutting through thoughts,
I, Samudra,[204] will become a nonentity
Through cultivating the subtle yoga, {43}
I behold[205] the siddhi of nonduality [6]

This concludes "The Practice of the Subtle Yoga" composed by master Samudra. {44}

(106) A Dohā Treasure Song on the View of the Nature of True Reality

In the language of India: *Tattvasvabhāvadṛṣṭidohakoṣagītikānāma*[206]
In the language of Tibet: *Rang bzhin gyi do ha mdzod kyi glu'i lta ba zhes bya ba*

I pay homage to Śrī Heruka

So that the means for making the stainless awakened mind,
view, conduct, and so on of the siddhas—the embodiment
of the nectar of nonduality—a living experience will benefit all,
I pay homage to the sugatas and shall explain it[207] [1]

It is neither being
nor arisen from[208] nonbeing—
so who will realize
this kind of nature? [2]

This is what Lūhipa declares:
something like that is so amazing
It sports[209] through the three realms' abodes,
but its very own abode cannot be realized [3]

Neither its color, nor its caste,
nor its shape[210] could I realize

As this kind of nature is not established
as an entity, how could it be shown? [4]

This is what Lūhipa declares:
something like that is so amazing
It sports through the three realms' abodes,
but its very own abode cannot be realized [5] {45}

This is what Lūhipa declares:
how could I ask anybody else?
The moon's reflection in the depths of the water
cannot be realized as being ultimate or illusory [6]

This is what Lūhipa declares:
something like that is amazing
It sports through the three realms' abodes,
but its very own abode cannot be realized [7]

This is what Lūhipa declares:
how could I ask anybody else?
Its nature cannot be realized [8]

This concludes "A Dohā Treasure Song on the View of the Nature [of True Reality]" composed by master Lūhipa. {46}

(107) A Dohā Song on View, Meditation, Conduct, and Fruition

In the language of India: *Bhāvanādṛṣṭicaryāphaladohagītikānāma*[211]
In the language of Tibet: *Lta sgom spyod pa 'bras bu'i do ha'i glu zhes bya ba*

I pay homage to noble Mañjuśrī

The diversity of entities is nothing but your own mind
All of saṃsāra and nirvāṇa is the undivided yoga
Buddhas and sentient beings do not exist as two,
just like in the example of water and its waves [1]

In the single instant of the yoga of realizing
this mind as such, devoid of being and nonbeing,
just as in the case of a small lamp and darkness,
the blurred vision that is the nature of saṃsāra's five poisons is
dispelled [2]

The mudrā[212] of unity, the greatness beyond mind,
is blissful, lucid, and nonconceptual, like space,
pervasive, vast, the essence[213] of great compassion,
appearing yet without nature, like a water-moon [3]

Though lucid, it is free of all conventions, extremes, and a middle,
untainted by anything, stainless, and free of hope and fear
Just like the dream of a mute, it cannot be expressed [4]

The wisdom whose nature is immeasurable great bliss,
just like the light of sun and moon, is without any bias[214]
Hey, this self-arising yoga is amazing! [5] {47}

Native uncontrived mind is the dharmakāya—
with a contrived mind, yoga will not be attained
Therefore, give it free rein in the sphere of bliss! [6]

Yogīs who attain the naturally accomplished path are blissful
Due to being free of thoughts, it is impossible for wanting to arise
This is what I, Saraha, who attained the siddhi of Hayagrīva, say [7]

Hey, yogīs, if you wish to familiarize with its nature
through making the view a living experience,
this mountain of your own body is the supreme abode [8]

Mind as such is the practitioner of the timely yoga,
binding the sense faculties, setting the boundary, being blissful
There isn't even any need to deliberately relinquish distractions [9]

If whatever is encountered[215] is known to be mind, it's the oath deity
Not withdrawing cognition, thoughts are gradually abandoned
If thinking springs forth in the mind, oh yogīs,
relax and let be, just like a ball of cotton wool! [10]

Abandon doing, let your own mind look at itself!
If wanting arises, understand it to be māra!
The root of thinking consists of the mind
Since it[216] does not exist, thinking doesn't either [11]

For yogīs who cultivate minding and nonminding,[217]
this mind is never established and dissolves in itself
Not desiring to meditate, the fruition of buddhahood is attained [12]

Yogīs are without thoughts, just like small children
They resemble bees tasting flowers in a garden
They wander from forest to forest, just like lions
They roam everywhere, just like all kinds of winds [13]

Mind as such endowed with heedfulness is the supreme conduct
Not blocking its nature, {48} behave like a lunatic,
not attached to the back and without clinging to the front![218] [14]

In brief, yogīs engage in whichever ways of conduct are beneficial
for making view, meditation, and conduct a living experience
This essence of the mind that appears as all kinds of things
is mahāmudrā, not established through a mere encounter [15]

Appearing yet nonappearing, the fruition—buddhahood—arises
If you think about that, it is the genuine siddhi
The connate of everything internal and external
resembles the nonconceptual river-stream yoga[219] [16]

This is not to be searched for anywhere else than the mind
Mental nonengagement[220] is the path of mahāmudrā
If realized without hoping for a fruition, it is mahāmudrā [17]

Realizing what was not realized is like the sky clear of clouds[221]
If realized, it is the true reality that is naturally empty,[222]
the connate of view, conduct, and fruition being inseparable
If their nondual nature[223] is realized, this is the supreme fruition [18]

This concludes "A Dohā Song on View, Meditation, Conduct, and Fruition" composed by master Saraha.[224] {49}

(108) A Song on True Reality That Is a Dohā Treasure

In the language of India: *Dohakoṣatattvagītikānāma*[225]
In the language of Tibet: *Do ha mdzod kyi de nyid kyi glu zhes bya ba*

I pay homage to Mañjuvajra

If examined, the entities of self and other do not exist—
they are similar to the dreams of a dumb fool
True reality is indeed very difficult to realize,
just like a fool who is playing a game of dice [1]

This is what Thagana has to declare:
true reality is hard to express through words
Not discarding thoughts of appearance and emptiness,
how could liberation possibly be attained? [2]

If it is not understood that body, speech, and mind
are all three equal as true reality in the expanse,
true reality is indeed very difficult to realize,
just like a fool who is playing a game of dice [3]

Things are difficult to express through words
Even if you are putting phenomena into words,
are they established through mere words, or what? [4]

Without realizing the true reality of mind,
there's no realization of everything being one
The ultimate is indeed very difficult to realize,
just like a fool who is playing a game of dice
This is what Thagana has to declare [5]

This concludes "A Song on True Reality That Is a Dohā Treasure" transmitted by master Kanari and composed by Thagana. {50}

(109) A Dohā Treasure Song on Conduct

In the language of India: *Cāryadohakoṣagītikānāma*[226]
In the language of Tibet: *Spyod pa'i do ha mdzod kyi glu zhes bya ba*

I pay homage to Śrī Heruka

Having produced tilakas with ruby sulphur,[227]
you then need to employ[228] khacārinī[229]
AHO! This play[230] overcomes the four māras [1]

Those who make an attempt to speak to yogīs
with their majestic splendor are unable to be
protected by Viṣṇu, Rudra,[231] or Brahmā [2]

AHO! If they were to converse with them,
they would be devoured by the lord of death
[Yogīs] are protected by the ferocious ḍākinīs' assembly [3]

AHO! What's the point for ignorant ḍākinīs
to scheme and look for their opportunity?
AHO! What's the point for animal ḍākinīs
to scheme and look for their opportunity? [4]

Hey, blazing lamps[232] are full of poison
Those who make an attempt to speak to yogīs

with their majestic splendor are unable to be
protected by Viṣṇu, Rudra, or Brahmā [5]

Like the blade of a razor or a sword,
just so are the feet of Kambala
The conduct of samaya is amazing [6]

Those who make an attempt to speak to yogīs
with their majestic splendor are unable to be
protected by Viṣṇu, Rudra, or Brahmā [7]

This concludes "A Dohā Treasure Song on Conduct" {51} *transmitted by master Kaṃkabala*[233] *and sung by master Kaṅkaṇa.* {52}

(110) The View in a Dohā Treasure Song of Connate Ecstasy

In the language of India: *Sahajānandadohakoṣagītikādṛṣṭināma*[234]
In the language of Tibet: *Lhan cig skyes dga'i do ha mdzod kyi glu'i lta ba zhes bya ba*

I pay homage to Śrī Heruka

Having folded[235] the tattered rag of dualistic engagement over his chest,
Bhadepa had been fallen asleep
How could any skilled thief[236]
carry away this tattered rag? [1]

When I had found sewing work—
passion, hatred, and ignorance pure in their place!
This sewing work cannot be interrupted
by any division or price numbers [2]

Now, this sewing work of mine
has become equal to the sky
When I had found sewing work—
passion, hatred, and ignorance pure in their place! [3]

Bhade went to search for sewing work
When I had searched everywhere,

I myself became unobservable as well
When I had found sewing work—
passion, hatred, and ignorance pure in their place! [4]

This concludes "The View in a Dohā Treasure Song of Connate Ecstasy" composed by master Bhandepa. {53}

(111) A Song on the View of the Sugatas

In the language of India: *Sugatadṛṣtigītikānāma*[237]
In the language of Tibet: *Bder gshegs kyi lta ba'i glu zhes bya ba*

I pay homage to the Three Jewels

To Buddha, dharma, and saṃgha,
I am paying homage in every respect
Free me from the suffering of arising and ceasing! [1]

This is what Dhamapa declares:
venerating the sugatas on the crown of my head,
I realize the ultimate true reality [2]

In the shrine room of the four brahmavihāras,
I go forth into homelessness right here
I realize the entirety of phenomena [3]

This is what Dhamapa declares:
venerating the sugatas on the crown of my head,
I realize the ultimate true reality [4]

How could Meru and the lushness
of greenery be gauged on a scale?

Likewise, could the views of all
outsiders be equal to this, or what? [5]

This is what Dhamapa declares:
venerating the sugatas on the crown of my head,
I realize the ultimate true reality [6][238]

Who would possibly pick up a trinket
while throwing away a precious gem?
If the Buddha, dharma, and saṃgha
are checked, I say they are the two realities [7] {54}

This is what Dhamapa declares:
venerating the sugatas on the crown of my head,
I realize the ultimate true reality [8]

This concludes "A Song on the View of the Sugatas" composed by master Dharmapa. {55}

(112) A Dohā Song on the True Reality of the Vāyus

In the language of India: *Vāyutattvadohagītikānāma*[239]
In the language of Tibet: *Rlung gi de nyid kyi do ha'i glu zhes bya ba*

I pay homage to nondual great bliss

In the vāyus' palace of the mobile and immobile,[240]
the vajra of mind resides on its throne
Within profound emptiness,
hey, my darling, you the connate,
may you please be my witness![241] [1]

If this existence is shaking violently,
how will we ever meet again?
Hey,[242] you beauty, you the connate,
may you please be my witness! [2]

If you are staying by my side,
how would I search elsewhere?
For one who wishes to be pulled out
from a ship that has already sunk,
hey, my darling, you the connate,
may you please be my witness! [3]

If this existence is shaking violently,
how will we ever meet again?
Even if I were to kill the assemblies
of the five families for your sake, [4]

I would not see your face
for even a single instant
Hey, my darling, you the connate,
may you please be my witness! [5]

If this existence is shaking violently, {56}
how will we ever meet again?
Hey, you beauty, you the connate,
may you please be my witness! [6]

It is for your sake that I need
mudrā, without the slightest
thinking of brahmans of bad family
Hey, my darling, you the connate,
may you please be my witness! [7]

If this existence is shaking violently,
how will we ever meet again?
From him with a ship in the ocean,
the kāpālika[243] who is Kaṇha, [8]

Mahi has received instructions
and severed the fetters of existence
Hey, you beauty, you the connate,
may you please be my witness! [9]

This concludes "A Dohā Song on the True Reality of the Vāyus" composed by master Mahipa. {57}

(113) A Song on the Four Vajras

In the language of India: *Caturvajragītikānāma*[244]
In the language of Tibet: *Rdo rje bzhi'i glu zhes bya ba*

I pay homage to the glorious Buddha.

Do not cultivate a dissonant mindset!
Do not cling to true reality's suchness!
Do not meditate with any hope for fruition!
Familiarize with nonreferential mahāmudrā![245] [1]

If there is defilement and no resting,
that is not the glorious Mahāyāna
Do not meditate with any hope for fruition!
Familiarize with nonreferential mahāmudrā! [2]

Skandhas and dhātus are mahāmudrā
The wheel of samaya has its nature
Do not meditate with any hope for fruition!
Familiarize with nonreferential mahāmudrā! [3]

This is the victor of nondual qualities,
the yogī of nondual qualities declares
Do not meditate with any hope for fruition!
Familiarize with nonreferential mahāmudrā! [4]

This concludes "A Song of Amarasiṃha"[246] *composed by Avadhūta Advayavajra, who was born in the land of Śāri.* {58}

(114) A Song by Guru Maitrīpa

There is no bondage through entities that neither arise nor cease
They appear to the deluded in the three realms without freedom
Their root, mind as such, has the nature of all kinds of delusion
If beginningless delusion's nature is scrutinized, it is not found [1]

What is the seeing that all entities are primordially unborn?
Think about who would be born, cease, and be bound!
Their root, mind as such, has the nature of all kinds of delusion
If the nature of beginningless delusion is scrutinized, it is not found [2]

The master says that mind resembles the stainless sky
It is the nature of all three existences that are of this kind
Their root, mind as such, has the nature of all kinds of delusion
If the nature of beginningless delusion is scrutinized, it is not found [3]

The thought-free nature is accomplished through self-aware experience
Why would the luminous nature be dulled down through delusion?
Their root, mind as such, has the nature of all kinds of delusion
If the nature of beginningless delusion is scrutinized, it is not found [4]

This concludes "A Song by Guru Maitrīpa."[247] {59}

(115)–(116) Two Songs by Saraha

I pay homage to the Buddha

The whole world talks about the profound, the profound,
but there are just a few who delight in the unborn
Hey, since the profundity of the mind is hard to get,
if the connate is scrutinized, it is simply not there [1]

The nonabiding mind is let be in nonreferentiality
Through the fire of yoga, all entities are burned up
Hey, since the profundity of the mind is hard to get,
if the connate is scrutinized, it is simply not there [2]

Desire for yoga cannot be taught by the guru
Absorb the unsurpassed blessing of the guru!
Hey, since the profundity of the mind is hard to get,
if the connate is scrutinized, it is simply not there [3]

If you have the desire to search for glorious great bliss,
wishing to seek a middle, you fall blindly down the well
Hey, since the profundity of the mind is hard to get,
if the connate is scrutinized, it is simply not there [4]

This concludes "A Song by Sarahapa."[248]

I pay homage to the Buddha

Intertwined is the nature of emptiness and compassion
Emptiness exists inseparably without interruption {60}
I can so clearly see the empty yoginī,
milking, milking, and drinking the sky [1]

Not seeing the sky uniting with the sky,
nor dwelling on the plane of saṃsāric bondage
I can so clearly see the empty yoginī,
milking, milking, and drinking the sky [2]

Such a yoginī moved out of her home that is her root
The great taste of compassion is without any stain
I can so clearly see the empty yoginī,
milking, milking, and drinking the sky [3]

Why should anybody else do what Saraha says?
Wandering day and night to milk the sky
I can so clearly see the empty yoginī,
milking, milking, and drinking the sky [4]

This concludes "A Song by Saraha."[249] {61}

(117) A Vajra Song by Virūkara

I pay homage to the Buddha

Once the vajrayogī has seized his arrow,[250]
knowing how to point out phenomena,
I am shooting the arrow of the connate
without a target, not even a single thing to hit [1]

Please listen to this talk on the connate!
It's the arrow uniting with the being of all
I am shooting the arrow of the connate
without a target, not even a single thing to hit [2]

There exists no feeling apart from those
"This is through that"[251] became nondual
I am shooting the arrow of the connate
without a target, not even a single thing to hit [3]

No twenty cowries due as wages—
that kind of servant is Virūkara
I am shooting the arrow of the connate
without a target, not even a single thing to hit [4]

This concludes "A Vajra Song by Virūkara."[252] {62}

(118) A Song by Kāṇhapa

I pay homage to the Buddha

Don't view maṇḍalas of colored sand, vases, vajras, and the like
as freedom—they are the means for the skandhas to have their fill![253]
This is what Kanapa declares—who would come up with such stuff?
Since its entirety consists of delusion, I proclaim it to be deceiving

This concludes "A Song by Kāṇhapa."[254] {63}

(119)–(121) Songs of Guru Dhiṣṭijñāna

I pay homage to the Buddha

Hey, brahman person with matted hair, Saṅghawa,
have belief in the Buddha as well as wisdom!
The mind of such a person is so full of joy,
the stainless jewel of everything mobile and immobile [1]

You bee with your restless nature, meditate!
Persevere in the pith instructions of the perfect guru!
The mind of such a person is so full of joy,
the stainless jewel of everything mobile and immobile [2]

You unborn bee with your restless nature
are as nonexistent as a woman in a dream
The mind of such a person is so full of joy,
the stainless jewel of everything mobile and immobile [3]

If that bee with its restless nature is understood,
the siddhi of a buddha is accomplished in this life
The mind of such a person is so full of joy,
the stainless jewel of everything mobile and immobile [4]

This concludes "A Vajra Song from the Mouth of the Venerable Guru Dhiṣṭijñāna, Who Realized the Actuality of Nonabiding."[255]

I pay homage to the Buddha

With nothing corresponding to any ways of looking being seen, {64}
it is nothing but delusion, the deception of what does not exist
I declare this to be established inconceivably, Heruka[256]
Through a weary[257] mind, natural form is not known [1]

Letting be within whatever pops up in whichever way,
how[258] could the spear of desire be piercing itself?
I declare this to be established inconceivably, Heruka
Through a weary mind, natural form is not known [2]

The connate is the body of space—the body of the sugata heart
The nondual is dual—the mind of emptiness and compassion
I declare this to be established inconceivably, Heruka
Through a weary mind, natural form is not known [3]

It is unborn, unceasing, and without conditions
If its nature is realized, the root mind is known
I declare this to be established inconceivably, Heruka
Through a weary mind, natural form is not known [4]

This concludes "A Song from the Mouth of the Guru Dhiṣṭijñāna."[259]

I pay homage to the Buddha

AHO! The sentient beings of the three realms,
tightly bound by the chains of their thoughts
in the swamp[260] of the misery of saṃsāra,
they keep roaming all ten directions [1]

AHO! The sugatas of the three realms
are the great freedom that is primordial
With their pure realm of Sukhāvatī,
they show the play of buddhahood [2]

AHO! The path of thoughts and suffering
is without a time of traveling, like a lunatic[261]
Desire without bliss is nothing but suffering—
stagger into the actuality of equality! [3]

AHO! The lack of any path is the supreme path
Being effortless just like a bird in the sky, {65}
without any hope or fear, this is mahāmudrā,
incorruptible under the sway of flaws or qualities [4]

AHO! [Even] through searching it for three
incalculable eons, true reality will not be found,
just like a halfwit searching for the end of the sky
What is called "buddhahood" is impossible to find [5]

AHO! It is in just one single instant that
the fruition, never separate, is found within yourself
It is the greatly powerful wisdom of self-awareness
that is the chief among all the mighty in the world [6]

This concludes [this song].[262] {66}

(122) A Song by Karṇari

The guru is the one who milks a cow in the sky
The calf that drinks it is your own mind as such
Kanapa, who is uninterruptedly milking the sky,
offers it up to the assembly of joined yogīs[263] [1]

Who's the one to take the milking pail? Māmakī!
The milking pail is the connate without any stain
Kanapa, who is uninterruptedly milking the sky,
offers it up to the assembly of joined yogīs [2]

Milking and milking the sky, the pail is filled and set down
It cannot be grasped at all; thus, the five bulls
Kanapa, who is uninterruptedly milking the sky,
offers it up to the assembly of joined yogīs [3]

One who milks a cow in the sky is not seen here
How come your inside is filled with water, Kalipa?
Kanapa, who is uninterruptedly milking the sky,
offers it up to the assembly of joined yogīs [4]

This concludes "A Song by Karṇaripa."[264] {67}

(123) A Song by Mātṛceṭa

I pay homage to the Buddha

A single flower blossoms with all kinds of colors
It bursts into open bloom on trees that are empty
This powerful incomparable flower is flourishing
Please, just smell this flower that is so priceless! [1]

It is without any stalk, root, branches, or leaves
Look! Eating,[265] lying, and walking are good times
This powerful incomparable flower is flourishing
Please, just smell this flower that is so priceless! [2]

The one skillful in cutting its anthers is the illusionist,
who offers them to Kuliśeśvara, the dharmadhātu
This powerful incomparable flower is flourishing
Please, just smell this flower that is so priceless! [3]

Supreme ecstasy and cessational ecstasy scrutinized, they're gone
Devote yourself to prostrating at the feet of the perfect guru!
This powerful incomparable flower is flourishing
Please, just smell this flower that is so priceless! [4]

This concludes "A Song by Mātṛiceṭa."[266] {68}

(124)–(125) Two Songs of Bada

I pay homage to the Buddha

You, don't entertain any likes or dislikes
about virtuous or nonvirtuous karmas
of the past, the present, or the future!
The wisdom that is fully itself is like a lion [1]

Profound dharmatā is the object of yoga
Meditation and nonmeditation are bodhicitta
You, don't try to possess or not possess them!
The wisdom that is fully itself is like a lion [2]

You, don't try to conform or not conform
with the avenues of conduct[267] of buddhas
and sentient beings being a certain way!
The wisdom that is fully itself is like a lion [3]

Happiness and suffering are resultant phenomena
You, do not give yourself over to any hope or fear
that has to do with either saṃsāra or nirvāṇa!
The wisdom that is fully itself is like a lion [4]

This concludes this song.[268]

I'm hanging out, without death or nondeath,
not a single matter to engage in my mind
Since Kana's sword has cut through the noose,[269]
now I do not entertain any hopes, Bada says [1]

When you place your feet on the bows of two boats,
your body keels over and suffering arises in your mind[270]
Since Kana's sword has cut through the noose, {69}
now I do not entertain any hopes, Bada says [2]

Even if some people surrounded its roots with a well,
two kinds of fruits will not grow on a single tree
Since Kana's sword has cut through the noose,
now I do not entertain any hopes, Bada says [3]

How slothful have I become about the siddhis
of eye lotion, pill, extracting the essence, and feet![271]
Since Kana's sword has cut through the noose,
now I do not entertain any hopes, Bada says [4]

This concludes [this song].[272] {70}

(126) A Song by Ācārya Vīravairocana

I pay homage to the Buddha

Hey, if you wish to view the entirety of all lands,
look at them from the surface of the great mountain!
If aware of your own mind, the land of phenomena's
being unborn and unceasing,[273] that is Meru's peak[274] [1]

If you wish to drink all waters,
drink the waters of the ocean!
Unborn bodhicitta's waters, though,
are the great ocean without middle or end [2]

If you wish to burn everything mobile and immobile,
ignite the huge fire of the time of destruction![275]
Everything mobile and immobile is thinking,
while effortless wisdom is the fire of the mind [3]

If you wish for a happy place without fear,
remain in a place that is greatly secluded!
The happy place of saṃsāra's utter purity
is the great secludedness of bodhicitta [4]

This concludes "A Song by Ācārya Vīravairocana."[276] {71}

(127) A Song by Paṇḍita Nāropa

I pay homage to the Buddha

This natural Nairātmyā
I made into a halo of fire[277]
By lacking attachment,
the afflictions are pacified [1]

Birth and death are existence
I relinquish their delusions
She who bestows great bliss
I adopt—this is not delusion [2]

She has neither color nor shape,
nor is she seen to have any extent
By virtue of being without desire,
I have no desire for pride to arise [3]

At the time when Nairātmyā
is residing here in my heart
I do not see any division there
between me and all others [4]

No coming and no going,
no abiding anywhere at all

Like the nature of the sky,
shining in utter lucidity [5]

Without exception, the ecstatic
yogīs of the great Sage[278]
thus speak of the lack of a self
as this Meli[279] Nairātmyā [6]

This concludes "A Song by Paṇḍita Nāropa."[280] {72}

(128) A Song by Lūhipa

I pay homage to the Buddha

Since beings are tormented by afflictions, you are the deity who travels the earth
Though such is the case, you do not shun the body of the consort of great bliss
Hey hey, you are filled with passion for the consort beyond compare
Not separated from her for innumerable eons, you are the world's chief deity [1]

You are far from accepting the utterly amazing consort of Māra
You are the deity of supreme form more distinguished than others
Hey hey, you are filled with passion for the consort beyond compare
Not separated from her for innumerable eons, you are the world's chief deity [2]

You surround many hundreds of beings who are struck by diseases
As the deity who grants them bliss, you are the mirror of the three realms
Hey hey, you are filled with passion for the consort beyond compare

Not separated from her for innumerable eons, you are the world's chief deity [3]

You are Matirohaṇa,[281] moved by[282] the bliss that is utterly unequaled,
the deity Khasarpaṇa[283] who is endowed with a victor's many qualities
Hey hey, you are filled with passion for the consort beyond compare
Not separated from her for innumerable eons, you are the world's chief deity [4]

This concludes "A Song by Lūhipa."[284] {73}

(129) A Song by Ḍombipa

I pay homage to the Buddha

In the abundance of illusory forests here and there,
Ḍombi the fool is wandering around to kill deer
I see where the deer of wrong views is heading
Ḍombi shoots sharp arrows, entering right inside [1]

Five arrows I have, loosing them in a straight shot
Ḍombi remains holding the drawn bow string
I see where the deer of wrong views is heading
Ḍombi shoots sharp arrows, entering right inside [2]

With neither bow, nor string, nor reed, nor tip
Ḍombi kills for sure without any shade of doubt
I see where the deer of wrong views is heading
Ḍombi shoots sharp arrows, entering right inside [3]

The five victor families serving as crown ornament,[285]
I have brought the deer I killed right back to life
I see where the deer of wrong views is heading
Ḍombi shoots sharp arrows, entering right inside [4]

This concludes "A Song by Ḍombipa."[286] {74}

(130) A Song by Virūpa

I pay homage to the Buddha

Though the entire world is blabbing that I am bad, so bad,
I possess profound stainless qualities to be cherished
When an utpala[287] forms in water, it is untouched by water
The one who creates many such illusions is Virūpa [1]

Be it marketplaces,[288] villages, or the banks of a river,
wherever I go, my body lies down, but they don't understand
When an utpala forms in water, it is untouched by water
The one who creates many such illusions is Virūpa [2]

That the world says I am bad is simply a lie
My anger has reversed the flow of the Ganges
When an utpala forms in water, it is untouched by water
The one who creates many such illusions is Virūpa [3]

Holding the sun as a pawn, I kept drinking beer
I destroyed[289] Aṇḍa,[290] crushing Bhīmeśvara[291]
When an utpala forms in water, it is untouched by water
The one who creates many such illusions is Virūpa [4]

This concludes "A Song by Virūpa."[292] {75}

(131) A Song by Lavapa

I pay homage to the Buddha

Look! When there is no arising and no abiding,
this is not different from connate great bliss
Having fully understood the nature of true reality,[293]
tell me how that could be disagreeable! [1]

Thus, think about what at that time could bind
the three realms as well as the five sugatas!
Having fully understood the nature of true reality,
tell me how that could be disagreeable! [2]

The basic nature of all this is not found but lost
At that point, the nature of space does not exist[294]
Having fully understood the nature of true reality,
tell me how that could be disagreeable! [3]

Don't make yourself stupid! Why would you tie up
an empty fist in lies with the knot of nonduality?[295]
Having fully understood the nature of true reality,
tell me how that could be disagreeable! [4]

This concludes "A Song by Lavapa."[296] {76}

(132) A Song by Mahāsukhatā

Just as sesame oil pervades sesame seeds,
so the three realms are filled with Mañjuśrī's body
Knowing that, through cultivating the effortless yoga,
sing this dharma song of genuine great bliss! [1]

The queen of all sugatas who is utterly nameless
has all kinds of forms and embodies compassion
If you are together with her, all suffering is dispelled
Sing this dharma song of genuine great bliss! [2]

Just as the characteristic of space is space,
so is the dharmatā of the mind, the guru says
Unaware of this unsurpassable actuality, you cannot meditate
Sing this dharma song of genuine great bliss! [3]

By relying on the scriptures and the pith instructions,
just as the sun, a sun crystal, and cotton wool come together,
the fire of self-aware wisdom will blaze forth
Sing this dharma song of genuine great bliss! [4]

The dharma in texts and the wealth lying in the hands of others
are not the dharma or wealth—they're not there when you need them
Leap into the great wealth of the noble ones—your own mind!
Sing this dharma song of genuine great bliss! [5]

In all situations of happiness as well as suffering, {77}
devote yourself day and night to Mañjuśrī, the guide of all,
the true reality that is like a wish-fulfilling jewel, bodhicitta!
Sing this dharma song of genuine great bliss! [6]

This concludes "A Song by Mahāsukhatā."[297] {78}

(133) A Song by the Yogī Prasara

I pay homage to the glorious Buddha

Here goes my utterly amazing discourse:
I'm like someone asleep after having sold an elephant
Those who have wealth employ watchmen at night[298]
I am the all-pervasive bold one, Prasara[299] [1]

I don't ask questions about dharma or nondharma
The nature that is self-arising is immovable
I'm like someone asleep after having sold an elephant
Those who have wealth employ watchmen at night
I am the all-pervasive bold one, Prasara [2]

Through the discerning knowledge of the yogī Maitri,[300]
I'm free of all flaws accrued since beginningless time
Those who have wealth employ watchmen at night
I am the all-pervasive bold one, Prasara [3]

This concludes "A Song by the Yogī Prasara."[301] {79}

(134) A Song by Nāgārjuna

Having the character of compassion dwelling in emptiness,
the accumulations of means and prajñā of those residing in pure realms
should be understood as being similar to a reflection
Through compassion's taste, drop disputes about differences! [1]

There, eat the flesh of the objects of the seeming!
Drink the beer of emptiness that is utterly pure!
Teach this actuality to living beings fortunate enough,
but keep it very secret from those lacking such fortune! [2]

Having moisturized the inner and the outer with liberation's ointment,
enjoy the pleasures of objects in just the way your heart desires!
You should not engage with either a pure or an impure mind
in phenomena that come toward and depart from each other [3]

Adorned[302] by the garland of bodhicitta,
you should enter into the secret maṇḍala
With means and prajñā uniting incessantly,
do not abandon the connate Ḍombinī![303] [4]

This concludes "A Song by Master Nāgārjuna.[304] {80}

(135)–(136) Two Dharma Songs by Dīpaṃkaraśrījñāna

I pay homage to the Buddha

If you know the fear of the destructive thieves of thoughts,
be a night watchman to guard the great wealth of discipline!
Hey, don't be lazy, act as the night watchman of the mind!
Due to the sleep of ignorance, the night of saṃsāra is long [1]

Hey, don't be lazy, act as the night watchman of the mind!
If you fall asleep, those thieves will enter your home
and will steal the great wealth of your discipline
Without the wealth of discipline, there is no samādhi
When this is missing, the sun will not shine [2]

Familiarizing with the sun of true reality, be a watchman!
Don't create any other trifling wealth for even an instant!
At that time, the sun of true reality will shine forth
Thus, at that point, this becomes the dawn of saṃsāra
Hey, don't be lazy, act as the night watchman of the mind! [3]

This concludes a dharma song by Dīpaṃkaraśrījñāna.[305]

Namo Buddhāya

Na—there is neither birth nor death,
neither form nor possessing form
This is what is thus expressed by *na* [1]

It's what destroys the ignorance about a self,
grants the bliss of the sole liberation, {81}
and crushes[306] māras, foes, and afflictions
This is what is thus expressed by *mo* [2]

Buddhahood means having gone beyond
This buddhahood is what benefits beings
Buddhahood is excellent, pure, and unafflicted
This is what is thus expressed by *bud* [3]

Relinquished are all dharmas held
within the genuine dharmadhātu
The supreme dharma is dharmatā
This is what is expressed by *dhā* [4]

Just as abiding, so is perishing
Just as perishing, so is abiding
Just as speaking, so is acting
This is what is expressed by *ya* [5]

Through the great dynamic energy of vajra skull garland's awareness,
this is for the sake of liberating all beings of excellent fortune
Uniting with the women of threefold existence at the same time,
having killed the men of the three realms in a single instant,
having burned the minds of threefold existence, such as temples, [6]

and having gathered all sense pleasures without exception,
I am dwelling within the center of the cloudless sky
Staring with the two wide-open eyes of great hatred,
the sphere without any reference points is to be beheld![307] [7] {82}

This concludes a dharma song by Dīpaṃkaraśrījñāna.

(137) The View in a Conduct Song Dohā

In the language of India: *Dohacaryāgītikādṛṣṭināma*[308]
In the language of Tibet: *Do ha spyod pa'i glu'i lta ba zhes bya ba*

I pay homage to the vajraḍākinī

Similar to lunatics are those yogīs
who cling to a peacock's spread-out parasol
and who hold on to all kinds of attires
Lūhi declares that there is no place
for the victor's path in the prideful
It is accomplished by guarding the body's tailoring[309] [1]

Having taken many granted empowerments,
you are deceived in a meaningless manner
If empowerments do not turn into realization,[310]
your time will certainly arrive some day[311]
Lūhi declares that there is no place
for the victor's path in the prideful
It is accomplished by guarding the body's tailoring [2]

Through sleep, beer, quarrels, and union,
how could yoga possibly be accomplished?
If it's prevented, the noose of existence binds you
Lūhi declares that there is no place

for the victor's path in the prideful
It is accomplished by guarding the body's tailoring [3]

When you are acting like a clay bowl
or a golden spoon in a marketplace,[312] {83}
you will encounter the buddhas
Lūhi declares that there is no place
for the victor's path in the prideful
It is accomplished by guarding the body's tailoring [4]

This concludes "The View in a Conduct Song Dohā" transmitted by master Lūhipa and sung by master Kirapāla. {84}

(138) The View of Emptiness

In the language of India: *Śūnyatādṛṣṭināma*[313]
In the language of Tibet: *Stong pa nyid kyi lta ba zhes bya ba*

I pay homage to Avalokiteśvara

With the hoe of mind, plow the expanse
of the sky for the seed of dharmatā![314]
Embraced by the young lady of no-self,
rest in the state of her waking you up!
Abandon it, cast it off—the self[315] is ignorant! [1]

Hey, all bondage without exception
is enjoyed by Śavari as great bliss
Embraced by the queen of emptiness,
hey, body, speech, and mind are matured [2]

By examining all the time,[316]
Śavari became intoxicated
In all kinds of ecstasy,
Śavari has fallen asleep,
fallen asleep in the sky's expanse [3]

Hey, I declare that my true reality
is the seed that is equal to the sky

The fruition is the morning star's dawning in the sky
Abandon it, cast it off—the self is ignorant! [4]

I killed the elephant of bondage by existence,
made oblations with[317] my five senses,
and relinquished the entirety of suffering
Abandon it, cast it off—the self is ignorant! [5] {85}

Without ever sleeping during day or night,
act as the watchman of your own mind
Then, oh you men and women,
go into solitude alone and stay there! [6]

Speaking with[318] the world's chief protector,[319]
abandon it, cast it off—the self is ignorant!
Embraced by the queen of emptiness,
Śavari remains resting in great bliss [7]

This concludes "The View of Emptiness" sung by master Śavaripa. {86}

(139) The View of Being Free of the Duality of Happiness and Suffering

In the language of India: *Sukhaduḥkhadvayaparityāgadṛṣṭināma*[320]
In the language of Tibet: *Bde sdug gnyis bral gyi lta ba zhes bya ba*

I pay homage to mother Prajñāpāramitā

What is beyond meditation cannot be practiced
Paying homage to the gurus of the siddhas
who have the character of being protectors,
I explain the view of being free of duality [1]

Since the nature cannot be meditated on,
yoga is completely beyond meditation
As it is free of both being and nonbeing,
the seeming is not established at all [2]

Not to be meditated on as being or nonbeing,
the inseparable nature is beyond any cause,
being natural wisdom at any and all times[321]
This is the nondual ecstasy of unity [3]

Mindlessness lacking mindfulness
constitutes the delusion of yogīs
As for the intention of other yogīs
about the unity of prajñā and means,

so as to cultivate the true state's[322] means,
a means that's not accomplished in the instant
of thought-free prajñā won't be accomplished
Not seeing this does not represent meditation [4]

If someone is familiarizing with the means,
due to possessing the guru's instructions
and with the means of the perfect mudrā, {87}
the nectar of all wisdom that is subtle
and naturally flowing rains down [5]

Within the instant of illustrating luminosity,
the intelligent cultivate it with a stable mind
Not accomplished by thinking, it's free of thought [6]

As in the example of a traveler visiting a country,
to arrive step by step through directing the mind
toward the dharmakāya's characteristics is not true reality
By being without characteristics, just as before,
great bliss free of thoughts is accomplished [7]

All the kinds of awareness are self-awareness
Something else could not be aware of them
This realized, day and night are equal as great bliss [8]

Blissful[323] are the yogīs who do not abide anywhere
and have relinquished duality and nonduality
This is the realization of prajñāpāramitā [9]

To realize that constitutes the view of no-self
The yogī free of the duality of happiness and suffering
is the yogī Śāntipa who is free of such duality
By realizing this, he has attained mahāmudrā [10]

This concludes "The View of Being Free of the Duality of Happiness and Suffering" composed by master Śāntipa. {88}

(140) The View of Nonconnection

In the language of India: *Asaṃbandhadṛṣṭināma*[324]
In the language of Tibet: *'Brel med kyi lta ba zhes bya ba*

I pay homage to the deity of the wisdom of nonconnection and discontinuation

As for the convention of perishing and support,
if something is a temporary support, it cannot perish,
so what's the point of perishing and support?
Consequently, there exists no positing
in terms of what is perishing and a support[325]
This is to be known as the assessing valid cognition [1]

In terms of an example of distinguishing
what entails and what is entailed,
the sun is to be known as "what entails"
and its light rays as "the entailed" [2]

For example, butter that is blended
with milk does not exist at first
Entailer and entailed are not different,[326]
nor do they possess any connection[327] [3]

What is the cause of fire and
how does a result arise from it?
The definition of fire is that which burns
This is referred to as "what entails"
and the entailed is seen to be smoke [4]

It is said that the father is the Buddha (what entails),
while the son is the genuine dharma (the entailed)
Now, take the example of a lamp[328] inside a vase—
it illuminates what is inside but not the outside [5]

Likewise, {89} the Buddha is the illuminator[329]
How could the dharma be the illuminator?
At first, [there] is neither dharma nor Buddha
How could what is unborn be connected?[330] [6]

[From] causes, results that are concordant arise
It is said, without causes, there are no[331] results
How are what entails and entailed established?
The perishing support of that which is mobile
and immobile is [established] by the elements,
but all four elements themselves are not established [7]

How is it that a tree exists as what entails
and its branches and roots as the entailed?
The names and name-bearers of the thoughts
of[332] "I" and "mine" arise from discursiveness
"Is the name-bearer or the name the first?"
Thus, with something coming to an end,
what it entails likewise comes to an end [8]

It is due to the arising in dependence
that there is ceasing in dependence
That childish beings act as they speak
is due to arising from a single factor[333]
If the entailed ceases, there is no contradiction

Thus, this is to be understood as
worldly assessing valid cognition [9]

Just as the horns of a rabbit
do not exist if examined,
so phenomena do not exist
while they are examined[334] [10]

Just as with the horns of a cow,
a meeting between east and west
will likewise not be perceived [11]

As in these examples, so are those with the six views,[335]
inner and outer tīrthikas, the liṅgins,[336]
those who are the inner Buddhist śrāvakas,
the Atis,[337] the Nirgranthas, those with tenets,
the Vaiṣṇavas, and those with the brahman thread [12]

The pair of inner and outer is not established
and they do not have any connection:
this is the intention of the Buddha, {90}
but the persons who do not possess it
are not to be called "supramundane" [13]

By virtue of examining in that regard,
there is no person as what is entailed,
that is, a person who is me or another
Higher and miserable realms (the activities)
and mind (the entailed) are seen as two,
just like mundane and supramundane [14]

Saṃsāra is due to the clinging to a self,
but it is free of that and is sugatahood:
free of desire, hatred, and ignorance,
with their flow severed, it is nirvāṇa [15]

Thus, the statement that buddhahood
is due to realization is unreasonable
Saṃsāra does not represent misery,
and nirvāṇa is without any misery [16]

They are awareness and unawareness
Thoughts[338] are what bind temporarily,
while nonthought is taught to be freedom
For the realized,[339] there is no difference [17]

As for coming and going, there is no convention
of being close to or far away from awakening
Those with the darkness of the afflictions purified
do not see such a thing, nor does it exist for them
This is what the Buddha said in the scriptures [18]

Just as hungry ghosts see the ocean
without beginning and end to be dry,
likewise, for those who are scorched
by ignorance's darkness, buddhahood
does not exist, nor do they see it [19]

The scriptures of great perfection declare
that basic[340] or uncontrived dharmatā
is what entails, while the six realms
that arise from it are the entailed[341] [20]

In phenomena that constitute a little bit of virtue,
buddhahood is not achieved, so what's their point?
For example, a blazing jewel that is placed
in the palm of a person who is blind {91}
is not seen, so what's the point of that? [21]

As far as the inner tīrthikas are concerned,
luminous self-awareness is what entails,
while cognizance—the entailed—is mind [22]

Take the example of milk blended
with water in the same container,
and geese who drink the milk
while leaving behind the water [23]

Likewise, wisdom that is mixed with
afflictions is in the same container
Thus, yogīs drink awareness,
leaving unawareness behind
It is the inner tīrthikas
who proclaim this view[342] [24]

As far as the answer to that is concerned,
the Buddha's scriptures declare this:
There is neither an agent nor an object
Without these two, there is no entailed
Without these three, how is connection established? [25]

If the external were really existent,
the internal would have a real nature
What is realized does not exist
in outer referents—nothing exists,
neither self-known nor by others
Hence, the three realms are unconnected [26]

In that way, awareness and entities
do not possess any characteristics
Like nonentities, entities are not known [27]

That which is unborn is lacking a self
and what lacks a self does not take birth
This is not reasonable as the seeming
If it were reasonable, the ultimate would not exist [28]

Without a cause to begin, arising is absent
Where there is no result, there is no arising

Since it neither arises from itself nor from others,
nor from both, it is not the seeming [29]

Lucid[343] self-awareness is what entails,
and, as mere cognizance, the three realms
and mind's desire {92} are the entailed [30]

Being explained in terms of this,
as far as the śrāvakas are concerned,
the ālaya consciousness[344] is what entails,
while the eighty-four thousand afflictions
and thoughts are the entailed [31]

For example, the sky is what entails,
whereas the sun as well as the moon,
clouds, lightning, water, and so on
are its ten incessant qualities entailed [32]

These kinds of examples are two, known
as the valid cognition assessing conventions
Now, with regard to the valid cognition
that is the means to assess the ultimate,
it's both the example and its meaning above
that represent the intention of Kambala [33]

As per what scriptures establishing the external say,
the Buddha as well as the siddhas clearly
discuss this through[345] experience and reasoning [34]

Among these, in terms of the scriptures,
it is stated there is no phenomenal identity,
the entirety of the three realms is empty,
and everything conditioned is not permanent [35]

These are the thoughts of mind as such,
and these very thoughts are saṃsāra
That which is thought-free is freedom [36]

Desire, hatred, as well as pride,
and furthermore the phenomena
of saṃsāra, nirvāṇa, and so forth,
as long as childish beings discuss them,
are to be understood as mind's thoughts
There isn't any difference at all
between good and bad thoughts [37]

For example, with regard to great trees,
there exists no difference for fire—
it burns down whatever it touches
Sandalwood, camphor, and so on
are burned alike by a blazing fire [38]

Hence, {93} yogīs who understand the view
relinquish even the slightest thoughts
Examined by reasoning, they are unestablished
There is no attachment to sense objects [39]

Inner and outer do not exist in the mind,
not abiding in others nor in yourself
For example, for those without realization,
lightning [seems to] arise from clouds
In the same way, hatred, pride, as well as
[other] afflictions and such arise from mind [40]

It is the very self that is empty of a self
The sense faculties too lack any support
Without them, the mind does not exist,
so how could a connection with matter be established?
Any connection between what entails

and the entailed means saying too much—
not even a single instant can be established [41]

As far as experience is concerned,
love and compassion are explained
in brief through not being established [42]

At the time when hatred arises
in its very first moment,
there is not even the name of love
At the time when love arises,
the darkness of hatred is no more [43]

Due to that, examination is threefold:
know that they arise from the mind;
ultimately, as the scriptures declare,
mind as such does not exist [either];
you sons or daughters of noble family,
mind as such is like an illusion or a dream [44]

The meaning of this is just as follows:
for example, it may be as one and as many
that the native nature of mind as such[346] is seen
These are the magical creations of mind as such
Neither mind as such nor discursiveness exist [45]

Take the example of a star's qualities—
if a blanket exists, its qualities exist,
but without it, its qualities do not exist
One and many {94} are not reasonable
This blanket does not exist at all [46]

Thus, in terms of such examples,
there is no mind as such, and love,
compassion, equanimity, joy,
and so on do not exist either [47]

Now, in terms of reasoning,
is the mindstream[347] one or different?
If the mindstream were one,
it would not be reasonable for love
to arise later once hatred arose first [48]

But does hatred arise later
from some previous love,
or are those three simultaneous,
or is this the result of karma? [49]

Connection occurs in impermanent phenomena[348]
For example, from the seeds of cotton wool,
how could cotton wool arise as being red?
In the same way, the skandhas that are other
than those that arise in just a single instant
are being connected through karma [50]

In line with rejecting such being reasonable,[349]
it is thus reasonable that there is a connection
for each one at just its very own time[350]
At the time of love, [there is only] love;
that hatred would arise at [love's] own time
is very flawed and thus unreasonable [51]

The karma committed by Devadatta
has no connection with that of Yajña
Likewise, there exists no connection
whatsoever between hatred and love
To think otherwise is unreasonable [52]

"How is it that this is unreasonable?"
It is because there exists no connection
between the types of Devadatta and Yajña
This is similar to the examples of kimpāka[351]
and such versus barley and rice grains [53]

Accordingly, just like[352] arisen skandhas,
the skandhas of others have no connection
Just so, {95} it is unreasonable for there to be
any connection between hatred and love [54]

"If mind as such is a single continuum,
it is reasonable that there is connection"
Just as in the example of heat and cold,
this is a case of being mutually exclusive [55]

If it were reasonable to say that
previous love is hatred's cause,[353]
a hot sensation of touch could arise
from a cold sensation of touch [56]

If you say its cause is something else,
the first moment's state is not[354] established
Except for the body and the mind,
there exists nothing further at all [57]

"Causes" cannot be refuted anywhere at all,
but if you say that they are simultaneous,
this represents a statement that is untenable
Beings do not maintain two mindstreams—
This is clear from experience and scripture [58]

The reasoning for that runs as follows:
the skandhas, the dhātus, and the āyatanas,
being immobile, pervasive, and mobile,
do not have the nature[355] of lacking those [59]

The self, the puruṣa, the skandhas, and such
that are propounded by the tīrthikas
do not exist as anything else devoid of mind
The diversity of those is impermanent;
others say that they are permanent [60]

The continua of love, compassion, and such
are interrupted in what arises with parts
Thus, a beginning or an end are unobservable
If they were permanent, this is flawed—
seed and sprout would be simultaneous [61]

Hence, in terms of the valid cognition
that is the means to assess the ultimate,
it is declared that not even an instant
of a perishing support, what entails,
the entailed, example, meaning, cause,
result, connection, and so on is established [62] {96}

As for the reasoning of not being established,
first, a connection between the pair
of fire and smoke is not established
The characteristics of burning and brightness
are not reasonable as the darkness in smoke [63]

If it were reasonable, lacking its brightness,[356]
such a fire would come to accrue[357] a flaw
If exactly that which is smoke were fire,[358]
it would have the flaw of untenable[359] brightness [64]

Without a cause to kindle it, there is no fire
It is not the case that fire is present in wood
For that reason, there exists no connection
Alternatively speaking, the connection of
same identity as well as that of causality
do not have any existence at all either [65]

If a connection of same identity did exist,
it would entail the flaw of mutual exclusiveness
This is the flaw of it following that just as fire
is what illuminates, so smoke would be too [66]

If a connection of causality did exist,
it would entail the flaws of it following
that just as fire burns, smoke burns too,
and that similar to smoke being black,
fire would likewise be black [67]

Therefore, there exists no connection
This is as in the example of there being
no connection between a blanket and yarn [68]

What is not the blanket is the yarn;
what is the yarn is not the blanket
What is the blanket is not the thread—
how could the thread be the blanket?
They are mutually exclusive [69]

Dharma and Buddha have no connection
First, what is not the dharma is the Buddha;
that which is the Buddha is not the dharma
This is not to deny them, but they are unborn
In what is unborn, there is no connection [70]

The same is to be explained for father and son
in accordance with scriptures and reasonings
Just as the east and the west are not established
in a wheel that is driven by the wind's force, {97}
any connection between a father and a son
likewise has no existence at all either [71]

It may be [said] that such a flaw
does not exist in seeming reality
This here is my, Kambala's,
reasoning of nonexistence [72]

What exists does not arise, because it exists
For example, a vase that is existent
cannot arise through a person's effort [73]

What does not exist is likewise not arising,
because there is neither cause nor result,
as in the example of a barren woman's child[360] [74]

The same goes for existents and nonexistents
[arising] neither from themselves nor from others
What has the nature of being unborn has no character [75]

So how would father and son be established?
In those two not being established,
there are no conventions of father or son [76]

As far as their conventions are concerned,
first, how could the convention of a father
arise without the son being established? [77]

At the time when the son is not established,
the characteristic of time is not established
Therefore, where would there be a convention
of a father and a connection with a son? [78]

Notwithstanding that the thinking of others
is not established if examined by reasoning,
they hold existents and nonexistents to be connected [79]

Now, my own thinking in this matter
is that there is no[361] connection here
of either same identity or causality [80]

There is no connection of same identity,
since a father's essence is not established
The connection that represents causality

is to be understood as in the example
of how butter arises from milk [81]

What you are propounding as conditioned
is due to the progression of arising, abiding, perishing, and such[362]
However, these are present separately [82]

Among them, within the state of arising,
neither perishing nor abiding do exist {98}
Since these don't exist,[363] there is no arising,
so how would any connection be established? [83]

In the case that the nature of abiding
is characterized by abiding separately,
how would connection be established?
When two entities are not established,
how could labeling any as "father" be right? [84]

You may say, "Exactly that which
[has arisen] from the first moment's
potential that is a nonentity is not
established as the convention 'son'"
Therefore, if two are not established,
nothing can be established by these two [85]

To declare that the result of a son is established,
although a cause-like "father" is not established,
is the flaw of it following that a nonexistent is an existent—
the flaw that a valid cognition of it performing a function exists
[86]

Hence, what entails and the entailed
are not established in this context
Just as these two are not established,
a connection is not established either [87]

Moments are likewise not established,
as in the example of a sprout and a seed
Given the flaw of there being no sprout,
based on what would a seed be posited? [88]

"We speak of it dependent on the sprout"
At the time when the sprout arises,
that seed is not established any more
The powerless potential of the arisen
seed is what covers up any result [89]

Hence, without the seed being established,
how could that nonexistent be connected?
"It is an existent that is connected"
That existent would be an immutable,
everlasting entity that has no result [90]

How could entailer and entailed be established?
What is not established is a nonentity,
which does not have any color or shape
This is the intention of the Buddha[364] [91]

Without those, correspondingly,
moments of time are not established
At the time of the past, the future {99}
is not established, nor is it a self [92]

In terms of an example and likewise its meaning,
that which entails is the person who is the self—
the permanent[365] [entity] that is the agent—and
the entailed is the higher and miserable realms [93]

If there existed a connection of same identity
or a connection of causality between those,[366]
[both] permanent [entities] with the name "agent"[367]

and the higher and miserable realms would be unreal—
the flaw of it following that the permanent is an agent[368] [94]

You may wonder, "Why is that the case?"
Because this level of identity is the same,
as in the example of declaring a blanket
to be impermanent by way of a vase [95]

"The sense faculties' referents are entities
The form of a vase is seen to be existent,
while nonexistent forms are not seen—
hence, to see forms is as with a vase" [96]

To say such a thing is not reasonable
Are a vase and the sense faculties
the same or are they not the same? [97]

If they are not the same,
the senses lack connection
and the vase is not seen [98]

However, if they are the same,
there are neither faculties nor a vase,
so there is no connection of same identity [99]

If you say, "The faculties are not
existent, but the vase does exist,"
then those two are not the same
Not being the same, they lack a connection [100]

"They have a connection of causality"
This entails the flaws of it following
that the agent—the self—always arises
from the higher and the miserable realms
and the higher and the miserable realms
always arise from that agent [101]

You may say, "There is no connection, {100}
but [the self] is single and permanent,"[369]
does this referent promote or not promote
the welfare of other sentient beings? [102]

If you say, "It does not promote such,"
it follows it is not different from a stone
If you say, "It promotes their welfare,"
does it promote it gradually or simultaneously? [103]

If you say, "It promotes it gradually,"
this has the flaw of it following that its permanence is ruined
If you say, "It promotes it simultaneously,"
it would follow[370] that when a single self
is born, all six kinds of beings are born
The same is to be applied as appropriate
to aging, death, arising, ceasing, and so on [104]

In this context, it is the tīrthikas who question
the view of there being no self and no connection
To the children of noble family, the omniscient one
taught that the skandhas have no connection [105]

Given that no self exists in these skandhas,
thoughts about how to come, go, laugh,
play cymbals, conch shells,[371] and so on
keep arising in such ways in us,[372]
and we wish for them to be liberated[373] [106]

There exists no self in the skandhas at all
For those with the Mahāyāna disposition,
how could a connection with no self be reasonable?
In these skandhas here, oh tīrthikas,
a self is not existent at all [107]

We do not speak of its existence,
nonexistence, or both of these
For those who say a self exists,
its nonexistence is not reasonable [108]

But if it did exist, how come that
its expression[374] is not seen in them?
Looking at the hair, the skin, the nails,
the head, the flesh, the bones,
the marrow, the fat, the ligaments,
the bile, the intestines,
the hands, the feet, and so on, {101}
in both the outer and inner domains,
a self is not to be seen [109]

Here, the question of the tīrthikas is:
With no self, how could a nonexistent and form[375] connect?
Those with the Mahāyāna disposition
say the following on no connection [110]

The eye of flesh is utterly nonexistent[376]
It is not seen by the eye of wisdom
How could it be reasonable to see
a connection of color, shape, or place? [111]

Here, the tīrthikas are venturing,
"Well then, they are nonexistent"
Those with the Mahāyāna disposition
say that using the word "nonexistent"
renders such existence unreasonable [112]

Again [they say,] "If they thus did not exist,
how could any valid cognition see them?"
That the hosts of the displays[377] that are
based on earth, water, fire, and wind

therefore do not exist is unreasonable,
[yet] their existence is not established either [113]

Here, the tīrthikas say the following:
"So by what are they supported then?"[378]
Just as those with the Mahāyāna disposition[379]
speak about no self and no connection,
there is no support whatsoever either [114]

The tīrthika opponents say this:
"So it's just empty space then"
That is what the mahāyānists say
and the liṅgins say the same [115]

The tīrthikas say the following:
"But how should these entities—
conches,[380] laughing, and the hosts
of displays—be understood?" [116]

The mahāyānists answer thus:
They should be understood
just like illusions, dreams,
and miraculous displays [117]

The tīrthikas utter the following:
"What is illusion- and dream-like?"[381]
The mahāyānists answer like this:
If illusions that are similar to space {102}
are apprehended by dreams,
their miraculous displays are delusive [118]

Subjects and objects are conditioned
Objects of expression are unestablished
As for how the liṅgins again perceive
the seeming with their hands and such,
ultimately, it is exactly the same [119]

What is named "the seeming" is thus:
it[382] consists of self and others,
minds, persons, and skandhas,
feelings, as well as agents,
wealth, children, youth, and such
Ultimately, those are unconnected [120]

Where there is no self and others,
there exists no mind, no person,
no agent, no feelings,
no wealth, and no youthful haughtiness
This is to be understood as the ultimate [121]

In any of those, there does not exist
a connection, nor is there a purpose
Since it is by relying on the seeming
that the afflictions gain their power,
you roam saṃsāra without number [122]

By being subjected to suffering and afflictions,
you have no knowledge of the path to travel
and keep circling in saṃsāra like worldlings,
following the sun's and moon's example day and night [123]

Ultimately speaking, bodhicitta
has no support and lacks a nature
In the all-empty, there is no ground
Connection is one of reference points [124]

In ultimate awakening's characteristic,[383]
there is nothing soft or hard,
nothing that is hot or cold,
nothing to be aware of, no awareness, no grasping,
nothing that is subtle or coarse—
this is bodhicitta's characteristic [125]

Unseen by tīrthikas, beyond meditation, {103}
not seen as a nonentity, free from any
clarity or unclarity in nonmeditation—
this lack of connection is bodhicitta [126]

Everything is like bubbles on the ocean,
without any pith, resembling foam,
impermanent, without a self, illusion-like,
similar to a mirage for deer [chasing it],
and resembling vases made out of clay—
in the midst of being filled with miraculous displays,
thousands of wheels are not established [127]

Thus, how could any connection between
the seeming and the ultimate be established?
In the dream-like thoughts[384] of the mind,
mind does not exist at all, just like space,
so how could mind as such be connected? [128]

This concludes "The View of Nonconnection"—the view of a yogī's scope of realization—composed by master Kambala. It was translated by guru Ratnaphala on his own. {104}

(141) The View of Being Unbound and Letting Go

In the language of India: *Asaṃbandhasargadṛṣṭināma*[385]
In the language of Tibet: *Zhen med kyi lta ba zhes bya ba*[386]

I pay homage to mother Vārāhī

On the racetrack[387] of threefold existence here,
I, the bold one, continue[388] racing on this track
I mounted the horses of the five sugatas
You do not find any rider in this world
who gallops as audaciously as I
Racing, I tamed the wild horses of the three poisons [1]

I saddled[389] them with the saddle of the four great gods
and put on the bridle of prajñā and means
You do not find any rider in this world
who gallops as audaciously as I
Racing, I tamed the wild horses of the three poisons [2]

I gave them the food of the ten afflictions
and put them in the stable of the six views' center
You do not find any rider in this world
who gallops as audaciously as I
Racing, I tamed the wild horses of the three poisons [3]

I brandish the sword of the guru's words
and ascend above the six pure abodes
You do not find any rider in this world
who gallops as audaciously as I
Racing, I tamed the wild horses of the three poisons [4] {105}

I galloped throughout the ten directions,
but the tracks of these horses are invisible
You do not find any rider in this world
who gallops as audaciously as I
Racing, I tamed the wild horse of the three poisons [5]

This concludes "The View of Being Unbound and Letting Go" composed by master Kambala. {106}

(142) The View of Emptiness and Compassion

In the language of India: *Śūnyatākaruṇādṛṣṭināma*[390]
In the language of Tibet: *Stong nyid snying rje'i lta ba zhes bya ba*

I pay homage to noble youthful Mañjuśrī

By analyzing and looking at
impure saṃsāric existence
and worldly people's conduct,
entities appear as emptiness [1]

AHO! The resounding of the ḍamaru[391]
of compassion is so very marvelous!
Āryadeva, there is no satisfaction
in the kingdom of nothing to observe [2]

Where the mind, the vāyus,
and the faculties do not abide,
I don't know where to go
nor where to stay [3]

AHO! The resounding of the ḍamaru
of compassion is so very marvelous!
Āryadeva, there is no satisfaction
in the kingdom of nothing to observe [4]

From the moon, its light rays
stream forth so very lucidly
The nature of the connate
is to merge with true reality [5]

AHO! The resounding of the ḍamaru
of compassion is so very marvelous!
Āryadeva, there is no satisfaction
in the kingdom of nothing to observe [6]

Oh Āryadeva, experience everything! {107}
By experiencing, its nature is unobservable [7]

AHO! The resounding of the ḍamaru
of compassion is so very marvelous
Āryadeva, there is no satisfaction
in the kingdom of nothing to observe [8]

This concludes "The View of Emptiness and Compassion" transmitted by master[392] *Āryadeva and composed by master Catrapa.* {108}

(143) The View of the Jewel of Mind

In the language of India: *Cittaratnadṛṣṭināma*[393]
In the language of Tibet: *Sems nyid rin chen gyi lta ba zhes bya ba*

I pay homage to Śrī Heruka

I am the essence of the Sugata, Viṣṇu, Mahādeva, Brahmā,
Ati,[394] Nirgranthas, the sun, and the tenet systems
I am the great hero, the sole one in this threefold world
Out of oblivion, worldlings don't get it, bound by ignorance's web
I am the great[395] hero, the sole one in the three worlds [1]

Existence is me, and the enjoyment of existence is my essence
Dancing, the unrivaled yogī rests in the spaciousness of equality
I am the great hero, the sole one in this threefold world
Out of oblivion, worldlings don't get it, bound by ignorance's web [2]

Though appearing as men and women, they are my emanations
The formations and destructions of existence are also my emanations
I am the great hero, the sole one in this threefold world
Out of oblivion, worldlings don't get it, {109} bound by ignorance's web [3]

Gurus and students are me, those who expound are me,
examples and their meanings are me, what protects from suffering is me
I am the great hero, the sole one in this threefold world
Out of oblivion, worldlings don't get it, bound by ignorance's web [4]

What appears as many colors also is my essence
Kana, a single speaker has the essence of many
I am the great hero, the sole one in this threefold world
Out of oblivion, worldlings don't get it, bound by ignorance's web
I am the great hero, the sole one in this threefold world [5]

This concludes "The View of the Jewel of Mind" transmitted by master Kāṇhapa and composed by master Dhetana. {110}

(144) The View of True Reality in Eight Stanzas

In the language of India: *Tattvāṣṭakadṛṣṭināma*[396]
In the language of Tibet: *De nyid brgyad kyi lta ba zhes bya ba*

I pay homage to noble youthful Mañjuśrī

These thoughts of the entities of saṃsāra and nirvāṇa
are not established, similar to a water-moon
By relying on the conventions of the seeming,
I explain the view of true reality in eight [stanzas] [1]

Mind with its stains is saṃsāra
Freedom from conventions is nirvāṇa
For example, the cloud-free sky
does not abide anywhere—mahāmudrā
This is what Indrabhūti says [2]

This saṃsāra as well as nirvāṇa,
any happiness and suffering too,
are burned up by the realization[397] of mind,
as in the example of camphor in fire [3]

Therefore, even the smallest thoughts
of yogīs are to be utterly relinquished
All entities, which are the entities[398]

of mind and mental factors[399] do not abide,
as in the example of a city of gandharvas[400] [4]

What's beyond[401] nonabiding is delusion's appearance
Indrabhūti is discussing nonduality
This is the true reality of Madhyamaka
and also identityless phenomena's nature [5]

Precisely this is the nature of beginning and end
The view of the sugatas is nothing but this, {111}
also to be understood as the actuality of emptiness
I say it is nonbeing, nonminding, and beyond mind [6]

For example, the sun, the moon,
the sky, the star constellations,
the earth, the water, the ocean,
and cardinal and intermediate directions are it too [7]

Meru and such are delusion's appearances
This is what Indrabhūti declares
They are not established as anything
Make nonduality's actuality a living experience! [8]

This concludes "The View of True Reality in Eight Stanzas" composed by master Indrabhūti. {112}

(145) The View of Overcoming Mind's Thoughts

In the language of India: *Cittakalpaparihāradṛṣṭināma*[402]
In the language of Tibet: *Sems nyid kyi rtog pa 'joms pa'i lta ba zhes bya ba*

I pay homage to Yamāntaka

Severing your head on fresh butter,
you break the blade of the axe
A frog will swallow an elephant
AHO! The woodcutter breaks into laughter [1]

AHO! Amazing, Mego,[403] hey!
Don't entertain doubts in your mind!
If you are stunned, Avadhūtipa,
don't create thoughts in your mind! [2]

He didn't explain; this one didn't understand
Flowers are growing out of the sky [3]

AHO! Amazing, Mego, hey!
Don't entertain doubts in your mind!
If you are stunned, Avadhūtipa,
what's the point of a mind with doubts? [4]

AHO! If a barren woman's child is born,
even a throne will break into dance
Since cotton wool is rare to obtain,
those wearing the sky as garment[404] weep [5]

AHO! Amazing, Mego, hey!
What's the point of doubts in the mind?
If you are stunned, Avadhūtipa,
don't entertain doubts in your mind! [6]

AHO! An elephant sits on a throne
that is supported by two bees
The blind leading the way—amazing!
The mute {113} give speeches [7]

AHO! Amazing, Mego, hey!
Don't entertain doubts in your mind!
If you are stunned, Avadhūtipa,
what's the point of a mind with doubts? [8]

A mouse chasing a cat—astounding!
Seeing that, amazement will arise
By seeing a drunken donkey,
even an elephant runs away [9]

AHO! Amazing, Mego, hey!
Don't entertain doubts in your mind!
If you are stunned, Avadhūtipa,
what's the point of a mind with doubts?[405] [10]

AHO! A famished monkey
gobbles down morsels of rock
AHO! The experience of the mind
cannot be expressed by anybody [11]

AHO! Amazing, Mego, hey!
Don't entertain doubts in your mind!
If you are stunned, Avadhūtipa,
what's the point of a mind with doubts? [12]

This concludes "The View of Overcoming Mind's Thoughts" transmitted by Kanakhalā[406] *and Mekhalā and composed by mastress Lakṣmī.* {114}

(146) The View of Driving Away Misery

In the language of India: *Śokavinodadṛṣṭināma*[407]
In the language of Tibet: *Mya ngan gyi lta ba zhes bya ba*

I pay homage to the gurus

Since these bad skandhas of mine
were separated from guru HAṂ,[408]
splendorous appearances vanished[409]
In my agony about the true guru,
Mahila, I[410] wallow in misery [1]

Since I lack the guru's wisdom eye,
I don't see anything in the cardinal or intermediate directions
In my agony about the true guru,
Maṇibhadra, I am awash with tears [2]

With compassion's small drums and open white parasols,[411]
he has the character of the handsome king of yogīs
He has been lured away by some evildoers,
so, Maṇibhadra, I am utterly distraught [3]

The siddhas, eighty-four in number,
rise as a maṇḍala in the sky's expanse
The gem of the guru resides in its midst[412]

My mind's anguish burns up my body
Dhama, Dhuma,[413] I'm utterly distraught [4]

Within a single instant, in Kāmarū,[414]
I saw the wealth of the guru dissolve
Within a single instant, I have seen
this variety to be complete nonbeing
As the guru left, I'm utterly distraught[415] [5]

With all my wealth and youthfulness left behind, {115}
the pride of attachment to existence is crushed
Maṇibhadra and Mahila as well,
Dhama, and Dhuma, as our guru,
who is so glorious, is now no more,
all cardinal and intermediate directions are covered in darkness[416] [6]

AHO! With the ḍamaru of nonduality
being played in the expanse of the sky,
as a result of our anguish, we the yogīs
smear our bodies with the guru's ashes [7]

Meditating on him on my head's crown,
I have slayed Bahuri out of compassion[417]
You, Bahuri, carried away by the māras,
you are the mortal enemy of the guru [8]

We have become obscured by your darkness
and our congregation has been destroyed[418]
Wearing tattered rags, having cut our hair,
and holding our staffs as well as skulls,
our miserable bodies[419] turned into skeletons [9]

AHO! Yogīs, this is impermanence![420]
We have annihilated this Bahuri
From Devībandhukoṭi[421]
to sīmika's[422] great site, it's two and a half[423] [10]

With the gaze of the guru Kṛṣṇa,[424]
it was the wrathful yogī Mahila
who terrified sixty-four ḍakinīs
Cleaving[425] sīmika, I killed Bahuri
AHO! The guru's foe liberated,
we proceed to Khecara's abode [11]

This concludes "The View of [Driving Away] Misery" transmitted by master Mahila and composed by Bhadrapa.[426] {116}

(147) The View of Mere Mind

In the language of India: *Cittamātradṛṣṭināma*[427]
In the language of Tibet: *Sems tsam gyi lta ba zhes bya ba*

I pay homage to Śrī Hevajra

In this ship that is called "space,"
body, speech, and mind act disturbed
Plant the central pillar of the guru's pith instructions! [1]

Mind's firmness takes its seat in this ship
and lets you cross to the other side
Thus, yogīs indeed do not possess
any means that are other than this [2]

There are no thoughts except this,
nor are there any oars either
It travels driven by just the wind[428]
Through the means, you stay in it, moving [3]

If this ship does not move swiftly,
on the way, the fear of pirates is great
Through the upsurge of the ocean's waves,
yogīs plunge into threefold existence's abyss [4]

Firmly seizing this ship of the mind,
you should cross to the other shore
Thus, yogīs indeed do not not possess
any means that are other than this [5]

All those without realization
say all kinds of different things
All the dharmas of the six views[429]
are contained in one place in this ship [6] {117}

Firmly seizing this ship of the mind,
you should cross to the other shore
Thus, yogīs indeed do not not possess
any means that are other than this [7]

Having been pulled out of an extreme,
this ship needs to travel upward[430]
This is what Saraha declares
Mind dissolves in the state of emptiness [8]

Firmly seizing this ship of the mind,
you should cross to the other shore
Thus, yogīs indeed do not not possess
any means that are other than this [9]

This concludes "The View of Mere Mind" transmitted by master Saraha and spoken by master Maitrīpa. {118}

(148) The View of the Skull of Compassionate Conduct

In the language of India: *Karuṇācaryākapāladṛṣṭināma*[431]
In the language of Tibet: *Snying rje spyod pa thod pa'i lta ba zhes bya ba*

I pay homage to Śrī Saṃvara

You who dwell in the sky,[432] holding a parasol
with a golden handle above[433] your head—
Vajraḍākinī, please approach! [1]

Dhari is the son of the ḍākinīs
If you wonder why, thanks to their kindness,
this yogī's intention is fulfilled [2]

I hold the clay cup of emptiness in my hand,
filling it up with the elixir of the means
Thus traveling to the buddha realms, I stay [3]

I cut the bondage of threefold existence at its root,
being guarded by the eight ḍākinīs at all times,
as well as stamping my seal onto the ten gates[434]
This is what Dhari has to proclaim [4]

Though it pervades all, if someone
does not realize its characteristics,
how could[435] I demonstrate it? [5]

Dhari is the son of the ḍākinīs
If you wonder why, through them,
my intention is fulfilled as I wish [6]

This concludes "The View of the Skull of Compassionate Conduct" transmitted by master Dārikapa and composed by master Sarvabhakṣa. {119}

(149) The View of Being Unbound

In the language of India: *Asaṃbandhadṛṣṭināma*[436]
In the language of Tibet: *'Brel med kyi lta ba zhes bya ba*

I pay homage to the gurus

Haughtiness due to wealth, youth, or ancestry—
at the time when I will have perished,
not even a single one of those will appear [1]

How could there ever be a meeting
of what are called "me" and "you"?
Will a ship destroyed in the ocean
ever be reassembled, or what?[437] [2]

Father, mother, children, and grandchildren
are like an audience come to watch a dance
Once the dancers have left, the show dissolves [3]

How could there ever be a meeting
of what are called "me" and "you"?
Will a ship destroyed in the ocean
ever be reassembled, or what? [4]

Be it at a market or in the streets,
on a mountain, a plain, or a river bank—
at which place my body and speech will perish,
that is something I don't know [5]

How could there ever be a meeting
of what are called "me" and "you"?
Will a ship destroyed in the ocean
ever be reassembled, or what? [6]

This is what Kanapa has to say: {120}
I have no realization except this
Through coming and going, I was crushed[438] [7]

How could there ever be a meeting
of what are called "me" and "you"?
Will a ship destroyed in the ocean
ever be reassembled, or what? [8]

This concludes "The View of Being Unbound" composed by master Kṛṣṇa. {121}

(150) The View of Suchness

In the language of India: *Tathatādṛṣṭināma*[439]
In the language of Tibet: *De bzhin nyid kyi lta ba zhes bya ba*

I pay homage to the tathāgatas

On this tree of suchness there,
roots and branches are unobservable,
but it always yields flowers and fruits [1]

AHO! This tree is amazing, look!
Without any seed or sprout,
its fruits grow beyond measure [2]

What is its nature like?
Just like breaking the sky
with your fists by slicing it up,[440]
so is breaking this tree [3]

This tree that has roots
and also has branches
appears to pervade the sky
AHO! Look at this tree!
Amazing how it pervades the sky! [4]

AHO! This tree is amazing, look!
Without any seed or sprout,
its fruits grow beyond measure [5]

You don't realize the characteristics
of this tree of suchness there,
but I do firmly[441] realize them [6]

This is what Dharipa declares:
through being lazy about this,
you will not reach the end
Thus, don't fail on the way! [7]

AHO! {122} This tree is amazing, look!
Without any seed or sprout,
its fruits grow beyond measure [8]

This concludes "The View of Suchness" composed by the great master Dārikapa. {123}

(151) A Conduct Song

In the language of India: *Caryāgīti*[442]
In the language of Tibet: *Spyod pa'i glu*

I pay homage to youthful Mañjuśrī
I pay homage to the glorious one on the vajra seat

Just like a reflection, so is being's saṃsāric existence
If its own essence is examined, it is free of any nature
As the knowledge of its own essence being like a reflection has not
dawned,
hey, benighted mind, may you not create unawareness! [1]

Myself and all beings who are clearly appearing
with stainless space and a huge gem or a mirror
are just like children deluded about their own reflections—
why do they dwell in the delusion of splitting self and others? [2]

Those always [trying to] know and conceptualize[443] reflections
resemble cattle, just fighting with [their own] shadows
You should stabilize familiarizing with the maṇḍala circle
The yogīs who understand true reality do not dwell on it [3]

The supremely great bliss to be pointed out is essential—
it is to be stabilized by condensing it in the maṇḍala

Whatever your approach of examining and analyzing[444] may be, {124}
how do you think the nature of true reality is in it? [4]

For as long as the nature of true reality is not understood,
how would unsurpassable awakening be accomplished?
Conceptual discursiveness without exception lacks any being,
possessing the nature of supreme great bliss [5]

Have an equal mind toward the eight worldly dharmas[445]
and remain[446] in the accumulation of samādhi!
If you remain in it, you will become utterly pure—
all discursive conduct without exception is relinquished [6]

Any entities created by various kinds of thoughts
Do not constitute the supremely pure nature
Without exception, discursiveness and thoughts don't exist
This is suchness—the very being of supreme purity [7]

The samādhi of suchness is a great blazing fire
that burns the afflictions' straws without exception
When the world is understood completely,
then all sentient beings become like space [8]

Don't be deluded[447] about beings' space-like nature
and don't be blinded by the blurred vision of thoughts!
Just as they are before, so sentient beings are thereafter,
There's no difference between before, after, and between [9]

Between seeing strands of hair in space due to having blurred vision
and seeing the world due to the blurred vision of thoughts, there's no difference
Without exception, familiarize with the nature of having examined
the nature of thoughts as being the nature that is equal to space! [10] {125}

Seeing the fearsome thieves who are the maturations of
wrongdoing,
hey, be a night watchman in order to guard the great wealth of
discipline!
Due to the sleep of ignorance in the long night of saṃsāric
existence,
hey, mind, do not be heedless; serve as a watchman at night! [11]

Similar to there being no daylight if there is no sun,
how could there be any dhyāna without the wealth of discipline?
With those thieves entering the house in which you sleep,
hey, the great wealth of your discipline will surely be stolen! [12]

Without being attached to negative deeds for even an instant,
be a night watchman until the sun of true reality will shine!
For as long as the pure sun of true reality is shining,
enjoy saṃsāric existence just like a gem, as you please![448] [13]

Just what I am, that is what you sentient beings are
Don't commit the inner harm of splitting yourself from others!
You need to overcome this inner damage of thinking
Like a poisonous snake, it is to be pacified by the taste of nectar
[14]

This inner damage resembles a many-headed venomous snake
If all beings without exception are known to be thought's[449]
diversity,
it is suchness that is called "the taste of the great nectar,"
which is the state of a great yogī's mind resting at ease [15]

If the taste of that great nectar is ingested all the time,
the supreme nirvāṇa of great bliss will be realized
Those naked and making fire offerings are not brahmans,
nor are they by wearing a tuft of hair, their caste, or their lineage
[16]

If someone is completely pure in body, speech, and mind,
that one represents a brahman, {126} the Buddha declared
The entirety of the ten wrongdoings needs to be relinquished,
and all ten virtues should be made into powerful qualities [17]

Even if you are born in a lower caste, at any time in this[450] [life]
until you die, you should abandon what is not the dharma
By seizing the dharma of patience, you need to be victorious over anger
You should relinquish every desire for pleasure related to objects [18]

You should always bathe in the lake of the dharma of bliss
and not give rise to craving's[451] flaws, fear,[452] or ignorance
Mounting the steed that is just a skeleton again and again,
don't you always feel you're exuding impurity through your oblivion? [19]

Abandon desire and ignorance, the paths to the miserable realms!
Hey, mind, you need to wash away your own stains by yourself!
With respect, you should rely on the wellspring of the true guru
and terminate being tainted by the stains of great ignorance [20]

Since the pith instructions of the guru are stainless water,
you need to know how to wash yourself by adopting them
You, mind, understand yourself completely, look
at yourself and purify the great darkness of ignorance! [21]

Persons who do not listen to the Sage's dharma speech
resemble persons [who are lost] in a flood or a forest
Since this world surely moves on to the next world,
the Sage's dharma speech should be listened to [22]

Having heard the dharma of the Sage, don't dwell in nondharma,
because nobody will be able to save you in the Avīci[453] realm!

Those who heard the dharma and familiarized with the dharma
according to its meaning {127}
will easily attain the fruitions of the higher realms and liberation
[23]

The dharma is the lamp for those in the darkness of ignorance—
the ship that carries them across the ocean of saṃsāric existence
[24]

This concludes "The Conduct of Discipline Put to Song" composed by the great master Dīpaṃkaraśrījñāna. It was translated, edited, and finalized by Paṇḍita Vajrapāṇi and lotsāwa bhikṣu Chökyi Sherab. {128}

(152) A Commentary on "A Conduct Song"

In the language of India: *Caryāgītivṛtti*[454]
In the language of Tibet: *Spyod pa'i glu'i 'grel pa*

I pay homage to youthful Mañjuśrī

> Having paid homage to the kāya of unity
> endowed with the supreme of all aspects,
> with a mindset of benefiting others, I wrote
> this elucidation of the meaning of *A Conduct Song*

Now, in terms of the two kinds of the correct view, after [my] vajra song has mainly taught luminosity, [the reality of] cessation, and ultimate reality, this conduct song teaches self-blessing, the reality of the path, and seeming reality.[455]

[1][456] In order to do so, I say, "**Just like a reflection** . . ." Here, the objects to be viewed by the eye of prajñā are two: [those whose nature is] to be nonexistent and those whose nature is to be existent.[457] What is nonexistent refers to what is not a given [phenomenon] but appears as that [phenomenon], just as in the example of the perception of someone with blurred vision. There are three phenomena[458] with regard to the phrase "just like a reflection": a mirror without tarnish, a face close by, and unobscured space. In [that situation], {129} a reflection appears. Likewise, in the miraculous creations of the mind and the vāyus that are specified by [distinct] karmas and ignorance, the **beings** of threefold

saṃsāric existence appear clearly, like reflections. Apart from their being mere appearances, there is nothing whatsoever that is established ultimately. Therefore I say, "**If its own essence is examined, it lacks any nature.**" "How do you understand through examination that they do not exist?" This is **the understanding** that your **own essence** and that of those in the three realms consists of mere appearances, **like reflections,** and the understanding that these [mere appearances] have not [really] arisen. Hence,[459] this is the instruction [that begins] by calling out "**hey**": "Do not create delusion about those reflections! Do **not create unawareness** about the nature of those reflections!"

[2] Having thus given a brief introduction, I shall teach the characteristics of the meaning of this example in detail. To do so, I say, "**Myself and all beings** . . ." Due to the coming together of the triad of **stainless space, a** pure **gem or mirror,** and a face, a reflection appears. Likewise, due to being specified by mind, vāyus, karma, and ignorance, your own reflection and those of the ones in the three realms **appear.** Those **deluded about** those **reflections** who then [try to] **conceptualize**[460] **and** fully **know** them **resemble** a lion who, through **fighting with** its own **shadow,** dies in the ocean—they are fools. Or, they resemble **children** not knowing representations who are scared[461] of the **reflections** of **their own** faces—just fools. Likewise, {130} [the text says,] "**Why** are **they deluded** about the reflection-like appearances of themselves and those in the three realms as being **self and others**? Don't create delusion!" The sūtras say:

> Just as on the surface of a mirror
> forms devoid of being one or many
> are appearing but do not exist,
> so is the essence of entities[462]

And:

> There are no referents—the mind
> seeing outer referents is mistaken
> . . .
> It is mentation agitated by latent tendencies
> that arises as what seem to be referents[463]

Thus, without exception, the entities of yourself and of those in the three realms—the cognitions and cognizable objects of those who see just this life—should be understood as being like flowers in the sky.

[3] In terms of seeing these [appearances] as having the nature of being existent, I say, "**You should stabilize familiarizing with the maṇḍala circle**." This has five parts: (1) dependent origination having power, (2) its being that, (3) understanding it as that, (4) familiarizing with it as that, and (5) the arising of blessing.

(1) Having thus dispensed with referents that do not exist, at the time when both the mind and the vāyus are rendered special through uncontaminated qualities, the support and the supported[464] appear as a circle of deities. Due to the coming together of the triad of mind as the substantial cause,[465] the vāyus as the cooperative conditions, and the uncontaminated qualities, a mental body appears, just like an illusion and so on.

(2) In order to teach that the [mind and the vāyus] have the nature of being that [maṇḍala], it is said that it has the nature of all qualities that are uncontaminated by nature; {131} for if they do not exist, it does not exist [either].[466]

(3) Through relying on a perfect spiritual friend who makes you understand this, it is illustrated and understood as having the nature of self-blessing by way of three and twelve examples.

(4) You familiarize with it by mastering it through the five faculties.[467]

(5) Through the blessings[468] [deriving] from that, the certainty that all phenomena appear like illusions arises. Furthermore, the benefits, such as being continuously protected by the deity, should be known from Āryadeva's explanation.[469] [Then, the text] says, "**Yogīs who understand true reality do not dwell on it**." Even if [this maṇḍala and phenomena] are understood as illusions, there may [still] be [some] clinging [to them], similar to attachment arising in an illusionist toward a woman created by him. Therefore, this is purified through luminosity.

[4] The two lines [that begin with] "**the supremely great bliss to be pointed out is essential**" are easy to understand. [The next two lines] beginning with "**whatever your approach of examining and analyzing may be**" repudiate [the approach of] yogīs who perform examinations[470] that do not possess the characteristics of the two realities, which is easy to understand.

[5] "**For as long as the nature of true reality is not understood, how would unsurpassable awakening be accomplished?**" refers to luminosity and unity.[471] "Well, what is the characteristic of great bliss?" "**Conceptual discursiveness without exception lacks a being**" refers to stopping[472] the one hundred and sixty mundane states of mind.[473] "**Possessing the nature of supreme great bliss**" refers to luminosity's {132} purification by itself.[474]

[6] "What is the cause of that?" "**Have an equal mind toward the eight worldly dharmas and remain in the accumulation of samādhi!**" This has two parts: common and uncommon.[475] The common accumulation consists of being endowed with discipline, not depending on possessions, being endowed with patience, firm oaths, abandoning hustle and bustle, being endowed with alertness, undistracted mindfulness with regard to the two realities, knowing what is to be done and what is not, relinquishing the five obscurations,[476] knowing the right amount of food, and resting mind in its native state within mundane behavior. The uncommon [accumulation] consists of the proper obtainment of the four empowerments, firm bodhicitta, and respect for the guru. **If you remain in** these kinds of accumulations, the triad of body, speech, and mind, as well as the three obscurations, **will become utterly pure—all discursive conduct without exception is relinquished**.

[7] The two lines [beginning with] "**any entities created**" repudiate yogas with discursiveness, which is easy to understand. Threefold saṃsāric existence, the worldly mind's **discursiveness**, however it may appear,[477] and **thoughts, without exception, don't exist** ultimately. Therefore this luminosity[478] **is the supremely pure nature** [called] "**suchness**."

[8] Now, **when** the **fire** of **the samādhi** that is mastered by the five faculties {133} **burns the afflictions' straws** (worldly states of mind), the threefold **world** and worldly states of mind **are completely understood** to be like the center of space. **Then**, with [all] thoughts about **sentient beings** without exception having vanished, they **become like space**.

[9] The instruction that stains with regard to the arising of the certainty that all phenomena appear **like space** in this way must be purified consists of "**do not be blinded by the blurred vision of thoughts!**" "Why is that?" Within the state of the pure nature of the three [kinds of]

beings, **there's no difference** whatsoever **between** any of them—they are differentiated by thoughts.

[10] The detailed teaching of the meaning of this consists of the lines that begin with "**between seeing strands of hair in space due to having blurred vision**," which are easy to understand.

[11–12] Now, in order to teach that **until** the arising of karmas and afflictions has been purified through the samādhi of luminosity it is necessary to refrain from even very subtle karmas,[479] there follow the lines beginning with "**seeing the fearsome thieves who are the maturations of wrongdoing**," which are easy to understand.

[13] Having severed the workings of karma with the samādhi of the luminous **sun of true reality**, through being endowed with the [ensuing] poised readiness,[480] the virtuous phenomena in your own mindstream are completed and so on.[481] At this point, since those [discipline, patience, and so on] are not needed [anymore], I state, "**for that long enjoy as you please!**" This is why it says, "for that long . . . ," which is easy to understand.[482]

[16cd–17] Those with such a view and conduct are called "**brahmans**," but not in terms of **their caste** and so on. {134} In order to teach that, I say, "**those naked and making fire offerings are not brahmans** . . . ," which is easy to understand.

[18] In order to teach that being endowed with the unmistaken path does not depend on caste, I say, "**Even if you are born in a lower caste** . . ."

[19–20a] The instruction to turn away from delusion, because it is under its sway that you always cycle [through saṃsāra], consists of the lines that begin with "**mounting the steed that is just a skeleton again and again**."

[20b–d] The instruction through a concluding summary[483] [begins with] exclaiming "**hey**" and then says, "**mind, you need to wash away your own stains by yourself!**" Once you look at the stains on your own face in a mirror,[484] you [are able to] remove them by washing it.[485] Likewise, through **a true guru** (who resembles a mirror) and his or her pith instructions (which resemble water), **you should terminate** [mind's] **being tainted by the stains of** ignorance, as well as by karma and the afflictions.[486]

[21] Therefore, **you need to wash** away the stains of thoughts with the **water** of **the pith instructions of the guru**. "In what manner are they washed away?" I say, "**you, mind, understand yourself completely, look at yourself, and purify the great darkness of ignorance!**" That is, understand completely that all phenomena are the miraculous creations of the mind and the vāyus. [Mind, look] for yourself at yourself—settle the mind and the vāyus into their own nature and regard them as being like space!

[22] The kind of **persons who do not listen to the Sage's dharma speech** and lack the fortune for it are [merely] a semblance of **persons.**[487] Therefore, **since** you **surely move on to the next world**, engage your mind in [the fact] that you must move on. {135} Since **the Sage's dharma speech should be listened to**, you need to listen to, and familiarize with, bodhicitta and so on.[488]

[23] **Having heard the** [dharma], **don't** commit any actions that contradict it. "**Because nobody will be able to save you in the Avīci realm**" means "because nothing whatsoever will be able to save you there, given that the [dharma] does not exist there."[489] **Those who heard the** [dharma] **and** trained in it in such a way **will attain the higher realms** (the temporary fruition) **and** awakening (the ultimate **fruition**).

[24] This **is the lamp** of **the dharma in the darkness of** ignorance: from taking refuge, bodhicitta, and so on up through the final samādhi of great bliss, it resembles a lamp because it naturally kindles luminosity.[490] Therefore, since it is **the** boat or **ship that carries** you **across the** great **ocean of saṃsāric existence**, you should definitely rely on and familiarize with it.

This concludes "A Perpetual Commentary on 'A Conduct Song'" composed by the great master Dīpaṃkaraśrījñāna. It was translated by this Indian upādhyāya himself and the Tibetan lotsāwa bhikṣu Tsültrim Gyalwa upon having been supplicated by the venerable Ngog Legpé Sherab[491] *on the meadowy plain at Nyetang Dashi Bal.*[492] *Later, Nagtso [Lotsāwa] provided interlinear editorial glosses.*[493] {136}

(153) A Song on Beholding the Dharmadhātu

In the language of India: *Dharmadhātudarśanagīti*[494]
In the language of Tibet: *Chos kyi dbyings su lta ba'i glu*

I pay homage to the omniscient one

Those completely ignorant about it
Circle through threefold existence—
I pay homage to the dharmadhātu
That dwells in all sentient beings[495] [1]

In their due order, I shall describe here
those seeing the dharmadhātu and others who don't
Profound peaceful suchness free of discursiveness,
which is luminous and unconditioned,[496]
is unborn, unceasing, and originally pure [2]

By virtue of being the natural nirvāṇa,
the dharmadhātu is without middle or end,
seen by insight's sharp eye free of thoughts,
without the blurriness of dullness and agitation [3]

Due to having purified[497] just that
which serves as saṃsāra's cause,
this very purity constitutes nirvāṇa
The dharmakāya too is nothing but this [4]

Just as clarified butter is not visible
due to being mixed in with milk,
the dharmadhātu is not seen
due to being mixed with afflictions [5]

Just as clarified butter becomes stainless
by virtue of being refined from milk, {137}
the dharmadhātu becomes utterly stainless
through being purified of the afflictions [6]

Just as a lamp that's sitting in a vase
does not illuminate even a little bit,
the dharmadhātu dwelling in the vase
of the afflictions does not shine [7]

From[498] whichever of its sides
holes are punched into this vase,
it is from just these very sides
that the nature of light beams forth [8]

Once the vajra of samādhi
has shattered this very vase,
the[499] [dharmadhātu] radiates
to the very limits of space [9]

Unborn is the dharmadhātu,
and never ever cease it will
At all times without afflictions,
stainless at the outset, middle, and end [10]

The jewel of a blue beryl[500]
is luminous at all times,
but if confined within its ore,
its light does not reveal its shine [11]

Just so, obscured by the afflictions,
the utterly stainless dharmadhātu
does not reveal its light in saṃsāra [12]

Just as a grain covered by its husks
is not asserted to be edible rice,
being covered by the afflictions,
this is not labeled "buddha" [13]

Just as rice becomes visible
once it has become free of chaff,
the dharmakāya clearly manifests
when it is free of the afflictions [14]

Just as there is a child in the womb
of a pregnant woman but is unseen,
the dharmadhātu is not beheld
due to being covered by afflictions[501] [15]

Since the dharmadhātu is not a self, {138}
neither a woman nor a man,
and free of all to be perceived,
how could it be conceived by a perceiver?[502] [16]

"Impurity," "impermanence," and "suffering"—
these three are the means to purify the mind[503]
The sūtras that teach about emptiness,
however many spoken[504] by the victor, [17]

all put an end to the afflictions,
but will never ruin this dhātu[505]
The dharma best purifying the mind
is the lack of any nature[506] [18]

Any horns there on a rabbit's head
are just imagined and not existent
Just so, all phenomena as well
are just imagined and do not exist [19]

The horns of an ox are also not observed
as having the nature of minute particles
Just as it was before, so it is after,
so what is to be imagined[507] there? [20]

If what arises in dependence,[508]
what ceases in dependence,
and what abides do not exist,
how can childish beings imagine them?[509] [21]

The nature of the dharmadhātu, like the element
of[510] space, is without any causes and conditions
Since[511] it is without birth, aging, abiding,
and ceasing, it is unconditioned[512] [22]

The buddha qualities are inseparable from it
and it accordingly bears their disposition
It is without delusion, deception, and harm
Hence, it is original natural peacefulness [23]

Just as in the case of the ocean,
through terms, examples, and minds,
its bottom or yonder shore are not found
Therefore, it is utter profundity [24]

Since the dharmadhātu is without divisions,
it is not suitable that there are different views
Still, I speak a little bit about different views
by virtue of the distinctions in the mind [25] {139}

Those who propound the very middle[513]
assert its meaning as the two realities,
which are the seeming and the ultimate [26]

Those knowing how to distinguish the two realities
are not ignorant about the words of the Sage
By gathering the accumulations without exception,
they proceed to the far shore of excellence[514] [27]

Whatever is projected as a self and what is mine,
permanence and extinction, afflictions and the purified,
causes and results, and perceiver and perceived—
that is what constitutes seeming reality [28]

What is emptiness, identitylessness, and peacefulness
is not tainted by any discursive reference points,
is without any difference, and is nonconceptual—
this is what constitutes ultimate reality [29]

By virtue of correct and incorrect,
as well as nominal and nonnominal,
those two are classified, respectively[515] [30]

Mere imputations,[516] entities that appear and resound,
conventions, magical creations,[517] illusions,
and the seeming itself represent synonyms [31]

Emptiness, the true end,
signlessness, the ultimate,
and the dharmadhātu are synonyms[518]
The seeming is such because it obscures
The ultimate is such because it is immutable [32]

[There] are two realities because there are the two
[types of] cognition that are correct and incorrect[519]
You may say, "There is no correct cognition"
This is true—it exists as a mere convention [33]

To begin, those searching for true reality
should be told that everything exists
Later, for those who realized the ultimate[520]
and lack attachment, it is voidness's actuality[521] [34]

The two realities are neither one nor different,
because four flaws for each were discussed
Those who think[522] they are one or different {140}
have not engaged them in a proper way[523] [35]

If there is any claim of [real] entities,
horrid views that arise from unbearable
desire and hatred are grasped firmly,
and disputes will arise from that[524] [36]

For those who entertain discursive notions,
there is no attainment and no clear realization
If they even lack approximate poised readiness,
what need is there to mention nirvāṇa?[525] [37]

If they have flawed views about emptiness,
those with little prajñā will be destroyed,
just as when incorrectly seizing a snake
or wrongly performing an awareness mantra[526] [38]

All the victors have declared
that emptiness eradicates all views
They said there is nothing to accomplish
for those who have views about emptiness[527] [39]

Those who see being and nonbeing
due to own-being and other-being
do not see the true reality
in the teachings of the Buddha[528] [40]

Nonexistence rests on its counterpart of existence
Existence rests on its counterpart of nonexistence
Hence, you should neither speak about nonexistence
nor entertain any thoughts about existence[529] [41]

Those who propound existence[530] go to the pleasant realms
Those who propound nonexistence[531] go to the miserable realms
Since they understand actual reality just as it is,
those who do not rely on either will be liberated[532] [42]

Those who mount the two approaches' chariot
and hold the reins of reasoning[533]
thus attain the status of a follower
of the Mahāyāna in the true sense[534] [43]

All phenomena, beginning with forms and such,
however they may appear, up through the sugatas,
exemplified by the horns of rabbits and of oxes, {141}
should be understood as the very middle[535] [44]

Neither existent, nor nonexistent, nor existent and nonexistent,
nor of a character that is neither of the two—
the true reality free of the four extremes
is asserted to be the middle by the wise[536] [45]

If the middle is free from extremes,
it lacks extremes, and[537] there is not even a middle
The view without middle and extremes
constitutes the view that is perfect [46]

This is the unsurpassable view,
always cultivated by the intelligent
Those who enter this view
will attain omniscience [47]

It is the Vijñaptimātravādins
who assert the three natures:
the imaginary, the dependent, and the perfect
For, in due order, these are what is imagined,
what arises from causes, and what is immutable [48]

Whichever entity is conceived
by whichever conception
is the imaginary nature,
which is nonexistent[538] [49]

The nature that is dependent
is conception arising from conditions
The perfect is the perpetual
absence of the former in it[539] [50]

Through the two extremes of existence and nonexistence,
it is therefore neither other nor
not other[540] than the dependent,
said to be like impermanence and such[541] [51]

Through the examples of a crystal or a blue beryl,
the three natures are to be understood
In due order, each one is twofold:
what is imagined as self and phenomena,
the pure one and the impure one,
and the changeless and the unmistaken [52]

All those who possess excellent insight
make efforts in reflecting on the internal[542] {142}
The consciousness that is free of perceiver
and perceived is what exists[543] ultimately[544] [53]

No phenomenon whatsoever
has the slightest arising or ceasing
It is solely cognition[545] alone
that will arise and cease[546] [54]

Those nonexistent phenomena do appear,
but neither from matter, nor from something other,
nor from nonexistence, since that has two flaws
Therefore, they have the character of cognition[547] [55]

Consciousness constitutes what arises
as the opposite of the nature of matter
That which is immaterial in its nature
is held to be known as having this character[548] [56]

The sky, the earth, the wind, the sun,
the ocean, directions,[549] and waterfalls[550]
are portions of real internal cognition,
appearing as if they were external[551] [57]

Since they appear as having the nature of lucidity,
their connection is not something hidden
Since that which is aware is connected
to the objects to be aware of, it is aware of them[552] [58]

You may say, "As with a sword's blade and a fingertip,
[the notion that] mind perceives itself is dismissed"[553]
In the *Saṃdhinirocana[sūtra]*, it is declared
that [mind] illuminating itself is not dismissed [59]

Hence, the characteristic of mind
is established as self-awareness[554]
Since suchness is hard to realize,[555]
its nature cannot be analyzed [60]

Since it is subtle, it is to be self-experienced
by the buddhas who behold what is subtle
Although it is dwelling within ourselves,
blockheads like myself do not see it[556] [61]

Mind and what is lucid have a connection
of same identity—hence, this is sheer mind[557]
The nature of cognition is something real, {143}
but aspects are deceptive and delusive[558] [62]

Mind is single but appears as duality,[559]
because it is confounded by aspects
due to its in every way very ingenious
split into perceiver and perceived [63]

Since the perceived aspect is unmoving,
it appears as if it were external,
but since the perceiving aspect is alive,
it appears as if it were internal[560] [64]

Having relinquished these characteristics,
familiarize with wisdom as being like space!
The nature of the mind is uncontaminated
With the seeds of contamination not exhausted,
they make up the state of the ālaya consciousness [65]

Having been exhausted, the uncontaminated dhātu
is what constitutes the vimuktikāya[561]
Since it always, like the sun and its rays,
is the abode of the buddha qualities,
it is the dharmakāya of the protectors[562] [66]

For those who entered the śrāvakayāna,
be it the skandhas, dhātus, and āyatanas
devoid of a self and what is mine,
the five bases,[563] or the three times,
all is existent and what is perceived [67]

They are perceived by what has them as focal objects[564]
They assert these two as ultimately [existent]
and explain that the afflictions are relinquished
by seeing and familiarizing with the realities[565] [68]

The realities are of four kinds:
suffering, likewise its origin,
cessation, as well as the path
Thus is their clear[566] realization's order[567] [69]

Suffering is the appropriating skandhas[568]
Its origin consists of karma and afflictions
Cessation consists of the two nirvāṇas[569]
The path is the thirty-seven concordant factors[570] [70]

Steeped in the conduct and {144} equipped with study and
reflection,
one then is engaging in meditation[571]
The approach of virtuous effort is the stainless path
Its results are conditioned and unconditioned [71]

Those that make up a total of eighty-nine
are the paths of liberation plus the terminations
Otherwise, they constitute the four results,
since five causes are contained [in each][572] [72]

The śrāvakas are of four types:
emanations, perfectly awakened ones,
travelers to peace, and tenet holders
The last are two, four, or eighteen [73]

The two are the Vaibhāṣikas
as well as the Sautrāntikas
Those holding that cognition without aspects
is aware of [outer] referents, such as forms,
represent the Vaibhāṣikas [74]

Those who assert an awareness of referents
through experiencing the reflections triggered
by [outer] referents constitute the Sautrāntikas [75]

The four are the Mahāsaṃghikas,
the Sarvāstivādins, the Sthaviras,
and the Saṃmatīyas; the eighteen: [76]

the Pūrvaśailas, the Aparaśailas, the Haimavatas,
the nikāya of the Lokottaravādins,
and the nikāya of the Prajñaptivādins[573]—
these five make up the Mahāsaṃghikas [77]

The Mūlasarvāstivādins, the Kāśyapīyanikāya,
the Mahīśāsakanikāya, the Dharmaguptakanikāya,
the Bahuśrutīyas, the Tāmraśātīyas,
and the nikāya of the Vibhajyavādins
constitute the Sarvāstivādins [78]

The Jetavanīyas, the Abhayagirivāsins,
and the Mahāvihāravāsins are the Sthaviras
The nikāyas of the Kaurukullakas, the Avantakas,
and the Vātsīputrīyas are the three kinds of Saṃmitīyas
Distinguished by distinct locations, topics, or masters,
these are the eighteen different kinds [of subschools][574] [79] {145}

Those striving for pratyekabuddha awakening
relinquish the thoughts about the perceived
but do not relinquish those about the perceiver
Hence, they [take] the rhino-like path as support [80]

By having meditated until they reach the end
of one hundred eons, they touch awakening
This refers to dependent origination
with its twelve links in three periods:[575] [81]

two for the first one, two for the last one,
and eight for the middling one, with all complete
Ignorance refers to the afflictions in a former state
Formations refer to that of former karmas[576] [82]

Consciousness refers to the skandhas at conception
Name-and-form refers to these from that time
onward, all the way up through the six āyatanas
Those extend up through the three gatherings [83]

Contact extends up to the ability[577] to know
the causes of happiness, suffering, and so on
Feelings extend up to intercourse, while craving
refers to those desiring enjoyments and intercourse [84]

Grasping refers to those who are running
around in order to obtain enjoyments
Becoming refers to performing actions
that have a future existence as their result [85]

Birth refers to connecting with rebirth
Aging and death extend up through feelings
They claim that this pertains to phases
They are named as links due to what is chief [86]

This is in order to put an end to ignorance
with regard to past, future, and in between
Three are afflictions, two constitute karma,
and seven are the bases[578] as well as the results [87]

Causes and results are comprised by two
due to inferring them from the middling one
Here, arising is held to be the cause,
while what has arisen is the result [88] {146}

From among these twelve links,
five are causes and seven results,
which are propelling, propelled,
completing, and completed [89]

As for the links that are shortcomings,
they are three, four, three, one, and one
The sufferings of formation, suffering,
and change are, in their due order,
five, two,[579] and five [90]

In the three realms, in their due order,
twelve, eleven, and ten are operating
Miraculous birth works through eleven links,
birth from a womb and an egg through eleven,
and birth from warmth and moisture as appropriate [91]

The same goes for the five states of existence
From the three, two arise
From two, seven arise, and from seven,
three arise—this cycle of existence
keeps spinning again and again[580] [92]

Saṃsāra's essence, aspects,
what, where,[581] and whereby,
how, how long, and shortcomings
operate through[582] infinite assemblies [93]

Make some effort and get out of it!
Enter the teachings of the Buddha!
Crush the hordes of the lord of death,
just like an elephant does a mud hut! [94]

Those who with heedfulness
engage in this dharmavinaya
relinquish the saṃsāra of birth
and will bring suffering to its end [95]

It is put to an end by nirvāṇa:
what, whereby, at what time,
where,[583] why, and in what way,
how long, essence, aspects,
what is to be attained, divisions, activity, {147}
and the assemblies of qualities [96]

The tīrthikas consist of two types:
those who are emanations and the actual ones
The latter acquired [their status] by birth or by training
Those by birth have the cut-off disposition and great desire
Those by training [practice] the dhyānas or are dialecticians [97]

Those in the dhyānas, by the power of supernatural knowledge,
entertain speculations in terms of the sixty-two [wrong] views:[584]
four kinds of proponents of permanence,
four who propound a partial permanence,
four of finiteness and so on, four evasive ones,
and two of causelessness[585]—these speculate about the past [98]

Sixteen proponents of discrimination existing,
eight proponents of it not existing, as well as
eight proponents of it neither existing nor nonexisting,
seven proponents of extinction, and five proponents
of a nirvāṇa in this present life here—
these are the views of speculating about the future [99]

The dialecticians are the Sāṃkhyas and so on,
who cling to tenets by way of valid cognition
The Sāṃkhyas discuss the three constituents[586]
that are lightness, motility, and darkness[587] [100]

States of mind of joy, satisfaction,
ecstasy, lust, and peacefulness
that are sometimes appearing
represent the signs of lightness [101]

Dissatisfaction and agony,
misery, as well as impatience,
for whatever reason they appear,
are held to be the signs of motility [102]

Oblivion, as well as dullness,
heedlessness, sleep, and indolence[588]
that appear at certain times[589]
represent the qualities of darkness[590] [103]

The three constituents' supreme primal substance[591]
does not represent the path of seeing[592]

What represents the path of seeing
is very hollow, just like an illusion [104] {148}

From the primal substance, the great one[593] arises,
and from that, the threefold I-consciousness[594]
From that originate the eleven faculties
and the five essential elements;[595] from those five,
the five [coarse] elements, making twenty-four:
the primal matter[596] itself and its modulations[597] [105]

These do not possess any consciousness
The person[598] experiencing all is conscious
If these twenty-five principles[599] are understood,
through a lock or[600] hair tuft at the crown of the head,
there is no doubt that one will become free
in the abode of repose that one desires[601] [106]

The Vaiśeṣikas assert six categories:
the six aspects of substance, quality, action,
generality, particular, and inherent relation[602] [107]

Substances are nine, qualities twenty-four,
actions five, generalities two, particulars two,
and inherence is likewise of two kinds
To understand these six principles is supreme knowledge,
going beyond the entirety of the Vedas[603] [108]

The Nirgranthas speak of nine categories:
soul, contamination, stoppage,
depletion,[604] bondage,[605]
karma, wrongdoing, merit,
and liberation[606] are the nine categories
Those who see them are completely pure[607] [109]

The Naiyāyikas assert sixteen categories:
valid cognition, the evaluated, doubt,

purpose, example, tenet,
parts, reasoning, ascertainment, [110]

debate, wrangling,[608] caviling,
fallacy,[609] deception,
wrong objection, and occasion for reproof[610]
Through these sixteen, one is delivered[611] [111]

The Mīmāṃśakas discuss four categories:
earth, water, fire, and wind
These are unconditioned,
always remaining without arising and ceasing [112]

Apart from those, karma {150} and its results do not exist,
nor are there any past or future existences
Those who conduct analysis in this way
will become liberated by mere seeing[612] [113]

Those who speak of Viṣṇu as creation's cause [say]:
"Among the Ādityas, I am Viṣṇu
Among lights, I am the radiant sun
Among the Maruts, I am Marīci[613]
Among the stars, I am the moon [114]

"Among the Vedas, I am the Sāmaveda
Among the gods, I am Vasava[614]
Among the senses, I am the mind
Among the elements, I am intention[615] [115]

"Among the Rudras, I am Śaṅkara[616]
Among yakṣas and rākṣasas, I am the lord of wealth
Among the gods of wealth, I am the god of fire
Among mountains, I am Meru
Among syllables, I am the letter A"[617] [116]

Matsya, Kūrma, Varāha,
Narasiṃha, Vāmana,
Paraśurāma, Rāma, Balarāma,[618] Kṛṣṇa,
the Buddha, and Kalki[619] are the ten [avatars]
If someone is constantly meditating on
Viṣṇu's qualities, they will attain bliss [117]

Those who speak of Īśvara[620] as creation's cause
[say that] Īśvara constitutes the creator
of the entirety of all sentient beings
and that he possesses eight qualities [118]

He is subtle, light, worthy of veneration,
the sovereign, the almighty,
obtains all, has irresistible will,
and also exists as he pleases [119]

By [just slightly moving] his hands or feet,
his eyes, his face, or his body,
he creates and destroys many [worlds]
Hence, he is said to be subtle [120]

Since he makes space, wind,
earth, water, and fire remain,
withdraw, {150} and also expand,
he is declared to have lightness [121]

He is venerated in the three realms
and revered by those who stay and go,
as well as the entirety of spirits
Hence, he is worthy of reverence [122]

He has power over all faculties[621]
and does whatever he wishes
with the[622] mobile and immobile
Hence, he is called "the sovereign" [123]

He is self-sufficient, independent,
never afraid of anything,
thus having power over all
Hence, he is called "the almighty"[623] [124]

Whichever place or food it may be
and whatever his mind is thinking,
his mind goes there and [his body] does not remain behind
Hence, he is called "obtaining all"[624] [125]

Lightness, motility, and darkness,
wherever they may be located,
he creates by merely opening his eyes
Hence, he is called "having irresistible will" [126]

Be it liberation or any divine bodies,
whichever he himself may desire,
he obtains it all by wishing so
Hence, he is called "existing as he pleases" [127]

He who is subtle[625] remains born alone
He creates and destroys all of this
Called "the powerful lord, the supreme god of highest generosity,"
he is the creator of qualities who attained utter peace [128]

Lacking any knowledge about this, living beings
have no control over their own happiness or suffering
It is Īśvara who sends it to them, and so they will either go
to the higher realms or simply plunge into the abysses [129]

If Īśvara, similar to a potter, were not the magical creator of all this diversity {151}
this Mount Meru would not be, nor would this ground of the earth, nor the ocean,
nor would the sun and the moon with the stars as they are arranged be objects of our eyes

But since they exist, Īśvara is the creator of beings, so some people propose [130]

He is subtle, peaceful, inconceivable, firm, creator, all-knowing, all-creating,
attained by being familiar with yoga, the dhyāna object of intelligent dhyānists,
and has the form of the sun, the moon, earth, water, fire, wind, space, and so on—
those who wish for the ecstatic bliss of peace should always meditate on Īśvara [131]

Those who say that [all] is contingent on time
[say that] all entities are changed by time
Since even the fearless wrathful one
whose maternal uncle is Vasava
and whose father is Vāsuki was killed,[626]
it is difficult to go beyond this time [132]

The elements are brought forth by time
The assembling of all beings is created by time
Time makes us fall asleep and wake up[627]
Hence, it is difficult to go beyond time [133]

The pit of the Tripura guardians,[628] the ocean,
soldiers, rākṣasas, riches, the efforts of Dhanada,[629]
as well as the śāstṛ Rāvaṇa with evenly measured
purification[630] are also ruined by the power of time [134]

Those who propound an essence as the cause[631]
[say that] entities are established by their essence
The three [features] of the redness of fire,
the righteous promoting others' welfare,
and the unrighteous lacking loving-kindness[632]
are established by their very essence [135]

Who has created the sharpness of thorns?
Who made the patterns of deer and birds? {152}
Take sweet sugar cane and the bitter nimba[633]—
all of these are established by their essence [136]

The sun being hot, the moon being cool,
people having passion, sages not having it,
satisfaction by pleasure, and torment by suffering—
those six are established by their essence [137]

Those who propound causelessness[634]
[say that] all is independent of causes
By what is the arising of entities—
their diversity, such as the sun
and the anthers of a lotus—produced? [138]

What is it that has created this diversity,
such as the eyes of peacock feathers?
Just as rain, wind, and such are regarded
as causeless, since they occur out of the blue,
so suffering and so on are without a cause [139]

Being indolent about what is very vast
and profound, being utterly unrefined,
and oblivious of themselves, others, and their foes,[635]
[those people] at present[636] denigrate the Mahāyāna [140]

It is better if you fall away from discipline,
but never, at any cost, do so from the view!
Through discipline, you proceed to the higher realms
Through the view, you do so to the supreme state [141]

Those obscured by the power of dullness
thus keep obstructing true actuality
They do not even have any virtuous existences,
so there is no need to mention lacking liberation [142]

Seeing the abundance of the tīrthikas
with their seeds of being harmful,
is there anyone not feeling compassion
for persons[637] wishing for liberation?
Hence, those who strive for liberation
should behold the dharmadhātu [143]

This concludes "A Song on Beholding the Dharmadhātu" composed by the great master Dīpaṃkara. {153} *It was translated by this Indian upādhyāya himself and the Tibetan translator bhikṣu Tsültrim Gyalwa.* {154}

(154) A Vajra Song on the Vajra Seat

In the language of India: *Vajrāsanavajragīti*[638]
In the language of Tibet: *Rdo rje gdan gyi rdo rje glu*

I pay homage to youthful Mañjuśrī

To the Buddha at the summit of the glorious vajra seat
and the guru who has the character of Vajradhara in person,
who taught this song endowed with the profound meaning,
and in whom all qualities are complete, I pay homage [1]

He who abandoned without exception the kind of activities
that lead to an emaciated body and a mind full of affliction
will thereby become awakened[639] on the vajra seat full of glory
in the form of the natural complete purity of all beings[640] [2]

Through swiftly practicing by bringing the beauty endowed with
what's supreme,
at the banks of the Nairañjanā, he unites by entering easily[641]
Residing on the vajra seat at the root of the bodhi tree,
exemplified by a vajra, he is resting in samādhi [3]

Through this path of unsurpassable samādhi, hey,[642]
he overcomes the[643] great fears of the four māras

By not abandoning form but playing in coexistence,
he is uniting with the natural Nairātmyā [4]

This queen with her persona[644] of ravishing nonbeing {155}
is without afflictions due to lacking attachment and being at peace,
by which existence's whirl of delusion of birth and death is
relinquished
and great bliss without delusion is seized and bestowed [5]

She does not have any color, shape, or size,
lacks activity, lacks desire,[645] lacks birth, and lacks pride
If the mind has entered this Nairātmyā,
without exception, divisions of self and others are not seen[646] [6]

She lacks any coming, going, or abiding anywhere
Just as the essence of space, as it truly is,
she is relished by the supreme yogī sages without exception
She is the queen Nairātmyā, I declare [7]

In a proper manner, make firm the bodhicitta of aspiration
that arises from love and compassion without attachment
The mind that is familiar with its nature does not dwell anywhere
Precisely this is the path to unsurpassable awakening [8]

Those with blurred vision say they see hairs in the sky
Those with blurred vision and all beings are not different
In fact, without arising and without abiding, all beings
definitely appear just like optical illusions [9]

Don't be attached to what is created by conceived discursiveness!
It does not serve as the path to unsurpassable awakening
There exists no bondage other than all kinds of thoughts
This saṃsāra of birth and death is nothing other than that [10]

I speak about the quintessence to beings who are yogīs
Do not look at any movements of thoughts![647]

Thoughts are not one thing, ignorance is not another one,
and attachment, hatred, fear, and wrath are nothing other[648] than
that [11]

Whatever is examined is delusive and mistaken
What is determined for sure is held to be great bliss {156}
I say that this kind of samādhi is great bliss
There is no harm anywhere through any fear of birth or death [12]

Though deer who see a mirage as water may rush there,
they will die from exhaustion, not finding pleasure anywhere
Hey, oh deer of the mind desiring the water of bliss,
don't rush[649] toward the mirages of objects! [13]

There is no water of bliss in any mirages of objects
Not understanding real entities, you rush by desiring something
Take an animal searching for enjoyment and pleasure in a
village—
that animal will come to be bound by a tight noose[650] [14]

Those who understand the essence delight in the inconceivable
play[651] of samādhi that is without going anywhere whatsoever
The tree on which the vulture of the mind relies and dwells[652]
does not bring forth the leaves and flowers of bliss [15]

If the vulture of the mind is bound and killed for good,
what bad things could it possibly do by moving and shifting?
When the vulture of the mind becomes free of its bondage,
it won't be hungry due to eating and drinking lots of meat and
blood [16]

By overcoming the dimension of seeing duality, you
do not make any effort anywhere[653] through anything
Rely[654] on emptiness—delusion cannot be relinquished!
Do not think that delusion is able to get rid of bondage! [17]

Closely look at what may arise from anything
and dispel it through nonconceptual samādhi!
Without exception, the great stains of thoughts are delusion[655]
Examine[656] entities as being equal, just like sky flowers [18]

A yogī's not seeing due to lacking training's latent tendencies {157}
is similar to seeing a bee sipping from a flower in the sky
The completely pure conduct of the samaya of training
is what counters living with worldly discursiveness [19]

Overcome the delusion of views about self and others
that resembles a bee sipping from a flower in the sky!
By letting the vajra swoop down on worldly discursiveness,
relinquish fear,[657] clinging, and shame through the avadhūtī! [20]

Through both the aspiration for awakening and compassion,
everything comes to be included in this training
The guru's instructions appear as precious jewels,
but what pleasure could arise from other jewels? [21]

The fruition does not arise from lacking the guru's pith instructions,
just as in the case of saffron color on a soiled piece of cotton
If you have experienced a yoginī, you will become a yogī
Thus, by a young woman's union with someone else, bliss is created [22]

Other than the guru's speech, through which you will be liberated
from the ocean of saṃsāric existence, what is there that's essential?
Benefiting others through compassion is the undertaking of a disciple
By virtue of seizing the orange robes, alms are not difficult to find [23]

The syllable *śrī* is nondual wisdom—
it shows that beings[658] are inseparable

Abandon all treatises that make the mind dull
and you will become the ultimate Śrī Heruka! [24]

The syllable *he* teaches that the oblivion that arose
without a cause and so on is stopped and given up
The syllable *ru* teaches that death is relinquished
because of being the ultimate free of examination and analysis [25]
{158}

The syllable *ka* teaches that, without abiding in any being
or nonbeing whatsoever, there's no existence or nirvāṇa[659]
The meaning that is thus taught by these four
constitutes the ultimate glorious Heruka [26]

This concludes a vajra song sung by Mahāpaṇḍita Dīpaṃkaraśrījñāna on the meadowy plain at Kyishö Nyetang Dashi Bal,[660] *when he had arrived at the state of Vajradhara in order to teach others the actual reality of being, just as he himself had seen it.*[661] {159}

(155) A Commentary on "A Vajra Song on the Vajra Seat"

In the language of India: *Vajrāsanavajragītivṛtti*[662]
In the language of Tibet: *Rdo rje gdan gyi rdo rje glu'i 'grel pa*

I pay homage to youthful Mañjuśrī

You dispel the suffering of saṃsāric existence
with its towering waves of birth and so on,
and out of compassion fulfill our hopes as we wish—[663]
to you, venerable Tārā, I pay homage

Resembling the moon in the water,
you possess the nine expressions of dance[664]
Prime teacher, glorious blood drinker,
king of vīras, may you always protect us!

In order to benefit those without eyes who are on the wrong
path
and forever cycle under the sway of delusion's unbearable
whirl,
I shall write down, in accordance with the words of the guru,
the line of transmission of the profound definitive meaning

[1][665] The lines that begin with "**to the Buddha at the summit of the glorious vajra seat**" are the expression of reverence. Its objects are two:

the three jewels and their cause—the guru. By speaking about the Buddha here, the jewel of the dharma (the path) and the jewel of the saṃgha (the support) should be understood implicitly. For they have the nature of cause and effect as well as support [and supported]. {160} Since the guru is the one on whom they depend,[666] I say, "**the guru who has the character of Vajradhara in person**," because there is no difference in their nature and [the guru] is their cause. As for "**who taught this song endowed with the profound meaning, and in whom all qualities are complete**," connate luminosity[667] is as profound as the ocean. Since its actuality is pointed out in its natural way, I speak of "song." I use the expression "in whom all qualities are complete," because all described qualities of the guru without exception are complete and [all] buddha qualities are naturally complete in him. Therefore[668] he is genuine, and this is my expression of reverence.

[2] Now, to explain the [actual] text, it [begins by] saying, "**He who abandoned without exception** . . ." In terms of refraining and engaging, this is twofold. The causes for **an emaciated body and a mind full of affliction** consist of the yogic disciplines of the outsiders, such as relying on the five fires.[669] Here, the deeds of the followers of this dharma that represent **activities** of **the** same **kind** are the twelve qualities of abstinence and so on.[670] Furthermore, [such activities] refer to everything that is not in accordance with samādhi. Having abandoned such activities to refrain from,[671] engagement [in what is appropriate] means that if someone properly makes efforts in the nature of connate luminosity and makes it a living experience, "**he will thereby become awakened on**[672] **the vajra seat full of glory in the form of the natural complete purity of all beings**." Here, purity is twofold: by virtue of the natural purity that is common to all beings {161} being excellently cleansed by prajñā and compassion, it enters its state of [also] being pure of [adventitious] stains. The words "in the form of" refer to [natural] purity's being without stains. The other [words] are easy to understand.[673]

[3] Having briefly introduced the means[674] of refraining and engaging, now, I teach them in detail by way of examples. To do so, I say, "**Through swiftly practicing** . . ." There are four examples here: the beauty, a river, the bodhi tree, and a vajra. Among these, the first example is the example of what is to be illustrated[675] and the illustrating symbol. The sec-

ond is the example of being uninterrupted like a river and not abiding in the two extremes. The third is the example of what is clearly manifest through having been purified. [The fourth is the example of the qualities.][676]

As for [the first example in] the line "**through swiftly practicing by bringing the beauty endowed with what's supreme**," in terms of Nairātmyā as the illustrating symbol, "the beauty" refers to her body. "What's supreme" refers to her speech and mind. She is endowed with the qualities of these three. "Bringing" refers to [taking these three] into solitude[677] and so on. There, you "swiftly practice."[678] "Through" means that through practicing in that way, connate luminosity is experienced. How it is experienced shall be explained below. The Nairātmyā that is to be illustrated consists of luminosity and the connate, which represent the supreme beauty.[679] "Endowed" refers to being endowed with the uncontaminated qualities. Through swiftly practicing these two [Nairātmyās] as a unity in such a way, the fruition of mahāmudrā is attained.

The second example consists of the line "**at the banks of the Nairañjanā,** {162} **he unites by entering easily**." The Nairañjanā has two attributes: its stream is uninterrupted and it does not flow beyond its two banks. Likewise, yogīs should focus on the actuality illustrated by the [first] example in an uninterrupted manner and without falling into the extremes of either permanence or extinction. It is because the path does not enter either of these two [extremes][680] that I say, "entering easily." "Unites" is twofold: practicing in the manner of uniting vajra and lotus as well as expanse and awareness.

In terms of the third example, I say, "**residing on the vajra seat at the root of the bodhi tree**." The bodhi tree has five attributes: roots, trunk, leaves, flowers, and fruits. Likewise, yogīs attain mastery and practice through the prajñā that resembles the roots, the confidence that resembles the trunk, the vigor that resembles the leaves, the mindfulness that resembles the flowers, and the samādhi that resembles the fruits.[681] That is, no matter where such yogīs dwell, they reside on the vajra seat.

In order to teach the meaning of the fourth example, I say, "**exemplified by a vajra, he is resting in samādhi**." A vajra has two [attributes]: being unsplittable and splitting. Likewise, by way of being endowed with the five faculties [just mentioned], yogīs practice in the manner of being unsplittable by the triad of the afflictive [obscurations], cognitive [obscurations], and the obscurations to meditative equipoise, {163} while splitting these [obscurations].

[4] "**Through this path of unsurpassable samādhi, hey**"[682] means "through this path of having mastered connate luminosity through the five faculties [just mentioned]." "Hey" refers to instructing by calling out. I say, "**He overcomes the**[683] **great fears of the four māras**." For, through the power of the arising of connate luminosity, the operations of such-and-such māras (such as the arising of karma and afflictions)[684] are seen like the surface of a pure sky.

Now, in order to teach in detail the actual Nairātmyā illustrated[685] by the first example, I say, "**by not abandoning form** . . ." *Rūpa* is used for both "form" and "nature." If the prefix *sva-* is added, it becomes *svarūpa*[686]—the Nairātmyā who is mind's luminosity. As for "**by not abandoning form but playing in coexistence**," this kind of Nairātmyā and awareness play in such a way that they are nondual. The two lines beginning with "**he is uniting with the natural** . . ." are easy to understand.

[5] To teach [this Nairātmyā's] characteristics and benefit, I say, "**is without afflictions due to lacking attachment and being at peace, by which**." "Lacking attachment" refers to the one hundred and sixty mundane states of mind. "Being at peace" refers to their arising and operating having been cut through. "Without afflictions . . . by which" is merely an illustration: it refers to the luminous wisdom free of [all] three obscurations, by which [saṃsāric] **existence's delusion of birth and death is** severed. {164} Is this merely a severing? [No,] without exception, the uncontaminated qualities of delusion having become exhausted are seized. Therefore, I say, "**great bliss without delusion is seized and bestowed**."

[6–7] To teach her characteristics in detail, I say, "**She does not have any color, shape, or size**." The meaning here is this: in terms of the illustrating Nairātmyā—the karmamudrā—there are [characteristics, such as her] excellent distinctions[687] in terms of color and shape, the length of her eyes and so on, being evenly proportioned, activity (the six samaya-cakras), the desire of[688] anticipating bliss, and, based on that, the birth of mind arising in the form of bliss as well as the pride of mantra, dharma, and so on. Based on that, by bringing the vāyus into the central nāḍī, the mind transforms into[689] the expression of bliss. Through that, once it has become stable, the familiarization with it as the **Nairātmyā** to be illustrated[690]—luminosity—occurs. Therefore, her [actual] characteristics are the nine,[691] such as not having any color: she has the characteristics of not having any color, not having any shape, not having any measure, **lacking activity**, **lacking desire**, **lacking birth**, **lacking pride**, **lacking any coming** and **going**, and lacking any **self and others**. The example of there being no difference between the [Nairātmyā] who has such characteristics and **the mind** is stated in the line "**just as the essence of space, as it truly is**." That is, {165} she appears like the center of a pure sky. Whose object is she? "**She is relished by the supreme yogī sages without exception**." It is the fortunate supreme[692] yogī sages who are the children of the Buddha, rely on true gurus, and gather the accumulations who see her as an object with the eye of prajñā and relish her in the manner of being certain by virtue of the four faculties. Why is that? I say,[693] "**She is the queen Nairātmyā**."

[8] By relishing that kind of natural Nairātmyā,[694] this is clearly both the severing of the arising of karma, afflictions, and so on at their root and the natural cessation that is to be manifested. However, if you do not complete all uncontaminated qualities in your own mindstream, do not fully mature sentient beings, and do not fully purify buddha fields through the bodhicitta that is propelled by love and compassion, but manifest the true end some time in between, you will fall into [the states of] a śrāvaka or pratyekabuddha.[695] Therefore, while being endowed with this poised readiness [of not leaving the bodhisattva path and shortcutting to the nirvāṇa of a śrāvaka or pratyekabuddha], you need to complete all virtuous qualities. To teach that, I say, "**In a proper manner, make firm the bodhicitta of aspiration that arises from love and compassion without attachment**." "Without attachment" refers to not clinging [to what is illusory], due to knowing its nature, just like an illusionist. The bodhicitta that is propelled by love and compassion has already been understood. {166}

Here, its progression is this. Upon having risen from their bed, yogīs first consider the following: While this body that is of a mental nature since beginningless time has not been established as a self and what belongs to that self, it is conceived as being real.[696] Therefore, it is [nothing but] thoughts. Through the power of [that consideration], they regard the stream of thoughts as blazing fires of suffering. Since the succession of births is countless, the number of [cases in which] just a single [sentient being] has been the mother[697] of a given sentient being cannot be determined. Hence, with the motivation of pulling out [all] beings who live in the entirety of saṃsāra, [yogīs] should first engage their minds in love and compassion. Then, they should make firm their bodhicitta of aspiration that consists of wishing, for the sake of those [beings], that they become Śrī Heruka. Next, they think that since all phenomena are the miraculous creations of the mind and the vāyus, there are no referents other than the mind. To imagine the sheer[698] vāyu-mind as the body of the deity represents the seeming reality that is self-blessing. Then, through the principle of recollecting previous bliss,[699] they should bring the mind and the vāyus into the central nāḍī and cultivate the samādhi of great emptiness, which is associated with bliss. Then, they think that they have entered the nature of the mind.

At that point, they should look at the characteristic of the [nature of the mind]—the appearance-free luminosity that is like the center of the sky—with the eye of prajñā, look undistractedly through mindfulness, look with trust through confidence, look in [a state of] having annihilated mundane states of mind through vigor, and {167} look in a one-pointed manner through[700] samādhi. Thereby, through resting based on the luminous nature of the mind, which is appearance-free, lucid, limpid, pure, and radiant,[701] certainty arises.

The example for looking undistractedly through mindfulness is to be like a person pursuing someone while carrying a stack of sesame seeds in their hand. The example for trust through confidence is to be like a young woman experiencing desire. The example for vigor is to be like a king's gatekeeper. The example for samādhi is to be like a lamp without wind. The example for certainty through prajñā is to be like someone seeing a person with whom they are already familiar. I do not adduce the oral tradition of these examples out of fear of [having to quote] too many scriptural passages.

[Yogīs] rest in this way for as long as the mind is able to rest. Then, from within that state, they should instantaneously rise as the illusion-like body of the deity,[702] think of all entities as having the characteristic of being mere appearances free of superimposition and denial, just like water-moons, and fully complete all virtuous phenomena propelled by love, compassion, and bodhicitta in the manner of [these phenomena] being free of superimposition and denial, just like water-moons. In that way, they should fully complete all virtuous phenomena in the manner of means and prajñā as well as emptiness and compassion[703] being inseparable. Otherwise, they will fall into [the states of] śrāvakas and so on. Therefore, the sūtras say:

> Without means and devoid of prajñā, they will fall into śrāvakahood.[704] {168}

What is means here? It consists of fully completing all virtuous phenomena by virtue of being propelled by bodhicitta, fully maturing sentient beings, and fully purifying buddha fields. What is prajñā? It consists of cutting through clinging and discursiveness with regard to that. For without means, prajñā therefore does not arise. The same is also stated in detail in other Mahāyāna sūtras [such as]:

> Through means, all virtuous phenomena are brought together.
> Through prajñā, they are distinguished

Such yogīs do not travel [the path] by dwelling in the two extremes. Therefore, I say, "**The mind that is familiar with its nature does not dwell anywhere. Precisely this is the path to unsurpassable awakening**."

[9] Now, to teach other objects viewed by the eye of prajñā, I say, "**Those with blurred vision say they see hairs in the sky**." The objects that are viewed are two: the pair of[705] what is nonexistent and what is existent. Seeing what is nonexistent refers to delusion in terms of all the cognitions and cognizable objects of those who see just this life without exception, which is understood to be similar to the example of **those with blurred vision** seeing strands of hairs and so on.[706] Seeing the nature of what is existent is twofold: seeing luminosity (the support) and the uncontaminated qualities (the supported). How is luminosity seen? It is seen as being without arising and without abiding. Therefore, I say, "**in fact, without arising and without abiding,** {169} **all beings**."

How are the uncontaminated qualities seen? They are seen as having the nature of mere appearances and mere experiences free of superimposition and denial, just like illusions, dreams, optical illusions, and water-moons. Therefore, I say, "**definitely appear just like optical illusions**."

[10] Now follows the ancillary repudiation of conceived yogas. To do so, I say, "**Don't be attached to what is created by conceived discursiveness!**" Conceived discursiveness refers to subtle bindus and so on. As for not being attached, though there is a subtle resting of the mind based on this [discursiveness], the defining characteristics of the [true] path are not complete [in that resting]. Therefore, it is repudiated in that **it is not the path to awakening**. Since this is not the path of cutting through the whirl of delusion of saṃsāra, it is rather taught to be the cause of saṃsāra: "**There exists no bondage other than all kinds of thoughts. This saṃsāra of birth and death is nothing other than that**." Though one may already be familiar with some means that lack the characteristic of cutting through the whirl of delusion of saṃsāric existence, since this very whirl of delusion is not severed [by such means], they are to be relinquished.

[11] To teach the instructions for yogīs who familiarize with the definitive meaning,[707] I say, "**I speak about the quintessence to beings who are yogīs**." This consists of [stating] who is instructed, in what are they instructed, and in which manner they are instructed. It refers to instructing yogīs in essential reality and in mindfulness. Who is instructed? Yogīs. In what {170} are they instructed? In the quintessence—luminosity. How are they instructed? In terms of mindfulness and so on. **Movements of thoughts** constitute the mundane states of mind. "**Do not look**" is the instruction not to follow them. You may wonder why that is. What cycles? The mind. Through what does it cycle? Through the vāyus. In which manner does it cycle? It cycles under the sway of the mundane states of mind inputting all kinds of latent tendencies throughout the day and night. Hence, the **thoughts** that represent the means[708] that cause this cycling **are not one thing**, and the ignorance that causes delusion **is not another one**. So what are they? They are [nothing but] mind and the vāyus. The explanation of the mundane states of mind consists of the line that begins with "**and attachment, hatred** . . . ," which is easy to understand.

[12] The instruction on prajñā consists of the lines that begin with "**whatever is examined is delusive** . . ." If whatever mundane states of mind that may arise based on the miraculous creations[709] of the mind and the vāyus are examined by prajñā, they are realized[710] to be delusive **and mistaken**. However, if essential reality **is determined for sure**, it **is . . . great bliss**. Therefore, "**I say that this kind of samādhi is great bliss**." Luminosity is mastered through the five faculties. By virtue of having severed the delusion of saṃsāric existence without exception, **there is no fear of birth or death**, as well as no suffering of any illness or **harm** whatsoever at all.

[13–14] Now, to teach that there is bondage through being attached to the five sense pleasures if their nature is not understood, {171} I say, "**Though deer who see a mirage** . . . ," which is easy to understand. The lines that begin with "**take an animal searching for enjoyment and pleasure . . .**" teach the example for being bound.

[15] Now, to teach that if someone understands the nature [of phenomena], they are free through that,[711] I say, "**Those who understand the essence delight in the inconceivable play**[712] **of samādhi that is without going anywhere whatsoever**." This occurs if all entities are understood to be the miraculous creations of the mind and the vāyus, and these are understood to be unborn.

Now, to teach that true reality is not seen if there is clinging to the illustrating bliss, I say, "**The tree on which the vulture** . . ." Here, there are two examples: the example of a tree that is the support of a vulture and the example of seeing a bee sipping from a flower in the sky [in stanza 19].

The first one has two parts: the example for being bound and the example for being released. Through the vulture dung, the roots of a tree on which a vulture sits rot, and its leaves and flowers do not grow because its bark is stripped off by the [vulture's] beak. Likewise, if there is clinging to the mind arising in the form of bliss due to the fusing of the mind and the vāyus of a yogī, luminosity (resembling flowers) is not seen and the kāya of unity (resembling leaves) is not seen [either]. Therefore, I say, "**The tree on which the vulture of the mind relies and dwells does not bring forth the leaves and flowers of bliss**." So through what are these two seen? Luminosity is seen by binding the mind and the vāyus and killing mundane states of mind. Unity is seen by releasing them. {172}

[16] "**If the vulture of the mind is bound and killed for good**" refers to the mind and the vāyus being bound and killed within the natural state of luminosity. What happens through that? The whirl of delusion is cut through: "**what bad things could it possibly do by moving and shifting?**" Since any movement through the vāyus and any shifting of the one hundred and sixty [mundane] states of mind are cut through, how could any bad things—that is, the input of virtuous and nonvirtuous latent tendencies—be done? They cannot [be done]. If a **vulture** is released **from its bondage, it won't be hungry** or thirsty[713] **due to eating and drinking meat and blood**.

[17] Similarly, **by overcoming the dimension of seeing duality** through prajñā, the mental body that is present like a water-moon becomes an aid of true reality. Perceiver and perceived **do not make any effort at any** place whatsoever in harming yogīs who understand appearing entities to be like water-moons. Therefore, apart from needing to rely on[714] luminous emptiness, delusion cannot be relinquished. Hence, I say, "**Rely**[715] **on emptiness—delusion cannot be relinquished!**" "**Do not think that delusion is able to get rid of bondage!**" Without realizing the connate yoga through luminosity, the bondage of the mundane states of mind is not relinquished through any yoga of delusion whatsoever.

[18] Therefore, I say, "**Closely look at what may arise from anything and dispel it through nonconceptual samādhi!**" Look with the eye of prajñā at any mundane states of mind[716] whatsoever that may arise and {173} dispel them. Through what? Through nonconceptual samādhi. Nonconceptuality (prajñā) and samādhi are explicitly mentioned [here]; the third [element] is to be understood implicitly, which consists of dispelling[717] [mundane states of mind] by being endowed with the five faculties. The instruction in the manner of a concluding summary says, "**Without exception, the great stains of thoughts are delusion.**[718] **Examine**[719] **entities as being equal, just like sky flowers**." [Through] the path that involves examining the stains of thoughts with prajñā as being entities of delusion within delusion and understands and familiarizes with them [in that way], they are to be examined as being equal in terms of unity.[720]

[19] In terms of examining[721] the second example, I say, "**A yogī's not seeing due to lacking training's latent tendencies is similar to seeing a bee sipping from a flower in the sky**." For, even if yogīs lack the latent tendencies of the movements of the mundane states of mind by virtue of having trained the mind in the illustrating bliss, they do not see the nonduality of expanse and awareness.[722] Without incorporating the vāyus and the mind into this nature [that consists of the nonduality of expanse and awareness], there is [still some] involvement in being ensnared by bliss without feeling,[723] and the clinging to that is similar to seeing a bee sipping from a flower in the sky. You may wonder why [this bliss] is then explained as what illustrates [that nature]. This is without flaw, because similar to a finger pointing at the moon, after the vāyu-mind has been transformed into having the form of bliss, {174} it must be stabilized, and this [stabilized] vāyu-mind must be incorporated into that nature. If there is clinging to true reality, this is called "being deceived and deluded about the ultimate," because it is posited through dependence. What then? The teaching by way of following the correct order [of practice] consists of the lines that begin with "**the completely pure** . . ." By having **trained** in the vāyu-mind [that manifests] in the form of bliss, the great empty[724]—being empty of the one hundred and sixty mundane states of mind—is incorporated into all-empty luminosity in accordance with the words[725] of the true gurus and the buddhas, and then the familiarization [with this luminosity] takes place. This is the completely pure **conduct**. From that [state], [luminosity] needs to arise as the illusion-like body of the deity[726] and complete all virtuous phenomena in the manner of understanding that this body of the deity is like a water-moon. You may then wonder what the point of any discursiveness apart from needing to familiarize with nothing but all-empty luminosity is. I say that though [the above steps] may look like discursiveness, they **counter living with worldly** people's **discursiveness**.

[20] Therefore, [both] the mudrā and **the delusion of views about self and others that resembles a bee sipping from a flower in the sky** are purified through luminosity. How are they purified[727] as luminosity? I say, "**by letting the vajra swoop down on worldly discursiveness**." The entirety of container and contents[728] melts into luminosity and is withdrawn into it. "**Relinquish fear,**[729] **clinging, and shame through**

the avadhūtī!" That is, the vāyus including the mind should be brought into the central nāḍī, and familiarization with luminosity should occur.

[21] To give a concluding summary of the fourth example, {175} I say, "**Through both the aspiration** . . . ," which has already been explained. For **everything** on the path of the Mahāyāna is **included in this training** in **compassion** and prajñā being nondual.

[22] This kind of path resembles the cursing mantras of the ḍākinīs. Where is it obtained? It is obtained from **the gurus**, because it **does not arise** if they are **lacking**. Therefore, I say, "**if you have experienced a yoginī, you will become a yogī**." The familiarization with compassion and prajñā, as well as expanse and awareness, as being nondual is contingent on the guru,[730] which resembles the example of the **bliss** of **a young woman** being contingent on a man.

[23] Hence, since the delusion **of saṃsāric existence** is severed **through** the means of a true guru in this lifetime, **there is** nothing **other** whatsoever **than** taking **the speech of** the [guru] to be **essential**. Therefore, the wise who wish excellency for themselves should rely on a genuine [guru]. The lines [beginning with] "**benefiting others through compassion** . . ." are easy to understand.

[24–26] Now,[731] to give a synopsis of the text, I say, "**The syllable** ***śrī*** **is nondual wisdom.**" This is the concluding summary of this path, which teaches the characteristics of the two realities and that they are a nondual unity. The synonyms of that are said to be "**the ultimate Heruka**," "Vajrasattva," "dwelling in the mode of being of the two realities," and so on.

With the motivation to benefit others, I wrote down
this ocean-like profound approach of dharma {176}
May the noble ones and the ḍākinīs be patient
about all mistakes that may have occurred here!

When the final times are upon us,
life is short, diseases are many, possessions few,[732]
and bad conditions and obstacles abound
Hence, being powerless to remain for long,

you are thus unable to ascertain the words,
but should rely on a genuine spiritual friend
With a mind full of great vigor,
be very mindful of distractions[733]

In order to free myself and others,[734]
I commented on this essential reality
Through the merit of commenting on it with love,
may the beings who entered inferior paths
come to dwell on the genuine path!

This concludes an elucidation of the meaning of "A Vajra Song on the Vajra Seat" composed by Mahāpaṇḍita Dīpaṃkaraśrījñāna. It was translated and finalized by this paṇḍita himself and the bhikṣu Tsültrim Gyalwa. {177}

(156) A Dhyāna Song

In the language of India: *Dhyānagīti*
In the language of Tibet: *Ting nge 'dzin gyi glu*

I pay homage to Śrī Heruka

It is to the actuality of the tantras,
very profound to me, Dīpaṃkaraśrī,
that I pay homage at the full moon's feet,
venerable, wise, and secret Rāhula [1]

HE HE PHEṂ PHEṂ HA HA

It is the excellent attire of E that
is adorned by WAṂ in its center
In its being the abode of all bliss,
it is the buddhas' jewel casket [2]

The pistil of the beautiful lotus—
delightful, pure, luminous space,
the dharmakāya of the buddhas—
is to be pointed out clearly by Heruka [3]

Through always concealing the vola,
the movement of sun and moon is overcome

Otherwise, meditate within great space
Bhairava will not enter [4]

Through the yogas of opening and entering,
you should invoke them fervently
The five buddhas and the four female deities
are to be burned up again and again [5]

The vīras and yoginīs of the ten directions
gather and dissolve into Jālandhara
The four bindus on the four lotuses
will arise as the sixteen kinds of bliss [6] {178}

They arise having the form of self-appearing wisdom
and dwell in the center of the lotus pistils
When dwelling at the tip of the jewel,
like a lamp, they become extinguished [7]

When becoming extinguished
at the tip of the jewel,
the hosts of thoughts about self, other, and so on
I do not see as anything whatsoever [8]

When sun and moon are seized by planets,
the mind and Bhairava are not moving
When thoughts without exception melt and dissolve,
they are within the natural state of mind's expanse [9]

In the expanse of space, there is no self
In the center of the self, there is no space
Thoughts without exception are space
Self and space are inseparable [10]

Realization is *he* and *ru* and *ka*
With mind contained in being empty,
if being empty is poured into the mind,

contrived thoughts about being empty,
nonempty, and so on dissolve into space [11]

On the bliss arising from kunduru[735]
through joining vola and kakkola,
the brahmacārins should not rely
To impair samaya means going to the lower realms [12]

The female deity residing in the heart
constitutes Prajñāpāramitā
Yogīs are giving rise to yoga
Vajradhātvīśvarī is the mother [13]

She on whom all the buddhas rely
is none other than Prajñāpāramitā,
the supreme queen of the tathāgatas
Her bhūmi is the thirteenth one [14]

The genuine dharma is explained as the bhaga
Śrī and *he* and *ru* as well as *ka*
Abiding as the four mudras and the four kāyas
or representing the expanse of wisdom,
it is the dharmakāya of the buddhas [15] {179}

Those who are taken care of by an excellent guru
with this yāna of secret mantra's great principle
become accomplished in six months and so on—
so who on earth would not enter it? [16]

We are greatly tormented by sufferings
in saṃsāra since time without beginning,
yet we do not enter this yāna of secret mantra
that terminates all suffering without exception [17]

The hosts of swords, such as the peaceful,
make the waves of the siddhis billow,
yet we do not enter this yāna of secret mantra [18]

Similar to geese on a lotus lake,
all the assemblies of vīras and yoginīs
bestow their blessings and their protection
Thus, which wise one would not enter here? [19]

Those for whom relinquishment, ruin,
and flaws have occurred in other yānas,
once they entered here, will see buddhahood
in this very lifetime without a doubt [20]

HE HE PHEṂ PHEṂ E HYE HI
E SARVAVĪRAYOGINĪ
OṂ ĀḤ HŪṂ MAHĀPRAJÑĀ PRA HŪṂ HŪṂ
OṂ PHEṂ GHAḤ OṂ PHEṂ GHE
OṂ PHEṂ OṂ GHAḤ GHAḤ GHAḤ HŪṂ

Śrāvakas as well as inferior people,
in very solitary places of relinquishment,
holding a small plate filled with offering cakes,
play the ḍamaru and sing this samādhi song [21]

At the time when Śrī Guhyajñānavajra[736] *was engaging in the conduct of yogic disciplines, the ḍākinīs in the secret land Śrī Oḍḍiyāna were singing [this song] in his dream, and he retained it in his mind. Later, at the time of a feast of vīras in Somapuri, he sang it as a song. [Hereby,] it is concluded. Since both Gya Dsöndrü Sengé*[737] *and* {180} *the bhikṣu Tsültrim Gyalwa requested him to write it down, he did so. Then, this guru himself and those two translators translated it as this very [rendering here].*[738] {181}

(157) A Meditation on the Sixteen Bindus

In the language of India: *Ṣoḍaśabindubhāvanānāma*[739]
In the language of Tibet: *Thig le bcu drug gi nyams len zhes bya ba*

I pay homage to mother Nairātmyā

Thinking of your own body as an empty house,
you should contemplate the four cakras
in the avadhūtī without characteristics [1]

The sixty-four letters
bless the nirmāṇacakra
Sugatas, male and female deities
are to be seated on eight-petaled lotuses [2]

So that the skandhas and dhātus become pure,
cultivate the experience of the sixteen vowels
Multiplied by two, at the crown of the head,
this is the pith instruction on guarding yourself [3]

The sixteen bindus are blazing brightly
Through[740] the eight nāḍī bindus moving,
Four are melting and playing, then two
The half of these two is Nairātmyā
These are the numbers of halving and halving sixteen [4]

Beginning with *ka* up through *ma*,
these are the twenty-five Vedas
Beginning with *ya* up through *ha*,
these are the eight named "untouchable"[741] [5]

Condensed, both the a-series and the ka-series[742]
are to be contemplated in the nirmāṇacakra {182}
When heated up by the light of the sun,
think that the three realms are burned and melt [6]

Following the progression of the date,[743]
the one with a hare[744] will be waxing
With the ḍākinīs' experience dissolving into me,
in the instant that has the character of ecstasy,
glorious and victorious great compassion arises [7]

By accomplishing perfect unity,
all obscurations will become pure
The yogī without birth and cessation,
I, Kaṃkali, have attained siddhi [8]

Hey, yogī free of distraction,
practice with your own mind! [9]

This concludes the instruction on practicing with the four cakras composed by master Kaṅkāripa. {183}

(158) A Pith Instruction on Binding Inner and Outer Bodhicitta

In the language of India: *Bāhyāntarabodhicittabandhopadeśanāma*[745]
In the language of Tibet: *Phyi nang byang chub kyi sems bcing ba'i man ngag zhes bya ba*

I pay homage to the bodhisattvas

Ultimate and conventional bodhicitta
are connate but obscured by darkness
The practice for their vivid arising
is what I shall explain here [1]

From the crown of the head down to the vola,
you should meditate on all kinds of nāḍīs
Then, in the mahāsukhacakra,
direct the mind toward the bodhicitta
resembling the hollow inside of an egg! [2]

It condenses[746] at the vola's tip,
lucid and the size of a lentil
From the nāḍī of the egg of great bliss,
The bodhicitta needs to drip [3]

By being filled up with the yogī's[747]
nectar of nonduality up to the navel,

cognition becomes the supreme bliss
Don't go out to a meditation object over there,
nor should you summon the mind in here! [4]

As in the example of knots in a snake,
the mind rests free in and by itself
Lacking activities involving things,
the clinging of the yogī's mind is severed
Since I, Mīna, realized this, {184} I'm free [5]

This concludes "A Pith Instruction on Binding Bodhicitta" composed by master Mīnapa. {185}

(159) A Pith Instruction on Familiarizing with the True Reality of the Vāyus

In the language of India: *Vāyutattvabhāvanopadeśanāma*[748]
In the language of Tibet: *Rlung gi de nyid sgom pa'i man ngag zhes bya ba*

I pay homage to the gurus

Ghorakha guards cattle,
a cowherd sustaining cows
Sustaining them, they become nondual [1]

The pair of sun and moon
blend into a single flavor
Gorakha, Rāhula swallows
the sun—very amazing! [2]

If the spine that's in the back
becomes forcefully bound, yogīs
are accomplished as dhātu in a mere instant
Invincible and utterly transparent,
the true state of emptiness is lucid[749] [3]

The pair of sun and moon
blend into a single flavor
Gorakha, Rāhula swallows
the sun—very amazing! [4]

A small wooden stick sinks to the ground,
while a large boulder will float up
I have practiced with ecstasy—
this is what Ghorakha declares [5]

The pair of sun and moon
blend into a single flavor
Gorakha, Rāhula swallows {186}
the sun—very amazing! [6]

A vajra pierces all gems
The yoga of Ghorakha
is accomplished by the guru's kindness [7]

The pair of sun and moon
blend into a single flavor
Gorakha, Rāhula swallows
the sun—very amazing! [8]

This concludes "A Pith Instruction on Familiarizing with the True Reality of the Vāyus" composed by master Gorakṣa. {187}

(160) Cultivating the Four Yogas

In the language of India: *Caturyogabhāvanānāma*[750]
In the language of Tibet: *Rnal 'byor bzhi'i nyams len gyi thabs zhes bya ba*

I pay homage to Śrī Vajrasattva

Mind and mind as such are without movement
What is to be accomplished and what accomplishes have the
essence of bindu
The fruition, not accomplished, is nirvāṇa
The glorious vīra is without syllables [1]

By relying on the a-series and ka-series
on the secret anthers in the navel,
I shall explain cultivating the four yogas [2]

In the wisdom cakra in the navel,
plant the bindus of the eight nāḍīs
Thinking that the a-series and ka-series are equal,
the flames of the eight ḍākinīs blaze [3]

As for the nature of bodhicitta,
by making the nondual unity drip
from the light of the sky's expanse,
it moves on the path of the vīras [4]

To lock it in it is the yoga without characteristics
By virtue of the stable yoga being accomplished,
the paths and bhūmis of the buddhas are attained
This is the yoga of the a-series and ka-series [5]

AHO! The yogīs who keep repeating this,
by becoming free of being and nonbeing,
dispel the forms of inner and outer poisons {188}
If this yoga is accomplished in a stable manner,
they will become equal with Vajrasatttva,
which will be accomplished in six months [6]

This is the yoga of awareness
Think of the lotus in mind's abode
as being equality and red!
With bindus on the four lotus leaves,
the unmoving bindu is in the center [7]

The colors of these [bindus]
are red in the east, yellow in the north,
white in the west, and black in the south
Multicolored luminosity radiates[751] from the center [8]

If meditating, together with the mantra
mentioned before, the mighty yogī lord
is perfect buddhahood in a single instant
This constitutes the yoga of equality [9]

Akṣobhya water[752] and Vairocana—
through fivefold inner and outer nectar,
hey,[753] the yogī with a māntrika's means,
I, Tantipa, have attained siddhi [10]

This concludes "The Means for Cultivating the Four Yogas" composed by master Tantipa. {189}

(161) Familiarizing with the True Reality of the Vāyus

In the language of India: *Vāyutattvabhāvananāma*[754]
In the language of Tibet: *Rlung gi de nyid sgom pa'i man ngag zhes bya ba*

I pay homage to the gurus

The charnel ground lady[755] lacks thoughts[756] of the connate
She is subtle, unobservable, and of a delightful nature,
playing in all kinds of ways in the middle of the lotus
Through the power of time, she is nondual with the vīra
Thus pervading space and dissolving, she is unobservable [1]

In the single instant of realizing equal bliss,
the three realms shake and the view of bliss is realized
Through the guru's speech, anything is connate [2]

If not realized through the guru, the connate isn't otherwise
Hey, do not give rise to pride about any qualities!
With the connate falling asleep, you become drunk
Thus, engage in samaya just like an elephant! [3]

Blocking the paths of the nine gates[757] with mantras,
by virtue of the stable vase, this constitutes nirvāṇa
If the coming and going of the vāyus is bound firmly
in the anthers of the lotus, the protector will confess [4]

With the vāyus dissolving, there is no change and no color
In empty mind as such without bond and mindfulness,[758] {190}
there is no meditation, nothing to meditate, and no meditator[759]
By virtue of the samādhi of moving mind as such,
the king of mind soars in the sky without support [5]

Press down evenly and perform yantras with your body!
By spreading the great bliss[760] of mind as such, this is nirvāṇa
Cut through the noose[761] of ignorance and relinquish the others!
In a single instant, there is freedom from saṃsāra's attachment [6]

Bound by true reality, there is freedom of things to do
and no rebirth in the six states of existence is assumed
Those who dwell without distraction at the nāḍī gates
do not become frightened by thieves who are fierce [7]

Those who lie and steal[762] are without misery
The mantra is dwelling in your own body
Be mindful of every bliss, oh yogī!
By realizing bliss, qualities will arise [8]

The mistress rests satisfying your own body's nature[763]
The vāyu mind as such resembles the water of a lotus
The elements will be experienced through that
Hence, apply yourself diligently to the moving mind
through locking the nine gates of the yogī! [9]

By virtue of yoga, cut through your ignorance!
Realizing the qualities of abiding, you'll be attachment-free
Having the nature of a cloud-like miraculous display,[764]
imaginative ignorance and basic ignorance are burned,
and the yogī dissolves into the state of the connate [10]

As everything vanishes, by locking the upper and lower gates,
saṃsāra is nirvāṇa by virtue of the experience of abiding
This is realized thanks to the kindness of the yogī's guru {191}

Meditating on the guru on the crown of the head day and night,
resting in the connate itself is what will take place [11]

Hence, ingest the nectar of space again and again
Attaining the kāya of stainless following and service,
the single pillar has nine gates beyond measure
I alone realized the illusory body of the path [12]

Since this dispels the obstructions of the four māras,
there is no need for virtue, generosity, discipline, and such
Śramaṇas[765] and dharma preachers meditate on deities,
but no one realizes the taste of the dharma [13]

If you desire the three kāyas to be firm, hey yogī,
familiarize with the inner and outer bodhicitta vāyus
By cutting through the branches of the five poisons,
you swiftly enter the path of bodhisattvas well,
attain stability in yoga, and will not be reborn [14]

This concludes "A Pith Instruction on Familiarizing with the True Reality of the Vāyus" composed by master Caurańgi. {192}

(162) The Perfection Process of the Vajraḍākinī

In the language of India: *Vajraḍākinīniṣpannakrama*[766]
In the language of Tibet: *Rdo rje mkha' 'gro'i rdzogs pa'i rim pa*

I pay homage to Vajravārāhī

While holding Vajrayoginī as your bow
and setting up all entities as the target,
shoot with the arrow of nonduality—
Meditation and something to meditate on are unseen! [1]

Through striking it, birth will not be observed
and the extremes of self and others are severed
Shoot with the arrow of nonduality—
neither meditation nor something to meditate on! [2]

By drawing the bow of emptiness,
the arrow that cannot miss strikes—
neither killing nor something to be killed
Shoot with the arrow of nonduality—
neither meditation nor something to meditate on! [3]

Having gathered the entirety of dharmatā
through the great miraculous display of space,

Shoot with the arrow of nonduality—
neither meditation nor something to meditate on! [4]

By Virū having cycled in this way,
from one all the way up to twenty,
without engaging in entities as anything at all,
empty syllables were provided as sustenance
Shoot with the arrow of nonduality— {193}
neither meditation nor something to meditate on! [5]

This concludes "The Perfection Process of the Vajraḍākinī" transmitted by master Virūpa and composed by master Vīṇāpa. {194}

(163) A Synopsis of Ascertaining Prajñā and Means

In the language of India: *Prajñopāyaviniścayasamudayanāma*[767]
In the language of Tibet: *Thabs dang shes rab gtan la dbab pa'i bsdus pa zhes bya ba*

I pay homage to Śrī Heruka

As the insiders' nondual dharmakāya unequaled by anything else[768]
that clears away thoughts like clouds and is naturally stainless
is the cause of all kinds of forms whose nature is the sambhogakāya,
I pay homage to the nirmāṇakāya of the nonduality of prajñā and means [1]

Having summarized this for the sake of myself and others, I, the awareness holder
who is a shoemaker, shall explain it without exception in order to benefit
sentient beings who lack realization—you intelligent ones, listen respectfully! [2]

Based on thoughts about being,
nonbeing and no-self emerge
Both are equal in being thoughts
but taught to guide the childish [3]

From those, all the afflictions originate,
and from these, birth, perishing, and suffering
By clinging to the duality of self and others,
liberation will not ever be attained [4]

Hence, being {195} is to be relinquished,
and nonbeing is not be relied on either
If yogīs are placing their stakes on being,
they are nowhere else than just saṃsāra[769] [5]

Since they are mutually connected, they are not those
Not being those, self and other are not established,
just like in the example of a flower in the sky
For that reason, being as well as nonbeing
are delusive miraculous displays to be abandoned [6]

A nature is not established, and there are no stains
Therefore, this is well-known as pāramitā
Inseparable from all-pervasive compassion,
This constitutes the means of yogīs [7]

Since means and prajñā are nondual,
similar to a blend of water and milk,
there's nothing to cling to, no clinger, no beginning, no end,
and no stains, and any characteristics of being are absent [8]

Duality and nonduality have the character of peace
Dwelling in them is the supreme bliss,
self-aware wisdom, the dharmadhātu,
and the peaceful and gentle pāramitā [9]

Possessing the three yānas and the three kāyas,
mantras beyond the sets of a hundred thousand in number,
the supreme kings of the maṇḍalas, mudrās,
the mundane and the supramundane, [10]

the gods, the asuras, as well as Kauśika,[770]
humans, hungry ghosts, animals, and such
resemble the example of waves on water—
they arise from it and merge back down [11]

Hence, familiarize with the nondual
actuality of means and prajñā!
Don't familiarize with emptiness
by means of unequal mantras!
Likewise, don't familiarize with being! [12]

Clinging to those two,
even nirvāṇa is saṃsāra
It is impermanent; by having relinquished it, {196}
nonreferential emptiness will be accomplished [13]

This is the inexpressible compassion of space,
which is just like a wish-fulfilling jewel[771]
The welfare of beings consists of love,
which is like pervading all of space [14]

The mind of nonduality is ecstasy
This is familiarization's equanimity
about the pair of being and nonbeing
Familiarize with ultimate nonbeing! [15]

The duality of what is to be done and a doer,
meditation and what is to be meditated on,
giving and what is to be given is not established,
nor is anything to be clung to and a clinger [16]

Being imaginary, afflictions have no being
Yogīs who are endowed with true reality
Will come to accomplish bodhicitta [17]

Being obscured by attachment is saṃsāra
What is like the sky without clouds
constitutes nirvāṇa free of thoughts
Hence, by making their minds firm,
the intelligent should meditate [18]

I wrote down the instructions received from the lotus of the guru's mouth
Through the result of any virtue that I have accomplished,
may the six classes [of beings] cross the afflictions' swamp,
be stainless,[772] abide in bodhicitta, and attain the siddhis [19]

This concludes "A Synopsis of the Siddhi of Ascertaining Prajñā and Means" spoken by master Cāmaripa. {197}

(164) A Pith Instruction Called "Nonestablishment of a Nature"

In the language of India: *Svabhāvāsiddhināmopadeśanāma*[773]
In the language of Tibet: *Rang bzhin grub pa med pa'i gzhi'i man ngag zhes bya ba*

I pay homage to venerable Tārā

AHO! How is it that experts
have constructed this temple?[774]
Which carpenters made it into a house
with a single pillar and nine doors? [1]

Since[775] it is not known in what way
and when this temple will perish,
where does the pigeon that dwells
in[776] this temple search for its abode? [2]

If it is not known in which manner
and when this temple will perish,
by whom was it covered and plastered? [3]

With its doors being closed firmly,
when its pillar is consumed by bugs,
it is not known in which manner
and when this temple will perish [4]

By whom was it covered and plastered?
Where does the pigeon that dwells
in this temple search for its abode? [5]

Even if they are fed butter and honey,
the conduct of those of bad descent stays the same,
and the same goes for the vajra approach [6]

It is not known in which manner
and when this temple will perish
Where does the pigeon inside {198}
this temple search for its abode? [7]

The pigeon with all kinds of colors,
having abandoned the temple's dome,
keeps cooing, full of courage [8]

It is not known in which manner
and when this temple will perish
Where does the pigeon that dwells
in this temple search for an abode? [9]

Having abandoned the temple's dome,
it keeps cooing, full of courage
This is mind's magical creation,
noble Nāgārjuna declares [10]

This concludes "A Pith Instruction on the Ground of the Nonestablishment of a Nature" composed by master Nāgārjuna. {199}

(165) The Jewel Garland

In the language of India: *Ratnamālānāma*[777]
In the language of Tibet: *Rin chen phreng ba zhes bya ba*

I pay homage to Śrī Heruka

Yours is the character of all protectors—
a nature of entities not being established—
Having paid homage to the lord guru,
I shall explain this *Jewel Garland* [1]

The thoughts of yogīs about meditation
and what is to be meditated on are not real
Since the two realities are not established,
they should not rely on meditation [2]

The realization of the nature of anything
as the dharmadhātu and suchness[778]
is peaceful nondual self-awareness—
this is the first[779] thought of the guru [3]

The prajñā that is without any characteristics
is the mudrā together with the guru's instructions
In the moment when it is subtle and not perfected
through[780] the wisdom in your own mindstream,

it will not be completely accomplished
This is the second thought of the guru [4]

Thinking is not something that is real
Through[781] being linked with nonthought,
gradually there is freedom from thinking
As exemplified by seizing a snake with a string,
yogīs without thoughts are greatly blissful
This is the third thought of the guru [5]

If these appearances of ignorance {200}
have been realized as self-aware wisdom,
appearances in dreams and during the day
are realized in their actual reality as equality
Hence, feelings and what feels them are nondual [6]

The yoga of not abiding in anything whatsoever,
in which duality and nonduality are relinquished,
is what constitutes prajñāpāramitā
This is the fourth thought of the guru [7]

These are the thoughts of myself, Śala:
yogīs who possess nonreferential compassion
and realize clinging to duality as nonduality's actuality,
by virtue of resting in profound dharmatā,
will come to attain the state of Vajrasattva [8]

If the thought-free and stainless view
and conduct that are the play of such yogīs
have been realized as the nature of phenomena,
happiness and suffering are realized to be nondual
Realized in that way, they will be free in themselves [9]

This concludes "The Jewel Garland" composed by the great[782] *master Śyalipa.* {201}

(166) The Blessing of Cultivating Compassion

In the language of India: *Karuṇābhāvanādhiṣṭhānanāma*[783]
In the language of Tibet: *Snying rje bsgom pa'i byin rlabs zhes bya ba*

I pay homage to the true guru

Having received the blessings of the guru,
equality is realized in a single instant
Since it is not clear in the tantra collections,
I explain the practice of cultivating compassion [1]

Yogīs, by being mindful of true reality,
should think of the tilaka in the middle
of their heart on top of a crescent moon[784]—
its[785] nature is with or without characteristics
and dispels the blurred vision of darkness [2]

He who is playing as the natural sovereign,
adorned with garlands of wrathful splendor,
is Heruka, the glorious great protector,
who is victorious over the four māras [3]

Dwelling in the charnel ground of the connate,
the sambhogakāya with bodhicitta relishes

the taste of great bliss, the supreme of ecstasies,
uttering syllables without any cause [4]

There is no need for deity meditation, rosaries, mantras,
setting boundaries, fire offerings, reading, and so forth
By way of having relinquished thoughts,
compassion without any fear is generated [5] {202}

Wisdom, having meditated [like this]
in the hearts of the disciples and myself,
will come to be omniscient and equal
It is attained through realizing true reality [6]

You attain the four miraculous powers and the ten bhūmis
Flying[786] through the sky, you accomplish invisibility
You recollect your births and realize your own mind [7]

In the past, in the present, and in the future,[787]
all self-awareness and other-awareness arises
Similar to the revolving circle of a firebrand,
experiences with[788] the nature of diverse states
of mind dawn, and the yogī attains the siddhis [8]

This concludes "A Pith Instruction on Cultivating Compassion" composed by master Tilopa. {203}

(167) Ascertaining the Basic Nature of the Mahāyāna

In the language of India: *Mahāyānasthitiniścayanāma*[789]
In the language of Tibet: *Theg pa chen po'i gnas lugs gtan la dbab pa zhes bya ba*

I pay homage to Śrī Heruka

The very character of the Mahāyāna
is[790] the nectar of the ocean of great bliss
Its size, with middle and periphery equal, dispels disease
I pay homage to the great vīra[791] [1]

The supreme among the yānas—
the wisdom of cognizers and cognizables—
in order to benefit others, not myself,
is what I shall ascertain here [2]

Awareness with perceiver and perceived
is endowed with its distinct karmas
It's the cause of entities with form being bound
Since inner and outer forms do not exist,
they're unestablished as such but are nonduality [3]

That which is perceived is form
As there is no perceiver, it's true reality

This constitutes genuine wisdom,
effortless and free of color and shape [4]

What the wise realize is self-awareness
That of which this is aware is empty—
it is not awareness of what is not empty
All these are ceasing on their own [5]

This view of being aware of emptiness
through the yoga free of the two realities {204}
constitutes the prajñā of great compassion [6]

Even the perfection process, deity practice, and such
that are discussed in the entirety of all tantras
are not the wisdom of ultimate true reality
Through the power of this ultimate wisdom,
the perfect deity will be accomplished [7]

It is for this reason that I, Dhokhandhi,
State the nonduality of ultimate and seeming,
which is not an object of those of inferior insight [8]

This concludes "Ascertaining the Basic Nature of the Mahāyāna" composed by the great master Dokhandhi. {205}

(168) Offering a Piece of Advice for the Mind

In the language of India: *Cittasaṃpradayavyavasthānanāma*[792]
In the language of Tibet: *Sems la gros 'debs pa zhes bya ba*

I pay homage to mother Vajravārāhī

Having paid homage at the feet of great Śrī Heruka,
who is being surrounded by vīras, vīrās, and bhūtas,
to dispel the obscurations of the beings in the three realms,
for myself and others, I shall give some advice benefiting the mind [1]

Being aware that desire is like lotus water, hey, you mind,[793]
remember the unsurpassable view, meditation, conduct, and fruition!
By that, you see the face of the glorious one and realize nonduality's actuality
Hence, to attain mahāmudrā by making effort in putting that into practice,
if you're not attached or cling to the diversity of forms, sounds, and so on,
there is no reason not to remain in saṃsāra while nirvāṇa is attained [2]

AHO! Why would you cling to the poisons of hatred and envy,
caused by the sense faculty of visual perception, beautiful like a lotus,
the ears impaired by echoes, and the mind that is oblivious?
Though you have seen white hairs, wrinkles, and so on, {206}
you keep searching, thus being bound by flaws due to clinging [3]

Through desire and hatred in their highest, middling, and lowest conducts,
the learned and venerable ones with pride wander through saṃsāric abodes
with their many sufferings of hungry ghosts, asuras, animals, and so on
Therefore, relinquish envy and focus on your own nature![794] [4]

Though gods, nāgas, and humans may obtain many instances of happiness,
it is greatly amazing that the king of mind is not satisfied through desire
The suffering of being separated from friends is even greater than the sea of tears
The skeletons amassed[795] in charnel ground locations are equal to Mount Meru
The blood flowing from wounds due to quarrels out of desire[796] resembles an ocean
AHO! Oh yogī, you king of the mind, why don't you abandon saṃsāric existence? [5]

Having obtained the desirable human body endowed with freedom,
you should consider [all] things as resembling water bubbles
and benefit yourself and others for as long as such is possible
Having sunk into saṃsāra's swamp, liberation is very difficult [6]

Hell beings have the sufferings of wailing, being hot, cold, burned, and crushed
Through their craving, hunger and thirst well up in envious hungry ghosts
Animals, obtaining a place of compassion, still have great hatred for one another
Even gods will tumble down from their abodes, and humans have many sufferings
You need to remember how those sentient beings suffer in these ways
Give up the plethora of conventions of the ultimate and the seeming! [7]

Possessions will be moved around, just as lightning does with cloud banks
The lifespan perishes just like lotus water stirred up by the wind {207}
Regarding those in the prime of youth as being impermanent like that,
those who are wise should then swiftly take their leave for the forests [8]

Envy arises through being attached to desired saṃsāric friends
In the end, you go to Yama's realm and will not attain victory
If you understand it's like this, you attain the path to liberation [9]

What is difficult to obtain again and again is a genuine human body
If you meditate on all kinds of delusive appearances, exemplified by the ocean's
waves appearing as vapor,[797] moon reflections, dreams, and optical illusions,
you are free of being fettered by saṃsāra's noose, like a bird sprung from[798] a trap [10]

Hence, oh mind, don't be attached, don't cling, and do your practice!
Those yogīs who have terminated delusion and have attained bliss
obtain the fruit of buddhahood through the hundred branches of mind's lucidity [11]

This concludes "A Piece of Advice for the Mind" composed by master Ajogi. {208}

(169) A Mahāmudrā Practice of Familiarizing with the Guru of Ground, Path, and Fruition

In the language of India:
Sthānamārgaphalaguru-bhāvanāmahāmudrābhāvanānāma[799]
In the language of Tibet: *Gzhi lam 'bras bu'i bla ma bsgom pa'i phyag rgya chen po'i nyams len zhes bya ba*

I pay homage to Śrī Heruka

This is the practice of the three nāḍīs,
the lineage gurus, and the three syllables
of the triad of ground, path, and fruition—
oh feeble ones, listen, I shall explain it [1]

From the nirmāṇacakra that is at the navel
up to the two nostrils and the brahmarandhra,
you should focus the mind on the three nāḍīs [2]

Within the white of the left, the red of the right nāḍī,
and the dark Akṣobhya-blue of the central one,
think of a HŪṂ in the right, an OṂ in the left,
and a syllable ĀḤ[800] in the brahmarandhra [3]

With dark blue, white, and red clear lights,
the three realms are pervaded by emanated light
Having guided those to be guided, they melt back in [4]

On the three syllables' crescent,
on top of a tilaka that is empty,
are the luminous lineage gurus [5]

On top of that, meditate in this way:
meditate that the guru of experiencing
trust on the syllable in the left nostril {209}
is luminous, similar to a star [6]

The guru of perceiving the fruition
is on top of the syllable HŪṂ's crescent
Cultivate dhyāna in a stable manner! [7]

With the three vāyus ceasing, dispel the three evil spirits!
You should be free of thoughts of the three poisons
Give up thoughts of causal and resultant phenomena! [8]

Through the hermitage of the body having become stable,
the actuality of the nonduality of self and others is realized
and the fears of charnel grounds are relinquished
Haricandra, the expanse of the sky
is enjoying the city of the gandharvas [9]

This concludes "A Mahāmudrā Practice of Familiarizing with the Guru of Ground, Path, and Fruition" composed by master Paṅkaja. {210}

(170) Yoginī Conduct by Way of Nāḍī and Bindu

In the language of India: *Nāḍībindudvāre yoginīcaryānāma*[801]
In the language of Tibet: *Rtsa rlung gi sgo nas rnal 'byor gyi spyod pa zhes bya ba*

I pay homage to mother Nairātmyā

I'm neither a harlot with fine complexion
nor am I a hooker who is well-shaped
This śramaṇa engaging in Hevajra
will come to be the lord of me
I shall be vanquished at this juncture,
crushed by the bandhaka[802] at the juncture[803] [1]

How should I possibly deal with him?
Looking in the four directions, nowhere to escape[804]
Looking everywhere, it's the expanse of space
I shall be vanquished at this juncture,
crushed by the bandhaka at the juncture [2]

Now the actuality of emptiness is realized
"Speak up, oh mind, what do you realize?"
Abandoning it,[805] something else is on its way
I shall be vanquished at this juncture,
crushed by the bandhaka at the juncture [3]

In the solitude of charnel grounds,
that is where I am dwelling now
Having cut the stream of birth and aging,
I stay in places of mountain training
I shall be vanquished at this juncture,
crushed by the bandhaka at the juncture [4] {211}

This bandhaka so greatly skilled
lets the mind of diversity dance,
naturally putting me under his spell
I shall be vanquished at this juncture,
crushed by the bandhaka at the juncture [5]

This concludes "Yoginī Conduct by Way of Nāḍī and Bindu" composed by master Ḍombipa.[806] {212}

(171) A Pith Instruction in Two Syllables

In the language of India: *Akṣaradvikopadeśanāma*[807]
In the language of Tibet: *Yi ge gnyis pa'i man ngag ces bya ba*

I pay homage to the venerable gurus

The Rigveda represents the pestle[808]
The Yajur[veda] is the musala[809] pounding the mortar
The Sāmaveda I employ as the mortar
The Athar[vaveda] I use for sweeping[810] [1]

Hey, I keep pounding this mortar here
[according to] the words of the true guru
[In line] with the guru's pith instructions,
I tread the wooden receptacle with my feet [2]

When I engage in the nature of entities,
I gladly devote myself to the six views
as this path of becoming a buddha[811]
AHO! I pound with a one-pointed mind [3]

In this way, from the black rice,
having been struck by both merit
and pounding, the husks fall away—
what remains is my own mind as emptiness [4]

Hey, I am pounding this mortar
Taking sun and moon as poles,[812]
I stay in the mortar with my feet[813]
This is like the dream of a mute—
how could I express it to anyone? [5]

Hey, this pestle of mine here
resounds with the sky's HE and HŪṂ {213}
Abandoning existence's two certainties,
in each instant throughout day and night,
I dwell in equality with the mortar [6]

This concludes "A Pith Instruction in Two Syllables" composed by master Ḍombipa. {214}

(172) A Pith Instruction on Cultivating the Yoga That Accords with Cultivating the Bliss of True Reality

In the language of India:
Tattvasukhabhāvanānusāriyogabhāvanopadeśanāma[814]
In the language of Tibet: *De nyid bde ba bsgom pa'i rjes su 'brang ba'i rnal 'byor bsgom pa'i man ngag ces bya ba*

I pay homage to the perfect yoginī

Within the center of a lotus united with the heart
is the mind, subtle, lucid, pervasive, and graceful,
through which all three realms will attain nonduality—
I pay homage to the equal, nondual dharmadhātu [1]

Dissolved into the wild horses of the moving faculties,
it is the vessel for the perfect wisdom of the victors
In it, the wise will attain nonduality and swiftly realize true actuality
Thereby, the view is accomplished like the glorious stainless sky [2]

Familiarizing with dharmas and dharmatā within the dharmadhātu,
yogīs who recollect the Buddha attain the nature of the dharmakāya

True reality being without minding, feeling, and awareness, wisdom is seen
This is the purpose of familiarization—luminosity without any doubt [3] {215}

The letterless bindu that abides in the heart
dawns as the wisdom of yogīs familiarizing with it
In it,[815] all vajraḍākinīs endowed with compassion dwell,
including buddhas, bodhisattvas, and the three realms [4]

Venerating true reality's nature, veneration is received from those worth venerating
The buddhas venerate those who are cultivating yoga
The Buddha said this cultivation of veneration is the fruition
The vajra yoga and the inner character are united [5]

Therefore, the wise venerate with the vajra veneration
The five wisdoms radiate; buddhahood will no doubt be accomplished
Meditate that in the nirmāṇacakra at the navel of the yogī,
in the center of the anthers of six lotuses, like banduka[816] fruits,
are A NṚI SU TRI PRE DU KA so as to end the six classes [of beings] [6]

By virtue of all six hollow syllables progressively dissolving
into KA in the middle, mind itself ceases and does not rearise
Your own mind—obscured and obscurer—is stainless and unobservable
This is taught so as to guide the mindstreams—it's not the ultimate yoga [7]

This is the great natural veneration that will accomplish all buddhas
The twenty great sites abide in yourself; paths and bhūmis are gradually attained

Therefore, do not look for true reality elsewhere—it dwells in yourself
What's the point if[817] yogīs roam around without realizing true reality? [8]

If true reality is realized, what's the point of anything else?
Good fortune's character is accomplished in yourself, true reality {216} attained
Those endowed with yogic discipline by virtue of this yoga
engage in the dhyāna of nonduality, just like lunatics [9]

Those who wear the sky as their garment or are not such yogīs
meditate on the reality that's the nature of the oath deity dwelling in the body
For six months, control your speech and meet the ḍākinīs!
A yogī who radiates the light of wisdom is equal to a buddha
Like an illusionist, this supreme guide promotes being's welfare [10]

This concludes "A Pith Instruction on Cultivating the Yoga That Accords with Cultivating the Bliss of True Reality" composed by master Kukkuripa. {217}

(173) The Means to Calm Mind and Thinking

In the language of India: *Cittacitiśamanopāyanāma*[818]
In the language of Tibet: *Sems dang sems nyid 'dul ba'i thabs zhes bya ba*

I pay homage to Śrī Heruka

The stag[819] who possesses fur in all kinds of colors
strikes out with his legs and roams the four directions
Having hunted him down,[820] I kill him in the sky [1]

It is in all respects that his own flesh
turns into an enemy for his own body
The hunter who is a bhusuku[821]
does not spare him for even an instant [2]

The doe is calling out to the stag:
"If you stay in the forest, you will be fine;
once you step out of it, you are killed" [3]

It is in all respects that his own flesh
turns into an enemy for his own body
The hunter who is a bhusuku
does not spare him for even an instant [4]

The stag speaks like this to the doe:
"I have not done any harm to anybody
and I have not eaten anything at all
If I haven't done any harm to anybody,
why would they shout, 'Kill him'?" [5]

It is in all respects that his own flesh
turns into an enemy for his own body
The hunter who is a bhusuku
does not spare him for even an instant [6]

With grass and water being undamaged,
wherever they stay, they are not hungry {218}
Though I always kept looking for them,
I never ever managed to find these two—
unfindable deer, the stag and the doe [7]

It is in all respects that his own flesh
turns into an enemy for his own body
The hunter who is a bhusuku
does not spare him for even an instant [8]

This stag who is running and walking—
his tracks are not to be found anywhere
Having hunted him down, I crush[822] him in the sky's expanse [9]

The hunter who is a bhusuku
does not spare him for even an instant [10]

This concludes "A Pith Instruction on Calming Mind and Thinking" that was transmitted by master Śāntadeva and sung by master Mekopa.[823] {219}

(174) The Path of the Perfection Process of All Deities

In the language of India: *Sarvadevatāniṣpannakramamārganāma*[824]
In the language of Tibet: *Lha kun gyi rdzogs pa'i rim pa'i lam zhes bya ba*

I pay homage to the ḍākinīs

Leaving unpleasant sounds and so on behind,
in a location that is secluded and secret,[825]
or alternatively in an agreeable hermitage,
meditate following these progressive stages! [1]

With a single tree being bodhicitta,
at the river banks of the avadhūtī
is caṇḍālī's charnel ground at the navel
In the mountain retreat[826] of the lotus at the heart
is the abode of the hermit Vairocana [2]

In the grove's secret of the lotus,
meditate on bhiḍa,[827] vajra water,
bodhicitta, excrements,
Ratnasambhava, and Amitābha
in the six places of bindu
This teaches the yogī's practice[828] [3]

Then, the maṇḍala of the body
consists of the nāḍīs of stainless nature,
entailing the experience of the connate
Being spherical just like space,
the size of a thumb, contemplate
Great bliss as either an OṂ or a HAṂ [6]

Having blessed this maṇḍala
with mirror-like wisdom, {220}
think that the wisdom of equality
is a smoke-colored[829] HŪṂ on top
of Rāhu in the yogī's heart [7]

In the ocean of Akṣobhya,
the OṂ resembles a star—
think of discriminating wisdom
as being the throat cakra
It is bodhicitta, rakta,
and the Akṣobhya water bindu [8]

Having thus contemplated the nāḍīs of blessings,
in order to gather the accumulation of merit,
the signless nāḍīs and the four cakras
are to be sealed with the four mudrās
Thus, practice with the four bindus!
The four immeasurables' experiences arise [9]

Having cultivated the four yogas like this,
think of the perfect HŪṂ, expelling obstacles
In the center of the dome at the heart,
a lotus springs forth from PAṂ, a sun
from RAṂ, and a blazing vajra from HŪṂ,
cutting off inner and outer obstacles [10]

Then, as for the emptiness[830] of yoga,
sit cross-legged, straighten the body,

and direct the eye faculty to the nose tip
Recollecting the entirety of entities,
with mind as such, which is like a star
in a sky that is without any stains,
contemplate self and others the size of an atom [11]

Having stabilized[831] the view of emptiness,
the perfect empowerment's stages are taught
Think[832] that through the union of vajra and bell,
the goddess who turns into the area of the palate—
the river stream of the moon of great bliss—
rains down, the empowerment satisfying the body [12]

What follows is the kāya embodying
any kind of glory of[833] vīras and vīrās
It is like a reflection in a stainless mirror
or a person who consists of space
Its nature is free of any color {221} or shape,
and it has the nature of the five wisdoms—
contemplate it as the expanse of space [13]

I have composed the perfection process
in this way for the sake of the fortunate
I dedicate the virtue obtained by this
so that beings may attain awakening [14]

This concludes "The Path of the Perfection Process of All Deities" composed by master Ghadhari. {222}

(175) Cultivating the Inconceivable

In the language of India: *Acintyaparibhāvanānāma*[834]
In the language of Tibet: *Bsam gyis mi khyab pa bsgom pa zhes bya ba*

I pay homage to the bodhisattvas

I pay homage to the gurus

I shall explain a yogī's inconceivable
practice of the four immeasurables
that epitomizes the awakened mind [1]

In the nature empty of cause and result,
insubstantial form, nondual speech,
and the unobservable fruition are effortless,
as in the example of rain without thunder [2]

Hence this diversity of possible appearances
of yogīs fortunate enough for yogic discipline
that consists of the natural lack of a self
is the lack of a self of empty entities,[835]
which is completely pure by nature [3]

Within this kind of compassion,
buddhas and beings do not exist as two

Not meditating, not thinking, [mind's] nature is lucid—
the middle's actuality free of center and fringe [4]

Familiarize with this nature of the mind!
Cultivate compassion dispelling illness
for sentient beings not realizing this! [5]

Whatever there may be in front of you,
resting in equipoise, {223} familiarize with equality
In this, the actuality of nonduality
in all respects will be accomplished [6]

As for the meditation instructions of the aural lineage,
contemplate that the kāya that embodies all buddhas—
a white syllable HŪṂ that is everyone's mind as such—
is residing in the hearts of yourself and others [7]

Meditate that there is a bindu on a sun seat
Think that due to its emanating and reabsorbing,[836]
the entirety of the afflictions is purified
This is the actuality of nonduality—
the deity's true reality of lacking a nature [8]

Having thus cultivated compassion,
think of inconceivable love[837]
in this way so as to benefit [all] [9]

In the heart of yourself, the yogī,
is an eight-petaled lotus the size of a pea
From it, white-and-red clear light [radiates]
In between is the syllable AṂ of Agnideva [10]

There is no yogī at all who is an entity
The yogī who familiarizes with being
inconceivable as anything whatsoever
will accomplish nondual wisdom [11]

Lacking clear awareness is the dharmakāya
Thus, with supernatural knowledge dawning,
the yogī who is subtle realizes nonduality
With the nature of ecstasy coming forth,
the fruition of equanimity is attained [12]

Some meditate on the four goddesses
and some rely on verbal[838] recitations,
not understanding nondual meditation [13]

Rāhula, in order to benefit others,
has explained the oral instructions
transmitted from mouth to mouth [14]

This concludes "Cultivating the Inconceivable Four Immeasurables" composed by master Rāhula. {224}

(176) A Pith Instruction on the View of Self-Aware Wisdom

In the language of India: *Ātmaparividjñānadṛṣṭyupadeśanāma*[839]
In the language of Tibet: *Rang rig ye shes kyi lta ba'i nyams len zhes bya ba*

I pay homage to mother Nairātmyā

If self-aware wisdom were an object,
there would be no agent and no object
Without these, there would be no activity
How could these three be nondual? [1]

If what is external were something real,
due to conventional connection, it would be expressed as internal
If the seeming were self-awareness,
awareness through awareness would be unawareness [2]

If yogīs are aware of themselves,[840]
the suffering of saṃsāra is overcome
By virtue of this[841] convention, a nature
of things is not established, and they are stainless [3]

Since things are not established,
there's nothing else to be established for me
Therefore, I definitely do not exist[842]

If words and their meanings were what is to be realized,
there would be no words or meanings in nature's actuality [4]

This yogī for whom entities are unestablished—
that is me, I am free from everything[843]
In duality's freedom, the darkness of ignorance is gone
Its absence represents stainless wisdom[844] [5]

In this way, the yogī's awareness
is freeing the bondage of saṃsāra
By lying on the back, {225} yoga arises[845]
Be mindful of the body's meditative equipoise! [6]

Open wide your eyes, offer up consciousness
Through looking at the sphere of space,
there's nothing to be seen, nothing to grasp in the mind
By being free[846] from thoughts about sides,
the faculties vanish, and nonduality is accomplished [7]

This concludes "Making the View of Self-Aware Wisdom a Living Experience" composed by master Campaka. {226}

(177) The Heart of the Realizations of the Eighty-Four Mahāsiddhas

In the language of India: *Caturaśītisiddhasambodhihṛdayanāma*[847]
In the language of Tibet: *Grub thob brgyad cu rtsa bzhi'i rtogs pa'i snying po zhes bya ba*

I pay homage to Vāgiśvara

Bowing respectfully at the feet of the buddha-like siddhas who realized actual reality,
in order to extract the sentient beings who are greatly distracted and led astray
by the sea monsters of their nonvirtuous deeds in the ocean of saṃsāra, the yogī Vīra
shall weave the views of the experiences and realizations of the siddhas into a garland

(1) Guru Lūhipa says:[848]

Just as a savage wild dog with honey rubbed on its nose gobbles up everything in all directions,
imparting the guru's pith instructions to the unfortunate of lesser insight sets their own mindstreams ablaze
The fortunate who realize the unborn vanquish thoughts merely upon encountering appearances,

as, for example, a steadfast drunken elephant with a sword
tied to his trunk crushes hostile ranks[849]

(2) Guru Līlapa says:

In the hermitage of the four immeasurables,
the king of yogīs is similar to a lion,
his head adorned with five tufts of turquoise color {227}
The yogī holds the five families as signs of empowerment
The lion's ten claws rip apart the flesh and bones of oxes[850]
and such
The ten pāramitās of the yogī tear adverse thoughts apart
Upon having realized this, Līla is free[851]

(3) Guru Virūpa says:

Let the connate within the natural state of mahāmudrā
be in no-self's own state, without thinking or awareness[852]
Not becoming extinct, experience is aware all by itself
Not becoming permanent, it is unity by virtue of no clinging[853]

(4) Guru Ḍombipa says:

Just as the power of a gold-making elixir
leads to transforming base metals into gold,
so the power of precious empowerments
transforms afflictions into nondual wisdom[854]

(5) Guru Śavaripa says:

Within the dense jungle of ignorance,
the deer of the duality of perceiver and perceived roams
Drawing the bow of both means and prajñā,
I shoot the single arrow of essential reality

Its death is the dying of thoughts
Its flesh is consumed as nonduality
Its taste is experienced as great bliss—
the fruition of mahāmudrā[855] is attained

(6) Guru Saraha says:

Hey, friends! This wisdom that is connate[856]
is not found elsewhere but on the true guru's lips
If the ultimate essence of his words is realized,
mind is without death and the body without extinction[857]

(7) Guru Kaṅkāripa says:

Just as form is devoid of the pair
of one and other in the empty sky,
the queen of self-appearing wisdom {228}
is without example and beyond all convention[858]

(8) Guru Mīnapa says:

The fisherman who was holding on to his iron hook
was carried away into the ocean under the sway of karma
Making his home in the body of the giant fish,
by practicing the instructions of the great god,
his qualities are such that earth and rocks
could not hold him—he is known as "Mīnapa"[859]

(9) Guru Gorakṣa says:

By the abiding cause in highest, middling, or lower
castes being associated with powerful conditions,
the fruition of unimpeded karmic power is truly amazing
Through the power of the conditions of having performed
bodhisattva services for Cauraṅgi, the dhātu's seed flourished[860]

Aciṅta[861] showed[862] me the nectar of immortality,
and Gorakṣa saw the true reality of nonduality
This cowherd king of threefold existence is amazing![863]

(10) Guru Cauraṅgipa says:

In saṃsāric existence that is beginningless,
for a long time, the roots of the tree of ignorance
were moistened well by the water of formations,
unfolding saṃsāric existence's plethora of branches[864]

As for this giant tree of ignorance,
with the axe[865] that consists of the genuine
guru's instructions and the three prajñās,
Cauraṅgi has cut it down to true reality[866]

(11) Guru Vīṇāpa says:

Having analyzed[867] with respect and effort
the sounds of habituation to mistakenness,
I was not free; by analyzing unborn sound,[868]
Vīṇāpa has realized the very lack of a self[869]

(12) Guru Śāntipa says:

Just as a small boy nourished by his mother
may come to possess the strength of a wrestler,
through the guru's pith instructions, those of little insight
[enter] the Mahāyāna by being guided[870] gradually

Just as medicine dispels diseases
of wind, bile, and phlegm constellations, {229}
it is this clinging to a "me" and a self
that's instantly burned by the guru's instructions[871]

(13) Guru Tantipa says:

Those weavers there in the world
keep weaving all kinds of yarns
I, through the guru's pith instructions,
weave the entirety of phenomena

With the emptiness of the five wisdoms
as my yarn, the pith instructions as comb,
and with the loom of prajñā as well,
I weave the nonduality of expanse and awareness into the
dharmakāya[872]

(14) Guru Cāmāripa says:

With this leather of thoughts and characteristics
on the mold[873] of the vajra of emptiness,
the continuous thread of abandoning the eight dharmas,
and the awl of the experience of prajñā, I stitch
Making the effortless shoe of the dharmakāya,
Cāmāripa is the supreme shoemaker[874]

(15) Guru Khaḍgapa says:

Though worldly heroes brandishing their weapons[875]
may continuously wage battles with their enemies,
it is themselves who come under the sway of suffering[876]
Having defeated the enemies of threefold existence
with the sword of the wisdom of immortality,
Khaḍgapa then keeps enjoying himself[877]

(16) Guru Nāgārjuna says:

Those without realization[878] should not engage in the conduct
If they do so, they are like subjects trying to seize a kingdom
The realized should not engage in the conduct of the
unrealized
If they do so, they resemble elephants who sink into the mud[879]

(17) Guru Kāṇhapa says:

Just as a chariot without a single[880] wheel cannot drive even if you pull it,
Even if you make efforts in generosity and such, without a guru, there's no genuine siddhi
Wide-winged vultures with perfect dexterity {230} cut[881] and soar through the sky
By absorbing the instructions of the empowerments, fortunate yogīs are blissful[882]

(18) Guru Karṇaripa says:

All buddhas in the three times have a single essence
If this is realized, its nature is your own mind
If you wish to realize it, uncontrived, let it be as it is
If there is familiarity with it, yoga is revealed[883]

(19) Guru Thaganapa says:

If some water has entered your ear,
it is water itself that will extract it
Likewise, reality is seen by familiarizing with
all possible delusive appearances as delusive[884]

(20) Guru Nāropa says:

Just as the armed forces of a cakravartin king
bring continents and islands under their power,
yogīs who embody the taste of the connate
exert their power over saṃsāra, which is great bliss[885]

(21) Guru Śyālipa says:

Visual artists who are very accomplished[886]
paint pictures that are very terrifying

When seeing them, they themselves become afraid
If examined, they are appearances of unreal images[887]

(22) Guru Tilopa says:

When a bird settles on Mount Meru's surface,
the nature of that bird appears to be golden
Likewise, if the wise realizing the unborn
cast off entities, they are greatly blissful[888]

(23) Guru Catrapa says:

Whatever appears to[889] yogīs represents their instructions
To realize what is seen to be unborn is the supreme master
By virtue of realizing the dualistic clinging of childish beings,
there, the results of virtue and wrongdoing do not arise as two[890] {231}

(24) Guru Bhadrapa says:

Realizing emptiness, delusion is at peace[891]
By cultivating love, conduct is perfected
Being familiar with the nonduality of diversity,
the single taste of the discordant[892] is realized as the fruition[893]

(25) Guru Dukhaṅdhi says:

The pair of the conventional creation process
as well as the ultimate perfection process—
familiarize with it as the mahāmudrā of unity
and the three kāyas dawn[894] as the fruition![895]

(26) Guru Ajogi says:

Through the instructions of the true guru,
familiarize with the bindu at the upper gate's tip

Through mind being held stable[896] on this,
the focus of white mustard with a trichiliocosm[897] is tossed
away[898]

(27) Guru Kālapa says:

These beings are deluded since beginningless time
Thus, the entire world is known to be imbalanced[899]
The ambrosial medicine of the guru's instructions
burns the diseases of delusion in just an instant[900]

(28) Guru Dhobīpa says:

Even if you wash its stains for a long time,
the nature of charcoal will never become white,
but naturally pure[901] emptiness will become pure
The guru's instructions are the supreme natural launderer[902]

(29) Guru Kaṅkaṇa says:

It is the wish-fulfilling jewel of realization[903]
that is bringing forth the colors of experience
By its activity's power, what's wanted and needed arises
This is accomplished by those with equal taste[904]

(30) Guru Kambala says:

Just as the deep and vast ocean is filled with jewels
and the nāga kings' enjoyment of this is very amazing, {232}
all appearances and sounds primordially are the dharmakāya,
and this being enjoyed by those with realization is very
amazing[905]

(31) Guru Ḍeṅgipa says:

If it resembles a horse, an elephant, and the ocean, this is supreme bliss
If it is like a monkey, a child, and a drawing on water, this is thought[906]
If it is similar to a river, the sun, and medicine, this is inseparability
Like a hair-knot, an eye, and a wheel, so is the attainment of the fruition[907]

(32) Guru Bhandepa says:

Nonclinging constitutes supreme love
Realizing the basic nature is compassion
The bliss that is uncontaminated is joy
Phenomena's[908] single taste is perfect equanimity[909]

(33) Guru Taṅtepa says:

Just as the entire plethora of discursive awareness
becomes exhausted and ceases in nonthought's expanse,
the entirety of phenomena that can possibly appear
becomes exhausted and ceases in emptiness's expanse[910]

(34) Guru Kukkuripa says:

Venerating buddhas[911] and so on yield no meaning
If there is wanting and effort, this is not buddhahood
Experiencing the blessings[912] of the true guru is splendid
It exists in ourselves in its entirety, but we don't see it[913]

(35) Guru Kucipa says:

If the connate within someone
arises as irritation, pain appears,
just as in the eye of an elephant—
not clinging while relaxing is supreme dhyāna[914]

Through the light rays of the guru's speech,
I don't find the extremes of existence and nonexistence
That which is not found represents the extreme[915]
If this extreme is realized, that is the ultimate[916]

(36) Guru Dharmapa says:

The person of awareness is continually in the grip
of the poison of ignorance by virtue of duality[917] {233}
It is the light rays[918] of the guru's speech that eliminate
the poisonous disease of the delusion of possible
appearances[919]

(37) Guru Mahipa says:

The wish-fulfilling jewel that is not realized
remains obscured by the pride of ignorance
Through the wish to act, what's wanted and needed arises
This is accomplished by those with equal taste[920]

(38) Guru Aciṅta says:

Within mahāmudrā devoid of focal objects,
the plethora of the deluded thinking mind[921] is cast off
Through the appearances of wisdom's awareness,
whatever appears[922] is seen as mahāmudrā[923]

(39) Guru Babhaha says:

Bliss! Bliss! This is insubstantial bliss!
Since there is no clinging, this is insubstantial bliss
To know everything imagined[924] as such is bliss
The secret of[925] there being nothing to accomplish is bliss[926]

(40) Guru Nalinapa says:

In the mud-born petals[927] at the crown of the head,
the movement of the seed constitutes ecstasy
At the heart and throat,[928] there are supreme ecstasy
and the connate, attaining unsurpassable cessational ecstasy[929]

(41) Guru Bhusuku says:

Until I had gained realization, flavors differed greatly
Likewise, those in saṃsāra were very different from buddhas
At the time of realization, saṃsāra constitutes great bliss,
just as in the example of flaming jewels in the ocean[930]

(42) Guru Indrabhūti says:

If the pivotal points in time are not endowed with blessing,
yogīs will not become buddhas by any inner or outer conduct
The nature of ecstatic bliss and buddhahood are not different
If clinging is let go, naturally arising experience is supreme
ecstasy[931]

(43) Guru Mekopa says: {234}

By virtue of true gurus, you should first realize your own
mind
Then, you should make this not different from all appearances
Being familiar with nonduality, you should run to[932] charnel
grounds
Having realized equality, behave with the yogic discipline of
a lunatic[933]

(44) Guru Koṭalipa says:

All happiness and suffering arise from the mind
With the guru's instructions, dig up mind's mountain
Though the intelligent may dig up a mountain,
they will not attain[934] the native great bliss

Ordinary mind wakes up in the center of the heart
In the objects of[935] the six collections, bliss is uninterrupted
Everything imagined is meaningless, the cause of suffering
With nothing to meditate and no meditation, let be in the
native state[936]

(45) Guru Kamparipa says:

In the furnace of the natural body[937]
are the coals of discursive thoughts
Fanned by the bellows of lalanā and rasanā
kindling the fire of wisdom in the avadhūtī,
I forge the three poisons' thoughts into the dharmakāya
Having realized this, Kamparipa is free[938]

(46) Guru Jālandhara says:

As for the entire plethora of the discursive thoughts
of the three realms' bodies, speeches, and minds,
why should you not bind the blessings[939]
in the lalanā, the rasanā, and the avadhūtī?[940]

(47) Guru Rāhula says:

The excellent Rāhu[941] that is on the outside
swallows the moon's light so they are not two
The Rāhu of expanse and awareness swallows
the conventional moon bindu so they are not two[942]

(48) Guru Dharmapa says:

Into the vessel of possibly appearing phenomena,
the clarified butter[943] of bodhicitta is poured
The wick of consciousness in its six collections {235}
is ignited through the fire of nondual wisdom,
overcoming the darkness of deluded thoughts[944]

(49) Guru Dhokaripa says:

Into the vessel that is the nature of the dharmadhātu,
the substance of the dharmakāya of awareness is placed
The fruition of the pair of expanse and awareness
is realized by the awareness of fortunate yogīs[945]

(50) Guru Medhini says:

Through the pair of the prajñā of native awareness
and the means of familiarity with the afflictions,[946]
out of the pure ground that is the natural basic nature,
the fruition of connately present bliss is realized[947]

(51) Guru Paṅkajapa says:

When not cared for by a guru and lacking realization,
a wish-fulfilling jewel and trinkets look the same
When fully embraced by the guru and realization,
these are as alike as the light of sun and moon and a firefly[948]

(52) Guru Ghaṇṭāpa says:

The triad of lalanā, rasanā, and avadhūtī
should be bound for the sake of self-blessing
It is on the triad of guru, mind, and appearances[949]
that the wise rely so as to give rise to realization[950]

(53) Guru Jogipa says:

By being familiar with the subtle lucid mind
that is similar to the tip of a flame in a lamp,
the entirety of mobile and immobile entities
keeps dissolving into the dharmadhātu[951]

(54) Guru Celukapa says:

Having long become familiar for a long time
with the instructions of the true guru,
with the progressions[952] of bhūmis and such dissolving,
self-appearances are becoming mahāmudrā[953]

(55) Guru Godhuripa says:

All inner and outer phenomena are contained in the mind
If the true actuality of lucid mind as such is realized,
revealing the realization of the four kinds of behavior {236}
as the dharmakāya constitutes perfect buddhahood[954]

(56) Guru Lucikapa says:

Some have been roaming the ocean of saṃsāra
for very long since time without beginning
By way of the true guru, the supreme ship,[955]
I crossed[956] the ocean difficult to cross today[957]

(57) Guru Nirguṇapa says:

Having stabilized wave-like experiences,
merge with conduct through the means[958]
Through the instructions of the true guru,
thoughts of desire and hatred subside on their own[959]

(58) Guru Jayānanda says:

The samādhi of wisdom awareness
rests in the native state since beginningless time[960]
If it is realized as it is, that is certainty
Discursive thinking is not true reality[961]

(59) Guru Pacaripa says:

Not looking anywhere, look at the center!
Supreme and cessational ecstasy—great bliss!
Expressing[962] the power of mantra's secret,
yogīs should be gathering[963] the signs[964]

(60) Guru Campaka says:

Within luminosity-like means and prajñā,
the guru's constant river flow pervades all
On the wish-fulfilling tree of the connate,
the fruits—the self-radiant three kāyas—are perfect[965]

(61) Guru Bhikṣanapa says:

Having been shown the difficult-to-travel path of the great bliss of unity
to the unsurpassable charnel ground, the great abode of awakening,[966]
the supreme yogī, the mighty lord who is free of bias and corruption,[967]
realizes true reality thanks to the kindness of the guru's instructions[968]

(62) Guru Dhilipa says:

It is my own original buddhahood that,
by the power of realization,[969] is dharmatā
Through the connate taken as empowerment, {237}
to be sealed by the unborn is Vajradhara[970]

(63) Guru Kumbharipa says:

The wheel of karma concordant with its cause
creates all kinds of saṃsāric songs and dances
It is the fire of the awareness of wisdom that
burns the stains of delusion without exception[971]

(64) Guru Carbaripa says:

The supreme oath of all māntrikas[972]
is not to cling to their own realization[973]
What's seen by mind realizing the native state[974]
is seen by all the buddhas as well[975]

(65) Guru Maṇibhadrā says:

At the time when I was without realization,[976]
all kinds of thoughts followed sounds outside
With the nature of true reality[977] being revealed,
whatever appears is the true reality of that nature[978]

(66) Guru Mekhalā says:

Everything inner and outer is contained in the mind
If there is no clinging, this is equal taste
If there is no effort, this is meditation supreme
Nondual great bliss is perfect buddhahood[979]

(67) Guru Kanakhalā says:

Having donned the great armors,
through gem-like perseverance,
I steered the ship of my own mind,
sailing to this human corpse's inner sanctum[980]

(68) Guru Kilakilapa says:

In the center of the sky of the pure dharmadhātu,
the thunder of birthlessness resounds excellently
All phenomena of delusion that can possibly appear
are beautiful as the fruition of the three kāyas' wisdom[981]

(69) Guru Kantalipa says:

With the needle of the true guru
as well as the thread of compassion,
I stitch the rags of all three realms together
This ragman yogī is very amazing![982]

(70) Guru Dhahulipa says:

The precious treasury of unity awareness {238}
is nonduality's natural state, not [found] by seeking
Like the mindset of letting go of your duties,
this is blissful to the extent that it is let be[983]

(71) Guru Udhilipa says:

The ways of chasing after thoughts are delusion[984]
Not following them,[985] don't discard their latent tendencies
but seize them!
Without abiding anywhere, seize movement!
Searching elsewhere, that's not it either![986]

(72) Guru Kapālapa says:

The nonduality of all entities is Vajradhara
The ornaments, the skull,[987] and such are adventitious
The delusion of clinging to "me" is also true reality
It is not found by myself searching for it[988]

(73) Guru Kirapālapa says:

Until[989] realization, thoughts about ourselves and others fetter
Upon realization, both ourselves and others are not
established
Hence, what is called "buddhahood " is our own appellation
Seize the nature[990] in uncontrived, nondiscursive true reality's
own place![991]

(74) Guru Sakara (Saroruha) says:

For beings tormented by suffering,
a rain of sense pleasures showers down
Within the great abode of suchness,
by squeezing the nāga king of awareness,
the rain of secret mantra's awareness is brought down
upon male and female fortunate awareness holders[992]

(75) Guru Sarvabhakṣa says:

At the time without realization, all kinds of flavors differ greatly
At the time of realization, the essence of flavors is without distinction
Likewise, if not realized, saṃsāra and nirvāṇa appear differently[993]
If true reality is realized, saṃsāra and nirvāṇa are not distinct[994]

(76) Guru Nāgabodhi says:

If you dwell on the ground, all is of excellent fortune
If going to the ocean's depths, {239} you are free of poverty
If you hold a sword in your hand, this is a great enjoyment
If you amble around without direction, you meet friends[995]

(77) Guru Dārikapa says:

Though great bliss lies within us, it is not realized and obscured by delusion
Those wishing to dispel it[996] should gather the accumulations of merit and wisdom
When not gathering the two accumulations, even if you strive for a hundred lives,
Without possessing any gurus, great bliss will not be realized[997]

(78) Guru Putalipa says:

All are endowed with the nature of a sugata
Relinquishing the wrong path established by mind,
if you make efforts on the path of pith,
the fruition of pith is beyond any doubt

Those with empowerments from the
true guru are pervaded everywhere
by the taste of the connate[998]—
to be sealed by the unborn is Vajradhara[999]

(79) Guru Upanaha says:

Through contemplating native essential reality,
it is realized in just the way it is contemplated
Hence, with true reality simply resting naturally,[1000]
everything desirable comes forth with ease[1001]

(80) Guru Kokilipa says:

Letting go of doing constitutes the pith instruction
Lacking any clinging or wanting[1002] is realization
Insubstantial bliss is what constitutes the meditation
If there is nothing to accomplish, this is the supreme fruition[1003]

(81) Guru Anaṅgapa says:

In saṃsāra, there exists no pith at all
If this body that resembles a rainbow
is in the grip of the poisons of ignorance,
clinging, and vanity, it fixates on happiness
Once the poisonous disease of clinging is healed,
it is saṃsāra itself that is the dharmakāya[1004]

(82) Guru Lakṣmī says: {240}

First, the intelligent give rise to realization
Second, they familiarize undistractedly with the basic nature
Then, once experiences have sprung forth,
they should gradually engage in the conduct[1005]

(83) Guru Samudra says:

Even if the unborn is realized but experience is lacking,
this is like a child carried away in the hands of a rākṣasī[1006]
If experience is disconnected from the basic nature,
this resembles an elephant who is stuck in the mud[1007]

(84) Guru Vyālipa says:

If you see the true guru, you are seeing true reality
If you meditate in the sky's expanse, this is solitude supreme
If you realize phenomena, there is nothing unfavorable
If you drink the sky's milk, this will be your livelihood[1008]

Through the vast merit I attained by well compiling with a boundless mind
the entire heart of the realizations of the gurus for the sake of the fortunate,
may [all] beings meet with gurus and may their blessings enter their true minds!
Realizing the true mind, basic nature's reality, may they dwell on the victor's bhūmi!

*This concludes "The Heart of the Realizations of the Eighty-Four Mahāsiddhas" compiled by master *Vīraprabhāsvara.* {241}

(178) Dohās of the Secret of Mind

In the language of India: *Cittaguhyadohanāma*[1009]
In the language of Tibet: *Thugs kyi gsang ba glur blangs pa zhes bya ba*

I pay homage to youthful Mañjuśrī

(1) The great brahman Saraha puts the realization of his mind to song:

> Hey! The root of all of saṃsāra and nirvāṇa is mind's nature
> If realized, there is nothing to meditate; let it be, uncontrived and loose!
> Leaving it behind in yourself and searching for it elsewhere—what delusion!
> There is no "this is it" or "this is not it"—all is the natural state

(2) Nāgārjuna says:

> If realized, you must say what is able to bind!
> What is bondage is primordial freedom per se
> If bondage and what is bound are not established anywhere,
> let the buffalo living in the forest run around as he likes!

(3) Prajñāphala says:

Who sits[1010] between the two of realization and nonrealization,
that one is me; there is nothing whatsoever elsewhere
That which is seen here is self-arising great bliss
You should know that all and everything is true reality

(4) Śāntarakṣita {242} says:

Not stirring from equality's expanse, diverse miraculous displays manifest
All kinds of inlets become one in the ocean, thus having a salty taste
In this single taste of the many, there is no difference whatsoever
If everything is pervaded by the taste of the native state, this is bliss

(5) Sthiramati says:

Like the moon king's[1011] dawning in the sky outshining constellations,
great nondual wisdom leads to the decay of the hosts of thoughts
Through this, all seeds of saṃsāra without exception are crushed
Now, may you not search for nirvāṇa anywhere else!

(6) Vāgīśvara says:

In the palace of the dharmadhātu of possible appearances,
it is the brilliantly radiant wisdom of awareness that
is residing on the throne[1012] of lucid and empty bliss
While offering you all kinds of sense pleasures,
I request you to enjoy them without blocking or creating

(7) Vajraghaṇṭāpa says:

If you are yearning to see the true reality of the mind
and wish to accomplish the desires of yourself and others,
you should venerate the gem at the crown of your head—
it is the entirety of all siddhis that springs forth from it

(8) Śaṅkara says:

A crystal ball that is so stainless and pure,
conditioned by colors, appears to be variegated
If you know how to place it within open space,
lasting bliss will come forth from that

(9) Śāntipa says:

If resting, let be; if moving, let go!
Don't supervise; wander freely!
To seize anything deliberately is delusion
Look at the crow flying from the ship!

(10) Virūpa says: {243}

Whatever may be seen is true reality
Not separated from the elixir of mindfulness,
practice with whatever may come up!
Look at the gold-making alchemist![1013]

(11) Jñānapāda says:

Just as timid[1014] persons are unable to move their limbs to and fro,
with mind as such lacking a root, it cannot be fettered by thoughts
Just as those with poison mantras transform poison itself into medicine,

with the proper means, the afflictions themselves are awakening's cause

(12) Śāntideva says:

From the root of both saṃsāra and nirvāṇa,
the trunk of both kinds of bodhicitta grows,
the flowers of both this and future lives bloom,
and the fruits of both myself and others ripen

(13) Jñānagarbha says:

Just like a banana tree[1015] lacking a core,
mind's true reality is lost by searching
Just as with the pictures of an illusionist,
all kinds of things appear but cannot be identified

(14) Nirupa says:

Leave the self-illuminating lamp alone!
Water and waves[1016] show no difference
The tracks of a bird need not be searched
The mind of a person awaking from sleep is happy

(15) Koṭalipa says:

Those in whom certainty arises seize the root
There is no other introduction superior to that
Among all appearing and possible phenomena,
there is not one that does not serve as the guru

(16) Kṛṣṇapāda says:

Just as bees combine the flavors
of all kinds of flowers into one,
those with realization combine

the flavors of all kinds of phenomena {244}
This flavor is the flavor of being unborn,
experienced without being identifiable

(17) Nāgabhusuku says:

The experience in which there is nothing to experience
is made a living experience due to being free of mind
It is determined without anything to be realized
It becomes revealed without anything to be attained

(18) Lūhipa says:

Once this immutable native mind has become revealed,
searching for buddhahood with effort elsewhere is so tiresome,
like searching for a buffalo's tracks once that buffalo has been found
Since I know that there is no buddhahood, I'm free of a mind desiring it

(19) Kṛṣṇapa says:

Having been introduced to the unidentifiable,
experience it within the state of emptiness!
Skilled in protecting it with mindfulness's sentry,
the thief of delusion will not find any opportunity
Through practicing this without any interruption,
it becomes revealed without meeting or parting

(20) Indrabhūti says:

Beings are under the sway of delusion while asleep,
but when they wake up, there is no delusion in objects
Likewise, those without realization suffer in saṃsāra,
but for those with realization, there is no saṃsāra in objects[1017]

(21) Ratnakīrti says:

That the sun's light rays with their all-encompassing web
overcome the accumulations of darkness is very amazing
That the web of a realized guru's light rays of compassion
dispels the mental darkness of those to be guided is very amazing

(22) Kaukata says:

Children matured by the four empowerments {245} have the instructions of experience
Those who cut through doubts through studying have the instructions of words
Those whom the gurus place in their minds have the instructions of the vital points
Those whose delusion has collapsed from within have the instructions of the true core

(23) Sahaja says:

Listen, son! Look at the center of the sky!
No southern clouds—they're the sky's display
Without clinging to this rainbow as being real,
mount the great river stream and gallop to the east!

(24) Elephant Garment says:

Just as the king of elixirs transforms grains into their quintessence,
through the elixir of experience, all possible appearances blaze as great bliss
Whatever may be seen is unborn and free of discursiveness
Since there is nothing to identify in this, emptiness need not be sought

(25) Bhasudhari says:

All sentient beings are sugatas
All appearances are the dharmakāya
All sense pleasures are mind's ornaments
All hosts of thoughts are great wisdom

(26) Herukapa says:

Great wisdom is what dwells in the body,
clearly realized from the guru's mouth
Not being expressed by others, this native
actuality is uncontrived and self-arising

(27) Kanakoti says:

Just as the fire of saṃsāric existence burns all entities,
the fire of realization incinerates the clinging to a self,
thus annihilating the entire fuel of saṃsāra for good
Then, it courses as it pleases for the welfare of beings {246}

(28) Power of the Sun says:

Diversity is the mind's magical display
Mind cannot be pointed out as "this"
Hence, saṃsāra and nirvāṇa lack a root
Understand exactly this as the dharmakāya!

(29) Ratnavajra says:

By virtue of certainty, the actuality is seen
By virtue of devotion, blessings well up
Through vigor, the purpose is accomplished

(30) Tréutrapa says:

If awareness does not awake from within,
it will not be realized by teaching it as "this"
As with the appearances of one with an eye disease,
first your own mindstream needs to be illuminated[1018]

(31) Anaṅgavajra says:

Just as the eye sense faculty does not see
an object, if what is to be seen is not manifest,
since the desired fruition does not arise [without it],
it is crucial to work on becoming familiar with it

(32) Javaripa[1019] says:

The three kāyas do not exist in outer objects—
it is out of the pellucid wisdom of awareness
that they dawn from within as mere reflections
You should not sully them through thoughts!

(33) Guṅdharipa[1020] says:

Possible appearances, primordially free, are the dharmadhātu
There is nothing to relinquish or to attain in mahāmudrā
The birds in the sky do not go anywhere at all
The efforts of children are so utterly exhausting

(34) Kambala says:

Not seen as anything—the eye of the blind
Not thought of as anything—dullness
Not having gone anywhere—the gait of the paralyzed
Nothing to attain at all—the treasure of a pauperess {247}

(35) Ḍombi Heruka says:

In the equality of saṃsāra and nirvāṇa free of discursiveness,
making efforts and accomplishing are so utterly exhausting
To cling to the unobstructed nonduality of objects and mind
as something involving difference—how afflicted this is!
To cling to the dharmakāya of the nonduality of self and others
as something involving good and bad—how pitiful that is!

(36) Ravigupta says:

Looking at objects, they are without arising
Looking at mind, it is free of discursiveness
This actuality of nonduality is beyond mind
I do not understand anything whatsoever

(37) Guṇati says:

Within the sky of being unborn and immovable,
all kinds of reflections are its magical display
Let unpretentious awareness be in its own seat!
To be bound by phenomena—how pitiful is that!

(38) Padmavajra says:

Letting completely go of all activities,
Let the buffalo of mind be in its own place!
Nonduality cannot be searched for
All and everything are true reality

(39) Tilopa says:

Pulling the rug out from under the unobstructed ālaya's feet
and casting off the clinging to a self within the expanse,
dishearten the mental consciousness from above!
Let the five gates be, loose[1021] and free in themselves!

(40) Prajñākara says:

Being free of discursiveness cannot be bound by thoughts
Seeing things as illusions cannot be bound by objects
Being free of wanting cannot be bound by conduct
Wishing for buddhahood cannot be bound by saṃsāra

(41) Jñānaśrī says:

Just like a trunk without any root,
my mind as such is lost in space {248}
Delight in deluded appearances as much as you can!
I am the yogī of space

(42) Parahita says:

Like a heron soaring through the sky,
saṃsāra and nirvāṇa are free in equal taste's expanse
Being free of all hopes and fears,
great bliss is the natural state of space

(43) Kāmaśrī says:

Without a body, it dwells within the body
Without support, it moves like the wind in the sky
Unobservable, it is beyond objects of speech or thought—
This is great,[1022] immutable[1023] self-arising wisdom

(44) Durjayacandra[1024] says:

Like searching the moon with a lamp,
thoughts[1025] themselves are nonthought
Just like searching space with space,
nonthought is beyond the mind

(45) Jālandhara says:

If there is no wisdom, seeing is great
If there are no thoughts, lucidity is great
If there is no clinging, bliss is great
Not abiding anywhere, abiding is great

(46) Maitrikamala says:

Mind as such, empty of a basis and rootless,
cannot be bound through karma,
nor is such the case by clinging to entities
Thus always look at your own mind!

(47) Padmavajra says:

The vajra of awareness is thrusting
into the bhaga of the expanse of space
If they unite in nonduality's natural state,
connate great bliss is dawning[1026]

(48) Nāgabodhi says:

Reign in the wind stirring in the sky!
Look at a dog's behavior in an empty house!
The child who sees the mother[1027] of the sky
Will for sure race onto her lap[1028] {249}

(49) Mañjuśrīmitra says:

If you travel to an island of jewels, you are free of poverty
If you obtain the guru's kindness, delusion collapses
If the true reality of saṃsāra is seen, there is no saṃsāra
If bodhicitta is perfected within, the welfare of beings arises

(50) Rājahasti says:

Those not promoting others' welfare after realization

resemble someone guarding a treasure in the ground
Isn't it that the yogīs who have assembled here
take care of sentient beings out of compassion?

(51) Bhadraśrī says:

Although I and sentient beings are inseparable,
since beings are suffering by virtue of their karmas,
I supplicate you to display for the welfare of beings
out of your compassion that's an unceasing stream

(52) Līlabhadra says:

Though it exists in us, it is not recognized,
like a poor woman deceived about a treasure
I supplicate you to lift the lamp of[1029] compassion
for sentient beings who do not see true reality

(53) Yoginī Dūtima says:

Water and ice show no difference
Appearance and emptiness are inseparable
The sky and the wind are not distinct
The same goes for mind and mental factors

(54) Taruparṇā says:

Who is uttering this sound of an echo?
Who draws the reflections in a mirror?
Where do the shows in a dream unfold?
They don't exist anywhere—that's mind's natural state

(55) Śmaśānikā says:

The pure ālaya is the dharmadhātu
Recognizing this to be so is wisdom

If self-clinging caves in, it is rootless
The five gates {250} free in themselves is to bring [all] onto the path

(56) *Nirgranthā says:

In what is free in itself and lacks mind,
loosely, let the uncontrived three gates be!
Let be without clinging, blocking, or creating!
Let be in immovable great equality!

(57) Vetālī says:

It is skillfulness, if you are practicing without
distraction where there is nothing to meditate
It is freedom, if you are bringing diversity
onto the path as great inexpressibility[1030]

(58) Mahāsiddhi says:

Don't meditate! Don't meditate! Don't meditate on mind!
Meditating on the mind is the whirl of delusion of thoughts
Through your thoughts, you are fettered in saṃsāra
Being free of the mind, there is nothing to meditate[1031]

(59) Vimalā says:

In primordially empty and void mind as such,
what's the point of meditating on being unborn?
In[1032] self-arising mental factors free in themselves,
what's the point of relinquishing any thoughts?

(60) Matighoṣā says:

The wisdom of space pervades everything
It's the path of[1033] supreme great primordial freedom,

immovable, immutable, beyond thought,
great nonconceptual self-aware wisdom

(61) Nairātmyā says:

Space, space—great equality
The sun, the sun—great primordial lucidity
Rivers, rivers—the uninterrupted flow
Rainbows—great bliss free in itself

(62) Prakāśā says:

If the actuality that cannot be understood is realized,
it becomes the narrative that cannot be expressed
Familiarizing with the actuality that cannot be thought,
the fruition that cannot be attained is emerging

(63) The One from Sandy Valley[1034] says:

Nondual great bliss is the supreme actuality {251}
Since it exists in us, why search elsewhere?
Preoccupied with terms due to our ignorant efforts—
how pitiful are sentient beings full of delusion!

(64) Ekavajrā says:

In the volume of the sky of emptiness,
write the letters of self-aware wisdom,
formulate the instructions on all kinds of means,
and proclaim the teachings as an incessant stream!

(65) Śyāmā says:

It is within the vajra of immutable space that
magical displays of moving and shaking arise,
performing their functions for all kinds of beings

and vanishing in the space[1035] of being free in
themselves

(66) Lady Brandishing a Sword says:

Through the one with many names yet free of any name,
realize the great one that is the primordial way of being,
the one free of mind in which clinging to such has caved in,
the one of utter freedom without anything at all to do!

(67) *Mārgajā says:

Devoid of the extremes of observed object and observer,
within the samādhi that is free of any support,
similar to the flowing stream of a great river,
you should practice without being distracted

(68) Mitrā says:

Just as a bird's path in the sky is without any trace,
so the conduct of yogīs does not leave any traces
If there is no clinging to independent existence,
even the ten nonvirtues are unable to fetter

(69) Kauṇapā says:

Just as when encountering a gold-making elixir,
due to possible appearances dawning in the sphere[1036] of
empty bliss,
there is freedom from all clinging to any entities—
the great wisdom of possible appearances free of discursiveness

(70) Padmaśrī says:

If the connate that is the native state
is not manipulated by a reflecting or meditating mind, {252}

the dharmakāya need not be searched elsewhere
It is inherent, so let it be in a loose manner!

(71) Padmarājñī says:

If this self-aware wisdom is found,
it is like a lamp in the darkness of eons
The delusion of karma is crushed for good,
as in a person waking up from sleep

(72) The ḍākinī *Sitā says:

What do persons seized by karma think?
Brahman, look at spinning your thread!
Who would be able to eat the sky?
You and me are not different at all

(73) Princess Glorious says:

Emptiness with a heart of compassion
constitutes the heritage of the sugatas
Since it is said to lack any chance to go astray,
you should be endowed with prajñā and means

(74) Vajrasukhā says:

The dhyāna that is vast and immovable
is the ground of all kinds of movements
Since moving and nonmoving are inseparable,
there's neither meditation nor nonmeditation here

(75) Jñānapādā says:

Those who do not see any phenomena anywhere
are the ones who see phenomena in their entirety

Beyond all objects to be seen and what sees them,
this constitutes the great wisdom of self-awareness

(76) Ghaghaśrī says:

If you know all perceptions, feelings, and experiences
anywhere to be empty of their individual essence,
the sense pleasures are ornaments of the mind—
you will not be bound, but you will be free

(77) Karmākarā says:

Those who see the wisdom of the mind {253}
will realize the true reality of the dharma
By realizing the dharma, bliss is attained

(78) Queen of Ornaments says:

You are the one without color and free of shape,
the one without meaning and free of any names,
the one without all kinds of awareness thinking,
the one with neither attainment nor relinquishment

(79) Ḍākinī Kambalā says:

This great nonreferential wisdom
cannot be pointed out by words
It is not realized by anything other
than relying[1037] on the guru's timely methods

*"A Garland of Pure Bindus" (*Śuddhabindumālā)—the expressions of the realizations of eighty*[1038] *male and female siddhas—was written down by the ḍākinīs and then remained in their secret treasury. After the principal ladies of the expanse had discussed the matter, they [eventually] gave [this text] to Tampa Gyagar.*[1039] *It was translated well by Shama Lotsāwa.* {254}

(179) Vajra Songs by Forty Siddhas, Called "A Garland of Gold"

I pay homage to the gurus

(1) Master Nāgārjuna says:

Those without realization[1040] should not engage in the conduct of the realized
If they do so, they are like subjects trying to break the law of the king
The realized ones should not engage in the conduct of the unrealized
If they do so, they resemble elephants who are sinking into the mud[1041]

(2) Master Saraha says:

Hey, friends, it is this connate here that
is not found elsewhere, so ask the guru's mouth![1042]
If the ultimate essence of his words[1043] is realized,
Where would mind be bound? The vāyus are without extinction[1044]

(3) Master Koṭalipa says:

Ordinary mind is waking up in the center of the heart

Once the six collections are pure, great bliss is uninterrupted
Everything imagined is meaningless, the cause of distraction
Since there is nothing to meditate, let be in the native state![1045]

(4) Master Samantavajra says:

Mahāmudrā is present within us in a connate manner
Without thinking, awareness, or effort, let it be on its own
Not becoming extinct, direct[1046] experience is aware by itself
Not becoming permanent, {255} it is unity without clinging[1047]

(5) Master Kāṇhapa says:

Just as a chariot without a single wheel is unable to drive,
Even if you make efforts in generosity and such, without the guru's pith instructions, there's no genuine siddhi
Vultures with their wings and perfect dexterity course and soar through the sky
Fortunate genuine yogīs absorb genuine empowerments and blessings, being blissful[1048]

(6) Master Kambala says:

The ocean in its depth and vastness is filled with jewels,
and the nāga kings' rule over this is very amazing
All appearances and sounds primordially are the dharmakāya—
those with realization and experience ruling over it is very amazing[1049]

(7) Master Lūhipa says:

A savage wild dog with honey rubbed on its nose gobbles up everything in all directions
Imparting empowerments and instructions to persons of

lesser insight and fortune sets their own mindstreams ablaze
A brave and steadfast elephant with a sword attached to his trunk crushes the hostile ranks
The intelligent of good fortune who realize the unborn vanquish thoughts upon encountering them[1050]

(8) Master Tilopa says:

A bird settling on Mount Meru's golden surface
casts off its bird nature and appears to be golden
If some wise people are realizing the unborn,
casting off the nature of an entity, they are very blissful[1051]

(9) Again, {256} Tilopa says:

Though it is since the very beginning that I am a buddha,
by the power of not realizing it, I don't see myself as a buddha
That through which nonduality is realized is mahāmudrā
At the time[1052] of realization, there's no seeing and no attainment

(10) Master Prajñābhadra says:

Just as a small child may come to possess the strength of a wrestler by being nourished,
being guided through the guru's instructions, even those of little insight [enter] the Mahāyāna
Just as medicine dispels diseases of wind, bile, and phlegm constellations,
the diseases of "me" and a self are instantly burned by the guru's instructions[1053]

(11) Master Nāropa says:

Just as the armed forces of a cakravartin king

bring all continents under their power,
through finding the taste of the connate,
you exert power over saṃsāra—very amazing![1054]

(12) The lesser master Ḍombipa says:

Just as the power of a gold-making elixir
leads to transforming base metals into gold,
so the power of precious empowerments
transforms afflictions into nondual wisdom[1055]

(13) Master Javari says:

Even if the unborn is realized but experience is lacking,
this is like a child carried away in the hands of a rākṣasī
Even if there is experience but the basic nature is not realized,
this resembles trying to rob an elephant with an iron hook[1056]

(14) Master Basudhara says: {257}

Until I gained realization, this corpse differed greatly from
cooked rice
Likewise, until gaining realization, I thought of buddhas and
beings as different
At the time of realization, even those who are in saṃsāra are
great buddhas
Hence, since realization and nonrealization are hard to distinguish, they do not differ[1057]

(15) Master Dignāga says:

Letting go of any activity is the pith instruction
If there is no wanting, this constitutes realization
If there is nothing to accomplish, this is conduct
If there is nothing to express, this is experience

If there is nothing to be adopted or rejected, this is the
fruition[1058]

(16) Master Ḍombi Heruka says:

Within the wish-fulfilling jewel of realization,
its colors are brought forth through experience
By its activity's power, what's wanted and needed arises
This is accomplished by those with equal taste[1059]

(17) Master Avadhūtī says:

Within the avajra[1060] of means and prajñā,
the guru's constant river flow is victorious
On the wish-fulfilling tree of the connate,
the fruits arise effortlessly, perfect in themselves[1061]

(18) Master Dārikapa says:

Though great bliss lies within us, it is not realized and
obscured by delusion
Those wishing for lucid great bliss should gather the two
accumulations
When not gathering the two accumulations, even if you strive
for a hundred eons,
without the actuality of no actuality, great bliss will not be
realized[1062]

(19) Master Kṛṣṇapāda says:

All buddhas in the three times have a single essence
The nature of this constitutes bodhicitta {258}
If you wish to realize it, let it be just as it is!
If there is familiarity with it, it will be revealed[1063]

(20) Master *Nirgranthapātra says:

By virtue of the gurus, you should first realize your own mind
Then, you should make this no different from all phenomena
To become familiar with nonduality, stay in charnel grounds!
Resting in equipoise, behave with the yogic disciplines of a lunatic![1064]

(21) Mastress Vetālīsukhā says:

If it resembles a horse, an elephant, and the ocean, this is supreme bliss
If it is like a monkey, a child, and a drawing on water, this is thought
If it is similar to a river, the sun, and medicine, this is inseparability
Like a hair-knot, an eye, and a wheel, the fruition is attained[1065]

(22) Master Rāmapala says:

Since the supreme samaya of all buddhas
is present as your very own realization,
that through which all buddhas are seen
is the realization of the native mind

(23) Master Kukkuripa says:

If you dwell on inseparability's ground, all is of good fortune
If you go to the ocean's depths, you are free of poverty
If you hold a sword in your hand, this is a great enjoyment
If you amble to places without direction, you meet friends[1066]

(24) Master *Cāryabalavān says:

All that appears to yogīs constitutes their instructions
Since by what is seen its being unborn is realized, this is the supreme master

Since the unborn is realized through all deeds, this is the means {259}
If persons are free of likes and dislikes, nonduality arises in them[1067]

(25) Master Kumāratrita says:

Those who have received empowerments
from[1068] the guru's instructions are pervaded
everywhere by the taste of the connate
To be sealed by the unborn is Vajradhara
By the blessing's dawning, there's inseparable, perfect buddhahood[1069]

(26) Master Bhatipa says:

Unite all dharmas with your mind so that they are nondual!
If realization's experience lacks the actuality of the definitive meaning's instructions,
There exists no great bliss in jewels that are nothing but trinkets
If possessing these dharmas, without hope or fear, let them be in their own place!

(27) Master Anaṅgavajra says:

If mind is not tormented, this is great bliss
If there is no wanting, this is equal taste
If there is no effort, this is meditation supreme
If free of duality, this is perfect buddhahood[1070]

(28) Master Indrabhūti says:

If the pivotal points in time are not endowed with self-blessing,

even if they perform inner or outer conduct, yogīs will not
become buddhas
There is no difference between inherent bliss and appearances
Once clinging is let go, the supreme experience[1071] will be
attained[1072]

(29) Master Padmavajra says:

Not looking anywhere, look at the center!
If free of the supreme, this is great ecstasy
If mantra knowers behave based on the secret,
yogīs should transform through the signs[1073]

(30) Princess Lakṣmīṃkarā says:

First, the intelligent give rise to realization {260}
Second, they meditate on the nose tip[1074] in jungles
Then, once experiences have sprung forth,
they should realize conduct's distinctive features[1075]

(31) Master Padmapāda says:

If the connate within someone
arises as irritation,[1076] it is painful,
just like in the eye of an elephant—
not clinging while relaxing is supreme dhyāna[1077]

(32) Master Garbhapāda says:

Once experiences present as a river stream are stable,
you should proceed through the points of conduct
It is by virtue of the instructions of the true guru
that thoughts of desire and hatred are to be pacified[1078]

(33) Master Vajrapāda says:

Bliss! Bliss! This is nonabiding bliss!
The nature of lacking desire is bliss
To know everything imagined[1079] as such is bliss
The buddhahood of nothing to accomplish is bliss[1080]

(34) Master Śāntipa says:

Similar to a turtle, the one who is untainted
by the flaws of saṃsāra and originally pure
is the guru, who is the lamp free of darkness
Thanks to his kindness, the wisdom sun is bliss[1081]

(35) Master Ghaṇṭāpāda says:

The triad of lalanā, rasanā, and avadhūtī
should be bound for the sake of self-blessing
It is on the triad of guru, mind, and appearances
that the wise rely so as to give rise to realization[1082]

(36) Master Mute One with a Spear says:

The four kāyas free of blocking and creating are inseparable
All phenomena without reference points have a single root
Nondistraction[1083] constitutes the path of all the buddhas
If there is no bias, this is the supreme of all the yogas {261}

(37) Master Kutibhirva says:

Venerating buddhas and so on yield no meaning
If there is wanting and effort, there will be no buddhahood
Through the words of a guru with blessings, experiences increase
This is due to the factor of the gurus' pith instructions, not through anything else[1084]

(38) Master Ajitakesarī says:

If relying on the genuine venerable one, you attain true reality
If you meditate in the midst of the jungle, you attain solitude
If you realize phenomena as mind, there is nothing unfavorable
If you drink the milk of the sky, you will be satisfied[1085]

(39) Master Śāntīśvara says:

If you realize the freedom of extremes of empty bliss,
you are free of flaws by relying on a wish-fulfilling tree
If a person knows to move around in a lake by swimming,
a son will be born to a brahman father and mother[1086]

(40) Yoginī Dharmā says:

Having donned the great armors,
through gem-like perseverance,
I steered the ship of[1087] my own mind,
Sailing to this human corpse's inner sanctum
If you eat the flesh of a seven-lifer,[1088]
you are similar to a bird in the sky[1089]

(41) Master Maitrīpa says:

Inseparable bliss and emptiness are perfect in the pure lotus in the heart
Mental engagement in the unborn is the mind of inconceivable great bliss
Yogīs experience all appearances and sounds as threefold equal taste
With the blessings of the venerable ones[1090] dawning, this is inseparable, perfect buddhahood[1091]

(42) Yoginī Ghaghā {262} says:

Don't look at objects! Don't look at mind either!
Don't entertain wanting! Don't perform any actions!
Without holding on to any fears or allowing decline,
Let go of native mind just as it pleases!

(43) Master Bhusuku says:

Activities amount to nothing but saṃsāric suffering
Yogīs who let go of activities realize their mind,
not abiding anywhere, beyond the extremes of permanence
and extinction
Since there is nothing to meditate, this is inconceivable

(44) Yoginī Kaṅkarā says:

Nondual mind is like water poured into water
Don't impair its nature, let it be like an elephant!
No matter how the monkeys of experience may come up,
How could they pervade the sky of realization?

(45) Master Thagana says:

If some water has entered your ear,
it is water itself that will extract it
Likewise, reality is seen by familiarizing with
all that is primordially delusive as delusive[1092]

This concludes the vajra songs that forty yogīs who had attained siddhi intoned at the time of performing a gaṇacakra in Śrī Oḍḍiyāna, being pith instructions from their experience, called "A Garland of Gold."[1093] {263}

(180) The Expressions of Realization of Thirty-Five Wisdom Ḍākinīs[1094]

Namo Ratnaguru

At the great charnel ground Śītavana, the ḍākinī Sukhakauṇapā had been holding a gaṇacakra for the principal [ḍākinīs] of the expanse. Later, inviting them with a ḍākinī receptacle full of wine, she asked each one for a song that expressed her realization.

(1) First, the ḍākinī Wearing a Topknot with a Golden Sun and Moon raised a song expressing her realization:

> Hey! If certainty arises about uncontrived
> natural[1095] mind, this is buddhahood
> If these appearances of white and red objects
> are understood as symbols, this is the guru

(2) The ḍākinī Wearing a Tuft Topknot expressed her realization:

> Hey! If there is no duality, there is no bondage or freedom
> If there is nothing to identify, there are no obscurations
> If there is no self and other,[1096] there is no desire or hatred
> If there is nothing to mind, there is no distraction

(3) The ḍākinī Wings of the Wind expressed her realization:

Hey! Baseless phenomena are similar to dreams
Arising as appearances through conditions is like a reflection
Self-arising and self-subsiding resemble a bubble
The great freedom of any root is similar to space {264}

(4) The ḍākinī Skull Garland of Sun and Moon expressed her realization:

Hey! For persons who experience true reality,
great bliss does not fit into the element of space
You tell me whether this can be pointed out!
I see without anything whatsoever to be seen

(5) The ḍākinī Clad in a Blanket expressed her realization:

The anthers of a lotus wake up in the center of my heart
Its vibrantly lucid flower is free of the stains of mud
It has scent and colors—what are the conditions for that?
Is there any blocking or creating here, or what?

(6) The ḍākinī Mekhalā expressed her realization:

Hey! Magical displays arising from the sky
are created by the sky itself and hence
they are self-arising within the sky
Don't cling to them as being flaws!

(7) The ḍākinī Vetālīsukhā expressed her realization:

Hey! Having found supreme great bliss thanks to the guru's kindness,
you must understand that relying[1097] on any other means is stupid[1098]
Any path to bliss that exists outside of that
cannot be found anywhere else by anybody

(8) The ḍākinī Jñānavajrā expressed her realization:

Hey! If you understand this magical display of all kinds
of appearances to be the perceiver and perceived of minding
and you know that minding is empty of an essence of its
own,
there is no need to search for the bliss of the expanse

(9) The ḍākinī Queen of Saṃsāric Existence expressed her realization:

Hey! If this king of self-awareness is seen,
all and everything is the path to liberation {265}
If this very self-awareness is not realized,
there will never ever be any freedom

(10) The ḍākinī Padmapādā expressed her realization:

Hey! Who would be able to examine or analyze
what is free of the extremes[1099] of existence and nonexistence?
Who would be able to reflect or meditate on
what is without minding and free of any mind?

(11) The ḍākinī Insight of the Victors expressed her realization:

Hey! Emptiness endowed with awareness's dynamic energy
demonstrates the magical display of the unborn being born
Without blocking or creating, this is free in its own place
I have not found anything that is to be done here

(12) The ḍākinī Lion Face expressed her realization:

Hey! If you say "It exists," there is nothing to identify
If you say "It does not exist," all kinds of things appear
What is beyond the extremes[1100] of existence and nonexistence
I am not able to point out by saying "It is this"

(13) The ḍākinī Queen of Splendor expressed her realization:

Don't be distracted from where[1101] there is nothing to mind!
Saṃsāra by virtue of distraction is similar to a dream
If realized, this is like a person waking up from sleep
As far as I am concerned, I have not seen any saṃsāra

(14) The ḍākinī Śrībhadrā expressed her realization:

Hey! These possible appearances are mahāmudrā
These sense pleasures are the locus of pellucidity[1102]
In native reality, there is no meeting or parting
I request that you run on the plain of great bliss!

(15) The ḍākinī Light Rays of Glory expressed her realization:

Hey! In the treasure vault of native reality,
there is the gem of mind for all wants and needs {266}
The one who holds the key is the true guru
Are you enthusiastic about following her?

(16) The ḍākinī Bhadrā expressed her realization:

Look! Look at your own mind!
Looking, nothing is found; smash its root!
Make up branches however you please!
My thoughts are free in themselves

(17) The ḍākinī Vajrasukhā expressed her realization:

Though beings have been deluded by their karma,
there is no bliss anywhere else than in themselves
Once more, look at your own true actuality,
and mind will be liberated from karma!

(18) The great being Mighty Lady of the Sun expressed her realization:

All possible appearances are illuminated and burned

through the majestic splendor of thousands of suns
Likewise, phenomena are illuminated and vanquished
through the great wisdom that is nondual

(19) The ḍākinī Devīśrījñānā expressed her realization:

Hey! I am neither born nor perishing
I am the changeless wisdom vajra
All phenomena that arise from me
are equally free as my own essence

(20) The ḍākinī Tiger Face expressed her realization:

Hey! Unborn, unceasing, beyond thought,
lacking words to describe it as "this,"
the path of great supreme primordial freedom
is inconceivable—let it be in its own place!

(21) The ḍākinī Śāntibhadrā expressed her realization:

Hey! The true reality of mind cannot be described
The true reality of the basic ground cannot be conceived
The true reality of the dharma cannot be identified
The true reality of the path cannot be meditated on {267}

(22) The ḍākinī Ghaghaśrī expressed her realization:

Hey, son, look at whatever you are thinking!
What is free of reference points[1103] cannot be seen
Who can meditate on what is inconceivable?[1104]
Make no efforts in this, let be in the ground!

(23) The ḍākinī Mighty Lady of Wisdom expressed her realization:

If someone is not seeing true reality,
even if performing virtuous actions of body and speech,

they will not encounter supreme great bliss
but solely[1105] happiness that's just temporary

(24) The ḍākinī Sukhavajrā expressed her realization:

Hey! The plethora of the distinct things
that may be seen, heard, thought, or felt
only appears as a mere reflection
in the pellucid wisdom of mind—
not established as any basis, empty of essence

(25) The ḍākinī Deity with the Sun Horse expressed her realization:

For those who see what cannot be seen,
mind is free in itself—the dharmakāya
Leaving the stallion of the vāyus behind,
the rider[1106] of mind courses through the sky

(26) The ḍākinī Lotus Sprout expressed her realization:

Sentient beings are bound by the garland of mind
By killing mind and cutting through this garland,
just like a poisonous snake wiped out by a weapon,
it cannot inflict any harm or provide any benefit

(27) The ḍākinī Queen of the Expanse expressed her realization:

Hey! Given space's pellucidity, colors cannot change it
Persons with realization cannot be bound by karma
Doing the job of a wrestler without confidence
is similar to a fox wearing the skin of a lion {268}

(28) The ḍākinī Moon Face expressed her realization:

Hey! Great wisdom is the supreme path
Don't travel! It's the ground of suchness

Don't practice! It's the effortless actuality
AHO! Yoginīs are fortunate indeed!

(29) The ḍākinī Blazing One with a Garland of Lightning expressed her realization:

Looking but not seeing—that's my eye
Thinking but not minding—that's my mind
Speaking but not expressing—that's my tongue
Traveling but not going—that's my path

(30) The ḍākinī Wearing a Crystal Topknot expressed her realization:

In the natural mind of not meditating,
there's nothing to seize or not to seize by mindfulness
In the loose three gates of lacking conduct,
there's nothing to block or create deliberately

(31) The ḍākinī Sun Queen expressed her realization:

Hey! This wisdom of self-arising great bliss
cannot be described without realization
Once realized, how could it be expressed?
Its experience is speechless—the mouth of a mute

(32) The ḍākinī Lion Face expressed her realization:

Don't look at him! Look at yourself!
I am embodying great wisdom
He is just an emanation of mine
Nondual wisdom is beyond mind

(33) The ḍākinī Blood Face expressed her realization:

Hey! At the border between minding and nonminding,
the mental consciousness is beyond thinking

Understand this from the mouth of the guru—
it will not be realized by anything else

(34) The ḍākinī {269} Lamp of Glory expressed her realization:

Hey! Since you are looking at this[1107]
wisdom of mind, how do you see?
It won't be realized by imagination
Don't search! Let be in suchness!

(35) The ḍākinī Queen of Clear Illumination expressed her realization:

Beings are bound by the tangle of their karma
Just like a brahman spinning his thread,
you should relax the tangle of your mind!
If you are free of karma, there is no bondage

This concludes the expressions of realization of thirty-five wisdom ḍākinīs that were [later] passed on to lord Tampa Gyagar from [the texts] that were lodged in the secret treasury of the ḍākinīs, after the principal [ḍākinīs] of the expanse had discussed the matter. It was translated by Shama Lotsāwa.[1108] {270}

(181) The All-Encompassing Song of the Ḍākinīs

In the language of India: *Ḍākinītanugītināma*[1109]
In the language of Tibet: *Mkha' 'gro ma'i 'byams glu zhes bya ba*

I pay homage to the bhagavatī Nairātmyā
At the time when the ḍākinī Sukhamahāsiddhi performed a gaṇacakra at the great charnel ground Nakṣatraśrīlalita in the abode of Oḍḍiyāna, the land of the ḍākinīs, the yogī Kamalaśrī[1110] gained confidence in realizing and fathoming the actuality of his own native wisdom of true reality. Through the power of the dynamic energy of experience dawning without any bias, saddling this great nondual wisdom onto the horse of pointing-out words, he raised a song in the rows of the gaṇacakra. This delighted the wisdom ḍākinīs and those coming about through karma. In the sky before him, they assembled like cloud banks and raised songs by calling out to him with their heart advice in the form of secret words:[1111]

Hey, oh powerful scion of a noble family,
dynamic vajra energy of goal-accomplishment,
fortunate one whose karma of training awakened,
mighty lord of qualities, sovereign of the treasury [1] {271}

Your body is adorned by the two siddhis,
supreme leader of humans, gaṇacakra lord,

you nourished[1112] causal dharmatā through conditions
Drink some sips of the karmic fortune of your training! [2]

You found the wish-fulfilling jewel of qualities
and rest in the radiance of great luminosity,
promoting beings' welfare as a mere illusion
You yogī of space who are incomparable,
there is no need at all to encourage you,
but please listen to this song of ours! [3]

In general, sentient beings are deluded by karma,
making their experiences in the realm of suffering
Let your flesh be struck by unbearable love for them!
If you do not consider them now with your compassion,
how will your parents in the six states of existence fare?
You, oh yogī, give rise to the mindset of benefiting them! [4]

Usually, the small child of awareness is stuck in distraction
The appearances of delusion are such a great spectacle
The thieves of perceiver and perceived upset your head
States of mind with doubt and indecision are many [5]

The watchmen of the remedies have little perseverance
Your armor of alertness and mindfulness is slack
There is the danger of losing the gem of mind as such
You, oh yogī, do not be distracted toward objects! [6]

The cancer[1113] of the five poisons of the afflictions is invading
the queen of the space that is the ground without any change,
being harmed by the nine evil spirit siblings of perceiver and perceived
and following the delusion of thoughts conditioned by good and bad [7]

Through inappropriate conduct due to attachment and aversion,

the chronic disease of perceiver and perceived rises from the
depths
and the well-being of your own body is lost and gone—
how pitiful are sentient beings who are full of delusion!
You, oh yogī, do promote the welfare of beings! [8]

Usually, the small child[1114] of the wisdom of mind {272}
keeps listening to the lies of the five sense gates
There's the danger of being hurled into the abyss of the six
classes [of beings]
You, oh yogī, dismantle the clinging to duality! [9]

The wild moving mind of discursive thinking,
instead of lying down uncontrived and naked
in the palace that is the expanse of the ālaya,
plays with the deception of illusory sense pleasures
by mingling with the friends of the five poisons [10]

Being distracted toward the two objects of desire and hatred,
there's the danger of plunging into the miserable realms'
abyss
Close the doors of the five sense gates
and lock the small child of mind in prison!
Stretch out on the bed of bliss, lucidity, and emptiness!
You, oh yogī, are headed for distraction![1115] [11]

In the river of birth, aging, sickness, and death,
the fools who cannot swim like to play around
While owning the ship of the freedoms and resources,
they do not rely on the ferryman[1116] of the guru lord
but chatter away[1117] in the waves of nonvirtuous actions [12]

Flee from the waves of suffering through the remedies!
Without being left behind in the mud of clinging,
pursue the dry shore of liberation as best as you can!
You, oh yogī, let go of your wanting! [13]

On the tree trunk of the poison of desire,
the branches of adopting and rejecting spread,
the foliage of clinging grows in the ten directions,
the flowers of effortful accomplishing fly into the sky,
and the fruits of suffering keep plunging down
Picking them up,[1118] the monkey of cowardice eats them—
there's the danger of being bound[1119] in saṃsāra's jungle [14]

Persons who do not cling to all kinds of things,
brandishing the weapon of immutable confidence,
knock down the tree of desire at its very foundation[1120]
and carry away the unripe dried-up fruits of the five poisons
Terminate the lethal power of this poison! {273}
You, oh yogī, relinquish your wanting! [15]

A deer being defeated by sounds[1121]
is the payback[1122] for doing things for fame
Oh yogī, do not cling in a biased way
to praise and blame that are like echoes! [16]

An elephant being captured with an iron hook
is the payback for being attached to the taste of wine
Oh yogī, do not entertain any clinging
to the troubled salt waters of the sense pleasures! [17]

A peacock's wasting away[1123] and dying
is the payback for it seeing feathers as ornaments
Oh yogī, do not[1124] see the skandhas
of the unclean elements as yourself! [18]

A bee being stuck in the mud
is the payback for it being attached to sweet scents
Oh yogī, do not torment yourself with affection
for relatives with whom you have a transient connection! [19]

A moth being burned by fire
is the payback for it being attached to a lamp's shine
Oh yogī, do not entertain any clinging to
appearances of illusion-like objects as such! [20]

A feathered creature's entrapment in a snare
is the payback for it pursuing sense pleasures as food
Oh yogī, do not entertain the hungry desire
for food with the iron hook of clinging! [21]

With the mirror of the pure ālaya
polished by the six collections' awareness,[1125]
the clear reflections of the six objects appear
Childish beings without realization cling to them as entities,
experiencing the happiness and suffering of desire and hatred
[22]

The uncontrived ālaya, the dharmadhātu,
lacks clinging to the ceaseless six collections as such
The six objects are clear yet empty of essence
Childish beings clinging to entities can't help but weep
The wise are free of clinging to self-appearances as such
You, oh yogī, annihilate any clinging to them as such! [23] {274}

In the sky of the ground that cannot be identified,
the southern clouds of the afflictions' five poisons gather,
the thunder of the clinging to a self resounds,
and the continuous rain of all kinds of karma falls,
stirring the filthy swamp of saṃsāra with its attachment
Thus, the crops of the sufferings of the six realms grow [24]

The sun of the awareness of superior insight
brings the sun of the expanse clearly to mind
The breeze of the mindfulness of equipoise and thereafter
dispels the southern clouds of discursive thinking in the
expanse,

and the thunder of clinging to a self vanishes in its own place [25]

The continuous rain of karma lacks any root
The sun dries up the filthy swamp of clinging
The seeds of the six classes [of beings] become parched
The unripe dried-up harvest of suffering is carried away—
You, oh yogī, do not entertain any doubts! [26]

The rightful prince who was cheated by his ministers
roamed as a beggar in lands without any friends,
soiled and barely making a living with tattered rags,
going unrecognized by either himself or others
A brahman expert in signs, realizing his pedigree,
queried this foolish young man with his insight [27]

Entrust the basic nature to the lord of awareness,
extract it by washing it with the two pure accumulations,
adorn it with the wish-fulfilling jewel of the instructions,
place it on the jeweled throne of realization,
and seize the royal seat of the buddhas of the three times!
You, oh yogī, must rely on the guru! [28]

The deer of the mind without any physical support
roams the intermediate state's plain through karma's force,
tormenting itself with the water of the mirage of clinging
The six classes [of beings] die in the extreme state of saṃsāra [29]

Mountains and valleys are full of the traces of their flesh and blood
Now,[1126] bind awareness without a physical support in space! {275}
Not traveling on the surface of the six collections' conditions,
race across the vast plain of great luminosity! [30]

Without entertaining any clinging to the river
of the mirage of the sense pleasures as such,
cut through the torment of wanting within!
Not traveling on the surface of the conditions of the six classes
[of beings],
stretch out within the expanse of great equality![1127] [31]

In the native state of inconceivable mind,
the arrow-maker of undistracted mindfulness
straightens it out as the uncontrived native essence
and cuts off the tip and the base of hope and fear [32]

She wraps it in the four ecstasies' attire,[1128]
inserts the arrowhead of the connate,
crafts[1129] the notch of means and prajñā,
attaches the feathers of the four moments,
and shoots it right at the clinging to a self [33]

Pierce the heart of the wild pig of ignorance!
Sever the life-force nāḍī of perceiver and perceived!
Now,[1130] don't move around in this abode of saṃsāra!
You, oh yogī, must seize the fortress! [34]

When objects appear as self-appearances without clinging,
the sense pleasures turn into the aids of the path
The colors of the lotus shine clearly in the mud
Oh yogī, sustain your experiences[1131] as you please! [35]

When phenomena are realized to be unreal,
this is the great unity of prāṇa and apāna
Loosening the buffalo's golden chain, he is happy
Oh yogī, just let your efforts be! [36]

With the stallion of the awareness of equality
not shackled with the chains of perceiver and perceived,

the bridle of clinging to self and other is loosened
Race across the plain without any direction as you please! [37]

When the lunatics in whom experiences keep bubbling up
spontaneously are not put into the irons of the remedies, {276}
they exit the house of fake discipline through the door
and freely wander around in places as they please [38]

With the garuḍa[1132] of the sky of realization
not attached to the food of tenet systems
and not afraid of the abyss of delusion,
let him soar through the sky without bias! [39]

With the wish-fulfilling jewel of the fruition
not tainted by the stains of hope and fear
and not left behind in the realm of wishful thinking,
persevere in facing the requests for all wants and needs![1133]
[40]

Having seized the fortress of immutability,
through the unbiased light rays of compassion,
you don the armor of your previous vows
for the six kinds of beings who were your parents
Now, this is the right time do so—samaya! [41]

These sounds of their great encouragement resounded like the thunder of an eon and then vanished as if to the end of space.

This concludes "The Great All-Encompassing Song of the Ḍākinīs." From among the eight special lineages, this is the fourfold cycle of true actuality including the all-encompassing song.[1134] {277}

(182) The Vajra Songs of All Siddhas, Called "The Light of the True Reality of All Yogīs"

In the language of India: *Sarvayogatattvālokānāmasakalasiddhavajragīti*[1135]
In the language of Tibet: *Rnal 'byor pa thams cad kyi de kho na nyid snang ba zhes bya ba grub pa rnams kyi rdo rje'i mgur*

I pay homage to the true gurus

The path that allows sentient beings (the cause) to attain buddhahood (the result) does not exist as anything outside of the two accumulations, and the ultimate accumulation of merit is the gaṇacakra. The locations where [such gaṇacakras] are turned consist of the eight great charnel grounds,[1136] which represent places difficult for people to travel to, paths where spirits and zombies wander, areas where the nonhuman beings of the world roam, and the abodes of the karma ḍākinīs who, by merely being seen, make the māras' hairs stand on end and fill the yakṣas with utter dread. After yogīs with ultimate realization and yoginīs whose minds are well-refined in unborn dharmatā have assembled at such [charnel grounds], in order to bless the gaṇa offerings, they raise songs of experience about that from which their certainty about ultimate reality (the object of engagement) arose in each of their mindstreams, how they were introduced to the wisdom of the connate of native reality that dwells in [all of] us, {278} and by which means their realization dawned. These are [the songs that] the ḍākinīs dwelling in these individual places, such as Sukhasiddhi and Subhagā, set down in writing on white paper[1137] through their power of total recall for the sake of later generations.

Lūhipa,[1138] he who completed hardships, says:

The means for greatness in this life are saṃsāra's cause
Be without many things to do—the path to liberation ends
Being free of the mindset of desire is the sphere of activity
It is in this location that awakening is close by [I.1]

Śrīsukhā, she who possesses the radiance of bliss, says:

Worldly activities represent the sphere of the māras
Turning the mind away from this life is the path of the noble
The traces of being harmed by the venomous snake
of desire consist of nothing but suffering itself [I.2]

Lalitavajra, he from the gem continent, says:

Samādhi and prajñā eliminate the stains
Self-aware wisdom is the kāya of luminosity
The means to attain bliss is the path of empowerment
At the time of it being revealed, thoughts are free [I.3]

Candravimalā, she who takes desire as the path, says:

Through samādhi, sharp powerful prajñā is not seen
and the shackles of saṃsāra are not cut through
Through the power of precious empowerments,
contamination turns into nothing but great bliss [I.4]

Virūpa,[1139] the ultimately powerful, says:

Just as in the case of a dried-up lotus lacking mud,
if the five poisons do not exist, wisdom {279} ends

Bringing sense pleasures onto the path, paths and bhūmis shorten[1140]
Wishing for freedom by relinquishing them is an inferior path [I.5]

Rurusukā, the benefactress of material goods, says:

Seers who are endowed with the eye of prajñā
transform the bases of disease into the body's strength
Likewise, by being endowed with the means,
the five poisons give rise to wisdom [I.6]

Nāgārjuna, the protector of beings, says:

Just as dreams lack any nature,
phenomena are empty of an own essence
Neither saṃsāra nor nirvāṇa
are established ultimately [I.7]

Jñānadhara, he who realized discriminating wisdom, says:

To be empty of essence is appearances' true core
What is without any nature of its own thus
has the character of being inexpressible
Without seeing unity, you cannot be free [I.8]

Saraha, the mighty lord of yogīs, says:

The vajra seat never recollected before
is the indescribable place of mind's defeat
Its character is luminosity without coming and going
Dualistic appearances being free is mahāmudrā [I.9]

Anukirā, the yoginī of vajra recitation, says:

Pellucid appearance-emptiness free of conditions
is not limited as the objects of the six collections
Within the native state without coming and going,
rest mind at ease in the gap between mindfulness and
forgetting! [I.10]

Saraha, the mighty lord of Śabaras,[1141] says:

The adventitious conditioned appearances of delusion
are empty of arising and ceasing in the three times,
not established in the ground {280} yet amazement's sphere
Seeing this is the sphere of freedom [I.11]

Sukabhau, the benefactress who is a refuge, says:

The thinking of discursive awareness
arises due to the power of ignorance
All kinds of nonexistents dawn, empty of essence,
with an aftermath[1142] of rootless space [I.12]

Āryadeva, he who transcends being human, says:

Originally pure luminosity's natural state,
this unconditioned self-abiding root
that is free from the four extremes
and nondiscursive is a great spectacle [I.13]

Bhasurikā, the single-minded yoginī, says:

The natural state of all-pervasive luminosity
with its character of lacking coming and going
is free from discursiveness—at all times,
the dharmakāya will not abandon beings [I.14]

Kalaaleba, the lion of speech, says:

The views of tenets are stated as names,
and names consist of thinking
Empty true reality is the dharmakāya
free of any names—mahāmudrā [I.15]

Karidharimā, the one-pointed yoginī, says:

It is the nameless queen of the sugatas
who is drinking down the milk of the sky
Thus, beyond the sphere of speech, thought, and mind,
she consumes dualistic appearances and milks the sky
Through seeing her, you will be free [I.16]

Śāntadeva, he with inexhaustible insight, says:

To turn the mind away from this life is the path to liberation
Without pursuing appearances, delusion is free
Severing the three times with a single stroke {281} is the vital core—
the mahāmudrā of stainless self-appearance [I.17]

Anutārā, the dharma benefactress, says:

Without being free of the shackles of the worldly
armor, the path of the noble will not be embraced
For that long, bliss will not be encountered
Once self-appearances are pure, pure realms dawn [I.18]

Ḍombipa, he who completed yogic discipline, says:

Cognizance that is not deliberately seized
by any focus is not scattered toward[1143] objects
Stainless bliss, lucidity, and nonthought
constitute pellucid mahāmudrā free of mind [I.19]

Jñānavimalā, the yoginī who turned her mind away from desire, says:

The striving of the meditating mind is a stain
Through just letting awareness be in its seat,
uncreated cognizance is free from flaws
Based on the focusing of clinging thoughts,
the freedom of discursiveness will not dawn [I.20]

Kamala, he who possesses the eye of prajñā, says:

The experience of the connate
of self-aware wisdom, the true state,
is not the experiential sphere of words
Pointing out by symbols is the lion's speech [I.21]

Padmadhanu, the lady with the roar of no-self, says:

The native basic ground that is the essence
does not dwell among the objects of mind
Impossible to be illustrated and unidentifiable,[1144]
it is known through the perfect guru's symbols [I.22]

Vīṇapa,[1145] he who is free[1146] of the shackles of delusion, says:

Similar to the disc of the moon in the water,
appearances' own core is to be empty of essence
The clinging to entities constitutes delusion
Free of clinging to such, {282} this is mahāmudrā [I.23]

Mekhalā, she with the discipline of vows, says:

Resembling the city of the gandharvas,
phenomena's nature is void if examined
With reality used up, falseness used up, letters used up,
the path of words is severed, it's beyond mind [I.24]

Gorakṣa, the hidden yogī, says:

Through dusting off the wish-fulfilling gem
of realization by becoming acquainted with it,
its color of having attaining stability comes forth[1147]
At that time, what is desired and needed manifests [I.25]

Kumalasūryā, she who is weary of saṃsāra, says:

If the interior of the clouds of self-appearances does not clear
up,
the light of the glorious knot does not become clearly manifest
If thinking is not kept at a great distance,
wisdom does not like to be close by [I.26]

Coborika, the mighty lord of the vāyus, says:

The workings of the letters present as unity
are eliminating the letters of consciousness
Through experience's lucidity, self-clinging is undone
This undoes the propelling and adopting by experiences[1148]
[I.27]

Umukara,[1149] the glorious one with the conduct of a lion among humans, says:

The letters that dwell in the hubs of the triad
of the mahāsukha-, dharma-, and nirmāṇacakras
represent the bodies, speech, and minds
of all the sugatas without any exception [I.28]

Naduba, he who sees his own face in symbols, says:

The supreme actuality taught by the guru
that is introduced in the center of the heart

is to recognize effortless presence's own face
Behold this crucial point with certainty! [I.29]

{283} Bhacala, he with the discipline of gathering virtuous dharmas, says:

The kāya of self-arising wisdom perfect in the ground
is not contingent on any conditions of contrivance[1150]
Self-aware luminosity—the basic ground of the true state—
is known through the means of specific auspicious
connection[1151] [I.30]

Tailopa, the mighty lord of the treasury of scripture and reasoning, says:

The speech of the guru dispels blindness[1152]
When looking at the piṭakas with the eyes
of seeing that, there is not even a single letter
to be cast away that does not serve as instruction [I.31]

Karmalikā, she who possesses lucid radiance, says:

This diversity of red and white letters
in the tome of the expanse of the sky
is mind's phenomena, the delusion of thoughts
Ultimately, this tome is empty of letters [I.32]

Dantipa, he who engages in the means to bring bliss onto the path, says:

By melting inner heat through outer conditions,
without making any effort, all on its own,
the dhātus align and the wisdom dwelling
within yourself dawns—thus, you are free of karma [I.33]

Nakara, he who takes bliss as the path, says:

Within the egg of the empowerments of the path of
maturation,
the wings of the path of liberation—creation and
perfection—spread
Through your devotion and faith cracking open this shell,
you are free from the trap of the delusion of ignorance [I.34]

Cara, he whose realization[1153] arose from blessings, says:

Through your fervent great love of keeping
the supreme precious gem in your hearts,
the glorious treasure vault is filled completely
Oh friends, keep cherishing this gem! [I.35]

{284} Bhikala, he with the discipline of promoting the welfare of sentient beings, says:

Just like not accomplishing your goal on the ocean's
most supreme island without having a captain,[1154]
though you may be adorned with many qualities,
without the guru, you're not at the end of existence [I.36]

Khagapa, he whose realization[1155] arose in his being a carpenter, says:

Entities are endowed with the nature of illusions
Regard them as unreal and delusion is undone!
Behold saṃsāra's true core—it lacks any nature!
Don't find anything to get rid of, cast out remedies! [I.37]

Morjunutara, he who realized all-accomplishing wisdom, says:

Saṃsāra is not established, being empty of a basis
Nirvāṇa is not established, being empty of a mind
Paths and bhūmis are not established, being empty of reality
The fruition is not established, being empty of a sphere[1156]
[I.38]

Kanapa, he who is free of the stains of hope and fear, says:

Due to their being baseless and without root,
in phenomena that are originally[1157] empty,
what would saṃsāra be and what nirvāṇa?
Without seeing a fruition, practicing is free [I.39]

Gadarā, the yoginī focusing on the mind, says:

How could there be any time when
the trunk of a banana tree has a pith?
At this time, the fruition is not seen
as anything else than lucidity [I.40]

Kanara, he who possesses the eye of wisdom, says:

Arising from pellucid awareness on the inside
but not from blessing of gods[1158] on the outside,
by clinging being severed, experiences blaze
Through the power of pellucid awareness,
all kinds of artistries will be brought forth[1159] [I.41] {285}

Vajrasiddhi, he who possesses the patience of gladly accepting suffering, says:

The surface of a crystal not affected by outer
conditions of impurity and pure of tarnish
assumes the colors of all kinds of silks—
it is just like that with volitional karma [I.42]

This is the first chapter, called "Cracking Open the Eggshell of Ignorance," in *Vajra Songs, [Called] "The Light of True Reality."*

Takana, he who brings wisdom onto the path, says:

Buddhahood free from the four extremes

lacks any stains of arising and ceasing
The natural state of thoughtless lucid bliss
free of dualistic appearances is mahāmudrā [II.1]

Hulukā, the yoginī of thoughts being free in themselves, says:

The dharmakāya that is not contrived
or affected by anything, and singular
as the inseparable expanse, is all-pervasive
No bondage by thinking will surface [II.2]

Tillipa, he who sees reality, says:

The ordinary mind of discursive thinking[1160]
will be afflicted by the entirety of bondage
When the stirring winds of discursive awareness
sever bliss, cognizance is not tainted by objects [II.3]

Matila, the river stream yogī, says:

The body of the deity makes
even ordinary thoughts true
The reality in vāyu speech
dispels ordinary thoughts of mentation[1161] [II.4]

Nāropa, he whom the guru's blessings entered, says: {286}

The ground of all glorious qualities
will not ever be found without this
Without devotion, a recipient for blessings[1162]
to enter is absent and will not mature [II.5]

Karmakari, he who possesses the patience of being unconcerned about harm being done, says:

The pair of the dharmakāya for your own welfare

and the form kāyas for the welfare of others
arises from relying on the guru's timely means
Without this, the supreme siddhi is lost [II.6]

Salipa, he whose power is adorned with compassion, says:

Without this love, compassion, and bodhicitta,
the path to supreme awakening
will never ever be encountered
Friends, don't give up cherishing them! [II.7]

Daraaliṅga, he who is warmed by the garment of bliss, says:

In the ground yielding the seeds of benefit and happiness
that is the soil[1163] of love, and the earth that is moistened[1164]
by the water of compassion, the sprouts of bodhicitta
will grow, but they will not do so anywhere else [II.8]

Catala, he in whose way of using terms nondiscursiveness arises, says:

By raising the eye that is sharp, vigorous, forceful,
clear, and pellucid, dullness and agitation are dispelled
The trace of thoughts having been cut through is that
dharmatā's[1165] own face is seized by subsequent cognition
[II.9]

Anusira, he in whom the ways of making a livelihood[1166] in this life became undone, says:

Switching alternate sustaining is the process in sections
By switching the two aspects of settling and dropping
the gaze, what is encountered within lacks identification
Through this, the native state's own face is seen [II.10]

Bhita, he who brings courageous confidence onto the path, {287} says:

The connate—the secret of the lion—
is not the sphere of speech, thought, or mind
The natural state of unborn and unceasing luminosity
is the mahāmudrā of nondiscursive self-awareness [II.11]

Rupata,[1167] he with poised readiness for the profound dharma, says:

Those intoxicated by the taste of drinking the fluid
of the native wisdom that dwells in themselves
are the ones who take up the behavior of a wrestler
The confident are free of the abyss[1168] of saṃsāra [II.12]

Takhontipa, the chief of humans, says:

The appearing phenomena that keep arising
from all kinds of conditions do not go beyond
being empty and are devoid of an essence of their own
This nonduality constitutes mahāmudrā [II.13]

Vigama, he with the behavior of a pig who has cast off clean and dirty,[1169] says:

There exist no external referents
that are other than mind as such[1170]
appearing as all kinds of entities
This is known by a river's sight [II.14]

Aluki, the great being, says:

Like a weapon brandished in a Caṇḍāla's hand,[1171]
through caṇḍālī,[1172] thoughts are vanquished
Being captured by the cry of bliss-lucidity,
stainless pellucidity increases in the mind [II.15]

Bhiturā, she who utters[1173] cries, says:

The sound of the bee, the melody of cries,
keeps resounding within the glorious knot
This vanquishes thoughts of perceiver and perceived
The light rays of thinking make the mind sad [II.16]

Phalavyadeva,[1174] he who brings the gaze onto the path, says:

Threefold saṃsāric existence—the realm that is arising
through immovable wisdom—is {288} the seat of bondage
The karaṇa[1175] of cutting through what is coarse and subtle
is originating from the glorious vajra eye [II.17]

Sukamala, he with armor-like[1176] vigor, says:

Resting in meditative equipoise on the right,
you are embraced by its compassion on the left
To direct your gaze straight ahead
constitutes the vajra-like samādhi [II.18]

Ratnaaliṅga, he who possesses the radiance of nonthought, says:

Not desiring the path through prajñā
embraced by means, you are not seized
by prajñā, and the same goes for means
Both coming together resembles garuḍa wings [II.19]

Kandhapa, he with the karmic fortune of prior training, says:

With the bow of means and the arrow of prajñā
being inseparable, and encouraged by devotion,
to gather the accumulations of merit and wisdom
represents the means to attain the two genuine ones[1177] [II.20]

Kampala,[1178] he who subdues movement within emptiness,[1179] says:

The kingdom[1180] of letting awareness be in its own seat is seized
Nonproliferating[1181] vāyus tame scatteredness[1182] and agitation
To calm down cognizance represents the eye of the peacock
To be embracing the awareness of the ultimate vital point
constitutes the means for attaining the two genuine ones [II.21]

Kumasitamo, she who takes pride as the path, says:

Through piercing straight ahead, the root is seized
The gaze of pouring remains immovable by conditions
Through the ever-seeing peacock, other-appearances cease
Holding cognizance's own seat is the path of nonthought [II.22]

Dhakisala, he who brings the accumulation of merit onto the path, says: {289}

The maturation of paying services and respect
at the feet of the stainless is like a shooting star
On the cloud-free path that dispels the darkness
of ignorance, the glorious knot is seen [II.23]

Bharidhara, he who possesses the vigor of application, says:

By merely bringing to mind
the supreme precious gem,
saṃsāra's continuous flow is quelled
and unsurpassable awakening attained [II.24]

Bhadodeva, he for whom, right within all kinds of circumstances, delusion is free, says:

Meeting thoughts head-on, not observing objects,
fresh cognizance is what eliminates delusion—

this is the support basis for the arising of the single-stroke
wisdom of awareness not pursuing any objects [II.25]

Surisaṅgāpā, she who realized mirror-like wisdom, says:

The fresh dynamic energy of cutting through discursive
appearances with a single stroke
eliminates any appearances of delusion upon encountering
them
This is the basis for grasping what is nonreferential and
baseless
The kingdom[1183] of letting awareness be in its own seat is
seized [II.26]

Tandhapa, he who turned his mind away from desire, says:

The nonreferentiality of the mindset of wanting to accomplish
being out of business represents the path pure of the three
spheres
To depend on any hopes for a result is the sphere of māra
Supreme actuality is accomplished by lacking fine distinctions
[II.27]

Kundhalī, the yoginī of illusory body, says:

The work of a machine and the deeds of
a wooden person are without any desire
Likewise, the freedom from a desirous mind
and the birth of nonclinging are the path of the noble [II.28]

Kukkuripa, he who brings space onto the path, says: {290}

Through nectar showering down from the sky,[1184]
all the many assertions of tenets are satisfied
Within uncontrived naturalness, piercing awareness
as if with a spear is to be free of clinging thoughts [II.29]

Vajravimala, he with utterly perfected vigor, says:

With cognizance not observing any ordinary objects,
the native state's essence lacks any clinging thoughts
The basic ground of the essence of being free in itself without clinging
constitutes the stage for the yoginī's spectacles [II.30]

The yogī Sukadhanu says:

The eyes of shellfish perceive without stain
Through stripping appearances bare,
self-aware[1185] experience is immutably lucid
When the essence is seen, self-appearances are free [II.31]

Dharmabhadra, he who recognizes luminosity's own face, says:

Luminous mind as such—the actual true state—
is the natural essence, the cause of buddhahood
When nonreferential originally pure
wisdom sees it, ignorance is dispelled [II.32]

Bhatali, the yogī for whom the many are of one taste, says:

The stainless essence free of discursiveness
abides naturally in all sentient beings,
obscured by adventitious deluded thoughts,
just like a crystal that is tainted by mud [II.33]

Matī, she with pellucid meditative equipoise, says:

The island of mindfulness within the center of the heart
is very clearly perceived with the eyes of a bat
With appearances of objects unobservable, subtle and coarse cease

The uncontrived natural way of being is the path of nondiscursiveness [II.34]

Aretalā, she who possesses the dhyāna of accomplishing qualities, {291} says:

Through the binding iron shackles of karaṇa,
threefold saṃsāric existence will not stir
By virtue of the king being held in prison,
he is not able to meet[1186] his subjects [II.35]

Abhita, he who identifies the appearances of objects as illusions, says:

Thoughts are cut through through the eyes of a turtle
At that time, phenomena have the natural state of space
Appearances of objects in the aftermath lack any nature
Through seeing the lack of reality, delusion is freed [II.36]

Candravimalā, the yoginī who sustains herself with the food of samādhi, says:

The upward gaze is the secret of Brahmā
The senses' self-appearances are mahāmudrā
The essence of dharmatā is embraced by means
The dawning of nondiscursiveness is the key point of letters [II.37]

Sahala, he who is not lazy about the welfare of others, says:

There is no being in threefold saṃsāric existence
who has not been your father or your mother
If compassion does not arise in you for those
who live in unreal[1187] saṃsāra, you are crazy! [II.38]

Rurusukā, she who devotes herself to practice, says:

The dawning of nondiscursiveness is the secret vital point
The center of the path of the noble ones is bodhicitta
Devotion to others' welfare is your own welfare complete
Here, the siddhis are close at hand [II.39]

Nilapa, he whose nāḍīs and vāyus are workable, says:

Through binding discursive thoughts in luminosity,
they are the radiance of the five self-aware wisdoms
It is the appearances of earth, water, fire, wind,
and space that are the signs of cause, path, and fruition [II.40]

{292} Jñānadhara, he with immovable dhyāna, says:

The light rays of pellucidity appear as smoke
What appears like a mirage is the light of bliss
Lucidity is the light of firefly insects
The light rays of nonthought shine like space [II.41]

This is the second chapter, called "Light of the Golden Sun," in *Vajra Songs, [Called] "The Light of True Reality."*

Indrabhūti, the powerful adept of the true mighty lords, says:

Desire embraces bliss
Hatred kindles lucidity
Ignorance showers down nonthought
Pride and envy are the causes of qualities [III.1]

Devaraśmi, the king of the gods, says:

The manure of the excrements of the cities
allows the grains to grow in the fields
Likewise, in the mindstreams of yogīs,
wisdom surges through the afflictions
Look at appearances free in themselves! [III.2]

Megoba, he who completed secret conduct, says:

Not keeping the hidden path of the supreme
siddhi secret, great obstacles will arise
The forms on it that are unrevealed
will further increase realization [III.3]

Anuśrī, he with the conduct of training the tongue throughout day and night, says:

Without the divine bindu being stable,[1188]
the mudrā's light rays do not radiate outside
If you drink the nectar through the behavior
of Caṇḍālas of bad family, it turns into elixir [III.4]

Koṭali,[1189] the hoe man with realization[1190] dawning in sickness, {293} says:

Thoughts are not to be abandoned!
By taking what is unfavorable as the path,
adverse conditions arise as aids
This method destroys the job of remedies [III.5]

Devasukha, he who puts EVAṂ to song, says:

Just as a fire that spreads in a forest
becomes greatly fanned by the wind,
at the time when yogīs attained stability,
bad circumstances turn into their aids [III.6]

Dharani, he who possesses the dhyāna of promoting the welfare of sentient beings, says:

The traces of mental appearances' erased pictures
that constitute the objects of mentation

are the ground of the dawning of pellucid wisdom
untainted by minding and free of fine distinctions [III.7]

Jālandhara, he in whom thoughts[1191] that time passes momentarily dawn as realization,[1192] says:

Since unconditioned nondiscursive nonthought
is without nature, it is devoid of arising and ceasing
True reality free of dualistic appearances
is the native state of connate naturalness [III.8]

Vikasurā, she who possesses the radiance of ecstasy, says:

In the center of the ground of the arising of uncontrived
prajñā
that is without the conditions of dualistic appearances,
characteristics are free in their very own place
In the gap between mindfulness and forgetting, mother and
child meet [III.9]

Rāhula, the yogī of activity, says:

Entities have the nature of illusions
Inner ablution ends the grasping at this life
By clinging to reality being free, delusion's path is blocked
This is what makes wisdom blaze [III.10]

Jakirī, she who takes envy as the path, {294} says:

Meaningless toils are for the sake of this life
Efforts that tire you out are the causes of suffering
By not relinquishing meaningless conduct,[1193]
delusion will not be put to an end [III.11]

Dharmapa, he who is free of bondage, says:

The essence of phenomena lacks any base or root[1194]
With the native state's own face untainted by the mud
of[1195] thoughts, it is the natural state of pellucidity
The basic nature is condition-free appearance-emptiness
[III.12]

Yogī Aliṅga, he with the prajñā of hearing, says:

Within the basic ground of diversity without nature,
the ground, the path, and the fruition are equal
Within the dharmatā that is without appearance,
appearances are displaying all by themselves [III.13]

Suvarṇadvīpapa, he who possesses the ornament of compassion, says:

Bodhicitta, which is like a wish-fulfilling jewel
that keeps bestowing any results you may desire,
is the kāya of uncontrived effortless buddhahood
It is naturally present within all beings [III.14]

Padmavimala, he who realized the wisdom of equality, says:

It is from the excellent vase of realization that
the pair of the dharmakāya and the form kāyas,
which do not entertain efforts or deliberate fixation,
arise naturally as the welfare of oneself and others [III.15]

Dhokaripa, he who lets mindfulness be in its seat, says:

Not pursuing conditions is the eye of Brahmā
Letting mindfulness be in its seat, clinging to it as such is
gone
Objects are not clung to by distracted cognizance
Being bound by karaṇa is the throne of bliss [III.16]

Karmasiddhi, the yoginī of luminosity, {295} says:

Lord of the three worlds, look up!
Look at the nondiscursive vajra crown,
the mahāmudrā that is without stains,
and the self-appearances of the faculties! [III.17]

Sagaja, he who is free through the four kinds of tantras, says:

To be free through studying is the vital point of words
To be content through seeing is the vital point of actuality
To not engage in what is dissimilar[1196] is the lion's secret
Being without Rudra's malice is freedom after maturation [III.18]

Salitasuka, he with the prajñā of reflection, says:

Sounds that appear but are without any nature
destroy delusion due to clinging in the heart
Knowing illusion's core, clinging to reality is gone
There is no brass[1197] in gold—it transforms into all that is desired [III.19]

Medini, he who possesses the eight great siddhis, says:

To drop meaningless activities, the burden of suffering,
is the path to liberation for those who desire happiness
Assiduous practice constitutes the cause of the siddhis
Through extending it, they will be revealed [III.20]

Anukirī, the yoginī of speech isolation, says:

Not discontinuing effort, the fruition is lost
Keep churning the water, don't pull out!
If tiredness is relinquished on the ground
of seeing gold's color, it will be revealed [III.21]

Ghaṅhaba,[1198] he in whom the wisdom of realization dawned through the experience of empowerment, says:

> The gaze that has the form of the uncontrived
> eye of the waxing moon is nondiscursiveness
> Holding the gentle vāyus is the native state
> This lets wisdom dawn in the mindstream [III.22]

{296} Sunidharī, the yoginī of the unity of great bliss, says:

> Smelting and refining subdue scatteredness[1199] and agitation
> Through that, clear pellucidity without any stains is sustained
> The eye of the waxing moon that does not behold coarse or subtle
> does not see appearances of objects and lacks clinging thoughts [III.23]

Anjuba,[1200] he who sees reality, says:

> If the native reality that is introduced by the guru
> is realized through the power of blessings entering
> the mindstream, this is the ground of all qualities
> By this,[1201] paths and bhūmis are shortened through the cakra [III.24]

Śrī Apaka, he with the prajñā of meditation, says:

> It is through the fiery heat of its mother that
> the garuḍa expands its egg tremendously
> As soon as its breath is freed from its trap,
> this chick will soar high through the sky [III.25]

Kambala, he in whom realization[1202] dawned through the symbols of the ḍākinīs, says:

> Just as Indra's bow[1203] that is [similar to] a web

appears in the sky, the pure essence of the elements
has the character of appearing yet being without nature
This demonstrates phenomena's very own characteristic
[III.26]

Bhinukarī, the yoginī who gained mastery over mind, says:

Phenomena—entities appearing as diversity—
are utterly devoid of any essence of their own[1204]
Just as with the moon appearing[1205] in water,
delusion collapses by virtue of realization [III.27]

Kundhari, he who brings the gaze onto the path, says:

Through the sharp and greatly powerful eye of Viṣṇu
looking at conditions, dualistic appearances are crushed
As the expanse of space without seeing appearances of objects
is free of any clinging to it as such [objects], it is nondiscursiveness [III.28]

{297} Lakṣmīṃkarā, she for whom appearances are purified as illusions, says:

In having the form of kumārī,[1206]
regard two people as evenly united!
Any kinds of above and below
will not be seen at that time [III.29]

Kṣana, he who made up his mind through hearing, says:

Seeing the definitive meaning, doubts are cut through
In the mindset of devotion that is unmistaken,
the dhātus are gathering all by themselves
In a single one, all qualities are infinite [III.30]

Sukabhiru, she who is skilled in keeping her own flaws under control, says:

> The end of hearing, meditating, and reflecting
> is the effort through awareness free of pride
> The cause of that[1207] is trusting confidence,
> springing from supreme devotion as its root [III.31]

Kulipa, he who identified the wisdom dwelling in himself, says:

> By[1208] letting be in its seat—cutting through the three times
> with a single stroke—
> appearances are not pursued, the three times are free,
> and the native state's own nondiscursive home is seized
> To be uncontrived constitutes the dharmakāya [III.32]

Jñānabinu,[1209] the lunatic-like yoginī without deliberate fixation, says:

> Just like catching a peacock in a trap,
> by letting awareness be in its seat,
> bliss and lucidity are put into chains,
> unmoved by the winds of thoughts [III.33]

Jayantipa, he in whom the wisdom of realization dawned through the experience of empowerment, says:

> By sustaining undistracted awareness with the glue
> of mindfulness during the four ways of conduct,
> the exhaustion of reality is the ultimate secret
> By seeing it, delusion collapses within objects [III.34]

{298} Audarā, she who blows a kāki conch, says:

> Don't be attached to being mindful of supreme actuality!
> The distracted mind is empty of true reality

Those who forget the true core of[1210] the lack
of a nature are tainted by delusion's stains [III.35]

Cabari, he in whom realization[1211] dawned through looking at scriptures, says:

With the four syllables, comment on the instruction lineage!
Through the three kinds of conduct of the Sage,
seize the lineage of the scriptures of the Sugata!
The secret treasury of the vital point's awareness overflows
[III.36]

Kulacandrā, she who is skilled in making the mind work, says:

Within the scope of objects with no-self's actuality seen,
the ground in which all phenomena are exhausted
is found by the brahman son, who holds the Vedas,
in the father's statements with their secret words [III.37]

Campaka, he who has cut through coarse and subtle, says:

That the triad of nāḍīs, vāyus, and what is aware
is bound above by the nondiscursive cognizance
carried by the vāyus[1212] is the secret vital point[1213]
After being undone, bliss, lucidity, and nonthought dawn
[III.38]

Śrīsiddhi, she who possesses the radiance of compassion, says:

In the experiences of bliss, emptiness, and lucidity,
free of the stirring and moving of thoughts,
by bringing awareness holding its own ground onto the path,
what's left after letting go of the gaze is the nondiscursive
state [III.39]

Riri, he who beholds beings, says:

The mind for which nonduality appears
as duality is the appearance of delusion
This is what links with saṃsāric existence
Look at appearances free in themselves! [III.40] {299}

Dharisukhā, the yoginī of unity, says:

When the mind with its stains of impurity
arises as a cognition of taking the shining
radiance of mother of pearl to be silver,
make this mother of pearl empty of silver! [III.41]

This is the third chapter, called "Utterly Clear Radiance of Wisdom," in *Vajra Songs, [Called] "The Light of True Reality."*

Tummala, he who lacks any mental engagement in fine distinctions, says:

In the natural state of freshness unimpaired by objects,
the faculties are translucent up through the ūrṇā hair[1214]
Through this letter-eye of appearances being free
in themselves, mental engagement becomes undone [IV.1]

Metita, he who is skilled in the means for swift and fully perfect awakening, says:

Cognizance without clinging to the unimpeded
lucidity dimension of objects as being such
is free from any propelling[1215] of thoughts,
dwelling at the place between the eyebrows [IV.2]

Mekhali, he for whom appearances dawn as scriptures, says:

The instructions on this process of dependent origination
that propels things onto the path are taught by objects
Through the six collections dawning as scriptures,
appearances incite the conditions for realization [IV.3]

Vimalasitī, she who realized dharmadhātu wisdom, says:

What serves as the aids for the path
is far from being absolutely certain
What serves as the support for
realization[1216] is the karmamudrā [IV.4]

{300} Kalipa, he who experiences nonreferentiality, says:

Don't repeat the equipoise, look at undoing's traces!
Cognizance that is devoid of focus is free of clinging
At that point, refrain from pursuing time!
Thinking is free within dharmatā's natural state [IV.5]

Bhatala, she who takes ignorance as the path, says:

Dullness and agitation are undone in the gap where clarity
and pellucidity are divided by the sentinel not having arrived
To then straighten this out represents meditation's vital point
Through this, eliminate coarse and subtle stains! [IV.6]

Kanapa, he who arrived at understanding through symbols, says:

The root—your own face—is realized through symbols
Certainty arises from the speech of the guru
By seeing true actuality, doubts are cut through
The power of the ḍākinīs eliminates obstacles [IV.7]

Moharisukā, she who dwells in aspiration prayers whose words are made into a continuum, says:

Within actual reality, there exist no letters at all
It's beyond objects of speech, thought, or expression
By virtue of the great symbolic means of the guru,
the gate of the arising of realization[1217] will be opened [IV.8]

Kantipa, he who is skilled in making realization into a ship,[1218] says:

Don't contrive any focus! Undo the support of the mind!
Characteristics being free in themselves lacks meditation
Clinging thoughts are nondiscursive and thinking vanishes
By virtue of practice being free, freedom is attained [IV.9]

Śrīmanurā, the yoginī of mind isolation, says:

Don't engage in the thoughts[1219] of the mind! The plethora
of ordinary states of mind constitutes the native state's
own condition as it is, without contrivance or impairment
This is inconceivable and free of any meditation [IV.10]

{301} Daubari, he in whom self-awareness is free of the support of mind, says:

In the ground of phenomena empty of any base,
cognizance is objectless and mind's support is undone
This expanse is devoid of any roots of thoughts,[1220]
without mental engagement, and beyond efforts[1221] [IV.11]

Kaṅkadharī, the yoginī of nondual wisdom, says:

Any beginning, end, and middle are not observable
The garuḍa of awareness does not search for any support
In those who obtain the traces of rootless space,
inconceivable experience is free of any focus [IV.12]

Utipa, he who sees that thoughts are baseless, says:

Baseless phenomena free of arising and ceasing
are devoid of thoughts, untainted by the mind,
and stainless—characteristics vanish[1222] in their own place
Just look at this naked awareness! [IV.13]

Śrīvisupā,[1223] she who holds the treasure of the wisdom that connects with mind's actuality, says:

Within the natural state of having tightened awareness
and then relaxing, coarse and subtle thoughts disappear
The expanse without fine distinctions and minding
is the ground of the dawning of stainless wisdom[1224] [IV.14]

Kambala, he who puts the native state to the test, says:

The state when cognizance with the unimpeded lucidity dimension
of objects is free of any clinging[1225] to itself as being such [objects]
is the ground of thoughts disappearing—wisdom dawns
on the avenue of being undistracted at the tip of the nose [IV.15]

Narutī, she who dwells in aspiration prayers, says:

In what is unborn, there isn't any dying
Phenomena are devoid of their own essence
There is no forgetting in not being mindful—
to be free of mind's[1226] extremes is mental nonengagement [IV.16]

{302} Dhakara, he who struck the vital point of introduction, says:

Mental nonengagement constitutes the native path
Fine distinctions are unobservable, thoughts severed
The stains of the support of mind are pure in the heart
Thoughts are free in the natural state of dharmatā [IV.17]

Śrīdhanā, she who is free of the eight dharmas, says:

With all kinds of object appearances washed clean inside

as being baseless, delusion turns away from objects
It is on the avenue of thrusting the spear of nondistraction's
spaciousness that the path of thoughts arising is blocked
[IV.18]

Sapakarapa, he who is pure of the stains of thoughts, says:

Within the aftermath of thoughts being free,
identifying mind's fine distinctions is gone
In this nonreferential state, mind's[1227] extremes are free
The native state awakens without any identifying [IV.19]

Sukasitā,[1228] she who is free of the shackles of delusion, says:

The nonminding of the six collections
not engaging objects is the path to nirvāṇa
Since the nonconceptual dharmadhātu
is free of mind, it is mahāmudrā [IV.20]

Sarvabhagala, he in whom attachment and aversion are free, says:

The true reality of the seeds of the path
of perceiver and perceived is the unborn state
Phenomena lack a root and are empty of a base
As dualistic appearances are free, there's no saṃsāra
or nirvāṇa [IV.21]

Vajrahalu, she who dwells in aspiration prayers that completely purify buddha realms, says:

Within the natural state of having tightened awareness
and then relaxing, settle the mind and let it rest at ease
Thoughts are free in the natural state of dharmatā
Through this, the five wisdoms are perfected [IV.22]

{303} Kambala, he who heard instructions from the gods, says:

Even though the nature of thinking has been free
as the dharmakāya that constitutes its essence,
this is not something that people will see
How to get to the self-secret's[1229] bottom through means
is known by relying on the guru's timely methods [IV.23]

Putrala, he who enjoys the taste of being free of thoughts, says:

The cause that creates worldly happiness and suffering
consists of karma, which is accumulated in the mind
The essence of that is the karma of the mind
Awareness—mind as such—is originally pure [IV.24]

Sukato, he who burned the seeds of karma, says:

In the gaps between remaining in distraction,
awareness seizes its seat, mindfulness swirls[1230]
The essence is free of clinging thoughts
Mind's appearances lack any base or root [IV.25]

Ahara, he with the roaring laughter "hahaha," says:

On the other side of giving up saṃsāra,
there exists no nirvāṇa at all—
it is the core of saṃsāra's lack
of nature that is nirvāṇa [IV.26]

Nāgabodhi, he who embraces beings with compassion, says:

The essence appears as anything whatsoever
and yet its nature isn't anything at all
Look at the unborn essence itself,
free of characteristics, base, or root! [IV.27]

Śrīsitī,[1231] she who has the power of action and engagement, says:

In the gap between mindfulness and forgetting,
the wisdom that is free of mind is present
In the center free of conditions, it is fulfilled[1232]
If it is seen, freedom will be right here [IV.28]

{304} Wangna,[1233] she who does not rely[1234] on clinging to reality, says:

All kinds of white and red appearances of objects,
at the very time of appearing through conditions,
are[1235] without any arising and devoid of it
Any reality is used up, being empty of an eye [IV.29]

Dharisukha, he who possesses the eye of wisdom, says:

By virtue of the essential point of a single entity
appearing as different ones, phenomenal entities
that constitute referents beyond and outside
of the mind have no existence at all [IV.30]

Ratana, he who is free of the extremes of mind, says:

The unborn true state that lacks any base or root—
the groundless true reality that is beyond mind—
is present within the expanse of nonminding
Don't impair this pellucid clarity with conditions! [IV.31]

Cadilā,[1236] she who possesses the power of not accumulating afflictions, says:

No matter in which ways the six collections may arise,
by severing the clinging to their reality, they leave no imprints
Don't accumulate the karma of freeing the causes of delusion,
and saṃsāra will be free in its very own place! [IV.32]

Akara, the heroic vajra, says:

From the causes of arising as saṃsāra,
it is brought about by the afflictions
Afflictions are mind, lacking a base or root
Seeing this, the wheel of existence is undone [IV.33]

Śrīparanā, she who possesses the light of miraculous powers, says:

Diversity arises from the state of being unborn
This very arising does not ever go beyond
being unborn, being similar to water and ice
If their inseparability is realized, this is mahāmudrā [IV.34]

Lalanta,[1237] he who sees appearances' own true core, says: {305}

Forms are empty of forms—
in phenomena without a nature,
saṃsāra as well as nirvāṇa
are not even seen in dreams [IV.35]

Tapasarī, she who possesses nonconceptual wisdom, says:

These appellations by way of the differences
between mothers, sisters, and daughters
that do not stem from the excellent essence
of beings are indeed objects of amazement! [IV.36]

Samudra, he who is free of effort, says:

In the traces of untying bringing about agreement,
appearances lack a root and are free of characteristics
Without clinging, undo the support of your own mind!
Look at this cognizance that is uncreated! [IV.37]

Vimalasitā, she who possesses the power of not being affected by māras and what others say, says:

Diverse universes originate from karma
Diversity is empty of any essence of its own,
just like stars and planets [reflected] in the ocean
The clinging to reality is the deluded mind [IV.38]

Vyatriva, he who realizes that phenomena are without nature, says:

Experiencing it, it is free of identification
Identify this mind as such that is rootless!
Diverse appearances are without any nature
Identify these phenomena without a base! [IV.39]

Ratnasiddhi, she who possesses the wisdom that pierces thinking, says:

Forms resemble the city of gandharvas
Sounds have the appearance of echoes
Mind is like being enveloped in a dream
Any nature whatsoever is not seen [IV.40]

{306} Jñānakara, he with the wisdom that does not transcend[1238] the means, says:

What is apprehended by focusing is mental karma
With it being undone, pellucidity will become clear,
just as in the example of a magical mirror
Don't rely on the stains of mental clinging! [IV.41]

Devasarī, the yoginī who is naturally familiar with prajñāpāramitā, says:

At the time when connate wisdom
arises in someone's mindstream,
this experience cannot be expressed
Pointing out through symbols is the means' vital point [IV.42]

Siranupā,[1239] she who holds the treasure of wisdom, says:

Within the natural state of having tightened awareness
and then relaxing, coarse and subtle thoughts disappear
The expanse without fine distinctions and minding
is the ground of the blazing of stainless wisdom[1240] [IV.43]

Rasinā, she who holds the treasure of glory, says:

Such a cognizance of the native state arising
within the mindstream cannot be expressed
The basic ground of phenomena that is devoid
of an essence is not an object of the mind [IV.44]

This is the fourth chapter, called "Seeing the Native State's Own Essence," in *Vajra Songs, [Called] "The Light of True Reality."*

Dārikapa, he who has let go of worldly activities and, as someone of the royal caste, assumed a lowly position, says:

The mind resting in this in such a way
is what makes up meditative equipoise
Intelligent brave ones, look at the key point
of the conditioned and the unconditioned! [V.1]

{307} Litapuki, he who possesses the glory of compassion, says:

AHO! When resting in what has no characteristics
after having undone any notions of characteristics,
this will lead to understanding that phenomena,
without any exception at all, are empty [V.2]

Unalana, he who has let go of worldly activities in their own place, says:

Your own originally unborn mind
possesses the nature of luminosity
AHO! It is the ultimate bodhicitta,
unconditioned just like space [V.3]

Śrīlalitā, she who is the source of bliss, says:

Just as illusory horses and elephants
are empty of essence when appearing,
AHO, these very objects of clinging
imagined by thinking are empty of a base [V.4]

Kambala, he whom the blessings of Tārā have entered, says:

Without first understanding that knowable objects
are thinking, saṃsāra will not become empty
In this baseless essence that lacks any root,
any nature of its own does not exist [V.5]

Sukaratnā, she with the power of devotion, says:

Just as with the pith of a banana tree,
phenomena do not have any pith at all
Realizing the lack of a self is supreme actuality
Seeing it tears saṃsāric existence into rags [V.6]

Kanayenapa, he who opened the eye of prajñā toward symbols, says:

AHO! Naturally uncontrived cognizance
that is self-sufficient does not change[1241]
The fresh cognizance that is uncreated
rests loosely, undivorced from the remedy [V.7]

Jñānasiddhi, she who absorbs the ocean's radiance, says: {308}

The cognizance that is naked, free of any owner,
and without support is unblemished by the mind
Cognizance just as it is, free of arising and ceasing,
is not tainted by thoughts and is without stains [V.8]

Ānanda, he in whom realization dawned through mudrā,[1242] says:

Since phenomena naturally lack any being,
but childish beings don't know this actuality,
the character of being naturally unborn
will be seen through the guru's words [V.9]

Jambhala, the light rays of glory, says:

If the notion that the unborn is an entity
with characteristics has become free,
there will be no engagement at all
in any internal or external āyatanas [V.10]

Utikupati, he in whom realization dawned through empowerment,[1243] says:

Forms, feelings, discriminations,
formations, and consciousnesses
are devoid of any essence of their own
Look at what is baseless and lacks a root!
Any clinging to reality or "I" is undone in the ground [V.11]

Śrīdukarī, she who is the source of prajñā, says:

The thoughts of discursive awareness that arise
from adventitious conditions are empty of any reality
Apart from[1244] this luminosity without coming and going,
how could there possibly be any saṃsāra or nirvāṇa in it?
[V.12]

Sagalapa, he who was blessed by Nairātmyā, says:

Just look into this mirror of the wisdom
of the glorious awakened mind's maṇḍala!
It will become clear that the phenomena
of the past, present, and future are empty [V.13]

Siṅgasiṅga, she who possesses the power of reality,[1245] says:

AHO! {309} The mind of complete weariness
is the supreme path of the unsurpassable unborn
It is for the reason that it has never been found
that you should develop revulsion for saṃsāra [V.14]

Narika,[1246] he who was uplifted by circumambulating Khasarpaṇa, says:

Since certainty is found through the guru's symbols,
phenomena are understood through that to be empty
Childish beings think about nonexistent phenomena
Through that, they will not be free from karma [V.15]

Dharmalaṅke, she who dispels the poisons of beings, says:

Through being aware of the true core of entities,
the lack of entities will be fully understood
Phenomena do not go beyond having the nature
of illusions—clinging to any reality is delusion[1247] [V.16]

Cantipa, he who happened upon luminosity within, says:

The inconceivability of luminosity without any
coming and going that is free of meditation
will dawn by virtue of putting the native state
to the test—it's not the sphere of anything else [V.17]

Bharaaralī, she who possesses the gem eye, says:

Binding the mind to the nose's tip is the secret of the vital
point
It is the ground of the arising of undistracted nonthought
Through karaṇa, the vāyus of bliss are seized
and the bindu of great bliss is allowed to rest [V.18]

Śrīkṣuti, he who is victorious over uncontaminated bliss, says:

It shows respect to make offerings to the victors with gold
for as many eons as there are sand grains in the Ganges,
but having given a massage to just a single pore
of the guru's skin is much more outstanding [V.19]

Sukadhana, he with the light rays of compassion, says:

Merit differs like a sesame seed and Mount Meru do {310}
Who wishes for the supreme city of liberation?
Venerate the guru on the crown of your head!
Forgetting this, the supreme siddhi disappears [V.20]

Alipa, he who cracks the eggshell[1248] of ignorance, says:

Appearances are empty of any essence of form
Make up your mind that phenomena are illusions!
Don't rely on clinging to reality in your mindstream!
Abandon the views and assertions of any tenets! [V.21]

Ridharu, she who possesses the power of vigor, says:

Rid yourself of this mind that entertains clinging
to anything possible! It is what māra is about
Once the cognition of dualistic appearances is free,
delusion is pellucid within dharmatā's natural state [V.22]

Sutalalipa, he who cuts through the shackles of delusion by seeing true actuality through symbols, says:

Through the dharma of the afflictions not serving as
the remedies, the path to buddhahood is not found
AHO! A view and a meditation that are not connected
to the mindstream are just names—what are they good for?[1249]
[V.23]

Surikari, he who is endowed with the ornament of merit, says:

Once the bindu of the uncontrived native state
has become stable in the heart, delusion is undone
and cognizance is not impaired by conditions
If you find yourself in pursuit of objects,
you are relying on scattered[1250] awareness [V.24]

Kumbaripa, he in whom realization dawned through seeing[1251] skeletons in charnel grounds, says:

No matter where you may be searching[1252]
for the name of the lord of gods, Śakra,
you will not find it in any direction—
the same goes for the self in the body [V.25]

She who possesses the light rays of profound glory {311} says:

By searching for what is not seen to exist
even in your dreams, you will not find it
It's fine to check whether it is the path to awakening
Meditate on the lack of a self, oh yogīs! [V.26]

Khaṅhagagati,[1253] he who gained mastery over his mind, says:

Just look at this dharmadhātu wisdom—
luminosity without being, empty of essence!
Its presence as the nature of the awareness
of emptiness is the dynamic play of its power:
this constitutes mirror-like wisdom [V.27]

Jñānavajrā, she who shows the path to liberation, says:

Take a hold of this mirror-like wisdom!
What does not go beyond the nonduality
of awareness and emptiness is wisdom

The dynamic play within discriminative
lucidity is all-accomplishing [wisdom] [V.28]

Ilapa, he with the isolation[1254] of nāḍīs and vāyus being workable, says:

Phenomena are naturally empty of any essence
Those who understand them to be like dreams
are free from the entirety of all bondage
and do not behold any birth or death [V.29]

Vasudharā,[1255] she who possesses the glory of realization,[1256] says:

The eye of not even seeing what is empty
beholds the means of letting entities rest
When the appearances of delusion have become pure,
the pure realms of the three kāyas will dawn [V.30]

Kedualapa, he who is free of the impregnations of negative tendencies, says:

Just as a captain does not accomplish his goal
on an island when not returning from the ocean,
without reversing the mindset of saṃsāra,
the path to liberation will not be found [V.31]

{312} Sukhakule, she who is the source of goodness, says:

Keeping their eyes on this life, childish beings
accomplish the means for worldly greatness—
the causes of maturations gathering in the next—
simply selling[1257] their own heads themselves [V.32]

Ganapa, he with distinguished realization,[1258] says:

The wisdom of the very essence
of the nonbeing of phenomena

has the nature of being originally
and naturally completely pure [V.33]

Bhagadharā,[1259] the heroine with excellent insight, says:

Without arising, without ceasing, without letters,
without any signs, without characteristics,
without seeing, and without observing,
thus fully perfect awakening is seen [V.34]

Cadurkipa, he with the karmic fortune that consists of the support of previous accumulation and purification, says:

This cognizance of unborn appearance
and emptiness that is free of conditions
is naturalness, not created by the mind—
the uncontrived nondiscursive native state [V.35]

Sudharā, she who is a lotus full of light, says:

This cannot be touched by tenet views,
such as permanence and extinction
Beyond mind, not an object of speech or thought,
empty[1260] of letters, and free of names this is [V.36]

Navā, she in whose mindstream the wisdom of the path of seeing has dawned, says:

That dharmas arise from nonbeing
is an amazing wondrous dharma
Look, fortunate son of noble family!
If you see, you have the supreme fortune [V.37]

Śrīsavarī, she who is a wish-fulfilling cow[1261] of bliss, says: {313}

This that has become absolutely stable for sure

is what constitutes the most supreme of paths
It completely perfects the unsurpassable wisdom
of buddhahood, the consummate relinquishment [V.38]

Ganakunupa,[1262] he who is able to transform appearances of lacking devotion, says:

From the perspective of deluded people,
saṃsāra seems to be independently existent
In what appears for the noble ones,
it is seen as a mere illusion [V.39]

Sukhadharī, the excellent lady who possesses the light of virtue, says:

The appearing duality of real and delusive
is free in what is appearing for yogīs
Therefore, saṃsāra will not be seen—
it's the expanse of original peace and purity [V.40]

Aṅjiṅpa,[1263] he who is pure of the stains of sleep, says:

The moon never ever transits
from the sky into the water
A water-moon is empty of its own essence
Knowing phenomena to be so, delusion is gone [V.41]

Asudhalā, the queen of awareness, says:

The mental clinging to existence
and nonexistence constitutes stains
Yogīs should abandon the two extremes
but not dwell in any middle either [V.42]

This is the fifth chapter, called "Pure Mirror of the Heart," in *Vajra Songs, [Called] "The Light of True Reality."*

Bodhinipa,[1264] he who attained the wisdom of heat, says:

Since people do not put an end[1265] to delusion,
they look at the duality of perceiver and perceived
By seizing the true characteristic through the dhātu
of mental events, wrong ideas are stopped [VI.1]

{314} Dhiridhalā, she who possesses the power of prajñā, says:

Due to being seized by thoughts, the āyatanas'
gateways open and the five kinds of faculties dawn
Due to the engagement in objects through that,
the five poisons arise and thus karma is accumulated
Thereby, the wheel of saṃsāric existence is all set [VI.2]

Siṃhapa, he who is free of the five fears, says:

In the same way as the illuminating sun
dispels[1266] the carpet of darkness,
phenomena will be pure in the natural state
of the connate free of discursiveness [VI.3]

Sukatā, she who possesses the glory of blessings, says:

At the time when they vanished from the sky,
clouds do not go into hiding anywhere else
Likewise, in the expanse of characteristics
free in their own place, there is no saṃsāra [VI.4]

Kilalaki, he who unraveled the knots of dualistic clinging, says:

Clinging to a self is the cause of saṃsāra
Clinging to a self is the afflictions' field
Clinging to a self is the seed of karma
Clinging to a self is the path of delusion [VI.5]

Jñānalitarā, the glorious lady of excellent prajñā, says:

Clinging to a self is the ground of thoughts
Clinging to a self is thinking's grandmother[1267]
Clinging to a self is the latent tendencies' vessel
Hence, without giving it up, nirvāṇa is not attained [VI.6]

Candhalipa, he who sees saṃsāric happiness as an object of compassion, says:

Thus, the nature of all
phenomena is equality
Know them to be illusion-like! {315}
Entities are dreams, mirages, and echoes [VI.7]

Dharamahā, she who possesses the strength of a wrestler, says:

Phenomena do not go beyond being optical illusions,
magical creations, water-moons, and reflections
If they have been understood to be just like space,
with the three times unobservable, nondiscursiveness dawns [VI.8]

Jalasipa, he whom the blessings of the ḍākinīs have entered, says:

Awareness without clinging is free of experiences
If you examine the mahāmudrā that is free of mind,
this is delusion; if you reflect on it, it is impaired;
if you meditate on it, it is cut off; if you search it, it is gone [VI.9]

Vimalasiddhi, she who holds the glory of auspiciousness, says:

If analyzed, they are empty and cease to be tangible
Appearing yet empty, they are free of conditions[1268]
Being inexpressible, they are expressed in words[1269]

Phenomena have no names and are free of letters,
clearly being way beyond the path of words [VI.10]

Sukhadharī, she who possesses the light of a gem, says:

With signs at peace on their own, free of arising and ceasing,
it has the characteristic of lacking any characteristic—
look at that which is bereft of the thinking mind!
This is such an amazing great spectacle! [VI.11]

Karmavajra, he who completed realization, says:

Any dhyāna created by the mind is a reflection
Thought's innermost seed is delusion's fortress[1270]
If you meditate, it's there; not meditating, it's not
Thus, it is contingent on circumstances [VI.12]

Bhasukamā,[1271] she who possesses the radiance of a lotus, says:

No matter to which side of the actual connate
you may cling, you are unable to be close to it {316}
Since the samādhi that is naturally native
is settled in its own flow, it is uninterrupted [VI.13]

Padmavajra, he in whom the stains of dualistic appearances are pure, says:

The cause for wandering through this saṃsāra
without any beginning over and over again
is that childish beings take thoughts to be referents
Thereby, they accumulate the stains[1272] of existence [VI.14]

Jñānasagā, she who possesses the ornament of bliss, says:

Phenomena naturally lack reference points
None of them have any existence at all,

just like a mirage devoid of water
Knowing phenomena to be so, freedom is here [VI.15]

Ānandavajra, he who expels the poisons of the afflictions through the seven-syllable one, says:

By binding the vāyu mind in luminosity,
the native state is put to the test,
awareness is not in pursuit of objects,
and clinging to an exterior is stopped [VI.16]

Sunivikā, the excellent lady who possesses the power of devotion, says:

The soaring bird of awareness is the vital point of sections
By alternately sustaining, placing, and dropping the gaze,
the pool of nonconceptuality becomes raised,
and thus ordinary clinging is put to an end [VI.17]

Vasudhara, he who recognizes actuality's own face through the symbols of the guru, says:

AHO! The dharma that is hard to see
has a subtle and peaceful character
You are not able to apply any letters
to phenomena that are unobservable [VI.18]

Sukadharakī,[1273] she who possesses the glory of miraculous powers, says:

In the state of being devoid of any mental engagement, {317}
without thoughts of clinging to such, and free of
discrimination,
no matter where a so-called "self" may be searched for,
it is not found, because it is empty of any essence [VI.19]

Prajñāphala, he whose thoughts coincide with the circumstances, says:

If the clinging to entities is free, it is great bliss
This medicine that is the supreme means
vanquishes the diseases of saṃsāra
There is no state of mind superior to this [VI.20]

Śrī Alitā, she who is the source of wisdom, says:

For as long as cherishing it is not undone,
there is no freedom from bondage's cause,
but with the clinging to a self being free,
the wheel of saṃsāric existence will cease [VI.21]

Cāryapa, he who sees that the fruition is connate, says:

It is the nature of all arising phenomena
without exception to lack coming and going
Nondiscursive nonthought—the true end—
is unconditioned and free of any effort [VI.22]

Siṅgadhalī, she who possesses the ornament of discipline, says:

It should not be ascertained through words,
but seen for sure through the guru's symbols
Experience is free of any identification
This constitutes the sphere of yoginīs [VI.23]

Avadhūtipa, he who found the basic actuality through the four empowerments, says:

By taking what is unfavorable as the path,
adverse conditions are turning into aids
This is taking all kinds of things as the path
Dispel obstacles, and appearances are free in their own place!
[VI.24]

Ghamalitā,[1274] lady of moonlight rays, says:

Piercing the sky as if with a spear {318} is dhyāna's fortress
Letting awareness be in its seat is the vital point's core
This permits lucid bliss to be an uninterrupted flow
Don't allow yourself to be distracted toward objects! [VI.25]

Kṛṣṇapa, he who is trained in the process of dependent origination, says:

AHO! Look at this nature of form
that is profound by its very essence!
With the characteristic of emptiness becoming clear,
form's true core is seen and true reality is known [VI.26]

Rapakiri, he who possesses the divine ornament, says:

Awareness of this is to realize nirvāṇa
For those with the focus of clinging
to nonbeing as being any being,
there will never be any liberation [VI.27]

Kośapa, he who identified nondiscursive wisdom, says:

The entirety of phenomena is empty of any essence
With reality used up, delusiveness used up, letters used up,
and referents used up, they have the nature of space,
cannot be conceived, and are free of meditation [VI.28]

Ratnalitī, she who holds the light of glory, says:

Being without any thoughts, not in pursuit of any objects,
and free of clinging to such due to immediate appearance
are the six relaxed collections as they are let be in their seat
In this natural state, the meditating mind's striving is a stain
[VI.29]

Āryasiṅga, he whose mindstream was matured through devotion, says:

Since all aspects of phenomena without exception
have [always] been empty of the two aspects
of expressing words and referents to be expressed,
they have the character of lacking any base or root [VI.30]

Natarā, she who possesses the power of goodness,[1275] says:

The appearances of the objects of the six collections {319}
are showing up by virtue of all kinds of circumstances
Conditioned appearances do not go beyond being illusions
Being without any nature, they are objects of amazement
[VI.31]

Ratnavajra, he who sees entities to be unreal, says:

As long as you are not free of a mind of desiring
a fruition, there is no passing into nirvāṇa
It is exactly this mind of trying to identify
the ultimate that constitutes thinking [VI.32]

Śrardhāna,[1276] the light rays of glory, says:

The stain of clinging to something as supreme
should be understood as the māra of the path
It is in the center of a heart free of any hope
that the unsurpassable precious gem abides [VI.33]

Jarana, he who cuts through treacherous passages by way of[1277] their remedies, says:

When the courageous endowed with insight
understand the nature of phenomena
to be peace, it will not take long for them
to undo the wheel of saṃsāric existence [VI.34]

Śrīkasutā, she who has the radiance of bliss, says:

That the piṭakas of the words of the sages
of the past, the present, and the future
are different formulations with the same meaning
is to be gathered through the symbols of the guru [VI.35]

Ratrita, he who strikes at theoretical understanding in the aftermath, says:

Pellucidity's natural state without mental engagement—
the native basic ground in which nothing at all arises—
constitutes the dharmakāya of uncontrived true actuality,
empty of phenomena comprised by the twofold no-self [VI.36]

Surisukā, she who is the source of blessings, says:

Seeing the true core, no deliberate fixation dawns in the mind
At the time of seeing that phenomena's reality
has exhausted itself, reality has become free {320}
This is what tears saṃsāric existence to rags [VI.37]

Candragomī, he who has undone hope and fear, says:

Form is empty of form:
like a banana tree, it has no pith
The dhātus devoid of any own essence
are similar to bubbles in water [VI.38]

Bhatarā,[1278] she who possesses the power of bliss, says:

Similar to mirages, the āyatanas
are natureless and empty of essence
Look at the very core of appearances
being free in their own place, oh yogīs! [VI.39]

Aśokara, he who is free of the mindset of bringing about a fruition, says:

Through searching for thoughts,
nonthought will never be found
Any time of searching does not go beyond
thoughts, being minding's fine distinctions [VI.40]

Sukato, she who possesses the light of glory, says:

AHO! When the nature of thoughts
is naturally empty of any essence,
without relinquishing these thoughts,
they will be naturally free [VI.41]

Śrīcandrapa says:

The essence of the mindset of wishing for
nonthought has the character of thinking[1279]
It is the nonduality of thought and nonthought[1280]
that constitutes fundamental actuality [VI.42]

This is the sixth chapter, called "The Dawning of the Light Rays of Glory," in *Vajra Songs of the Siddhas, [Called] "The Light of the True Reality of All Yogīs."*

Bhuta, he in whom experience is surrounded by the six collections, says: {321}

In mahāmudrā, there is nothing to meditate
Not relying on the striving of the mind,
entrust meditation to its owner! [VII.1]

Siṅgali, he with the light rays of bliss, says:

Look at the cognizance of not mediating!
This cognizance that is not created and
lacks arising, ceasing, increase, or decrease
is the sphere of an amazing spectacle [VII.2]

Jaitāri, he who sees the vital point of dependent origination in pellucid awareness, says:

Just as a king is ruined,[1281] if he performs
the conduct of someone of a bad caste,
practitioners relinquish any meaningless
conduct, including its foundation [VII.3]

Madharohā, she who is the source of realization, says:

Just as extracting the essence of nectar is the supreme
medicine but turns into a disease if it is vomited up,
by speaking nonsense about meditative experiences,
they will disappear without even a single trace [VII.4]

Bhitakama, he who dispels dullness and torpor through powerful sharpness, says:

The eye of seeing appearances
to be free as their empty essence
is the stainless essence's dynamic play
This is the confidence[1282] of realization [VII.5]

Bugadhalā, she who possesses the power of mightiness, says:

The intelligent who understand
that the nature of being empty
arises incessantly are fortunate
Not to lack such is what liberates [VII.6]

Ratnajala, he who seizes emptiness's own essence in the aftermath, says:

In the first moment of an arisen lucid
cognizance that has not yet ceased, {322}
by examining[1283] it while it encounters
objects and appearances,[1284] it has no nature [VII.7]

Ajulī, she who possesses the radiance[1285] of bliss, says:

> Being completely embraced by emptiness,
> awareness is unconditioned nondiscursiveness
> In the nonconceptual essence of the mind,
> saṃsāra and nirvāṇa are not established [VII.8]

Bhavabhadra,[1286] he in whom the assertions of tenets are undone through the view free of names, says:

> With mind bound at the nose tip, movement[1287] is pellucid
> Not seeing any appearances of objects, clinging to such is gone
> At the time of not mentally engaging in the three times,
> the paintings of minding keep just fading away [VII.9]

Siridhinā, she who possesses the radiance of bliss, says:

> Piercing cognizance as if with a spear, discursiveness is at peace
> Through this, the coming and going of thoughts[1288] is severed
> In that way, the self-appearing objects of the sense faculties
> are indeed inconceivable and free of meditation [VII.10]

Kunduru, he who binds the vāyu mind through the gaze, says:

> Since the path to liberation will not be without foes,
> don't let go of practicing due to circumstances!
> Don't have wrong aims of your actions; cherished
> friends are the causes of desire and hatred arising [VII.11]

Sukapa, the lamp of the glory of compassion, says:

> Similar to a deer who has been wounded,
> Upa should remain all alone by herself

In people's midst, realization dwindles
Striving for supreme actuality, the end is reached [VII.12]

Jambuta, he who is always unfazed due to forcefully cutting through afflictions with powerful remedies, says:

AHO! The methods for greatness in the world {323}
are incompatible with practicing the path to liberation,
similar to the heads of the supreme nāgas
being the basis of just as many[1289] sufferings [VII.13]

Sūryakhadhī, the powerful queen, says:

Clinging to entities is the cause of saṃsāra
Being free of clinging is the path to nirvāṇa
A mind with desire throws liberation away
Being free of desire is the supreme bliss [VII.14]

Jinamitra, he who has cut through the shackles of delusion by the afflictions being free in their own place, says:

Coarse and subtle being cut off is the lion's eye
It is within this that the nonconceptual wisdom
that is self-aware and stainless has its place
This eye should never ever be closed [VII.15]

Bhanudhara, he with the light rays of blessings, says:

Clinging to the stainless entity is bondage's key point
When the vāyu mind is entering luminosity,
it is the path of the supreme king of great bliss
This constitutes the king of methods [VII.16]

Sonaśrī, he who is aware of the ultimate vital point through appearances dawning as symbols, says:

If there is no arising of certainty,
the seeing of reality will not take place
The jewel pure of doubt dispelling pride
is the treasure to be cherished most [VII.17]

Jñānarohā, the principal lady of the expanse, says:

Yogīs, you need to cherish certainty
Uncertainty is the blessing of māra
Doubts are throwing the siddhis away
Trust is the basis for all qualities [VII.18]

Javaripa, he in whom lucid bliss is an uninterrupted flow through letting awareness be in its seat, says: {324}

By way of putting awareness to the test[1290]
through the qualities of karaṇa bondage,
objects' unimpeded lucidity dimension
frees the cognizance of clinging to such[1291] [VII.19]

Padmakhadā, the glorious lady, says:

Give up coarse and subtle thoughts through this!
It is of the essence to shift the fresh gaze
within this vital point of seizing bliss, vāyus,
and awareness in a lightning-like manner [VII.20]

Śrīsāgara, he in whom nondiscursiveness arose from gathering the accumulation of wisdom, says:

Nonthought by having eliminated thoughts
is delusion and in opposition to the mindstream[1292]
If there are no thoughts, there are no means
for wisdom to arise, and wisdom ceases [VII.21]

Bhigasī, the excellent lady who possesses the light of a gem, says:

By experiencing whatever thoughts may arise
in a nonobserving manner, prajñā becomes food
This method is what allows the dynamic energy
of thinking to appear as great wisdom [VII.22]

Sūryaśrījñāna, he who, through being struck by being introduced [to mind's nature] all at once, attained the bhūmi of irreversibility as true reality, says:

The bow of emptiness without the arrow of compassion
will not allow experiences to arise in the mindstream
The prajñā that is divorced from compassion
will tumble into theoretical understanding [VII.23]

Salijadhari,[1293] he who is the source of glory, says:

With compassion's arrow missing its bow,
you are also unable to perform any function
With means that are divorced from prajñā,
there is nothing that is accomplished [VII.24]

Śrītari, he who, through taking[1294] cognizance to be unreal, is free of the conditions of delusion, {325} says:

Through the eye of the Sage, the vāyu mind is bound,
appearances are unobservable, and clinging to such is free
At that time, cognizance is not carried away by objects,
the three times are cut with a single stroke, and there is no
coming or going [VII.25]

Bulakhadhā,[1295] the queen of great bliss, says:

The natural state of immovable one-pointed pellucidity
is the dharmakāya of thoughts being free in themselves—
naked awareness free of any obscurations or veils,
cognizance's own natural condition, mahāmudrā [VII.26]

Ghudheripa, he who, through the elixir of being completely pure of the three spheres, is free of the mindset of desiring a fruition, says:

> The obstacle that prevents attaining
> the four kāyas is the mind of desire
> With it present, obscurations are not purified
> Hence, the pure realms will not manifest [VII.27]

Sukhacandha, the lamp of glory, says:

> Create great bliss free of the mind of desire!
> At that time, this is what removes suffering
> With the mindsets of desire coming to an end,
> the swamp of the contaminations will dry up [VII.28]

Śrīparanā,[1296] she who dispels the stains of doubts through certainty, says:

> The dharmakāya that pervades everything
> has the characteristic of nondiscursiveness
> that is naturally without arising or ceasing—
> self-abiding wisdom is an uninterrupted flow [VII.29]

Dhanurohā,[1297] she who holds the treasure[1298] of bliss, says:

> With the radiance of space, originally pure,
> completely free of the four extremes,
> and not contained within any time of past,
> present, or future—this is mahāmudrā [VII.30]

{326} Saradhipa, he in whom the watchman of the remedies has perished due to the afflictions being free right within themselves, says:

> Look at this greatly powerful[1299] cognizance!
> Resting in the center of the expanse of space,

stainless awareness is the supreme of paths
Once the bindu is free, it will be seen [VII.31]

Madhalā, the liberatress of bliss,[1300] says:

It is within the mind that wisdom will arise
Alert[1301] awareness represents the wrathful eye
Thoughts let be in their seat don't stir the vāyus
This is achieved through auspicious connection[1302] [VII.32]

Nāgavajra, he in whom setting up meditation sessions is gone thanks to experience being free of appearances, says:

In a mindstream where the blessings of the guru
have not entered, realization[1303] does not arise
If there is no certainty that springs forth,
the actuality of profound true reality is not seen [VII.33]

Amakapālī, the principal blazing lady, says:

The greatness of auspicious connection[1304] not shunning
the native state consists of the symbols of the guru
When the certainty about this has become lost,
there will be a great many letters to illustrate this [VII.34]

Padmavajra, he in whom thinking is pellucid[1305] in its own place through being aware that the three times are empty of arising and ceasing, says:

Through the seeing of actual reality,[1306] dismantle
the mind of delusion as well as genuine reality!
Through this, the views of mental extremes are free
Thereby, dualistic appearances do not remain [VII.35]

Siritirā, the excellent glorious lady, says:

Having arrived at[1307] dependent origination's root,

the seeds of saṃsāra will not remain anymore
Saṃsāra is empty of dependent origination,
from ignorance up through aging and death [VII.36]

{327} Vajrajñāna, he in whose aftermath of being embraced[1308] by the mindfulness[1309] of the actuality of nondiscursiveness there is no connection with any traces of objects, says:

In a support in which ordinary thinking
is gone, the path of means is not needed
In a cognizance that is pure of delusion,
it is not necessary to look at this [VII.37]

Sukaralī, the queen of glory, says:

In a cognizance in which thoughts' fine distinctions
have been relinquished, meditation is not needed
Where self-appearances have become free,
there is no need to engage in any practice [VII.38]

Vimalaghiti, he in whom the clinging to cognizance as being such[1310] has become undone by having identified the appearances of objects as illusions, says:

With the six collections not scattered toward objects,
the three times will be free in their own place
Those who wish for the supreme state of great bliss
must not lapse from the stability[1311] of one-pointedness
[VII.39]

Padmavati, he with the light rays of miraculous powers, says:

If distracted, true reality will not be seen
Nondistraction is the key point of the means
Through this, that which has the nature
of being empty lucid bliss will be found [VII.40]

Gīrtijñāna, he in whom delusion has been severed based on objects by realizing the meaning of symbols, says:

> Through these deluded appearances of laziness
> that are blended with the city, the path to liberation
> will never ever be found within the three times
> If examined, delusion does not have any basis [VII.41]

Saridharī, she who bestows glorious bliss, says:

> These are adventitious self-appearances
> Oh yogīs, look at this true core
> that is rootless and lacks a nature! {328}
> Seeing it, delusion will be undone [VII.42]

This is the seventh chapter, called "The Overflowing Inexhaustible Jewel Treasury," in *Vajra Songs of the Siddhas, [Called] "The Light of the True Reality of All Yogīs."*

Śrīvajrabala, he for whom adverse conditions arise as aids by taking what is unfavorable as the path, says:

> There is no happiness in this place of saṃsāra
> Just as in the case of ripples on the water,
> one suffering arrives because of another one
> What's this life good for? It's the cause of suffering [VIII.1]

Bhugalamī, she who is intoxicated by the taste of bliss, says:

> If what cannot be looked at is seen,
> it is identified as being ungraspable[1312]
> Through this, free of the disease of effort,
> the king[1313] of great bliss is attained [VIII.2]

Jñānacakra, he in whom cognizance without meditation has become nondiscursive by not examining whether thoughts arrive earlier or later, says:

If it is realized, not realizing its qualities is a flaw
This self-arising wisdom that is unconditioned
and cannot be tainted by anything whatsoever
is the basic ground of the entity of nondual cognizance[1314]
[VIII.3]

Bhanuharī, she[1315] who is not tainted by the flaws of the afflictions, says:

The clinging to thoughts is what appropriates
It puts us into the wheel of saṃsāric existence
through being ignorant about all phenomena
Being empty, they are taken to be a self [VIII.4]

Prajñācandra, he in whom clinging thoughts are free by being aware of the ultimate vital point, says: {329}

Within the connate of native reality,
uncontrived, natural, and just as it is,
don't rely on minding's fine distinctions!
If mind's analysis slips in, it's the basis of thoughts [VIII.5]

Sukale, she who is free of the shackles of delusion, says:

The foundation of[1316] karma, afflictions,
and latent tendencies is not established
In baseless[1317] saṃsāra that's free in itself,
how could any nirvāṇa be established? [VIII.6]

Śrīratnamati, he in whom wisdom has dawned by the shackles of delusion having been cut through, says:

What is it that divides baseless phenomena that are empty
of their own essence into the pair of ultimate and seeming?

If saṃsāra and nirvāṇa have no existence even in a dream,
how could a view of tenets having perished be uttered?
[VIII.7]

Ralidharī, she who has arrived at understanding through symbols,[1318] says:

What is without discursiveness, without birth,
without thoughts, without contrivance,
and has the nature of great compassion—
that realize as the essence of the connate! [VIII.8]

Kamoro, he whose cognizance is free of conditions by seeing the true core of appearances, says:

Perceiver and perceived[1319] appearing as diversity
do not ever find their way beyond the essence
of the connate, which is without contrivance,
possessing the nature of the dharmakāya [VIII.9]

Ghajudharī, the excellent lady who seizes ultimate glory,[1320] says:

Everything that appears as coarse[1321] entities
is endowed with the nature of emptiness
At the very time of its naked appearance,
mahāmudrā is right there by seeing this [VIII.10]

{330} Rāja Flower Hali,[1322] he for whom there is nothing to be bound by thoughts through having seen the native state's own face, says:

All entities[1323] that appear as they do
possess the essence of mahāmudrā
With their character of having no nature,
they resemble the orb of a water-moon [VIII.11]

Rukalī, she who possesses the radiance of uncontaminated bliss, says:

Through the connate of the illustrating example,
the actual connate to be illustrated is realized
It possesses the nature of native mind as such
with its character of lacking any coming or going [VIII.12]

Śrījñāna, he in whom uncontaminated cognizance is not carried away by objects, says:

The guru of appearances shows entities to be instructions,
just as a person familiar from before is recognized by seeing
Through the guru's introduction striking the vital point,
phenomena are realized to be naturally unborn [VIII.13]

Gaṅgale, she with the radiance of self-aware luminosity, says:

Since whichever entities that may appear
as the objects of the six sense faculties
are utterly devoid of any real nature,
why is it that you do not see emptiness?[1324] [VIII.14]

Candrasiṅha, he with revulsion for this life, says:

Through the power of the guru's blessings entering,
E and VAṂ are melting in the center of the heart
It is through this that these entities that appear
enter the natural state of unborn realization[1325] [VIII.15]

Bhagadharā, the heroine who spirited away the radiance of wisdom, says:

Identifying the appearances of the objects of the six
collections as illusions, delusion turns away from objects
By seeing the true core of the baseless empty nature, {331}
their latent tendencies are vanquished in their place [VIII.16]

Prajñāphala,[1326] he who grasps the welfare of others through disregarding his own happiness and suffering, says:

> Thereafter, destroy the watchman of remedies!
> When attached to the corpse of happiness,
> meditation is fettered through experiences—
> the deities will fall down as māras [VIII.17]

Ratnarohā, the excellent lady with the light rays of glory, says:

> Since any thoughts about phenomena
> that are characterized by hope and fear
> represent the flaw of lacking experience,
> seize them with the elixir of nonduality!
> Allow self-appearances to be free in their own place! [VIII.18]

Devaśrīsūrya, he who sees the essence of the native state through the true core of appearances, says:

> When the pair of hope and fear has arisen
> in the mindstream of a person on the path,
> this is the flaw of not realizing the view
> Therefore, do make up your mind that
> saṃsāra and nirvāṇa are your own mind! [VIII.19]

Bhagajulu, the heroine divine liberatress, says:

> If the pair of what is to be adopted and to be rejected arises,
> this constitutes the flaw of not having equal taste,
> in that you have failed to familiarize with conduct
> Hence, understand that there is no saṃsāra or nirvāṇa
> that lies outside of this mind that is so precious![1327] [VIII.20]

Dānaśrīrāja, he who is not bound by thoughts due to cognizance being free of conditions, says:

If during this time of traveling on the path of the noble ones
the pair of something to meditate on and a meditator
arises,
this constitutes[1328] the solid stains of[1329] the conditions
For failing to identify the essence of the basic nature—
you need to recognize the unborn essence of mind [VIII.21]

{332} Bhavadeva, he who possesses the ornament of nondiscursiveness, says:

If you entertain any hope for the supreme fruition,
you go astray due to the flaw of nonrealization
AHO! Without abandoning hope for anything,
the stains will not be purified, and therefore
being without any hope is the supreme bliss [VIII.22]

Vajraraśmi, he who fulfills the hopes of those to be guided through his enlightened activity, says:

If you happen to have become attached to appearances,
it's the flaw of not knowing how to carry them onto the path
Hence, look at phenomena that are real or delusive entities!
This cause of bondage due to clinging to something—[1330]
get a grip on it through casting it far away! [VIII.23]

Ratnakhadha, he with the mudrā of irreversibility, says:

Due to hoping for your own joy, you may anticipate
the signs that you may see on the path and thus
the impure state free of mind that is not seized
by the elixir of nonreferentiality constitutes a flaw
Hence, come to a final resolve about cognizance! [VIII.24]

Candratṛda, he who made a firm decision on the purport of what he heard, says:

If you become weary by the fear of seeing
saṃsāra as suffering, you are going astray
Since this is the flaw of objects being unpurified,
when the wise have relinquished their fear,
they are ushered into the lair of bliss [VIII.25]

Haradhanā, she for whom delusion dawns as dharmatā, says:

It is through the vigor that is without any effort
that experience free of identification is sustained
Though dullness, agitation, and so on may arise,
while recognizing what their flaws consist of,
simply let the mind be in true reality! [VIII.26]

Vajradhalipa, he who has cut through the doubts of reflection through being aware of the ultimate vital point, {333} says:

AHO! AHO! Do identify
uncontrived ordinary mind!
Look at its very own nature!
At this time, you need to drop
scrutinizing self-appearing dharmas [VIII.27]

Rasabhī, she in whom the mind of desire has come to its end, says:

Since whatever may appear is naturally free in itself,
it is not tainted by afflictions or their latent tendencies
Since phenomena and mind are of the same equal taste,
diversity is free as formlessness without any root,
and therefore this means being similar to a lunatic [VIII.28]

Raśmisūrya, he for whom meditation arises in lightning-like suddenness through the blazing experience of blessing, says:

Everything does not go beyond being an illusion
By understanding the true core of lacking a nature,

the inside is bestowing blessings onto the outside
Thus, just like ice spreading and perishing on a lake,
appearances will be free in their own place [VIII.29]

Bhakadanu, he whose awareness is free of haughtiness, says:

Due to realizing saṃsāra and nirvāṇa as one taste,
the cognizance of clinging to duality is thereby free
Without any effort, the welfare of those to be guided
springs forth, just like with a wish-fulfilling jewel
The fruition will be found within yourself [VIII.30]

Ratnapali, he for whom whatever he does has become the dharma through having undone the deliberations of this life, says:

The fruition that abides within the ground,
AHO, is self-arising and inconceivable
By recognizing your own unborn mind,
striving to accomplish the two kāyas is free
There is no fruition to be attained outside [VIII.31]

Rabhinada,[1331] he who overcomes afflictions right within themselves, says: {334}

Since it is not endowed with any form,
it remains immutable throughout the three times
The phenomena of saṃsāra and nirvāṇa
are never going beyond mahāmudrā—
it has the character of pervading all [VIII.32]

Gīrtisiṅha,[1332] he who seizes the gentle vāyus in lightning-like suddenness through constraining his gaze, says:

Originally empty and without self,
this precious mind is mahāmudrā,
unarisen from causes, unborn, and unceasing

Through seeing this unborn essence,
saṃsāra's beginning and end are severed [VIII.33]

Bhagatā, she for whom the three times are free in their own place, says:

Luminous[1333] mind as such devoid of essence
does not exhibit any differences at all
between buddhas and sentient beings,
which is similar to a lamp and its light
Knowing this, thoughts of clinging to saṃsāra or nirvāṇa are gone [VIII.34]

Candraprajñā, she in whom realization[1334] arose through blessings, says:

In this actuality of mental nonengagement,
there is no arising, ceasing, coming, or going
Self-appearances are your own mind,
not conceived of as being different
If free of dualistic clinging, this is mahāmudrā [VIII.35]

Rabhina, he in whom thoughts are free in themselves, says:

Letting the mindset of reality be within emptiness,
the knot of the clinging to a self will be untied[1335]
Through identifying the agent, delusion is undone
This is the instruction that is the vital point [VIII.36]

Ratnabodha,[1336] he in whom certainty about the vital point of introduction arose, says:

Abandon clinging to realization's actuality as supreme! {335}
Those stains that are so very difficult to purify
are the connate state of seeing the essence—
This is the view that is free of extremes [VIII.37]

Bhacalā, she who is drunk[1337] by the experience of empowerment, says:

The thinking of discursive awareness
that arises from adventitious conditions
has the baseless essence of true reality
When the ground of being naturally unborn
is seen, the appearances of delusion perish [VIII.38]

Kandharipa, he who recognized luminosity's own face through the symbols of the ḍākinīs, says:

The ignorance about thinking being dharmatā
constitutes the wisdom of the expanse,
unidentified due to not seeing the true core
AHO! Hey, look at nothing but this! [VIII.39]

Siṅgadhanā, she who awoke from thoughtless[1338] sleep, says:

The unconditioned essence of true reality
is characterized by lacking coming and going
Look at this originally pure natural state[1339]
of luminosity with discursiveness at peace! [VIII.40]

Vīryajala, he in whom the cognizance of dualistic appearances is free, says:

It was not born, is not born, and will not be born
What stems from emptiness is without any birth
The unborn is empty of any essence of being born
Causes and conditions are not established as a creator
[VIII.41]

Ghajulī, she who is intoxicated by the taste of bliss, says:

Phenomena arising from the unborn expanse
possess the character of being unborn
They are not going beyond this nature—
entities are without any being born [VIII.42]

Vilita, he who holds the glory of virtue, says:

Persons who let go of things to do are happy {336}
The noble ones will never come to see
any entity at all that does not end up
in suffering for beings in the world [VIII.43]

This is the eighth chapter, called "The Dripping Quintessence of the Glorious Knot," in *Vajra Songs of the Siddhas, [Called] "The Light of the True Reality of All Yogīs."*

Sarjana, he in whose mindstream appearances gave rise to certainty,[1340] says:

Karmamudrā is that which illustrates
Dharmamudrā is the path of meditation
Mahāmudrā constitutes the fruition
Samayamudrā is enlightened activity [IX.1]

Siddhana, he who possesses the prowess of a lion, says:

If there is no means to illustrate, actuality is not seen
If there is nothing to meditate, the path is lacking
If there is no fruition, what's the point of practicing?
If there is no enlightened activity, the purpose is lost [IX.2]

Devaśari, he who has cut through doubts about the lineage of true reality, says:

The experience of bliss represents ecstasy
The experience of being free of clinging is supreme ecstasy
The inseparability of bliss and emptiness
constitutes the ecstasy that is connate
If free of experience, this is cessational ecstasy [IX.3]

Vimaladhana, he with the light rays of bliss, says:

Through experience, body and mind are taken into
naturalness
Experience without clinging is to be free of grasping
Empty nondiscursiveness is the experience of bliss,
cognizance lacking any clinging to being such [IX.4]

Śrīsaraba, he in whom the lineage of blessings has dispelled obstacles, says:

The root that is self-abiding and unconditioned
is known through the true core of the moment
Spur-of-the-moment cognizance lacks any earlier or later
{337}
In it, the knots of dualistic appearances are unraveled [IX.5]

Dhanalā, the excellent lady who possesses the light of a gem, says:

If the thinking of discursive awareness
is not cut through in a nonreferential way,
the support where latent tendencies lie is not undone
Look at characteristics being free in themselves! [IX.6]

Gajudhara, he in whom characteristics are free in their own place through not assuming any mental support, says:

The five skandhas that are appropriating
lack any characteristics, just like illusions
That which is without any nature of its own
has the sole characteristic of no characteristics [IX.7]

Ratrita,[1341] he with the light rays of miraculous powers, says:

Although there does not exist[1342] any nature
in phenomena whose essence is that of illusions,
if delusion is not eliminated on the path,

[just] seeing them as illusions is not freedom—
illusions will be fettered by illusions [IX.8]

Tharindhapa, he in whom thoughts are severed through not observing the three times, says:

Undoing after having intensified is the path of prajñā
This is the ground of nondiscursive dharmatā dawning
To tighten and relax[1343] awareness is the core of means
By meditating on unawareness,[1344] the key point is not realized [IX.9]

Sukarī, she who bestows glorious bliss, says:

Don't push! You won't contract[1345] into the vital point
Don't undo! Any thereafter will not be identified
Don't tighten![1346] Wrong cognition is not annihilated
Don't relax![1347] This is the path of nondiscursiveness dawning [IX.10]

Gagadhara, he in whom dualistic clinging is free through having seen it to be without root or base,[1348] says:

Understand that phenomena are names!
Thereby, {338} clinging to reality is free
Behold this basic nature without any base!
Thereby, the pain of contamination is free [IX.11]

Kanalī, the lamp of glory, says:

You need to behold saṃsāra's own true core![1349]
This leads to the desire for nirvāṇa being free
See discursive awareness as having the essence of wisdom!
This undoes the mindset of accomplishing buddhahood [IX.12]

Śrīsūrya, he in whom uncontaminated bliss blazes through desire having perished in the mind, says:

> Though it is undoubtedly the case
> that oil pervades sesame seeds,
> don't press a dry one—it has no fluid
> Sesame cannot function as its oil does[1350] [IX.13]

Dhanaru, she who holds a vase, says:

> Likewise,[1351] though the sugata heart exists
> in saṃsāric sentient beings of the six classes,
> without practicing, freedom will not be attained [IX.14]

Sukadeva, he who is free of the watchman of remedies through seeing that thinking is baseless, says:

> To carry awareness's spear is the key point of meditation
> Cognizance without meditation is the natural native state
> Since meditation and nonmeditation are not dual,
> the unity of cognizance is so greatly amazing [IX.15]

Abharadhā,[1352] she who possesses the radiance of bliss, says:

> Cognizance free of extremes is the key point of the view
> Ordinary mind is lacking any thinking state of mind
> Being uncontrived is what constitutes the dharmakāya
> The accomplishing mind having perished is amazing!
> [IX.16]

Bhanasūrya, he for whom appearances dawn as scriptures through knowing how to demonstrate whatever benefits the path as an aid, says: {339}

> Just as leaves, fruits, and flowers do not grow
> on a tree that has been turned into charcoal,

so the gem of qualities will not come forth
in those who are without devotion [IX.17]

Dhanā, the cotton-clad lady who possesses the eye of wisdom, says:

Just as an elephant paralyzed in the womb
does not arrive in a grove full of mud,
due to not possessing any natural vigor,
you will not go to the city of liberation [IX.18]

Daraca, he whose awareness is pellucid by virtue of the lion's gaze, says:

Just as is the case with dreams and illusions,
the nature of seeming appearances is empty
Similar to a city of gandharvas,
just so arising and abiding are [IX.19]

Manilā, she who spirited away the radiance[1353] of the gods, says:

Since the three realms are not actual reality,
they are completely devoid of any essence
Since phenomena are not established ultimately,
Their pure nature is so greatly amazing! [IX.20]

Caṇḍali, he in whom the essence arose from the dynamic energy[1354] of mindfulness, says:

With phenomena being naturally pure,
this saṃsāra that is causeless is not seen
Its being unseen is the key point of nirvāṇa
Through realizing that, freedom is attained
AHO! This is the ḍākinīs' secret key point [IX.21]

Bhanuhiri, the principal blazing lady, says:

Lacking the mind's extremes is the natural native state,

free from meditation and something to meditate on
In mahāmudrā, there is nothing to meditate at all
The uncreated cognizance that possesses[1355] power
is awareness without any support, just like space [IX.22]

Asuradhe, he in whom thoughts are severed through cognizance not proliferating toward objects, {340} says:

On the level of the fruition of consummate realization,[1356]
hope, fear, and chances to go astray[1357] are pure in the expanse
Yogīs who realize actuality are free of any anxiety
Saṃsāra being free in itself is so greatly amazing! [IX.23]

Bhanuharī, she who possesses the eye of wisdom, says:

The two realities that are not different in essence
are the unity of appearance and emptiness inseparable
For yogīs in whom appearance-emptiness is free,
there is no saṃsāra or nirvāṇa—how greatly amazing! [IX.24]

Ghacalipa, he who, by virtue of the fundamental vital point, recognizes his own face through symbols, says:

Those in whom the knowledge of certainty has arisen
are free of doubt, uncertainty, and being of two minds
Within the wisdom that is an uninterrupted flow,
momentary phenomena have no place to stay [IX.25]

Sukadhanā, she who is a wish-fulfilling cow,[1358] says:

In the dharmatā that is without any gap,
coming and going phenomena do not abide
Within the wisdom that is free of mind,
the stains of delusion are completely pure [IX.26]

Candhepa, he in whom, through letting cognizance be in its seat, the shackles are severed within the appearances of delusion, says:

> Just as the essence of iron embraced
> by an elixir turns into pure gold,
> embraced by[1359] bliss, lucidity, and nonthought,
> discursive awareness turns into wisdom itself [IX.27]

Bhatahā, the principal lady of the expanse, says:

> When this is known as the key point's essence,
> the darkness of ignorance becomes pellucid
> Those in whom delusion's appearances are pure
> understand "the pure realms of the three kāyas" [IX.28]

Śoporipa,[1360] he for whom the actuality of the lineage of oral instructions is free through the vital point of the a-series and the ka-series, says: {341}

> Where there is a well with a treasure,
> there arises a mind full of attachment
> But without any treasure, there is no attached mind
> Cormorants do not pursue the middle of the forest [IX.29]

Thanamo, he who is endowed with the ornament of miraculous powers, says:

> Bees without any honey live happily
> The minds of herons letting go of fish rest at ease
> An insatiable mind is destitute [IX.30]

Ratnadeva, he who holds the lineage of the noble ones through having finished the path of hardships, says:

> The causal yoga consists of the avoidance of conditions
> The yoga of those on the path is the freedom of conditions

The fruitional yoga is conditions' lightning-like suddenness,
Nothing at all has become a condition for realization [IX.31]

Suridhanā, she who possesses the light of compassion, says:

Among sentient beings within the ocean,
there is none who is not food for makaras[1361]
Likewise, for those who attained stability,
there is nothing at all that is not an aid [IX.32]

Amoghacandra, he for whom, through identifying delusion, the six collections dawn as conditions that evoke realization,[1362] says:

In what is without view and lacks any view,
how could you say, "This is the view?"
Just like the bliss of a young woman,
its experience cannot be expressed [IX.33]

Sanalī, she who possesses the power of bliss, says:

Someone who pours water onto their cheeks
is not able to speak or express anything
The yogīs who drank the elixir of actuality
do not know how to express mahāmudrā [IX.34]

Sukhajñāna, he who exercises the dynamic energy of awareness through understanding the vital point's own core, says: {342}

Just as all waters are the same
in their salty taste in the ocean,
in the introduction to the instructions' vital point,
phenomena are understood as the single actuality [IX.35]

Ranudhara, he who gained mastery over the mind, says:

Just as a person[1363] plagued by jaundice

may see the ground of the earth as gold,
by having drunk the elixir of actuality,
whatever appears is seen as instruction [IX.36]

Bimadeva, he who identifies wisdom in the aftermath of having been undone, says:

When a person is carried away by the māras,
they praise themselves and put down others
Those who are clinging to benighted tenets
constitute the māras of the view indeed [IX.37]

Balibadā, the heroine who possesses feathers of the garuḍa bird, says:

The assertions of the learned should be relinquished
Those whose own mindstreams are composed by study
cast the need for qualities [of erudition] into the wind[1364]
The ultimate Veda is to be peaceful and composed [IX.38]

Ranucanda,[1365] he who puts movement[1366] to the test by binding mind at the tip of the nose, says:

Just as a vase and so on are not visible
behind a curtain that has been closed,
likewise, by closing the eyes of desire,
contamination will not be seen outside [IX.39]

Bhagasuna, he who possesses gorgeous peacock feathers, says:

Once clinging to duality is free in someone,
at that time, delusion is pure in its own place
Appearances of dharmatā dawning on their own
is designated as "the seeing of reality" [IX.40]

{343} Ciradevī,[1367] she in whom mahāmudrā dawns in lightning-like suddenness through hitting the vital point of introduction,[1368] says:

> The view of not seeing any extremes of mind at all,
> due to all knowable objects having perished by being free
> and appearance-emptiness lacking any conditions,
> consists of being bound by the mudrā of being unborn [IX.41]

Patamī, the lady endowed with bliss who wears a conch topknot, says:

> Drop the clinging mind, and thoughts are cut!
> To be rid of the eight[1369] within the equal taste
> of phenomena in the ground[1370] constitutes yoga
> The kāya of wisdom is free from karma [IX.42]

Ghajudeva, he who is aware of the actuality of all phenomena based on a single introduction, says:

> Just as an eye with its pellucid faculty
> does not see forms if it has gone blind,
> likewise, if there is no mind of desire,
> you will not see due to being obscured [IX.43]

Bitalā, the fiery lady with a coat of dragon skin, says:

> Just as a shadow accompanies
> everything up to what is formless,
> so, since the mind of desire exists,
> the obscurations will not be given up
> Oh friends, be rid of the mind of desire! [IX.44]

This is the ninth chapter, called "The Rain Shower of Nectar," from the tradition of experiential pith instructions increasing [as if] from one lamp flame to another, which points out true reality in its native state.

This was translated by precious Tampa Gyagar, the lion among humans who is a son of the victors, on his own.

This mahāmudrā that is arranged in sections
has few words but wraps up the meaning
These vajra songs that arise from experience
are the lamp dispelling the darkness of ignorance {344}

In those not embraced by the mindset of insatiably
gazing with the eye sense faculties of the fortunate,
their doubts are cut through by merely reading this
AHO! This is amazing and hereby completed

May it be the welfare of all sentient beings! Virtue! {345}

(183) A Golden Garland of Mahāmudrā

In the language of India: *Mahāmudrākanakamālānāma*[1371]
In the language of Tibet: *Phyag rgya chen po gser phreng zhes bya ba*

I pay homage to the true gurus

The flowers and leaves of trees having blossomed, their sweet fruits are many
The dharma kings guide the trichiliocosm realms[1372] and adorn them with ornaments
The sky is filled with the dance of suns and moons and the dance of the constellations
The nāga kings' crowns of the head are adorned with the ornaments of precious jewels
Ravishing persons full of beauty are bedecked with the finest of pearls
Authentic buddhas clearly manifest among the assemblies of gods and humans [I.1]

Although precious jewels are endowed with an abundance of qualities,
without a captain, you are not able to make any travels on the ocean
You may have studied a lot and possess all the qualities of the piṭakas,

but[1373] without blessing, you will not realize the unborn true actuality [I.2]

Just as greenery will grow in the summertime,
but there will be no harvest without planting a field, {346}
sentient beings in the six realms have the nature of buddhas,
but they don't see the wisdom of freedom without meditation [I.3]

With the path obstructed by optical illusions and doubts,
travelers[1374] will not arrive at the lands they desire
Likewise, with a distrusting mind full of doubts,
the state of the awakening of great bliss will not be found [I.4]

Meditation and nonmeditation are the sphere of the thinking mind
Free of thinking about nonmeditation, the ground without distraction
is the path of the mahāmudrā of mental nonengagement
Hey, this is free of any doing, unborn, and beyond mind! [I.5]

The dharmatā wisdom lamp of lucid and empty luminous awareness
is the king of the great bliss of uncontaminated bliss and emptiness
There, the dharmatā eye of nonconceptual appearance and emptiness,
AHO, takes in the sight of this amazing reality of dharmatā [I.6]

With the luminosity of illusions guiding their light into the dharmakāya,
seize the luminosity of the illusory body as the dharmakāya's appearance!
By having this encounter with nondual connate dharmatā,
AHO, the guru is the buddha—isn't that the truth?[1375] [I.7]

Nāgā[rjuna], Sara[ha], Cāryapa,

Śavari, Sara,[1376] Kamaya,[1377]
Śānti[pa], Bhusu[ku], Virūpa,
Deṅgi[pa],[1378] Una[pa],[1379] Mīnapa,
Pudhri,[1380] Catra[pa], Bhadrapa,
Ārya[deva], Mekha[lā], *Karopa,[1381]
Ravi,[1382] Dito,[1383] Koṅkali[pa],[1384]
Bhaga,[1385] Vīra,[1386] Nīlapa,[1387]
Kaṅka[na], Koki[lipa], Anaṅga[pa],
Candra,[1388] Sarva[bhakṣa], Koṭali[pa],
Bhade[pa], Kāṇha[pa],[1389] Kambala,
Ḍombi Heru[ka], Dārika[pa],
Kṛṣṇa, Nāga[bodhi], Prabhaka[ra],[1390]
Kukku[ripa], Canu,[1391] and Ghaṇṭāpa[1392] [I.8]

Those without realization should not engage in the conduct of the realized
If they do so, they are like subjects trying to break the law of the king
The realized ones should not engage in the conduct of the unrealized
If they do so, they resemble steadfast elephants stuck in the mud[1393] [I.9]

Hey, you friends! {347} This connate here
is not found elsewhere, so ask the guru's mouth!
If the ultimate essence of his words is realized,
mind is without death and the vāyus without extinction[1394] [I.10]

Those not realizing the kāya of the uncontaminated
nirvāṇa of the great bliss of luminous dharmatā
cannot be taught the path of nonconceptuality—
this constitutes the supreme quintessence [I.11]

In the maṇḍala of the victors that is your own body,
there is no effort at all in terms of any maṇḍalas—
inner, outer, with or without colored powders, and such—
that cuts off the life force of the path to liberation [I.12]

The lamp of the blessings of the guru who experiences
nondual bliss and emptiness is self-arising dharmatā
It was not realized, is not realized, and lacks anything to meditate on
Unable to describe it as "this" or "that," just remain silent [I.13]

The path of the unborn native state that
neither comes from anywhere nor goes anywhere,
dharmatā's awakening, the dharmakāya's sun,
is free of the darkness of ignorance [I.14]

Similar to a tortoise, this is not tainted
by saṃsāra's flaws and is originally pure
Thanks to the guru's kindness, the lamp
free of darkness, this is the sun of wisdom [I.15]

Don't look! There is nothing to see by looking
Don't scrutinize![1395] It's not an object of examination
Don't ponder! There is nothing to think about
Don't hope! It's beyond any object of hope or fear [I.16]

Since it is not an object that is seen by looking,
meditation refers to seeing dharmatā's actuality
by the blessings of the guru; don't think of it as anything—
this is the freedom without anything to identify [I.17]

A person who has let go of activities
is action-free, has nothing to do, and lacks perceiver and perceived
In the practice that is free of hope and fear,
there is nothing at all to cultivate as nonthought [I.18]

AHO! {348} The amazing reality of dharmatā is seen
AHO! The lamp of experiencing blessings blazes
AHO! Faith in and respect for the guru are without distraction
AHO! The fruition is lucid self-luminous blessing [I.19]

Self-awareness is originally unborn,
empty, uncontrived, and effortless
The self-aware and self-luminous gem
of mind as such is clear, pellucid, and unimpeded [I.20]

The luminosity that is natural will not be found
by[1396] conceptual meditation or nonmeditation
It is the uncontrived and undistracted relaxation
within nonmeditation, without anything to distract [I.21]

The dharmatā of connate self-awareness—
the great bliss that cannot be described—
transcends self, other, happiness, suffering, and mind
Seeing the reality of dharmatā is the dharmakāya's spaciousness [I.22]

Self-awareness is what is realized by itself
It is like the water element, gold, and space
Buddhas and sentient beings, saṃsāra and nirvana,
and what to reject and to adopt are not different [I.23]

In the three poisons[1397] free in themselves—the nondual bliss-emptiness
of the nāḍīs and vāyus that represents the lamp of the dharma—
the knots of attachment and aversion of ordinary thoughts' clinging
to entities are free from perceiver and perceived in their own place [I.24]

Since wisdom—the clear and pellucid dharmatā of living beings—
is free of extremes, without support, and unobservable,
delusion, nondelusion, the basis of delusion, and the root of delusion
are severed in the unborn natural state free of any doing [I.25]

The illusory body that is similar to a rainbow

represents the samayamudrā; by encountering
the self-appearances of the sense faculties
without clinging, dharmatā's reality is seen [I.26]

Uncontaminated great bliss—the karmamudrā that is the sun
of dharmatā—is the lamp of the wisdom of dharmatā {349}
through unborn awakening that is free of imagination,
saṃsāra's suffering is dispelled in great bliss's spaciousness [I.27]

The vīras, ḍākinīs, and dharma protectors[1398]
in your own body—the maṇḍala of the victors—
are the mudrās, nāḍīs, vāyus, and bodhicitta
The native state is unobservable as anything at all [I.28]

Blissful and empty mind as such is dharmatā's actuality
To realize it constitutes the path of mahāmudrā:
the lack of observed object, observer, and observation
cannot be conceived of as anything whatsoever [I.29]

The lamp of the samādhi of the emptiness
that[1399] resounds as the lion's roar of no-self
dispels all obscurations without exception,
such as happiness, suffering, permanence, and extinction [I.30]

Virtuous and nonvirtuous actions
dissolve in the native state without clinging
The mahāsukhakāya of dharmatā
is attained in the state of nondual self-awareness [I.31]

Since there is no bliss when lacking the lamp
of samaya, resembling the sound of a vīṇā,
the sun of samaya and the sun of[1400] wisdom
are beheld as the sun of dharmatā [I.32]

Going through the four empowerments, the four paths are seen
The four kāyas are free as the four mudrās

The vajra body of unity endowed with means
is perfected in the victor's state in your own body [I.33]

In latent tendencies being free in themselves as wisdom,
there is no permanence, extinction, adopting, rejecting, superimposition, or denial
In the native state of dharmatā that is originally pure,
there is no obscuring dullness, agitation, hope, or fear at all [I.34]

In the inconceivable luminosity of self-awareness,
there is no seizing by mindfulness, no perceiver, and no perceived
In afflictions being self-pellucid and thoughts being the dharmakāya,
the buddhas of the three times cannot be searched for at all [I.35] {350}

Just as in the case of a gold-making elixir, the three realms
are filled with the taste[1401] of the dharmatā of great bliss
Ultimately, the seeming [reality] of saṃsāra is pure
and the dharmatā free of extremes is the middle way [I.36]

The low-caste[1402] thoughts of purity and impurity
represent the saṃsāra of perceiver and perceived
Due to this delusion, great bliss is not seen
Yogīs who do not see this, do not find it [I.37]

Ordinary mind wakes up in the center of the heart
Once the six collections are pure, bliss is uninterrupted
Everything imagined is meaningless, the cause of suffering
Since there is nothing to meditate, let be in the native state[1403] [I.38]

Mahāmudrā is connately present within us
Not thinking or being aware, let be in its effortless state!
Not becoming extinct, direct[1404] experience is experienced by itself
Not becoming permanent, it is unity without clinging[1405] [I.39]

Similar to a chariot without its two wheels, unable to drive anywhere,
even if you make effort in generosity and such, without a guru, there's no genuine siddhi
Vultures with their wings and perfect dexterity cut and soar through the sky
By absorbing empowerments, blessings, and instructions, the fortunate are blissful[1406] [I.40]

The ocean in its depth and vastness is filled with jewels,
and the rule of the nāga kings over this is very amazing
All appearances and sounds primordially are the immutable dharmakāya—
this being enjoyed by yogīs with realization and experience is very amazing[1407] [I.41]

Just as the power of a gold-making elixir {351}
leads to transforming base metals into gold,
so the power of precious empowerments
transforms afflictions into nondual wisdom[1408] [I.42]

Since in the wish-fulfilling jewel of realization[1409]
the colors of experience are brought forth,
by its activity's power, what's wanted and needed arises
This is accomplished by those with equal taste[1410] [I.43]

Though great bliss lies within us, it is not realized and obscured by delusion
Those wishing to dispel it should gather the accumulations of merit and wisdom
When not gathering the two accumulations, even if you strive for a hundred lives,
without having a guru, great bliss will not be realized[1411] [I.44]

The buddhas of the three times have a single essence
It is your own mind that is their nature

If you wish to realize it, let it be as it is!
Once familiar with it, it will become revealed[1412] [I.45]

By virtue of the gurus, you should first realize your own mind
Then, you should make this not different from all phenomena
Having realized nonduality and staying in charnel grounds,
with experience and realization, behave spontaneously with a lunatic's yogic discipline[1413] [I.46]

If it resembles a horse, an elephant, and the ocean, this is the bliss of equality
If it is like a monkey drawing a picture on water, this is discursiveness
If it is similar to a river, the sun, and medicine, this is inseparability
Like a hair-knot, an eye,[1414] and a cakravartin, this is attainment[1415] [I.47]

If you dwell on the ground, everything is of good fortune
If you go to the depths of the ocean, you are free of poverty
If you hold a sword in your hand, this is a great enjoyment
If you amble around places without direction, you meet friends[1416] [I.48]

If the mind is not tormented, the view is great
If there is no clinging, {352} this is equal taste
If free of exertion, this is meditation supreme
If free of dualistic appearances, this is perfect buddhahood [I.49]

The triad of lalanā, rasanā, and avadhūtī
needs to be self-blessed and bound
It is on the triad of guru, mind, and appearances
that you should rely to give rise to realization[1417] [I.50]

This is the first chapter, the one of the first gaṇacakra (naturally arising blessings), in *A Golden Garland of Mahāmudrā*.

Lūhi[pa], Jālan[dhara], Virūpa,
Kama,[1418] Indra[bhūti], Kharabha,[1419]
Viku,[1420] Nātha Gorakṣa,
Toka,[1421] Bheni,[1422] Vinasi,[1423]
Ghuna[pa],[1424] Ajogi, Kantali[pa],
Dhahu[lipa], Tapa,[1425] Teli,[1426]
Oḍra,[1427] Saka[ra],[1428] Nidrayi,[1429]
Kaṅka[na], Sana[ka],[1430] Ganasi,[1431]
Capa[ripa],[1432] [Bhu]suku, Śyali[pa],
Suta[pa],[1433] Dharma[pa], Kuruna,[1434]
Rāhu[la], Kusu[lī],[1435] Kumari[pa],[1436]
Lakha[pa],[1437] Dhakha[pa],[1438] Parapu,[1439]
Dhoka[ripa], Viḍa,[1440] Ṇerapa,[1441]
Cāmā[ripa], Dhakha[pa], and Nyingpopa[1442] [II.1]

Just as a savage wild dog with honey rubbed on its nose gobbles up everything in all directions,
imparting the guru's pith instructions to the unfortunate of lesser insight sets their own mindstreams ablaze
A steadfast and brave elephant with a sword tied to his trunk crushes all the hostile ranks
The intelligent of good fortune vanquish thoughts upon encountering appearances realized as unborn[1443] [II.2]

Even if the unborn is realized but experience is lacking,
this is like a child being carried in the hands of a rākṣasī
Even if there is experience but the basic nature is not realized,
this is like trying to work the trunk of an elephant with an iron hook[1444] [II.3]

Venerating buddhas and so on yield no meaning
If there is wanting and effort, there will be no buddhahood
Through the words of a guru with blessings, experiences increase {353}
This is [only] so from the point of view of mind, but not ultimately[1445] [II.4]

Not looking anywhere, look at the center!
Supreme and cessational ecstasy—great bliss!
With mantra knowers behaving secretly and crazily,
yogīs should transform through the signs[1446] [II.5]

If the pivotal points in time are not endowed with[1447] self-blessing,
through any inner or outer conduct, you will not become a buddha
If there is no difference between fully flourishing bliss and appearances,
by letting go of clinging, the supreme experience will be attained[1448] [II.6]

If you rely on the wise venerable one, you see true reality
If you meditate in the midst of the jungle, you attain solitude
If you realize phenomena as mind, there is nothing unfavorable
If you drink the milk of the sky, you will be satisfied[1449] [II.7]

If you realize the blissful and empty freedom of extremes,
you are doing fine[1450] by relying on a wish-fulfilling tree
If a person knows how to move around in a lake by swimming,[1451]
a son will be born to a brahman father and mother[1452] [II.8]

It is through desire, hatred, and ignorance themselves that
the attachment and aversion of perceiver and perceived are severed in their own place
By not clinging to them in that they are like dreams and illusions,
experience is unobstructed and lucid emptiness[1453] [II.9]

Lucid, so lucid! The guru of great bliss,
the guide on the path to awakening, is lucid
The experience of the nondual, lucid, and pellucid
dharmadhātu is lucid in the native state [II.10]

Bliss, oh guru, great bliss, bliss!
Not clinging to bliss, not thinking of it as anything—bliss!

Perceiver and perceived free in themselves, clinging pellucid in itself—bliss!
An action-free person has nothing to do and is beyond mind—bliss! [II.11]

Empty, so empty—the ordinary body!
The illusory body is empty in the expanse without clinging {354}
Their unity is empty within the state of being unborn
Self-awareness is empty as the sahajakāya[1454] [II.12]

Awareness, awareness—your own mind!
Not clinging to anything at all—nonconceptual awareness!
Not analyzing anything at all—inexpressible awareness!
Awareness beyond any object of examination and analysis [II.13]

Nonconceptual, without thought, beyond the reach of examination and analysis,
not conceiving, inconceivable, not conceivable as anything at all,
without support or supported, free of coming, going, and staying—
saṃsāra, nirvāṇa, happiness, and suffering wake up in great bliss's spaciousness [II.14]

Within the relaxed nature that is uncontrived and undistracted,
the flow of mental factors stops—luminosity free of coming and going
Appearances are inexpressible—the master cannot be distracted[1455]
Dharmatā's self-lucid awareness is encountered as the dharmakāya [II.15]

Mind as such is not seen—there is nothing there at all
Right now, it cannot be looked at and cannot be shown
It is not distracted, there is no distraction, and nothing to be distracted
There is no meditation and nothing to meditate on [II.16]

Free! Free! Free of saṃsāra and nirvāṇa!
Great bliss is free in the spaciousness of dharmatā
Awareness is free within the state of inexpressibility
Meditation is free in the expanse without clinging
Doing rests on the dry shore of not needing to do anything [II.17]

AHO, dharmatā! Dharmatā is seen!
AHO, buddhahood! Hey, buddhahood!
Hey! The state of awakening is attained!
AHO! Amazing! There is nothing to die![1456] [II.18]

What can possibly appear is not real but primordially delusive
Friends and foes[1457] never existed,[1458] being appearances of delusion
All that has been done is meaningless, the state[1459] of suffering
Once free of attachment and aversion, this is buddhahood [II.19]

The entirety of actions is meaningless, the cause of suffering
Not needing to do anything is bliss, effortless yoga is bliss
No matter what you think of, {355} your wants and needs won't arise
Hence, bliss is in the native state where there is nothing to think [II.20]

Mind as such is the kāya of the bindu of great bliss
The inseparability of bliss and emptiness is mind's continuum
Like the sky, the dharmatā that's[1460] inexpressible
cannot be looked at and cannot be shown [II.21]

AHO! Amazing! The kāya of the guru
is the state of nonconceptual emptiness free of discursiveness,
the empty expanse of inseparable appearance and emptiness,
possessing the continuum of the unborn dharmakāya [II.22]

Appearances and mind, buddhas and sentient beings too,
are similar to the sun and its rays of light

Free of relinquishment and attainment, without wanting—
wherever these are absent, that is buddhahood [II.23]

Knowable objects appear but lack a nature
Knowledge is lucid yet nonconceptual
Being undistracted from uncontaminated great bliss—
mind as such—there is nothing to meditate at all [II.24]

Mind as such is the guru, the kāya of the buddha
The mind of appearances is conditioned virtue's basis
The dharmakāya is the path of samādhi in the lower realms
Pride is endowed with the bodhicitta that is nondual [II.25]

Uncontrived dharmatā is free of [all] thinking[1461] in terms of
a beginning and an end of saṃsāra, as well as hope and fear,
and devoid of an object of meditation, a meditator, adopting, and rejecting
The fruition is supreme self-lucid self-awareness[1462] [II.26]

It is the sahajakāya of self-awareness,
the buddha nature of the six [kinds of] beings,
whose essence is self-lucid awareness,
that wears the ornament of nonconceptual samaya [II.27]

The dharmatā of mind and appearances is the dharmakāya[1463]
The illusory body that is pure, unequalled,
and nonconceptual is the path to awakening
Unborn unity is the pleasant realms' ornament [II.28]

Appearances and mind are self-aware, nondiscursive great bliss
Illusory nāḍīs and vāyus are the vāyu mind that's inexpressible {356}
Dreams and luminosity constitute the unity of great bliss where
the clear illumination of the four kāyas' wisdom is unobstructed [II.29]

There is nothing to look at—your own pure mind
that cannot be looked at appears as the guru
Empty appearances are the mahāsukhakāya
Inseparable bliss-emptiness is blessings' ornament [II.30]

Mind as such cannot be looked at, and its root
beyond mind is lucid and empty, the ḍākinīs' secret
Appearances are emptiness, the mahāsukhakāya[1464]
Inseparable appearance-emptiness is the ḍākinīs' ornament [II.31]

The appearances of the action-free nonconceptual
vāyu mind are empty and free of discursiveness
This emptiness is inexpressible great bliss
Bliss-emptiness free of extremes is the vāyus' ornament [II.32]

Your own mind is great bliss, bodhicitta
Uncontaminated great bliss is the dharmakāya
Appearances are the spaciousness of empty luminosity
The wisdom of bliss-emptiness is awakening's ornament [II.33]

Appearances consist of dreams empty of reality
Perceiver, perceived, attachment, and aversion are objects of delusion's appearance
The imaginary is [like] a banana tree without any pith
Any appearances without clinging are the path's ornament [II.34]

What neither comes from anywhere nor goes
anywhere is nonconceptual mind as such,
which cannot be looked at and cannot be shown
Its dharmatā is the ornament of seeing the essence [II.35]

Although saṃsāra is suffering and without bliss,
[bliss] is introduced through the blessings of the guru,
while dullness and agitation—the enemies of meditation and experience—
become the ornaments of seeing luminous self-awareness[1465] [II.36]

The meditation of action-free experience beyond mind
is free of focus, thoughts, perceiver, and perceived
In the effortlessness of not conceptualizing anything at all,
it is the ornament of hope, fear, blocking, and creating being free
in themselves [II.37]

The emptiness that possesses the nature of wisdom
and has compassion as its ornament is the path of unity[1466] {357}
Since emptiness and compassion are inseparable,
this is great bliss, the kāya of mahāmudrā [II.38]

The beyond-the-mind experience of naturally arising bliss[1467]
without clinging is the spaciousness[1468] of the native state
The dharmatā of the meditation that cannot be distracted,
which possesses the ornament of wisdom, is bliss [II.39]

Not thinking anything, not pondering over anything,
not clinging to anything, and free of examination and analysis,
self-lucid[1469] awareness without anything to do
is the ornament of being free in itself, without anything to
fabricate [II.40]

This is bliss—nonconceptual experience as you please
This is empty—dharmatā's natural state[1470] beyond mind
This is conduct—the path of naturally arising equal taste
This is freedom—the ornament of hope and fear being free in
themselves [II.41]

This does not exist as anything at all. Possibly appearing objects
are empty anywhere. There exists neither an identifying mind
nor examination and analysis. The paths of saṃsāra and nirvāṇa
are the ornament of the native state without meditation and
analysis [II.42]

If the experience of resting [like] a river became stable,
you should gradually transition into the conduct

Through the pith instructions of the true guru,
thoughts of attachment and aversion are pacified [II.43]

This is the second chapter, the one of the second gaṇacakra (experiencing the actuality of meditation), in *A Golden Garland of Mahāmudrā*.

Tilo[pa], Nāro[pa], Bhasutra,[1471]
Candana,[1472] [Ava]dhūtī[pa], Ramaya,[1473]
Cārya[pa], Rātrī,[1474] Maitrīpa,
the Tibetan Legjin,[1475] Padmapāda,[1476]
Vajra,[1477] Dharma[pa], Joginī,[1478]
Kāhna[pa], Mekha[lā], Mahāla,[1479]
Rari[pa],[1480] Raṅka, Kasauri,
Jāla,[1481] Cindha,[1482] Virūpa,
Jnāna,[1483] Vajra, Medhapa,[1484]
Ḍombi [Heruka], Bhata,[1485] Riwopa,
Kama, Krita, Prajnārū[pa],
Vajra, Kana[pa], Namase,
Hora, Siti, Karana,
Bhūti, Mata, Bramana [III.1]

A bird settling on Mount Meru's golden surface
casts off its bird nature and appears to be golden
Once some wise ones {358} realize the unborn,
they cast off the nature of an entity, being greatly blissful[1486] [III.2]

I have been a buddha from the very beginning
but did not see this buddha under the sway of thoughts
At the time of realization, there's nothing to see or to hear[1487]
That through which nonduality is realized is mahāmudrā [III.3]

Just as small children may come to possess strength by being nourished by their mothers,
through the guru's instructions, even those of little insight gradually [enter] the Mahāyāna

Just as the power of medicine dispels all diseases of wind, bile,
and phlegm constellations,
all diseases of clinging to "I" and a self are burned by the instructions of the guru[1488] [III.4]

Just as an entire group of blind people
is guided by a person who has eyes,
those lost[1489] on the path of wisdom
are led to awakening by the guru's eyes [III.5]

Just as the armed forces of a cakravartin king
bring all continents under their power,
through finding the taste of the connate,
you exert power over saṃsāra—great bliss![1490] [III.6]

Being of noble family, supreme family, and the lord of the family,
the gurus, the ḍākinīs, and dharmatā constitute their aids,
the actuality of view, conduct, and meditation is connate,
and the reality of exemplary and actual wisdom is seen [III.7]

The path of fortunate mighty yogīs consists of
the fire[1491] of the three kāyas' luminous dharmatā,
the illusory body of clear and pellucid mind as such,
the very unity of the mudrā of utter freedom [III.8]

The three vows arisen in the beings of the six realms are ornaments
View, meditation, and conduct without clinging represent the ladder
Being aware that your own body has the essence of great bliss,
being free of experiences of blocking, creating, adopting, and rejecting, {359}
and hope and fear being self-luminous are all the guru's kindness [III.9]

Before I gained realization, cooked rice differed greatly from this corpse
Having realization, sweet cooked rice and this rotten corpse are not different
Just so, when lacking realization, I took saṃsāric beings and buddhas to be distinct
At the time of realization, saṃsāric beings have the primordial great buddha's kāya[1492] [III.10]

If letting go of doing, this is the pith instruction
If lacking any wanting, this is realization
Insubstantial bliss constitutes the meditation
If there is nothing to accomplish, this is conduct[1493] [III.11]

The avajra[1494] of means and prajñā is the view,
pervaded by the guru's constant river flow
On the wish-fulfilling tree of the connate,
the fruits are perfect in the state of effortlessness[1495] [III.12]

Since the supreme vow of all buddhas
is your own mind not dwelling in thoughts,[1496]
what is realized by the native mind
is what is beheld by all the buddhas [III.13]

Everything that is heard [and seen] by yogīs is genuinely real
Since they realize the unborn by such seeing, it is the supreme master
Since nonduality is clear through all they do, this is the means
For such persons, the results of virtue and wrongdoing will not be two [III.14]

It is this taste of the connate [stemming]
from the empowerment of the genuine
guru that keeps pervading everything
To be sealed by the unborn is Vajradhara[1497] [III.15]

Inseparable bliss and emptiness are perfect in the pure lotus of the heart
Mental engagement in the unborn is the mind of inconceivable great bliss
Yogīs experience all appearances and sounds as threefold equal taste {360}
With the venerable ones' blessings dawning, this is inseparable, perfect buddhahood[1498] [III.16]

Analyze the entirety of phenomena and your own mind many times!
If your entire understanding is devoid of experiential instructions[1499]
and you are happy about gems that are trinkets as being the true nature,
with dharmas accompanied by that, the inborn bliss with neither hope nor fear perishes [III.17]

First, the intelligent give rise to realization
Second, they meditate on their nose tips in jungles
Once experiences have sprung forth,
they need to become distinguished through conduct[1500] [III.18]

If the connate in someone
causes irritation, pain arises,
just like in the eye of an elephant—
not clinging while relaxing is supreme dhyāna[1501] [III.19]

Bliss! Bliss! This is nonabiding bliss!
The nature of lacking desire is bliss
To know everything imagined as such is bliss
The buddhahood of nothing to accomplish is bliss[1502] [III.20]

Having donned the great armors,
through gem-like perseverance,
steering the ship of my own mind,
great bliss entered this human corpse's inner sanctum[1503] [III.21]

It is by virtue of the mindset of examining and analyzing
anything at any time through anything whatsoever that
we fell under the sway of the evil spirit of clinging to entities
Hence, to not cling to anything at all is the supreme insight [III.22]

It is within the sun of the dharmatā of appearances that
we are thrown into the dark prison of perceiver and perceived
Luminous mind as such—the very dharmakāya itself—
is covered by the web of the darkness of ignorance [III.23]

Nondual great bliss constitutes the kindness of the guru
Naturally arising nonclinging is experience's spaciousness
The nature of being free in itself is the way conduct works
To be free of any hope and fear constitutes the dharmakāya [III.24] {361}

By virtue of being unborn and devoid of imagination,
the great path to awakening is free of thoughts,
nonconceptual, without clinging, and beyond mind
Wherever you search, it is the thought-free state [III.25]

Thanks to the kindness of the guru, the genuine dharma sun,
look at this treasure that consists of the priceless, precious
qualities of a buddha [that are manifesting] from this mind,
with its nature of[1504] naturally stainless means and prajñā! [III.26]

The friend who transcended the reality of delusion,
has cut through the shackles of the afflictions,
and gained mastery over the reality of dharmatā
is the one to see the luminosity that is unborn [III.27]

Eyeless prajñā crushes the evil spirit of entities
Myself and others are the mahāsukhakāya
The experience of not thinking about anything
and being action-free is wisdom's bright lamp [III.28]

Since for those who cling to being and nonbeing
it is difficult to relinquish what, unlike a lamp,
is not an object of the mind, go beyond the mind
and undo the entangled knot of fabrication! [III.29]

The lamp of prajñā that is divorced from means
is just a flower in the sky; the path of prajñā
lacks a mind of clinging to extremes to be relinquished
that are as meaningless as the horns of a rabbit [III.30]

If the actuality of nonduality is realized thereby,
this is not [just] seeing dharmatā; the sun of dharmatā
that is the dharmakāya cannot be distracted at all
It is precisely this that is mahāmudrā [III.31]

The luminous emptiness of saṃsāra and nirvāṇa
that is free of knowledge and knowable objects
constitutes the lamp of prajñā beyond the mind
that cannot be looked at and cannot be shown [III.32]

It is the ship[1505] of incessant compassion
that frees sentient beings without exception
from the great ocean of saṃsāric suffering
so unbearable—{362} it's the ladder of means [III.33]

Appearances and mind not being two, as well as means
and prajñā being inseparable, is the path to awakening
Similar to the case of milk [being mixed] with water,
the experience of equal taste is simply indivisible [III.34]

The nondual wisdom that naturally lacks the stains
of existence, nonexistence, perceiver, perceived,
characteristics, and characterized is dharmatā's lamp
It is the secret of all buddhas in the three times [III.35]

The ground of beings' happiness, suffering,

faults, and qualities, like clouds in the sky,
dwells in all sentient beings without exception,
being similar to a wish-fulfilling jewel [III.36]

Experience free of blocking, creating, hope, and fear
can neither be looked at nor can it be shown
Those who see the true reality of genuine actuality
as being just this genuine actuality are free[1506] [III.37]

To experience appearances with the mind of suffering
of the six classes [of beings] constitutes great bliss
What appears in it, without any common appearances,
is seen thanks to the guru's kindness—this is freedom [III.38]

It is with[1507] the wisdom eye of the sun
of the great goal—awakening's dharmatā—
that the actuality of the ineffable great bliss
of all lamps of experience is seen—bliss! [III.39]

Clinging-free is the experience of those receiving the kindness
of the guru who cuts through the shackles of imagination
Those who remain without having set up the watchman
will never manage to find any bliss within saṃsāra [III.40]

Having heard terms not disconnected from the meaning,
the [resultant] prajñā[1508] is beyond any object; hence,
it is thanks to the kindness of the guru that the mind
comes to possess the qualities of a precious jewel [III.41]

The lamp of the samaya of undistracted faith and respect
represents the treasure of the victors in my own body
It is the source of the arising of the qualities of great bliss {363}
Seeing the actuality that cannot be looked at is very amazing
[III.42]

Not having come from anywhere and being free

of coming or going anywhere, the experience[1509]
of the native state is ineffable, undistractable,
not divorced from meditation, and beyond mind [III.43]

The mind of pure and luminous dharmatā,
awakening's clear illumination, is the dharmadhātu
Find this utterly stainless jewel of the mind
with its kāya of the wisdom of great bliss! [III.44]

Don't look! Great bliss cannot be seen
Don't think! Experience is beyond mind
Don't ponder! Realization is dharmatā's spaciousness
Free of anything to be done, there's nothing to distract [III.45]

The precious experience of resting in what is supreme right now
is[1510] not imaginary but the native state that cannot be distracted
The undistracted basic nature overcoming entities due to clinging to an identity of form
cannot be conceived as any virtue to be adopted or any wrongdoing to be rejected [III.46]

The lamp of wisdom is nonreferential, does not engage mentally,
and cuts through the bondage of the imagination of mindfulness
Flux is cut off within the spaciousness of dharmatā's dharmakāya [III.47]

Since it is not an object seen by the blind without meditation,
to taste this nectar through meditation is the guru's kindness
Within the taste of bliss in the experience of the native state[1511]
of the lineage of blessings, there is nothing to be identified at all [III.48]

Saṃsāra as well as nirvāṇa are without any thoughts
and beyond the sphere of examination and analysis
There is no meditation or object of meditation at all

Abandon the delusion of thoughts of clinging and nonclinging![1512]
[III.49]

Those with the dharmakāya that has the eye
of the dharma are the lamps of the dharma
The two accumulations are the drum of the dharma
The great path to awakening is the conch of the dharma—
the conch[1513] that resounds with luminous selflessness [III.50]
{364}

It is the precious jewel, the wish-fulfilling cow,
the nectar of immortality, the essence-extraction,
the tree that is endowed with flowers and fruits,[1514]
the ocean, Mount Meru, the excellent vase,[1515]
the sky, the sun, the moon, song, dance, and play [III.51]

Having been examined with perception and inference,
true actuality is known; through the trust of seeing
this actuality, as this is accompanied by certainty,
the bond of mother and child, previously acquainted, is faced
[III.52]

Though the dharma and what is not the dharma are equality,
the delusive minds of beings for which they are different
cut off the life force of liberation; the thoughts of this life
are without liberation, being [like] a sea monster's maw [III.53]

For as long as compassion and emptiness are
separate and different, true actuality is not seen
The path of inseparable emptiness and compassion
means not to abide in either saṃsāra or nirvāṇa [III.54]

Nobody wants the entangled knot of objects
due to the thoughts[1516] of the clinging mind
The path of the unborn is filled with the taste
of the connate bliss of sense pleasures [III.55]

Given that experiencing the taste of naturally virtuous
mind as such—the connate that is the directly manifest
great bliss of the native state—cannot be expressed,
the actuality of true reality is not found through signs [III.56]

Since the ignorant with their minds that think
of great bliss as saṃsāra and nirvāṇa are bound,
no matter as what you might be viewing it,
true reality is beyond being an object of mind [III.57]

The path of the great bliss of self-awareness that cannot be pointed out—
the taste of the native state that involves connate mind—is realized
thanks to the guru's kindness; due to the experience of familiarizing
with the unborn, true actuality is seen—the unborn is very amazing! [III.58]

To know the actuality of being free of[1517] the karma
that puts beings into bondage—the realization
of self-aware mind—constitutes supreme nirvāṇa {365}
True reality is free of objects of discursiveness [III.59]

Mind as such, which represents a treasure of precious jewels,
is saṃsāra, nirvāṇa, the nirvāṇa [beyond] existence and peace,
the root of the seminal latent tendencies of virtue and wrongdoing,
and the kāya of finding the path to liberation and awakening [III.60]

Once your own mind is free in the spaciousness
of the sky of dharmatā, all sentient beings
[dawn as] the sun of completely pure wisdom
There is no awakening other than this freedom [III.61]

Though those in saṃsāra are filled with the taste of great bliss,

lacking the means, they do not see the actuality of true reality
In those beings who possess the means and are free of doing,
immortality transcends any objects of coming and going [III.62]

Those who entertain clinging are under the sway
of the evil spirits of entities; for those ignorant ones,
there is no path of becoming liberated from bondage
Hence, to show the path to liberation depends on not clinging [III.63]

The one who mounts the horse of the vāyus is the child of the thinking mind
The bees of perceiver and perceived keep pursuing the sense pleasures,
but what they pursue lacks bliss; cut through saṃsāric roaming and wandering[1518]
and seize the awakening of wisdom—the dharmatā of nāḍīs and vāyus! [III.64]

For those who become empowered by the realization[1519]
of an awareness holder, the sense pleasures are a show
Apart from seeing what is not contingent on self and other,
a mindstream of their own[1520] is not seen, and desire is not satisfied [III.65]

Since phenomena without being and free of being
constitute neither any entities nor [non]entities,
the clinging to them as being such and such
is a mental object, because it is a clinging thought [III.66]

Being empty and emptiness are suitable as fruition
If being under the influence of the great demon
of clinging to entities is not treated like being a slave,
when being stuck in it, this [emptiness] is not seen [III.67]

With a mind full of devotion and supreme, respectful insight, {366}
by[1521] seeing the actuality of the dharmatā of what has a mental body,
the root of the latent tendencies for connecting with rebirth through karma,
the welfare of others is seen like a jewel and a wish-fulfilling tree [III.68]

You are free of the dullness and agitation of samādhi, not agitated
by the winds of thoughts, and endowed with the dharmakāya
free of thoughts—oh guru, you mountain and sun of dharmatā
and the dharmakāya, free us from the darkness of ignorance! [III.69]

Your mind loves beings and you are an immovable
ocean full of compassion—oh glorious vajra holder,
mighty sovereign of compassion, let the wisdom lamp
from your mind's treasure vault be our guide on the path to awakening! [III.70]

You are an immutable wish-fulfilling tree full of flowers and fruits
and filled with the taste of the nectar of immortality—oh kusali,[1522]
through[1523] your playfulness of selfless, nondiscursive great bliss,
show us changeless actuality and vanquish the evil spirit of entities! [III.71]

You are the glorious source of glory who is endowed
with all the qualities of the precious jewel that radiates
the light of unborn luminous emptiness—oh you ācaryā,
utter the sound of nondual emptiness free of discursiveness! [III.72]

You are great bliss, the source of bliss, the secret of all buddhas—
oh you lion so fearless, you mahāpaṇḍita who are free of fear,

like a bee[1524] extracting honey from flowers with nutritious
essence,
show us the actuality of the lamp of the thought-free nature
beyond mind! [III.73]

You inexhaustible treasury of space[-like] qualities
who are adorned with the most supreme of merit,
you fourfold dharma of the wisdom of a buddha,
let us attain the dharma of the dhātu's awakening! [III.74]

You possess the space-like properties of those with insight
into the unborn—{367} unconditioned luminous emptiness,
the dharmakāya free of extremes, selfless, and nondiscursive—
through this sun with such provisions, may we realize wisdom's
actuality! [III.75]

You are the connate nature—the sahajakāya of sentient beings,
the expanse of the nirvāṇa of completely pure properties,[1525]
the thought-free buddha eye with the effortless two
accumulations—
lord of the assembly, chief of the gathering, may we see dhar-
matā's actuality! [III.76]

The union of all buddhas, the union of the bhagavatī ḍākinīs,
the source of bliss, the sun of great bliss, and the glory of all
bliss—
the guru's secret treasury, the treasury with the secret of the
instructions' essential reality—
is selfless great bliss—may we possess this host of great bliss!
[III.77]

Being the principal one with the maṇḍala of the equal taste
that consists of the complete purity of existence and peace,
you are the supreme one within the gaṇacakra assembly—
lord of the assembly, chief of the gathering, may we be glorious!
[III.78]

The emptiness of phenomena's nonbeing,
which is nondual and free from clinging,
is the gaṇacakra of luminous dharmatā—
the actuality of awakening—may we see it! [III.79]

By virtue of the assembly of this gaṇacakra here
that cuts through the bondage of the imagination
of observing an object of meditation and a meditator,
may we possess the transmission of the protector Maitreya! [III.80]

The insight of peace constitutes the expanse of the nirvāṇa of no-self
As long as there is the quintessence of secret mantra's essential reality
that has the continuity of great bliss, supreme bodhicitta, and compassion,
the great[1526] illusory path to awakening is the light of buddha awakening [III.81]

Clinging[1527] to the dualities of being and nonbeing, mobile and immobile, {368}
the path is lost; the all-pervasive lord bhagavān, the lion among humans,
in this city of buddhahood, the most supreme town of the gaṇacakra,
is endowed with the lamp of awakening, the lamplight of wisdom [III.82]

Sentient beings with their pure nature of being buddhas primordially,
due to the cloud banks of the darkness of ignorance of the dull six classes [of beings],
are lacking the correct path, and the sun of the sugata has set for them
It is for them that the blazing wisdom light of gaṇacakra is a huge fire [III.83]

You possess the root of the path to the awakening that is great bliss—
the dharmatā of the nirvāṇa of phenomena being naturally nondiscursive—
you protector of beings who enjoys the bliss of the uncontaminated nirvāṇa[1528]
of the undeclining luminosity of nonduality—may you keep us in mind! [III.84]

You light of awakening of the wisdom sun dispelling the darkness of ignorance,
the awakening of the glorious dharma, the wisdom that is the lamp
of the dharma, oh spiritual friend of awakening, Ātmakṛta,[1529]
with your dharma insight, may you hold us with the dhāraṇī of dharmatā![1530] [III.85]

Oh sole friend of all qualities with a mind that is full of virtue,
firmly rooted in compassion, you are the lion among humans,
the tree of love, the precious gem who is the spiritual friend,
and the inexhaustible great treasure—may your shade[1531] protect us! [III.86]

Glorious principal of all qualities of threefold worldly existence,[1532]
supreme king of humans, crown jewel of all gods and nongods,
genuine foremost lord who is endowed with all qualities—
may we possess the ornaments of the precious gems of the field-born![1533] [III.87]

You are free from thoughts, bhagavān, physician of effortless dharma, {369}
the protector of sentient beings who removes the pain of the afflictions—
oh venerable one, we supplicate you to eradicate the fortunate ones'

unbearable pain of the karmic afflictions brought about by karma [III.88]

Being the dharmatā that is the sugatas' sun, you are endowed with the dharma eye
You are mantra-born through the lamp of the immortal nectar stream of the guru,
[resembling] a stainless, clear, and pellucid crystal [reflecting] the light of the moon—
please purify the entirety of the stains of saṃsāra without any exception at all! [III.89]

Brave one, father of the lamp that dispels the entirety of suffering of beings out of compassion,
glorious one who is the cause of stainless means and prajñā benefiting yourself and others,
incomparable courageous guru with a lineage, the treasury of the entirety of qualities,
free of the ocean of existence, you play as the great hero who interrupts saṃsāra's vicious circle [III.90]

You son who venerates the assembly of the glorious victors and possesses the eye of dharma,
you son who dries up the ocean of saṃsāric existence by venerating the assembly and its lord,
you son who venerates the sugatas and is like an ornament of all the qualities of a great wish-fulfilling tree,
You are the son of the ḍākinīs' secret words and the unborn gaṇacakra of all[1534] buddhas [III.91]

Mother, mother, sole mother! Mother of the bhagavāns, lady of the gaṇacakra's great bliss,
guide to nondual awakening, lady with the eye of the dharma of no-self of the gaṇacakra,
you are the sunlight that opens up the lotus of our minds through your kindness,

the lamp of seeing, hearing, and thinking, and the lamp of awakening that is the wisdom dispelling the darkness of ignorance [III.92] {370}

This garland of precious pearls excellently boosts the extent of the experience, expertise, and realization of yogīs
At the time when the six realms are lacking any of the qualities of these precious jewels,
the children of the buddhas with their eye of the sugata dharma and the family lineage of precious qualities
sever the roots of their latent tendencies through[1535] the path to awakening that is the mahāmudrā of mental nonengagement [III.93]

The great path of the supreme dharma that bears the true actuality of the dharma—dharmatā—and possesses this delightful golden garland
is the dharma treasure that is the precious jewel of the protectors of beings who are the all-embracing sovereigns born from nondual wisdom,
the very intention of their pure minds that behold the way of being of what is meaningful and see the actuality of the freedom of the piṭakas
Since it is thanks to their kindness that the unseen is seen, the actuality of great bliss as on the path of seeing is seen,
the lamp of trust free of a mind with doubts is the clear, pellucid, and stainless awakening that is free of thoughts,
and the clinging-free experience of the native state—the sun of luminous dharmatā—clears away the darkness of ignorance [III.94]

With its roots of latent tendencies and karma linked by the aspiration prayers for encountering it,
the tree of awakening that is endowed with the beautiful trunk of the motivation as well as

the flowers and fruits of accomplishment [casts] its cool shade of
trust in karma and its results,
so why should the children of aspiration prayers not come across
it, just like meeting their mother with whom they have been
familiar from before? [III.95]

This is the third chapter, the one of the third gaṇacakra (nondual self-lucid trust], in *A Golden Garland of Mahāmudrā.*

This concludes "A Precious Golden Garland of Mahāmudrā Vajra Songs." {371} *It consists of teachings by many yogīs and paṇḍitas who had attained siddhi, instructions that were compiled into a single text by the venerable mighty adept Maitrīpa. It was translated by this paṇḍita himself and lotsāwa Marpa Chökyi Lodrö.* {372}

(184) A Letter to Prajñā

In the language of India: *Prajñālekhanāma*[1536]
In the language of Tibet: *Shes rab kyi phrin yig ces bya ba*

I pay homage to venerable Avalokiteśvara and the goddess Tārā

You are the completely pure jewel of threefold true reality,
more secret than secret, appearing as the learned and monastics
Oh goddess, ground of omnipresent and supreme great bliss,
you represent the ultimate prajñā—to you, I pay homage [1]

May this be the cause for attaining the outcome of the buddha state!
What appears like a wish-fulfilling jewel and the excellent vase
is this letter about very secret true reality[1537] worth listening to
I shall send this explanation of the state of true reality's actuality [2]

Then, in order to benefit practitioners,
Padmavajra, in this letter to prajñā,
shall clearly elucidate the true reality
that is much more secret than secret [3]

Svasti, pure and completely free,
you are unborn, similar to space,

to be known by sheer self-awareness,
the lady bestowing supreme ecstasy [4]

Without characteristics, without appearance,
devoid of any being and nonbeing, {373}
you are the supremely stainless state
that is called "dharmadhātu's nature" [5]

Devoid of all that is not the characteristics,
with all characteristics being fully perfect,
you are the ground of stainless selflessness,
the immaculate source of the three vajras [6]

You are the locus of the intended goal,
arising just like a wish-fulfilling jewel
Similar to the gods' wish-fulfilling tree,
you are the object of supreme veneration [7]

This goddess who has taken up residence there
is the goddess of prajñā who is unsurpassable
Through the union of the inseparable three vajras,
she is endowed with the lotus of true reality [8]

You lady who bestow supreme ecstasy
through the nature of the inner abode,
Please understand us in a complete way
through the nature of being and nonbeing! [9]

Though you dwell in my own body
without waves and without appearance,
great blazing lady, it's at this very time[1538]
that I fail to perceive you [10]

Oh lady who embodies supreme ecstasy,
you are ravishing because you lack a nature

Since you are unborn, you are the lady
whose omniscience pervades everything [11]

With the five excellent sense pleasures,
you are omnipresent in bodies over bodies
It is in all places, such as in the hells,
that you play through secret conduct [12]

You are devoid of any color and limbs,
being so much more secret than secret
I have realized you thanks to the kindness
stemming from glorious great bliss [13]

Oh all-pervasive lady who is immaculate,
your sole characteristic is self-awareness
In order to realize you, I am resting {374}
right within the unborn, just as it is [14]

In order to terminate any clinging to being
or nonbeing as supreme, I rest just as it is
Thanks to the kindness coming from the guru,
I realized you lady of virtue just as you are
and, by virtue of possessing perfect respect,
I also familiarized with you as much as I could [15]

Though all that is true, why is it that
we did not become one until now?
Or is it that I don't have the fortune?
Why is it that you do not reside in my
mindstream through perfect union,
just as you have declared you would? [16]

Pure by virtue of your own nature,
oh lady leading to full awakening,
in the five skandhas, three vajras,
and such, true actuality is present [17]

The mouth of the glorious master,
with a mind steeped in compassion,
tells me about true actuality just as it is
to make me completely realize it thus [18]

The protector of glorious great bliss
lets my mind arise in your true state
By granting your speech and abiding,
there is no doubt about this here [19]

Though I meditated day and night
after I clearly realized true reality,
since reality is not appearing
clearly, is it empty or what? [20]

Like[1539] a wish-fulfilling jewel and space,
the perfect Buddha described this indeed
The words that he spoke in such a way
are true and not true, respectively [21]

Though its being similar to space is true,
and some meditate by understanding this,
since the true state doesn't manifest clearly, {375}
its being like a wish-fulfilling jewel is a lie [22]

I do understand that ultimately
you are appearing everywhere
Still, since I do not perceive you,
I cling to forms that are illusory clusters [23]

The perfect Buddha said that ultimately,
both flaws and qualities are certainly
like what comes from friends gathering
This statement of his rings true [24]

Oh prajñā, you who speak the truth,
those for whom the nature of realization
is combined with fourfold identitylessness
are resting in concordance with that [25]

Oh excellent lady who blazes stainlessly,
nevertheless, those who know your character
may then analyze you for a long time and yet
not perceive you—where do you hide? [26]

Embodiment of bestowing supreme ecstasy,
you are the one leading to full awakening
Through raising the brilliance of the lamp
of wisdom clearly in the ten directions,
you are the lady displaying scents, garlands,
and so on, clothes, food, and likewise others [27]

Though I have relied on prajñā
all the time without interruption
through the union of nonduality,
there's not even an instant of change [28]

You who allow for stainless clear realization,
it is by way of maintaining the samaya
of your pure realization of suchness
that you show the path to awakening [29]

Just as we find it said in the tantras,
by continuously and uninterruptedly
relying on all five sense pleasures,
beginning with the children of mine,
it is by relying on and familiarizing with you
through being very aware of your character {376}
that you serve as the very ground of virtue,
so why do you not have any trust in me? [30]

"Who[1540] would develop any trust
in a woman who is of two minds?"
This statement by the perfect protector
is one that is based squarely on the truth
From among the entirety of all illusions,
the most distinguished one is a woman[1541] [31]

Though some have served you in all respects
by way of benefiting you in numerous ways
and looked in the entirety of the three realms,
you don't even appear—where do you dwell? [32]

If some childish beings meditate on you
without being mindful of your essential point,
they will be ruined in a meaningless manner
and you won't be there as awakening's cause [33]

If those who know this essential point
properly have familiarized with you,
they abide in order to become buddhas
until the very heart of awakening [34]

Even those who know you directly, excellent lady,
but who have not managed to familiarize with you,
end up with you, lady friend, joining hands with them
No matter whether they are of low or high caste,
if they know the key point, they become your beloved,
and so you, excellent lady, also illuminate them within [35]

Although it is the nature of the vile,
whose being is not that of a beloved,[1542]
to commit faults at times, it is certain
that you will look at the lotus faces
of such persons and restrain them [36]

Exactly this is the path to be entered
by people who are of noble descent too
Even if they omit some mere words,
nothing changes, even when they die [37]

Both do spring from this pure family, {377}
being born as people of noble descent
Do's and don'ts are not different here,
nor are being a vessel or a nonvessel [38]

At times, making offerings to you
in all respects, I did not take a look
Thus, I now comprehended this
sphere of your family, oh prajñā [39]

The nature of women is to be
utterly tempting and deceitful
With lips, palate, and so on dry,
what's the point of exposing many hidden flaws? [40]

If one familiarizes with you day and night,
not being distracted for even an instant,
it is in just an instant that you let them
attain the state that is unsurpassable [41]

Those who closely familiarized with you
did not know before this kind of conduct
of yours that is the cause of the state
of buddhahood, just as it was taught [42]

What's the purpose of saying much?
There's nothing for the mind to rely on
If those who are ignorant due to regret,
sleep, and oblivion do not know you,
you must speak up in a clear manner
about that which is your own nature! [43]

Since the three vajras arise from seeds,
they are undoubtedly produced by three
Since all sentient beings are oblivious
due to stains such as desire and hatred,
even among many billions of them,
there is nobody who knows you [44]

What's the purpose of saying a great deal?
Just like being surrounded by cunning harlots,
there is nothing that is established ultimately,
so you're the lady assuming supreme illusion's form [45]

I have not known you by being oblivious
for billions of eons that are countless {378}
By being attached to food, drink, and so on,
I plunge into saṃsāric existence's dungeon [46]

Through being very attached to such things,
I keep forgetting you who bestow wealth
Through engaging in the passion of a mudrā,
I'll be victorious, supreme vajra-bearing lady [47]

Thanks to the venerable guru's kindness,
I will come to know the entirety
of your nature, oh excellent lady,
in exactly the way that it truly is [48]

Through having realized the entirety
of your nature without any exception,
I cannot be deceived even in dreams
Therefore, turn your mind toward me! [49]

It is your path that is the one and only
The wise who entered it through training
according to procedure meet the buddhas—
this was taught by the victorious ones [50]

For as long as I have not
trained in this profundity,
I do not find the bliss arising
from the touch of your body [51]

Due to the pit of dullness's density,
the rising of the tree log of hatred,
and the pathetic thorn of desire,
the path to awakening is hard to travel [52]

The tree of the skandhas lacks beginning and end
With the sense pleasures' branches reaching upward,
the vast expanse of the sky is becoming shrouded
Thus, they are in place tightly blocking that path [53]

Being surrounded by the great abundance
of the skandhas, the afflictions, and likewise
the lord of death, gods, māras, and robbers,
so hateful, is the jungle with saṃsāric existence's
plants, twigs, kings of stones,[1543] and such
that keeps growing from great thoughts [54]

Being very vast and so difficult to cross, {379}
by relying on the chariot of the skandhas,
the pit of oblivion is a place hard to traverse,
being completely hidden in the sanctuary
of imagination's grass, greenery, and such [55]

Gods, māras, robbers, and so forth
dwell in this kind of place
Travelers who entered the correct path
are vanquished out of utter hatred
by those who rob the gem of the mind [56]

As the great treasury of the three jewels
that is full of the wealth of qualities

becomes spotted by the watchman
dwelling on the path to awakening,
with the axe of the vajra of wisdom
that has such a sharply grinded blade,
he cuts down the tree of the skandhas
that blocks the path to awakening [57]

Having been cut up according to procedure,
the logs[1544] of the afflictions with their thorns
that grow out of the tree of the mind
are to be burned in the fire of selflessness [58]

The mound of the stones of pride
is pulverized by the vajra of prajñā
The density of the pit of oblivion
is filled[1545] by incessant bodhicitta [59]

The lord of death, māras, robbers, and so on,
all of whom are difficult to tame and who harm
the travelers who have entered the correct path,
will take flight by virtue of being defeated [60]

Once the path to awakening is wide open,
the hateful dwelling in the ten directions,
who linger in order to obstruct awakening,
are vanquished through making efforts
with the body of means without stains
as well as the sharp sword of prajñā
Then, having entered this excellent path,
they all proceed on it as they please [61] {380}

Having thus trained in the path to awakening,
they become utterly and completely stainless
Hence, having trained in you, oh lady friend,
who are so wonderful as well as inconceivable,
they are naturally stainless, pure, and peaceful [62]

Being granted the desired goal's fruition,
the equality of selfless self-awareness,
they will attain the unsurpassable state
If your nature's taste is experienced,
even the buddhas cannot express it
by proclaiming, "It is like that" [63]

What's attained is unborn self-awareness,
to which all the buddhas pay homage
and which is beyond the sense faculties
Arising from supreme ecstasy, it is pure [64]

The state that is very hard to find,
inconceivable, unsurpassable,
and called "the abode of nirvāṇa,"
is what leads to full awakening [65]

It will be attained through the single dharma
of meditating throughout day and night
on the kindness from the guru's mouth
It will not be attained by anything other
than such meditating with utter respect [66]

This is pure by its nature,
unconditioned at all times,
devoid of permanence and extinction,
stainless means and prajñā [67]

Those realizing this as being unborn
should know it to be the unsurpassable
and inconceivable buddha awakening
that's fully present in all sentient beings [68]

It is this state of the entirety of all buddhas
that allows for the attainment of buddhahood
Having realized the nature of the actuality

of[1546] mind and mental factors in that way,
unite with the three stainless vajras!
If this is understood and familiarized with,
through uniting with the vajra of wisdom, {381}
the lady friend will be accomplished by that [69]

Being beyond being and nonbeing,
you are all-pervasive, just like space—
the guide declared, "You should rely
on stainless peace including means!" [70]

Neither through you, if you lack the means,
nor through the means, if they lack you—
through any of these two lacking the other,
there will never be any accomplishment [71]

Being endowed with the means,
you, my beloved, are as you should be
If I already realized you completely,
other than this, what is there to say? [72]

If I, until the essence of awakening,
rely on[1547] the kindness from the guru's
mouth as being the buddha's in person,
I will thus be covered in such kindness [73]

From the mouth of glorious great bliss,
to you, oh lady of great insight
who is endowed with the means,
the cause for me becoming a buddha,
Padmavajra, in accord with the words
of the message that the buddha spoke
with certainty, and for the sake of providing
my supreme lady friend with the means,
the vajra holder of glorious great bliss
sends his letter with these words here;

accordingly, serve swiftly as the cause
for me becoming a buddha in this way! [74]

As clear as can be, swiftly bestow your
instantaneous awakened activity upon me!
Do not make me live this life of mine[1548]
while you abandon or forget me! [75]

With dullness and agitation relinquished,
during all times throughout the day and night,
I remember you in each and every moment,
continuously and without any interruption, {382}
so grant me the entire actuality of the siddhis!
In case that does not come to pass,
at such a time, I will be downcast,
so please look at how you're doing! [76]

Having bound me with the rope[1549]
of the mindstream's suchness as it is,
oh virtuous lady, you place me
in the home of true actuality [77]

Through having completely guarded me
with the nature of the mind and mental factors
that realize this to be unborn,
on the supreme buddhabhūmi of true reality,
you bind me with the iron chains of the means
and drive home the vajra nail of wisdom,
placing me in the fortress of selflessness—
it is then that I shall gain accomplishment! [78]

Thus, I have sent you the message
that needed to be sent just as it is
Avoiding restraint[1550] and flattery,
oh excellent lady, I said it all to you,
but if you still don't feel love for me,

what more is there to say at this point?
But if it isn't so, oh vajra-holding lady,
in your heart, just let these bad omens be! [79]

I am aware of the specific features
of your path and your training;
your family, your form's nature,
your source, and your ultimate state
I am understanding as well—
hence, turn your mind toward me! [80]

Being endowed with the supreme of means
thanks to the kindness from the guru's mouth,
Since I have already seized and shackled
that which makes me rush here and there
with the solid rope of what is to be known,
where would there be a place to escape to now? [81]

Hence, oh goddess, since you are fond of me,
please consider your samaya of mastery {383}
and protect me with the ocean of qualities
of the words coming from glorious great bliss! [82]

Being aware of your ungraspable
and wonderful nature, just as it is,
following your words, I shall engage
in the conduct of glorious great bliss [83]

It is thanks to the kindness of the words
from the mouth of glorious great bliss
that I have composed a letter to prajñā,
unequaled and with secret vajra words [84]

It is this self-arising nectar of wisdom,
born from churning knowable objects' milk ocean
with the churning rod of the mountain of prajñā,
that allows us to perceive buddhahood directly[1551] [85]

Those persons who have understood
this letter to prajñā completely and
familiarized themselves fully with it
will become genuine vajra holders [86]

This concludes "A Letter to Prajñā" composed by the great master Padmavajra. It was translated, edited, and finalized by Mahāpaṇḍita Śāntabhadra and the Tibetan editor-lotsāwa Gö Lhedsé. {384}

(185) Dispelling the Obstacles of the Thoughts of Yogīs[1552]

I pay homage to the venerable true gurus and Śrī Vajrasattva

You may wonder about the why, who, with what, and how of meditation,
its signs, qualities, hindrances and obstacles, and the dispelling of flaws
Through gaining familiarity while knowing those, awakening is attained
Not having heard and knowing them, there's no accomplishment, or it's tardy [1]

First, why meditate? Even if yogīs who do not relinquish the duality
of perceiver and perceived and do not meditate in a proper way
pay homage, make offerings, confess, and practice generosity a lot,[1553]
their merit may increase, but their wisdom will not be perfected [2]

Second, who [meditates]? Those who are endowed with yoga,
are well-studied and vigorous, keep their samayas and oaths,
make offerings, are generous, have faith, and possess bodhicitta
represent the vessels of the secret Mahāyāna and meditate [3]

Third, with what [do they meditate]? They are always resting,
without any distraction, in their own mind, in just the way it is,
which is uncontrived, primordially pure, free of discursiveness,
lacking the extremes of existence, nonexistence, permanence, and extinction [4]

Fourth, how is it that they meditate? Within the very own essence
of the nonduality of something to meditate on and meditation, {385}
there is nothing whatsoever and yet it appears as anything whatsoever—
they meditate lucidly without dullness, oblivion, or discursive thoughts [5]

Fifth, its signs are that in yogīs who are endowed with vigor,
first, it is sleep and greedy craving that will become diminished
Then, gradually, [the same goes for] desire and so on in their dreams,
and they show forms of miraculous displays according to their realization [6]

Sixth, their qualities arise in terms of thinking, expression,
direct perception, a prolonged life, healing sicknesses,
dispelling obstacles, and many qualities other than these
Accordingly, they progressively enter the path to awakening [7]

Seventh, as for hindrances and obstacles, if yogīs wish to go
somewhere else by leaving one place and seeking another,
they simply desire to go from one yakṣa to another
Once yogīs entered their minds, they cast off other places [8]

If yogīs who remain in a certain place while meditating
stopped speaking but then, when others enter or exit,
start seeking food and wealth due to haughtiness and craving,
the evil spirit of a greedy hungry ghost has entered their mind [9]

If yogīs whose minds are disturbed wish to quarrel,
Scold their retinues and revile others,
it is indeed the lord of the bhūtas, Yavaṣonapa,
who has entered the heart of such practitioners [10]

Should yogīs take pleasure in lying around and sleeping,
crave food and drink, and make no effort in chanting,
the mahoraga[1554] called "the slothful one vigorous in sleep"
entered the minds of such yogīs, making them hang out [11]

Should yogīs guard the conditions of their own possessions {386}
and daily necessities, appoint guardians[1555] to stake their claims,
seek sense pleasures to accumulate them, and wish to give them to others,
the yakṣa named Dhanarakṣa has entered their mind [12]

Should yogīs, out of attachment to their parents and the assemblies
of their siblings, protect them with aspiration prayers and services,
it is by virtue of their innate latent tendencies not becoming purified
that their afflictions are not relinquished, and awakening will be far [13]

If yogīs calculate courses and powers of stars and planets,
as well as positive and negative times, years, and months,
since they are in contradiction to inseparable equality,
it will be very difficult for them to attain awakening [14]

Should yogīs who are vastly erudite, are endowed with great realization,
and strive in meditation praise themselves and disparage others out of arrogance,
since they do not relinquish their afflictions and their pride will increase,

they will suffer downfalls later as well, and awakening will be far away [15]

If hatred arises in yogīs, thinking, "I am harmed
by others in the past, at present, or in the future,"
and they cast awareness mantras so as to kill them,
under the sway of hatred, awakening will be far off [16]

Should their minds become delighted in others providing offerings
and services to them, praising them profusely, and extolling them,
they become partial toward beings; due to such an attached mind,
they will thus also be very distant from[1556] the path to awakening [17]

If yogīs who are surrounded by the clamor of many retinues
rely on large crowds of people, similar to a king,
their haughtiness causes their meditation to be distracted
and they will be very far from the path to awakening [18]

Eighth, as for the means to dispel[1557] flaws, {387} if the signs
of any kinds of hindrances emerge in the minds of yogīs,
they need to dispel thoughts about such signs by thinking thus:
however it may appear as phenomena, there's nothing else than mind [19]

When in the nature of the mind, whose essence is dharmatā,
obstacles arise under the sway of thoughts over thoughts[1558]
about good, bad, adopting, rejecting, greed, love, hate, and such,
if mind is looked at, nothing whatsoever is appearing [20]

So how could there be thoughts or signs in a mind without appearances?
Since it is a flaw to take mind as being thoughts about a self or signs,

abandon the entirety of thoughts and keep resting without any
thoughts,
but there exists no resting within some absence of thoughts either
[21]

If resting like that for a long time, the obstacles of thoughts
will swiftly subside;[1559] in those who meditate accordingly,
the thoughts of mind that are hindrances will not emerge
and the fruition of awakening will quickly be attained [22]

This concludes "Dispelling the Obstacles of the Thoughts of Yogīs" composed by the great master and paṇḍita Buddhaguhya who had attained[1560] *siddhi.*[1561] {388}

(186) The Inconceivable and Supremely Secret Hidden Path of the Five Poisons

I pay homage to Śrī Cakrasaṃvara

It is after the childish that the childish keep following
Since it is the childish who will destroy[1562] the childish,
here, in order to liberate the childish, I shall explain
delivering[1563] the bondage of the childish onto the path

Thus is my motivation to explain this.

Here, as for "the vinaya being accomplished fruitfully," the mahāyoga tantras say:

Those who are fettered by their oblivion
and at their wailing's end become certain,
are exactly the ones who will become free
and attain bliss through the power of prajñā[1564]

The wise should rely on the meaning of this. Since they are the supreme to be instructed in this, I shall first examine the tantras.[1565]

Here, as for [persons who have] proportionate [afflictions], though afflictions such as desire may not arise for a long time, it is not [the case] that through a given thing desire and so on toward this [thing] will not emerge [ever again]. As for those with small afflictions, afflictions arise slowly toward desirable things and so on that are big, multiple, excessive, and [directly] encountered and manifest. {389} Toward medium and small [such things], [their afflictions] are very subtle.

As for persons who engage in desire, if they have great desire even for small and bad desirable things, forget about the opposites of those [things]—they are attached to them for a long time. Their faculties are supple, gentle, and not rude;[1566] they do not inflict harm on others through body or speech; they have difficulties making decisions; they are interested in what is inferior; they are tolerant; they are not withdrawn and are without unhappy states of mind; they have many joys, do not scowl, and have a radiant complexion; their smile precedes them; their skin color is rosy; they walk swiftly; they speak with sighs; and all kinds of erratic ways of thinking stir in them.

As for persons who possess hatred, their skin color is dark, they are strong, walk forcefully, speak rudely, and have malice for all. If they become ensnared intensely and many times by anger, hating small things, what need is there to mention medium and big [things]—they make them remain [angry] for a long time. Their faculties are not supple and not gentle, they inflict harm on others, it is easy for them to make decisions and easy to become weary, they talk nonsense, are very impudent, are disinterested in many things, have strict actions and strict spiritual disciplines, have many unhappy states of mind, are often disturbed, are difficult to stop, live doing harm, scowl, {390} and their facial complexion is not radiant.

As for persons who possess ignorance, if they become ensnared intensely and many times by ignorance over small things that one should be oblivious to, what need is there to mention medium and big [things] that make them remain [ignorant] for a long time. Their faculties are slow, dull, and weak; their physical actions are lax and their verbal actions are lax [too]; they think mistakenly, speak mistakenly, and commit mistaken actions; they are very lazy, unable to accomplish things; their speaking is weak; they don't apply their mind; due to forgetfulness, they do not engage in alertness; they misperceive; it is difficult for them to make decisions and difficult to become weary; they are interested in what is inferior; they are dense, stutter, and are stupid; they gesture with their hands; they are unable to understand any meanings of dharmas that are excellently delivered or explained in a flawed manner; they are carried away by conditions;[1567] they depend on the kindness of others; their complexion is uncertain; and they move slowly.

As for persons who possess pride, if they become ensnared intensely and many times by pride, being haughty over small things, forget about medium and big [things]—they make them remain [proud] for a long time. Their faculties are agitated, their faculties are as high as reed; they are haughty; they make efforts in greatly adorning their bodies; [they] use strong words and do not bow down; they do not venerate persons like parents, relatives, and gurus appropriately in a given situation in the three times; they do not bow with their bodies; they speak in a straightforward manner; {391} they do not have the character of paying homage, standing up out of respect, folding their hands, or prostrating; they cling to themselves; they praise themselves and disparage others, desire gain, homage, and services; they desire fame; they represent dull vessels; it is difficult for them to make decisions and they become weary; they are not interested in what is vast; they have little compassion; they prioritize views about the self, the sentient being, the life force, the soul,[1568] and the person; they have a very fierce wrath; and they possess delusion. The signs of pride accord with such [characteristics].

As for persons who possess envy, it is said that their skin color is dark bluish, they move around where [people] do not gather, speak in harmful ways to others, and all kinds of erratic ways of thinking stir in them. A master should definitely examine these [signs] and provide instructions on them. The following is said:

> [Bhikṣus, just as experts do with gold,]
> by burning, cutting, and rubbing it,
> accept my words after examining them,
> but not merely out of respect[1569]

Since this is stated, to assert direct[1570] liberation to be inconceivable, to assert impure causes to be inconceivable, to assert a mere fraction to be inconceivable, and to assert utter extinction to be inconceivable constitute the signs of the reality[1571] of the oblivious ones—they are what is to be completely relinquished by the wise. What is to be adopted is the inconceivable highest secret, which {392} is sixfold: the inconceivable secret, the inconceivable patience, the inconceivable means, the inconceivable sleep,[1572] the inconceivable transition, and the inconceivable fruition. The inconceivable secret consists of the unsurpassable instructions.[1573] The inconceivable patience consists of bringing the five poisons onto the hidden path. Though some [elements] of the inconceivable secret and so on are no doubt included in the five poisons,[1574] this is something that has an underlying intention.

How are the five poisons brought onto the path? It is declared:

> What is the emptiness of one,
> that is the emptiness of all[1575]

Therefore, just as it is with the emptiness of desire, so it is with [the emptiness of] hatred and so on. Now, since the attachment that arises for a single pleasant inner or outer form and so on is not established as any color and so on, the extreme of permanence is eliminated. Just as [one arrives at the existence of] cognition due to inferring it from [the existence of] the vāyus, it is by way of its unceasing cognizant awareness that [that attachment] is not something extinct [either]. Nor is there any entity in between these two that has the character of both of them. Hence, a fourth [possibility]—a true reality that is to be inferred by a cognition during subsequent attainment—does not exist as any kind of discursiveness in time whatsoever either. That desire is not relinquished but is completely pure is also said with regard to hatred and so on. This is not contradictory in terms of being mutually exclusive. It is stated that through realizing the dharmadhātu, {393} all objects without exception are to be rendered poison-free.[1576] As mentioned before, emptiness is to be applied to everything.[1577]

The means of searching for the five poisons are to be regarded just as in the [following] case of searching for hatred. When the morning rises, make the following aspiration prayer: "Today, since any of my[1578] entities of hatred, whether they arose through myself[1579] or consist of the mutual fighting or arising of hatred between [me and my] opponents or between others, are expedients to attain the supreme siddhi, may I feel any hatred that may emerge!" At the time it is felt, this very hatred is to be treated as being inconceivable. If hatred does not emerge on this day, give rise to a memory of some hatred that arose previously in yourself, some [previous arising of] mutual hatred, or some [previous] arising of hatred between others, and then treat it as lacking any nature of its own. Thus, [in this case too,] make an aspiration prayer like the one in the morning. By dealing with it in that way, the poison of hatred is to be rendered harmless. When you understand all instances of arising hatred to be the path, you should understand the same with regard to the other poisons as well.

By virtue of persons with hateful minds taking hatred as their commitment, this [hatred] becomes workable, and the same will come easily with desire and so on. Accordingly, whatever is the biggest stain[1580] should be made a commitment first. Then, to apply this to the other [afflictions] is just as [with the ones] before. As for the proportionate and small afflictions, at the beginning, {394} any one can be taken as a commitment and they should be made workable and gradually be removed. Why is that? If some persons who are beginners are not instructed in [the point that one of the afflictions is] the foremost [to tackle],[1581] since [all] the five poisons arise in many [instances], they may not have the heartfelt desire to direct their minds [toward all of these afflictions right away], and thus their engagement will grow lax. [All] those [instructions] are not to be taught prior [to the individual practice]; at the time of meditating [in this way], it is precisely the point of the teaching that precedes [this meditation]—the instruction for a certain [affliction] to begin with—that constitutes the instruction about the [specific] commitment [during that time of meditation].

This very [point of] entering fearlessness by taming the fears of the five poisons is the highest secret. [Only] very excellent vessels are to be instructed in this, not bad vessels who behave heedlessly by relying on mere words.

As for the inconceivable means, it is said:

> Be it oblations or chanting,
> maṇḍalas, fire or water activities,
> mudrās, offering parasols and such,[1582]
> prostrations, circumambulations,

something casted or painted and so on,
or composition such as writing sacred words,
at all times, yogīs should treat
everything as nonconceptual by nature

They do not fall asleep heedlessly,
similar to the case of a closed lotus
being closed under the sway of shadow
yet unfolding by virtue of the shadow gone

Lucidity[1583] having passed constitutes unawareness
By the power of the rarified[1584] becoming dense,
similar to breaths condensing on a mirror's orb,
gradual withdrawal is what represents unawareness

Having been purified by means of prajñā,
it is definitely absorbed into the other one {395}
This is familiarity with the mind of strong effort,
without becoming weary of not being familiar
and without any doubts due to being familiar

The *Guhyasamāja[tantra]* states:

What is inconceivable at the time of transition
is the transition through the force of karma
and the pith instruction for yogīs seeking death

After having seen the object of meditation
to be a mirage and so on, rest in true reality,
and the vajra body is naturally accomplished

Having relinquished the transition of seven,
saṃsāric existence is not entered, the two extremes are cast off
By preparing with the mindset of application,
you will rise by seeing and be made not to enter
There's no going beyond, the supreme is accomplished

Whether it is the feet, the mouth, or the navel,
the heart, the crown of the head, or the eyes,
from wherever the vāyus will be transiting,
according to this order, rebirth is obtained
as hell beings, hungry ghosts, animals,
human beings, gods, or wisdom

Then, having blocked the other gates,
the vāyus are to be expelled through the eyes,
coming to rest in the face of the guru
Likewise, death seekers rest on that face

The persons who do not know this yoga
should make their minds that assumed
births as humans or gods one-pointed

It is among the vajraḍākinīs as well that
the mind at the point of death is chief
Thus, however you think, so it will be[1585]

"Will it also be like that for those with wrongdoings?" It will not:

Due to the karma of great wrongdoing, you may wish
for the pith instructions but not encounter them for eons,
and even if you were to encounter them, due to strokes,
insanity, and so forth, you will not remember them[1586] {396}

You may say, "But even if those who gathered the accumulations lack this [particular] state of mind at the point of passing, they are born in the pleasant realms." Even if you have gathered a lot of accumulations, if a bad state of mind arises at the point of death, this is just as in the case of King Ajātaśatru.[1587] Therefore you should make great efforts with regard to the inconceivable at the point of passing.

The inconceivable fruition consists of the kāyas and wisdoms. It is said:

Just as gold's shining nature never diminishes[1588]
even when it has been placed within excrement,
the honorable[1589] never let go of their thinking's nature,
even when they are engaging in worldly dharmas[1590]

Therefore even when the form kāyas promote the welfare of beings, they lack any bad worldly activities. Thus, though cause and result are in all respects nothing but nondual and the five poisons are to be sought out very much, under the sway of being habituated since beginningless time to what is mistaken, you lack [genuine] prajñā, and thus wrong prajñā stirs. Hence, [as a beginner you need to] dwell in solitude. Once the power of nonconceptuality has been found, even if you walk into the middle of a crowd and are neither divorced from mindfulness [there] nor fall under the sway of others, no matter what may arise—hatred and so on—the time has come [to leave your solitude]. Or, you should become a mendicant—don't dwell in a single place for a long time: humans and dogs are similar. Hence, just as dogs are very strong in their own place but will become subdued in other locations, it is difficult for humans to subdue their afflictions in their own place but in other locations it is easier for the afflictions {397} to become workable. Therefore you should keep to the way of life of a mendicant.

Through the merit I achieved,
may all be without any harm!
No matter which path is traveled,
may this accomplish buddhahood!

This concludes "The Inconceivable and Supremely Secret Hidden Path of the Five Poisons" composed by master Āryadeva.[1591] {398}

(187) The Reality of the Characteristics of Yoga

In the language of India: *Yogalakṣaṇasatya*[1592]
In the language of Tibet: *Rnal 'byor gyi mtshan nyid bden pa*

I pay homage to venerable Tārā

To the buddhas of all directions and times,[1593]
plus the dharma and the saṃgha assemblies,
I respectfully pay homage with folded hands
and then shall explain in a brief manner
this pith instruction on cultivating yoga,
resembling a collection[1594] of assorted jewels,
in order to lead yogīs to liberation [1]

Waking up in the last part of the night,
first of all, I shall cultivate compassion
for all sentient beings other than myself
Thereafter, by looking at myself,
throughout this very day today,
I shall not be tainted by any stains
of miserliness toward begging beings,
no matter how long they approach [2]

If I am not to engage in my thinking
in even the subtlest mental movement

that is in contradiction to the trainings,
what need to mention body and speech? [3]

Today, may anger, beating,
and so forth happen to me!
I shall not be disturbed even by that,
but if laziness dawns, through alertness, {399}
I cast it out as if my head were ablaze [4]

No matter whether I walk, lie down, or sit,
however I may be involved in any conduct,
without being separated for even an instant
from the pride of the deity in my mind,
I shall always think that I myself am it [5]

Cognitions and objects of cognition,
within saṃsāra as well as nirvāṇa,
I shall examine from today on [6]

Praise and blame, fame and disgrace,
no matter how others may voice them,
I shall take them to be like echoes
and myself to be like a deaf person [7]

Wherever objects of consciousness becoming scattered
toward the five sense pleasures—forms, sounds, smells,
tastes, and tangibles to be attached to—may be emerging,
not letting them emerge in speech, I stop them in between [8]

What appears as form makes up the kāya
Sounds I examine to be awakened speech
Since beings are the cause of awakening,
it is their cognitions that are wisdom [9]

However I may see sentient beings,
I shall pay homage to them in my mind

Since it is through relying on them
that I will accomplish buddhahood,
they are genuine spiritual friends [10]

When crowds of people have gathered,
I regard them as corpses in charnel grounds
When I am stepping into a village,
I regard it as a prison or a dungeon [11]

When I go the palace of a king,
I regard it as the miserable realms,
a disease, a bondage, and a great abyss [12]

If I come to see an assembly of women,
I think they consist of the thirty impure
substances and are the guides to saṃsāra [13]

I abandon attachment to my ancestors, parents, children,
and grandchildren, {400} thinking of them with equanimity
If I happen to see enemies, I will think that the patience
that I owe to them constitutes perfect awakening [14]

What I think about these material possessions of mine
is that they are the causes of dispute in this very life
and will lead me to the miserable realms in the next [15]

Even if praises are uttered for me,
since they are boosting my pride,
they lead me to the miserable realms
Even if I encounter any disparaging,
I cultivate patience, thinking that even
awakening's marks are complete in it [16]

If clinging to a place has arisen,
yogīs shall meditate on its being
similar to a city in a dream [17]

Throughout this very day today,[1595]
I shall do my chants and recitations
Not contradicting the trainings such as reading,
I shall be speaking on this present day [18]

The entirety of my physical movements,
such as offering and circumambulating,
I shall render a meaningful resting at ease [19]

If thoughts are not controlled by remedies,[1596]
what's accomplished by speaking them out loud?
For that reason, in each and every respect,
I shall raise this army of the remedies
and thus eradicate the afflictions [20]

When consuming delicious food and drink,
I shall relinquish clinging to their taste
and think they arise from impure causes,
just turning into body waste in the end [21]

When I am feeling soft tangible objects,
I shall reflect on what tangibles are like
What need is there to say any more here? [22]

Be it householders or those who left their home
toward whom my afflictions are increasing,
I shall thoroughly relinquish them {401}
On any supreme companions in practice
through whom my afflictions do not soar,
I shall rely and treat them like my eyes [23]

Beginning with today and onward,
until reaching the heart of awakening,
I shall always go into homelessness
and engage in conduct that is pure [24]

At day and at night, not letting time slip by,
I shall meditate in three sessions and breaks
What I need to do is stop prāṇa and apāna,
and, similar to a lamp without any wind,
always cultivate nondiscursiveness [25]

Then, at the time of rising, full of pride,
I resolutely think of the pride of the deity's
body with the major and the minor marks
During the time of the nightly periods,
just as the Sugata has been lying down,
I abandon worldly thoughts and sleep [26]

In brief, the entirety of all phenomena
I shall examine as being like dreams
I shall make yoga cultivations my priority,
but not put physical or verbal virtues first [27]

Full of effort and concentration, I shall practice
the ten kinds of dharma activities[1597] and so on
without being distracted by any afflictions
Always thinking of death and, with a detached mind,
not entertaining any clinging to any things at all,
I meditate, no matter how I engage in conduct [28]

I dedicate my merit to all sentient beings
May I and all beings without exception,
through the stainless moon rays of my,
Bodhibhadra's, virtuous action of
composing this cultivation of yoga,
come to accomplish Śrī Vajradhara [29]

This concludes "The Reality of the Characteristics of Yoga" composed by the glorious Mahāpaṇḍita Bodhibhadra. {402}

(188) A Timely Discourse on Making Effort in Prajñā

In the language of India: *Prajñārambhāvadhiparikathānāma*[1598]
In the language of Tibet: *Shes rab brtsam pa dus kyi gtam zhe bya ba*

I pay homage to the bodhisattva Kṣitigarbha

The kāyas and dharmas of the uncontaminated mahāsukhacakra's vast excellence,
the fields of accumulations and the roots of the siddhis—to them, I pay homage
It might well be that it is [sometimes] not the time for the pāramitā of vigor,
but at the times[1599] with the signs that such is the case, make irresistible efforts! [1]

Masters searching for their disciples,
practicing to acquire precious substances,
students returning[1600] the kindness again,
lacking empowerments, yet desiring them again, [2]

walking around with bad clothing,
sustaining oneself with heavy food,
disputing such as having found the indivisible,
wishing to overpower others forcefully, [3]

destroying bodies through quarrels,
rivals who are envious disputing,
bhikṣus disputing about abodes,
invalidating tenets through denial, [4]

judging the conduct of beings,
ḍākinīs transiting to the fruition, {403}
overstating a well-known value,[1601]
making a living through hypocrisy and deceiving people, [5]

summoning trees with hand signals,
mountains uttering lamentations,
water emitting the light of fire,
and badmouthing the fortunate [6]

Through these twenty signs of dispute being complete,
this resembles the lamp of a brahman woman [7]

Hey, when the time of gods and seers being alive has passed,
or[1602] when the moon of taking care of the lowly with compassion
dawns,
if you lack[1603] the support of genuinely taking refuge,
at the time of death, suffering and so on will happen [8]

Hey, if men[1604] and women who attained an excellent birth
don't remain, in a loving and nonobserving manner, in the bond
with the three supreme vows of body, speech, and mind
and lack the way of being genuine, they are bound for sure [9]

Hey, if you do not search for the siddhi that is found close by,
through making effort, your own great bliss will not be realized
Without finding luminosity, afflictions will not become the path
and the sealing with the dharmatā that is speechless will be
lacking [10]

By virtue of lacking solitude, deliverance is not found
Not engaging diligently[1605] in yogic disciplines, lucidity is not food
Due to lacking the watchman of the mind, the supreme is not attained [11]

Yogīs in whom the sense faculties arise without distraction
are not distracted by desire and do not engage in any doing
The pith instruction: don't be distracted toward beings, don't fall asleep,
don't let the genuine lineage dry out, and don't cut off the fruition! [12]

Hey, AHO, always regard inside and outside as being equal!
If you do not complete this within the short time [you have],[1606]
due to the changes of time,[1607] you won't find the best time
Therefore, {404} muster your vigor in a timely fashion! [13]

Realized buddhas are what brahmans are—
you're attached to what's desirable, Bhabhiti,[1608]
you lack the experience of insatiability, Bhelośa[1609] [14]

Now, being just like the sun of times past,
this instruction is what I have written down
May this lead to gradual efforts on the path! [15]

This concludes "A Timely Discourse on Making Effort in Prajñā," an instruction by the Bengali Paṇḍita glorious and well-trained Śrīman Advayavajra for the brahman Bhalo. {405}

(189) A Chapter on Samādhi Equipment

In the language of India: *Samādhisambhāraparivarta*[1610]
In the language of Tibet: *Ting nge 'dzin gyi tshogs kyi le'u*

I pay homage to the protector of the world

First,[1611] make the mindset for perfect awakening
that springs from the power of compassion firm!
Don't be attached to the pleasures of existence's enjoyments
but turn your back on[1612] this clinging of yours [1]

With the excellent riches of devotion and so on,
revere the guru as being equal to the Buddha!
Make great effort in fully maintaining
the samaya conduct that he has taught! [2]

The bestowal of the secret vase's empowerment
is obtained thanks to the kindness of the guru
Practitioners with pure body, speech, and mind
do constitute the vessels for the siddhis [3]

Through fully completing the accumulation
that arises from the branches of samādhi,
the siddhis will be attained in a swift manner
Such[1613] is abiding in the way of secret mantra [4]

If the branches of samādhi have deteriorated
and you remain in what is discordant with it,
even through tens of billions of births,
you will not fully accomplish samādhi [5]

In order to fully accomplish samādhi,
yogīs abiding in secret mantra's conduct {406}
should avoid any states of mind other than it
and thus strive with undistracted effort [6]

To ascertain what is discordant
with the branches of samādhi,
it shall be explained in brief what
accords[1614] with samādhi's branches [7]

Possessing excellent discipline,
utter disregard for possessions,
as well as patience, firm oaths,
avoiding people's hustle and bustle, [8]

showing alertness with regard to
the actions of body, speech, and mind,
having correct recollection of the body
by[1615] recollecting terms for the Buddha's body, [9]

being steadfast in the mindfulness
of what is to be done[1616] at what time,
relinquishing the five obscurations,
knowing the right amount of food, proper conduct, [10]

an ever-equanimous state of mind
toward all these worldly phenomena,
and few necessities—these are the branches
Their opposites are what is discordant [11]

By the merit of articulating *The Chapter on Samādhi Equipment,*
may [all] sentient beings attain the samādhi that is vajra-like! [12]

This concludes "A Chapter on Samādhi Equipment" composed by the great master and paṇḍita Dīpaṃkaraśrījñāna. It was translated, edited, and finalized by this Indian upādhyāya himself and the editor-lotsāwa bhikṣu Śākya Lodrö. {407}

(190) The Supramundane Ritual of the Seven Branches

In the language of India: *Lokātītasaptāṅgavidhi*[1617]
In the language of Tibet: *'Jig rten las 'das pa'i yan lag bdun pa'i cho ga*

I pay homage to all buddhas and bodhisattvas
I pay homage to Śrī Vajrasattva

Object of homage, payer of homage, and homage—
when they are not observed to be different,
this is the paying of homage praised here,
which is expressed as "the vajra homage" [1]

Object of offering, offerer, and offering—
when they are not observed to be diverse,
then this constitutes the great offering,
which is expressed as "the vajra offering" [2]

Object of confession, confessor, and confession—
at the time when yogīs do not see these,
they are rightly seen as the pure nature
This is the supreme confession here [3]

All that they need to rejoice in,
themselves, and the rejoicing—

yogīs see these as being equal
This is the genuine rejoicing [4]

Buddhas miraculously created by illusion,
for the sake of beings created by illusion,
are being properly entreated to impart
the dharmas that are similar to echoes [5] {408}

In accordance with such miraculous creations,
to entreat them by folding your hands
and to see this as equal to the vajra yoga
is held to be the supreme entreaty [6]

In accordance with the buddhas who are wishing
for nirvāṇa miraculously manifesting in saṃsāra,
know[1618] the true reality of the supplication to remain
for the welfare of miraculously created sentient beings [7]

This is held to be the supreme supplication
here for the sake of transcending the world
Any engagements that involve focal objects
are in their entirety nothing but mundane [8]

Perfect awakening is similar to a dream
Knowing true reality, it's known as dream-like
If through benefiting the sentient beings
who live in dream-like saṃsāric existence [9]

the entirety of all virtue is fully dedicated
in a way as immeasurable as the dharmadhātu,
this constitutes the genuine dedication here,
which is greatly praised by all buddhas [10]

This concludes "The Supramundane Ritual of the Seven Branches" composed by the great master and paṇḍita Dīpaṃkaraśrījñāna in the great temple of Glorious Samyé Lhüngyi Trubpa.[1619] {409}

(191) The Ship of the Precious Teachings of the Sugata

In the language of India: *Sugataśāsanaratnavohitthanāma*[1620]
In the language of Tibet: *Bde bar gshes pa'i bstan pa rin po che'i gru bo zhes bya ba*

I pay homage to the Bhagavān Lokeśvara

He possesses loving-kindness and realization,[1621] is rich in scriptures,
is an expert in speaking, lacks weariness, and has a disciplined mind
His refinement,[1622] his vows, and his faculties are very peaceful—
I bow before the guru and shall explain that which he has taught [1]

The freedoms very difficult to find, their being like clouds, the connection of actions and their results, and what is filled with suffering;
supreme confidence in the proper objects, loving-kindness for beings, thorough discrimination of phenomena, and vigor;
supplicating the supreme with respect, possessing the superb ritual, effort in meditative equipoise, and excellent dedication—
to engage in what is to be contemplated, what is to be accomplished,[1623] and the supreme yogas constitutes the ship that crosses the ocean of saṃsāric existence and peace[1624] [2]

It is said that just like a turtle in a yoke,
mustard seeds on the eye of a needle,
and dried peas on the surface of a wall,[1625]
the freedoms are very difficult to find[1626] [3]

Since it is the karma of all beings[1627]
to plunge downward like a stream, {410}
since nonvirtue increases during that,
and since virtuous conduct is hard even if not, [4]

this support is difficult to obtain; accordingly,
it is to the same degree that it is hard to find
that we need to search for the genuine pith
within this body that is without any pith [5]

Hence, so that persons wishing[1628] the very best
for themselves are able to accomplish their goals,
they should use this body in a way that is similar
to finding a ship[1629] when drowning in the ocean [6]

Since this life force is something conditioned,
since it doesn't last, since conditions are many,
and since it accordingly is without any pith,
it is certain the lord of death will devour us swiftly [7]

Our bodies, possessions, and beautiful
loved ones will not follow after us—
unprotected, all alone, and ordinary,
we shall proceed to the next world [8]

If gaining the confidence that we will not
be afflicted in some lifetime for a while
doesn't ever[1630] dawn in us at all,
why would our minds dwell in happiness? [9]

For that reason, it is by means of all their efforts,

while disregarding the necessities of this life
and as concentrated as if their heads were ablaze,
that the wise should achieve the goal of the hereafter [10]

The maturations of experiencing what is seen and not seen
constitute the karmas through the power of natural outflow
The undeceiving connection of actions and results is held
to be like sweet, sour, and bitter having specific causes [11]

Within mind as such, which is as unobstructed as space,
the cloud banks of all sorts of latent tendencies gather
Their continuous stream of rainfall that will mature
ripens the harvest that is experienced thereafter [12]

Phenomena in their entirety are dependent origination
That which is without support[1631] {411} is their support,
since it is the ground of the causes and results it supports—
this is the connection of black and white causes and results [13]

Since this is certain in an undeceiving individual way,
since something big arises from something small,
and since what happened before will still be experienced,
the intelligent do well to make effort in adopting and rejecting [14]

All these beings who are thus tormented
by the inconceivable sufferings that are
the results of such and such karmas
resemble a charcoal kiln[1632] in flames [15]

This includes the sufferings of conditionedness,
change, suffering, and so forth, as well as
those such as birth, aging, sickness, frailty, death,
what has met separating, [what is obtained] being hard to keep,
and searching [16]

Just as Maṅgala has black ears,

has a bad smell, and is unclean,
we are always innately linked
with appropriating suffering [17]

While afraid of suffering, the ignorant
engage in its causes with great delight
Just as with poison for a person ill from it,
it is wise to dispel both through knowledge [18]

Excellently finding the freedoms hard to find for many eons is like an uḍumbara[1633] on a bare rock
This life that's been obtained is incapable of lasting, like a river stream in the midst of a steep cliff
The black and the white karmas of sentient beings are similar to seeds and their harvests
The torments of suffering within these [beings] are like flames in a blazing pit of fire [19]

This is a summary of the dharmas that are the four[1634] points to be contemplated.

Supreme [confidence] in, longing for, and trusting in
the three refuges, liberation, and actions and results,
as well as the certainty of stainless perspicacity {412}
are without doubt the causes of devoted training [20]

Based on the understanding of their qualities,
seeing the flaws of their counterparts, weariness,
and comprehending the experience of the signs,
in this way, confidence[1635] will be attained [21]

Since this precedes everything that is to be done
and since it is the very cause of doing anything,
similar to a sprout [growing] from a burned seed,
it is not so in those lacking zest for all dharmas [22]

Those who possess supreme confidence[1636]
will accomplish anything hard to accomplish
in a manner that is even much easier
than what can be done easily by others [23]

With regard to sentient beings, phenomena, and dharmatā, respectively,
the featureless realization of loving-kindness, the manifestation
of unbearable compassion, and the understanding of the actuality
of nonthought are the causes of the training to exhaust the stains [24]

You remember seeing the sufferings of your friends' assemblies
and also behold the lack of an identity of persons and phenomena
through the corpus of reasonings,[1637] scriptures, and pith instructions
Therefore, usher in others and give rise to loving-kindness! [25]

Since it is the cause of the effortless two kāyas,
since it is the cause of the mind that is precious,
in order to keep attracting sentient beings,
just as in the case of a magnet and a needle, [26]

and in order to fully complete the activities
of the victor's children through such distinct features,
you should give rise to consummate compassion
that bears a similarity with the rattan tree[1638] [27]

In the city that is magically created by illusion,
these people are joyful as well as tormented
Know appearances to be very similar in all
places, times, and kinds—unestablished ultimately [28]

Since they reach no end of unimpededness
and are born from that which is unborn,
any appearances that are born are unborn
and empty, since dependent origination's root is used up [29]

Because of what appears there and so on, {413}
it is this very saṃsāra; if it is analyzed,
at that time, it is just as void as space—
this is expressed as the natural nirvāṇa [30]

When not realized, it is difficult to realize,
but if realized, it will certainly be freedom
Thus, it is greatly profound and very amazing[1639]—
the wise ones scrutinize their clinging [31]

Since seeing the results that are excellent
and accomplishing them depend on effort,
we know that the goal is attained by ongoing familiarity
This is the vigor of irreversible motivation and endeavor [32]

Knowing the flaws of the other and the qualities of this,[1640]
being free of idleness such as sleep, not being fainthearted,
training in the means, and having a firm heart, courage, and valor,
the enthusiasm of those who are fortunate will increase [33]

Just as movement does not occur when there is no wind,
how could there be virtuous conduct without any vigor?
Those endowed with enthusiasm give rise to the mindset
of reducing even Mount Meru to dust in just an instant [34]

AHO! There is nothing to be relied on anywhere else
When connecting with being reborn, there is no leisure
The time of being alive is like a lamp in a cool house
Why is it that my mind keeps dawdling around?[1641] [35]

With the blazing red and lucid sun rays of very joyful stainless
confidence having opened the lotus of your true character,
and the moistening water of loving-kindness for infinite beings
having stirred the eyelashes of the utpala of affection,
realize the emptiness that is the nature of the dependent origina-

tion of the maṇḍala of all kinds of appearances and minds to be known,
and, afraid of the many flaws of the hosts of foes in saṃsāric existence, engage in vigor similar to making every effort when a snake has slithered onto the lawn [36]

This is a summary of the dharmas that are the four[1642] points to be accomplished. {414}

Remembering saṃsāric existence's flaws and peace's qualities,
in order to accomplish the welfare of both yourself and others,
just as in the case when polishing a wish-fulfilling jewel,
you need to request the supreme siddhi from them [37]

Since you don't find even a mere fraction of it
though you make efforts for hundreds of eons,
whereas they allow you to attain great bliss
in just an instant, thanks to their kindness, [38]

having perceived them just as they are
through the ritual of continuous yoga,
supplicate the two supports with hope,
intense longing, as well as respect [39]

At the time when the blessings of the guru
as well as the deity flow into your heart,
you will attain a state of mind as pellucid
as a crystal and be overwhelmed by joy [40]

Having transformed this through threefold purity,
you should make it stainless through luminosity
It is through their unity that this becomes wisdom
By training in mastery, enlightened activity is accomplished [41]

It is the deity, mantra, and samādhi that constitute
the very lack of appearance, sound, and minding

While devoid of diversity, everything appears
Whatever appears depends on something else [42]

Since these are what wash away the stains
of body, speech, and mind, respectively,
since they make them supreme and of one taste,
and since they accomplish the goal, perform them![1643] [43]

Since it is that which causes your own realization,
since you're free through that realization, and since this
very freedom miraculously manifests as others' welfare,
this path is so much more distinguished than other yānas [44]

Because the great yoga is that which is rendering
your own mind stainless, pellucid, and serene, {415}
like[1644] seeing the reality of the sky and moon light,
this is called nonthought, luminosity,[1645] and great bliss [45]

Just like an illusion itself, that as which it appears,
and its true character,[1646] all phenomena are mind
For the reason that this very [mind] is luminosity,
the state of mind that is supreme is nonthinking [46]

Its own nature is to be completely unobstructed
It is self-appearing as all kinds of manifestations
It is characterized by being all-pervasive and taintless,
said to be the samādhi of luminosity of the fortunate [47]

Because of seeing the supreme, because of being stainless,
and because of awakening[1647] within the entity free of entity,
it is held to be the great bliss that is free from attachment,
without contamination, utterly peaceful, and serene [48]

Thus, the virtues that arise in this
lack any characteristics and yet are vast

The supreme conduct by a mind endowed with emptiness
and compassion is to be dedicated well to the two kāyas [49]

Just as with the formations of dream objects,
what is accomplished, why, where, by what,
and how is unobservable—for that reason,
virtue is stated to be without characteristics [50]

The unobservable is very clear as what is observed
The essence is linked to the lack of any essence
The ground that appears as five kinds of facets
is the supreme accumulation of the victor's children [51]

The prajñā and means by which phenomena[1648] and persons
are understood constitute the attachment free of attachment
The dedication to the nirvāṇa that is the nonabiding one
constitutes the most amazing wonder of great beings [52]

Those who are marked by the supreme deity and adorned by the protector with thousands of perfect buddhas on red blossoming lotuses at their heart and crown,
who perform the display of connate wisdom—the stainless sovereign of the outer, the inner, and the secret—through the training of light, {416}
who have an utterly serene mind of pure and very lucid great bliss, similar to a sky free of clouds and the rays of the full moon,
and who, propelled[1649] by the bow of loving-kindness, shoot the precious arrows of any accumulations of virtue that may arise at beings are courageous [53]

This is a summary of the dharmas that are the four[1650] points of what is to be practiced as yoga.

This represents the excellent supreme ship of the precious teachings that are the means to liberate

from both the utterly black[1651] ocean of saṃsāric existence—which
houses the gaping-mouthed sea monsters of the afflictions,[1652]
is stirred up by the waves of suffering, is bottomless in its depths,
and is absolutely terrifying—
and also the white and swirling enormous sea of peace that contains [all kinds of] trinkets [54]

By this virtue of having made efforts in composing this well
with a very clear and joyful mind, compassion, and perspicacity,
may I become the supreme leader who excellently liberates those
beings who have not yet been liberated by any previous victors!
[55]

This concludes "The Ship of the Precious Teachings of the Sugata" composed by Mahāpaṇḍita Ajitamitragupta who had attained siddhi.[1653] {417}

(192) A Treatise on the Glorious Liberation from Bondage

In the language of India: *Śrībandhavimuktaśāstra*[1654]
In the language of Tibet: *Dpal 'ching ba rnam grol gyi bstan bcos*

I pay homage to the Bhagavān Lokeśvara

If what is not realized and hard to realize is realized, at that time,
you will be free from the unbearable fetters so hard to be free of
In order to liberate beings, I shall explain this wondrous path
to perfect buddhahood—the utmost welfare of myself and others [1]

Just like the wrestler's jewel and so on,
this pith does not dwell anywhere else,[1655]
since all bind themselves by themselves
and will become free[1656] by themselves [2]

Here, there is no bondage whatsoever
Freedom comes through that which binds
It's just the work of emptiness and dependent origination
Therefore, the ignorant[1657] do not realize it [3]

It is difficult to be realized by people
who are seized by inferior and false
friends, have feeble merit and vigor,
and little training, power, and insight [4]

You need to search for spiritual friends who are genuine,
and have realization, compassion, and skill in pith instructions {418}
Rely on them with the stainless respect of all the aspects
of your life, your body, your possessions, and so forth! [5]

For as long as your mind remains stable,
for that long, like a body and its shadow,
the teachings given by them are the nectar
of dependent origination and emptiness [6]

Just like cool water for those tormented by thirst,
drink it with inexhaustible delight and openness
Other paths lack consummate deliverance
To understand that is means and prajñā [7]

This is the door to all the doors of dharma—
the genuine path to realize what's hard to realize
Just as it is mere dependent origination,
how could it therefore not be empty? [8]

Since it is just as unobstructed
as space is, if it is emptiness,
why would it not be dependent origination?
Therefore, these two are not two [9]

"What is dependent origination like,
and what constitutes its emptiness?"
Listen! These entities thus appearing
are as vividly clear as Indra's bow [10]

All kinds of happiness, suffering, and so forth
neither arise from themselves, nor causelessly,
nor from other causes, nor from uncertain ones,
just as sweet, sour, and bitter have specific causes

Mind as such and dependent origination
are similar to clouds in the sky [11]

AHO! Within this dense jungle of saṃsāric existence,
the trees lush with the foliage and fruits of suffering
are endowed with the branches of flawed conduct
and their flowers of clinging are simply dazzling [12]

The trunks of their causes—improper desire and hatred—
are resting on the stable roots of the views about a self
The warmth and moisture of ignorance and latent tendencies
let them grow from the element that is the great earth [13]

Similar to the world that is the container in space,
AHO, what lacks support {419} has become a support[1658]
What is free of support is the supreme of what is supported[1659]
Given that a support is not established in the first place,
how could positing something supported be viable? [14]

If the lack of any identity were thus not true,
as what and how should what is created by it—
attachment, karmas, and so on—be ascertained?
If those are not established, then what is suffering
and who would express its being experienced? [15]

Just as the action of severing is established,
if the roots of a tree have been eradicated,
it's by ending thoughts about a self as its basis
that the wise dismantle saṃsāric existence [16]

Like burning, cutting, and filing gold and such,
what are called "self" and "other" should thus
be examined in terms of what their supports,
abodes, essences, and characteristics are like [17]

Nobody at all is able to be certain
that the body, speech, vāyus, mind,
outside, inside, in between, and such
ever function as supports or abodes [18]

If the self were something that is suitable to appear,
it would be observed, but since it is unobservable,
name some mind or non-mind that does not appear! [19]

Mind has the character of being empty by nature
The character of what's not mind is impermanent dependent
origination
If analyzed, they are without any reference points
Since activity is contradictory to being permanent,[1660]
please show us a self of any sorts anywhere! [20]

In brief, not much needs to be said about this
If the self were other than your own three gates,
what would any harm to it possibly matter? [21]

Flaws such as a wound through a weapon
are nothing but childish beings' own reasons[1661]
and disputes by people with misplaced desire
If the things that are not other are analyzed,
how could any among them be a self? [22] {420}

Through this approach here of[1662] analyzing
any of its supports and its abodes that are not it,
and the dimensions of its supports and its abodes,
any entity of a self or characteristics of a self
are shown to be well established as illusion-like [23]

Look! If in this body like a banana tree,
echo-like speech, and space-like mind,
there is not even a speck to be observed,
how could they be designated as a self?[1663] [24]

The outer is outside and the inner is other
Hence, the in between is not a self[1664] either
You cannot[1665] be certain about its features,
whether it is "white" and so on,
"long," "short," "large," "skinny,"
"thick," or "thin," and so forth [25]

"But just as with creeping vines on a tree,
based on the latent tendencies of[1666] the ālaya,
it is present without being visibly manifest"
Analyzing its appearing or not appearing
and examining mind and what's not mind
apply in just the same way as above [26]

"But what is called 'the self'
is nothing but this very mind"
This mind is unobservable and luminous
Hence, the self has now become no-self [27]

AHO! This is the state so hard to realize
AHO! AHO! It is so utterly amazing!
AHO! It is suitable to be known by the wise
AHO! The expanse of knowing free of knowing [28]

Thus, there is no self in this world,
but what about these crazy beings
possessed by the perceiver "me"
and the perceived "mine"? [29]

Still, with its eyes obscured by mistakenness,
the world is putting perceiver and perceived
forward in exactly the ways they are appearing
Attachment to appearances as they appear is saṃsāric existence
[30] {421}

"Isn't the cause of the turning of the wheel
of suffering something beyond ourselves?
Though a self as such may not be established,
it is really existent as the very clinging to it" [31]

Since exactly this, AHO, is all beings'
unbearable bondage in mistakenness,
as concentrated as if your head were ablaze,
you should end it promptly and swiftly [32]

Oh friends, since thus this self
is not established through the eye
of directly perceiving awareness,
there is also nothing called "other" here [33]

Thus, these wrong ideas we all have,
thinking "me," thinking "I am,"
thinking "other," and "other's"—
how and about what are they afraid? [34]

Take the example of a son dying in a dream:
if there exists no son, his death as well
is not anything that is really existent,
and the very same goes for our clinging[1667] [35]

AHO! The utterly amazing state!
By realizing just this single thing,
all will become completely free,
so who could fear doubts about it? [36]

The phenomena of saṃsāra and nirvāṇa,
skandhas, dhātus, āyatanas, and so forth,
the three yānas, the three yānas' deliverances, and their paths
without exception are neither a self nor what is others'[1668] [37]

The characteristic of no-self is to be empty
Since it is nonexistent, AHO, what flaw
is there for you in properly ascertaining
its nonexistence to be nonexistence? [38]

All these bondages of clinging
to anything as "me" or "mine"
are not outer, inner, or in between,
Just so, not being body, speech, or mind,
they don't [arise] from or abide in them [39] {422}

Likewise, if all mental engagements
through attachment, hatred, and so on
are analyzed, how could there be any
attachment or hatred for a bit anywhere[1669]
toward anything through anything? [40]

Beautiful forms, pleasant sounds, fragrant scents, sweet tastes,
what is soft to the touch, and the conditions for a happy mind—
what kind of beneficial connection by virtue of any of these
could there possibly be for those who understand this? [41]

Through understanding this, what would
attachment and strong attachment for these
be—something outer, inner, or in between,
or maybe some entity such as the body? [42]

A given relying on something that is not it,
as well as arising, abiding, and ceasing,
just like illusory elephants and horses,
are not at all established ultimately [43]

As for the mental factors of hatred and strong hatred,
which are the causes for self-contempt and so forth,
and for actions such as beating inferior ones,
just as before, your own mind as well as

the minds of anybody else out there
lack any characteristics, just like space [44]

Likewise, if others' speech and bodies
are like knives,[1670] sounds, and wood,
just like an illusion striking an illusion,[1671]
what harm[1672] could they do to me here? [45]

My own speech and body are just like that
Thus, the same goes for those of all beings
Hence, neither their arising, nor their abiding,
nor their ceasing are observable at all [46]

Since they are not connected with one another,
since all are free of reference points if analyzed,
and since all places, times, and kinds are stainless,
they are like the tracks of a bird flying in the sky [47]

In that way, in this dimension of being empty,
as with sounds[1673] and rainbows in a dream, {423}
what would be attached to what in what way?
Likewise, what would hatred be afraid of? [48]

Fathers, mothers, wives, children,
relatives, friends, and likewise foes[1674]
are simply like illusions; therefore,
you should scrutinize all clinging [49]

By virtue of that, what would the functions
performed by attachment and so on be like?
It is by way of their firm prajñā that the wise
need to examine this again and again as above [50]

Therefore, happiness and suffering
are not experienced by matter

Awareness is without any entity—
wrongly trained since beginningless time [51]

This trifle clinging due to delusion
is indeed without any entity as well
If those of excellent insight familiarize
with its nonexistence as nonexistence, [52]

this bondage by those unbearable fetters,
akin to lunatics[1675] taking friends to be foes,
will most certainly become complete freedom,
like knots in a snake becoming untied on their own [53]

This freedom as well as the effortless
result that emerges from this freedom
are the two amazing consummate welfares
They are similar to the excellent vase [54]

This concludes "A Treatise on the Glorious Liberation from Bondage" composed by the great Indian master Śrī Niṣkalaṅka who had attained siddhi. After having been finalized by the great lord of yogīs Śrī Jaganmitrānanda and the Kashmiri Mahāpaṇḍita Buddhaśrībhadra, it was translated by the junior Tibetan lotsāwa Nub Tsültrim Sherab.[1676] {424}

(193) A Pith Instruction on Pure View and Conduct

In the language of India: *Viśuddhadarśanacaryopadeśanāma*[1677]
In the language of Tibet: *Lta spyod rnam dag gi man ngag ces bya ba*

I pay homage to the Bhagavān, the lion of the Śākyas

Just like in a dream, there is nothing outside
Just like in an illusion, there are no real referents
Just like with space, characteristics are lacking
All phenomena are natural luminosity [1]

Bodhicitta without coming, going, and remaining
is the expert in the vast welfare of sentient beings
The two accumulations' inseparability is the supreme path
Familiarize with the emptiness whose heart is compassion! [2]

This concludes "A Pith Instruction on Pure View and Conduct" composed by the mahāpaṇḍita of Kashmiri origin who was the glorious dharma lord[1678] *Śākyaśrībhadra. It was translated in front of this mahāpaṇḍita by lotsāwa Jampé Bal in the excellent valley of Tropu.* {425}

(194) The Path and Fruition of Purifying the Jewel of the Mind

In the language of India: *Cittaratnavisōdhanamārgaphala*[1679]
In the language of Tibet: *Sems rin po che sbyangs pa'i lam 'bras*

I pay homage to the venerable protector Ajita[1680]

The freedoms and resources hard to find swiftly perish
Actions and their results are what constitute suffering
Cultivate the prajñā and compassion that relinquish them!
Through the three individuals' paths, three goals are attained [1]

Through the three excellencies,[1681] merit is gathered
Through extensive means, it is increased perfectly
Through profound prajñā, it is to be made fully pure
Through the dedication of unity, it becomes sealed [2]

This concludes "The Path and Fruition of Purifying the Jewel of the Mind" spoken by the mahāpaṇḍita who was born in a Kashmiri family in Nepal, the glorious supreme one who knows the five fields [of knowledge], Buddhaśrījñāna. It was translated in front of this mahāpaṇḍita by lotsāwa Jampé Bal in the Yamgal[1682] *temple in Nepal.* {426}

(195) A Pith Instruction on the Liberation of Bondage

In the language of India: *Bandhavimuktopadeśanāma*[1683]
In the language of Tibet: *'Ching ba rnam grol gyi man ngag ces bya ba*

I pay homage to noble Avalokiteśvara

Hey!
The very cause that creates bondage
is the path that leads you to freedom
Here, there is no bondage whatsoever
Freedom comes through that which binds[1684] [1]

Desire is pure as great bliss
Hatred blazes as luminosity's flame
Ignorance is simply nonthought—
the three poisons are the effortless three kāyas [2]

This concludes "A Pith Instruction on the Liberation of Bondage" spoken by the mighty lord of yogīs Śrī Jaganmitrānanda. It was translated in front of this mighty lord of yogīs by lotsāwa Jampé Bal in Śivahemagṛha[1685] *in Nepal.* {427}

(196) Certainty about the Genuine Path to Accomplishment

In the language of India: *Siddhisanmārganirṇaya*[1686]
In the language of Tibet: *Grub pa dam pa'i lam nges pa*[1687]

I pay homage to the bhagavān Lokeśvara

Khasarpaṇa,[1688] you who are the world's glory,
by the power of demonstrating great compassion,
in the taming of your own mind difficult to tame,
you attained the threefold unsurpassable quintessence [1]

AHO! People of Jambudvīpa, listen!
The friend of beings declares this:
the very cause that creates bondage
is the path that leads to freedom[1689] [2]

The ship crossing the ocean of suffering
consists of the Sage's precious teachings
Its essence, its path, as well as its means
are the instructions delighting all friends [3]

AHO!
The precious human body is difficult to obtain
The hard-to-find freedoms and resources are as fleeting as
clouds

The entirety of saṃsāra consists of suffering
It is your own mind that constitutes nirvāṇa [4]

Like a ship found when drowning in the ocean,
a courageous person in a roaring river stream,
a nest that is teeming with poisonous snakes,
and the center of the autumn sky, so these [four] are [5]

What are possessions like? A woolen tent[1690] as a home
What is consciousness like? A person in a shop
What is your own body like? {428} The skin of a snake
What is the life force like? A rushing waterfall [6]

AHO! For as long as you are not swallowed
by the mouth of the rākṣasa of impermanence,
oh you friends, please pull yourselves together
Do turn away from saṃsāric existence, good sirs! [7]

In the immense city of illusion,
dream people enjoy themselves
Mind as such is dependent origination—
thus appearances and mind should be known[1691] [8]

Look! If in this body like a banana tree,
echo-like speech, and space-like mind,
there is not even a speck to be observed,
oh sons, who would be bound in what?[1692] [9]

These wrong ideas we all have,
thinking "me," thinking "I am,"
thinking "other," and "other's"—
how and about what are they afraid? [10]

Just as when a son dies in a dream,
if there exists no son, his death too

is not something that really exists,
and the same goes for our clinging[1693] [11]

Since all phenomena are like dreams,
all these various appearances, such as
food, clothing, wealth, friends, and foes,
are like illusory horses and elephants [12]

Letting whatever arises be in its own place is mindfulness[1694]
Mindfulness being free in itself is what constitutes release
Release is what represents equal taste without any effort
These make up the threefold hidden trail of the essence[1695] [13]
{429}

(197) A Pith Instruction on Untying the Knots in the Yogī's Own Mind

In the language of India: *Svacittayogigranthamocakopadeśa*[1696]
In the language of Tibet: *Rnal 'byor pa rang gi sems kyi mdud pa dgrol ba'i man ngag*

I pay homage to the bhagavān noble Avalokiteśvara

AHO! That which is primordially unborn
is the cause that creates saṃsāra and nirvāṇa
Abiding nowhere else but in your own heart's center,
it will be known from the mouth of the guru[1697] [1]

Hey, good sirs, please listen to me!
The very cause that creates bondage
is the path that leads you to freedom
Here, there is no bondage whatsoever[1698] [2]

In the immense city of illusion,
dream people enjoy themselves
At the time of enjoyment, there is no enjoyment
Thus appearances and mind should be known[1699] [3]

Diverse appearances are your own mind,
being similar to an assembly of snakes

Your own mind, being like Indra's bow,
is the native state—effortless luminosity [4]

Everything that arises is just that,
but it doesn't arise as anything at all
Hence, what has been born is unborn
This being unborn is the mode of being born[1700] [5]

Just as with the forms in a mirror, the sound of a vīṇā,
bhikṣus, magical creations, and miraculous {430} formations,
realize the characteristics of existence, nonexistence,
arising, ceasing, coming, and going as well [6]

Just like illusory horses and elephants,
appearances are dependent origination
True reality,[1701] just like the autumn sky,
is to be joined with luminosity's three dharmas [7]

AHO! The great king of yogīs
AHO! Neither bound nor free
AHO! No relinquishment, effortless
AHO! AHO! Great bliss [8]

In all beings lacking realization, independently
and through the power of great compassion,
the merit and wisdom that are nonreferential
and complete in all aspects shall be excellent [9]

This concludes "An Instruction on Untying the Knots in One's Own Mind." At the time when the guru named Mitrānanda, the hidden buddha, had arrived at Gurmo Rinpoche Ling in the great market place Dashi[1702] in the middle of Snowy Tibet, he sang this dohā of single-stroke mahāmudrā for the sake of the six great lords of sūtra and mantra—Gya, Dré, Lam, Lo, Tro, and Shen[1703]—who had requested it. It was translated by Nub Lotsāwa. {431}

(198) The Empowerment of Samādhi

In the language of India: *Samādhyabhiṣeka*[1704]
In the language of Tibet: *Ting nge 'dzin gyi dbang bskur ba*

I pay homage to the glorious cakravartin Lokeśvara

Glorious one, you have overcome the foes of the four māras and
gained mastery over supreme awakening
Through your compassion, you bestow the empowerment that
also matures other beings who are not forgetful
on the excellent path to unsurpassable peace—I bow to the lord of
the three planes, Avalokiteśvara
Having done so, I explain the ritual of the empowerment of the
pure mental conduct of the samādhi wisdom of the fortunate [1]

The assembly of conditions for happiness in a pleasant place
constitutes being endowed with the entirety of samaya
Hence, place great compassion in front of yourself
and begin by supplicating in a respectful manner [2]

Elevated as many arm spans in space as possible,
meditate that the great Sage and Cakravartin
arises in union with his consort of great bliss,
together with their children beyond measure [3]

Having presented offering clouds of all kinds
of things, just as in Samantabhadra's conduct,
eliminate all wrongdoing, and following that
request the completely pure empowerment [4]

In the three kinds of places of the deity and yourself, {432}
bring the three vajra syllables clearly to your mind
By virtue of devotion, compassion, and samaya,[1705]
colored light rays radiate in a threefold progression [5]

From OṂ—the essence of the supreme body—white light rays
Likewise, from ĀḤ—the stainless stream of speech—red light
From HŪṂ—the character of the pure mind—blue rays radiate
Touching the three places of your own body, speech, and mind,
they dispel the three stains [6]

Subsequent to that, white, red, and blue nectar [streams forth]
according to the pith instruction on threefold purification
Then follows the anointment with the three kinds of wisdom
Finally, nonduality is what constitutes the fourth one[1706] [7]

The great bliss that is extraordinarily secret
is the union of the flow of the three bindus
Subsequently, cultivate it with great insight
Having received empowerment, enjoy[1707] it well! [8]

This concludes "The Empowerment of Samādhi." It was translated by[1708] *Nub Lotsāwa.* {433}

(199) A Commentary on "Namo Buddhāya"

Namo Buddhāya

Na
There is neither birth nor cessation,
neither form nor possession of form,
neither any saṃsāra nor any nirvāṇa
This is what the syllable *na* expresses [1]

Mo
It's what constantly destroys ignorance,
excellently grants the sole liberation,
and overcomes māras and afflictions
This is what the syllable *mo* expresses [2]

Bud
Through buddhahood, you're gone beyond
Buddhahood is the very benefit of beings[1709]
Buddhahood is the purity of the afflictions
This is what the syllable *bud* expresses [3]

Dhā
Being endowed with the dharmadhātu
by virtue of it embracing all dharmas,

the very dharmas are the supreme dharma
This is what the syllable *dhā* expresses [4]

Ya
Just as abiding, so is perishing
Just as perishing, so is abiding
Just as speaking, so is acting
This is what the syllable *ya* expresses [5]

This concludes "A Commentary on Namo Buddhāya."[1710] {434}

(200) The Accomplishment of Glorious Great Bliss

In the language of India: *Śrīmahāsukhasiddhināma*[1711]
In the language of Tibet: *Dpal bde chen grub pa zhes bya ba*

I pay homage to Śrī Heruka

Without example, luminous, beyond being an object,
inexpressible,
without something characterized and characterizing, stainless,
baseless,
nondual, free from expression, and inseparable is the dharmakāya
Through the power of compassion that relies on the seeming,
I shall explain the Buddha's words in order to benefit the ignorant[1712]
[1]

The dharmakāya beyond cause and result,
unestablished, without meditation or anything to meditate,
beginningless, and free of middle and end,
in the center of the pistils of the sixteen
lotuses in the dharma and the navel [cakras],
has the colors of the bindus of the five elements [2]

In the center of the vajra of sun and moon kissing,
the light rays of the lotuses represent prajñā
and the luminosity of the vajra is the means

Successively looking at the six maṇḍalas,
the seventh's nature dawns within experience
and the five poisons' obscurations will be pure [3]

Some assert it as being the essence
of bindus and some as emptiness
Some as having the form of Viṣṇu[1713] [4]

Some are assuming a peaceful air,
[some] are true mudrās, rattling, shaking,
song, {435} dance, as well as music,
deities, and recitations, complete, [5]

some are the drawings of maṇḍalas
or the progression of empowerments
of past, present, and future, and so on
Displayed for devotion's sake, they're not actual reality [6]

The stainless nature is free of middle and end
The maṇḍala of your own body is mind as such
As for the three aspects of body, speech, and mind,
by virtue of the paints of the skandhas and dhātus,
their nature is the maṇḍala of colored sand [7]

In the navel's center is the natural dharmadhātu
In the east is mirror-like wisdom,
abiding as the nature of a bindu moon
The wisdom of discrimination
is in the west as a round bindu [8]

The great wisdom that is equality
beyond mind is in the south as a triangle
All-accomplishing [wisdom] is a square
dwelling in the north—the deity meditation [9]

Hence, this makes up the square palace

with the four mindfulnesses and the four gates
In the center that possesses the nature
of Akṣobhya, there are eight light rays [10]

This is the nature of body, speech, and mind
It is the bodhicitta that is without duality
Having taught the maṇḍala, I shall explain
the fire offering in order to satisfy the deities [11]

This mind as such that is without duality
is to be understood as the natural homa[1714] pit
Once the fire of the mind has been set alight
with the firewood of the five skandhas and the self,
the thoughts of the five poisons are burned [12]

Having thus explained the fire offering,
I shall now teach consecration[1715]
In the center of the skandhas' palace,
mind as such that is utterly stable
is of immovable nature and unestablished {436}
The nature of that is consecration [13]

As for the characteristic of yoga mantra,
it is free of being, nonbeing, and features
The secret of body, speech, and mind
constitutes the mantra of empty mind as such [14]

As for the basic nature of natural yoga,
being supported by the five skandhas,
that which liberates yourself or others
is this mind as such pointed out by mind
This is what constitutes the natural deity [15]

It is the true reality of mahāmudrā
that seals body, speech, and mind
Focusing the eyes on the nose tip, cross-legged,

and with the mudrā of meditative equipoise,
the intelligent should utter mantras and practice [16]

If some yogīs have realized
this nonconceptual mind as such,
they, in that very instant,
will meet the buddhas [17]

Since I have explained in the beginning
the bindu at the tip of the nose and so on,
that is the seeming, not the ultimate [18]

Rakta, śukra, māṃsa,[1716] as well as
Akṣobhya, Vairocana, the sugatas,
are the talk of barbarians of uncivilized areas,
since they dispel the samaya of nonthought [19]

This concludes "The Yoga of Accomplishing Glorious Great Bliss" spoken by master Kālapa. These seven sādhanas were translated by Ratnaphala on his own.[1717] {437}

(201) Twenty-Five Stanzas of Pith Instructions on Letting Your Own Mind Take a Rest

In the language of India: *Svacittaviśrāmopadeśapañcaviṃśatikāgāthānāma*[1718]
In the language of Tibet: *Rang gi sems ngal bso ba'i man ngag gi tshigs su bcad pa nyi shu rtsa lnga pa zhes bya ba*

I pay homage to Śrī Vajrasattva

AHO! That which is primordially unborn[1719]
is the cause that creates saṃsāra and nirvāṇa
Abiding nowhere else but in your own heart's center,
it will be known from the mouth of the guru[1720] [1]

Since whatever arises is the native state itself,
if whatever dawns is not forgotten by mindfulness,
it is the character[1721] of that dawning's emptiness
that without question represents the king of yoga [2]

Everything that arises is just that,
but it doesn't arise as anything at all
Hence, what has been born is unborn
This being unborn is the mode of being born[1722] [3]

By extending the right, pulling in the left, thrusting out
the threatening gesture, and looking with the vajra gaze,
the supreme steed comes and goes leisurely
If remaining there, the many are to be made one [4]

You should put your feet into the great ocean,
let your hands wander all over the earth,
and have your two eyes look into the sky—
the mind does not move anywhere at all [5]

Like a dancing girl's mirror, a powerful wrestler,
a dungeon,[1723] {438} the queen of a king,
a dung sweeper, as well as a prostitute,
associate with the sole companion![1724] [6]

Resembling a tiger, a lion, an elephant,
a camel, a spotted antelope, a monkey,
sandalwood, a trunk, and a human corpse,
the wise should make emptiness their yoga [7]

Like water over a steep cliff, a great ocean,
a single son's mother, an elephant keeper,
a snow mountain, as well as a pure crystal—
if[1725] free of focus, the foundation is firmly laid [8]

In the beginning, middle, and end, respectively,
this is free of a root, an essence, and an activity
Just as it is the case with a lamp in a dream,
it's accomplished by familiarity with unwavering compassion [9]

Coming, going, and staying are arising, abiding, and ceasing
In the three aspects of completely pure emptiness—
great bliss, luminosity, and nonthought—
those of excellent insight rest in equipoise [10]

Placing great compassion in front of you,
always look at true reality without distraction
Through this and training in deity and guru,
the practitioner should take a rest [11]

Listen, son! Because none of your thoughts
neither bind a self here nor set it free,
undistracted, uncontrived,[1726] and simply natural,
hey, take a rest from tiring yourself out! [12]

The mind, remembering reflections and forms,
echoes and sounds,[1727] what is actual and dreams,
possesses a connection with samādhi and
trains in becoming familiar with exhaustion[1728] [13]

Discrimination, the lack of any support,
and constant uninterrupted meditation—
just like gold, like a fire, and like space—
make known, make subside, and make pure [14]

Nonappearance, appearance as something, and conditioned
appearance
are similar to space, a mirror, and a crystal {439}
The gates of samādhi, wisdom, and dhāraṇī
are the means for the realization of that [15]

Seeing is the luminosity of meditative equipoise
At that time, seeing something does not arise
This utterly thought-free one-pointed resting
is the freedom from the dust of distraction [16]

Wherever the vāyus go, there the mind goes
If the person of the mind[1729] has been killed
by keeping them imprisoned in the body's house,
where does the mind go without them? [17]

The nature of everything is uncontrived
All imagination is under the sway of conditions
If this is understood through the three natures,
imagination is turned into imagination's lack [18]

"Established through seeing" and "nonexistent
once[1730] destroyed" are nothing but thoughts
Primordially, there is nothing at all in this
Hey, son, you shall contemplate the sky! [19]

When it comes to both camphor and its smell,
without the one, the other does not exist either
Likewise, conditions and conditions' lack
are not distinct—simply meditate naturally! [20]

Stop movement through the even mind!
Bind what is not even with mindfulness!
At that point, rest in equipoise free of that!
This is the means for killing thoughts [21]

Having washed, put on the sky's garment!
Make the fire offering[1731] of thoughts!
At the ford, the ashes of what comes to mind,
cleanse them with water and wind combined![1732] [22]

Through vessel, contents, vāyus, stream (static and moving),
and the examples of space, the sun, the moon,
Rāhu's seizing,[1733] fireflies, rain, and bees,
the samayamudrā will come to be mastered [23]

Extracting the elixir of fourfold ecstasy
from the flowers of various states of mind,
the taste of the connate is experienced,[1734]
thus satisfying the person of the mind [24] {440}

With the mudrās of body, vāyus, and great nāḍīs,
body, speech, and mind need to be bound
There is no obstruction to generating heat,
and your conduct should not be made rigid [25]

*This concludes "Twenty-Five Stanzas of Pith Instructions on Yogīs Letting Their Own Minds Take A Rest," the dohā that naturally points out true reality. Having heard these very stanzas of pith instructions directly from lord Avalokiteśvara, they were translated by Śrī Jaganmitrānanda, the great mighty lord of yogīs who had attained siddhi, and lotsāwa Jampé Bal in the summer residence *Ambaraparvata*[1735] *at the forest hermitage of Śrī Śivahemagṛha.* {441}

(202) An Expression of Realization in Thirty Stanzas

In the language of India: *Triṃśatyavabhāṣa*[1736]
In the language of Tibet: *Rtogs pa brjod pa sum cu pa zhes bya ba*

I pay homage to lord Avalokiteśvara

Oh vajra holder, the head of Brahmā and Indra,
the world's protector in the center of a huge lotus,
by bestowing empowerment through a stream of rays,
AHO, you purify the three stains—how marvelous! [1]

The immobile[1737] body is like a mountain
The mind free of discursiveness is the sky
The moving[1738] mind is bound by the vāyus' flow
Through this approach, I, the yogī, am super-free [2]

The mind that is all-pervasive space,
the body with its nature of five cakras,
and prāṇāyāma's pair of sun and moon
are bound by the vajra noose of great bliss [3]

The five stains are purified by the wisdoms[1739]
Body, speech, mind are awakened body, speech, mind
These are without contrivance and unborn
AHO! What is there to meditate in this?[1740] [4]

Through the blazing fire of the ocean's essence,[1741]
a chariot courses through Mount Meru's life-pillar
Brahmā and Indra shower down rains from the top
Through the means, look at what is free of means![1742] [5]

That which is ignorance is emptiness
Utter ensnarement is a pleasure grove
Blazing hate {442} magnifies luminosity
What binds a person who is a supreme deity? [6]

The lamp at the navel dispels darkness
At the heart, the lotus of prajñā blooms
The great bliss of wisdom at the head's crown drips
Now my own body turns into siddhi [7]

In the center of the cakras meeting the three nāḍīs
dwells the pellucid bindu of great bliss
Its center is the stainless single eye
of nonconceptual wisdom itself [8]

In the darkness of perceiver and perceived,
realization's light is like the sun shining in the sky
Neither abiding there nor anywhere else—
hey, that is the utterly profound abiding! [9]

The whole world is bound by space
and space is obscured by clouds
When it's pure of the clouds of thoughts,
then what appears in it? [10]

An illusion conquers an illusory city
Mind as such is deceived by the mind
From him, one like me knows the undeceiving—
AHO! AHO! The kindness of the guru! [11]

The below is bound by the karmacakra
The in-between is tied by the vajra knot
Above, the syllable turns upward
These means I find within myself [12]

With the body being made mountain-like,
speech being bound like wind currents,
and mind having the essence of space,
inseparable dharmatā is the entity of all [13]

With the immobile body in the posture of a chariot,
what is mobile is inserted into the life-pillar's path
The samādhi of being bound in such a way
attains the siddhi of the space of immortality [14]

The yoga of space is nonthought
The utterly pure deity is great bliss
Their unity is nothing but luminosity
Take a rest in this state, oh wise ones! [15] {443}

Vajra holder, Vajradhara,
vajra king, vajra bliss,
Vajrasattva empty of sattva
AHO! The omniscient vajra! [16]

You see the flower but don't see the honey
You see the ice but not the water
Seeing the body, extract the bliss!
There is no seeing the mind[1743] [17]

Whose child is a person in the water?
A dream city is without any owner
Where did forms in a mirror come from?
This whole world is just like that [18]

What arises somewhere, is abiding,
and ceases lacks a place, cause, and time
Hey, what fear[1744] could there be of these
phenomena whose characteristic is space? [19]

Their appearances are mere reflections
Awareness too is devoid of awareness
All is [merely] feeling aware, feeling conscious
Even feeling "mere"[1745] lacks that very feeling [20]

In this person with all goals accomplished,
the sun of hatred is the deity of luminosity,
the moon of desire is experienced with bliss,
and ignorance's Rāhu is defeated by nonthought [21]

Like clouds in the sky, waves on the ocean,
honey in a flower, the smell of camphor,
forms in a mirror, and white in a crystal,
thought and nonthought are indeed inseparable [22]

These beings are born from their karma
As for karma,[1746] afflictions are its cause
They are characteristics; if that is understood,
a person without characteristics is free [23]

The elephant is reigned in with an iron hook
The bee of mind is attracted with honey
The goose[1747] of samādhi frolics in a lake
The lotus of prajñā is opened by sun rays [24]

The lamp of mind dispels darkness
The bee suckles at the flower of bliss {444}
The waves of clinging dissolve into the ocean
The clouds of happiness and suffering vanish in the sky [25]

Illustrated by the symbols of the three letters,
I understand and[1748] realize the letterless
The king of yoga is the supreme letter
There is nothing other than the mind [26]

Where there is no going, how could this
going possibly become any "abiding"?
What does not abide is the dharmadhātu
Think how there could be any ceasing in it! [27]

To always be free of doing and without ignorance,
having crushed anger's[1749] latent tendencies for good,[1750]
constitutes the nirvāṇa that represents genuine peace
I understand that this great treasure exists in myself [28]

Yet the world is formed by illusory karma,
and illusions are so by the illusory mind
If all this is understood to be but illusion,
you are free in an illusion-like way [29]

Realizing this illusion crushes thoughts of reality
Not abiding in the illusion of nonthought,
by striving to benefit nonabiding beings,
AHO, this precious jewel is found [30]

This concludes "An Expression of Realization in Thirty Stanzas." It was translated in front of the great mighty lord of yogīs Mitrayogī himself by Nub Lotsāwa Jampé Bal.[1751]

Appendix

Jamyang Kyentsé Wangpo's and Jamyang Kyentsé Wangchug's *Commentaries on Mitrayogī's Letting Your Own Mind Take a Rest* (Text 201) and *Pith Instructions on Threefold Essential Reality*

A Synopsis of the Essence of the Textual Commentaries on Mahāmudrā: Letting Mind as Such Take a Rest Spoken by Noble Avalokita to the Mahāsiddha Mitrayogī (Jamyang Kyentsé Wangpo)[1752]

{526} OṂ svasti siddhaṃ

Having bowed full of respect before the supreme guru,
the treasury of the compassion of the world's protector,
I give a brief synopsis of the essence of the textual
  commentaries
on *Letting Your Own Mind as Such Take a Rest*

This has two parts:

1. The history[1753]
2. The actual instructions

. . . {531}

2. The explanation of the actual instructions has three parts:

1. The introductory points
2. The points of the text
3. The concluding points

1. The introductory points

This has two parts:

1. Teaching on the title
2. Homage by the translators

1.1. Teaching on the title

In the language of India: *Svacitta* . . . In the language of Tibet: *Rang gi sems ngal bso ba'i man ngag tshigs su bcad pa nyi shu rtsa lnga pa zhes bya ba*. As for its meaning, though the connate wisdom of **your own mind** as such is naturally pure from the very beginning, through not realizing this, {532} you have tired yourself out for a long time in the ocean of saṃsāra by being under the sway of perceiver and perceived. This text is what **lets you take a rest** on the island of precious mahāmudrā—the native state. It represents the **pith instructions** that teach the great actuality hard to fathom in an easy manner with just a few words. Since the size of this text consists of **twenty-five stanzas**, it is named in that way.

1.2. Homage by the translators

"**I pay homage to Śrī Vajrasatta**" is easy to understand.

2. The points of the text

This has two parts:

1. Introduction into the native state that is the ground
2. The path—bringing thoughts onto the path

2.1. Introduction into the native state that is the ground

This has two parts:
1. The general topic
2. The points that are the branches

2.1.1. The general topic

In general, the great [Tropu] Lotsāwa himself has condensed the essence of the manner of being introduced to and making these profound instructions a living experience by saying the following. The introduction into the actuality of this has three parts:
1. The preliminaries
2. The main practice
3. The concluding activities

2.1.1.1. The preliminaries

This has three parts: purifying the mindstream through the common preliminaries (the seven-branch [prayer] and so on), blessing it through the uncommon preliminaries (the meditation and recitation of Vajrasattva's hundred syllables and so on), and becoming the ruler of your stream of consciousness through the special preliminaries (supplicating with the fifty syllables and so on).[1754]

2.1.1.2. The main practice

The mudrā of the body consists of sitting on a comfortable seat in a solitary place and assuming the posture with the branches of dhyāna. The mudrā of speech consists of letting the breath move on its own accord. The mudrā of the mind consists of (1) relaxing at ease at first, (2) settling while being wide awake in the middle, and (3) letting go in a serenely even way in the end.

(1) The first—relaxing—has three parts: (a) the positive quality of relaxing, (b) the flaw of not relaxing, and (c) the manner of relaxing. (a)

As for the positive quality of relaxing, since the way in which mind's basic nature abides is to be without contrivance, it courses right within this way of abiding if it relaxes. {533} Therefore, [relaxing] has the purpose of realizing what this basic nature is like. (b) The flaw of not relaxing is the opposite of that: by not relaxing due to your own pushiness, mistaken appearances proliferate out of [mind's own] way of being and thus it will helplessly experience itself spinning and being deluded.

(c) The manner in which to relax has two parts: (a) the means to settle by relaxing and (b) the ancillary [point] of dispelling obstacles. (a) Turn your back on worldly activities. Never entertain any hope for the light of samādhi, nor any fear of it not occurring. Don't perform any mental examination or analysis. Don't cling to any kind of joy, nonjoy, characteristics, or signs. Since examination, analysis, and hope are thoughts that consist of layers on layers of delusion, it is [simply] mind as such that relaxes right within itself. By letting it be through itself relaxing in itself, this true reality has a mode of appearing. What is this mode of appearing? It is simply being without any fabrication and without anything to do. This is also the reason for the profound method of relaxing in an uncontrived manner in the realization[1755] of the uncontrived.

Don't think, "What should be the benefit of relaxing in what cannot be contrived?" Just as an arrow hitting the target is said to be archery, relaxing right within the uncontrived is called "being settled." As it is said:

> If you wish to clearly[1756] realize the true reality
> that is the ground of all uncontrived phenomena,
> without the mind straying off toward any object,
> relax at ease and let be without any artifice

(b) As for dispelling obstacles, to merely arrive at some state of not thinking that is still, in that the moving and proliferating of thoughts has become cut off by settling in a relaxed manner, in such a way is the fool's meditation of preventing the two [nonthought and awareness] from coming together. Therefore, without settling in that [kind of state], as its remedy, bring forth alert awareness, thus settling in a vividly aware, crisp, vibrant, and heightened manner. Since at that point awareness's own radiance dawns, you may not be able to bear being separated from this dimension of lucidity that arises. [However,] this is {534} the dualistic phenomenon of clinging to lucidity as having some characteristics. Therefore, without settling in that [kind of state], as its remedy, settle without mixing [lucid] cognizance with any fine distinctions in terms of boosting or dimming. At that point, within the state of awareness being of even strength while not thinking anything about it at all, vibrant bliss dawns. However, this is called "a mentally fabricated experience of self-arising bliss." Therefore, without resting in that [kind of state] either, in a serenely even way, let mental experiences freely go on their own as they please.

Even now, though you may think, "Don't cling to any experience of bliss that arises," a cause for bondage by clinging in the manner of not being able to bear being separated from this dimension of bliss may arise. If there is clinging, the [coarse] afflictions of saṃsāric existence will expand due to internally clinging to and desiring subtle phenomena of clinging. This is called "falling into the desire realm by clinging to bliss."

[Likewise,] though you may think, "Don't cling to any experience of lucidity that arises," a cause for bondage by clinging in the manner of not being able to bear being separated from the dimension of lucidity may arise. If there is clinging, the saṃsāric existences of the form realm will be accomplished due to the karma that involves inwardly oriented clinging in terms of subtle phenomena of clinging. This is called "straying into the form realms by clinging to lucidity."

[Likewise,] though you may think, "Don't cling to any experience of nonthought that arises," a cause for clinging by clinging in the manner of not being able to bear being separated from the dimension of lucidity may arise. Hence, since then inwardly oriented [clinging] to subtle phenomena of clinging is impossible, the saṃsāric existences of the formless realm will be accomplished through this subtle karma that involves clinging. This is called "going to the formless [realms] by clinging to having become habituated to nonthought." If there is thus any clinging to the triad of bliss, lucidity, and nonthought, a time of becoming liberated from the three [kinds of] saṃsāric existence is impossible. Therefore, no matter what may arise during a day, it is crucial to allow awareness to settle at ease without any contrivance by not clinging to anything that may arise.

There is nothing to be settled by settling—this is the great resting without settling. Even when resting, there is no resting—this is the genuine meditation without any resting. Even when meditating, there is no one who meditates—this is the unsurpassable samādhi of nonmeditation. {535}

Thereafter, (2) settling while being wide awake in the middle and (3) letting go in a serenely even way in the end should be understood by the approach [discussed] above.

Thus, as for beginners resting in meditative equipoise, the following is taught. It is within resting evenly without any highs or lows (unlike a person's face being manipulated by wrinkling it up) and balanced (like a scale made well by someone [whose job it is] to weigh gold) that they will identify the naturally uncontrived native state of their own mind. They will recognize it by virtue of true gurus taking care of them through their blessings and the nectar of their speech, as well as by themselves gathering the merit of having practiced well for a long time.

2.1.1.3. The concluding activities

It is taught that you need to be endowed with the following three [methods]: (1) the methods for not being separated [from mind's native state] for a long time after it has been recognized, (2) the methods for taking appearances as the path, and (3) the methods for whatever you do becoming the welfare of others. (1) Embrace the experience of having been introduced [to mind's nature] during the main practice and [continue to] make this a living experience by joining it with any of the various appearances that keep coming up. (2) Within the state of self-recognition by [mind] recognizing its own face, exercise and do not block the dynamic energy of just the [experiences of] happiness, suffering, and so on that may arise. (3) Dedicate [mind's] being free in itself by recognizing its own face, [thinking,] "May all sentient beings equal [in number] to [the vastness of] space also be free in themselves." Out of the natural state of all activities of the triad of body, speech, and mind being without clinging, earnestly apply yourself to the welfare of others with ever-present compassion. In detail, this is to be understood [as described] in the guiding manuals.

2.1.2. The points that are the branches

In general, due to the differences in terms of those with highest, medium, and lowest faculties, distinct ways of introducing [mind's nature] are taught.

2.1.2.1. [Brief] introduction for those of highest faculties through threefold settling in its own place

[1][1757] The first [point here] is this single stanza "**AHO! Your own mind** . . ." By virtue of not realizing the basic nature of mind in such a way, it is bound in saṃsāra, and if it is realized, it is set free. Therefore, since this is amazing, {536} "**AHO**" is uttered at the beginning. What is it that is amazing? It is the basic nature of **your mind that is primordially unborn** and not established as the essence of anything whatsoever. No matter whether the buddhas of the three times arrive or do not arrive, no matter whether it is introduced or not introduced by the gurus, and no matter whether it is realized or not realized by some persons, it is **abiding** in such a way. If not realized, it **is the cause** or seed **that creates saṃsāra, and** if realized, that of **nirvāṇa**. Apart from this essence, there is **no**thing to be searched for any**where else**. **In your own heart's center** (the place), whenever any kind of awareness dawns (the time), **it will be known** by virtue of making it a living experience by relying on the instructions **from the mouth of the** true **guru** (the means).

2.1.2.2. [Detailed introductions for those of higher, medium, and lowest faculties][1758]

This has two parts:

1. The pith instructions on those with a gradual path becoming free by way of symbols
2. The pith instructions on the instantaneous ones becoming free through the power of blessings

2.1.2.2.1. The pith instructions on those with a gradual path becoming free by way of symbols

This has two parts:

1. Those of highest faculties exhausting movement in its own place
2. Those of medium and lowest faculties allowing movement to be free through other methods

2.1.2.2.1.1. Those of highest faculties exhausting movement in its own place

[2] [Here,] introducing by way of threefold letting be in its own place is twofold: (1) The introduction in terms of being mindful of whatever may arise and whatever may dawn consists of "**Since whatever arises** . . ." **Since whatever** thoughts that may **arise** do not go beyond **the native state itself** that is free of coming and going, just like waves not going beyond the ocean, **if** everything **that dawns is not forgotten by** the **mindfulness** of recognizing its own face, though it may be **dawning** as this or **that** aspect, **it** has **the character of** the essence that is **emptiness**. It is **without question that this represents the king of yoga**—for sure there is no doubt about it. The way of not forgetting by mindfulness is threefold: first, not forgetting that which appears; in between, not forgetting that which perceives; in the end, {537} not forgetting that which clings.

[3] (2) The second [introduction] consists of "**Everything that arises** . . ." **Every** thought **that arises is** not moving away from **just that** true reality—the actuality of the native state. While **that** native state of your own mind **doesn't arise as any** essence **at all**, it appears as any kind of form, similar to a water moon. **Hence**, the lucid appearances **that** seem to **have been born** from the perspective of delusion **are unborn** from the perspective of awareness. However, **this being unborn** and **the** seeming **mode of being born** are not contradictory, just as there is no contradiction [in the example of] it being true that a child is not born in a dream but seems to be born from the perspective of [mind] being impaired by sleep.

The three stanzas up to here are also referred to as "introduction into the unborn native state," "introduction into its being pure of what is adventitious," and "introduction into their inseparable union."

2.1.2.2.1.2. Those of medium and lowest faculties allowing movement to be free through other methods

This has two parts:

1. Introducing those of medium faculties
2. Introducing those of lowest faculties

2.1.2.2.1.2.1. Introducing those of medium faculties

This has three parts:

1. Introducing the highest of those with medium faculties through the examples of three activities
2. Introducing the medium of those with medium faculties through outer, inner, and in between examples
3. Introducing the lowest of those with medium faculties through threefold lightning-like suddenness

2.1.2.2.1.2.1.1. Introducing the highest of those with medium faculties through the examples of three activities

This has three parts:

2.1.2.2.1.2.1.1.1. The examples of the wrathful expressions of celestial beings above the earth

[4] This consists of "**By extending the right** . . ." **Extending the right** [leg] refers to providing the mental backup of great compassion. **Pulling in the left** refers to withdrawing the mind inside through prajñā and emptiness. **Thrusting out the threatening gesture** refers to identifying the one who familiarizes with the pair of emptiness and compassion.

The vajra gaze refers to **looking with** the approach of not observing anything at the actuality of something to be looked at and something that looks not being two. **By** [doing so and then] training in the manner of **the supreme steed** of the vāyus that serves as the mount of thoughts **coming and going leisurely** on the outside and the inside and **remaining** in the profound vajra recitation, **the many** adventitious thoughts {538} **are to be made** a living experience as being of **one** taste within the native state of mind as such.

2.1.2.2.1.2.1.1.2. The examples of the play of the kings of nāgas below the earth

[5] This consists of "**You should put your feet** . . ." When the kings of the nāgas play and frolic during holidays, though they extend their feet into the ocean, roam on the earth with their hands, and let their eyes look into the sky, their minds do not move away from their own place. Likewise, to **put your feet into the great ocean** refers to cultivating the calm abiding of one-pointedly resting within the state of the uncontrived mind. To **let your hands wander all over the earth** refers to cultivating the superior insight of enjoying the appearing of various displays of the unimpeded appearances of [awareness's] dynamic energy by realizing them to be the inseparability of appearance and emptiness. To **have your eyes look into the sky** refers to undistractedly looking, in the manner of [not] engaging in anything whatsoever, at the lack of any focal object in terms of agent and object, and doing so within the state of calm abiding and superior insight being united. By making this a living experience, during all times and circumstances, **the mind** should **not move anywhere at all** from its own domain that is beyond mind and in which there is nothing to do.

2.1.2.2.1.2.1.1.3. The examples of the entourages of kings on the earth

[6] This consists of "**Like a dancing girl's mirror** . . ." It is taught by two examples for the preparation, two examples for the main practice, and two examples for the conclusion. The manner of [teaching this] by

way of these six [examples] is as follows. To look again and again into the mirror of stainless awareness resembles **a dancing girl** looking into her **mirror**. To be endowed with the **power** of overcoming all thoughts clinging to characteristics so that they are free in themselves resembles **a wrestler**. Not being separated during any time of the day and night from the wish to be liberated from all the bondages of afflictions and thoughts resembles **a dungeon**. Every conduct of body, speech, and mind is taken as the means to please the king of the wisdom of mind as such through practicing, {539} while there is no [attempt at] saving face at all, such as listening and explaining in terms of ordinary dharma activities that are similar to the ordinary subjects [of a king]. This resembles **the queen of a king**. To make efforts in sweeping away all thoughts of virtue, wrongdoing, and so on as being free in themselves, without any difference in terms of their being good or bad, resembles **a dung sweeper**. To unite [all] appearances that may arise and be encountered with the dynamic energy of realization, while not excessively striving for the greatest and most excellent dharmas is to be **like a prostitute**. These are the six [examples]. To **associate with the sole companion** refers to the following instruction: "Exercise the prowess of samādhi by associating with mindfulness as the sole companion of the variety of appearances!"

2.1.2.2.1.2.1.2. Introducing the medium of those with medium faculties

This has three parts:

2.1.2.2.1.2.1.2.1 The nine outer examples

[7] This consists of "**Resembling a tiger** . . . " It comprises the three means for giving rise to samādhi that has not yet arisen, the three branches of that arisen [samādhi] becoming the path, and the three essential points of completing the path, which are taught through nine examples. First, to be courageous and not fainthearted with regard to overcoming all thoughts and afflictions **resembles a tiger**. In between, not to be timid and afraid, no matter which inner and outer obstacles or close encounters with death may occur, resembles **a lion**. In the end, not to turn away

from the path due to any among the plethora of adverse conditions, such as dullness and agitation, resembles **an elephant** who has entered the water. These three are the three means for giving rise to samādhi.

For that arisen samādhi to become the path of the Mahāyāna, one needs the distinct feature of being skilled in the means to benefit others, and that in turn is contingent on the power to benefit others, the deity, and the guru. Therefore, the three [branches of arisen samādhi becoming the path] are as follows. The intense longing of devotion resembles **a camel**. Compassion arising on its own through the motivation of benefiting others {540} resembles **a spotted antelope**. To bring all kinds of discursiveness onto the path through means that benefit others and guide whoever is suitable in whatever way suitable resembles **a monkey**.

As for the three essential points of completing the path, to possess the following three features resembles **sandalwood**: cooling the fiery torment of wanting, dispelling the hot disease of the afflictions, and being the supreme among the great dharmas. To possess the following three features resembles the **trunk** of a tree: its root not being moved by adverse conditions, its tip not being bent by favorable conditions, and such a mindstream being way more exalted than all ordinary ones. To possess the following three features resembles **a human corpse**: the faculties that cling to characteristics having ceased, being free of the life force of clinging, and lacking the deliberations of what is to be adopted and rejected. As thus illustrated by these three examples, **the wise** who engage in the profound definitive meaning **should make emptiness** into **their yoga**.

2.1.2.2.1.2.1.2.2. The six examples in between

[8] This consists of "**Like water over a steep cliff** . . ." To possess the following three features resembles **water** that falls **over a steep cliff**: giving rise to many different kinds of thoughts with intense force, their not being interrupted by nonthought or equanimity, and their moving very swiftly like lightning. To possess the following three features resembles **a great ocean**: all the movements of thoughts being of equal taste within the natural state of dharmatā, resting in the natural state of nonthought while not moving, and all kinds of outer movements, no matter how

they may arise, subsiding within the natural state of being without contrivance. These two examples and their meanings represent the means to allow the mind to rest.

To possess the following three features resembles the **mother** of **a single son**: cherishing perfect realization even more than your own heart, being unable to bear ever being separated from this realization, and {541} not taking whatever arises through the dynamic energy of this realization as a flaw. To possess the following three features resembles **an elephant keeper**: being an expert in being taut in the center, in being temporarily relaxed, and in the characteristics of what works and what doesn't. These two represent the branches of stabilizing [mind's] resting.

To possess the following three features resembles **a snow mountain**: [mind] being elevated by virtue of not clinging to lower views, being cool by virtue of being free of the burning torment of perceiver and perceived, and holding its own ground without change no matter which obstacles and flaws may arise. To possess the following three features is **like a pure crystal** globe: being pure by virtue of being free of the stains of clinging, being lucid by virtue of not being obscured by any outer appearances of objects or any inner phenomena of awareness, and being unchangeable into anything whatsoever through conditions such as devotion, compassion, or the path of means. These two represent the essential points of perfecting [mind's] stabilization. **If** by having meditated in that way mind is naturally resting on its own **free of** any deliberately held point of **focus**, this is called "**the foundation** of samādhi **is firmly laid**."

2.1.2.2.1.2.1.2.3. The one inner example

[9] Having arrived in the beginning, all the thoughts that thus occur are as follows **in the beginning, the middle, and the end, respectively**. [In the beginning,] they **are free of a root** of the four conditions (object [condition], dominant [condition], causal [condition], and immediate [condition]), thus resembling horses and elephants in an illusion. [In the middle,] since their own **essence** is not established as such, they are nothing but mere imputations by names but empty of any referents [for these names], thus resembling the child of a barren woman. [In the end,] they

are free of **an active** function, resembling a dream axe cutting down a dream tree. In brief, all phenomena that appear and are imagined in this way are similar to appearances **in a dream**. As for the congruent features [of phenomena and a dream], {542} though **a lamp** may shine brightly during the state of a dream, this lamp's four causes or roots (an oil lamp, a wick, oil, and fire), this lamp's own essence (blazing brightly red), and this lamp's function[1759] (its light that is the means to dispel [darkness] and the darkness to be dispelled) are all not established by any nature of their own. **Just as it is the case with** [this example], **by being familiar** in an **unwavering** manner **with** great nonreferential **compassion** within the state of knowing that all phenomena that appear and are imagined in this way are empty in that they are not established by any nature of their own, all characteristics will become free in their own place and pure enlightened activity will be **accomplished** effortlessly.

2.1.2.2.1.2.1.3. Introducing the Lowest of Those with Medium Faculties

This has three parts:

2.1.2.2.1.2.1.3.1. The Introduction into Awakening Insight (What Is to Be Accomplished) in a Stainless Manner through the Threefold Lightning-like Suddenness in Terms of Experience

[10] This consists of "**Coming, going** . . ." The phenomena to be accomplished consist of the triad of bliss, lucidity, and nonthought. The characteristics of these three phenomena consist of the triad of their being free of **coming, going, and staying**. Their basic nature consists of the three doors to liberation—emptiness, signlessness, and wishlessness. As for the triad of thoughts coming, going, and staying, the **emptiness** of being empty of all thoughts that have a cause of **arising** at first, an essence of **abiding** in between, **and** a result of **ceasing** in the end is **completely pure** as **the three** doors to liberation. It is within [that emptiness] that the following fruition of bliss, lucidity, and nonthought—(1) uncontaminated **great bliss**, (2) natural **luminosity**, and (3) **not thinking** anything

whatsoever—is revealed. Within that state, **excellent** yogīs with the completely pure eye of **insight** into profound actuality should always **rest in equipoise**.

2.1.2.2.1.2.1.3.2. The introduction into consummate meditation (the means to accomplish that) through the threefold lightning-like suddenness in terms of training

[11] This consists of "**Placing great compassion** . . ." (1) The training in means: {543} **placing great compassion** as the ocean-like motivation for beings equal [in number] to [the vastness of] space **in front of you**, [make it] the preliminary. Doing so, make the oath to accomplish the extensive conduct of a bodhisattva that is equal to Mount Meru. (2) The training in prajñā: **always look without distraction at** the knowledge of how to analyze and focus on the essence of the **true reality** of that motivation and application through the prajñā that discriminates it. (3) The training in blessing: supplicate by way of meditating on the oath **deity and guru** yoga. **Through** these kinds of **trainings, practitioners should** let their own mind that has tired itself out through its discursiveness **take a rest** in the natural state of great bliss.

2.1.2.2.1.2.1.3.3. Taking adverse conditions of accomplishing that as the path through threefold lightning-like suddenness in terms of thoughts

[12] This consists of "**Listen, son!** . . ." "**Son**" refers to calling [someone] with a name that [indicates their] being close to one's own son. "You **listen!**" refers to what [that person] should listen to when instructed, without being distracted toward anything else. (1) What is to be taken as the path consists of the entirety of **any** of the **thoughts** that keep coming up in **your** mindstream. (2) The reason for their power if they are taken as the path is **because** those thoughts **neither bind a self** in this great ocean of saṃsāra **here** at the beginning **nor** do they **set** such a self **free** at the end. The reason for this is as follows. For example, when a reflection of the moon appears in a water container, this reflection is not bound by the

water container, nor does the reflection of the moon become free when the water container breaks and its water flows out—that is, [this reflection] never moves away from the nature of the moon in the sky. Likewise, from the very moment of their arising, thoughts do not move away from dharmatā's own domain. (3) As for the practice of how to take [thoughts as the path], first, settling in an **undistracted** manner resembles a skilled swordsman having entered a battle. Being skilled in sustaining this in an **uncontrived** manner in between resembles a skilled elephant herder guarding an elephant. {544} Being skilled in **simply** letting go **naturally** in the end resembles a bird flying off from a ship.[1760]

In detail, these [teachings] are as they are found in the guiding manuals. Since this instruction is the quintessence of this text here, the special means for taking thoughts as the path, a word of amazement—"**Hey**"—connects [this and the following] instruction: "By relying on such a method, all you sentient beings whose own mind has been **tiring itself out** in this ocean of saṃsāric suffering since beginningless [time], **take a rest** in the expanse of natural luminosity that is the native state!"

2.1.2.2.1.2.2. Introducing those of lowest faculties

This has three parts:

1. Introducing the highest of those with lowest faculties to the three trainings—teaching that self-awareness is stainless
2. Introducing the medium of those with lowest faculties to the three gateways—severing the root of perceiver and perceived
3. Introducing the lowest of those with lowest faculties to threefold stopping and accomplishing—letting characteristics dissolve in the expanse

2.1.2.2.1.2.2.1. Introducing the highest of those with lowest faculties to the three trainings—teaching that self-awareness is stainless

This has three parts:

2.1.2.2.1.2.2.1.1. Three examples and their meanings showing equal taste—the union of calm abiding and superior insight

[13] This consists of "**The mind** . . ." By analyzing well the mind **re**collecting **reflections and** actual **forms, echoes and** actual **sounds, what is actually** seen by the sense faculties **and** what is experienced in the state of **dreams**, [the following is understood]. In terms of the aspects as which they manifest, [just like actual forms and such], reflections and so on are also something that appears. In terms of their essence, [just like reflections and such,] actual forms and so on are also not established through any nature of their own. From the very moment of their appearing, all phenomena are unreal. Having understood this, since all objects toward which attachment or aversion arise are not established through any nature of their own, once they are known to be unreal by the cognition that is the [perceiving] subject, the entirety of perceiver and perceived will be free in its own place. It is based on this [understanding] that the calm abiding of one-pointedly abiding **samādhi** {545} is accomplished. Therefore, [this understanding] is established as **possessing a** causal **connection with** [samādhi], **and** you should [also] practice the **training in** cultivating superior insight by [letting] the means to relinquish characteristics [eventually] **exhaust** themselves. That is, first place the entity to meditate on in front of you in a one-pointed manner. In between, let this very one-pointedness be in its own place by way of recognizing its own face. In the end, by not even observing that either, allow the fine distinctions of the mind to become exhausted.

2.1.2.2.1.2.2.1.2. Dispelling the darkness of obscurations and veils by lighting the lamp of the three prajñās

[14] This consists of "**Discrimination** . . ." By analyzing all noticed movements through **discriminating** prajñā, they are understood to be without any nature of their own. Finally, that discriminating prajñā itself is understood as **lacking any support**. Within the state of the clinging to what is known and the insight that is the knower having subsided, in

a **constant uninterrupted** manner, rely on the continuum of the prajñā arising from **meditation**. These three kinds of prajñā are **just like gold** being burned, cut, and filed; **like a fire** when its fuel has become exhausted; **and like space** unchangeable by clouds, mist, and so on. In due order, they [are the means that] **make** the basic nature of what is perceived (that which is to be relinquished) **known** just as it is, **make** the perceiving thoughts that are [considered as] the remedies **subside** on their own accord, **and make** the two adventitious obscurations including their latent tendencies **pure**.

2.1.2.2.1.2.2.1.3. Opening the Gates to Precious Qualities by Awakening the Wisdom of Threefold Appearance

[15] This consists of "**Nonappearance, appearance as something** . . ." Though the ground is by its own nature without appearance,[1761] it still appears through the power of this path, and the fruition is to appear as all kinds of things by virtue of being changed by [certain] conditions. In due order, the examples for these three [kinds of] appearance are that they are similar to **space** being without any nature of its own, reflections appearing in **a mirror**, and **a** pure **crystal** globe appearing as all kinds of colors through the conditions of [certain] objects [reflected in it]. {546} Through the power of resting in meditative equipoise by bringing such modes of being into your experience, the gates to the treasury of [all] precious qualities are opened. By awakening **nonappearance** within the natural state without contrivance, [the gate of] the **samādhi** of one-pointedly abiding in that state [is opened]. By awakening **appearance as something** as being [nothing but the ground's] self-appearances, [the gate of] the **wisdom**[1762] of self-appearances being free in their own place [is opened]. By awakening **conditioned appearance** as dependently originating appearances, **the gate of** the **dhāraṇī** of pure dependent origination is opened. Thus, it is by virtue of the ground of samādhi that the essence of wisdom is accomplished, which is retained without being separated from it through dhāraṇī. It is the power of those [three gates] that **is the means for the realizations of the** dharmakāya, sam-

bhogakāya, and nirmāṇakāya to ultimately appear in the mindstream in their due order.

2.1.2.2.1.2.2.2. Introducing the medium of those with lowest faculties [to the three gateways—severing the root of perceiver and perceived]

This has three parts:

2.1.2.2.1.2.2.2.1. Relinquishing the dust of the perceived and distraction by relying on the gateways of the body (the five sense faculties)

[16] This consists of "**Seeing is the luminosity** . . ." When **seeing** the five objects based on the sense faculties that are the five gateways [of the body], relax at ease in the intrinsic natural state of that which sees and rests in **meditative equipoise** in a wide-awake manner. Through that, the appearing object does not cease, while the **luminosity** free of clinging to it dawns. **At that time**, the reason for that which is such **seeing** actually being nonseeing is because the clinging to perceiver and perceived **does not arise** in it. By **resting one-pointedly** in **utterly thought-free** luminosity in that way, this **is the freedom from the dust of** the **distraction** of characteristics.

2.1.2.2.1.2.2.2.2. Killing the person of the mind (the perceiver) by relying on the gateways of speech (the vāyus)

[17] This consists of "**Wherever the vāyus go** . . ." Since the mind has the vāyus as its mount, **wherever the vāyus go, there the mind goes** and stays. Therefore, **by keeping them imprisoned in the body's house** within the central [nāḍī] through applying vase [breathing], **the person of the mind is** {547} pierced by the weapon of recognizing its own face and thus **killed** in the expanse free of doing and effort. By virtue of **having** done so, **if** it is **without the** mount of the vāyus, **where does the**

mind go? Just like a handicapped person, it will simply remain in its own place.

2.1.2.2.1.2.2.2.3. Overcoming the latent tendencies of both perceiver and perceived by realizing the nature of the gateway of the mind (imagination)

[18] This consists of "**The nature of everything** . . ." Since **the nature of every** imagination **is** not transcending the essence of the **uncontrived** native state, **all imaginations** in their [individual] manifestations arise **under the sway of** extrinsic **conditions**. Therefore, **if this** true reality of **the three natures is understood** well, at the very moment of **imagination** appearing, this very **imagination is turned into** the **lack of** any nature of its own. As for the three natures here, the nature of the essence is that there is nothing to be contrived. The nature of conditions is its appearing as many. The nature of nonduality is their being of the same taste.

2.1.2.2.1.2.2.3. Introducing the lowest of those with lowest faculties [to threefold stopping and accomplishing—letting characteristics dissolve in the expanse]

This has three approaches:

2.1.2.2.1.2.2.3.1. Letting the characteristics of being established and being eliminated dissolve by relying on the yoga of contemplating the sky

[19] This consists of "**Established through seeing** . . ." The position that these objects to be known are **established through seeing and** the position that they are **nonexistent once** they have been **destroyed** through prajñā **are nothing but** what is imagined by **thoughts**. **Primordially, there is nothing** that is established as anything **at all in this** fundamental ground of mind as such. Hence, after having called out with the phrase "**Hey, son**" that [indicates] closeness, the instruction is "**You shall con-**

template the sky!" The manner of contemplating the sky is threefold: looking at the outer unobscured sky with an unwavering gaze, letting the active mind settle within [the nature of] the mind without contrivance (the inner sky), and simply meditating naturally within [the state of] neither inside nor outside being observable as anything whatsoever (the secret sky). {548}

2.1.2.2.1.2.2.3.2. Letting the characteristic of being free of conditions dissolve by relying on the yoga of simply meditating naturally

[20] This consists of "**When it comes to both camphor** . . ." **When it comes to** the pair of **camphor and its smell**, they **both** depend on each other. Therefore, though their isolates are differentiated, they are inseparable in essence. **Without the** camphor, its smell **does not exist either**; without the smell, the camphor does also not exist and is unobservable. **Likewise**, in mind's nature, the pair of the delusion of adventitious appearances [through] **conditions and** the self-arising fresh wisdom that **lacks** any **conditions are not distinct** and not different from each other. Therefore, the instruction is "**Simply meditate naturally!**" The manner in which to simply meditate naturally is threefold: simply letting the native state that is the fundamental ground be in a manner that is natural, uncontrived, and fresh; simply letting the thoughts that are its dynamic energy go, no matter how they may keep arising naturally; and not observing anything to arise from the very moment when the unarisen essence simply arises naturally, thus being the equal taste of [everything] being unarisen.

2.1.2.2.1.2.2.3.3. Letting the characteristics of being equal and not being equal dissolve into the expanse by relying on the yoga of killing thoughts

[21] This consists of "**Stop movement** . . ." Internally, **stop** the adventitious **moving** mind **through the mind** of great all-embracing **equality!** Externally, **bind** the multitude **that is not equal** and the variety of appearances and experiences such as mirages **with** the rope of the

mindfulness of the instruction on great equality! To be **free of the** clinging to both—being equal or not being equal—**at** some **point** by having practiced like that represents the great **resting in equipoise**. **This is the means for killing** all **thoughts**. The way of killing thoughts is threefold: killing ordinary thoughts through mindfulness, killing the thoughts of mindfulness through recognizing their own face, and killing the thoughts of recognizing their own face through equality. {549}

2.1.2.2.2. The pith instructions on introducing the instantaneous ones into becoming free through the power of blessings

This has four parts:

2.1.2.2.2.1. Fully purifying thinking through the vase empowerment (the means to purify)

[22] This consists of "**Having washed** . . ." The instruction [here] is as follows. Externally, wash with the water in the vase. Internally, cleanse with the "svabhāva . . ." mantra. Secretly, understand that there is not even a sesame seed's worth of impurity in the true reality all phenomena. **Having washed** [in these three ways], [any impurity] has been purified within the natural state of naked awareness, and therefore even the stains[1763] of clinging to purity are no more: [this is what it means to] **put on the sky's garment**. By familiarizing with **thoughts** being without any support, **make the fire offering of** burning them such that they are free in themselves! **At the ford of** experiencing bliss, the ford of lucid wisdom, and the ford of thoughtfree samādhi, **cleanse the ashes of what comes to mind** due to subtle latent tendencies **with** the **water** of dhyāna **and** the **wind** of wisdom **together!**

2.1.2.2.2.2. Mastering the samayamudrā through the secret empowerment of the messengers

[23] This consists of "**Through vessel, contents** . . ." What is similar to a **vessel** and its **contents** are the body and the **vāyus**, because the vāyus

abide by being supported by the body. What is associated with the vāyus is the mind**stream**. Thus, the former (the body) is **static and** the latter (both vāyus and mind) are **moving**. **Space** refers to the expanse of natural luminosity, **the sun** to the fire of caṇḍalī, **the moon** to kunda, and "**seized by Rāhu**" to vāyus and mind uniting. **Fireflies** refer to the luminous experience arising from that: the dawning of the appearance of signs such as this. **Rain** refers to nonthought: just as heavy rains shower down from clouds in an unimpeded manner, [nonthought] arises from the dynamic energy of bliss and luminosity fusing. **Bees** refer to bliss: just as bees extract the honey that is the elixir [of flowers], [bliss] arises from experiencing the actuality of the unity of luminosity and nonthought. {550} **Through the** wisdom of the secret empowerment that is illustrated by those [examples], **the samayamudrā**—nāḍīs, vāyus, and bindus—**will come to be mastered**.

2.1.2.2.2.3. Experiencing the taste of the connate through the prajñā-jñāna empowerment

[24] This consists of "**Extracting the elixir** . . ." **The flowers of various states of mind** refer to the inner, outer, and secret [mudrās] as well as the mudrā of true reality. By relying on them in the proper manner, **the elixir of fourfold** [ecstasy]—**ecstasy**, supreme ecstasy, special ecstasy, and connate ecstasy—is **extracted**. Thus, by relying on **experiencing the taste of the connate** melting bliss, it is the wisdom illustrated by this example that **satisfies the person of** the practitioner's **mind**.

2.1.2.2.2.4. Engaging in carefree[1764] conduct through the empowerment of mudrā play

[25] The meaning of "**With the mudrās** . . ." is as follows. Here, the **body** refers to the pure body (familiarizing with [the body] as being the body of a deity),[1765] the supreme body (having faith in its being an illusion), and the consummate body (its being pure as luminosity). As for the **vāyus**, by being able to apply the [appropriate] activities to the moving vāyus, internal and external drawing in, guiding, and so on are accomplished. By being able to hold the stable vāyus like a vajra, the

elements do not inflict any harm. At the time when the indivisible vāyu is seized, the ability to induce the wisdom of the unity of bliss and emptiness [is gained]. As for the nāḍīs, the **great nāḍī** of illusion (the avadhūtī) is purified, the great nāḍī of space (the true reality of all phenomena) is familiarized with, and the great nāḍī that is inconceivable (the dharmadhātu) is revealed. By having sealed and **bound body, speech, and mind with** these kinds of **mudrās**, [the state of] **there being no obstruction to attaining heat** arises. Heat is fourfold: the heat of bliss, lucidity, nonthought, and equal taste. Having attained heat, **conduct should not be made** categorically **determinate**; rather, {551} it is through behaving without any reference points that unbiased enlightened activity should be sustained in the manner of pervading space.

2.3. The concluding points

This has two parts:

1. The colophon about the completion of the text
2. The translation colophon of the lotsāwas

2.3.1. The colophon about the completion of the text

This consists of "*This concludes . . .*" [These are the] "*Twenty-Five Stanzas of Pith Instructions on Yogīs* who join their minds with the profound actuality of the unity of means and prajñā *Letting Their Own Mind* that has tired itself out with all kinds of discursiveness in terms of perceiver and perceived *Take a Rest.*" They represent the means *that naturally point out* what is to be expressed—the *true reality* that is the basic nature of all phenomena just as it is. They constitute a *dohā*, because their means of expression is to express this in an uncontrived and loose manner. Since such a text of vajra words has been taught without any remainder [to be taught] being left over, [the colophon] says "*This concludes.*"

2.3.2. The translation colophon of the lotsāwas

The meaning of "*Having heard these* . . ." is as follows. When deriving "*lord*" from the term "ārya,"[1766] it applies to the expression "noble venerable one," which refers to "[Śrī Jaganmitrānanda's] own supreme deity." Who is that [lord]? Since he is the foremost one among the children of the victor who at all times beholds all beings with his eyes of great compassion, he is greatly renowned as *Avalokiteśvara*.[1767] In accordance with all topics of prajñāpāramitā being summarized in the twenty-five doors of samādhi in the chapter of Dharmodgata,[1768] [Avalokiteśvara] *directly* bestowed *this very* dohā in twenty-five vajra *stanzas* upon *Śrī Jaganmitrānanda* ("Glorious Joyful Friend of the World"), the person *who attained* the supreme *siddhi* of mahāmudrā right then and there. [Not only] being a *yogī* by virtue of having joined his mind with the actuality of unity, he was *the mighty lord* [of all yogīs] due to his being foremost among them, as well as *great* because he had attained the bhūmis of the noble ones. {552} When he was born as a prince, all divine and human beings were very joyful about his father meeting him as his son [for the first time] in the middle of a great marketplace, which was the reason for his being given that name. [These stanzas] *were translated* from their Sanskrit text into Tibetan *by* him and the *lotsāwa* in the lineage of the lords [descending from] Nub Namké Nyingpo,[1769] the eye of the world whose name is renowned as *Jampé Bal, in* a particular [place] in Nepal, *the summer residence* that is an open spacious place known as **Ambaraparvarta*[1770] *at the forest hermitage of Śrī Śivahemagṛha.*

For this text, there appeared the detailed and concise explications by the great Tropu Lotsāwa, the [texts] by the omniscient Butön Rinpoche that match it with quotes from the sūtras and the tantras, as well as some intermediate explications. From among [these texts], I summarized the quintessence of the meaning of Tro[pu] Lo[tsāwa]'s statements, thus writing [this commentary] in the manner of primarily extracting his comments on the words [of the stanzas themselves]. To ascertain this particularly distinguished instruction that arose in the tradition of the unrivaled great chief of siddhas [Śrī Jaganmitrānanda] by studying it and reflecting on it, and to make it a living experience by meditating, should be understood as being the supreme means to extract the very essence of the support that consists of the freedoms and resources [of a precious human body].

By having well accomplished a synopsis of the essence
of the textual commentaries on "Letting Mind As Such Take a Rest"—
the most sublime of all the instructions on mahāmudrā—
may all beings attain the state of supreme unity!

The erudite carefree renunciant Jamyang Lama Gyépé Bang Kyentsé Wangpo[1771] *composed this as a commentary in the form of notes by summarizing the intention of the essence of the textual commentaries [on these stanzas] without impairing it by muddying it through making up anything on his own. May virtue and excellence increase!*

Instructions on how to practice stanzas 12–16 by Jamyang Kyentsé Wangchug[1772]

The manner of making the yoga of the guiding instruction renowned as "Letting Mind as Such Take a Rest" a living experience has three parts:

1. The preliminaries
2. The main practice
3. The conclusion

.... {574}

2. The main practice

The main practice consists of making the meaning of the five stanzas among the twenty-five vajra stanzas that represent the methods to introduce into the native state [of the mind] a living experience. The meaning of "the native state of mind as such" is as follows. Just as one speaks of the saṃgha that continuously resides in a monastery as "the native resident saṃgha," mind as such is primordially uncontrived and resides in a naturally pure manner. Therefore it is called "native, uncontrived, fresh, or ordinary mind."

In terms of its essence, there is no change of state, but in terms of its aspects of manifestation, there is a change of state. In a single piece of copper in its three states of [having been made into] a bowl for a dog, an ornament, or a statue of a deity, there is not even a sesame seed's worth of the essence of this piece of copper having become any better or worse. However, in dependence on its different situational aspects [of how it manifests], it functions, respectively, as something nauseating, something that is understood to be an ornament, and an object that is venerated by all.

Likewise, from the Avīci hell all the way to buddhahood, in its own essence, mind has not become any better or worse. However, it is just differentiated by saying that during the state of not recognizing its own face, it is saṃsāra; at the time of its stains being thinned out a bit through the pith instructions of a true guru, it is what is on the path; and when all stains have been relinquished, it is buddhahood. {575} [The *Hevajratantra* states]:

> Sentient beings are buddhas indeed
> but obscured by adventitious stains[1773]

Though the luminous nature of the mind represents the buddhahood at the time of the ground, due to not recognizing that this is indeed the case, it arises as all kinds of appearances. By virtue of engaging in clinging to the real existence of what arises, the appearances of the delusion of saṃsāra are experienced while not existing. The inability of buddhahood to perform the activities of buddhahood is called "the causal tantra." The cause [here] is what serves as the continuum of both saṃsāra and nirvāṇa. Since that very [continuum] remains in an uninterrupted manner from sentient beings up through buddhas, it is called "tantra."

"Due to the removal of these [stains]" refers to thinning out the appearances of delusion by practicing the means to purify the adventitious stains due to the pith instructions of a true guru. This is the method tantra.

"[Beings] are definitely buddhas" refers to all that is to be relinquished having been relinquished and all that is to be attained having been attained through the path—that is, the buddhahood that is endowed with twofold purity having become revealed. This is called "resultant tantra."[1774]

Therefore, practicing the means to reveal [this buddhahood] is twofold:

1. Coming to a resolve through the view with prajñā
2. Making this a living experience through cultivating the means

2.1. Coming to a resolve through the view with prajñā

In this regard, we find the two [approaches] of letting objects be as being pleasant in their nature and letting the subject be as the view of nondual wisdom. Among these, here, [I discuss] the latter one. As taught above, the means to reveal your own naturally luminous mind are twofold:

1. Training in relaxing
2. Eliminating the obstacles to that[1775]

2.1.1. Training in relaxing

In accordance with the conventional expressions "the three solitudes," "the three immobilities," or here "the three mudrās," the mudrā of the body consists of properly assuming the sevenfold [posture] of Vairocana, with the hands in [the gesture of] meditative equipoise and the thumbs joined at the belly. The mudrā of speech {576} consists of letting the coming and going of the vāyus be in their own place. The mudrā of mind consists of directing the gaze toward a point about seven spans[1776] from the spot between the eyebrows by relinquishing all thoughts of mentally engaging in the three times. Then, settle in the gap, letting the mind be, mainly by relaxing internally.

The flaw of not relaxing is that agitation, such as hoping for meditation to happen, becomes the condition for the mind being distracted again. As for the positive quality of relaxing, when letting be by relaxing at ease in that way, mind itself will come to recognize its own face in a naked and radiant manner. This is similar to the following example. If you manipulate muddy water a lot in the hope for it to become clear, its muddiness will increase again. By letting it settle on its own, it will become clear quickly.

Thus, assume all three mudrās with vibrant lucidity; without mentally engaging in any thoughts of hope or fear whatsoever, such as pondering whether meditation will or will not happen, let mind relax by letting it settle on its own, thus letting it be in a still manner. When letting it be like that, without waiting, suddenly arising thoughts are dharmatā. Therefore, without following no matter which thoughts may arise, cut through them completely. In the gap between the previous thought having passed and the next thought not having arisen yet, right within ordinary mind dawning easily in a naked manner, allow the mind to be. By practicing like this without being distracted for even an instant, at some point after the clinging to the real existence of all kinds of outer appearances has perished, a realization that all these appearances are [nothing but] your own mind arises. In that way, the view of the Mere Mentalists has arisen in your mindstream. Here, this is said to be the recognition of the first point of letting your tired-out mind take a rest.

When looking nakedly at the essence of this knowing that appearances and mind are inseparable, first, any arising of a certain kind of shape from a certain object at a certain time is unobservable. In between, as illustrated by your own inner and outer body from the crown of your head to the soles of your feet, {577} the container and its contents as well as saṃsāra and nirvāṇa are not found to abide in certain kinds of ways or to have certain shapes, colors, or characteristics. Therefore, any abiding in-between is not established. Since arising and abiding are thus not established, any ceasing that is dependent on them is not established either: any ceasing or having become exhausted in a certain kind of way at a certain time is unfindable. In brief, the realization that [mind] is empty of the triad of arising, abiding, and ceasing and, as illustrated by this, that it is free of the four or eight extremes (such as existence, nonexistence, permanence, and extinction) occurs. This is said to be the arising of the Madhyamaka view in the mindstream or the recognition of the second point of letting your tired-out [mind] take a rest.

At the time of resting in meditative equipoise like that, if the mind is not able to rest just as it is, such as when a lot of agitated proliferations of thoughts occur, supplicate by again cultivating the guru yoga as explained above until your body and mind have become exhausted. [Then,] relax and let be without contrivance right within the state of the guru, inseparable from your own mind, having vanished into space. In brief, if you supplicate the guru with fierce devotion from the bottom of your heart not just once, the blessings will enter your mindstream: there arises a naked realization of the basic nature that is the native state of your own mind, in the manner of appearing to itself from within. If the guru's blessings have not entered [your mindstream], no matter how much you may meditate, what will dawn is [nothing but] some vague aspect of an object generality as a mere object of understanding, whereas [genuine] realization will not arise in an unmistaken way. Therefore, it is said that it is crucial to earnestly devote yourself to nothing but devotion for the guru.

> Within the consummation of the path, devotion to the guru,
> by continuously practicing[1777] it as not just some lip service,
> wouldn't it be great if the time came to nakedly see the
> self-arising
> supreme excellent face of the uncontrived native state of your
> own mind?

2.2. Making this a living experience through cultivating the means

Though the essence of the mind may be seen in that way, {578} if the continuum of that is not sustained, through the latent tendencies of being habituated to saṃsāra since beginningless [time], the recognition of the basic nature's own face will be obscured, just like the sun disappearing between clouds. Therefore, so that this does not happen, it must be sustained without distraction at all times and in all situations.

The manner in which to sustain it is threefold: (1) To be skilled in undistractedly training in the means to let [the mind] that does not rest rest is said to resemble a skilled swordsman having entered a battle. In India, when [swordsmen] didn't do battle, they still engaged in distinct combat [styles, ranging] from wielding a sword to using a slingshot. Therefore, since such skilled swordsmen swung their swords in an undistracted manner without being detracted by any doubt, no one could stab them on one side while they defeated everyone on the other side. Thus it was certain that they would win the battle. If some distraction or doubt lingered in their minds, in that gap [of indecision, such swordsmen] themselves would not only die by being pierced by others but also lose the battle.[1778]

Likewise, if yogīs who see the essence of the mind make that a living experience right within that very [seeing] without being distracted for even an instant, they will not only not be stabbed by any thoughts on this side but will also defeat all thoughts on the other side. If they are unable to let be right within that due to doubts or distractions, they fall under the sway of very extensive delusions by virtue of distraction. Having plunged into this ocean of saṃsāra, there is then no time to become liberated from it. Therefore it is said that undistracted mindfulness is crucial at all times and in all respects.

The above applies to [everything] starting from going for refuge up through letting be in the natural state of your own mind free of discursiveness. Settle right within that in the gap without ever being distracted. Completely cut through whichever thoughts may arise. By becoming familiar again and again with this kind of letting be without any clinging, a still resting of mind free of discursiveness takes place. {579} This is said to be the recognition of the third point of letting your tired-out [mind] take a rest.

(2) The means to stabilize [mind's] resting consists of being skilled in protecting it without contrivance in between, which resembles a skilled elephant herder guarding an elephant. Take the example of elephants, who are very powerful and unruly animals. When you guard them, you need someone who is skilled in what works and what doesn't. Whereas if you agitate [elephants] a lot with a whip, an iron hook, and so on, they become angry and just carry on as they like. But if they are not reigned in, they are not brought onto the path either. Therefore, when they walk on the path, let them be in their own place. When they enter what is not the path, guide them with a whip, an iron hook, and so on. Through that, they will walk as desired.

Likewise, if this mind is just left to its own devices, delusion will be extensive. If you agitate it a lot with remedies, this will just add to its delusion. Therefore, if mind itself is resting settled on its own by having set up the spy of nondistraction, without becoming too dull or too excited, in the manner of being relaxed externally but taut internally, simply let be in exactly that state in an expansive manner. If it is moving, seize it firmly with mindfulness, but let be right within the very thought that arises, without clinging and in an expansive manner. Through letting be in that way, [if] a thought arises, by looking at the essence of just that [thought], the single face of mind's native state is seen nakedly without clinging. However, as illustrated by this, since you are not able to block the movement of thoughts, settle right within whatever may arise, in an expansive manner that does not involve any clinging. By meditating in that way, no matter which thoughts may arise, to recognize their own face nakedly is called "movement being free in its own place." This is said to be the recognition of the fourth point of letting your tired-out [mind] take a rest.

(3) [The means to] enhance [mind's resting] after it has become stable consists of being skilled in simply letting go naturally in the end, which is said to resemble a bird flying off from a ship. In India, groups of ocean travelers {580} would bring pigeons, crows, and so on with them in order to investigate mountains and sea monsters. At that time, [when sailing] in areas close to Jambudvīpa, the keepers of these birds and other [people] did an excellent job in keeping [them on board]. Had they not made sure [the birds] did not get lost no matter what happened, [the birds] would have returned to Jambudvīpa. In that case, any investigation of mountains and sea monsters would not have come to pass, and thus bringing along [these birds] would have become useless. Therefore [the bird keepers] needed to apply certain methods so that the [birds] did not fly away. Upon arrival in the middle of the ocean, however, and not finding any limit in [the expanse] that looked like the union of the ocean and the sky, at that point, not needing to keep [the birds on board], they let them go so they could simply fly around naturally. Since [the birds] could neither find any place to go nor manage to stay on the water, they circled around [for a while] and then again landed on the ship.

Likewise, until mind's movement has become free in itself, reign it in without being distracted. No matter which thought may arise, if [its nature] is not sustained right within that [thought] without any clinging and if mind roams toward objects, apart[1779] from just a state of mind of having trained in virtue, you will not be able to practice the path to liberation and omniscience. Therefore [your practice] becomes useless. Thus, once it is known that movement is free in itself, in order to investigate whether this is stable or not, let the mind loose in a pervasive manner by deliberately letting it proliferate toward objects that give rise to afflictions such as desire and hatred. Thus, by bringing the dynamic energy of such and such [afflictions] to perfection, though their aspects [in which they manifest] are vividly present as such and such afflictions, their essence is present nakedly as nondual wisdom. Without dwelling on a given object, mind itself comes to rest within its inexpressible natural state. If there is familiarity with that, [this very] resting has become the remedy, being fused with the miraculous play of [all kinds of] obstacles. By fusing it gradually with fire, water, weapons, and so on, on top of such and such [obstacles] not being able to cause any harm, enormous enhancements of experience and realization will take place. This is said to be the recognition of the fifth point of letting your tired-out [mind] take a rest. {581}

Sustained for a long time by the nanny of undistracted
mindfulness,
all phenomena are free in the expanse of the uncontrived
native state
Through the vast avenue[1780] of recognizing their own face
without bondage,
wouldn't it be great if the time of realizing the unerring basic
nature came?

2.3. Eliminating obstacles

Thus, the actuality about which you have come to a resolve through the view with prajñā is made a living experience by way of the [above] three points of cultivating the means, without being distracted for even an instant. Through that, the experiences of bliss, lucidity, and nonthought will arise at some point, and if you cling to them, they become the causes of saṃsāra with its three realms. However, since that does not become the path to omniscience, such obstacles need to be eliminated. Still, if those experiences do not arise, that does not become the path either. Therefore, in the beginning, [the practice as described above] is sustained until they arise. If you cling to these experiences, that does not become the path either. Therefore they need to be elevated into being the path.

This bears some similarity with the following example. On the road that goes to the vajra seat in India, there are both delightful plains to become infatuated with (such as Glorious Baltang)[1781] and frightful [parts of the] path (such as toll gates, dangerous passages, and ravines). Unless you go to these [places], you will not be able to arrive at the vajra seat. Given that, if you either stay at the [former places] out of attachment to them or simply return [from whence you came] because you are unable to go to the [latter places] due to being fearful of them, these [places] become obstacles for arriving at the vajra seat.

At the time of resting in meditative equipoise like that, [there may occur] the dimness of failing to nakedly recognize mind's own face even if all movement of thoughts has ceased. This is called "stagnant calm abiding" or "the experience of nonthought." If you cling to that, you will only be born as a god in the formless realm, but it will not become the path to omniscience. Therefore, to eliminate that [clinging], tighten up the essential points of the body, intensify the power of your gaze, rouse your awareness, and uplift your cognizance. Vividly clear, vibrant, and crisp, let mind be in its natural state of being uncontrived. Through that, [mind] becomes the unity of lucidity and emptiness. {582}

By having thus become familiar with this again and again, the experience of lucidity is wide awake and crisp. [However,] if this lucidity dimension is associated with any clinging to its real existence, [an experience] like not being able to bear being separated from this lucid and blissful state of mind arises, and you cling to it, you will be born as a god in the form realm. To eliminate such a [rebirth], allowing the essential points of the body to be relaxed from within, lowering your gaze, and allowing cognizance to be relaxed from within, let [cognizance] be in an expansive manner, settled in its own natural flow. Through that, nonthought and lucidity become a unity.

When lucidity and emptiness thus are a unity, by virtue of the dependent origination of means and prajñā, inexpressible bliss arises vividly, [but] don't entertain any clinging to any experience of bliss. If you cling to it, you will only be born in a place in the desire realm, as appropriate, but this will not become the path to omniscience. Therefore, without clinging to the essence of that bliss, let the mind go in a pervasive manner until it reaches the end of space, expanding your cognizance. By letting [mind] be without grasping, bliss and emptiness will become a unity.

In brief, just like elevating load after load, if lucidity is predominant, [use the methods for] nonthought. If nonthought is predominant, [use] the methods for lucidity. If bliss is predominant, elevate it within the state of emptiness. Through this, all clinging and grasping becomes pure, and thus resting right within the native state of mind takes place.

Thus the very abiding of mind in its uncontrived native state (the dharmakāya at the time of the ground) is made a living experience through the means of letting it be in an uncontrived manner (the dharmakāya at the time of the path). The naked recognition of uncontrived mind's own face as such (the dharmakāya at the time of the fruition) through that is called "buddhahood." However, if a dharmakāya other than the mind existed anywhere, even if we [tried to] seize it, we would not be able to. And even if we had seized it, it would be difficult to blend with. In brief, it is said that [finally] all adventitious stains of not recognizing your own mind's own face have dissolved into the expanse, while mind as such endowed with twofold purity has become revealed. This is referred to with the conventional expression "buddhahood."

These {583} are the notes on what you should familiarize with during the progressive stages of the main practice.

> The experiences of lucidity, nonthought, and bliss arise in the mindstream
> Without clinging to them being distinct, make their unity a living experience
> Your own mind in its native state beyond mind constitutes mahāmudrā
> Wouldn't it be great if the time of realizing twofold purity came?

3. The conclusion

As for the means of resting for an extended period, through being undistractedly mindful of the actuality free of discursiveness, as taught above, it is made a living experience without being distracted for even an instant. Thus the training in virtue is embraced even at night in dreams. In brief, this means to practice with intense effort throughout day and night. It is also the method to bring appearances onto the path: no matter which diseases, evil spirits, afflictions, and so on may arise, nakedly direct the mind right into them. Once the dynamic energy of whatever it may be is brought to perfection, awareness is let be in an expansive manner without any fabrications and so on. In short, without analyzing the appearing of the very appearance that arises, let it be while relaxing right within its essence.

The means for whatever you do turning into the welfare[1782] of beings are said to consist of making efforts in these means so that whatever you do serves as the welfare of sentient beings by thinking: "Though the basic nature of the mind free of all discursiveness is inherently present in all sentient beings, due to their adventitious stains, they do not recognize this presence to be the case. Therefore they experience nothing but the appearances of delusion. Aren't they to be pitied? Thus, I shall benefit them as much as I can."

In the state of what appears and is possible arising as the dharmakāya of great bliss
due to having continuously trained in virtue, free of any equipoise and a thereafter,
wouldn't it be great if the time of bestowing extensive benefit and happiness
on to our mothers, who were so kind to us in direct and indirect ways, came?

Inseparably fastening the toenails of the embodiment of all victors,
the lord of Tsarpa,[1783] to the crown of my head as a jeweled diadem,

the one named Kyentsé, who gained mastery over the kingdom of dharma,
has written down [those instructions] into letters by phrasing them like that {584}

By this virtue, may our mothers who greatly tired themselves out by roaming
the paths of saṃsāric existence take a rest in the cradle of the native state
and attain the uncontaminated great bliss beyond the extent of space—
the state of unity of Lokeśvara, the mighty lord of the world!

Sarva maṅgalam

The Vajra Stanzas of Pith Instructions on Threefold Essential Reality[1784]

Namo gurave

The explanation of this instruction has three points:[1785]

1. *Brief introduction*

During this life, continuously meditate on the oath
When about to die, meditate on the instructions on transference
In the intermediate state, you should do the meditation of fusion
To continuously meditate is the essential point of all

2. *Detailed explanation*

This has three parts:

1. *The essence of practice in this life: continuously meditating on the oath*

2. *The essence of practice when about to die: meditating on the instructions on transference*
3. *The essence of practice in the intermediate state: the meditation of fusion*

2.1. The essence of practice in this life: continuously meditating on the oath

This has four parts:

2.1.1. The pith instruction on exhortation (the condition)

By recollecting impermanence and suffering

2.1.2. Giving rise to the mindset for supreme awakening (the cause)

as well as giving rise to great compassion,

2.1.3. The pith instruction on supplicating the guru and the oath [deity]

with the guru on the crown of your head and the deity in
your heart,

2.1.4. The pith instruction on familiarizing with your own mind being unborn (the essence)

you should familiarize with your own mind being unborn[1786]

2.2. The essence of practice when about to die: meditating on the instructions on transference

This also has four parts:

2.2.1. Offering the illusory body as a gaṇacakra offering

Having given away your own body as an offering

2.2.2. Severing [all] mental ties

and relinquished all dependencies by yourself,

2.2.3. Opening up the great path to liberation

through training with the tube of light,

2.2.4. Transferring your consciousness upward

shoot your mind to the abode of Tuṣita[1787]

2.3. The essence of practice in the intermediate state: the meditation of fusion

This also has four parts:

2.3.1. Mentally engaging in the remedy for not recognizing the intermediate state

Having understood this here to be the intermediate state

2.3.2. *Mentally engaging in the remedy for clinging to the intermediate state as something ordinary*

and having transformed what is outer, inner, and secret,

2.3.3. *Mentally engaging in the remedy for being reborn through attachment and aversion*

through the yoga of emptiness and compassion,

2.3.4. *Mentally engaging in the remedy for an uncertain birth*

you will be reborn through being skillful[1788]

3. *Concluding summary through the pith instruction on the triad of view, meditation, and conduct*

Identifying whatever arises is the essential point of the view
Being undistracted within that is the essential point of meditation
Equal taste through mindfulness[1789] is the essential point of conduct
This is the instruction of the great siddha[1790]

Thus, this instruction was taught by including the manner in which it originated. The first of its stanzas consists of the direct words of the mahāsiddha,[1791] *while the remaining ones were composed by Tropu Lotsāwa Nub Jampé Bal in the style of a commentary on its meaning. Śubham*

Notes

1. The most widely accepted hermeneutical etymology of "ḍākinī" says that it derives from the root *ḍī* or *ḍai* ("to fly"), as explained in Kaṅha's *Yogaratnamālā* (a commentary on the *Hevajratantra*), Jayabhadra's *Cakrasaṃvarapañjikā*, and others. Earlier Indian and Buddhist literature represents ḍākinīs (*mkha' 'gro ma*) as malevolent devourers of humans. This aspect still survives as the class of ḍākinīs known as "flesh eaters." In popular North Indian belief to this day, as one of the "shadows" of the traditional Hinduist view of women, ḍākinīs are understood close to the Western notion of human and nonhuman witches. In tantric Buddhism, there is a division into "mundane ḍākinīs" (Skt. *lokaḍākinī*), usually representing a negative force inimical to Buddhism that needs to be subdued and converted, and supramundane "wisdom ḍākinīs" (Skt. *jñānaḍākinī*), who embody the wisdom as well as the inner impetus that leads to buddhahood. They may appear in human or nonhuman forms, offering guidance to tantric practitioners and serving as the guardians of secret teachings.
2. Excerpted from *Do ha skor gsum gyi Ti ka 'bring po sems kyi rnam thar ston pa'i me long* by Karma Trinleypa (1456–1539); translation by Dzogchen Ponlop Rinpoche. The text preceding the quotation, as well as the paragraph that immediately follows it, also closely follows Karma Trinleypa's text.
3. Tib. *Nges don phyag rgya chen po'i rgya gzhung*. In the blockprints of Palpung Monastery (GZ1), this collection consists of three large volumes, while the modern Tibetan book edition (GZ3) has six volumes.
4. Tib. Chos grags rgya mtsho (1456–1539).
5. The Tengyur consists of the canonical texts of Tibetan Buddhism by Indian (and some Tibetan) authors other than the Buddha.
6. As Roger Jackson (2009, 3–4 and 12–13) says, the *Anāvilatantra* was probably included in GZ and other mahāmudrā collections as the only tantra because it was included in the old list of "the ten dharmas of mahāmudrā" (Tib. *phyag rgya chen po'i chos bcu*) that is mentioned in BA (865) as going back to Maitrīpa and as having been transmitted by his student Vajrapāṇi.
7. Tib. Karma bkra shis chos 'phel blo gros rgya mtsho'i sgra dbyangs (born nineteenth century). This catalogue also includes a description of the general background of the collection and the diverse lineages through which its texts were transmitted.

8. Tib. 'Jam mgon kong sprul blo gros mtha' yas (1813–99).
9. Tib. *Grub pa sde bdun* (different sources have varying lists of seven or eight "siddhi texts").
10. Thematically, and as indicated by their names, these two texts as well as Kerali's *Tattvasiddhi* at the beginning of volume 2 are also considered as belonging to the corpus of "siddhi texts."
11. Tib. *Snying po skor drug*; again, different sources have varying lists of the texts in this cycle.
12. Except for Saraha's *Dohakoṣa* and Sahajavajra's *Sthitisamāsa* (a doxography), the remaining texts of this cycle discuss the perfection process. I translate *utpattikrama* (Tib. *bskyed rim*) and *utpannakrama* (or *niṣpannakrama*; Tib. *rdzogs rim*) as "creation process" and "perfection process," respectively, rather than more familiar but somewhat misleading terms such as "creation stage" (or "generation stage") and "completion stage" (the term **saṃpannakrama*, which is still very common in contemporary secondary literature, is not attested in any known Indian text and appears to be nothing but a wrong back-translation of Tib. *rdzogs rim*). As for the reasons, Skt. *utpatti* means "arising" and "production," while *utpanna* means "arisen," "produced," and "ready" (*niṣpanna* means "arisen," "brought about," "completed," and "ready"). *Krama* means "an uninterrupted or regular progress, order, series, or succession," but also "method." Merriam-Webster defines "process" as "a series of actions or operations conducing to an end," which is exactly what *utpattikrama* and *utpannakrama* are: increasingly refined progressive sequences (and not just one stage) of visualization, recitation, and meditation that have clearly defined goals. The process of the *utpannakrama* is based on the readily available fruition of having sufficiently cultivated the *utpattikrama* (in that sense, more literally, the *utpannakrama* means further meditative training based on "what has been produced" before during the *utpattikrama*).
13. Both the names and the numbers (ranging from twenty-four to twenty-six) of the texts in "The Cycle of Twenty-Five Dharmas of Mental Nonengagement" (Tib. *Yid la mi byed pa'i chos skor nyi shu rtsa lnga*) vary in different sources. The classification of Indian Mahāmudrā texts into "The Seven Siddhi Texts," "The Sixfold Pith Cycle," and "The Cycle of Twenty-Five Dharmas of Mental Nonengagement" existed at least since the time of Butön Rinchen Drub (Tib. Bu ston rin chen grub; 1290–1364). For more details, see Jackson 2008 and Mathes 2011.
14. In addition, Saraha's "Queen Dohā" and another commentary on his "People Dohā" by Advaya Avadhūtīpa are found in appendices.
15. Alias Ajitamitragupta and Mitrayogī (twelfth century); though he is hardly known in the later Tibetan tradition, he also taught extensively in Tibet and was undoubtedly one of the most realized masters to ever visit there.
16. Maitrīpa's main works (many under his aliases Advayavajra and Avadhūta/Avadhūtipa) included here add up to about thirty-five (plus eight by his direct students), while more than twenty are attributed to Saraha. In addition, further songs attributed to these two masters are

found in some of the anthologies of dohās and vajra songs in volumes 4 and 5.

17. For more details, see Robinson 1979 and Dowman 1985.
18. These people are said to have originated from the union of a Brahman (the highest of the four castes) woman and a Śūdra (the lowest caste) man.
19. I am fully aware that other contemporary authors choose a different approach, providing detailed explanations of virtually every practice that the Indo-Tibetan tradition used to keep confidential.
20. This text is closely related to Maitrīpa's *Tattvaratnāvalī* (text 34) and *Sekanirdeśa* (text 42), as well as Rāmapāla's *Sekanirdeśapañjikā* (text 45).
21. The colophon of the latter text ascribes it to Ḍombi Heruka, but its contents leave no doubt that it was sung by his female consort.
22. P5092, N3874. This text is probably a record of the spoken commentary on these songs by Abhayadatta, the oral transmitter of the life stories of the eighty-four mahāsiddhas (translated in Robinson 1979 and Dowman 1985 and 1989) as they had been compiled earlier by *Vīraprabhāsvara/Vīraprakāśa.
23. Tib. Khro phu lo tsā ba byams pa dpal (the founder of the Tropu Kagyü); 1173–1236.
24. Tib. Ma gcig sangs rgyas ras ma; died ca. 1223.
25. These are not to be confused with the more well-known sets of the Six Dharmas of Nāropa, Niguma, or Sukhasiddhi.
26. Tib. Zha lu.
27. Tib. Bu ston rin chen grub; 1290–1364.
28. Tib. 'Jam dbyangs mkhyen brtse dbang po; 1820–92.
29. 'Jam dbyangs mkhyen brtse dbang po 1999b, 531. For more details on Mitrayogī's life and teachings, see BA (1030–43), Tanaka 2013, the final note on text 191 in NG, and the final note on the Tropu Kagyü in the appendix on the major and minor Kagyü lineages (both vol. 1).
30. Tib. 'Jam dbyangs mkhyen brtse dbang phyug.
31. Though Advayavajra and Avadhūtipa are indeed attested as aliases of Maitrīpa, it is not clear in each work whether these two names are indeed simply used as his aliases. There is evidence that there was at least one other tantric Advayavajra, and Avadhūtipa (more correctly Avadhūta) is a rather common generic epithet of tantric practitioners. The Sanskrit words *avadhūta* (male) and *avadhūtikā* (female) from the root "to shake (off)" are used in both Buddhist and non-Buddhist traditions, referring to persons who have reached a level on their spiritual path where they are beyond any ego-based consciousness, duality, and common worldly concerns as well as standard social norms. In the specific case of Maitrīpa, though he is commonly referred to as Avadhūtipa (or Avadhūtīpa) these days, this is the Tibetan "transliteration" of the term *avadhūta(pāda)*, as is confirmed by the colophons of the texts in the *Advayavajrasaṃgraha* (the Sanskrit edition of Maitrīpa's "Cycle of Works on Mental Nonengagement") always using the proper term Avadhūta, usually combined with Advayavajra. Thus, though Avadhūtīpa (or Avadhūtipa) may suggest otherwise, on its own, *avadhūta* has nothing to do with the avadhūtī (the central nāḍī),

though some persons may have reached the level of an avadhūta through avadhūtī-related practices.

32. Karma phrin las pa; 1456–1539.
33. Karma phrin las pa phyogs las rnam rgyal 2009, 8–10.
34. In this context, the term "conduct" (*caryā*) is either used in a general way or for the specific form of practice that is only reserved for highly advanced practitioners and consists of all kinds of antinomian behaviors as an enhancement to induce the nonconceptual nondual wisdom that is free of all reference points (on the latter, see Wedemeyer 2011 and 2013). Thus whenever we encounter the word "conduct" in our text, we need to keep in mind that, depending on the context, this term may either refer to mainstream Mahāyāna and Vajrayāna conduct or to the transgressive yogic practices that aim at going beyond all reference points, including the precepts of the classical Mahāyāna and Vajrayāna (these latter practices are sometimes also called "the conduct of a lunatic," "crazy wisdom," and so on).
35. This has led many to render *caryāgīti* as "performance song." However, this appears to confuse the contents of these songs (yogic conduct) with how they became used later (as songs performed with accompanying music and dance).
36. Jackson 2004, 10.
37. *Dohakoṣahṛdayārthagītaṭīkā*, D2268, fol. 66a.4–5.
38. Schaeffer 2005, 97–98.
39. I follow GZ CD *thur ma* against NP *phrul ma*.
40. I follow GZ CD *tshos* against NP *chos* ("dharma").
41. I follow GZ *ya shu ha* against CDNP *ya shu lta*.
42. I follow GZ *'dzi na pa* against CDNP *'dzin na pa*.
43. I follow GZ *dang gis grol 'dod ko sa la* against CDNP *dbang gis bu grol 'dod kos la*.
44. I follow GZ *thang bzang glu* against CD *thang bzangs glu* NP *thang bzangs krung*.
45. I follow GZ CD *dza* against NP *mdza'*.
46. The name of the text stems from these four and a half stanzas together with the following stories (each line in the first four stanzas refers to one of the sixteen episodes below).
47. Numbers in { } refer to the page numbers of GZ3, vol. 5.
48. I follow GZ *gnyis dang nyin gsum* against CDNP *gnyis dang gnyis gsum*.
49. CDNP omit *bstan pas* ("saw").
50. GZ *'gro bas bsten pa* CDNP *'gro bas rten pa*.
51. This is the full given name of the Buddha when he was a prince.
52. I follow GZ NP *slog* against CD *srog* ("life-force").
53. The poisonous plant Hālāhala (not to be confused with the poison called halāhala that the god Śiva swallowed) has fruits like a cow's udder, and its tuber is blue on the inside and white on the outside. No other plant grows in the vicinity of this very poisonous plant.
54. This is another name of the god Indra.

55. This is white coral.
56. GZ *na se* CDNP *na dpe.*
57. Throughout, I use "mistress" (Skt. *gṛhasvāminī*, Tib. *khyim bdag mo*; lit. "the lady of the house") in the sense of the female head of a household and not with its other meanings (such as a woman with whom a married man has an affair or the mistress of a school or brothel). Of course, here, the Brahman did have an affair with Samantā, but the Indian and Tibetan terms clearly indicate that she is his new wife now.
58. GZ CDNP *sgrub pa 'dis* emended to *sgrub par gyis.*
59. GZ CDNP *bas* emended to *ba'i.*
60. Tib. Dga' sbyangs mdangs.
61. GZ NP *sems* CD *khyod* ("you").
62. "The meditative absorption of cessation" (Skt. *nirodhasamāpatti*, Tib. *'gog pa'i snyoms 'jug*; also known as "the meditative absorption in which discrimination and feeling cease") represents the meditative state in which all primary minds and mental factors with an unstable continuum, as well as some with a stable continuum, have temporarily ceased. That is, the five sense consciousnesses, the mental consciousness, the afflicted mind, and all their accompanying mental factors do not operate in this state. By contrast, the latent tendencies in the ālaya consciousness are still present and will manifest as further instances of the other seven consciousnesses, including their objects, as soon as one rises from this meditative absorption. Note throughout that the term "ālaya consciousness" is different from "ālaya" on its own. The former is the deepest and most subtle substratum of all saṃsāric kinds of consciousness, serving as the basis from which they arise and into which they merge back, being stored as latent tendencies. By contrast, "ālaya" refers to the ultimate nature of the mind, also called "buddha nature."
63. I follow GZ *skur ba btab* against CD *skur pa btab* NP *skul ba btab.*
64. Technically speaking, "the meditative absorption without discrimination" (Skt. *asaṃjñisamāpatti*, Tib. *'du shes med pa'i snyoms 'jug*) is the highest type of meditative absorption within the fourth dhyāna (when performed for a long time, it leads to rebirth on the highest level of the gods of the form realm). During it, primary minds and mental factors with an unstable continuum (the five sense consciousnesses, the mental consciousness, and their accompanying mental factors) temporarily cease, while the afflicted mind and the ālaya consciousness remain active. Thus the latent tendencies for the arising of the first six consciousnesses remain and appearances of delusion will occur again once one rises from this meditative absorption.
65. I follow GZ *sa mthongs* against CDNP *sas thongs.*
66. I follow NP *de las* against GZ CD *las.*
67. CDNP omit everything from here up through "Hey, brahman Jinapa."
68. "The Peak of Existence" (also known as "Neither Discrimination nor Nondiscrimination") is the name of the highest level of the formless realm, which is the highest state of existence within saṃsāra.

69. As this episode speaks about this nun as the foremost one in the assembly of nuns, she appears to be the famous Prajāpatī who was the aunt and stepmother of the Buddha and who, upon her insistence on receiving ordination, became the first Buddhist nun.
70. GZ *tshogs kyi bdag mor lam rtags bcu gsum* CDNP *tshogs kyi lam rtags bcu gsum* ("the thirteen signs of the path of accumulation"). For those thirteen signs, see Nor brang o rgyan 2008, 2:2837.
71. GZ CDNP *dga' ba rnams* ("joys") emended to *dge ba rnams*.
72. I follow GZ *gsang* against CDNP *gsung* ("words" or "speech").
73. GZ CD *'bras bu 'dod pa'i dka' thub dag* NP *bya dka' byas pas 'bras 'dod pa* ("desiring results by doing what is difficult to do").
74. I follow GZ *chog par 'dzin pa dang bral bar bya ba* against CD *chog par 'dzin par bya ba* NP *chog par 'dzin pa dang bar bya ba*.
75. I could not locate this stanza in that tantra or any other text in Kg.
76. I follow GZ *rgyal po indra bhu ti las dbang lan bcu bdun du zhus* against CDNP *rgyal po indra bhu ti la / dbang lan bcu bdun du byas* ("bestowed empowerment on king Indrabhūti seventeen times").
77. CDNP omit *sgom pa* ("familiarizing with").
78. I follow GZ *sngon gyi lung gis nges par blo bsgyur du ma btub* against CD *sngon gyi lung gis nges par kha lo bsgyur du ma btub* ("due to the above scriptural passage, [the king] was not able to steer") NP *sngon gyi lung gi nges par blo bsgyur du ma btub*.
79. I follow GZ CD *rtogs pa* against NP *rtags pa*.
80. "One with misplaced desire" is the literal meaning of Tib. *log sred can*, though the Tibetan usually renders Skt. *icchantika* ("one with great desire"). *Icchantika* is often understood as, or equated with, "those whose disposition is cut off," in the sense of people who do not possess any disposition for nirvāṇa or buddhahood (St. *agotraka*) and thus will never attain it. However, if "disposition" (*gotra*) is understood as an equivalent of buddha nature, many sūtras and treatises explain that there is no sentient being who does not possess it. On the other hand, if "disposition" is understood as roots of virtue (as in some other sūtras and Yogācāra texts such as the *Mahāyānasūtrālaṃkāra*), one speaks of beings who have no disposition for nirvāṇa because they lack any roots of virtue (still, there are different opinions as to whether this means that these beings will never attain nirvāṇa or are eventually able to attain it once they accumulate sufficient virtue at some point in the future).
81. GZ *sel ba* CD *sos pa* NP *gsos pa* ("cured").
82. I follow GZ NP *mi rigs pa'i phyir* against CD *ma rig pa'i phyir* ("Since [all of this] is ignorance . . .").
83. I follow GZ *blun po* against CDNP *srun po* ("tame," "gentle").
84. "Outsiders" (versus "insiders") is a term for non-Buddhists, as Buddhists consider themselves as the ones who primarily deal with the workings of the inner mind as opposed to what seems to be outside.
85. Rākṣasas are fierce demons in Indian mythology who are of giant size, have two fangs protruding from the upper jaw, sharp claw-like finger-

nails, and eat human flesh. They usually are able to fly, vanish, change size, and assume the form of any creature.

86. GZ CDNP *karṇa*. According to Narendra Bhattacharyya 1991 (175), this is one of the fifty-six countries mentioned in the *Śaktisaṅgama*.
87. I follow GZ CD *kṛṣṇa* against NP *srid sna*.
88. Yakṣas (Tib. *gnod sbyin*) are a class of spirits normally portrayed as benevolent and helpful but somewhat fickle, who live on the earth (often in forests), in the air, and in the lower divine realms. Exceptions to their benevolence are that they may cause epidemics or possess humans, and some of them even eat human flesh.
89. CD *na ro pa* NP *nā ro pa*.
90. GZ CDNP *legs smin ka ra* is a corrupt form of princess Lakṣmīṃkarā, one of the eighty-four mahāsiddhas.
91. I follow GZ *gtan med* against CDNP *brten med* ("without being supported").
92. Only the last six stories involve siddhas. The text seems to refer to the future here because its author Nāgārjuna is regarded as one of the earliest mahāsiddhas (if not the earliest) and speaks here about later mahāsiddhas (though all the stories are written in the past tense).
93. I follow GZ NP *skyon* against CD *rkyen* ("conditions").
94. CD omit *(de)'i 'grel pa* ("a commentary on").
95. I follow GZ *ri khrod zhabs la* against CDNP *ri khrod kyis* ("by Śavari").
96. CDNP omit the last sentence. PDMT, 26:1288–1301.
97. PDMT, 26:1525–33. This text bears a close relationship with Maitrīpa's *Tattvaratnāvalī* (text 34) and *Sekanirdeśa* (text 42), as well as Rāmapāla's *Sekanirdeśapañjikā* (text 45). Note that with texts whose title is given in both Sanskrit and Tibetan, the English title always corresponds to the Sanskrit. The Tibetan title may sometimes vary, thus sometimes also varying in the colophon.
98. GZ *rang gi dpyod pa la* NP *rang gi spyod pa la* ("in their specific conduct"). CD omits this phrase.
99. Given the above outline, I follow GZ *dpyod pa* against CDNP *spyod pa* ("conduct").
100. GZ *don gyi ngo bor cir yang mi gnas pa* CDNP *don gyi ngo bo cir yang mi gnas pa* ("its ultimate essence does not abide as anything whatsoever").
101. GZ *aḥ* CDNP *a*.
102. GZ CD *badzra yo gi nī a dhi tiṣṭha* NP *badzri yi gi ni a bhi tiṣṭha*.
103. "Oath deity" (instead of the commonly used hybrid expression "yidam deity"; Tib. *yi dam kyi lha*) refers to one's personal meditation deity due to the samaya one received through an empowerment. Such a deity serves then as the focus of one's continuous daily practice.
104. As pointed out in Isaacson and Sferra 2014 (393n232), this refers most probably to Maitrīpa's *Tattvaratnāvalī* (Mathes 2015, 59–74 and 343–64), which uses the same ninefold classification of three kinds of śrāvakas up through the two kinds of Mādhyamikas.
105. CD omit this phrase.
106. The same threefold division as in this sentence (with regard to

buddhas lacking any blurred vision) is also found in Atiśa's *Ratnakaraṇḍodghāṭanāmamadhyamakopadeśa* (D3930, fol. 111a.7–111b.1; see Apple 2018, 101).

107. As pointed out in Isaacson and Sferra 2014 (393n232), the three kinds of compassion are also discussed in greater detail in the respective sections of the *Tattvaratnāvalī*.

108. That is, Aspectarians, Nonaspectarians, and the two kinds of Mādhyamikas.

109. D3707, fol. 16b.3–4 (Skt. in *Tattvaratnāvalī*: Mathes 2015, 364; *Nayatrayapradīpa*: *sngags kyi bstan bcos*; *Tattvaratnāvalī*: *mantraśāstra* instead of "Mantrayāna").

110. Skt. *utpattikrama*, *gambhīrotpattikrama*, *utpannakrama* (lit. "process of the arisen," but mostly used as an equivalent of the not-so-frequent *niṣpannakrama*), *pariniṣpannakrama*, *svabhāvikakrama*. The term **saṃpannakrama*, which is still very common in the secondary literature, appears to be nothing but a wrong back-translation of Tib. *rdzogs rim*, but is not attested in any known Indian text. See the introduction in the forthcoming vol. 1 of this series for the reasons for translating *utpattikrama* and *utpannakrama*/*niṣpannakrama* as "creation process" and "perfection process" rather than the more familiar but somewhat misleading "creation stage" and "completion stage."

111. Skt. *haṭha*, *duḥ*, and *su*. Compare also the expression "forceful yoga" (Skt. *haṭhayoga*) below as an equivalent of "forceful empowerment." However, as is clear in the following, here the term *haṭhayoga* does not have its usual well-known meaning, but specifically refers to the approach of those who, according to this text, are mistaken about the sequence of the four ecstasies (that is, taking cessational ecstasy and connate ecstasy to be the third and the fourth, respectively, instead of the reverse).

112. These two lines of unknown origin are quoted in a number of tantric treatises, sometimes with variant readings. For a number of references, see Isaacson and Sferra 2014 (275n120); see also Kambala's *Śrīcakraśambaramaṇḍalopāyikāratnapradīpodyota* (D1444, fol. 271a.4–5; second line: "Stabilize it by examining what is to be pointed out"). I follow the emendation of GZ CDNP *brtag(s)* ("examine") to *brtan* ("stabilize") in Isaacson and Sferra 2014 (394n236), since *brtan* is more or less certain in light of the quote's versions in Sanskrit texts, confirmed by the Tibetan of Kumāracandra's *Ratnāvalī* (D1921, fol. 297a.6; P2784, fol. 355a.1: *bstan*), and makes more sense in the given context.

113. *Hevajratantra* II.5.66b. Compare also II.2.40:

> I possess the nature of connate ecstasy,
> the one at the supreme's end and cessation's beginning.

114. This is found in the *Caturmudrānvaya* (D2225, fol. 77a.7) and the *Mudrācaturaṭīkāratnahṛdaya* (D2259, fols. 293b.1–2 and 316a.6–7).

115. I follow GZ *des na* against CDNP *de nas*.

116. As mentioned before, the most common sequence of the four ecstasies in the Indian Buddhist tantras and treatises consists of ecstasy, supreme ecstasy, cessational ecstasy, and connate ecstasy. In due order, these four ecstasies are matched with the four moments—variety, maturation, consummation, and lack of characteristics. The alternative sequence of these two sets of four switches the order of the last two ecstasies as well as the last two moments (interestingly, the *Hevajratantra* provides both of these two sequences in different passages). The latter sequence is generally followed by Ratnākaraśānti, Maitrīpa (as in this text here), Bhitakarma (text 44), Kumāracandra (text 2), a few times Munidatta (text 90), apparently Tilopa's *Dohakoṣa* 31 (at least in its Tibetan version), the latter's commentary on stanza 28, and (indirectly) the Tibetan of Kṛṣṇa's *Dohakoṣa* 24. For more details, see Mathes 2008, Isaacson and Sferra 2014 (96–100), Callahan 2014 (357–59 and 613–14), and Stenzel 2015.
117. *Mañjuśrīnāmasaṃgīti* I.3b.
118. GZ CDNP *rnam pa med pa* ("without aspect") emended to *rnam par nyed pa.*
119. *Hevajratantra* II.3.13. For the rich symbolism of the vajra and the bell in tantric Buddhism, see Beer 1999 (233–45) as well as Willson and Brauen 2000 (556–57).
120. *Hevajratantra* II.3.10cd.
121. As Isaacson and Sferra 2014 (396n242) point out, this stanza is not found in the Tibetan version of this tantra (D481), nor is it commented on in Ratnākaraśānti's *Sarvarahasyanibandha* (D2623). However, the lines of this stanza are found as parts of longer quotes in Abhayākaragupta's *Śrīsaṃpuṭatantrarājaṭīkāmnāyamañjarī* (D1198, fol. 68a.6), Rāmapāla's *Sekanirdesapañjikā* on stanza 22 (D2253, fol. 151a.4–5; two stanzas in Apabhraṃśa; for details, see Isaacson and Sferra 2014, 399–409), Vajrapāṇi's *Guruparamparākrama* (D3716, fol. 176b.2–3), and Vitakarma's *Mudrācaturaṭīkāratnahṛdaya* (D2259, fol. 294b.4–5 and 313b.6).
122. According to Isaacson and Sferra 2014 (396n243), it is likely that the work referred to here as *Dbang gi 'grel pa* is the *Sekanirdeśa/Sekanirnaya*, though the title of this work is usually rendered into Tibetan as *Dbang bskur ba nges par bstan pa.*
123. For further brief and detailed discussions of the differences between the forceful, poor, and excellent bestowings of empowerment, see Bhitakarma's *Mudrācaturaṭīkā* (text 44, 263, 286–87, and 341–44). As Isaacson and Sferra 2014 (101n27) point out, this topic is also treated similarly, though without reference to the distinction of forceful, poor, and excellent, in Puṇḍarīka's *Paramākṣarajñānasiddhi.* In addition, compare the *Caturmudropadeśa*'s section on karmamudrā here with the one in the **Sarvadharmāprasahadeśakatattvārdhagāthāvṛtti* (text 73, 188ff.).
124. Compare this description of the karmamudrā with Saraha's *Kāyakoṣāmṛtavajragīti* 90 (text 53).
125. "Sights and sounds" (Tib. *snang grags*) is a generic expression for all five sensory perceptions.
126. I follow GZ *gnyis su med* against CDNP *nyid du med.*

127. "The nature of the uncontrived true state" here appears to refer to the above (d), "thoughts of both variety and the connate not being observable," as the culmination of the dharmamudrā. Compare this description of the dharmamudrā with Saraha's *Kāyakoṣāmṛtavajragīti* 90 and 94 (text 53).
128. CD omit *rdzogs par* ("perfect").
129. Compare this description of mahāmudrā with Saraha's *Kāyakośāmṛtavajragīti* 69–71 and 91 (text 53).
130. GZ CD *rim pa* NP *rim par*.
131. As mentioned before, for the background and details of the Buddhist deity Heruka and his Śaivaite counterpart Bhairava, see Davidson 1991 and 2002b (211ff.) as well as Gray 2001 (473–505), 2007 (39–54), and 2016. Furthermore, the word "Heruka" is used to indicate the wrathful forms of the five principal buddhas of the five buddha families (such as Buddha Heruka, Vajra Heruka, and so on). It is also found generically as an epithet of many *yogānuttaratantra* deities, especially wrathful ones, such as Cakrasaṃvara, Yamāntaka, and Hevajra. Finally, Heruka can also signify a male realized tantric practitioner. The etymologies of Heruka vary greatly in different texts but the term is generally understood as signifying the embodiment of inseparable bliss and emptiness or inseparable expanse and wisdom. The Tibetan rendering *khrag 'thung* ("blood drinker") refers to drinking the blood of ego-clinging, doubt, and dualistic delusion. Having drunk that blood, Heruka experiences great bliss and all other awakened qualities of the mind (for an explanation of the meaning of the four syllables of "Śrī Heruka," see stanzas 24–26 of text 154).
132. Compare the presentation of the four ecstasies of the samayamudrā in Bhitakarma's *Mudrācaturaṭīkā* (text 44, 344–45).
133. Compare this description of the samayamudrā with Saraha's *Kāyakoṣāmṛtavajragīti* 92 (text 53).
134. This sentence obviously contradicts what was said above about mahāmudrā lacking any division into the four moments or the four ecstasies, as well as parallel passages in *Sekanirdeśa* 27b and its commentary. Thus, Isaacson and Sferra 2014 (398n248) suggest that it may be a later addition, since the division of the four ecstasies into sixteen is found in the Kālacakra literature. There, however, this division is made in terms of the fourfold distinction of body, speech, mind, and wisdom and not in terms of the four seals (also, the resultant sixteen ecstasies are further correlated with the sixteen digits of the black and white fortnights).
135. PDMT, 26:1364–65.
136. Skt. *vikalpa* (Tib. *rnam par rtog pa*) and its cognates are usually translated as "thought" or "conception." However, in its more general sense in Mahāyāna Buddhism, this term, as well as the similar *kalpana*/*rtog pa* and *parikalpa*/*kun rtog*, does not just refer to conceptual thinking but encompasses the entire—fundamentally deluded and dualistic—constructive activity of the mind that can imagine and project all kinds of appearances and

experiences, both conceptual and nonconceptual. In other words, mind continually imagines or constructs its own world and becomes immediately trapped in its own creation.

137. I follow GZ *yis* against CD *yi* and NP *yin*.
138. PDMT, 26:1366–67.
139. I follow CD *rnam par 'bral* and NP *rnam par bral* against GZ *rnam par 'brel* ("connected").
140. GZ *de ni su yis shes pa min* CDNP *de ni su yis shes pa yin* ("Who understands this?").
141. GZ CDNP *ma hā yo ga* emended to *ma hā yo gī*.
142. PDMT, 26:1368–69.
143. PDMT, 26:1370–71.
144. This could also be read as "Without abiding as anything, Kṛṣṇa's mind appears topsy-turvy in everything."
145. PDMT, 27:3–4.
146. Tib. Rdo rje dbang phyug; an epithet of Vajradhara.
147. Note that this song is very similar to text 123.
148. PDMT, 27:7–8.
149. GZ *bo la* NP *bho la*. In the *sandhyābhāṣā* chapter of the *Hevajratantra* (II.3.56–61), *vola* ("gum myrrh") is glossed as *vajra* (understood as "penis"; it can also mean "male," Śiva, Puruṣa, and "means" [*upāya*]).
150. The three main *nāḍīs* or subtle channels, through which flow the *vāyus* ("winds") that are mentally manipulated as part of tantric practice, are the *rasanā* on the right , the *lalanā* on the left , and the *avadhūtī* in the center, running parallel to the spine.
151. In the *sandhyābhāṣā* chapter of the *Hevajratantra*, *kakkolaka* ("perfume") is glossed as *padma* ("lotus"; here understood as a name for the female genitals).
152. GZ CDNP *re ni* appears to render Skt. *aṅga*, a particle implying attention, assent, or desire.
153. CDNP GZ *krī pi ta*. In the *sandhyābhāṣā* chapter of the *Hevajratantra*, *kṛpīṭa* ("wood") is glossed as *ḍamaruka* ("handheld drum").
154. In the *sandhyābhāṣā* chapter of the *Hevajratantra*, *karpūraka* ("camphor") is glossed as *śūkra* ("semen").
155. GZ *ka liṃ dzā ra* CDNP *ka li dze ra*. In the *sandhyābhāṣā* chapter of the *Hevajratantra*, *kāliñjara* (name of a mountain) is glossed as *bhavya* (among its many meanings, "suitable," "fortunate," and "potential" in terms of becoming awakened are the relevant ones here; it can also mean "gentleman," *vāyu*, and *samayinaḥ*).
156. GZ *dundura* CD *'dhu dhura* NP *du dhura*. In the *sandhyābhāṣā* chapter of the *Hevajratantra*, *dundura* ("emission") is glossed as *abhavya* (the opposite of *bhavya*; it can also mean *durguṇī* and *rāgādayaḥ kleṣāḥ-asamayinaḥ*).
157. In the *sandhyābhāṣā* chapter of the *Hevajratantra*, *catuḥsama* ("a potion of the four ingredients sandalwood, agallochum, saffron, and musk") is glossed as *gūtha* ("feces") and *kasturikā* ("musk") as *mūtra* ("urine").
158. GZ CDNP *ma la* appears to render Skt. *hanta* (or *bata*), an exclamation or

inceptive particle expressing an exhortation to do something or asking attention (often translatable as "come on!" or "here!" or "look!").

159. GZ CD *sha wa* NP *sha wang*. In the *sandhyābhāṣā* chapter of the *Hevajratantra*, *śava* ("corpse") is glossed as *śrāya* ("refuge," "reliance," "shelter," "protection").

160. I follow CDNP *rigs skyes* against GZ *rigs kyis*.

161. This could also be read as "self-awareness focusing on the sky." A common Buddhist definition of the often-misunderstood notion of self-awareness is "a nonconceptual, nonmistaken awareness that experiences itself." "Self-awareness" is sometimes understood slightly differently in the traditions of Pramāṇa, Yogācāra, Vajrayāna, and Mahāmudrā. In the texts in this collection, it usually refers to the nonconceptual and nondual wisdom that is aware of its own nature—that is, mind's ultimate nature being cognizant or aware of itself. This is in line with Dharmakīrti's "*saṃvedana* argument" in his *Pramāṇaviniścaya* (slightly elaborated paraphrase): "'Awareness' is simply appearing as such (or in a certain way) because it has that nature. This awareness is not of anything else, just like the awareness of awareness itself is not of anything else. For this reason, too, it is not reasonable for awareness to apply to any referent other than awareness itself" (1.42, 3–6: *saṃvedanam ity api tasya tādātmyāt tathāprathanam, na tad anyasya kasyacid ātmasaṃvedanavat. tato 'pi na tad arthāntare yuktam*). That is, by its very nature, cognition cannot be of some external entity. Thus awareness of any object is fundamentally not different from cognition's reflexive awareness of itself because by its own nature cognition is just an intransitive "appearing in a certain way" as opposed to a transitive apprehending of something else. It is important to acknowledge that "to appear" (*prathate*) is an intransitive verb of occurrence, as opposed to transitive activities such as someone cutting down a tree with an axe. The treatment of cognition by Dharmakīrti's opponents (such as different Hindu schools and Sarvāstivāda Buddhists) in a transitive sense appears to be in line with ordinary language but it is not correct when analyzed. When people such as Dharmakīrti or the mahāsiddhas use expressions like "cognition cognizes itself" (*dhīr ātmavedinī*) or "self-awareness," this is only in terms of speaking in a conventional or metaphorical sense. Actually, cognition simply arises with an intrinsic awareness of its own nature, similar to light having luminosity as its nature. Therefore, unlike someone shining a flashlight on something else or themselves, it is not that cognition actively illuminates itself or others within the framework of an agent, an object, and their interaction. Consequently, the well-known Madhyamaka arguments against self-awareness, such as a sword being unable to cut itself or a fingertip not being able to touch itself, entirely miss the point for two reasons: self-awareness neither operates within the triad of agent, object, and action, nor is it something material that has any physical dimensions in terms of space, shape, color, weight, density, resistance, and so on.

162. This could also be read as "attaining the siddhi of thoughtfree yoga."

163. PDMT, 27:9–10. "Caṇḍālikā" literally means "a passionate woman" or

"a woman who practices caṇḍālī," and "karma" refers to her being a karmamudrā. As Loseries 2015 (54) says, "This name indicates also her social status as Caṇḍāla, a class of people in India generally considered to be outcastes and untouchables. According to the ancient law code of the *Manu-smṛti*, the class originated from the union of a Brahman (the highest class within the four-class system) woman and a Śūdra (the lowest class) man." The term "Caṇḍāla" is also used in modern times for a specific caste of agriculturists, fishermen, and boatmen in Bengal, more commonly referred to as Namaśūdra. Figuratively speaking, the names of outcaste people, such as Caṇḍāla, Ḍombi, and so on also refer to any vile, wicked, filthy, loathsome, abominable, criminal, ferocious, or lascivious persons or deeds. Furthermore, as White 1996 (199 and 454n90) explains, in both Hindu and Buddhist tantric practices, outcaste Caṇḍāla or Ḍomba (wandering troubadours and dancers) women play a significant role in the worship of the female sexual organ and the subsequent production of a fluid, powerful substance (the *yonitattva*) through sexual intercourse with them. (For the origin, function, and significance of the *vajrolīmudrā* in that context, see White 1996, 199ff., and Mallinson 2018.) "Caṇḍālī" is also a term for a woman in the first day of her menses, as well as the female energy located in the abdomen. A fifteenth-century Bengali commentary on the Buddhist *Laghukālacakratantra* states that the part of the female sexual organ which resembles the beak of a bird is called "bird mouth." The channel that carries semen down from the bird mouth is called *caṇḍālī* when, instead of semen, it carries menstrual flow. "Ḍombī" is that channel which points upward during the menses. At the time of the discharge of semen, this *ḍombī* becomes *āvadhūtī*. In addition, among the "divine herbs" (*divyauṣadhi*) that are said to grow in places where Śiva and his wife once made love, the *cāṇḍālī* plant is obviously named for those outcaste women whose menstrual blood has perennially been prized by tantric practitioners for its transformative powers. The root of this plant exudes a red milk *(kṣīra)* that, similar to sulfur and menstrual blood, is used for the alchemistic fixing of mercury.

164. GZ CD *don thams cad grub pa* NP *don thams cad grub ma*. As mentioned before, Sarvārthasiddhi is the given name of Buddha Śākyamuni. However, as per NP, it may refer here to a female figure.
165. I follow CDNP *bgos pa* against GZ *bsgos pa* ("smear" or "taint").
166. GZ CDNP *rin chen gsal ba*.
167. CDNP *bi rū* GZ *birwa*.
168. CDNP *bi rū pa* GZ *birwa pa*.
169. PDMT, 27:26–27. The standard meanings of Skt. *vasantatilaka* are "the ornament of spring," "the blossom of the tilaka flower," and the name of a particular meter. However, in the *Sampuṭatantra*, its commentaries, and other tantric texts, this term refers to the practice of caṇḍālī (and also the related practice of karmamudrā). Specifically, *vasanta* is said to refer to the bhagavān or the moon (the white bindu), and *tilaka* to the bhagavatī, the sun, or the fire of caṇḍālī, with *vasantatilaka* referring to their blissful union. There

is also a *Vasantatilakanāma* by Kṛṣṇa Paṇḍita (D1448) with a *ṭīkā* by Vanaratna (D1449), both of which relate this practice to the *Cakrasaṃvaratantra*. According to those two texts, the white bindu is called "spring" because just like the season of spring, it delights the heart of all beings. The fire of caṇḍālī is called "tilaka" because it blazes with the fire of wisdom. The white bindu and the fire are also referred to as Heruka and Vārāhī, respectively. Furthermore, there is an anonymous *Śrīvasantatilakanāma* (P4667, N3642). For more details, see Kongtrul Lodrö Tayé 2005, 181–82.

170. GZ CDNP *se bhu* is probably a name (Sebhu is a present-day Indian name; but also "mucus" or "spittle" in Old Indoarian). Or, given the context of spring, it may be a misspelling of Tib. *se 'bru*, which renders either *dāḍima* or *karaka*, names for the pomegranate tree (*karaka* also can refer to *Pongamiag glabra*, *Butea frondosa*, *Bauhinia variegata*, *Mimusops elengi*, and *Capparis aphylla*).
171. I follow CDNP *aṃ bha ka ru ṇa* against GZ *aṃ bha kā ru ṇa*.
172. GZ CDNP *sha ris pa* is neither identifiable as Tibetan nor Sanskrit. Given the words "keeps the drum beat," the term must refer to one among the many types of Indian drums (the closest one in terms of spelling would be the ghat singhari).
173. I follow GZ CD *ri mo* against NP *re mo*.
174. I follow GZ NP *me* against CD *mo*.
175. PDMT, 27:158–60.
176. GZ *bsgrubs pas* CD *bsgribs pas* NP *sgrib pas* ("by having been obscured").
177. A literal rendering of Tib. *dran med* would be "lacking mindfulness" or even "being unconscious." However, in a mahāmudrā context, especially in Saraha's dohās and a number of stanzas in text 182, this term has the positive connotation of mind completely letting go of its tendency to think, project, grasp, and cling, similar to Maitrīpa's term "mental nonengagement" (Skt. *amanasikāra*, Tib. *yid la mi byed pa*). For nonminding's counterpart "minding" (Tib. *dran pa*), see note 217 below.
178. The titles of text may sometimes differ from the way they are referred to in their colophons.
179. PDMT, 27:161–64.
180. As also seen in the colophon, the Sanskrit and Tibetan titles of this text differ.
181. As mentioned before, in texts such as Nāgārjuna's *Pañcakrama* and other literatures related to the *Guhyasamājatantra* according to the Ārya school, the four kinds of being empty—empty, very empty, greatly empty, and all-empty—correspond to illumination, increase of illumination, culmination of illumination, and luminosity, respectively. These four are furthermore matched with the four ecstasies, the four moments, and sometimes the four empowerments. In due order, the first three kinds of being empty are also said to consist of the dependent (Skt. *paratantra*), the imaginary (Skt. *parikalpita*), and the perfect (Skt. *pariniṣpanna*), as well as being related to the ceasing of the thirty-three obscuring thoughts of hatred, the forty obscuring thoughts of desire, and the seven obscuring thoughts

of ignorance. For details, see Dasgupta 1946 (51ff.), Kongtrul Lodrö Tayé 2005 (251–72) and 2008 (109 and 128), Wedemeyer 2007, and Tsongkhapa 2013.

182. GZ *rjes su 'breng* CDNP *rjes su 'brang*.

183. DPR: "peace" refers to the past because it is gone, "passion" to anticipating the future, and "thoughts" to thinking about the present.

184. The tantric literature describes eighty thoughts or mental events (Skt. *prakṛti*; in this case meaning "character," "constitution," "temper," "disposition") that obscure the three stages of illumination that culminate in natural luminosity: (1) the thirty-three thoughts of aversion or hatred that obscure and are indicative of illumination (some of these thoughts are listed in stanzas 8–9), (2) the forty thoughts of desire that obscure and are indicative of the increase of illumination, and (3) the seven thoughts of ignorance that obscure and are indicative of the culmination of illumination. In the final stages of the process of dying or during the realization of luminosity via these three stages, these eighty thoughts dissolve progressively. They are listed and discussed extensively in relation to the three stages of illumination in Kongtrul Lodrö Tayé 2005 (251–72).

185. DPR: GZ CDNP *zung 'jug bral* is analogous to *dga' bral* ("cessational ecstasy").

186. I follow GZ CD *me* against NP *mi*.

187. DPR: "symbols" refers to the practices of the second and third empowerment and "the effortless" to mahāmudrā.

188. DPR: "threefold luminosity" refers to contaminated luminosity, uncontaminated luminosity, and the fusion of the two.

189. I follow GZ CD *dga' ba* against NP *dka' bar* ("difficult").

190. PDMT, 27:207–8.

191. I follow CD *'das pa ni smra* against GZ NP *'das pa na smra*.

192. GZ *skyed* CDNP *spyad* ("engage in").

193. GZ CD *kunydza na* NP *kunytsa na*. Skt. *kuñja* refers to a place overrun with plants or creepers (*kuñcana* means "curving," "bending," or "contracting"; *Khunjanā* is a common Hindi female name: "forest girl"). Given the combination with "garlands," *kuñjana* seems to refer to some kind of (creeping) plant or flower.

194. GZ CDNP *pu ri ma lar*. Pullīramalaya is the name of one of the twenty-four power places in the *Cakrasaṃvaratantra*, as well as a nāḍī in the head that is called "indivisible," and it produces teeth and nails (see Sugiki 2009, 515–62, Kongtrul Lodrö Tayé 2011, 138–39, and Callahan 2014, 309–17 and 630).

195. PDMT, 27:217–19.

196. Probably the siddha Nīlapāda (see von Schroeder 2006, 184–85, 206: Nilakhapa, Nīlapa, Nilapa, Nilipa). Or, this could also be Nīlakaṇṭha ("Blue-necked"), a common name and also an epithet of Śiva.

197. GZ NP *mkha' yis bdag nyid mgul nas 'khyud* CD *mkha' yi bdag nyid mgul nas mkhyud* ("I conceal the nature of the sky in my neck/throat").

198. GZ *gzhon nu lo ni bcu gnyis mar / cir yang bdag gis rtog pa med* CDNP *gzhon*

nu lo ni bcu gnyis ma / ci yang bdag gis rtogs pa med ("I don't realize anything at all").

199. GZ *cis kyang bdag la dgos pa med* CDNP *gcig kyang bdag la dgos pa med* ("I don't need a single one").
200. I follow CDNP *yis* against GZ *yi*.
201. PDMT, 27:220–21.
202. GZ *tshad dang gzung du med pa la* CDNP *tshad kyang gzung du med pa la* ("in that whose measure cannot be gauged").
203. The mahāsiddha Samudra was an outcaste pearl diver (thus the reference to caste). The three worlds are the celestial realms above the earth, the human realm on the earth, and the nāga realm below the earth. In terms of true reality being immeasurable and pervading everything, this stanza also seems to play on the meaning of the author's name (Samudra means "ocean").
204. GZ CD *sa mu dra dag* NP *su mu dra dag* emended to *sa mu dra bdag*.
205. GZ *mthong* CDNP *thob* ("attain").
206. PDMT, 27:5–6. GZ *tattvaṃ sva bhā va dṛṣṭi gī ti ko ṣa do ha nā ma* CD *tattvā sva bhā va dṛṣṭi gī ti ka do ha nā ma* NP *tattvaṃ sva bhā va* . . . AIBS *Tattvasvabhāva-dohakoṣagītikādṛṣṭināma*, Basu 1927 *Tattvasvabhāvadṛṣṭigītikādohā*. The compounds *gītikādoha(koṣa)* or *gītikoṣadoha* as opposed to *doha(koṣa)gītikā* are not attested elsewhere. The Tibetan title correctly renders *dohakoṣagītikā* but omits *tattva* and places *dṛṣṭi* at the very end, which does not make much sense (AIBS appears to follow the Tibetan except for not omitting *tattva*). For all these reasons, I emended the Sanskrit title to *Tattvasvabhāva dṛṣṭidohakoṣagītikānāma*.
207. The Old Bengali version of this song in Basu 1927 (678) does not contain this opening stanza. Basu already pointed out that the remainder of this song is very similar to song 29 of the *Caryāgītikoṣa* (text 90).
208. GZ *las* ("from") CDNP *la* ("in"). The Bengali says, "It is neither being, nor is it nonbeing" (*bhāva na hoi abhāva ṇa jāi*; obviously, GZ CDNP *skyes pa* is a misreading of *jāi* as "arisen").
209. GZ CDNP *longs spyod* Bengali *vilasai* (Skt. *vilāsa*).
210. GZ CDNP *rigs* ("caste") could also be understood as "type." The Bengali has *bāṇa cihna rūpa* ("color, characteristics, and form"). Kvaerne 2010 (190) says: "one suspects that *rigs* functions as an alternative translation of *bāṇa*, meaning not 'colour' but '(social) class')."
211. PDMT, 27:11–14.
212. I follow GZ CD *phyag rgya* against NP *bya brgya* ("hundred activities").
213. I follow CDNP *ngo* against GZ *ngor* ("from the perspective of"), though this would also make sense.
214. CDNP GZ *phyogs med min* ("is not without bias"); TRP (29) has *phyogs dang bral* "(free of bias"), which makes more sense here.
215. GZ *thug phrad* CDNP *tug phrad*.
216. I follow CDNP *de* against GZ *nga*.
217. The literal rendering and common meaning of Tib. *dran pa* would be "mindfulness," "recollection," or "memory." However, in a mahāmudrā

context, especially in Saraha's dohās and a number of stanzas in text 182, this term often has the connotation of the dualistic mind's natural tendency to think, project, grasp, and cling. Thus I chose the rendering "minding," with its counterpart being "nonminding" (Tib. *dran med*).

218. As this stanza shows, "conduct" in a tantric or mahāmudrā context does not just refer to any ordinary activities that one performs outside of one's meditation sessions but is the specific practice of testing and enhancing one's realization through engaging in all kinds of unconventional and even transgressive behaviors while constantly looking at one's mind.

219. This is a literal rendering of *rnam rtog chu bo'i rnal 'byor 'dra*; however, it seems that "Is the nonconceptual yoga that resembles a river stream" would make more sense.

220. I follow GZ *yid la mi byed* against CD *yid la mi gzhag* NP *yid la mi bzhag*. The term "mental nonengagement" (or "mental disengagement"; Skt. *amanasikāra*) in its mahāmudrā meaning of not only being the process of letting go of dualistic conceptualization but also being a direct nonanalytical approach to realizing mind's natural luminosity is primarily known from several of Saraha's dohās and also appears in some dohās by Tilopā and others. Still, Maitrīpa is certainly the one who discusses this term in the greatest detail, due to which his entire approach later came to be identified with this term. Maitrīpa's *Amanasikārādhāra* justifies its use in the Buddhist teachings and clearly explains its meaning, combining a broad range of Indian scholarly approaches with the Vajrayāna language of meditative experience, which is so typical of many of Maitrīpa's works. After having presented some grammatical considerations and then tracing the term back to both the sūtras and tantras, he says that mental nonengagement is not a nonimplicative negation, since it refers to negating all mental engagement that exists in terms of apprehender and apprehended and so on but does not negate mind as such. What that term teaches is the complete transcending of all conceptions. Nevertheless, to regard it as an implicative negation is without flaw—referring to an awareness that lacks any nature is the understanding of those Mādhyamikas who speak of illusion-like nonduality. When one calls that awareness "illusion-like" or "not truly established," this is not a wholesale negation of its existence. Then, Maitrīpa gives two very special etymologies of *amanasikāra*. (1) He says that the (correct) mental engagement (*manasikāra*) in primarily the letter "A" is mental nonengagement (*a-manasikāra*). That kind of mental engagement means that everything is "A"—primordially unborn, since "A" is the seed syllable of identitylessness. Hence, all such mental engagement refers to the lack of nature. (2) Alternatively, the meaning of *amanasikāra* is as follows. "A" stands for luminosity, and "mental engagement" (*manasikāra*) is a word for self-blessing. In this way, the state of *amanasikāra* means to bring forth the pure awareness that is the continuous flow of the nondual inseparable union of prajñā and compassion, which has the character of self-blessing with or within inconceivable luminosity. Thus, in other words, Maitrīpa's key notion of "mental nonengagement"

is just the subjective side of emptiness or what is called "freedom from discursiveness or reference points." The only way in which the mind can engage in the "object" that is the absence of discursiveness is precisely by not engaging in or fueling any reference points, but rather letting it naturally settle of its own accord. In other words, it is only by a nonreferential mind that the absence of reference points can be realized, since that is the only cognitive mode that exactly corresponds to it. At the same time, when the mind rests in its own natural state, free from all discursiveness and reference points, this is not like a coma or being spaced out, but it is vivid and luminous intrinsic awareness. Maitrīpa's above two etymologies of "mental nonengagement" highlight the two crucial features of his mahāmudrā approach explicitly spelled out by his student Sahajavajra and others later. Maitrīpa's linking mental nonengagement with the syllable "A" is an indication that his mahāmudrā corresponds to prajñāpāramitā (in the prajñāpāramitā sūtras, the letter "A" stands for emptiness, or that "everything is primordially unborn"). To connect mental nonengagement with the three highest levels of the perfection process of the *Guhyasamājatantra* ("self-blessing," "luminosity," and "union") is a clear sign that this mahāmudrā also entails Vajrayāna elements—not in terms of tantric rituals or techniques but in terms of inner experiences that represent the essence of the former and can be cultivated in Maitrīpa's sūtra-based approach with the help of the pith instructions of a guru. Sahajavajra's *Tattvadaśakaṭīkā* on 7cd (P3099, fols. 190b.1–191a.2) explains that mental nonengagement does not refer to a complete absence of mental engagement, such as closing one's eyes and then not seeing anything like a vase or a blanket at all. Rather, mental nonengagement refers to the very nonobservation of a nature of entities, be it through analysis or the guru's pith instructions. Therefore, mental nonengagement with regard to characteristics means nothing but fully penetrating the very lack of characteristics. To think "This is unthinkable and nonconceptual" is just thinking, but mental nonengagement does not mean that there is absolutely no cognition of the lack of nature. Padma dkar po (2005, 38–42) gives three meanings of *amanasikāra*. (1) The letter *i* in that term represents a locative case (referring to a place or a basis), with a location or basis being what is negated by the first letter *a*. Thus the term refers to there being no location, basis, or support on which to focus. Hence, to hold one's mind firmly on its focal object through the mode of apprehension of the mental factor of mental engagement is necessary during the practice of ordinary forms of calm abiding, but here this is to be stopped. (2) Without considering the locative *i*, what is negated through the first letter *a* is mental engagement—that is, mental activity. This refers to eagerly engaging in the mode of apprehension of the mental factor, impulse, or intention (Skt. *cetanā*), which is the mental activity of mental formation—mind's engaging in virtue, nonvirtue, and what is neutral. The eight formations or applications are needed in order to remove the five flaws in ordinary calm abiding, but mahāmudrā meditation is free from doing and does not arise from accumulating. All mental activities are presented here as entailing reference points or focal objects, so what is taught by this is the utter peace of all reference points or focal objects. Therefore, it is said:

> To the one who does not think through imagination,
> whose mind does not abide at all,
> who is without mindfulness, is without mental engagement,
> And is without focus, I pay homage.
>
> (This unidentified quote is attributed to Nāgārjuna in Atiśa's *Bodhipathapradīpapañjikā*; D3948, fol. 285a.5.)

(3) The initial *a* in *amanasikāra* stands for prajñāpāramitā and all expressions for nonduality, such as nonarising (Skt. *anutpanna*) and nonceasing (Skt. *anirodha*). Thus the term means to mentally engage in a proper manner in this meaning of the letter *a*. In terms of the Vajrayāna, nonduality refers to the union of prajñā and means, which has the nature of great bliss since this bliss arises from that union. In terms of the Pāramitāyāna, duality refers to apprehender and apprehended, me and what is mine, or cognition and what is to be cognized, which will always be dual for as long as there is mental flux. The identitylessness of all phenomena that is free from all flux and without any reference points arises as the kāya whose character is the nature of phenomena, which is nondual in essence. This arising of nonduality is specified by the aspect of nonarising and therefore is called "the dharma of nonarising." Thus, in brief, *amanasikāra* can be understood as either (1) no engagement in the mind, (2) no engagement of or by the mind, or (3) proper mental engagement in the meaning of prajñāpāramitā.

221. This line could also be read as "nonrealization and realization are like the sky when clouded and clear."
222. GZ *ma rtogs rtogs pa nam mkha' sprin dvangs 'dra / rtogs na de nyid rang bzhin stong pa yin /* (the second line could also be read as ". . . is the empty nature") CDNP *ma rtogs rtog pa nam mkha'i sprin dang 'dra /. . .* ("Thoughts of nonrealization resemble clouds in the sky. If realized, the nature of those very [thoughts] is empty") TRP (31) *ma rtog rtogs na nam mkha'i sprin dang 'dra /. . . .*
223. GZ NP *rang bzhin gnyis med* (which could also be read as "their natural nonduality") CD *rang bzhin dbyer med* ("their natural inseparability" or "their inseparable nature").
224. TRP (31): "This concludes 'A Dohā Song on View, Meditation, Conduct, and Fruition.' Coming from the mouth of the Indian upādhyāya and mighty adept Maitrīpa, it was translated by the Tibetan lotsāwa and great scholar Martön Chökyi Lodrö."
225. PDMT, 27:15–16.
226. PDMT, 27:17–18.
227. "Ruby sulphur" (also known as "ruby of arsenic") refers to realgar (α-As_4S_4), an arsenic sulfide mineral that is orange-red in color and is

used to create a colored dot (tilaka) or stripes usually worn on the center of the forehead (sometimes also on other parts of the body) by certain Indian spiritual practitioners. This is not to be confused with the red dot (called "bindu") made with vermillion that used to be worn only by married women but is nowadays also worn by unmarried women in all kinds of different colors as an ornament.

228. GZ *bsten* CDNP *bstan* ("teach," "demonstrate," "display").
229. GZ *ka tsi ri ni* CDNP *ka tsa ri ni*. Skt. *khacārinī* means a female who moves or flies in the air. The term is related to *khecarī*, a common designation for ḍākinīs.
230. GZ CD *rtsed mo* NP *rtse mo* ("peak," "tip").
231. In the post-Vedic period, Rudra is an epithet of the god Śiva.
232. GZ *mar me* CDNP *mer ma* ("a portable fire-vessel").
233. NP *kaṃ ba la*.
234. PDMT, 27:19–20.
235. I follow GZ *bltabs* against CDNP *bstabs* ("offering").
236. GZ *rkun ma mkhas pa* against CDNP *kun la mkhas pa* ("one skilled in everything").
237. PDMT, 27:21–22.
238. NP omit stanzas 5–6.
239. PDMT, 27:23–25.
240. "Mobile and immobile" refers to the outer world as the container and the sentient beings who are its contents.
241. Throughout, I follow CDNP *dpang* against GZ *dbang* ("power," "empowerment").
242. I follow GZ *kye ho* against CNDP *skye bo* ("person").
243. The Kāpālī or Kāpālika tradition is a form of Shaivism in India (probably originated around the fifth century CE). The word "kāpālika" is derived from *kapāla* ("skull"), literally meaning "one with a skull" or "skull-man." The Kāpālikas traditionally carry a skull-topped trident (*khaṭvāṅga*) and an empty skull as a begging bowl. They furthermore smear their bodies with ashes from charnel grounds, wear bone ornaments, revere the god Bhairava (a fierce form of Śiva), and engage in rituals with blood, meat, alcohol, and sexual fluids. At present, this tradition appears to have merged with the Nāth tradition. Many elements of the Kāpālika approach, such as the outer appearance of practitioners and the ritual aspects, are also found in tantric Buddhism, particularly among the mahāsiddhas, though with a nontheistic view. For more details on the Kāpālikas and the symbolism of the *khaṭvāṅga* and skull (cup) in tantric Buddhism, see Beer 1999 (249–58, 263–67, 280–82, and 285–87) as well as Willson and Brauen 2000 (558–59, 560, and 563).
244. PDMT, 27:28–29.
245. In this stanza, "cultivate," "meditate," and "familiarize" show the range of the different meanings of the same word *sgom pa* (Skt. *bhāvanā*).
246. GZ CDNP *a ma ra sing*.
247. PDMT, 27:30–31.
248. PDMT, 27:32–33.

249. PDMT, 27:34–35. For the theme of milking and drinking the sky, see also songs 122 (which can be understood as a commentary on song 116), 177 (84), 179 (38), 182 (I.16), and 183 (II.7).
250. For the rich symbolism of bow and arrow in tantric Buddhism, see the introduction in vol. 1, Beer 1999 (267–76), as well as Willson and Brauen 2000 (561–62).
251. GZ *de yis* CDNP *de yi* ("of that").
252. PDMT, 27:36–37.
253. I follow CDNP *'grangs pa* against GZ *'grong ba* ("to die").
254. PDMT, 27:38–39.
255. PDMT, 27:40–41.
256. GZ CDNP *he ru pa.*
257. Here and in the parallel instances in the remaining stanzas, I follow GZ *skyo ba* against CDNP *skyob pa* ("protect")
258. GZ *ji ltar* CD *ci ste* ("why") NP *ci ta.*
259. PDMT, 27:42–43.
260. I follow GZ CD *'dam bu* against NP *snam bu* ("blanket").
261. I follow GZ *smyon pa* against CDNP *smon pa* ("aspiration").
262. PDMT, 27:44–45.
263. This could also be read as "assembly of yogic vows."
264. PDMT, 27:46–47.
265. GZ CDNP *zla* ("moon") emended to *za.*
266. PDMT, 27:48–49. Note that this song is very similar to text 97.
267. GZ *spyod pa'i las* CDNP *spyod pa'i lam.*
268. CD omit *glu* ("this song"). PDMT, 27:50–51.
269. For the symbolism of the sword and the noose in tantric Buddhism, see Beer 1999 (276–80 and 294–95), as well as Willson and Brauen 2000 (562 and 564).
270. DPR: if one stands with one foot each on the bows of two boats facing each other, these boats will drift apart and one will fall into the water.
271. A general distinction is made between the common siddhis and the uncommon or supreme siddhi of mahāmudrā (attaining perfect buddhahood). In different sources, there are varying lists of either five or eight common siddhis. The set of five consists of the abilities to (1) create copies of one's own body, (2) walk through solid objects, (3) walk on water, (4) fly in the lotus posture, and (5) touch the sun and the moon. As for the set of eight common siddhis, there are several different lists and also different interpretations of what each one of these siddhis consists of. One version simply adds three more siddhis to the above five: the abilities to become invisible, sink into and move below the earth, and ascend to the divine realms of Brahmā. An often-quoted list from the *Ḍākinīvajrapañjaratantra* includes the eight siddhis of (1) the eye lotion that enables one to see the entirety of the three realms of saṃsāra (or things, such as treasures, beneath the earth), (2) fleet-footedness through applying a lotion to the feet (or wearing blessed boots), (3) the sword that enables one to fly (or to overcome a hostile army), (4) seeing underground in order to discover treasures (or traveling beneath the earth), (5) the pill that enables one to assume any form one wishes (or

to become invisible), (6) traveling to and dwelling in celestial realms, (7) invisibility through applying a substance to the forehead, and (8) extracting the essence in order to extend one's life and rejuvenate the body through elixirs (or extracting nourishment from inanimate things such as stones and even space). According to Lopez 2019 (4), another list of eight common siddhis consists of (1) flying to celestial realms, (2) the sword that defeats all enemies, (3) producing magical pills that make one invisible, (4) walking with great speed over long distances by putting a magical substance on one's feet, (5) making a vessel whose contents are inexhaustible, (6) making yakṣas into one's servants, (7) concocting an elixir that bestows longevity, and (8) seeing treasures beneath the surface of the earth. Referring to both Hindu and Buddhist sources, White 2003 (199) lists (1) magical sword (*khaḍga*), (2) invisibility lotion (*añjana*), (3) foot-paint (*pādalepa*), (4) disappearance (*antardhāna*), (5) elixir of immortality (*rasa-rasāyana*), (6) flight (*khecara*), (7) telekinesis (*bhūcara*), and (8) ability to see into the netherworlds (*pātāla*).

272. PDMT, 27:52–53. Given the words "Kana's sword" and "Bada" in the chorus of this song and the reference to the common siddhis, both of these songs are most probably by Kṛṣṇa's main disciple Bhadrapa (mahāsiddha no. 24). Kṛṣṇa was renowned for both having accomplished and teaching on how to achieve the common siddhis (such as the one of the sword), and there is also an episode about a sword in his biography. Similarly, Bhadrapa had a magical sword with which he slayed the malicious ḍākinī who had caused Kṛṣṇa's death (see song 146).

273. GZ *chos rnams skye 'gag med pa'i yul* CD *chos rnams thams cad skye 'gag med* NP *chos rnams thams cad skye 'gag med pa'i yul.*

274. I follow GZ NP *ri rab* against CD *ra rab*. "Meru's peak" (Skt. *meruśikhara*) is a common symbol for the mahāsukhacakra at the crown of the head.

275. In Indian cosmology, this refers to the cosmic fire at the end of an eon that consumes an entire universe.

276. PDMT, 27:54–55.

277. DPR: NP *bdag gi[s] me rir byed* is the preferred reading against GZ *bdag gis mi rig byed* ("I made imperceptible"). That is, "halo of fire" (DPR gloss: *me'i gong bu*) here refers to visualizing such a halo around wrathful tantric deities during the creation process. CD *bdag gi go rims* ("the stages of a self") thus also refers to the creation process. However, compare the more straightforward variant reading of this line ("I wish to be my harlot") in the quote of this stanza in text 73 (202).

278. "The (great) Sage" [Skt. *(mahā)muni*] is a common epithet of the Buddha.

279. In Eastern Apa. (Old Bengali), *meli* can mean either "uniting" or "abandoning" (the former seems more likely here). However, GZ CDNP *me li* could also be a misspelling of NP *me ri*, as in line 2 of the first stanza (or yet something else altogether).

280. PDMT, 27:56–57.

281. GZ NP *ma ti ro ha na* CD *ma ti do ha na* (Skt. *mati* means "mind," "intention," or "wish," and *rohaṇa* "mounting," "riding," "healing," "semen," or "sandalwood").

282. GZ *g.yos* CDNP *gsol* ("consuming," "relishing").
283. GZ *kārṣa pa ṇi* CDNP *kārṣa pa ṇa*. Khasarpaṇa (in Tibetan texts often spelled Khasarpāṇi, Khasarpaṇi, Karsapāṇi, Karṣapaṇi, Kharsapāṇi, or Kharṣapāṇi) is a form of Avalokiteśvara. It is said that he received this name after he provided money and resources (*paṇa*) to an upasaka named Śāntivarman. Later, when these resources had become exhausted, Avalokiteśvara flew through the sky (*khasar*) to meet Śāntivarman. The name is also explained as "exhaustion of the paṇas." It is often used generically for any form of Avalokiteśvara with one face and two hands, with the right hand in the mudrā of supreme generosity and the left in the mudrā of teaching the dharma and holding a lotus with a long stem blooming at the level of his left ear. With his right leg pendant, the right foot rests on a separate smaller lotus. Thus, this form of Avalokiteśvara represents a male version of the typical appearance of Green Tārā and is consequently often confused with her depictions. More specifically, the term is applied to Khasarpaṇa Amoghapāśa ("The Fruitful Noose"), Lokeśvara "Resting in the Nature of the Mind" (both kriyātantra), and Lokeśvara in the *Sarvadurgatipariśodhanatantra* (a yogatantra).
284. PDMT, 27:58–59.
285. For the symbolism of the crown of five jewels or five skulls as the five buddhas, see Beer 1999 (318–20).
286. PDMT, 27:60–61.
287. According to Desi Sangyé Gyatso 2010 (578), Skt. *utpala* can refer to *Meconopsis*, of four varieties: white, blue, yellow, and red (Clark, Pasang); blue lotus, *Nelumbo nucifera* (Clark); species of *Nymphaea* including white *kumuda*, *Nymphaea lotus*; blue *nilopala*, *Nymphaea stellata*; and red *raktopala*, *Nymphaea rubra* (Dutt). Here, since this refers to a flower in water, it must be either the blue lotus or one of the *Nymphaea*.
288. NP *tshong 'dus* GZ CD *tshong dus*.
289. I follow GZ *'jig* against CDNP *'jigs* ("feared").
290. GZ CDNP *anda*.
291. GZ CDNP *bhe me'i sa ra*. The song refers to several of the miracles that Virūpa performed throughout his life. For example, he was expelled from his monastery because he was seen to consume meat and alcohol, to be surrounded by many women in his cell, and also to frequent bars and brothels. Having left the monastery, he put butterflies and other insects into his mouth, so everyone, including those insects, said he was bad and cruel. However, Virūpa did not harm these beings but liberated their minds, also making people who engaged in animal sacrifices recognize their own cruelty. One day, Virūpa arrived at the Ganges and said, "I am the bad one, so I don't want to pollute you, sacred river. Please provide a path for me!" Upon this, the Ganges parted and he crossed it without becoming wet. At another time, he managed to reverse the flow of the Ganges. Later, he was drinking heavily in a bar, saying he would pay his bill once the sun set. However, he stopped the sun's course for many days so he could continue drinking for free. Finally, the king of the country

paid his bill. As for Aṇḍa ("Egg") and Bhīmeśvara ("Terrifying Lord"), they are epithets of Śiva. This refers to the episode of Vīrupa refusing to prostrate to a huge Śiva statue called Bhīmeśvara (at Drākṣārāma in the present-day Indian federal state Telangana), cracking it down the middle instead. Though he subsequently brought it back to its original form, he placed a statue of Avalokiteśvara on its head and urged all people to pay homage to it.

292. PDMT, 27:62–63.

293. CD omit this line.

294. GZ *nam mkha'i rang bzhin ma mchis so* CDNP *nam mkha'i rang bzhin mi 'chi'am* ("did the nature of space not die?").

295. DPR: "lies" and "the knot of nonduality" refer to elaborate discussions of the concept of "nonduality" in a number of Hinduist spiritual traditions that, from the Buddhist point of view, tie up and obscure the true realization of nonduality beyond all concepts.

296. PDMT, 27:64–65.

297. PDMT, 27:66–67.

298. DPR: "I'm like someone asleep after having sold an elephant" means that just as someone is able to sleep soundly without any worries about their wealth, the carefree yogī Prasara is free of any concerns about possessions or other worldly ties. By contrast, "those who have wealth employ watchmen at night," that is, those who still possess wealth (or have other worldly concerns) need to guard it at night because they worry about losing it, and thus are unable to sleep peacefully.

299. Skt. *prasara* means "boldness" or "courage."

300. This appears to refer to Prasara's guru, possibly Maitrīpa.

301. PDMT, 27:68–69.

302. GZ CDNP *rnam brgyan la* emended to *rnam brgyan pa*.

303. *Ḍombī* or *Ḍombinī* (Tib. *g.yung mo*) refers to a woman from the low caste of wandering troubadours and dancers. It is common in tantric texts for the avadhūtī, Nairātmyā, luminosity, the connate, and so on to be referred to as an outcaste woman, such as Caṇḍāla, Ḍombī, Rajakī ("dyer woman"), Śuṇḍinī ("liquor-seller"), and Nartakī ("dancing girl"), following the antinomian tantric approach of often labeling the highest and purest spiritual principles with the most despicable and impure names. In addition, as Ḍombīs and so on are outcastes or "untouchables," this symbolizes that the connate and so on cannot be touched by the ordinary dualistic mind.

304. PDMT, 27:70–71.

305. PDMT, 27:72–73. The three stanzas of this song resemble stanzas 11–13 of text 151.

306. In accordance with the very similar text 199, GZ *rmongs pa* ("ignorance") is emended to *'joms pa*.

307. This song is not contained in Tg, but its first five stanzas are very similar to the **Namobuddhāyavṛtti* (D2300; text 199). It could be that this text originally continued further, since it ends in *zhing* ("and").

308. PDMT, 27:226–27. Following AIBS and the Tibetan title, which makes

more sense, GZ *tsā rya dṛṣṭi do ha gī ti ka nā ma* CDNP *tsa rya dṛṣṭi do ha gī ti ka nā ma* are emended to *Dohacaryāgītikādṛṣṭināma*.

309. I follow GZ *tshems bu* NP *tshem bu* against CD *tshim bu*. "Guarding the body's tailoring" appears to refer to working with the subtle body of nāḍīs, vāyus, and bindus in the practices of the perfection process. In that vein, according to DPR, "tailoring" could also mean "numbers" (Tib. *'tshems*), referring to the set numbers of the movements of the breath and the vāyus in the nāḍis throughout a day, a month, a year, and so on.
310. I follow CDNP *rtogs pa* against GZ *rtog pa* ("thoughts").
311. DPR: you will die without having accomplished anything meaningful.
312. I follow GZ *tshong dus* against CDNP *tshang dus*.
313. PDMT, 27:228–29.
314. GZ *sems kyi rtog rtse'i chos nyid ni / sa bon nam mkha'i dbyings su smos /* CDNP *sems kyi rtog rtse . . .* emended to *sems kyi tog tses chos nyid kyi / sa bon nam mkha'i dbyings su rmos /*.
315. DPR glosses "the self" as "the clinging to a self."
316. GZ NP *thams cad du ni* CD *thams cad dus su*.
317. I follow CDNP *yi* against GZ *yis*.
318. GZ NP *dang* CD *la*.
319. "Protector of the world" (Skt. *lokanātha*) is an epithet of both Avalokiteśvara and the Buddha.
320. PDMT, 27:230–32.
321. I follow CDNP *nam yang* against GZ *rnams kyang*.
322. DPR: GZ *dngos po* is the preferred reading versus CDNP *dang po* ("first").
323. GZ *rnal 'byor bde* CDNP *rnal 'byor de* ("the yogīs . . .").
324. PDMT, 27:233–47.
325. This stanza is a play on the two words "perishing" and "support" (Skt. *dhvaṃsabhāk*; Tib. *'jig dang rten*). In Tibetan, *'jig rten* usually renders Skt. *loka* ("the world"; lit. "the perishing/perishable support"); thus, "what is perishing and a support" usually just means "worldly" or "mundane."
326. GZ *tha dad min* CD *'thad min la* ("are not tenable") NP *thad min la*.
327. I follow CDNP *'brel ba* against GZ *'bral ba* ("separation").
328. GZ *mar me* CDNP *me de* ("the fire").
329. GZ *gsal byed de* CDNP *gsal byed me* ("the illuminating fire").
330. I follow CDNP *'brel* against GZ *'bral* ("separated").
331. I follow GZ CNP *med* against D *me* ("fire").
332. I follow GZ *gi rtog pa yi* against CD *gis rtogs pa yis* NP *gi rtog pa yis*.
333. This seems to say that childish beings fail to recognize that phenomena arise in dependence on a multitude of causes and conditions, but rather think that one cause has one result (such as a sprout arising from a seed), thus acting accordingly (such as planting a seed with the notion that it is the only cause of the sprout, disregarding the many other conditions necessary for its growth, such as water, warmth, and soil).
334. I follow CDNP *brtags* against GZ *rtogs* ("realized").
335. "The six views" (Skt. *ṣaḍdarśana*) refer to the six major "orthodox" (Skt. *āstika*) tenet systems of Hinduism—that is, those that accept the Vedas as

authoritative: Sāṃkhya, Yoga, Nyāya, Vaiśeṣika, Mīmāṃśā, and Vedānta. Among the six "heterodox" doctrines besides Buddhism that were popular during the Buddha's time (all but Jainism do not exist anymore), four—headed by Pūraṇa Kāśyapa, Ajita Keśakambala, Kakuda Kātyāyana, and Saṃjāyin Vairaṭīputra—were materialistic, denying causality, the value of virtuous actions, and any kind of afterlife. Maskarin Gośālīputra (supreme head of the Ājīvikas) propounded a strict determinism over many lifetimes. Vardhamāna, called Nirgrantha Jnātaputra, but better known as Mahāvīra and Jina, was the founder of Jainism (for details on all these schools, see for example Frauwallner 1956 and Hiriyanna 1973).

336. Tib. *phyi nang mu stegs rtags can* could also be understood as "those with the signs of inner and outer tīrthikas." However, since *rtags can* occurs twice on its own below, it appears to render Skt. *liṅgin*, which is a name for brahmans of a particular order or the name of a Śiva sect. The term can also refer to logicians (one of the meanings of Skt. *liṅga* is "reason") or can simply mean "hypocrite" or "pretender."
337. It is not clear what "Ati" refers to here (possibly the Lokāyatas or some other "heterodox" Indian philosophical system).
338. I follow GZ NP *rtog pa* against CD *rtogs pa*.
339. I follow GZ *rtogs pa* against CDNP *rtog pa* ("thoughts are without difference").
340. I follow GZ CD *gzhi* against NP *bzhi* ("four").
341. I follow GZ NP *khyab byar* against CD *khyab par*.
342. This could be a reference to this example being used in *Mahāyānasaṃgraha* I.49 as a metaphor for "the supramundane mind" and the ālaya consciousness at first coexisting and the ālaya-consciousness then fading away through the path.
343. GZ *gsal bar* CDNP *bde gsal* ("blissful lucid").
344. I follow GZ CD *kun gzhi rnam shes* against NP *kun bzhi rnam shes*.
345. GZ *rig pas* ("through awareness") CDNP *rig pa* emended to *rigs pas*.
346. GZ *sems nyid rang bzhin rnal ma* CDNP *sems nyid rang bzhin chos rnams* ("the phenomena whose nature is mind as such").
347. I follow GZ CD *rgyun* against NP *rgyu* ("cause").
348. I follow GZ NP *mi rtag* against CD *mi rtog* ("nonconceptual").
349. GZ *ji ltar rigs pa spong ba yis* CDNP *ji ltar rigs pa yod pa yis* ("in line with such being reasonable").
350. Here and in the next stanza, GZ CDNP *'dus* is emended to *dus*.
351. GZ *kimpa* CDNP *kim pa*. Kimpāka refers to the poisonous *Strychnos nux vomica*.
352. GZ NP *bzhin* CD *gzhan* ("arisen skandhas that are other have no connection with the skandhas of others").
353. I follow GZ *rgyu* against CDNP *rgyun* ("continuum").
354. I follow GZ *mi* against CDNP *ni*.
355. I follow GZ NP *rang bzhin min* against CD *gzhan ma ni*.
356. GZ *gsal ba med pa yis* CDNP *gsal ba med pa yi*.
357. GZ *'brel ba* CDNP *'gel ba*.

358. GZ *me nyid ni* CDNP *me yin na.*
359. I follow CDNP *mi rigs pa yi* against GZ *mi rigs pa yis.*
360. GZ *mo gsham bu* CD *me long sku* ("a statue in a mirror") NP *me long sbu.*
361. Given everything so far and what follows about these two kinds of connection not existing, GZ CDNP *yod* ("there is") is emended to *med.*
362. I follow GZ *sogs* against CDNP *so.*
363. I follow GZ *med pas* against CDNP *med pa'i.*
364. NP omit this line.
365. I follow GZ *rtag pa* against CDNP *brtags pa* ("labeled").
366. I follow NP *'brel yod na* against CD *'brel pa yod* (GZ mistakenly repeats this line without "if").
367. I follow NP *rtag pa byed pa'i ming can rnams* against GZ *rtag par byed pa ming can rnams* CD *brtag pa byed pa ming can rnams.*
368. I follow NP *rtag pa byed par* against GZ *rtag par byed par* CD *brtag pa byed par.*
369. I follow GZ NP *rtag pa* against CD *brtag pa* ("imputed").
370. GZ NP *thal* CD *mthong* ("see").
371. I follow GZ *dung dang rol mo 'khrol* against CDNP *ngu dang rol mo khro.*
372. GZ *dgrol ba* CDNP *sgrol ba.*
373. This could also be read as:

    If there is no self in these skandhas,
    how can there be coming, going, laughing,
    playing cymbals, conch shells, and so on?
    Thoughts about such keep arising in us,
    and we wish for them to be liberated.

374. GZ *rnam pa* CDNP *gnas pa* ("its abiding in these is not seen").
375. I follow GZ *bdag med med gzugs* against CDNP *bdag med mi gzugs.*
376. GZ *ha rdang med* CDNP *ha rdang mes* emended to *ha cang med.*
377. Here and in line four of stanza 116, GZ CDNP *rol mo* ("cymbals") is emended to *rol pa.*
378. GZ *der brten* CDNP *de brten* NP *de rten.*
379. GZ CDNP *rigs can no* emended to *rigs can ni.*
380. I follow GZ *dung* against CDNP *ngu* ("weep").
381. GZ CDNP *sgyu ma lta bu'i rmi lam dang* emended to *sgyu ma lta bu rmi lam gang.*
382. GZ *'di ni* CDNP *'di na* ("in it").
383. GZ *don dam byang chub mtshan nyid* CD *don dam byang chub sems nyid* ("ultimate bodhicitta") NP *byang chub tshad nyid.*
384. I follow NP *rtog* against GZ CD *rtogs.*
385. PDMT, 27:248–49.
386. Note that though the Sanskrit title here is almost the same as that of text 140, the Tibetan for *asaṃbandha* here is *zhen med* versus *'brel med.* Given the contents of these two texts, the meaning of *asaṃbandha* in them obviously differs.

387. GZ *dkyus sa 'dir* CD *rgyu las 'di* NP *dkyus sa 'di.*
388. GZ *'thung* CDNP *thungs* ("drink") emended to *'thud.*
389. I follow GZ CD *bstad* against NP *gtad.*
390. PDMT, 27:250–51.
391. For the symbolism of the ḍamaru in tantric Buddhism, see Beer 1999 (258–59) as well as Willson and Brauen 2000 (559–60).
392. CD "the great master."
393. PDMT, 27:252–54.
394. Given the parallel phrase "Atis, Nirgranthas" in stanza 12 of text 140, I follow CDNP *a ti* against GZ *a tig*, but the meaning of this is as unclear as there. Given the context, it could be a corrupt name of a Hindu deity or a non-Buddhist school other than the Nirgranthas (Jains).
395. Here and in the parallel line in stanza 3, NP omit *chen po* ("great").
396. PDMT, 27:255–56.
397. I follow GZ and P *rtogs pa* against CDN *rtog pa* ("thoughts").
398. I follow GZ *dngos po yi* against CDNP *dngos po'o.*
399. GZ and CDNP *sems dang sems nyid* has its parallel in the title of text 173, where the Sanskrit *cittacaitanya-* given by AIBS appears to refer to mind and mental factors (*caitanya* derives from *cetana*), which also seems to make more sense here (rather than following just the Tibetan "mind and mind as such"). However, the title of text 173 in GZ CDNP has *cittaciti-* ("mind and thinking"), with *citi* maybe also used in the sense of mental factors. There is no attested Sanskrit equivalent of *sems nyid* other than *citta*; the single exception is *yac cit vetti na cittatām* in Maitrīpa's *Tattvaratnāvalī* 29d (text 34), but the Tibetan curiously renders this as *sems ni sems kyis rig ma yin.* Thus the specific Tibetan mahāmudrā distinction between *sems* ("mind") and *sems nyid* ("mind as such") seems not to appear in that way in Indian texts.
400. Gandharvas are the celestial musicians of Indra, who sustain themselves only through smells and live in the air and the heavenly waters. "A city of gandharvas" is an ancient Indian expression for a mirage, indicating that some part of the lowest heavenly realms in which the gandharvas live could occasionally be seen down on earth as a marvelous, shimmering castle floating in the sky at a distance.
401. I follow GZ *las 'das* against CDNP *mi 'das.*
402. PDMT, 27:257–59.
403. In this and all parallel lines, GZ *mi go* CDNP *me go.* As the colophon lists the sisters Mekhalā and Kanakhalā as the transmitters of this song (and thus in all likelihood her disciples), "Mego" seems to refer to Mekhalā.
404. This expression renders Skt. *digambara,* which refers to naked Jaina ascetics.
405. NP omit stanzas 9 and 10.
406. GZ *kang ka la* CDNP *kaṃ ka la.*
407. PDMT, 27:260–62.
408. I follow CDNP *haṃ* against GZ *hom.* The first two lines in Kun dga' grol mchog 1982 (henceforth abbreviated KG) read:

Since my own merit that is inferior
is separated from the guru's moonlight.

409. GZ CDNP *snang ba rnams* (plural) is ambiguous here, since it can render a wide range of Sanskrit terms, most of them meaning "(false) appearance," "reflection," "splendor," or "light" (many of these Sanskrit words also have a sense of seeming or treacherous appearances). Thus, this line can either refer to the guru's guiding light or splendor having disappeared after his passing or, as per KG's reading of the preceding line as "separated from the guru's moonlight," the author feeling completely lost after his guru's passing away, as if not seeing any appearances in a dark night without moonshine. Though it is impossible to cover both meanings in a single English translation, I opted for "splendorous appearances" as a phrase that can be read as including both of these possibilities.
410. I follow GZ *bdag* against CDNP *dag*. According to Tāranātha's biography of Kṛṣṇa (Templeman 1989, 5), there were six disciples of the mahāsiddha Kṛṣṇa who attained the highest siddhi of mahāmudrā: Bhadrapa (mahāsiddha no. 24), Mahilapa (an alias of Mahipa; mahāsiddha no. 37), Dhamapa (a variant of Dharmapa; mahāsiddha no. 36), Dhumapa, Cimbupa (also known as Maṇibhadra; not to be conflated with the female mahāsiddha Maṇibhadrā; no. 65), and Eyalapa.
411. This line in KG reads "The guru with small drums and open white parasols."
412. This line in KG reads: "The gem of his cremains resides in its midst."
413. GZ CDNP *dha ma dhū ma* KG *dha ma dhu ma*. In a Tibetan text related to a number of mahāsiddhas translated in Kapstein 2000 (57, 59), Dhamadhūmā is the name of a ḍākinī. However, given the context, it is clear that this song refers to Kṛṣṇa's two students Dhamapa and Dhumapa.
414. Skt. *kāmarūpa* means "a shape assumed at will" and "assuming any shape at will." It is also the name of a god, the abode of Kāmākhyā (the goddess of desire), and the first historical kingdom in Assam. In a tantric context, it is the name of one of the twenty-four power places in the *Cakrasaṃvaratantra* and can also refer to the mahāsukhacakra at the crown of the head.
415. This stanza in KG reads:

In Devīkoṭa, within a single instant,
I saw the wealth of the guru dissolve
Within just that brief single instant,
since I have seen complete nonbeing,
with the guru gone, I'm very distraught.

416. The fourth and fifth lines in KG read (the sixth line is omitted):

Dhama, and Dhuma, all of us,
the supreme guru is now no more.

417. GZ CDNP *bha hu ri*. (Yoginī) Bhahuri is another attested form of Ghahurī (corrupt for Gaurī), which is an alias of mahāsiddhā Maṇibhadra (no. 65). However, Tāranātha's biography of Kṛṣṇa (Templeman 1989, 38, 56) says that the malicious ḍākinī who had murdered him first miraculously manifested in the form of a householder called Bahuri, while her actual name was Kāladaṇḍibhartākālī. After Kṛṣṇa's death, Bhadrapa resolved to kill that ḍākinī and finally found her hiding in a tree. He split the tree asunder with his magical sword, chopped up the ḍākinī's body, and fed her to the vajraḍākinīs (in the song below, he seems to have had Mahila's help, who scared away a group of other evil ḍākinīs). Thus, it is that ḍākinī who is referred to here, and it is Bhadrapa who slayed her and then sang this song.

418. I follow KG *'dun ma gtor* against GZ *'dun ma byas* CDNP *mdun ma byas* (Skt. *apuraskṛta* "not hold in esteem"; *byas* may be a typo for *'byed* "split").

419. KG replaces *lus rnams* with *lhag rnams* ("remainders"), but other editions of KG also read *lus rnams*.

420. I follow CDNP and KG *mi rtag go* against GZ *mi rtog go* ("this is nonthought" or "yogīs do not think").

421. GZ *de bhi bhandu ko ti* CDNP *de bhi bhantu ko ti* are not attested; KG has the correct name Devīkoṭa (*de vi ko ṭa'i gnas nyid*), where Kṛṣṇa passed away. Devīkoṭa is an area in Bengal as well as one of the twenty-four power sites in the *Cakrasaṃvaratantra*.

422. GZ CDNP *sri mi li* KG *sre mi bar/sre mi li*. Given that the next stanza speaks of cleaving *sri mi li* and that Tāranātha's biography also says that Bhadrapa found the malicious ḍākinī hiding in a hollow tree called "simili" (*si mi li zer ba'i shing zhig gi khong stong*), split that tree, and killed her, this must be the location referred to here. The expression *sri mi li* is unattested elsewhere but given this context, it appears to be a misspelling of Skt. *sīmika*, which refers to a certain kind of tree.

423. In KG, the last two lines are replaced by the following three:

> From this very site of Devīkoṭa
> toward the great site of Sīmika,
> we crossed two and a half yojanas.

424. KG omits this line.

425. I follow CDNP *bshags* against GZ *bshig* ("destroyed") KG *gshegs* ("go" but most probably a typo for *gshags*).

426. GZ *bha hu ri* CDNP *dha'u ri*. As mentioned before, Bhahuri is an alias of the mahāsiddhā Maṇibhadra, while Dha(h)uri is an alias of the mahāsiddha Dhahulipa (no. 70). Since neither is the author of this song, these aliases are replaced by the name of actual author.

427. PDMT, 27:263–65.

428. I follow GZ *rlung nyid* against CDNP *rlung gnyis* ("two vāyus").

429. GZ *lta drug chos rnams thams cad kyang* CDNP *(b)rtags shing lta drug thams cad kyang*.

430. DPR: this refers to the extreme of saṃsāric existence, and the ship of mind needs to travel upward toward liberation from saṃsāra.
431. PDMT, 27:266–67.
432. I follow CDNP *nam mkhar* against GZ *nam mkha'*.
433. GZ *rting* CDNP *steng*.
434. The ten gates of the body are (1) the brahmarandra at the crown of the head, (2)–(3) the eyes, (4)–(5) the ears, (6)–(7) the nostrils, (8) the mouth, (9) the urethral opening, and (10) the anus.
435. I follow GZ *bya* against CDNP *byas*.
436. PDMT, 27:268–69.
437. GZ inserts the last two lines of this stanza also between the second and third lines of stanza 1.
438. This line has its parallel in the fourth stanza of song 7 in text 90.
439. PDMT, 27:270–71.
440. I follow CDNP *chad pa* against GZ *chang pa*.
441. I follow GZ *brtan par* against CDNP *bstan par*.
442. PDMT, 11:1606–10.
443. GZ *rtog* CDNP *rtogs* ("realize").
444. I follow GZ *dpyod pa* against CDNP *bskyed pa*.
445. These eight are gain, loss, fame, disgrace, praise, blame, happiness, and suffering.
446. I follow GZ CD *gnas par 'gyur bar gyis* against NP *gnas par 'gyur ba na*.
447. I follow GZ *mi 'khrul* against CDNP *mig 'phrul*.
448. Stanzas 11–13 resemble the three stanzas of text 135.
449. I follow GZ NP *rtog par shes* against CD *rtogs shing shes*.
450. I follow GZ *'di na* against CDNP *'di ni*.
451. I follow GZ *'dun pa* against CDNP *'dus pa*.
452. GZ *'jigs sngang* CDNP *'jigs dang*.
453. The Avīci hell is the lowest and worst of all the eight hot hells. According to the *Abhidharmakośabhāṣya* on III.58, two reasons are given for its name: unlike in other hells, there is never any interruption (*vīci*) of suffering, nor is there ever any agreeable state (*vīci*) at all. The suffering is greater than in any other hell, where, though there are no pleasant feelings that are the results of maturation, there might at least be pleasant feelings that are the results of concordant outflow.
454. PDMT, 11:1611–17.
455. Most probably, the vajra song that Atiśa refers to here is his *Vajrāsanavajragīti* (text 154), which is the only vajra song by this author in Tg and GZ. Its opening stanzas say: "I shall write down, in accordance with the guru's words, the line of transmission of the profound definitive meaning," and its colophon says: "In order to free myself and others, I commented on this essential reality." Technically speaking, self-blessing is the third of the five stages of the perfection process practices in the *Guhyasamājatantra* literature in the tradition of Nāgārjuna and Āryadeva.
456. Numbers in [ ] indicate the numbers of the stanzas of text 151 on which text 152 comments.

457. I follow CDNP *yod pa'i* against GZ *yod par bya ba'i*.
458. CDNP omit *chos* ("phenomena").
459. CDNP omit *de'i phyir* ("therefore").
460. Following text 151, GZ CDNP *rtag pa dang* is emended to *rtog pa dang*.
461. I follow GZ *bred pa* against CDNP *'brad pa* ("scratching").
462. I could not locate this quote in Kg. However, with slight variations, it also appears in Abhayākaragupta's *Śrīsampuṭatantrarājaṭīkāmnāyamañjarī* (D1198; attributed to the sūtras) and Kamalaśīla's *Madhyamakālokā* (D3887, fol. 222a.6–7; attributed to the Buddha).
463. In the *Laṅkāvatārasūtra* (X.153cd and X.155ab; H110, fol. 264b.1–2 and 264b.3), the first two lines read:

> Seeing outer referents is mistaken—
> there are no referents, solely mind.

464. "Support and supported" refers to the outer environment and the beings that live in and are supported by it.
465. GZ here mistakenly adds *gsum* ("three").
466. In this sentence, CDNP omit "In order to teach . . . that [maṇḍala]" and replace *rang bzhin zhes bya ba de med na* by *rang bzhin yin pa shes pa med na*, thus reading "If the understanding that it has the nature of all qualities that are uncontaminated by nature does not exist, it does not exist [either]."
467. These five pure faculties are confidence, vigor, mindfulness, samādhi, and prajñā. Specifically speaking, among the thirty-seven dharmas concordant with awakening that constitute the entire Mahāyāna path, the five faculties only pertain to the first two levels of heat and peak on the path of preparation (as the five powers, the same five constitute the remaining two levels of poised readiness and supreme dharma). However, twenty-eight among the thirty-seven dharmas actually consist of these same five factors: confidence appears twice, vigor nine times, mindfulness eight times, samādhi four times (in addition, it participates in all four limbs of miraculous powers), and prajñā five times. Thus the contents of the seven sets within the thirty-seven dharmas overlap greatly and are inextricably interwoven. When the same factors are named differently in different sets, this just serves to highlight their different functions, while their (often repetitive) arrangement in different sets indicates their progressive perfection and also shows how these factors cooperate in various patterns of mutual support. Also, as the boundary lines of these seven sets show, though they represent the main practices on their respective sections of the path, they remain to be practiced until the final attainment of buddhahood. In sum, in a general way, the five faculties can be said to represent the main factors that constitute all levels of the entire Mahāyāna path. For overviews of the seven sets of the thirty-seven dharmas in relation to the paths of accumulation, preparation, seeing, and familiarization, see chart 14 in Brunnhölzl 2010 and appendix I4C in Brunnhölzl 2011.

468. I follow GZ *byin gyi rlabs kyis* against CD *byin gyi rlabs* NP *byin gyi rlabs kyi.*

469. Since the comments below on stanza 5 refer to the perfection process practices of the *Guhyasamājatantra*, the reference to Āryadeva here probably is his *Caryāmelāpakapradīpa*, a treatise related to that tantra (translated in Wedemeyer 2007).

470. I follow CDNP *brtags pa* against GZ *rtag pa.*

471. Luminosity and unity are the fourth and fifth of the five stages of the perfection process practices in the *Guhyasamājatantra* literature in the tradition of Nāgārjuna and Āryadeva.

472. CDNP omit *'gag pa* ("stopping").

473. This appears to refer to the set of eighty thoughts of anger, desire, and ignorance mentioned in note 181, here multiplied by two (eighty by day and eighty by night). Alternatively, it could also refer to sixty basic states of mind (such as desire, hatred, and ignorance) that through a complex system of partial multiplications result in one hundred and sixty. These sixty are listed, and briefly glossed, in the *Mahāvairocanābhisambodhivikurvatyadhiṣṭhānavaipulyasūtrendrarājānāmadharmaparyāya* (H462, fols. 183b.5–186a.7) and the manner of calculating is explained in detail in Buddhaguhya's *Vairocanābhisambodhitantrapiṇḍārtha* (D2662, fols. 8a.2–9b.1). Furthermore, these one hundred and sixty mundane states of mind are declared to be the factors to be relinquished through the realizations of both personal and phenomenal identitylessness.

474. CDNP read *de dag mchog tu bde ba chen po 'od gsal gyi rang bzhin gyis sbyangs pa yin* ("They are purified by the nature of luminosity—supreme great bliss").

475. CDNP omit "common and uncommon."

476. BGTC (612) provides the two most common lists of five obscurations (with some pairs counted as one): (1) agitation and regret, malice, dullness and sleep, desire, and doubt, or (2) desire, dullness and sleep, regret, distraction, and doubt. Nāgārjuna's *Dharmadhātustava* 18–19 speaks of mind's luminosity being obscured by the five stains of desire, malice, laziness, agitation, and doubt, comparing them to clouds, smoke, mist, Rāhu's face (in ancient Indian cosmology, solar and lunar eclipses are regarded as the sun or moon being swallowed by the demon Rāhu, since he envies them for their light), and dust, respectively. The *Aṅguttaranikāya* (I.253–54, 275; III.16) also speaks about mind needing to be freed from the same five obscuring stains in order to regain its natural state. Vasubandhu's *Mahāyānasūtrālaṃkārabhāṣya* says that mind is similar to the sky by virtue of its luminosity, since all manifold phenomena are as adventitious with regard to the mind as are dust, smoke, clouds, and mist with regard to the sky (Nagao ed., 18.43–44).

477. GZ *ci'i phyir srid pa gsum dang / ji ltar snang ba 'jig rten pa'i sems spros pa dang* / CDNP *ji srid srid pa gsum dang / cir snang 'jig rten pa'i sems spros pa dang* / ("Threefold saṃsāric existence as long as it lasts, the worldly mind's discursiveness as whatever they may appear . . .").

478. I follow GZ *'od gsal ba* against CDNP *bsal ba* ("eliminated").

479. CDNP *las 'bras* ("karmas and their results").

480. In a general Buddhist sense, "poised readiness" (Skt. *kṣānti*, Tib. *bzod pa*; lit. "patience," "endurance") refers to the undeclining readiness or openness for the impact or purport of the four realities. In a general Mahāyāna sense, the term means to be mentally ready for the direct realization of emptiness, also known as "the dharma of nonarising" (Skt. *anutpattidharmakṣānti*, Tib. *mi skye ba'i chos la bzod pa*). Thus, "poised or open readiness" does not mean passively enduring or bearing something, but rather indicates an active willingness and receptiveness to integrate the experience of emptiness into one's mindstream and to be able to live within its utter groundlessness. Nāgārjuna's *Bodhisaṃbhāra* 28–29 says:

> Neither arising nor ceasing,
> neither nonarising nor unceasing,
> neither both nor neither,
> neither empty nor nonempty
> when not straying from the view of the middle
> with regard to any phenomena whatsoever,
> there is poised readiness for nonarising,
> because all conceptions are eliminated

In a more specific sense, "poised readiness" refers to the third of the four levels of the path of preparation, on which the practitioner newly attains some degree of openness and calm, in the sense of not being afraid of profound emptiness. Strictly speaking, the complete extent of this kind of poised readiness is only attained from the path of seeing onward, when the nature of phenomena is directly seen for the first time. For the most part, the path of familiarization then consists of increasing and stabilizing one's familiarity with this realization in all situations. Here, "poised readiness" refers to being open and ready to accommodate the realization of luminous true reality, whose power is too overwhelming for ordinary beings.

481. CDNP *bzod pa de dang ldan pa bzhin du rang gi rgyud la dge ba'i sems rdzogs par byed pa* (". . . while endowed with the [ensuing] poised readiness, the virtuous states of mind in your own mindstream are completed").

482. The current versions of Atiśa's text do not contain any comments on stanzas 14–16ab. Given the distinct theme in those stanzas, the original may have commented on them.

483. I follow GZ *la sogs pa'o/ mjug bsdus te gdams pa* against CD *la sogs pas mjug bsdus te gdams pa* NP *la sogs pa'i mjug bsdus te gdams pa.*

484. I follow GZ CD *me long* against NP *med nga.*

485. In this sentence, CDNP omit *rang gi* ("your own") and *'khrud pas* ("by washing it").

486. CDNP omit *las dang nyon mongs* ("as well as by karma and the afflictions").

487. I follow GZ *mi ltar snang ba* against CDNP *me ltar snang ba.*

488. CDNP *thub pa'i chos kyi gtam byang chub kyi sems la sogs pa mnyan zhing goms*

par bya'o ("You should listen to, and familiarize with, the Sage's dharma speech, such as bodhicitta").

489. CDNP *mnar med par 'gro ba la de min pa gang gis kyang 'dzin par mi nus pa'i phyir* ("because nothing whatsoever that is not the [dharma] is able to save those gone to Avīci").

490. The final phrase here could also be read as "because it brings natural luminosity." CDNP *ma rig pa'i mun pa la chos te skyabs su 'gro ba dang / tha ma bde ba chen po'i ting nge 'dzin gyi bar ni sgron ma ste* ("In the darkness of ignorance, the dharma—from taking refuge . . . the final samādhi of great bliss—is a lamp . . .").

491. Tib. Rngog legs pa'i shes rab (tenth century). He was a student of Atiśa and an uncle of the famous translator Ngog Lotsāwa Loden Sherab (Tib. Rngog lo tsā ba blo ldan shes rab; 1059–1109). In 1072, he founded the important Kadampa monastery Sangpu Nëutog (Tib. Gsang phu ne'u thog).

492. Tib. Snye thang bkra shis dpal. Located about forty kilometers south of Lhasa in the Kyichu valley, this is the monastery in which Atiśa stayed for many years and then eventually passed away in 1054.

493. CDNP's colophon simply says, "*This concludes* A Commentary on 'A Conduct Song.'"

494. PDMT, 26:1661–77 (first partially translated in Brunnhölzl 2007). This text is a good example of Atiśa's broad-minded approach to all Buddhist schools and to the two schools of the Mahāyāna (Yogācāra and Madhyamaka) in particular. Many of the text's stanzas are actually taken from works by various other masters throughout the history of Indian Buddhism (such as the Mādhyamikas Nāgārjuna, Āryadeva, Bhāviveka, Candrakīrti, Jñānagarbha, and Śāntarakṣita, Maitreya, the Yogācāras Vasubandhu, Kambala, and Ratnākaraśānti, and the *Laṅkāvatārasūtra*). What is particularly unique about this composition is that it explicitly and repeatedly combines an affirmative (or kataphatic) and a negative (or apophatic) approach to the dharmadhātu. Significantly, Atiśa begins by extensively describing the dharmadhātu in positive terms as the buddha nature that is endowed with all its qualities and exists in all sentient beings, along the lines of the affirmative approach to it found in texts such as Nāgārjuna's *Dharmadhātustava* (that Atiśa considered this text essential for understanding Nāgārjuna's thought is confirmed in Apple 2018, 14, 53, and 106), Maitreya's *Uttaratantra*, and certain Yogācāra works. Thereafter, Atiśa presents the Madhyamaka way of speaking about this very same dharmadhātu through exclusion or negation (as presented in the classical Madhyamaka texts by Nāgārjuna and so on). Thus Atiśa not only describes the dharmadhātu as being unborn, unceasing, lacking a nature of its own, free of discursiveness, and so on, but right from the start identifies it as the primordially pure nature of the mind that is luminous and inseparable from the qualities of awakening. In this way, we have the teachings on buddha nature and Madhyamaka right next to each other, like two sides of the same coin. Given this and that Atiśa also speaks quite favorably of some elements of Yogācāra (or Vijñaptimātravāda), he

cannot be classified as an exclusivist staunch Prāsaṅgika Mādhyamika, let alone as a Kadampa forefather of the later Gelugpa version of Prāsaṅgika Madhyamaka (that this is true for Atiśa's Madhyamaka approach in general is confirmed by the detailed account in Apple 2018). In sum, Atiśa's text here can be considered as a kind of "reader's digest" of more than a millennium of Buddhist and non-Buddhist thought in India. Thus the major part of its stanzas is laid out like a classical doxographical text that presents different tenet systems. Usually, such texts start with the systems that are considered to be lower and then ascend to the highest. Atiśa, however, takes the reverse approach: he starts with the proper characterization of the dharmadhātu as that which is to be realized or revealed as perfect buddhahood. As he says, though there cannot be different views about this indivisible dharmadhātu ultimately, relatively speaking, distinct positions about it are held due to different mindsets. Among these, Atiśa presents Madhyamaka as the supreme view and then descends through the Buddhist schools of the Vijñaptivādins, the Sautrāntikas, and the Vaibhāṣikas to the various non-Buddhist Indian schools. In particular, the stanzas about Madhyamaka give a good overview of the essential points and the development of ideas within this system in India throughout the centuries. A brief outline of the text is as follows (stanza numbers in parentheses):

(A) General presentation of the dharmadhātu (1–25)
(B) Buddhist tenet systems
  1. Mādhyamikas (26–47)
  2. Vijñaptimātravādins (48–66)
  3. Śrāvakas (67–79)
  4. Pratyekabuddhas (80–96)
(C) Non-Buddhist tenet systems (97–139)
(D) Conclusion (140–143)

495. Stanzas 1 and 4–14 correspond almost literally to Nāgārjuna's *Dharmadhātustava* 1, 2–10, and 12–13.

496. The last two lines allude to a stanza in the *Lalitavistarasūtra* (H96, fols. 305b.7–306a.1), which the Buddha is said to have uttered right after having attained enlightenment:

> I have found a nectarlike dharma,
> profound, peaceful, stainless, luminous, and unconditioned
> Even if I were to teach it, others would not understand it
> Thus, I think I shall stay silent in the middle of the forest

497. I follow GZ NP *sbyang bar byas pa* against CD *bya ba byas pa* ("having done what needs to be done").

498. I follow GZ *nas* against CDNP *gnas* ("abide").

499. I follow GZ *de ni* against CDNP *de yi*.

500. Skt. *vaiḍūrya*. This term is still often wrongly translated as "lapis lazuli." The Western name "beryl" ($Be_3Al_2[SiO_3]_6$) derives from Latin *beryllus*

and Greek *beryllos*, which come from the Prakrit *veruliya* and the Sanskrit *vaiḍūrya*. This word is actually of Dravidian origin and means "to become pale" (interestingly, the word "brilliance" also derives from *beryllus*). Originally, this term referred to "a precious blue-green color-of-sea-water stone" (usually some kind of aquamarine) but later became used for the mineral beryl in general. Pure beryl is colorless (which is very rare), but there are many varieties of different colors due to its being mixed with other minerals. Beryl crystals range from very small to several meters in size and many tons in weight. The main varieties are aquamarine (blue), emerald (green), golden beryl (pale yellow to brilliant gold), heliodor (green-yellow), Morganite (pink or rose-colored), and red beryl.

501. This stanza corresponds to *Dharmadhātustava* 27 and is similar to *Uttaratantra* I.121–123.
502. GZ *'dzin pas brtag* CDNP *'dzin par brtag* ("conceived as a perceiver"). This stanza corresponds to *Dharmadhātustava* 24 (there, the last line has "as 'self'" instead of "by/as a perceiver").
503. Lines 17ab correspond to *Dharmadhātustava* 26ab (there, the first line says, "'impermanence,' 'suffering,' and 'empty'").
504. GZ *ji snyed* CDNP *ji skad* ("just as they were spoken").
505. Lines 17cd–18ab correspond to *Dharmadhātustava* 22.
506. Lines 18cd correspond to *Dharmadhātustava* 26cd.
507. I follow GZ CD *brtag par bya* against NP *brtan par bya* ("to be solidified").
508. I follow CDNP *dang* against GZ *min* ("not").
509. Stanzas 19–20 correspond to *Dharmadhātustava* 30–32.
510. I follow GZ *yi* against CDNP *yin* ("is").
511. GZ *med pas* CD *med pa* NP *med par*.
512. This stanza resembles *Uttaratantra* I.62.
513. I follow GZ CD *dbu ma* against NP *dbu ba*.
514. This stanza corresponds to Jñānagarbha's *Satyadvayavibhāga* 2.
515. In Madhyamaka, seeming reality is classified as correct (such as a table) and false (such as a mirage), while ultimate reality is divided into nominal (the conceptual image of ultimate reality as a nonimplicative negation) and nonnominal (actual ultimate reality as such). Most Tibetan doxographers maintain that the above twofold classification is made only by Svātantrika Mādhyamikas and that its use is a criterion to define someone as a Svātantrika. However, despite being typified as a Prāsaṅgika by most Tibetans, Atiśa himself obviously has no problem in using this classification. He also employs the same classification in his *Satyadvayāvatāra* 2–3.
516. I follow GZ *brtags* against CD *rtags* ("signs") NP *gtags*.
517. GZ *sprul pa* CDNP *'khrul pa* ("delusion").
518. Lines 32ac correspond to *Madhyāntavibhāga* I.14.
519. Lines 33ab summarize Candrakīrti's *Madhyamakāvatāra* VI.23.
520. GZ *don dam* CDNP *don rnams* ("the actualities").
521. This stanza corresponds to Nāgārjuna's *Yuktiṣaṣṭikā* 30.
522. I follow GZ *rtog pa* against CDNP *rtogs pa*.
523. The detailed presentation of these eight flaws makes up the third chapter

of the *Saṃdhinirmocanasūtra*, called "The Questions of Suviśuddhamati." The last two lines of stanza 35 here correspond to the last two lines of the concluding stanza of that chapter (for details, see Brunnhölzl 2004, 88–94).

524. This stanza corresponds almost literally to *Yuktiṣaṣṭikā* 46.

525. The content of this stanza is discussed very similarly in many of the prajñāpāramitā sūtras and also in Śāntideva's *Bodhicāryāvatāra* IX.44cd.

526. This stanza corresponds to *Mūlamadhyamakakārikā* XXIV.11. "Awareness mantras" (Skt. *vidyāmantra*, Tib. *rig sngags*) can be used to propitiate mundane and supramundane deities in order to partake of their activity. However, if these mantras are used improperly, those deities might turn against the persons who supplicate them. The Buddhist explanation of the awareness mantra is that it overcomes the darkness of desire and the afflictions, thus countering unawareness (*avidyā*). It pacifies the hosts of flaws such as suffering and desire that are experienced in saṃsāra. It demonstrates extinguishing the afflictions through the syllables and meanings that teach the six pāramitās, the realities of the noble ones, and the factors conducive to awakening. Since it frees one from one's own unawareness, it also gives rise to awareness in others and thus pacifies wrongdoing and its bases. It represents an utterance that embodies the female deity.

527. In prose, the contents of this stanza is found in the *Kāśyapaparivarta*, and Nāgārjuna's *Lokātītastava* 23 expresses the same idea in slightly different words.

528. This stanza corresponds to *Mūlamadhyamakakārikā* XV.6 (there, the second line has "and" instead of "due to").

529. This stanza corresponds to *Laṅkāvatārasūtra* III.85 (there, the third line has "know" instead of "speak").

530. I follow CDNP *yod pa pa ni* against GZ *yod pa las ni* ("by virtue of existence, you go . . .").

531. I follow CDNP *med pa pa ni* against GZ *med pa las ni* ("by virtue of nonexistence, you go . . .").

532. This stanza corresponds to Nāgārjuna's *Ratnāvalī* I.57 (the first and second lines are switched).

533. I follow NP *rigs pa* against GZ CD *rig pa* ("awareness").

534. This stanza is identical with Śāntarakṣita's *Madhyamakālaṃkāra* 93. It is quite remarkable that this stanza is found in a text by Atiśa, since it is the very epitome of Śāntarakṣita's synthesis of Yogācāra and Madhyamaka ("the two approaches' chariot"). According to most Tibetan sources, Atiśa belongs to the Prāsaṅgika branch of Madhyamaka, which not only does not rely on any Yogācāra teachings but actually refutes their ideas.

535. GZ *go bar bya* CDNP *goms par bya* ("should be familiarized with"). Lines 44cd correspond to *Dharmadhātustava* 33ac (33bc in the Tibetan, which only has three lines).

536. With minor variations, these lines appear as *Jñānasārasamuccaya* 28 (ascribed to Āryadeva), Jetāri's *Sugatamatavibhāgakārikā* 1 (D3899, fol. 7b.5), and in the *Vimalaprabhā* commentary on the *Kālacakratantra* (D1347,

fol. 196b.3). The first two lines are also found in the *Śālistambasūtra* (see *Mahāyānasūtrasaṃgraha*, ed. P. L. Vaidya [Darbhanga: Mithila Institute, 1961], 1:115).

537. GZ *mtha' dang bral zhing* CDNP *mtha' dang bral phyir* ("since it lacks extremes, there is . . .").

538. This stanza corresponds to Vasubandhu's *Triṃśikākārikā* 20 and also echoes Kambala's *Ālokamālā* 40ab (in rendering stanzas from this work, I rely on the Sanskrit edition in Lindtner 2003; the Tibetan translation is often corrupt).

539. This stanza corresponds to *Triṃśikākārikā* 21.

540. I follow GZ *gzhan ma yin* against CDNP *gzhan pa yin* ("other").

541. Lines 51bcd correspond to *Triṃśikākārikā* 22abc. The impermanence of a book is neither the same as the book nor is it something completely other—that is, totally unrelated to the book. Likewise, the perfect nature is not identical to the dependent nature, but it is also not something altogether extrinsic to it, since it is its true nature.

542. Lines 53ab correspond to lines 3cd of the *Ālokamālā* and also resemble Āryadeva's *Catuḥśataka* VIII.21cd. According to the *Ālokamālā*'s autocommentary, "reflecting on the internal" refers to studying, reflecting, and meditating on the inner mind (as opposed to external things studied in other sciences).

543. I follow CDNP *yod* against GZ *'dod* ("is asserted").

544. Lines 53cd correspond to *Jñānasārasamuccaya* 26ab.

545. I follow GZ *shes pa* against CDNP *skyes pa* ("what has arisen").

546. This stanza is quoted in Ratnākaraśānti's *Prajñāpāramitopadeśa* (D4079, fol. 152a.2–3) and attributed to Nāgārjuna, but I could not locate it anywhere in Tg or Kg.

547. This stanza corresponds to one in Ratnākaraśānti's *Madhyamakālaṃkāravṛttimadhyamapratipadāsiddhi* (D4072, fol. 105b.3). According to this text (fol. 105b.5–6), the two flaws are that a nonexistent (1) cannot be an entity of cognition that entails causes, and (2) cannot arise intermittently, because it is not contingent on time and not subject to dependent origination.

548. This stanza is found as both Śāntarakṣita's *Madhyamakālaṃkāra* 16 and a stanza in his *Tattvasaṃgaha* (D4266, fol. 73a.3–4); accordingly, GZ *deng 'dir* CDNP *de 'dir* in the last line are emended to *de 'di'i*. The autocommentary on the *Madhyamakālaṃkāra* (D3885, fols. 60b.2–4) says that it is not suitable for cognition to have a character of experiencing any referents that are different from itself. Cognition is presented as having the nature of self-awareness, because it has the character of being lucid by nature, which is the opposite of the awarenessless nature of a chariot and so on. Since what cognition is aware of is its own nature, unlike objects such as blue, it does not depend on any other factor that is aware of it. This point of cognition not lacking awareness is called "self-awareness."

549. I follow CDNP *rgya mtsho phyogs* against GZ *rgya mtsho'i phyogs*.

550. I follow GZ *'babs chu* NP *'bab chu* against CD *'dab chu*.

551. Asvabhāva's *Mahāyānasūtrālaṃkāraṭīkā* on XI.5 (D4029, fol. 81a.2)

and *Mahāyānasaṃgrahopanibandhana* on I.25 (D4051, fol. 207a.7), as well as Cilupa's *Ratnavṛkṣanāmarahasyasamājavṛtti* (D1846, fol. 102b.5) and Vitapāda's *Sukusumanāmadvikramatattvabhāvanāmukhāgamavṛtti* (D1866, fol. 96a.6–7) quote this stanza in virtually the same form. The *Mahāyānasūtrālaṃkāraṭīkā* attributes it to a Bhadrihari (Tibetan translations sometimes mistakenly refer to the non-Buddhist grammarian and poet Bhartṛhari as Bhadrahari or Bhadrihari, but I could not locate the verse in Bhartṛhari's famous *Śatakatraya*). Cilupa attributes it to the *Saṃdhinirmocanasūtra* (where it is not found), while Vitapāda just says that it is from the sūtras. This stanza also echoes *Ālokamālā* 20.

552. This means that the appearances of both objects and subjects are mere appearances within the mind and thus related in the most direct sense, with no other linking factors in between. This is one of the two major arguments in Yogācāra texts (especially those of Dignāga and Dharmakīrti) for there being no external objects, but only mind, which is aware of its own appearances. In modern scholarship, this is often referred to as "the *saṃvedana* inference"—using the reason that appearances appear to the mind in a way that is as lucid and insubstantial as mind itself (thus they cannot be substantial and dense matter). This is one of the two classical reasonings that Yogācāras use to establish that appearances are nothing other than mind. The other one is the reasoning of the "invariable co-observation" of appearances and mind: any perceived object is nothing but mind appearing in the form of an object, which is not different from the perceiving cognizance, because they are necessarily observed simultaneously (there is never an object without an observer). Both reasonings are found, for example, in Dignāga's *Pramāṇasamuccaya* I.9–10 and its autocommentary as well as in Dharmakīrti's *Pramāṇaviniścaya* I.55bff. The first one also appears in Śāntarakṣita's *Tattvasaṃgraha* (lines 2001, 2003, and 2029–33) and the second one in the Dharmakīrti's *Pramāṇavārttika* III.388–91. Moreover, the word "hidden" (Skt. *parokṣa*, Tib. *lkog gyur*) in line 58b here suggests the rejection of any outer but imperceptible material objects that (especially in the Sautrāntika school) are said to trigger the perceived immaterial aspects that directly appear to consciousness.

553. Some sources refute the notion that mind is able to see or cognize itself, just as a blade cannot cut itself and a finger cannot touch its own tip. For example, the *Laṅkāvatārasūtra* (X.335, gātha 568), the *Ratnacūḍaparipṛcchasūtra* (H96, fols. 375b.7ff.), and Śāntideva's *Bodhicāryāvatāra* (IX.17cd–18ab) use these similes. However, they only apply to material things with spatial extension or some truly existent kind of mind. As both the preceding stanzas in the *Laṅkāvatārasūtra* and the passage in the *Ratnacūḍasūtra* that immediately follows these examples point out, when self-awareness, or *cittamātra*, is ultimately understood as the nature of the mind—the nondual unity of awareness and emptiness beyond subject and object that cannot be pinpointed as anything—it cannot be compared to such examples of reification. The same is also suggested by Atiśa in the next two stanzas.

554. Lines 58–60ab correspond to stanzas in Ratnākaraśānti's *Prajñāpāramitopadeśa* (D4079, fol. 154a.5–6).
555. I follow NP *rtogs par dka' bas na* against GZ *brtag par dka' bas na* ("since . . . examine/imagine") and CD *rtogs par dka' ba na.*
556. Lines 60cd–61 correspond to *Ālokamālā* 12cd–13.
557. I follow GZ *blo tsam* against CDNP *don tsam* ("sheer referent").
558. This stanza corresponds to Ratnākaraśānti's *Prajñāpāramitopadeśa* (D4079, fol. 154a.6–7); there, "mind" in the first line is replaced by "that," and the last two lines read:

> The nature of cognition is immediate
> but deluded by deceptive appearances

Moreover, these two lines closely echo a prose sentence in the same author's *Madhyamakālaṃkāravṛttimadhyamapratipadāsiddhi* (D4072, fol. 105b.7).
559. I follow GZ *gcig nyid gnyis* against CDNP *gcig gnyis gnyis.*
560. Stanzas 63–64 correspond to *Ālokamālā* 25–26. There, the last two lines read slightly differently:

> But since the perceiver is alive,
> it is as if it throbs internally

561. In the Yogācāra system in general, as exemplified by *Mahāyānasaṃgraha* I.48, the usual distinction between the vimuktikāya and the dharmakāya is that the former designates the removal of only the afflictive obscurations as attained by śrāvaka and pratyekabuddha arhats, while the latter represents the removal of both afflictive and cognitive obscurations as well as the possession of all buddha qualities. Thus when speaking about the dharmakāya as the actual state of buddhahood in a general sense, it is understood that both types of obscurations have been relinquished in it, and it is in this sense that it can be said that the dharmakāya includes the vimuktikāya. *Uttaratantra* II.21–26 describes these two kāyas as the two aspects of relinquishment (purity) and realization (wisdom), respectively, of unconditioned perfect buddhahood, without relating them to any distinction between buddhas and arhats (more commonly, it is the svābhāvikakāya that is said to represent the aspect of the purity or the relinquishment of all obscurations). Most Tibetan commentaries on these stanzas agree that the nonconceptual wisdom of meditative equipoise (familiarizing with the wisdom of knowing suchness) perfects the vimuktikāya (the ultimate relinquishment), while the wisdom of its aftermath or subsequent attainment (training in the wisdom of knowing variety) purifies the stains of the dharmakāya (the ultimate realization).
562. With slight variations, stanzas 65–66 correspond to lines in the *Prajñāpāramitopadeśa* (D4079, fol. 154a.7–154b.1). Moreover, stanza 66 condenses *Uttaratantra* I.94cd and II.21–23ab. These two stanzas here clearly

present the notion of buddha nature as the primordially pure nature of the mind that is only obscured by adventitious stains and appears as buddhahood with all its qualities once these fleeting stains have been realized for what they are—mere illusions of a deluded outlook.

563. This is another way to classify all phenomena, mainly employed by the Vaibhāṣikas. The five bases (Skt. *pañcavastu*, Tib. *gzhi lnga*) are (1) appearing forms (Skt. *rūpa*, Tib. *snang ba gzugs*), (2) primary minds (Skt. *citta*, Tib. *gtso sems*), (3) accompanying mental factors (Skt. *caitta*, Tib. *'khor sems 'byung*), (4) nonassociated formations (Skt. *viprayuktasaṃskāra*, Tib. *ldan min 'du byed*), and (5) unconditioned phenomena (Skt. *asaṃskrita*, Tib. *'dus ma byas*).

564. Lines 67e–68a correspond to *Abhidharmakośa* VII.12dc.

565. Lines 68cd correspond to *Abhidharmakośa* VI.1ab.

566. I follow GZ NP *mngon* against CD *gdon*.

567. This stanza corresponds to *Abhidharmakośa* VI.2.

568. Skt. *upādānaskandha*, Tib. *nyer len gyi phung po*. This means that, on the one hand, the five skandhas are appropriated through past karma and afflictions and, on the other hand, themselves appropriate the karma and afflictions that result in the skandhas of future lifetimes.

569. These are the nirvāṇa with remainder (while still alive and possessing the five skandhas) and the nirvāṇa without remainder (attaining nirvāṇa after death).

570. These are "the thirty-seven dharmas concordant with awakening": the four foundations of mindfulness (Skt. *catvāri smṛtyupasthānāni*, Tib. *dran pa nye bar bzhag pa bzhi*), the four correct exertions (Skt. *catvāri samyakprahāṇāni*, Tib. *yang dag spong ba bzhi*), the four limbs of miraculous powers (Skt. *catvāra ṛddhipādāḥ*, Tib. *rdzu 'phrul gyi rkang pa bzhi*), the five faculties (Skt. *pañcendriyāṇi*, Tib. *dbang po lnga*), the five powers (Skt. *pañcabalāni*, Tib. *stobs lnga*), the seven branches of enlightenment (Skt. *saptasaṃbodhyaṅgāni*, Tib. *byang chub kyi yan lag bdun*), and the eightfold path of the noble ones (Skt. *āryāṣṭāṅgamārga*, Tib. *'phags pa'i lam yan lag brgyad*).

571. Lines 71ab correspond to *Abhidharmakośa* VI.5ab.

572. Lines 71cd–72c correspond to *Abhidharmakośa* VI.51–52ab. According to Vasubandhu's autocommentary (D4090, vol. khu, fol. 29b.1–4), the eighty-nine results are actually three sets of eighty-nine results. The path of seeing entails eight uninterrupted paths (Skt. *ānantaryamārga*, Tib. *bar chad med lam*) and eight paths of liberation (Skt. *vimuktimārga*, Tib. *rnam grol lam*) as the remedies against the afflictions to be relinquished through seeing. The path of familiarization has eighty-one of each of these paths as the remedies against the afflictions to be relinquished through familiarization. In sum, during the paths of seeing and familiarization, there are (1) eighty-nine uninterrupted paths, and (2) eighty-nine paths of liberation. Finally, there is (3) the irreversible relinquishment or the "analytical cessation" (Skt. *pratisaṃkyānirodha*, Tib. *so sor brtags 'gog*) of the related eighty-nine categories of afflictions. In due order, the eighty-nine uninterrupted paths constitute the above "approach of virtuous effort," the paths of liberation are the conditioned results of this "approach of virtuous ef-

fort," and the irreversible relinquishments are its unconditioned results. In brief, these three sets of eighty-nine results can be summarized into four: (1) stream-enterer, (2) once-returner, (3) nonreturner, and (4) arhat. Each one of these four results contains five causes that lead to it. The details of these various causes, results, remedial paths, and the factors to be relinquished by them (especially in their relations to the four realities of the noble ones and the three realms of saṃsāra) as presented in the commentaries on the *Abhidharmakośa* are very complex.

573. GZ CDNP *rtag par smra ba* ("proponents of permanence") emended to *btags par smra ba*.
574. There exist several differing classifications of the four major and eighteen minor subsects of the śrāvakas (see Hopkins 1983, 340, 713–19; and Bareau 2013). The one given here corresponds with Vinītadeva's presentation in his *Samayabhedoparacanacakre nikāyabhedopadeśanasaṃgraha* (D4140).
575. I follow GZ NP *cha* against CD *chags* ("attachment"). Stanzas 81cd–88 correspond to *Abhidharmakośa* III.20–26 and 28ab. For explanations of this terse yet complex presentation of dependent origination, see the commentaries on the *Abhidharmakośa*.
576. GZ *gnas* CDNP *'das* emended to *las*.
577. I follow CDNP *nus pa* against GZ *nub pa* ("vanish").
578. GZ CDNP *bzhi* ("four") emended to *gzhi*.
579. I follow GZ NP *lnga dang gnyis* against CD *ldang dang bhzi*.
580. I follow GZ NP *yang dang yang du* against CD *yid dang yid du*.
581. I follow CDNP *gang du* against GZ *gang dang*.
582. I follow CDNP *tshogs kyis rab tu 'jug* against GZ *tshogs kyi bar du 'jug*.
583. I follow GZ NP *gang du* against CD *gang gis*.
584. These sixty-two wrong views about a self and the world are described in detail in the *Brahmajālasūtra* (*Dīgha Nikāya* I.12–I.46; Walshe 1987, 73–90).
585. I follow GZ *rgyu med* against CDNP *rgyud med* ("lack of continuity").
586. Skt. *guṇa*.
587. Skt. *sattva, rajas, tamas*.
588. I follow NP *g.yel ba* against GZ *g.yem pa* ("illicit sex") CD *gsal ba* ("lucidity").
589. I follow GZ *lan 'ga'* against CD *len 'ga'*. NP omit this line.
590. Stanzas 101–103 correspond to *Mahābhārata* XII, 247.20–25, 287.29–31, and 287.25b–28 (see Frauwallner 1956, 1:291).
591. Skt. *prakṛti*.
592. I follow CDNP *yon tan gsum gyi rang bzhin mchog / mthong ba'i lam du 'gyur ma yin* against GZ *yon tan gsum gyi rang bzhin can / mthong ba'i lam du 'gyur ba yin* ("What has the nature of the three qualities represents the path of seeing").
593. Skt. *mahat*.
594. Skt. *ahaṃkāra* (lit. "I-maker"). I follow GZ CD *de las nga rgyal rnam gsum 'byung* against NP *de la sangs rgyas rnams su'byung*.
595. Skt. *tanmātra*.
596. Skt. *pradhāna*.
597. Skt. *pariṇāma*.

598. Skt. *puruṣa*.
599. Skt. *tattva*.
600. I follow GZ *ral pa'am* against CD *ral pa* NP *ral pa'ang*.
601. For details on the Sāṃkhya system, see for example Frauwallner 1956 (1:275–408) and Hiriyanna 1973 (267–97).
602. Skt. *dravya, guṇa, karma, sāmānya, viśeṣa, samavāya*. Later, a seventh category "negation" (*abhāva*) was added.
603. For details on the Naiyāyika-Vaiśeṣika system, see for example Frauwallner 1956 (2:15–250) and Hiriyanna 1973 (225–66).
604. I follow NP *nges par rga* against GZ CD *nges par dga'* ("joy").
605. GZ CDNP *'chi ba* ("death") emended to *'ching ba*.
606. Skt. *jīva, āsrava, saṃvara, nirjara, bandha, karma, pāpa, puṇya, mokṣa*. Usually, the nine categories do not include *karma* but *ajīva* ("the insentient").
607. For details on the Jaina system, see for example Frauwallner 1956 (1:247–72 and 2:251–94) and Hiriyanna 1973 (155–73).
608. I follow CD *brjod* NP *rjod* against CDNP *bstod* ("praise").
609. I follow CD *rgyu ltar snang ba* against GZ *rgyu dang snang ba* ("cause and appearance") NP *rgyu skar snang ba'i* ("appearing as planets and stars").
610. Skt. *pramāṇa, prameya, saṃśaya, prayojana, dṛṣṭānta, siddhānta, avavaya, tarka, nirṇaya, vāda, jalpa, vitaṇḍā, hetvābhāsa, chala, jāti, nrigrahasthāna*.
611. For details on these categories in the Naiyāyika system, see for example Hiriyanna 1973 (245–60).
612. Except for the last two lines, this description rather fits the above-mentioned heterodox and materialistic position of Ajita Keśakambala. By contrast, the orthodox Mīmāṃśakas attempt to establish the Vedas on epistemological grounds and believe in karma (cause and result), virtuous actions, and liberation. For details on the Mīmāṃśā system, see for example Frauwallner 1956 (2:22–25, 33, 59–61, 185–86) and Hiriyanna 1973 (298–335).
613. "Ādityas" (plural) refers to all divine beings as the offspring of the mother goddess Aditi and her husband, the sage Kāśyapa. Āditya in the singular refers to the Sun God, Sūrya. The Maruts are the Vedic gods of storm and companions of Indra. Marīci is a mind-born son of Brahmā at the beginning of creation (in Mahāyāna Buddhism, Marīcī is the goddess of dawn).
614. This is another name of Indra.
615. GZ CDNP *sa* emended to *bsam*.
616. "The Rudras" is another name for the Maruts, the Vedic gods of storm and companions of Indra (their number varies from two to sixty, sometimes also enumerated as eleven, thirty-three, or one hundred and eighty). Śaṅkara is another name of Śiva.
617. The quotes in stanzas 114–16 correspond to *Bhagavadgītā* X.21–23 and X.33a (GZ CDNP have minor variations and switch the second and fourth lines of the quote in 114).
618. GZ CD *ṇa* NP *na*.
619. GZ CDNP *tsar ti ka*.
620. In general, the term *Īśvara* has a very wide range of meanings in Hinduism, depending on the era and the school. In ancient Indian philosophy,

Īśvara can mean supreme soul, ruler, lord, king, or husband. In medieval texts, Īśvara means God, the supreme being, a personal god, or the special Self (*Ātman*). In Śaivism and for most Hindus, Īśvara (also Maheśvara or Parameśvara) is synonymous with Śiva, "the Supreme Lord." For some, the term refers to Viṣṇu, and it can also refer to a chosen personal meditation deity (*iṣṭadevatā*). In traditional Bhakti movements, Īśvara refers to one or more individually chosen gods from among the many in Hinduism. In the Yoga school, it means any personal deity or spiritual inspiration. In Advaita Vedānta, Īśvara is the monistic universal absolute that is the oneness in everything and connects everything. In Atiśa's text here, Īśvara refers to Śiva.

621. GZ *dbang po* CDNP *'byung po* ("evil spirits").
622. I follow GZ NP *dag* against CD *bdag* ("self").
623. I follow GZ CD *thams cad dbang du gyur pas na / des na dbang du gyur ces bya* against NP *thams cad dbang du gyur ces bya*.
624. Instead of GZ *yul dang bcas pa bza' ba dang / gzhan yang yid kyis gang bsam pa / yid kyi rjes 'gror mi sdod pas /*, CDNP only has the one line *mtho ris ngan song kun khyab pas /* ("since he pervades all higher and miserable realms"). In the last line, Tib. *gar yang phyin pa* literally means "having gone anywhere," but according to the *Mahāvyutpatti*, this renders Skt. *prāpti* (thus, the two different explanations in GZ and CDNP).
625. I follow CDNP *gang zhig phra gyur* against *gang zhig phrad gyur* ("whatever he encounters, he . . .").
626. Both Vasava and Vāsuki are powerful nāgas. In a famous episode of the ancient Indian myth of creation, the gods and the asuras used the nāga king Vāsuki as a churning rope around the churning rod of Mount Maṃdara. Pulling Vāsuki's head and tail back and forth, the mountain rotated and thus churned the ocean of milk. In this way, first, a lethal poison (Skt. *halāhala*) that even the gods could not withstand was produced, and later the nectar of immortality (Skt. *amṛta*). Eventually, Śiva swallowed the poison to save the gods, upon which his throat turned blue (thus his epithet *Nīlakaṇṭha*). Since that time Śiva wears Vāsuki around his neck. "The fearless wrathful one" here refers to Vāsuki's son Mānava.
627. I follow GZ CD *sad pa* against NP *gsad pa* ("kill").
628. "Tripura guardians" refers to the three powerful asuras Tārākṣa, Vīryāvana, and Vidyunmālin, for whom Brahmā had three forts of gold, silver, and iron built in the heavens, in the sky, and on earth, respectively.
629. This is another name of the god of wealth, Kubera.
630. Rāvaṇa was the king of the rākṣasas in Laṅkā, renowned as a great scholar, capable ruler (*śāstṛ* can mean both), vīṇā player, ascetic, and foremost devotee of Śiva.
631. This refers to the Cārvākas.
632. NP omit this line.
633. The nimba tree (*Azadirachta indica*) has bitter fruits.
634. This refers to materialists like Pūraṇa Kāśyapa.
635. I follow GZ *bdag gzhan dgra dag* against CDNP *bdag bzhin sgra dag*.

636. GZ CD *da ltar* NP *de ltar* ("in those ways").
637. GZ *skye bo pa rnams* CDNP *skye bo 'dod rnams* ("desirous persons").
638. PDMT, 11:1585–89.
639. I follow GZ *sangs rgyas 'gyur* against CDNP *sangs rgyas gyur*.
640. As the commentary shows, this and the next two stanzas are not only an account of the deeds of the historical Buddha Śākyamuni but also describe what applies for everyone who properly practices the Buddhist path.
641. I follow CDNP *bde bar 'jug pas 'dus* against GZ *bde bas 'jug pa 'dus*.
642. I follow CDNP *kye* against GZ *skyes*.
643. GZ *gang des* CDNP *gang de*.
644. GZ CDNP *bdag gi* could also simply be read as "my." However, since this and the following lines still speak about Nairātmyā, rather than saying "my queen," it is more likely that *bdag gi* renders *ātma(ka)-* ("[having a] self/character"), which is also a nice play on words in relation to Nairātmyā ("the lady without a self").
645. I follow CDNP and the commentary *'dod med* against GZ *don med*.
646. I follow CDNP *bdag gzhan dbye ba ma lus mi mthong* against GZ *bdag gzhan dbye bas ma nus mi mthong*.
647. Following the commentary, GZ CDNP *rnam rtog rgyu bas gang yang* is emended to *rnam rtog rgyu ba gang yang*. As it stands, this line reads, "Do not look at anything through the movements of thoughts."
648. I follow CD *gzhan* against GZ NP *bzhin*.
649. I follow CD *rgyug dang* against GZ *rgyug par* NP *brgyug dang*.
650. Tib. *skra yi zhags pa* usually renders Skt. *keśapāśa* ("much or ornamented hair," "tuft") or *keśapāśī* ("a lock of hair hanging down from the top of the head"), but neither of these make sense here (Skt. *pāśa*, Tib. *zhags pa* means "noose" or "snare").
651. GZ NP *rol pa* CD *rol pas* ("are delighted in an inconceivable manner by the play").
652. I follow GZ *brten cing gnas pa* against CDNP *rten pa*.
653. "Anywhere" (*gang la*) could also be read as "for anything," but the commentary says "at any place whatsoever."
654. GZ *bsten gyis* CDNP *brtan gyis* ("stabilize").
655. GZ *'khrul* CDNP *khrus* ("wash away!").
656. I follow GZ NP *rtog* against CD *rtogs*.
657. I follow NP *'jigs* against GZ CD *'jig* ("destruction," "perishing").
658. I follow CDNP *'gro ba* against GZ *'gro bar*.
659. I follow GZ CD *mya ngan 'das* against NP *mya ngan*.
660. Tib. Skyi shod snye thang bkra shis dpal.
661. GZ *mar me mdzad ye shes kyi zhal snga nas dngos po'i don ji lta ba nyid gzigs* CDNP *mar me mdzad ye shes kyi dngos po'i don nyid kyis ji ltar gzigs*.
662. PDMT, 11:1590–1605.
663. GZ *yid bzhin* CDNP *yid bzhin nor ltar* ("like a wish-fulfilling jewel").
664. The nine expressive moods of wrathful deities are charming, dauntless, threatening (body); laughing, fierce, frightening (speech); and compassionate, ferocious, and peaceful (mind).

665. Numbers in [ ] indicate the numbers of the stanzas of text 154 on which text 155 comments.
666. I follow GZ CD *rag las sa* against NP *rag las pa*.
667. I follow GZ *'od gsal ba* against CDNP *don gsal ba* ("luminous actuality").
668. I follow GZ CD *de'i phyir dam pa* against NP *de'i dam pa*.
669. The five fires refer to the practice in certain Hindu schools to sit naked in the center of four fires, with the sun shining from above as the fifth one, in order to purify the negative karma and impurities of the body.
670. I follow the common *sbyangs pa'i yon tan bcu gynis* (Skt. *dvadaśadhūtaguṇa*) in CDNP against GZ *sbyangs pa'i yi dam bcu gnyis* ("the twelve oaths of abstinence"). These twelve qualities or oaths consist of (1) wearing the dress of a dung sweeper (that is, only clothes that other people have thrown away), (2) owning only three robes, (3) wearing clothes made only out of one kind of material, such as wool, (4) begging for alms, (5) eating only while sitting at one's eating place (that is, not getting up and returning to eat), (6) not eating food after noon, (7) living in isolated places, (8) living under trees, (9) living in places without a roof, (10) living in charnel grounds, (11) sleeping in a sitting position, and (12) being content to stay anywhere (that is, without manipulating the ground in any way to make it more comfortable).
671. GZ NP *ldog pa'i byed pa* CD *lhag pa'i byed pa* ("excessive activities").
672. Following the root text, GZ CDNP *las* is emended to *la*.
673. CDNP omit this sentence.
674. GZ *thabs* CDNP *sgra'i don* ("meanings of the terms").
675. I follow GZ CD *mtshon bya* against NP *mtshon dang*.
676. GZ omits this sentence.
677. I follow GZ CD *dben pa* against NP *bden pa*.
678. I follow GZ *rab tu myur bar bsgrub* CDNP *rab tu sgrub myur du sgrub*.
679. GZ *mdzes ma mchog gi* CDNP *mdzes ma mchog ni*.
680. CD *lam de gnyis kar 'jug pa ma yin pas* CDNP *lam de dka' bas 'jug pa ma yin pas* ("It is because the path is not entered with difficulty . . .").
681. As in Atiśa's text 152, these are the five pure faculties of confidence, vigor, mindfulness, samādhi, and prajñā that embody the entire path.
682. I follow CDNP *kye* against GZ *skyes*.
683. I follow CDNP *gang de* against GZ *gang des*.
684. GZ *las dang nyon mongs pa skye ba* CD *las dang nyon mongs pa'i skye ba* NP *las dang nyon mongs kyis skye ba* ("birth through karma and afflictions").
685. I follow GZ CD *mtshon bya* against NP *mtshon cha*.
686. GZ *sū ni rū pa* CD *svā ni rū pa* NP *sva vi rū pa* are all corrupt. Given the preceding phrase and the context, the Sanskrit here must be *svarūpa* ("one's own nature").
687. CDNP omit *dbye ba* ("distinctions").
688. CDNP omit *'i 'dod pa* ("the desire of").
689. GZ CD *brlabs pa* NP *blangs pa* ("assumes").
690. I follow GZ CD *mtshon bya'i* against NP *mtshon cha'i*.
691. CDNP adds *mtshan nyid* ("characteristics").
692. CDNP omit *mchog* ("supreme").

693. CDNP *de'i phyir . . . zhes bya'o* ("Therefore, I say, . . .").
694. I follow GZ CD *bdag med ma de* against NP *bdag med bde*.
695. The triad of perfection, maturation, and purification refers to (1) the perfection of a bodhisattva's aspiration prayers, (2) the maturation of sentient beings, and (3) the purification of buddha realms that bodhisattvas have to accomplish on their path in order to attain the fruition of the infinite enlightened activity of a perfect buddha (versus the state of the individual nirvāṇa of arhats, in which no such activity for others happens). (1) The full extent of the perfection or completion of aspiration prayers is the consummate perfection of the power of the virtues that are the causes for the ability to effortlessly and spontaneously promote the welfare of others while one-pointedly resting in meditative equipoise within the nature of phenomena. (2) The full extent of the maturation of sentient beings is the complete perfection of the power of the virtues that are the causes for the ability to display millions of physical manifestations in millions of buddha realms and to establish the retinue in front of each such manifestation—countless sentient beings—on the path of the noble ones by virtue of teaching them just a single stanza of dharma. (3) The full extent of the purification of buddha realms is the complete perfection of the power of the virtues that are the causes for accomplishing the particular buddha realm in which one will become enlightened, just as the full extent of the ripening of fruits is their being ready to be enjoyed.
696. GZ *bden par brtags pa* CDNP *der brtags pa* ("conceived as such").
697. GZ *ma byas pa* CDNP *ma lta bu byas pa* ("has been someone like the mother").
698. I follow CDNP *tsam la* against GZ *tsam las*.
699. GZ *sngar gyi bde ba dran pa'i tshul gyis* CDNP *sngar gyi bde ba dang dran pa'i thabs kyis*.
700. GZ omits *gyis* ("through").
701. GZ *dag pa / snang ba* CDNP *dag par snang ba* ("appear/shine/radiate in a pure manner").
702. I follow CDNP *lha'i skur* against GZ *skur*.
703. I follow GZ *thabs dang shes rab dang/ stong pa dang snying rje* against CDNP *thabs shes rab dang/ snying rje dang / shes rab* ("means and prajñā as well as compassion and prajñā").
704. This line of a stanza appears in both the *Aṣṭādaśasāhasrikāprajñāpāramitāsūtra* (H12, fols. 265b.7–266a.1) and the *Ratnaguṇasaṃcayagāthā* (XVI.5d, H17, fol. 201a.3–4).
705. CDNP omit *gnyis* ("the pair of").
706. CDNP replaces *ma lus par 'khrul pa ste /* with *ma lus pa ste med pa mthong ba* and *rab rib can gyis skra shad la sogs pa mthong ba* with *rab rib can gyi skra la sogs pa* ("Seeing what is nonexistent refers to all the cognitions and cognizable objects of those who see just this life without exception; seeing what is nonexistent is understood to be similar to the example of [seeing] the hairs and so on of those with blurred vision").
707. GZ CDNP *des don* emended to *nges don*.
708. CDNP omit *thabs* ("the means").

709. I follow GZ *rnam par 'phrul pa* against CDNP *rnam par 'khrul pa.*
710. I follow CDNP *rtogs* against GZ *rtog.*
711. GZ *des grol bar 'gyur ba* CDNP *grol ba'i rgyur* ("this is the cause of being free").
712. GZ NP *rol pa* CD *rol pas* ("are delighted in an inconceivable manner by the play."
713. CDNP omit *skom* ("thirsty").
714. GZ *bsten pa* CDNP *brtan pa* ("to stabilize").
715. GZ *bsten gyis* CDNP *brtan gyis* ("stabilize").
716. NP omit *sems* ("states of mind").
717. I follow GZ NP *bsal ba* against CD *gsal ba* ("illuminating," "elucidating").
718. GZ *'khrul* CDNP *khrus* ("wash away!").
719. I follow GZ NP *rtog* against CD *rtogs.*
720. CDNP *rtog pa'i dri ma 'khru ba la . . . brtags pa dang shes shing goms par bya ba'i lam* . . . ("For washing away the stains of thoughts, [through] the path on which the stains of thoughts are to be examined with prajñā as being entities of delusion and are to be understood and familiarized with [in that way], they are to be examined as being equal in terms of unity").
721. GZ *rtog pa* CDNP *ldog pa.*
722. GZ *rnal 'byor pas de ma rig pa dang dbyings gnyis med par mthong ba* CDNP *rnal 'byor te / dbyings dang rig pa gnyis med ma mthong ba* emended to *rnal 'byor pas dbyings dang rig pa gnyis med ma mthong ba.*
723. GZ *tshor ba med pa'i bde ba* CDNP *tshor ba bde ba* ("the bliss that is a [mere] feeling"—as opposed to the transcendent bliss of the nonduality of expanse and awareness—which appears to make more sense here).
724. I follow CDNP *stong pa chen po de* against GZ *stong pa chen pos.*
725. GZ *gsungs* CDNP *tshig.*
726. GZ omits *lha'i* ("of the deity").
727. GZ *sbyong* CDNP *bsgom* ("familiarized with").
728. "Container and contents" refers to the outer environment and the sentient beings that live in it.
729. I follow NP *'jigs* against GZ CD *'jig* ("destruction," "perishing").
730. GZ *snying rje . . . bsgom pa'ang de bla ma . . .* CDNP *snying rje . . . bsgom pa la bya la de bla ma . . .* ("You should engage in the familiarization . . . nondual, which is contingent on the guru").
731. I follow CDNP *da ni* against GZ *de'i.*
732. GZ *longs spyod dbul* CDNP *longs spyod dman* ("possessions inferior").
733. GZ *g.yeng ba* CDNP *g.yang sa* ("abyss").
734. GZ *bdag gzhan* CDNP *gzhan dag* ("others").
735. Ordinarily, Skt. *kunduru* refers to *Boswellia thurifera* as well as its resin, known as frankincense. In tantric texts, the term is often used as a synonym for *kunda,* one of the many epithets of semen. As applies in this case here, it is also glossed as "the union of the two faculties (male and female sex organs)" (Skt. *dvīndriyasamāpatti*)—that is, sexual intercourse. According to Davidson 2002b (268), the term is probably derived from the Dravidian root √*kund* (to pierce, to prick, to prod).

736. According to Tibetan sources, this was Atiśa's tantric name.
737. Tib. Rgya brtson 'grus seng ge (born tenth century).
738. This text is not found in Tg.
739. PDMT, 27:74–76.
740. I follow GZ *yis* against CDNP *yin*.
741. I follow GZ CD *mi reg* against NP *mi rig(s)*.
742. Skt. *āli kāli*, Tib. *a phreng ka phreng* (GZ CDNP *ā phreng kā phreng*). With reference to the *Sādhanamālā*, Edgerton 1953 (1:106, 181) explains *āli* as "*a-series* (i.e., a plus āli), name for a series of syllables (chiefly vowels and combinations of a or ā with semivowels) . . . ," and *kāli* as "(ka plus āli), *ka-series*, name for a series of syllables beginning with ka (consonants plus a or ā) . . ." As Miller 1966 (138) points out, these two terms are unknown in conventional Sanskrit grammatical and lexical sources or in the *Mahāvyutpatti*. The *Sādhanamālā* has at least twelve citations of the two terms as "vowel" and "consonant," but their main use in Vajrayāna texts is to indicate the following two series of syllables: a ā / i ī / u ū / ṛ ṝ / ḷ ḹ / e ai / o au / aṃ aḥ / and k kh g gh ṅ / c ch j jh ñ / ṭ ṭh ḍ ḍh ṇ / t th d dh n / p ph b bh m / y r l v ś ṣ s h kṣ / ka kā / ki kī / ku kū / ke kai / ko kau / kaṃ kaḥ /. *Āli* and *kāli* also are names for the lalanā and rasanā. As the most probable etymology of the two terms, Miller (1966, 146–47) suggests *a* + *ādi* ("beginning with a") and *ka* + *ādi* ("beginning with ka"), given that later Buddhist hybrid Sanskrit at times resulted in replacing intervocalic *-l-* for *-ḍ-* as well as *-d-*.
743. I follow GZ *tshes* against NP *chos*.
744. This is an epithet of the moon.
745. PDMT, 27:77–78.
746. I follow CDNP *rgyal lo* against GZ *rgyal po* ("king").
747. I follow GZ *gyi* against CDNP *kye*.
748. PDMT, 27:79–80.
749. NP omit the last two lines.
750. PDMT, 27:87–89.
751. GZ CD *'phro* NP *'gro*.
752. Tib. *mi bskyod chu* could also mean "immovable water."
753. I follow GZ NP *kye* against D *kyi*.
754. PDMT, 27:81–84.
755. An epithet of the deity Śrīdevī (Tib. Dpal ldan lha mo).
756. I follow NP *rtog pa* against GZ CD *rtogs pa*.
757. There are varying lists of the nine gates or orifices of the body: (1)–(2) eyes, (3)–(4) ears, (5)–(6) nostrils, (7) mouth, (8) urethral opening, and (9) anus; (1)–(2) eyes, (3)–(4) ears, (5)–(6) nostrils, (7) navel, (8) urethral opening, and (9) anus; and (1) forehead, (2) navel, (3) crown of the head, (4) eyes, (5) ears, (6) nostrils, (7) mouth, (8) urethral opening, and (9) anus.
758. I follow GZ *'brel med dran med sems nyid* against CDNP *'brel med dran sems nyid ni*.
759. I follow CD *bsgom rgyu sgom byed* against GZ NP *sgom rgyu bsgom bya*.
760. GZ *bde can* ("blissful") CDNP *bde chen*.

761. I follow GZ NP *zhags pa bcad cing* against CD *zhags pas bcings shing* ("fettered by the noose").
762. I follow GZ *rdzun rku na ni* against CD *brdzun rku brdzun mi* NP *brdzun brku brdzun ni.*
763. NP omit *rang bzhin* ("nature").
764. I follow GZ CD *cho 'phrul* against NP *mi 'phrul.*
765. Śramaṇas are mendicants from non-Brahmanic castes on spiritual paths not related to the Vedas, such as the Buddha (the general name for wandering mendicants of Brahmanic origin, following orthodox Vedic teachings or heterodox paths, is Parivrājaka).
766. PDMT, 27:85–86.
767. PDMT, 27:90–93.
768. I follow GZ NP *gzhan dang mi mnyam* against CD *mnyam dang mi mnyam* ("unequaled").
769. GZ *'khor ba nyid las gzhan du med* CDNP *'khor ba nyid las gzhan du min* ("This is nothing else than just saṃsāra").
770. This is an epithet of the god Indra.
771. This could also be read as "true reality is just like a wish-fulfilling jewel."
772. GZ CD *(b)rgal zhing dri med pa* NP *brgal phyir dri med pa* ("be stainless because of having crossed the afflictions' swamp").
773. PDMT, 27:94–96.
774. GZ *bzhengs par byas* CDNP *bzhengs par bya* ("should build").
775. GZ *pas* CDNP *na* ("if").
776. GZ *nang gnas* CDNP here and below *nang nas* ("from within").
777. PDMT, 27:110–12.
778. This could also be read as "The dharmadhātu, suchness, and the realization of the nature of anything are . . ."
779. I follow GZ *dang po* against CDNP *dam pa* ("genuine").
780. GZ *kyis* CDNP *kyi.*
781. I follow GZ *yis* against CDNP *yi.*
782. CDNP omit *chen po* ("great").
783. PDMT, 27:113–15.
784. GZ CDNP *zla rtse'i* emended to *zla tshes.*
785. I follow NP *gyi* against GZ CD *gyis.*
786. GZ *bskyod* CDNP *spyod.*
787. I follow GZ CD *skye* against NP *kye.*
788. I follow CDNP *gyi* against GZ *gyis.*
789. PDMT, 27:116–17.
790. I follow GZ *yin* against CD *ni* NP *yis.*
791. GZ *dpa' bo che* (which could also be read as "great courage") CDNP *dga' ba che* ("great ecstasy," which seems to make more sense here).
792. PDMT, 27:118–20.
793. I follow GZ NP *sems nyid kye* against CD *sems nyid kyi* ("remember the . . . fruition of the mind").
794. GZ *rang bzhin* CDNP *rang nyid* ("yourself").
795. I follow CDNP *bsags pa* against GZ *bsags pas.*

796. GZ *'dod pa'i 'khrugs pas rma byung khrag* CDNP *'dod pa'i rma phyung 'khrugs pa'i khrag*.
797. I follow GZ NP *rlangs* against CD *brlabs*.
798. I follow GZ *las* against CDNP *la* ("in").
799. PDMT, 27:121–23.
800. I follow GZ *āḥ yig* against CDNP *a yig*.
801. PDMT, 27:124–25.
802. I follow GZ *bandha pa* against CDNP *bhandha pa*. Skt. *bhandaka* can mean "violator" or "ravisher," "tie," "pledge," and "confinement." The feminine form *bhandakī* is a term for a harlot or courtesan, so it could be used here in the same sense for the author's male counterpart. Thus, the author somewhat playfully speaks about her male consort (probably Ḍombi Heruka) as someone who engages in conventionally inappropriate behavior, especially sexual yoga, but at the same time shares a strict tantric commitment with her.
803. Tib. *mtshams* renders a long list of Sanskrit words, each one of which in turn can mean a lot of different things, including "junction," "connection," "union," "sexual intercourse," "agreement," "alliance," "boundary (line)," "retreat," "critical juncture," "opportune moment," "interval," "twilight," "pause," "gap," and "vagina." Strange as it may sound, here this term may be understood as including all of these meanings. Given the initial two lines and the author speaking of practicing with a consort, as well as the mention of "charnel grounds" and "places of mountain training" in stanza 4, the term seems to refer to their agreed-upon practice of karmamudrā due to their mutual connection and tantric commitment after having set their boundaries by dwelling in solitary retreat places. This is considered a very opportune moment in that it represents a gap, pause, or "twilight zone" between mundane or dualistic states of mind. "Vanquished" and "crushed" appears to refer to overcoming any dualistic and ego-based perception as well as any illusory sense of a true personality through the realization of great bliss in this practice.
804. GZ *thar sa med* CDNP *thar pa med* ("no escape").
805. GZ *de dor* CDNP *de ngor* ("from that perspective").
806. As the word yoginī in the Sanskrit title suggests and the content of this song clearly shows, it was sung by a woman. The colophon's association with Ḍombipa suggests that she was the woman from the Ḍombi caste whom he married. However, this yoginī was not 'just' Ḍombipa's consort but a prodigious female guru in her own right (for details on her life and activities, see Shaw 1994, 63–72, and 79). Thus, this appears to be another typical case of a teaching being attributed to a male master instead of his female counterpart or even guru. In part, this may be due to omitted feminine endings of words in Tibetan (such as *rnal byor gyi spyod pa* instead of *rnal 'byor ma'i spyod pa* in the title, or *ḍom bi pa* instead of *ḍom bi ma*). However, the fact that such a misattribution happens even when the content of the song is clearly from a first-person female perspective just shows how the male-dominated Indo-Tibetan Buddhist tradition pushed many great female masters into obscurity.

807. PDMT, 27:126–27.
808. Throughout this text, I follow GZ CD *gtun* ("mortar") and *gtun shing* ("pestle") against NP *brtun* ("effort") and *brtun shing*.
809. Skt. *musala* refers to a wooden pestle used for cleaning rice. It is also the name for a mace or club, especially ones used by gods or other mythological figures, such as Balarāma, one of Viṣṇu's avatars.
810. I follow GZ *bdar* against CD *brdar* NP *rdar*. This whole stanza appears quite corrupt: GZ *rig byed dang ni gtun shing yin / dzā dang mu sal gtun rdung yin / sa ma bhe dang gtun du byas / a thar shim mas phyad bdar byas /*.
811. I follow CDNP *lta ba drug ni* against *zla ba drug na* ("I gladly devote myself to this path of becoming a buddha in six months").
812. Tib. *'gram shing* literally means "stile." For the use of poles (which may have looked somewhat similar to a stile in India) in the process of pounding paddy, see the following note.
813. This song uses the pounding of paddy to remove all its husks and make it edible as an analogy for the process of purifying the mind through both one's past merit and present vigor (pounding), so that its obscurations fall away and the "kernel" of buddhahood—mind's true nature of luminosity and emptiness inseparable—remains. This analogy here greatly resembles the process of parching and pounding rice as described in Densmore 2012 for the Chippewa in North America (315–16 and plates 41 and 42). In brief, after parching the paddy in the sun or over a fire, it is put into a wooden mortar and carefully pounded with a large wooden pestle several feet long in order to loosen the husks without breaking the kernel. After the rice was winnowed, the final step was to tread it with one's feet in order to dislodge the last fragments of the husks but not break the kernels. For this purpose, the rice was put in another wooden receptacle partially sunk in the ground. On either side of it, a stout pole was placed, with one end fastened to a tree about four feet above the ground and the other end resting on the ground. During the treading, these poles served as supports to hold on to with one's hands.
814. PDMT, 27:128–30.
815. GZ CDNP *las* emended to *la*.
816. This probably refers to *bandhura* (*Pentapetes phoenicea*), commonly known as midday flower or scarlet mallow.
817. GZ *nas* CDNP *na*.
818. PDMT, 27:139–41.
819. NP omit *ri dvags* ("stag").
820. Here and in the parallel line in stanza 9, I follow GZ *bdas* against CDNP *brdas*.
821. Torricelli 2018 (8–9) points out that according to Vibhūticandra's *Bodhicaryāvatāratātparyapañjikāviśeṣadyotanī* (D3880, fol. 194a.2–3), the term *bhusuku* is a Sanskrit acronym for an outwardly lazy person who does nothing but eat (*bhuñjāna*), sleep (*supta*), and stroll around (*kuṭiṃ gata*) but actually dwells in a profound inner samādhi: "Since he [Śāntideva] was dwelling in the 'Bhusuku' samādhi through continuously

cultivating luminosity, no matter whether he was eating, sleeping, or moving around, he was well-known by the name 'Bhusuku.'" This explanation is followed by Butön in his *History of the Dharma* (Butön Rinchen Drup 2013, 258). However, the more popular interpretation of *ku* has been "going to the toilet," which is possibly based on Skt. *kuṣṭhikā* ("contents of the entrails"), *kuth* ("stink"), or *ku* ("bad," "inferior"; another option would be *kuṣīda* "lazy").

822. GZ NP *gtor* (which can also mean "destroy" or "scatter") CD *stor* (which can also mean "lose").

823. For a strikingly similar contemporary version of a Bāul song (sung by Parvathy Baul), called "Kaahe Re" (*kāhere* is the first word of this song here in Old Bengali), which is said to have been composed by a Bhusuku in the seventh century, see https://www.youtube.com/watch?v=7JZ4_GTbjA. As mentioned before, song 6 in text 90 (attributed to a Bhusuku), though shorter, has very similar content, and the symbolism explained in text 90 certainly applies to text 173 as well. It is not clear whether this Bhusuku was identical to Śāntideva, who was born as Prince Śāntivarman in Saurāṣṭra (present-day Gujarat) and then called Bhusuku (which of course is a very generic epithet) by his fellow monks at Nālandā University. However, there are some indications for their identity, mainly around the shared theme of killing deer. The traditional Indo-Tibetan hagiographies say that Bhusuku was renamed Śāntideva in honor of having delivered his *Bodhicaryāvatāra* at Nālandā University, but then he took up the lifestyle of a wandering mahāsiddha. One episode during that later time (Abhayadatta's **Caturaśītisiddhapravṛtti*; N3873, fol. 38a.4–5) reports that Bhusuku/Śāntideva was seen to kill deer and eat their flesh while living in a mountain cave. When he was asked why he kills sentient beings, all the animals he had killed streamed out of his cave restored to life, multiplying as they ran and finally vanishing into thin air. Upon that, the fortunate people present realized that all phenomena are mere dreams and illusions and thus pursued the path. Then, Bhusuku/Śāntideva sang this song to them:

> The deer who have been killed by me
> did not come from anywhere at first,
> do not dwell anywhere in between,
> and will not cease anywhere in the end
>
> In primordially unestablished phenomena,
> how could killed and killer be established?
> This is what Bhusuku declares:
> AHO! Sentient beings are so pitiful!

The same theme of hunting deer is also found in song 23 by Bhusuku in text 90. In addition, the comments on song 46 in text 90 quote Śāntideva's *Bodhicaryāvatāra* by attributing it to Bhusuku, thus clearly considering the two to be identical.

824. PDMT, 27:142–44.
825. GZ *gsang ba* CD *gtsang ba* ("clean").
826. GZ *ri khrod* CDNP *ri thod* ("mountain peak").
827. Hindi *bhiḍa* means "hornet," while *bhīḍa* means "crowd." Skt. *bhidā* means "splitting," "destruction," "separation," "difference," "species," and "coriander." However, even if the spelling *bhiḍa* is correct, it is unlikely that any of these meanings apply here. Given that the retaining of Indic words in our texts often refers to sexual organs, sexual fluids, or human excrements (urine or feces), and given the following elements in this list here, *bhiḍa* could refer to female sexual fluids or blood.
828. GZ *sgrub pa* CDNP *sgrub sa* ("place of practice").
829. GZ CDNP *dud ka* renders Skt. *dhūmra*, which can also mean dark-colored, gray, dark red, or purple.
830. I follow GZ CD *stong nyid* against NP *snying nyid*.
831. GZ NP *brtan* against CD *bstan* ("taught").
832. I follow NP *bsam* against GZ CD *sam* ("or").
833. GZ CDNP *yis* emended to *yi*.
834. PDMT, 27:149–51.
835. This could also be read as "the lack of a self of the empty entity (in the sense of the true state)."
836. I follow GZ CD *'phro 'dus las* against N *'phro 'du la* P *'phro 'dul ba'i*.
837. I follow GZ NP *byams pa* against CD *bsam pa* ("thinking").
838. I follow GZ *ngag* against CD *dag*.
839. PDMT, 27:188–89.
840. This could also be read as "If I, the yogī, am aware."
841. I follow CDNP *'di yis* against GZ *'di yi*.
842. GZ *bdag ni gtan med pa* CDNP *bdag ni rten med pa* ("I am without support"; given the preceding two lines, this seems the more likely reading here).
843. I follow GZ CD *thams cad* against NP *gzhan ma*.
844. I follow GZ NP *ye shes te* against CD *ye shes med* ("the nonexistence of wisdom").
845. GZ CD *rnal 'byor skye* NP *rnal 'byor gyis* ("do yoga").
846. GZ *yis* CDNP *yin* ("this is being free").
847. PDMT, 26:1372–88.
848. GZ CDNP have many misspellings or variants of the names of the eighty-four mahāsiddhas; I use their names as given in Dowman 1985. Note also that Dowman's renderings of these stanzas are mostly very free and elaborated paraphrases, sometimes significantly recasting them.
849. Compare with stanzas 7 in text 179 and II.2 in text 183. In the following, I will add the comments (slightly paraphrased) on each stanza in the anonymous **Dohāvṛttisahitacaturaśītisiddhāvadāna* (P5092, N3874; henceforth abbr. DVS) that is not included in GZ. On Lūhipa's stanza, DVS (fols. 68a.7–69a.8) comments that it has two parts. (1) The example of a hunting dog, on whose nose a savage hunter has rubbed honey, gobbling up everything in all directions demonstrates that it is not suitable to teach the profound dharma to people of inferior insight. In a country called Sutari there

once was a man who made his livelihood by hunting. One time, a great heat wave occurred and all the deer fled. All dogs were tormented by the heat and lost their hair, but still kept searching for deer with their burning noses. The hunter rubbed some wild honey on the nose and paws of his dog, who licked it up, became intoxicated by it, and went mad. Thus, the dog ate up all the stones, sticks, and so on everywhere. He even devoured his owner and then his own limbs. Similarly, those of lesser insight are those who lack the propensities of having trained in study, reflection, and meditation in previous lives. "Unfortunate" refers to sentient beings who lack a master and pith instructions to instruct them. "Pith instructions" are the special means through which a great purpose is accomplished with little difficulty. If such instructions are given to those who are not proper vessels for them, their mindstreams will be burned: since these instructions are not an object to be realized by them, they lead them to going astray. (2) The example of king Bimbisāra's elephant demonstrates that thoughts do not harm those who are proper vessels. When king Bimbisāra of Māgadha waged war against the kings of Kośala and Campaka, he made five elephants drunk with rice beer, tied swords to their trunks, and sent them as battle fortresses against the hostile armies, which were thus defeated. "The fortunate" are those who trained in study, reflection, and meditation lifetime after lifetime and have a guru. Through these causes, their mindstreams are ripened so that wisdom will arise in their practice of samādhi at the time of the path and the three kāyas will become manifest as the fruition. They vanquish thoughts merely upon encountering appearances: through realizing the unborn, thoughts awaken as dharmatā. If appearances arise as the guru, this is like a fire breaking out in a storehouse of sesame seeds: everything in that storehouse becomes an aid to that fire. Likewise, merely by encountering appearances, all thoughts become exhausted and cease in the unborn natural state.

850. I follow CDNP DVS *glang po* against GZ *klad pa* ("brain").

851. DVS (fols. 69b.1–70b.8) says that similar to a lion as the king of all beasts of prey, yogīs who perfected their power and abilities are the kings among persons on the path. Similar to a lion's tufts of turquoise color, such yogīs hold the five buddha families as signs of empowerment on the crowns of their heads. Based on the vase empowerment, the five kinds of afflictions are brought under control. Thus they undergo a fundamental change as the five kāyas (the forms of the five buddha families) and the five wisdoms, while all adverse afflictions are at peace. It is said that a lion who has perfected his prowess has these kinds of qualities. Through possessing physical strength, he is able to tear apart all flesh and bones in an instant and overpowers all other beasts of prey. Through possessing the prowess of courage, he is free of all adverse circumstances. Likewise, the ten pāramitās of the yogī tear adverse thoughts apart. Lacking desire for any object, yogīs practice generosity by separating themselves from the adversity of miserliness. Lacking the heat of the afflictions, they attain the coolness of discipline by separating themselves from the adversity

of corrupt discipline. With the five poisons serving as the path, they attain patience by separating themselves from adversities such as hatred and anger. Not being distracted from profound actuality, they practice the vigor of making effort toward the supreme goal by separating themselves from the adversity of laziness. Lacking a state of mind other than solely the samādhis of the creation and perfection processes, they hold the mind of dhyāna by separating themselves from the adversity of being distracted by afflictions. Through that, ignorance is awakened as wisdom, which is the pāramitā of prajñā: true reality becomes manifest by being separated from the adversity of unawareness and so on. By virtue of the afflictions being the path of purified phenomena, aspects of the kāyas and wisdom, or the path of great bliss, this is the pāramitā of means: by separating themselves from the adversity of stupidity, yogīs become smart and skilled. From within this mahāmudrā, the dharmadhātu, the welfare of others is unimpeded, which is the pāramitā of aspiration prayers: by separating themselves from the adversity of intermittent compassion, they accomplish all kinds of welfare due to their enlightened activity being uninterrupted. When all these qualities are perfected, this is the pāramitā of power: by separating themselves from the adversities of miraculous powers and magic, they outshine all adversities. The pāramitā of omniscient wisdom with all consummate qualities means to give rise to the wisdom that is as uninterrupted as the flow of a river by separating themselves from the adversity of fragmentary samādhi. "Pāramitā" means to have gone to the other shore of saṃsāra—the expanse of nirvāṇa. When summarized, the ten pāramitās are six: with prajñā as the factor of meditative equipoise, its aftermath (or subsequent attainment) consists of the four pāramitās of means, aspiration prayers, power, and wisdom. Also, the ten pāramitās are contained in the three trainings and the two accumulations. Generosity, discipline, and patience represent the training in discipline. Dhyāna is the training in samādhi. Means, aspiration prayers, power, and wisdom constitute the training in prajñā. Vigor is the aid of all these, and prajñā is the factor of meditative equipoise. Generosity, discipline, patience, vigor, and dhyāna represent the accumulation of merit. The result of prajñā is the accumulation of wisdom. Thus, "having realized this, Līla is free" means that by separating themselves from the adversities of the ten pāramitās, yogīs realize true actuality just as it is.

852. GZ NP *rig* CD *rigs* DVS *dpyad*.

853. Compare this stanza with stanzas 4 in text 179 and I.39 in text 183. DVS (fols. 70b.8–71b.7) says that there are three kinds of mudrā. Persons who train in the samayamudrā (text: dharmamudrā; I follow the format of the comments on Ḍombipa's stanza below) see the kāya as a mudrā having form and characteristics. Persons who train in the karmamudrā see the kāya as a mudrā adorned by all kinds of qualities. Persons who train in the dharmamudrā see the kāya as a mudrā that is the birth of a great vidyādhara and the lineage of vidyādharas. Bodhisattvas who first give rise to bodhicitta see buddhas as having a body and characteristics.

Bodhisattvas who engage in the conduct of bodhisattvas see buddhas as being adorned with all qualities. Irreversible bodhisattvas see buddhas as taking birth and holding their family lineage. "Mahāmudrā" is the fourth mudrā. Persons who realize it realize the essence of buddhas as mahāmudrā—the unity of the connate. Bodhisattvas in their last birth neither see nor do not see buddhas. The eye of prajñā is without projecting and withdrawing. What is without projecting and withdrawing is free of the two extremes. What is free of the two extremes means seeing the true character. Seeing the true character means seeing the Buddha. Thus, since oneself is pure, buddhas are pure. Since buddhas are pure, phenomena are pure. Since phenomena are pure, omniscience is pure. Therefore, the text speaks of "the connate within the natural state of mahāmudrā." Within the natural state of the connate, all phenomena of saṃsāra and nirvāṇa are naturally pure. This is described as "within true reality, there is no mental engagement in diversity." Its essence is without desire for anything, but it appears as anything whatsoever due to conditions. Therefore, it is without any partiality or bias. Since it is beyond being an object that can be thought of, it is without thinking. Since it is not an object of examination, analysis, or discursive awareness, it is without analysis. Therefore, mahāmudrā's own way of being is fresh, loose, or free of effort, with the fruition being inherent. Therefore, without effort, let it be on its own. "Not becoming extinct, it is experienced by self-awareness" (note that, as in this case, the phrasings of certain lines of the stanzas commented on in DVS sometimes differ between how they appear at the outset of each section and how they appear in the following comments). Since the connate abides in the dhyāna of its own continuum not being interrupted, it does not become extinct. Since the wisdom of realization becomes manifest in itself, it is uninterrupted. Therefore, it is aware of its own. There is no clinging to this uninterrupted dhyāna, which refers to being free of clinging to entities being real. Mahāmudrā is "unity" because it is free of all views.

854. Compare this with stanzas 12 in text 179 and I.42 in text 183. DVS (fols. 71b.7–72b.7) says that a yogī who attained the siddhi of alchemy step by step creates an elixir through whose power other metals are turned into gold (in Indian alchemy [*rasāyana*], this was specially prepared mercury). Likewise, first, the psychophysical support must be ripened through empowerments (the cause). "By virtue of precious empowerments" means that by virtue of the power of the four kinds of empowerments, afflictions and wisdom are nondual. First, the vase empowerment empowers you to meditate on the samayamudrā. It is referred to as "samaya" because of not transgressing the welfare of sentient beings, beginning with generating bodhicitta up through the dharmakāya and the two form kāyas at the end. It is referred to as "mudrā" because of not transcending the deity or the form kāya. Through what do the afflictions turn into wisdom? In terms of the nature of means, the five afflictions are the male buddhas of the five families. In terms of the nature of prajñā, they are the four female

buddhas Buddhalocanā, Māmakī, Pāṇḍaravāsinī, and Tārā. Therefore, the afflictions are transformed into nondual wisdom. Second, the secret empowerment empowers you to meditate with the karmamudrā. Its hermeneutical etymology means that based on the sixteen emptinesses, your own mind is introduced as the dharmakāya. As for karma, there is empty karma, the karma of means, and nondual karma. "Mahāmudrā" means to realize unborn actuality due to these three. Thus, by virtue of the union of the male and the female consorts, the afflictions turn into the nature of nonduality—the unborn expanse. Thereby, the afflictions are transformed into nondual wisdom. Third, the prajñā-jñāna empowerment empowers you to meditate on the dharmamudrā. "Dharma" refers to the phenomena of saṃsāra and nirvāṇa. "Mudrā" means that through practicing by mentally engaging in the emptiness of cultivating the path and in the triad of nāḍīs, vāyus, and bindus, unborn actuality—the dharmakāya—is revealed. Through meditating by taking the afflictions as the path, they turn into nondual wisdom. Thus afflictions and wisdom are nondual. The fourth empowerment is called "the precious word empowerment." It is taught through four points. The cause of bestowing empowerment is that which abides inherently in the mindstreams of yogīs. The condition is that the empowerment, including its blessings, is bestowed through the gate of a single maṇḍala. Thus the means to practice the path tantra refers to the instructions on the four mudrās, including the certainty about them. By virtue of that, the appropriate fruition of mahāmudrā is the dharmakāya, which is the nature of all that. In it, there are no afflictions from the very ground up: this is the nature of the great affliction-free wisdom of not being distracted. Therefore, the afflictions become nondual wisdom.

855. GZ CDNP *phyag rgya chen po* DVS *sku gsum ye shes* ("the wisdom of the three kāyas"). DVS (fols. 72b.7–73b.1) says that since connate and imaginative ignorance give rise to all afflictions, they resemble a dense jungle. In it, the mind that is bound by the duality of perceiver and perceived is similar to a deer. Thus, this is the cause. How is this deer of perceiver and perceived hunted? "By drawing the bow of both means and prajñā." "Means" refers to appearances: not blocking them, appearances arise as the guru. "Prajñā" refers to emptiness: the nonconceptual empty luminosity that has the essence of identitylessness and formlessness. By drawing such a bow, what kind of arrow is shot? "I shoot the single arrow of essential reality." "Essential reality" refers to exactly this nonduality of appearance and emptiness. It is beyond any thoughts of perceiver and perceived, its essence is free of objects to be thought of, and it is not the sphere of mind or mentation. At what is that arrow shot? It is shot at the deer-like mind bound by the duality of perceiver and perceived. What dies? It is the thoughts that dwell in the jungle of ignorance, including the clinging to appearances being something that they are not. Since realization occurs in this single nondual actuality, this is the meaning of "its flesh is consumed as nonduality." Since bliss is uninterrupted in this nonduality, this is the meaning of "its taste is experienced as great bliss." Since true reality

abides as what is attained inherently and primordially, "the fruition that is the wisdom of the three kāyas is attained."

856. CDNP DVS omit *ye shes* ("wisdom").

857. GZ CDNP *'chad pa* DVS *rgas pa* ("aging"). Compare this with stanzas 2 in text 179 and I.10 in text 183. According to DVS (fols. 73b.1–74a.3), "Hey, friends!" addresses those who have the fortune for mahāmudrā. "The connate" means mental nonengagement. The connate essence need not be searched elsewhere, but dwells within us primordially in an inherent manner. Therefore it is connate. "It is not found elsewhere" means that it is not found by ascertaining it through conventional superimpositions such as words, letters, or reasons. "It is found on the true guru's lips." This means that by relying on a single guru with the three feats, awareness can be understood within. "A guru with the three feats" means one who possesses the blessings of the lineage gurus, has trust in the personal pith instructions, and has cut through doubts by virtue of having been introduced to mind's nature by his or her actual guru. Or, this means bestowing empowerments with blessings; explaining the tantras, including understanding and realization; and giving instructions with certainty. "Actual guru" means the one who nakedly shows your own mind as such by cutting through doubts. Based on these three feats, the realization of the connate is found at the feet of such a true guru. "The ultimate" is the connate, which is unmistaken. "Essence" means that once unborn actuality is realized, mind is without death. Since the mind of thoughts and afflictions turns into uninterrupted unborn actuality, there is no death. As for "the body is without aging," by virtue of the latent tendencies of thoughts, a body may be assumed as desired, but the body of wisdom is without aging.

858. According to DVS (fol. 74a.3–74b.1), within this unconditioned empty space, "one" or "itself" refers to appearance. "Other" refers to emptiness. Form devoid of both appearance and emptiness means that space's own essence is the inseparability of appearance and emptiness. As in this example, within mind as such that is like empty space, "itself" refers to the external wife, possessing things such as flesh and blood, whose nature is conditioned. "Other" refers to the internal wife—forms, sounds, smells, tastes, and tangible objects whose nature is emptiness. Mind as such is devoid of these external and internal wives. "Form" refers to your own mind as such, whose own essence is luminous great bliss—that is, the great wisdom inherent in yourself. This wife is called "the queen of self-appearing wisdom." Since this is the wisdom that abides inherently and need not to be searched for elsewhere, it is called "self-appearing." This wife of wisdom cannot be illustrated by examples and cannot be measured by conventions.

859. DVS (fol. 74b.2–6) says that the first two lines refer to the story of Mīnapa being swallowed by a giant fish. "Practicing the instructions of the great god" refers to the instructions of wearing the elements as one's garment: the instruction on the six collections of consciousness vanishing within

being like a lamp within a vase. The instructions on eating the character of bodhicitta as food are contained within the dohās. Mīnapa's qualities—the common siddhis—consist of overpowering the elements—that is, even earth and rocks could not bear or hold him.

860. GZ CDNP *brtas* DVS *btab* ("were planted").

861. GZ *ma tsin dha ris* CD *ma tsindhi yis* NP *ma tsindha yis* DVS *a tsindha yis*. As Gorakṣa's story informs us, Aciṅta is an alias of his guru Mīnapa.

862. GZ CDNP *brtan* DVS *bstan*.

863. According to DVS (fols. 74b.6–75b.4), the highest caste refers to the royal caste, the middling to the nobility or the brahmans, and the lower to the castes of common people or that of cowherds and so on. "The abiding cause" refers to native mind as such. Its essence is to be empty and its characteristic is to be free of discursiveness. It is the ground from which everything arises and it provides space for everything, similar to unconditioned space. Without needing to be searched for elsewhere, it primordially exists within ourselves in an inherent manner. Therefore it is called "abiding cause." "Powerful conditions" are three. The condition of giving rise to confidence (the preliminary) consists of turning your mind away from the world. The condition of being fortunate consists of meeting a guru with siddhis. The condition of practicing the path consists of the arising of trust in the dharma instructions and the revealing of nonreferential prajñā. By being associated with these three conditions, there are no obstacles. As for the fruition of these three conditions, when what exists within us is realized, the awakened mind of a buddha dawns within us in an inherent manner. Therefore, there is nothing to be impeded by others. For example, with fire existing inherently in a fire crystal, that fire is ignited through the condition of the sun, while other conditions, such as the moon, cannot impede it. Likewise, since the awakened mind of a buddha that exists inherently within us is clearly realized through the three conditions here, what is other—wrong ideas—cannot impede it. That this exists within us is truly amazing. "Having performed bodhisattva services for Cauraṅgi" means that, as Gorakṣa's story tells us, he performed menial services for prince Cauraṅgi through the four immeasurables for twelve years. Through those conditions, the seed of his basic element (dhātu) was planted. This means that by being free of the seeds of the common dhātus, āyatanas, and so on through conditions such as love, the seed of bodhicitta was planted. "Aciṅta showed me the nectar of immortality" means that his guru introduced him to the actuality without birth and death. "Threefold existence" refers to either body, speech, and mind or the three main mental poisons. Since Gorakṣa herded them like cattle in the expanse of the dharmakāya, this is amazing.

864. GZ CDNP *yan lag* DVS *yal 'dab* ("branches and leaves").

865. For the symbolism of the axe in tantric Buddhism, see Beer 1999 (300–302) as well as Willson and Brauen 2000 (565).

866. DVS (fols. 75b.4–76a.4) says that saṃsāra has neither a beginning nor an end that can be identified. By virtue of ignorance, it is called "saṃsāric

existence": the appropriated skandhas cycle or roam for a long time based on this saṃsāric existence. Its root is ignorance because formations, consciousness, name-and-form, the six āyatanas, contact, and feelings arise from it. This tree of ignorance grows by being moistened by becoming, from which craving, grasping, birth, as well as aging and death arise. Thus saṃsāric existence's plethora of branches and leaves unfolds. How is this great tree of ignorance cut down? The pith instructions of cutting ignorance at its root are clear in the dohās. The prajñā arising from study is the axe that depends on words. The prajñā arising from reflection is the axe that depends on both words and their meanings. The prajñā arising from meditation is the axe that depends solely on the meaning. "Cauraṅgi has cut it down today" means that the time of his realization occurred today.

867. GZ CDNP *dpyad* DVS *spyad* ("engage").

868. GZ CDNP *ma grol skye med sgra dpyad pas* DVS *ma skyes skye med sgra bcad pas* ("by scrutinizing unarisen unborn sound").

869. DVS (fol. 76a.4–8) says that "the sounds of habituation to mistakenness" refers to clinging to the sounds of a tanpura as being independently existent. As for "having engaged with respect and effort," without his mind entering any other activities of the world, such as the kingdom, Vīṇāpa engaged in sounds themselves with respect or one-pointedly. Therefore he says, "I was not free." As for "by scrutinizing unarisen born sound," both outer sounds, such as those of a tanpura, and the prajñā that perceives them within are minding awareness. Unborn actuality is the sound of nonminding, or selflessness. Therefore, by engaging in the actuality of sound of recognizing it as the lack of sound, Vīṇāpa realized the very lack of a self.

870. I follow DVS *khrid pas* against GZ CDNP *brid pas* "(by being deceived").

871. Compare this with stanzas 10 in text 179 and III.4 in text 183. DVS (fols. 76a.8–77a.2) says that the example of a small boy who is gradually nourished by his mother until his body has grown so much that he possesses the strength of a wrestler teaches the progressive journey through the yānas. The small boy represents those who lack the propensities of previous progressive training in the yānas, have not been ripened through empowerments, and have little prajñā. What is to be traveled through the instructions of the lineage gurus is the dharma of the path. Since this path is traveled in a progressive manner based on discriminating prajñā, it eventually becomes the Mahāyāna. Second, the example of medicine teaches the instantaneous realization of the path. Just as medicine dispels diseases of wind, bile, or phlegm constellations, the clinging to a "me" and a "self"—the 84,000 afflictions in persons who possess a self as well as the perceiver and perceived—is similar to a disease. The six inner and outer instructions by a guru with a lineage are clear in the dohās. The wisdom of realizing the view—true reality—that resembles a wall of fire burns the afflictions that are like firewood in the very instant of such a realization.

872. DVS (fol. 77a.2–77b.3) says that weaving yarn represents seeming reality.

"I, through the guru's pith instructions, weave the entirety of phenomena" refers to the ultimate weaving. How does this weaving take place? Outer perceived objects are empty of any essence and the inner perceiving consciousness is empty of any nature. Thus, emptiness's own nature is not established either, which is the location where this weaving takes place. When the five main afflictions and so on become exhausted and cease within the natural state of their empty essence not being established, the five wisdoms automatically dawn in an unceasing manner, just like the rays of the sun. This is what is taken as the yarn for the weaving here. These wisdoms depend on the instructions of the guru who points them out. Prajñā is what causes the realization of wisdom—it functions as the loom that threads the woof of wisdom. What is woven here? The nonduality of expanse and awareness is woven into the dharmakāya. "Expanse" refers to the dharmadhātu and "awareness" to self-aware wisdom. The realization of the nonduality of expanse and awareness is called "dharmakāya." Compare these two stanzas with song 25 by Tantipa and its comments in text 90, which share some of the above themes.

873. GZ *sbang* CDNP *sbyangs* DVS *sbangs*.

874. DVS (fols. 77b.3–78a.2) says that the guru gives instructions in tune with the constitutions, motivations, and latencies of students. Accordingly, they need to practice them by joining them with their own karma. Just as stiff leather is formed on a shoe mold, thoughts and characteristics that resemble stiff leather are formed by the wisdom of emptiness free of doing and effort. Through the power of aspiration prayers, great unceasing compassion arises. Thus the text says, "is put on the mold of emptiness and compassion." Its thread refers to matching the eight dharmas (gain, loss, fame, disgrace, praise, blame, happiness, and suffering) and so on with likes and dislikes. The awl of the experience that is based on discriminating prajñā means that in nonreferential experience, all of saṃsāra and nirvāṇa is effortlessly present as the great bliss of the dharmakāya. The one who sews the effortless shoe of the dharmakāya with this kind of awl and thread is Cāmāripa, the supreme shoemaker. There is no other shoe superior to the shoe of the dharmakāya.

875. GZ CDNP *'jig rten mtshon thogs dpa' bo* DVS *mtshon cha med pa'i dpa' bo* ("heroes without weapons").

876. GZ CDNP *sdug bsngal* DVS *dgra'i* ("enemies").

877. DVS (fol. 78a.3–78b.2) says that "without weapons" refers to weapons to gain victory over enemies or subdue them, such as a sword. Without weapons, even if you continuously wage battles with your enemies, you are not able to gain victory over them. Therefore it is yourself who comes under the sway of your enemies. The weapon to gain victory over the enemies of the afflictions as well as the perceiver and perceived is the wisdom of realization, which resembles a sword. Since it cuts through birth and death at their root, the text speaks of "immortality." "Threefold existence" refers to the three realms of saṃsāra. The outer three realms are the desire realm, the form realm, and the formless realm. The inner three realms

are the three poisons (desire, hatred, and ignorance) based on the triad of body, speech, and mind. These two sets of three realms causing death resemble enemies. The sword of the wisdom of immortality that gains victory over these three realms defeats them by cutting their root. "Enjoying himself" means that based on the common siddhi of the sword in Khaḍgapa's hand, he enjoys the supreme siddhi—the sword of wisdom cutting through the root of the three realms.

878. I follow GZ CDNP *ma rtogs* against DVS *ma gtogs* ("except").

879. Compare this with stanzas 1 in text 179 and I.9 in text 183. DVS (fols. 78b.2–79a.5) says that (1) the sambhogakāya is taught to be like a king and that (2) not having doubts about the dynamic energy of the dharmakāya resembles an elephant. (1) A person of middling faculties attains the king-like qualities of the sambhogakāya. First, through the two paths of accumulation, they are linked to the kāya just as it is through immersion in samādhi. Through the power of that, the wisdom of the ten bhūmis is seen. This wisdom has two names, as it is also called "pure mundane wisdom." Through meditating on shapes and colors based on syllables, "the wisdom of nonbeing" constitutes the path of seeing. Having familiarized with that, ultimately, bodhisattvas on the tenth bhūmi attain the sambhogakāya that is adorned with the major and minor marks. Since this is similar to the example of a cakravartin king over a chiliocosm, "those" refers to wisdom. Not realizing (text: *ma gtogs* emended to *ma rtogs*) the nonconceptual wisdom of the buddhabhūmi on the tenth bhūmi but pretending so, one may say that there is no need to cultivate the dharmakāya that is beyond mind and thus become indifferent about it. Therefore, lacking the samādhi of the king-like sambhogakāya, the dharmakāya is not attained. This is similar to losing a kingdom. (2) "The realized" refers to realizing the wisdom of the buddhabhūmi. This wisdom has a number of names: it is called "nonconceptual wisdom" and "the luminosity of the wisdom of terminating the continuum." This means that since all afflictions and thoughts have become exhausted and ceased, the causes of all minds and mental factors have been terminated. Thus, when this wisdom is free of all speech and expression and is beyond the reach of mind and thinking, on the buddhabhūmi, there is no doubt or qualm. If with such a realization you still take causes as the path and wish to attain a fruition later, this constitutes the conduct of the unrealized, which resembles an elephant sunk into the mud. This means that if you don't pull yourself out by yourself, others will not pull you out.

880. I follow GZ CDNP *gcig* against DVS *bzhi* ("four").

881. GZ CDNP *gcod* DVS *spyod* ("course").

882. Compare this with stanzas 5 in text 179 and I.40 in text 183. DVS (fol. 79a.6–79b.8) says that the example of a chariot illustrates not obtaining siddhis if one does not possess insight. If a chariot does not have four wheels, it cannot drive; this is equally true even if it lacks just a single one. Likewise, "even when making efforts in generosity and such," that is, even when making efforts in the causes (however many accumulations

of merit or however many vows of body and speech and so on), only the common siddhis or the states of gods or humans will be attained but not the supreme siddhi. The example of a vulture with its wings complete means that if you have a true guru, you will be joined with the supreme fruition by relying on the profound method of empowerment. "Vultures with perfect dexterity" refers to vultures in the prime of their youth. "With their wings complete" means having all six portions of their wings. Without becoming tired, such a vulture courses and soars through the sky for its entire lifetime. Likewise, "fortunate" refers to the fortunate who have siddhis or are cared for by a special guru with the three feats (DVS here repeats the description of the three feats in its comments on Saraha's stanza above). Since "genuine yogīs" unite with the three kinds of pith instructions of such a guru, they are genuine. "Absorbing the pith instructions of the empowerments" means that they absorb the pith instructions on attaining the supreme siddhi by relying on empowerments. Since they absorb the manner in which the three empowerments such as the vase empowerment (the empowerments that bestow) are bestowed, the text says they are "blissful." Since their own mind is introduced as the dharmakāya (the actuality to be bestowed), the wisdom of uncontaminated actuality is referred to as "great."

883. Compare with stanzas 19 in text 179 and I.45 in text 183. DVS (fol. 80a.1–80b.5) says that the qualities of each single buddha in the three times are inexpressible. The dharmakāya cannot be known through examples or mind: it possesses the qualities of the unceasing stream of compassion, illustrated by the example of space. Though the dharmakāya has no marks, the sambhogakāya is adorned by the major and minor marks, illustrated by the example of a cakravartin king over a chiliocosm. The qualities of the unceasing self-appearances of the nirmāṇakāya are illustrated by the example of a gem. Thus, since the three kāyas promote the welfare of beings, their qualities of taking on all kinds of forms appear. Since the essence of all these does not move away from nonconceptual wisdom—the dharmadhātu—they have a single essence. As for the buddhas in the three times, your own mind as such also involves the three times. In the past, under the sway of delusion arising in the first moment in the beginning, delusion in the form of all kinds of thoughts constitutes the cause of wisdom. The present delusion of the second moment is also wisdom, and the future delusion of the third moment is wisdom as well. What is the essential point of all that? When the essence of all of this is realized without any artifice as nonconceptual wisdom, no matter how many thoughts of the three times there may be, since all three times are the same in the natural state of nonconceptual wisdom, this is the meaning of "a single essence." As for "its essence is your own mind," the essence of all buddhas in the three times or the essence of all delusion in the three times constitutes the great dharmakāya that is your own mind. All of this need not be searched for anywhere else, but does not go beyond the essence of your own mind. Ultimately, this means that it does not go beyond mind as such whose

essence is wisdom. "If you wish to realize it, uncontrived, let it be as it is." "As it is" refers to wisdom's own way of being. It is not found through searching for it, so just let it be, because effort is mind, and mind is seeming reality. How do you practice or familiarize with what is free of effort and how does essential reality thus become manifest? There is nothing to familiarize with in the mind or in effort. However, by familiarizing with effortless wisdom's own way of being—the dhyāna of uninterrupted experience without anything to be experienced—essential reality is revealed and thus becomes the sphere of buddhas.

884. Compare this with stanza 45 in text 179. DVS (fols. 80b.5–81a.2) says that water may enter your ear and be retained in the earwax and hairs of the ear, causing a headache and even wind diseases. Someone skilled in extracting it will pour more water into the ear and thus the water itself will remove itself. Likewise, reality is seen by familiarizing with all delusive phenomena that appear and are possible as being delusive. When all phenomena of saṃsāra and nirvāṇa are seen as being delusive, they are found to be without any pith, hollow and vain. Exactly this is called "seeing reality."

885. Compare this with stanzas 11 in text 179 and III.6 in text 183. DVS (fol. 81a.2–81b.1) says that "the connate" refers to the native luminous self-awareness that primordially dwells within us in an inherent manner. It is called "the connate" because it need not be searched elsewhere. "Having found its taste" refers to yogīs who realized the dharmakāya that is the native state. They exert their power over luminosity, because all phenomena of saṃsāra and nirvāṇa do not go beyond the essence of the native state. Since all thoughts of saṃsāra are realized as the status or the nature of the native state, this is great bliss.

886. GZ CDNP *legs byas* DVS *legs sbyangs*.

887. DVS (fols. 81b.1–82a.2) presents the background story of the example here as follows. In India, a rich estate owner who wanted to protect his many treasure houses ordered a very skilled painter of deities to adorn the doors of his treasure houses with a painting of a terrifying protector, a black yakṣa called Ekajaṭā. After eight months, when the painter returned to collect his fee and looked at his painting together with the wealthy man, both were terrified and fainted. Once the painter awoke from his swoon, he examined the painting due to the latent tendencies of having painted it himself. His recognition that this terrifying image was not real then served as the antidote for both his own and the other man's fear. Similarly, the deluded thoughts of saṃsāra are like an accomplished painter. The forms of the outer container that arises from the elements and its inner contents (the forms of the beings who arise due to dependent origination) resemble the terrifying image. At the time of being deluded, when ordinary beings, śrāvakas and pratyekabuddhas in the lower yānas, and those bodhisattvas who cling to any object as being a real entity see the forms of the container and its contents, they become afraid. When persons who realize the basic nature as unborn luminosity examine them, they see that

the terrifying phenomena that consist of the outer container and its inner contents are not established as such, because they do not cling to any entity whatsoever. "Is there a remedy for this or not?" There is none, because both what is to be relinquished and its remedies are not established when examined.

888. Compare this with stanzas 8 in text 179 and III.2 in text 183. DVS (fol. 82a.2–82b.1) says that the golden ground of the earth is reflected on the sides of Mount Meru (thus, a bird landing on its surface also looks golden). Likewise, those who are wise in both words and meaning and realize the unborn cast away any nature of entities. That is, by realizing them to be unborn, they cast off the entities that function as inner and outer perceiver and perceived. Therefore there is the great bliss of lacking the duality of perceiver and perceived.
889. GZ CDNP *snang* DVS *mthong* ("is seen by").
890. GZ *byis pa rnams kyis* (CDNP *kyi*) *rtog pa yin / dge dang sdig pa'i 'bras bu de la gnyis su 'byung* ("The dualistic clinging of childish beings is thinking: there, the results of virtue and wrongdoing arise as two") DVS *byis pa rnams kyis rtog pa yis / dge dang sdig pa'i 'bras bu de la gnyis mi 'byung*. Following the comments in DVS, my translation follows DVS, but I emend *rtog pa* to *rtogs pa*. Compare this with stanza 24 in text 179. DVS (fols. 82b.1–83a.3) says that for the fortunate who realize the unborn, all phenomena of dualistic clinging, such as the two of appearance and emptiness, the two of happiness and suffering, the two of calm abiding and superior insight, the two of being and not being, the two of hither and thither, and the two of cause and result, are instructions. Why? Since all dualistically appearing phenomena are not established in unborn actuality, everything that is perceived is of the same taste in that it is unborn. Therefore everything becomes an instruction. Since what is seen is realized to be unborn, this is the supreme master, because it is the means for realizing that any dualistic appearances are unborn. "Childish beings" refers to ordinary beings who are ignorant and foolish. Once the unborn fruition is realized, the results of virtue (the higher realms) and wrongdoing (the lower realms) do not arise there as two and cannot be attained anymore.
891. GZ CDNP *zhi* DVS *dag* ("pure").
892. GZ CDNP *mi mthun* DVS *bzhi mthun* (following the comments, this should be *gzhi mthun*: "common ground").
893. DVS (fol. 83a.3–83b.2) says that Bhadrapa's stanza teaches four points in terms of view, meditation, conduct, and fruition. "Realizing emptiness, delusion is pure" represents the view. Emptiness is realized as being like vast space. Just as space has four qualities, so the wisdom of realizing emptiness has the essence of space. "By cultivating love, conduct is perfected." Since emptiness is the ground for the arising of everything, by engaging in love and so on without blocking or accomplishing anything, there is neither bondage nor freedom. Therefore conduct is perfected. As for "familiarizing with the nonduality of diversity," though all substances arise from emptiness, they are nondual with emptiness itself. Therefore this is

called "familiarizing with true reality." "The single taste of the common ground is the fruition." Though emptiness is the ground for the arising of diversity, it is of the same taste in that its essence is empty. Therefore, since that ground too has in common that it is empty, all is of a single taste. This is called "the fruition of nothing to be attained in true reality." Since it is uncommon, it is said to be supreme.

894. I follow CDNP DVS *'char* against GZ *'chang* ("hold").

895. DVS (fol. 83b.2–8) says that here the creation process and the perfection process are unified. The conventional creation process is the meditation by transforming all the hosts of thoughts into the male and female deities within a single maṇḍala. "Mahāmudrā" is the ultimate view. One speaks of "mudrā" ("seal") because it seals appearance, emptiness, the creation process, the perfection process, or all phenomena of saṃsāra and nirvāṇa. "Mahā" ("great") means that there is nothing else that is higher than it. This mahāmudrā is also called "unity," because there are no dualistic appearances of saṃsāric and nirvāṇic phenomena in its basic nature. Which fruition arises in it? The fruition that has the character of the three kāyas and the five wisdoms abides as the fruition in which there is nothing to be attained. It abides as the kāya in which there is nothing to be grasped by anything at all.

896. GZ CDNP *brtan pa* DVS *btad pa* ("directed").

897. GZ CD DVS *yungs kar stong nyid* NP *yul las dkar stong* DVS in its comments *yungs kar stong gsum*. Based on the commentary, my translation follows the latter; also, the other versions are hard to make sense of.

898. DVS (fol. 84a.1–7) says that "the instructions of the true guru" refers to the initial instructions on the creation and perfection processes. How are these taught? "Familiarize with the bindu at the upper gate's tip." The upper gate has the nature of means, and the lower gate the nature of prajñā. Therefore, at the tip of the cakra of bliss at the upper gate, there is the bindu of bodhicitta the size of a mustard seed. Meditate that a trichiliocosm is in it. Which fruition arises through that? To direct the mind toward this white mustard seed with a trichiliocosm means to meditate on it without distraction. What is attained here? Having meditated with a focus, the focus of the white mustard seed with a trichiliocosm is eventually tossed away within emptiness, emptiness is realized as mahāmudrā, and the absence of any focus is realized as being like vast space. "Is there a fruition called 'mahāmudrā' that is separate from emptiness?" No; in its very own time, emptiness is mahāmudrā, and it is nothing but mahāmudrā that is emptiness.

899. GZ CDNP *ma snyoms* DVS *smyon par* ("crazy").

900. DVS (fol. 84a.7–84b.8) says that "beings" (Skt. *gati*) are so called because they keep going without staying for a single moment. "These" refers to the three realms. "Beginningless" means since the time of eons without beginning. "Deluded" means being deluded since exactly this time without beginning. How are beings deluded? All phenomena of saṃsāra and nirvāṇa have the nature of empty luminosity—the nature of the nondu-

al great bliss of unity. Since beings do not recognize this to be the case, they are ignorant and labeled with the name "ignorant." Thus they are deluded by clinging to real entities. "The nature of delusion is known to be craziness." The nature of delusion resembles the example of having ingested poisonous hyoscyamus, which deludes the senses so that they seem to perceive all kinds of forms. "The world is known to be crazy." That this craziness resembles the ingestion of poisonous hyoscyamus is linked to the story of this siddha ("the handsome madman"). "The ambrosial medicine of the guru's instructions" means that by familiarizing with the creation and perfection processes in union, any focal objects of self and others are tossed away in that state and the view of the mahāmudrā of unity—the uninterrupted and steady basic element—appears as a matter of course. As this entails loose conduct, it is known to be crazy. The lack of the focal objects of self and others (resembling ambrosial medicine) burns the disease of craziness (resembling the ingestion of poisonous hyoscyamus) in a single instant.

901. GZ CDNP *rnam dag* DVS *rnam rtog* ("thoughts") but comments *rnam dag*.

902. DVS (fols. 84b.8–85a.7) says that since Dhobīpa was a laundryman, he was always washing dirty clothes. Here, he uses the example of charcoal never becoming white, no matter how much you may clean it. Likewise, even if you launder external stains for a long time, the inner stains of the mind or the stains of body and speech cannot be purified and thus do not become white. As for "for the pure garment of naturally pure emptiness," inner mind as such has a primordially pure nature, which is as pure as vast space. No matter how many adventitious things may arise in space, it will not be obscured or covered by any of them. Just like this natural purity of space, naturally pure mind as such is not tainted by any stains of adventitious thoughts. Thus it is called "a pure garment." Who launders this pure garment? "The guru's instructions are the supreme natural launderer." How is it laundered? Merely through guru Badha's teaching, all wrongdoings of body and speech became pure in an instant. Therefore this is called "laundering."

903. I follow GZ DVS *rtogs pa* against CDNP *rtog pa* ("thoughts").

904. Compare this with stanzas 16 in text 179 and I.43 in text 183. DVS (fol. 85a.7–85b.4) says that when you do not recognize a precious wish-fulfilling jewel, you do not realize that it has qualities. Once you recognize it as such, its colors are brought forth. By polishing it, venerating it, and so on, the colors of all wants and needs arise. Likewise, with the arising of the colors of experience in mind as such, everything that is wanted and needed arises through the power of its activity. "Its activity's power" means being able to act upon the actuality of realization. "What is wanted and needed arises" refers to the arising of all the qualities of the greatness of buddhahood. As for "this is accomplished by those with equal taste," in realization being of equal taste as dharmatā, the qualities of the greatness of buddhahood are accomplished as wisdom.

905. Compare this with stanzas 6 in text 179 and I.41 in text 183. DVS (fols.

85b.4–86b.1) says that all the precious jewels in the wondrous deep and vast ocean are enjoyed by all the great nāga kings. Likewise, "all appearances and sounds primordially are the dharmakāya." "Appearances" refers to outer perceived objects, including the inner deluded mind that is their perceiver. "Sounds" are mere imputations. All present appearances and sounds are primordially the dharmakāya. Appearances are not established by any nature of their own. Since they are established by virtue of the dependent origination produced by the four causal elements, they are naturally empty. Imputations merely have the essence of the thinking mind. Since they split off from any of the twelve āyatanas, they are also naturally empty. How is it that they primordially are the dharmakāya due to not being separate from it? Since the dharmakāya cannot be touched by mind or examples, it is the true entity or actuality. The enjoyment of this resembles the enjoyment of the nāga kings. "Those with realization" refers to realizing all phenomena of saṃsāra and nirvāṇa as the āyatanas. "Yogīs with experience" refers to experiencing true actuality. Since the sambhogakāya ("body of enjoyment") arises like an ocean of qualities, it means enjoyment, which is amazing or marvelous.

906. I follow GZ CD and DVS's comments *rtog pa* against NP DVS *rtogs pa* ("realization").

907. Compare this with stanzas 21 in text 179 and I.47 in text 183. DVS (fols. 86b.1–87b.4) says that this stanza teaches four points through twelve examples. (1) To ascertain what the basic nature is like is taught by three examples. (a) At the time of this basic nature being ascertained by the three kinds of guru, trust will naturally arise in oneself. At the time of seeing the qualities of mind as such, one proceeds on the path to be traveled without impediment. The example for that is the supreme horse that is attained through miraculous powers. By seeing the path of the basic nature (the qualities of mind as such), which resembles such a horse unimpededly journeying from one place to another, the paths and bhūmis to be traveled are completed in a single instant, which is blissful. (b) The example for having attained stability in this is an elephant (note that in DVS the explanation of this and the next example, as well as the first sentence under [2], is mistakenly inserted in the middle of its comments on the preceding stanza by Kambala). A stable and well-tamed elephant in the prime of its youth cannot be moved by the power of others. Likewise, when the qualities of mind as such—the basic nature—are seen, this cannot be agitated by any afflictions or thoughts. Therefore, this is the meaning of "being blissful by virtue of having attained stability." (c) Thus, when the qualities of realizing mind as such are internalized, the example for this not being stirred by thoughts is the ocean. When the ocean is stirred by the wind, no matter how waves may arise, the ocean does not become agitated below a depth of seven full arm spans. Likewise, since the realization of the basic nature does not become agitated by afflictions or thoughts, it is great bliss. (2) By realizing the qualities of the basic nature, thoughts arise in a self-arising manner, which is taught by three examples. (a) When the

qualities of the basic nature—mind as such—are internalized, thoughts arise in the mindstream in a self-arising manner. If appearances dawn as the guru, this is like a monkey who behaves in all kinds of ways and does not cling. Therefore, since exactly that lack of clinging to conduct is the supreme kind of thought, this is the meaning of "this is thought." (b) When such is the case, though there is no certainty about what appears, mind does not approach it, which is similar to the perception of a child. (c) The arising of this play of thoughts dawns as all kinds of appearances, resembling ripples on water, and the consciousness that subsequently expresses feelings vanishes without a trace. Therefore, like ripples on water, the play of thoughts disappears without any trace. (3) As for inseparability, (a) when all rivers flow into the ocean, they become indistinct, that is, they all have the same salty taste. Likewise, in dharmatā, all thoughts as all kinds of appearances are inseparable and of a single taste. (b) Though there is only a single sun shining in the sky, there are eight different ways in which the sun appears for the eight kinds of animals living in Varānasī, Candradvīpa (an island in the Ganges delta), the seven cool lakes of the nāgas, and so on: it may appear as mere light, blood, rainbows, a wall of fire, a golden wheel, the shine of all kinds of gems, or even darkness. Nevertheless, in the sun's own essence, all of these different ways of appearing are inseparable. Likewise, though all kinds of welfares are promoted by the two form kāyas in the dharmakāya of realizing mind as such, in this dharmakāya they are not different and inseparable. (c) By virtue of the eight ḍākinīs, medicine may appear as the eight common siddhis for practitioners, such as the eye lotion to see everything underground. Though it may appear as different things by virtue of conditions, in medicine's own essence, these are inseparable. Likewise, though the essence of realizing mind may appear as all kinds of discursive thoughts, these are inseparable in this essence itself. (4) The fruition that is attained is the dharmakāya that is the essence. (a) This dharmakāya is invisible, similar to the hair-knot on the head of a tathāgata. (b) "But if it is not manifest, is it unclear?" No, it resembles the eye faculty, which is not manifest but illuminates all objects. The dharmakāya's sheer lucidity constitutes the wisdom of knowing suchness and variety. (c) Since this wisdom of realization cuts through all the blurs of the afflictions, it is like a wheel.

908. GZ CDNP *chos rnams* DVS *gzhi mthun* ("the common ground's").

909. DVS (fols. 87b.4–88a.6) says that master Bhadepa presents the four immeasurables in terms of familiarizing with them as view, meditation, conduct, and fruition. (1) True reality is not established as any characteristics or any connection between support and supported. Since it is not established as such, it is free of all thoughts of minds and mental factors that are produced in terms of a producer and something produced. This essence of true reality is called "dharmakāya." However, this is just a designation, while ultimately the dharmakāya itself does not exist either. Such is called "the primordial dharmakāya." It is similar to the example of the ocean possessing four characteristics: though all kinds of waves may

stir on it, the ocean itself is immovable below a depth of seven full arm spans; it is the source of all precious gems; it eventually discharges all filth; and all its water is of equal taste. The same goes for the dharmakāya. Thus, in terms of the view, "realizing the basic nature is compassion." This means that if the view is realized, immeasurable compassion arises, which means it is not an object of meditation but unceasing. (2) This is due to its being uninterrupted within nothing but uncontaminated wisdom: "the bliss that is uncontaminated is joy." Nondistraction within nothing but this uncontaminated wisdom that is the view is uninterrupted meditation. Exactly this is the meaning of "immeasurable joy." (3) What is called "conduct" consists of nothing but this uncontaminated wisdom that is the view being free of all extremes of clinging. This is the meaning of "immeasurable love." (4) "The common ground's single taste is perfect equanimity" is the meaning of the fruition. "Ground refers to the common ground that dwells in the mindstreams of all sentient beings in the three realms—the common ground in terms of being a buddha." It is of equal taste as dharmatā. Exactly this kind of fruition constitutes the meaning of "immeasurable equanimity."

910. According to DVS (fol. 88a.7–88b.2), "become exhausted" means that discursive awareness vanishes in the empty expanse of nonminding. Likewise, all phenomena of saṃsāra and nirvāṇa that can possibly appear become exhausted and cease in the expanse of emptiness.

911. I follow CDNP DVS *mchod* against GZ *chos* ("dharma").

912. DVS switches the order of "experience" and "blessings."

913. Compare this with stanzas 37 in text 179 and II.4 in text 183. DVS (fols. 88b.2–89a.3) asks "Why do venerating buddhas and so on yield no meaning?" Such things may give rise to some trifling common siddhis, which leads to hopes about having attained buddhahood. However, the supreme siddhi is not attained through that. This matches the story of master Kukkuripa himself. When we regard trifling common siddhis as being like buddhahood, due to being venerated and so on, we may think, "I am also like a buddha," which actually turns into obstacles for becoming a buddha; as in the case of Kukkuripa himself, when the gods created such obstacles for him. If there is wanting for the common and supreme siddhis or the qualities of a buddha's greatness and if there is any corresponding effort by taking these as mental objects, this is not buddhahood. "So what is buddhahood like?" "Experiencing blessings from the mouth of the guru is splendid." "Blessings" refers to ripening our own mindstream, and the only blessings come from the mouth of the guru. Just as the ḍākinī (who first manifested as his dog) removed the obstacles for Kukkuripa, the blessings that ripen our own mindstream come from the mouth of the guru. Since what is taught by the guru is thus experienced by ourselves, it is revealed. Therefore, this is "splendid." However, what experiences and realizes this within us is the mind, and the aware mind is a conglomerate of a multitude (this is an explanation of Skt. *sakala*, Tib. *cha ldan*; lit. "possessing parts"). Therefore this refers to the parts of the mind but not the parts of objects.

914. Compare this with stanzas 31 in text 179 and III.19 in text 183.
915. I follow GZ NP DVS *mtha'o* against CD *mthong ngo* ("is seen").
916. DVS (fol. 89a.3–89b.5) says that "the connate" refers to appearance and emptiness—that is, the uncontrived native connate. How is it the connate? For example, though clouds, mist, vapor, and so on may appear in vast unconditioned space, they arise from nothing but space itself, and when they dissolve, they dissolve back into it. Likewise, though all kinds of discursive thoughts may arise from the essence of mind as such, they arise from this very essence, and when they dissolve, they dissolve back into it. This is called "connate appearances." The very location where appearances and discursive awareness vanish or dissolve is called "the connate." The essence or inconceivability of emptiness is called "connate true reality." Since this is the meaning of abiding in its own way of being without contrivance, it means it cannot be pointed out or contrived by any examples or counterparts, such as enemies and friends. The example of an elephant's eye refers to an elephant trying to sleep in a cave while counting with one eye open how many cubits he himself and his lower lip and so on may measure. When a breeze then drives many particles of dust into his eye, it becomes irritated and painful. Likewise, in the inconceivable essence of mahāmudrā called "the connate," there are no discursive thoughts to be made a living experience. Therefore, Kukkuripa says, "If I relax, there is no clinging, and hence this is the supreme dhyāna." Through what is he introduced into this? "Through the light rays of the guru's speech." Kucipa's guru was Nāgārjuna, and the light rays of his speech are his instructions. "I do not find the extremes of existence and nonexistence" refers to Kucipa not finding them. Exactly that which is not found represents the extreme of mahāmudrā. If this very extreme is realized, this is the ultimate—that is, the unsurpassable true actuality.
917. GZ CDNP *gnyis las* DVS *gnyis 'dzin* ("dualistic clinging").
918. GZ CDNP *'od zer* DVS *byin rlabs* ("blessings").
919. DVS (fols. 89b.6–90b.1) says that dualistic clinging refers to the ignorance that anything arising from causes and conditions is duality or to all thoughts of dualistic appearances. This clinging appears due to being obscured by the condition of ignorance. For example, when some persons eat poisonous food without recognizing that the poison will kill them, such persons come to be in the grip of that poison. Likewise, by not recognizing the nondual essence by virtue of it being obscured by the condition of ignorance, the thoughts of dualistic clinging resemble poison, since they are the poison that binds everything. The one held in the grip of that poison is the person of awareness. How is awareness gripped? The nondual essence is naturally free of discursiveness, and it is by not recognizing this that the person of awareness is held in a firm grip. For how long is it held? It is held continuously, which here refers to a very long time—that is, a duration without beginning or end. As for "the blessings of the guru's speech," "the guru" refers to the one who shows or identifies the poison of dualistic clinging as nonduality. How is it identified? It is identified

through the blessings of the speech of the guru who points out the person of awareness that is to be pointed out. How is awareness pointed out? All dualistic clinging is delusion, and delusion resembles a disease caused by poison. Since the essence of awareness is the freedom of discursiveness, this freedom is not tainted by any dualistic clinging. Therefore, the blessings of the guru's speech enter the person of awareness to be pointed out. "The blessings of the guru's speech" refers to realizing the view of self-lucid nonduality. What is eliminated by these blessings is the poisonous disease of the delusion of all possible appearances. "Appearances" refers to the outer container and its objects, while "possible" refers to the contents, such as the skandhas, dhātus, and āyatanas. Though delusion primordially is nonduality, it appears as delusion by virtue of being linked (text: *bral* emended to *'brel*) with dualistic clinging through the power of ignorance. For example, a skilled physician eliminates a disease caused by poison with a compound medicine. Likewise, the blessings of the guru's pointing-out instructions eliminate the entire poison of delusion.

920. Note that the last two lines here are virtually identical with the last two lines of Kaṅkaṇa's stanza above. DVS (fols. 90b.2–91a.5) says that ignorance is that which obscures seeing true reality. Based on this ignorance, many millions of afflictions such as pride arise. In their entirety, they resemble a huge mountain that obscures the wish-fulfilling jewel of realization. Realization means that this mountain of pride and so on that obscures the wish-fulfilling jewel of mahāmudrā is destroyed within the natural state of emptiness. "Through the power to act, what's wanted and needed arises" refers to the power to engage the wish-fulfilling jewel of realization. Since this wish-fulfilling jewel is the ground for the arising of everything that is wanted and needed, the tenfold wisdom of great ecstasy or the ultimate reality of the bhūmi of nonreferential wisdom—the entirety of suchness and variety—is accomplished. How is it accomplished? "This is accomplished by those with equal taste." "Equal taste" refers to realizing that in the natural state of mahāmudrā, all feelings of happiness and suffering are inseparable and of a single taste. "Accomplished" refers to the accomplishment of nirvāṇa.

921. GZ CDNP *dran yid* DVS *dran 'dzin* ("clinging thinking").

922. GZ CDNP *gang snang* DVS *rang snang* ("self-appearance").

923. DVS (fol. 91a.5–91b.5) says that "mahāmudrā devoid of focal objects" refers to the state of empty dharmatā being naturally free of any object to be focused on. Focal objects consist of wrong ideas and what is correct. "Nonrealization" means delusion in the form of the objects of the consciousnesses of childish ordinary beings. Under the sway of perceiver and perceived, they entertain all kinds of forms of discursive awareness, such as subject and object, clinging to a self and what is mine, and an agent and what is acted upon. These are the focal objects that involve delusion. "Mahāmudrā devoid of focal objects" refers to that whose essence is inconceivable, which lacks a nature of its own, and which seals everything in saṃsāra and nirvāṇa. "The plethora of the deluded thinking mind is

cast off." "Delusion" consists of the forms of discursive awareness listed above. "Plethora" refers to thinking without any direction. "Cast off" means that mahāmudrā casts out any focal objects of discursive awareness. In mahāmudrā, there are no appearances of the delusion of discursive awareness. Through the unceasing appearances of wisdom's awareness, self-appearance is seen as mahāmudrā. How is it seen? Without needing to search elsewhere, wisdom's awareness sees what primordially exists within ourselves in an inherent manner.

924. GZ CDNP *brtags pa* DVS *rtog pa* ("thought").

925. I follow CDNP DVS *pa'i* against GZ *pas*.

926. Compare with stanzas 33 in text 179 and III.20 in text 183. DVS (fols. 91b.5–92a.2) says that the cause is bodhicitta—that is, the true reality whose essence is originally unborn and whose nature is great bliss. Therefore Babhaha says "bliss!" How is this unborn bliss blissful? It is blissful because it is free of all the pain of substantial entities. Since the perceiver, entities, minds, and mental factors create pain, they are like poisonous snakes. Since this bliss here is the bliss that is free of all these and lacks any nature of its own, it is insubstantial bliss. This insubstantiality lacks any characteristics of substantial entities, minds, mental factors, discursive thinking, their desires, any nature of its own, and any clinging. Therefore it is insubstantial bliss without clinging.

927. GZ CD *'dab ma 'dam skyes* NP *'dab ma 'dab skyes* DVS *padma 'dab skyes* ("in the growing lotus petals").

928. I follow DVS *snying ka mgrin pa* against GZ CDNP *snying po 'byin pa* ("emitting the quintessence").

929. DVS (fol. 92a.2–92b.3) says that by cultivating the four ecstasies based on focusing on the four cakras, cessational ecstasy is not tainted by the flaws of focal objects. The example for this is a lotus that is not tainted by the flaws of mud. On the crown of the head, there is the nāḍī cakra that resembles the ocean or mud. The lotus refers to the seed of bodhicitta that is not tainted by the flaws of that. The first movement of this seed is the seed of heat. Since "ecstasy" need not to be searched elsewhere but exists within us, it is called "connate ecstasy." "At the heart and throat" refers to the second and third cakras, respectively. Based on them, due to the movement of the seed of bodhicitta and the wisdom of heat, the stability of the special path of seeing is attained (text: *brten pa thos* emended to *brtan pa thob*), which serves as the support of the path of familiarization. This is called "supreme ecstasy." As for "attaining unsurpassable cessational ecstasy," the nature of the bodhicitta of the fourth cakra—the essence of the native state—that resembles a lotus flower is not tainted by the flaws of the focal objects in the four cakras. Thus it is like a lotus untainted by mud: though a lotus grows in the midst of all kinds of muddy filth, it is untainted by these flaws but is endowed with its own consummate qualities of color, scent, and so on. Likewise, though the contaminated bliss of the upper three cakras is experienced in the wisdom of cessational ecstasy, the latter is not tainted by any flaws of contamination. Rather, based on this very

ecstasy, the mahāmudrā of nondiscursive wisdom whose essence is uncontaminated is attained. Therefore, cessational ecstasy is unsurpassable.

930. Compare with stanza 75 below by Sarvabhakṣa, stanza 14 in text 179, and stanza III.10 in text 183. DVS (fols. 92b.3–93a.2) says that "until I had gained realization" refers to being a childish ordinary being who is not versed in words and their meanings. When one is an ordinary being without realization, as with the conventional sense that things have many different flavors, saṃsāra and nirvāṇa are thought of as having different natures. At the time of realization, saṃsāra and nirvāṇa are great bliss. How is that? Beyond having relinquished saṃsāra, there is nothing separate called "buddhahood." What is called "saṃsāra" has the nature of buddhahood. How so? Since saṃsāra arises from the afflictions as its root, these afflictions are in fact the aspects of the kāyas and wisdoms that are the qualities of the greatness of buddhahood.

931. GZ CDNP *mchog tu dga'* DVS *mchog tu 'gyur* ("will be supreme"). Compare this with stanzas 28 in text 179 and II.6 in text 183. DVS (fol. 93a.2–93b.3) says that "time" refers to the four sessions of meditation within a day. "Pivot" (lit. "tip of the nose") refers to the objects of meditation, such as the four cakras or the tip of the nose. What is the blessing of that? Similar to the tip of the nose, the essence of buddhahood as the sole principal of all outer perceived objects is single, and the inner perceiving consciousness is also exactly that. Thus the cognition of the nonduality of the inner and the outer is called "the nondual essence of buddhahood—mahāmudrā." Without that, "yogīs will not become buddhas by any inner or outer conduct." That is, they will not become buddhas by outer objects to be relinquished and inner remedies that eliminate them being purified as wisdom. So through what do they become buddhas? They become buddhas through "the nature of ecstatic bliss and buddhahood not being different." The appearances that consist of all kinds of examination and analysis are also bliss, and these two and empty wisdom are not different. Therefore this is called "buddhahood." What is the means to attain that? "If clinging is let go, naturally arising experience will be supreme." What is clinging? "When any clinging to the outer and the inner or any wrong clinging to the inseparability of the two realities is let go, this is called 'mahāmudrā'—mental nonengagement." The nature of the view is that there is nothing to view. The nature of meditation is that there is nothing to meditate. To be free of any state of mind of clinging to that is the experience that cannot be experienced. This is the means to attain buddhahood, or "the supreme experience."

932. GZ *brgyug pa* CDNP DVS *'dug pa* ("stay").

933. Compare this with stanzas 20 in text 179 and I.46 in text 183. DVS (fols. 93b.3–94a.4) says that first, at the time of being an ordinary being, by relying on your own mind, you should realize what exists within you but is not recognized. You should realize this by realizing what is not realized, understanding what is not understood, knowing what is not known, and freeing what is not free. Since all of this is done by relying on the

guru, the text says, "by virtue of gurus, you should first realize your own mind." "Then, you should make this not different from all aspects." Within the natural state of that realization, you should render anything else not different from it. By realizing all phenomena as equality or nonduality, "you should stay in charnel grounds." That is, you should sleep in charnel grounds while realizing all phenomena as emptiness or equality at the time when appearances rise as enemies, and then familiarizing with the nonduality of appearance and emptiness at the time when emptiness rises as enemy. This means "the equal taste of appearance and emptiness." Having realized all phenomena as nonduality or equality, engage in the yogic discipline of a lunatic without clinging to anything whatsoever, just like quicksilver placed on the palm of your hand. Don't let your mind precede anything whatsoever, just like a small child. Without deliberating on anything whatsoever, engage in the yogic discipline of a lunatic.

934. GZ CDNP *thob* DVS *rtogs* ("realize").

935. GZ *tshogs drug yul la* CDNP DVS *tshogs drug dag na* (either "in the six collections" or "if the six collections are pure").

936. Compare this with stanza 3 in text 179. DVS (fol. 94a.4–94b.7) says that all happiness of thinking you will be fine by searching certain objects and all suffering of lacking certain objects arise from your own mind and do not come from anywhere else. "With the guru's instructions, dig up mind's mountain," that is, turning away from the six mistaken places yonder (digging the earth and so on), dig with the six correct places yonder (the six pāramitās). "Though the intelligent may dig up a mountain, they will not attain the native great bliss" refers to Koṭalipa's story. As for "ordinary mind wakes up in the center of the heart," "ordinary mind" here refers to mistaken states of mind—that is, the consciousnesses of childish ordinary beings who do not realize mahāmudrā. This ordinary mind first awakens in the middle of the heart. This is understood as the heart of all entities—the basic nature that is the heart of all phenomena, mahāmudrā—that is called "the nature of essential reality" and "the middle free of all extremes." That ordinary mind wakes up in the center of the heart means that ordinary thoughts become exhausted and cease within the natural state of mahāmudrā that is the nature of essential reality. With such thoughts having become exhausted, all thoughts of the six collections of consciousness are naturally pure. Since all hosts of thoughts of the six collections arise within the perspective (text: *mor* emended to *ngor*) of mahāmudrā, this is the great bliss that abides as "the uninterrupted dhyāna." If there are any imaginations in this natural state, all discursive awareness of mind and mental factors is meaningless, serving as the cause of suffering. For those with realization, exactly this will dawn as the guru. "Taking this as the guru, is there then something to meditate?" No, if it is meditation, there is nothing to meditate. "But if there is nothing to meditate, do you then not meditate?" "Let be in the native state" means "let be in the natural state of that without any contrivance." Note that, contrary to what the commentary says, a more straightforward reading of the

second verse here seems to suggest that the term "ordinary mind" (Skt. **prākṛtajñāna*, Tib. *tha mal gyi shes pa*), which later became such a hallmark of Tibetan Kagyü mahāmudrā, is used as an equivalent of mahāmudrā, or mind's native state. However, the commentary here represents one of several examples of this term not being used in this way in Indian works, but rather in its literal sense of the discursive states of mind of ordinary beings. For this term clearly being used as a synonym of mind's true nature, or mahāmudrā, see texts 44, 49, 56, 58, 70, 182 (VIII.27 and IX.16), 183 (I.38), as well as Siddharājñī's *'Phags pa 'jig rten dbang phyug gsang ba'i sgrub thabs* (D2140, fol. 208b.7), and Niguma's *Mahāmudrā* (N3422, fol. 138a.6 and N3435, fol. 155a.3).

937. GZ CDNP *gzugs* DVS *lus* ("body").

938. DVS (fols. 94b.8–95a.6) says that since the avadhūtī—the nāḍī of emptiness—in your own body is the support of consciousness, its natural emptiness functions like a furnace. In it, the entirety of adventitious discursive thoughts resembles the coals that are fanned by the bellow-like rasanā and lalanā (having the natures of means and prajñā, respectively). Through that, the fire of wisdom (the support of emptiness) that realizes appearance and emptiness to be nondual is kindled in the avadhūtī (the furnace of mind). In that furnace of emptiness, the nature of the mind is luminosity-emptiness. It is the wisdom of realizing the emptiness of the furnace and the appearances of discursive awareness as the nonduality of means and prajñā that forges the thoughts of the three poisons into the dharmakāya. Having realized this, Kamparipa is free of saṃsāra.

939. GZ CDNP *byin brlabs ci phyir bcing mi bgyi* DVS *bdag byin rlabs phyir bcing bar bya* ("You should bind them for the sake of self-blessing").

940. GZ CDNP *dhū tī* DVS *dbu ma* ("madhyamā"). DVS (fol. 95a.6–95b.4) says that the outer three realms are the desire, form, and formless realms, while the inner three realms are body, speech, and mind. The entire plethora of the discursive thoughts that consists of these three realms is contained in the three main nāḍīs: the rasanā on the right (having the nature of means), the lalanā on the left (having the nature of prajñā), and the avadhūtī in the middle (the nāḍī of nonduality). The latter is called "avadhūtī" because the nāḍīs of means and prajñā merge into it. As for "you should bind them for the sake of self-blessing," "self-blessing" refers to realization based on the nāḍī of nonduality and "binding" means to bind the plethora of discursive awareness as the nonduality of appearance and emptiness. The true reality of their inseparability is called "the mahāmudrā that is the basic nature."

941. Rāhu is the demon in ancient Indian mythology who is held to occasionally swallow the sun or the moon, thus being the cause of solar and lunar eclipses.

942. DVS (fols. 95b.4–96a.1) says that "the conventional moon bindu" refers to meditating on all thoughts of saṃsāra and nirvāṇa that can possibly appear (or the entirety of the discursive awareness of minds and mental factors) within a visualized moon disc that arises from an AH at the crown

of your own head. The one who swallows this is the excellent Rāhu of expanse and awareness. How does it swallow it? The great expanse is the dharmadhātu, and "awareness" means that the dharmadhātu is primordially pure. This is called "the inseparability of expanse and wisdom." The conventional moon bindu—the plethora of discursive thoughts—is swallowed within this inseparability of expanse and wisdom so that it is nondual with it.

943. GZ CDNP *mar zhun* DVS *mar khu*.

944. DVS (fol. 96a.1–5) says that all phenomena of saṃsāra and nirvāṇa constitute the vessel of dharmatā, while the uncontrived natural state of dharmatā is like an ocean. Bodhicitta, which is like clarified butter because it lacks the solid impurities of the afflictions, is poured into the vessel of dharmatā. By igniting the wick-like thoughts of the six collections of consciousness through the fire of nondual wisdom, the fuel of the darkness of deluded thoughts is burned up and dissolves into the natural state of insubstantial wisdom.

945. DVS (fol. 96a.5–96b.2) says that the dharmadhātu is not to be made pure or lucid by anything else. Like space, it is primordially and naturally pure in itself. Since there is nothing that does not fit into it, it is the source or vessel of everything. What is placed or poured into it is the substance of the dharmakāya of awareness. The fruition of this is the realization that the uncontrived expanse and the dharmakāya of awareness are nondual.

946. I follow GZ *goms pa* against CDNP *gos pa* ("tainted by"); DVS *nyams myong goms pa* ("familiarity with experience").

947. DVS (fol. 96b.2–6) says that "awareness" refers to your own mind and "native" means that this very mind is uncontrived. "Prajñā" refers to the nonreferential prajñā that realizes this native awareness. "Means" refers to "familiarity with experience." What is realized by the prajñā and the means of familiarizing with the native state? It is realized that what is called "native great bliss" exists as the great connately present fruition within the great basic nature that is the primordial ground.

948. DVS (fols. 96b.6–97a.4) says that not being cared for by a guru is like not recognizing a wish-fulfilling jewel and thus regarding it as being equal to trinkets. When lacking the realization of true actuality, you do not understand (text: *go* emended to *ma go*) that there is a difference between attaining the qualities of the buddhabhūmi and the states of gods and humans as results. Thus, by relying on the aspirations and applications of trifling paths, you strive for the trinkets that are the resultant states of gods and humans. As for "fully embraced by the guru and realization," the ultimate guru is your own mind as such. If the basic nature of mind as such—mahāmudrā—is fully identified, the awakened mind of a buddha is realized, which means that all qualities that resemble a wish-fulfilling jewel are perfectly complete. The difference between those with realization and those without realization is like the light of sun and moon compared with the light of a firefly. Their only commonality is that they emit light rays, but otherwise they are vastly different. Likewise, the only

commonality between those with realization and those without realization is that they engage in the path, but otherwise they are vastly different.

949. I follow DVS *bdag byin rlabs phyir bcing bar bya / bla ma sems dang snang ba gsum* against GZ CDNP *bla mas byin brlabs bcing bar byas / bdag dang sems dang snang ba gsum* ("bound by the guru's blessings, it is on the triad of self, mind, and appearances . . .").

950. Compare this with stanzas 35 in text 179 and I.50 in text 183. DVS (fol. 97a.4–97b.4) says that "should be bound for the sake of self-blessing" refers to blessing the three main nāḍīs as supports for your own realization. In what way are they bound for that sake? The rasanā and lalanā are bound to the avadhūtī so that they are nondual. That is, the white A—the letter of nonconceptuality—needs to be bound in the avadhūtī—the essence of mind as such—as the mahāmudrā that has the nature of bliss. Through what method? Through "the triad of guru, mind, and appearances." "Guru" refers to the guru who points out the dharmakāya in your own mindstream. "Mind" refers to naturally realizing the native state of your own mind as such. "Appearances" means that the sense faculties follow the six collections of consciousness, the support of outer objects, and thus appear as all kinds of things through the power of realization. That is, through the guru's instructions, diverse appearances all appear as mahāmudrā. Thus "mind" refers to the nature of the native state and "appearances" to the mahāmudrā of self-appearances. "The wise" means that those who are experts in the native state of essential reality realize all kinds of appearances to be mahāmudrā. "Rely" refers to the pith instructions to be realized by relying on certain symbols and methods. "So as to give rise to realization" means needing to familiarize with this very path here.

951. DVS (fols. 97b.4–98a.4) says that the tip of a flame is an example for being subtle and lucid. As for becoming familiar with subtle and very subtle qualities, the subtle essence—mind as such as the basic nature—that is not established as any entity or characteristic is subtle because it is difficult to examine and not established as anything at all. As for being very subtle, what abides as the dharmakāya is this very mind as such that is not established as anything at all. This dharmakāya is subtle and uncontaminated, resembling a causal seed. Since it is not contingent on any other conditions, its fruition is without any hope or fear, and it is utterly profound, very subtle. "Mind" refers to the subtle and uncontaminated mind as such whose essence consists of the nature of the dharmakāya. Which fruition arises from being familiar with that? "Immobile" refers to the outer world that is the container and "mobile" to the sentient beings who are its contents. "The entirety of entities" refers to all entities that consist of the hosts of thoughts of the twelve āyatanas that are contingent on those mobile and immobile entities. As for "is dissolving into the dharmadhātu," what is designated as just "dharmadhātu" is not to think any subtle or very subtle thoughts at all. Since the dharmadhātu lacks any entities that are clung to as independent thoughts, the text speaks of "dissolving."

952. GZ DVS *sa sogs rim par* NP *sa sogs rims pas* CD *sa sogs rig pas* (". . . through awareness"). Though *rim par/rim pas* suggests "gradually" and *sa* could be understood as "earth" (as Dowman does), DVS's comments make it very clear that what is at stake here is the progressive stages of the bhūmis themselves dissolving in an instant.
953. DVS (fol. 98a.4–98b.2) says that "true guru" here refers to the gurus who plant the first instructions into the mindstream. What are their instructions like? Since the rasanā and lalanā have the natures of means and prajñā, respectively, by inserting the thoughts of these two into the avadhūtī so that they are nondual, body and mind become of the nature of nonduality. Meditate that this nonduality—the dharmadhātu—is like an ocean. Meditate that in this ocean-like dharmadhātu, the wisdom of awareness is like a fish leaping out of the water. By having familiarized with this for a long time, which qualities arise? As for "the progressions of bhūmis and such dissolving," the realization of expanse and awareness as being nondual represents the fourteenth bhūmi of buddhahood—the bhūmi of Vajradhara. Therefore, since there is no need to travel through the progressive stages of paths and bhūmis at that point, they dissolve instantly. What happens then? "Self-appearances become mahāmudrā." In the self-appearances of the nonduality of expanse and awareness, all discursive thoughts become nondual mahāmudrā. This is what "attaining the fruition" refers to.
954. DVS (fols. 98b.2–99a.1) says that outer phenomena consist of the twelve (!) outer āyatanas, and the plethora of objects of thoughts that ensue from them does not go beyond the essence of mind either. Thus outer objects are not real. The twelve (!) inner āyatanas are not established as anything other than the essence of mind as such either. Also, the twelve inner and outer āyatanas are said to be the root of mind in the piṭakas of the Tathāgata. Therefore, "all inner and outer phenomena are contained in the mind." To realize all inner and outer phenomena contained in the mind as the true actuality of lucid mind as such means to realize that naturally luminous mind is like unconditioned space. At the time of such a realization, no matter how the four kinds of behavior (walking, standing, lying, and sitting) may be present within the inner and outer āyatanas, they do not move away from the dharmakāya. When such a realization is revealed, this constitutes perfect buddhahood.
955. I follow CDNP *gru mchog* and DVS's comments against GZ *grub thob* ("siddha") DVS *grub mchog* ("supreme siddha").
956. GZ NP *brgal* CD *rgal* DVS *thar* ("was liberated").
957. DVS (fol. 99a.1–6) says that "some" refers to sentient beings without realization. "Since time without beginning" means that there is no distinct entity of time in saṃsāra so that one could establish for how long a certain being has been circling in it. Saṃsāra is like the waters of an ocean; since it is very difficult to become liberated from it, beings have been roaming it for a very long time. Here "guru" refers to gurus with a lineage whose instructions cut through the root of saṃsāra. Since such gurus set us free

from the ocean of saṃsāra or the waters of the friends and relatives we crave, they are called "a ship." Since it is difficult to be liberated from or cross saṃsāra, it is called "an ocean." Who crossed it? Lucikapa found the ship of the guru's instructions and crossed it today.

958. GZ CDNP *spyod pa thabs kyis gzhol ba bya* DVS *spyod pa bag chags kyis 'gro bar bya* ("should proceed in their conduct through latent tendencies").

959. Compare this with stanza 32 in text 179. DVS (fol. 99a.6–99b.7) says that when a ship that has the nature of an entity becomes destroyed on the ocean, its parts become scattered in all directions but the ocean itself retains its own clarity and is not moved by that. Likewise, "wave-like experiences" refer to the three experiences of emptiness, compassion, and lucidity. As for the experience of empty being, your own mind as such is empty of an essence, being present like unconditioned space free of any characteristics. By familiarizing with worldly activities as having the nature of being empty, impermanent, suffering, and without a self, the wave-like experience of all possible appearances being empty arises. By thus realizing all inner and outer phenomena to be nonreferential emptiness, it is realized that self and others are not established; thus the wave-like experience of nonreferential compassion arises. Once the realization of the luminosity of the nonduality of emptiness and compassion is realized, all ships of ignorance are destroyed; thus the experience and realization of wave-like delusion vanishing within native luminosity that is like a transparent and immovable ocean dawns. This is taught "through the instructions of the true guru." How is this teaching to be practiced? "Conduct" refers to experience. "Proceed through latent tendencies" means that the experiences of yogīs proceed according to the paths and bhūmis of bodhisattvas through their latent tendencies. What is the sign of that? "Thoughts of desire and hatred subside on their own." At the time of further higher qualities including lower ones, in the luminosity of native dharmatā, thoughts of desire and hatred are neither relinquished nor owned. Therefore a yogī's own mind is clear and transparent in its own place. The example for this is the body of someone with an infectious disease having become cleared by medicine.

960. GZ CDNP *thog ma med nas* DVS *tha dad med de* ("without any difference").

961. DVS (fols. 99b.7–100a.8) says that with regard to "the samādhi of wisdom awareness," we need to think about the understanding of awareness, unawareness, and wisdom. In Sanskrit, *vidyā* means "awareness," while *avidyā*—*vidyā* with a prefix *a*—means "unawareness." This *a* is the white letter AH that signifies the nature of mind as such that is primordially present in all sentient beings in an inherent manner. Once this nature is recognized, the term "wisdom" is applied to it. Through what is it recognized? Through recognizing that the three times of wisdom awareness do not go beyond true actuality. If AH is not understood as the dharma, it is posited by the mind of ordinary beings. As for recognition or wisdom awareness, since it is not distracted toward the three times, it is called "samādhi." Do unawareness and wisdom exist as something different

or not? At the time of realizing that nondifference, this is wisdom itself. When it is not realized, this is unawareness itself. Therefore they are said not (text omits "not") to be different. "But if this native state is both unawareness and wisdom, wouldn't it be both a buddha and a sentient being?" For example, even if you do not know that a white mustard seed is the cause of mustard oil, it is still pervaded by oil. Likewise, for those without realization (text: *gtogs* emended to *rtogs*), the native state appears as if it were a sentient being or unawareness, but at the time of it being realized or being certain about it just as it is, it is buddhahood. If those who are unaware of this true actuality as it is realize wisdom awareness or realize the native state in an instant, they are certainly buddhas. Likewise, when it is not realized, discursive thinking is not the actuality that is the dharmakāya or the wisdom of true reality.

962. GZ CDNP *brjod nas* DVS *spyad na* ("if experiencing").

963. GZ CDNP *dgu ba* DVS *bsdu ba*.

964. Compare this with stanzas 29 in text 179 and II.5 in text 183. DVS (fol. 100a.8–100b.7) says that "not looking anywhere" means not looking at any mentally imputed outer aspects nor any inner appearances such as the four cakras. So where to look? "Look at the center!" What is the center? "Look at the avadhūtī!" What happens when looking at it? In the four cakras of the avadhūtī, there are the four kinds of bliss: the four wisdoms of ecstasy, supreme ecstasy, connate ecstasy, and cessational ecstasy arise progressively. With cessational ecstasy at the end being free of contamination, it abides as nothing but wisdom. Therefore it is called "great bliss." Through what is this experienced? Through "the power of the secret of mantra." The secret mantra is the special support. "Secret" means that certain special elements of the path of means are secret. "Its power" means that if the power of the uncontaminated wisdom of the bliss of cessational ecstasy is experienced, it is able to be concentrated as the locus of awakening. How do you know this? "Yogīs should be gathering the signs." To gather the signs of resting in the four ecstasies and mastering uncontaminated wisdom within the body refers to turning it into bodhicitta or a buddha realm.

965. Compare this with stanzas 17 in text 179 and III.12 in text 183. DVS (fols. 100b.7–101a.6) says that "means and prajñā" means that the basic nature free of flaws is taught to be like a campaka flower (*Magnolia champaca*) adorned by all the qualities of its scent and colors. "Means" refers to determining the location of this flower. "Prajñā" refers to your own mind as such, which is like a bee. What is the function of what is determined here by means and prajñā? It has the benefit of attaining the fruit of great awakening, which is like honey. This is "avajra" (this stanza does not contain that word, but see the first line of stanza 17 in text 179). "A" refers to the essence of the unborn basic nature (as the first letter of Skt. *anutpanna*, "a" stands for "being unborn"). "Vajra" refers to it possessing the four characteristics of being indestructible and unassailable. "How do you know that this basic nature exists in us in an inherent manner?" "The guru's constant

river flow pervades all." The guru is the one who determines the campaka flower. By the guru determining it, your own bee-like mind realizes the basic nature that is like honey. This is a constant river flow because it is uninterruptedly present everywhere in an inherent manner. "But does it not exist in others?" It does; it pervades all.

966. GZ CDNP *bla med dur khrod byang chub gnas chen du* DVS *bla med bgrod dka'i byang chub gnas chen du* ("in the unsurpassable and difficult-to-reach great abode of awakening").

967. GZ *phyogs 'chal* CDNP *phyag mtshan* ("hand-held insignia") DVS *phyogs cha* ("bias").

968. DVS (fol. 101a.6–101b.7) says that "the unsurpassable and difficult-to-reach great abode of awakening" refers to the bhūmi or abode of the nirvāṇa that is unsurpassable liberation. As for "awakening," through consummate relinquishment, the two obscurations are purified (Tib. *byang*). Consummate wisdom fully realizes (Tib. *chub pa*) something like the great realm of Akaniṣṭha. This great realm is very difficult to reach. "If it is that difficult to reach, is there no path toward it?" Bhikṣanapa teaches that there is a path by virtue of the great path of means of secret mantra: "Having been shown the difficult-to-travel path of the great bliss of unity." Since all unified appearance and emptiness, saṃsāra and nirvāṇa, happiness and suffering, calm abiding and superior insight, and so on are inseparable, this is called "the greatness of unity mahāmudrā." It is based on the mindstream that this path is traveled to the difficult-to-reach abode. When does this path appear in the mindstream? It appears in "the supreme yogī, the mighty lord who is free of bias." Such a yogī is mighty because of mastering and enjoying this path. How is this realized? "Realizes true reality thanks to the kindness of the guru's instructions." The guru here is a ḍākinī and the instructions that come from her kind mouth consist of the instructions on unity mahāmudrā. Therefore true reality is realized due to her kindness.

969. I follow CDNP DVS *rtogs pa* against GZ *rtog pa* ("thoughts").

970. Compare this with stanzas 78 below by Putalipa, as well as stanzas 25 in text 179 and III.15 in text 183. DVS (fols. 101b.8–102a.6) says that "original" means that when the basic nature of entities is not realized, it appears to be present as all kinds of branches of saṃsāra. When it is realized, without needing any agent who has purified it or is purifying it, it is primordially pure. This is buddhahood, because the afflictions are primordially cleared away (Tib. *sangs*) and wisdom has unfolded (Tib. *rgyas*) naturally on its own. "By the power of realization, this is dharmatā." Through which means is this realized? Through the means of "the connate being taken as empowerment," that is, through taking the empowerment that makes you realize the connate by virtue of it being introduced for the first time by the guru with a lineage. When doubts about your own unborn mind are thereby cut through, the bhūmi of Vajradhara is attained by sealing unborn saṃsāra and nirvāṇa both.

971. DVS (fol. 102a.6–102b.5) says that the first two lines present two exam-

ples for the way in which the wheel of saṃsāra cycles. Just as the yogī Khumbaripa performs his work as a potter by turning his potter wheel, "the wheel of karma concordant with its cause" keeps spinning. "Cause" refers to ignorance, and what is concordant with it are the remaining links of dependent origination up through aging and death. "Karma" refers to the karma that is accumulated by those links. Saṃsāra is referred to as a wheel because of the six kinds of mindstreams (text: *rgyu* emended to *rgyud*) cycling through the three realms. Through the darkness of the karma concordant with that, the mind of saṃsāric existence arises and cycles. Just as the body of an actor performs all kinds of songs and dances, the saṃsāric mind acts out all kinds of delusions involving the contaminations of appropriating all kinds of existences. Through what is this delusion purified? Through wisdom, the five afflictions such as ignorance (their concordant cause) awake as the wisdom of awareness. This wisdom is similar to a fire in that it burns the fuel of all branches of saṃsāric existence, such as ignorance.

972. GZ CDNP *sngags pa* DVS *sangs rgyas* ("buddhas").
973. GZ CDNP *rang gi rtogs la zhen med de* DVS *rang gis rtogs las gzhan med de* ("is that there is nothing other than their own realization").
974. GZ NP *gnyug ma sems kyi rtogs pas gang* CD *gnyug ma sems kyi rtog pas gang* DVS *gnyug ma sems kyis rtogs pa gang* ("the native state that is realized by the mind").
975. DVS (fols. 102b.5–103a.3) says that "buddhas" are those who see everything in the three times. "Oath" means to completely abide in the nature of the secrets of the bodies, speech, and minds of all buddhas. "Supreme" means that unborn true reality is the supreme one among all oaths. Where is such an oath to be sought? "There is nothing other than their own realization." There is nothing other than your own primordial connate's own face being realized by itself, while there is nothing to be found anywhere else. "The native state" refers to its continuum or own way of being that is uncontrived and loose. This native state being embraced or realized by the mind—awareness—is the essence of buddhahood. Since all others do not see it, it is only "seen by all the buddhas."
976. I follow GZ DVS *ma rtogs* against CDNP *mi rtog* ("no thinking").
977. I follow DVS *de nyid* against GZ CDNP *de phyir* ("therefore").
978. According to DVS (fol. 103a.3–7), "at the time when I was without realization" means that at the time of beginningless saṃsāra, who is it that feels following after everything, such as the nature of delusion and the nature of realization? "True reality" refers to the looseness of the nature of the native state. When Maṇibhadra had been taught by guru Kukkuripa and then her true nature realized itself, "whatever may appear is the true reality of this nature"—that is, any extent of realization as well as the nature of any delusion are the true reality of nothing but the native state.
979. Compare this with stanza 27 in text 179. DVS (fol. 103a.7–103b.4) says that all these mountains of thoughts—the phenomena of saṃsāra that consist of the outer world as the container and sentient beings as the inner

contents—are contained in the mind. What is mind's own nature? It is the unconditioned essence of self-awareness. This is said to be the unconditioned luminosity-emptiness in which awareness and bliss are inseparable. Thus, if there is some conduct based on that view, all forms of conduct are of equal taste as one. "If there is no clinging, this is equal taste." As for "clinging," all inner and outer phenomena are mind, and mind is the mind of seeming reality. Therefore, it is this mind that clings. Without any clinging, "when abiding free of effort, this is meditation supreme."

980. I follow DVS *mi ro* against GZ CDNP *ri mo* ("picture"). Compare this with stanzas 40 in text 179 and III.21 in text 183. DVS (fols. 103b.4–104b.1) says that there are four armors, and one armor opens all four: the armor of connecting with rebirth through latent tendencies, the armor of separating the pure essence of the elements from the dross, the armor of the equal taste of the elements, and the armor of single existence. These four great armors liberate from the four great floods of birth, aging, sickness, and death. When the completely perfect Buddha was born, he made seven steps in each of the four directions and spoke this stanza in the east:

On the other side of this world,
the suffering of birth does not occur
All suffering of birth is limited to here
This is the instruction on connecting with rebirth through latent tendencies

In the south, he said:

On the other side of this world,
the suffering of aging does not occur
All suffering of aging is limited to here
This is the instruction on separating the pure essence of the elements from the dross

In the west, he said:

On the other side of this world,
the suffering of sickness does not occur
All suffering of sickness is limited to here
This is the instruction on the equal taste of the elements

In the north, he said:

On the other side of this world,
the suffering of death does not occur
All suffering of death is limited to here
This is the instruction on single existence

There are six instructions here: luminosity (the view), illusory body (the body), dreams and the intermediate state (the connection), the transference of samādhi, and consciousness entering a corpse. The instructions on those are found in the *Ratnamālā* (there are many texts of this name in Tg, but this could refer to the anonymous text P5093 that directly follows this commentary in NP). Having donned these four great armors, what is "gem-like perseverance"? "Gem" refers to the example of a wish-fulfilling jewel that provides everything one may want and need. The basis for all this to happen is the perseverance that is like the ocean: the ocean does not become agitated below a depth of seven full arm spans, all rivers become of the same salty taste, and it is the locus of all kinds of gems. Where does such perseverance exist? It exists in mind as such. Therefore Kanakhalā says, "I steered the ship of my own mind." That is, she seized her own mind and became liberated from the floods of birth, aging, sickness, and death. "Sailing to the inner sanctum of this human corpse" means that the supports of the sense faculties still exist in a human corpse but there is no mind and all thoughts have become exhausted. If its inner sanctum of bliss, nonthought, and lucidity is entered, by becoming liberated from the sufferings of birth, aging, sickness, and death for sure, the body free of discursiveness is entered.

981. DVS (fol. 104b.2–6) says that the example of the sky is like a wish-fulfilling tree that grows the fruits of all kinds of trees. That is, from the clouds, the lightning, and the thunder in the sky, rain falls down and makes fruits grow. Likewise, "in the center of the sky of the pure dharmadhātu," that is, in the nature of the primordially pure uncontrived dharmadhātu that resembles the expanse of the sky, "the thunder of birthlessness—dharmatā—resounds" and thus the great rain of uncontaminated wisdom falls down. What fruits are ripened through that? "All phenomena of delusion that can possibly appear." Here, "appear" refers to the appearances of delusion and "possibly" to all phenomena of saṃsāra.

982. DVS (fols. 104b.6–105a.4) says that Kantalipa's guru was the great ḍākinī Veṭālī. Her instruction is to determine all three realms to be emptiness, which functions as "the needle." "The thread of compassion" means that the wisdom of the nonduality of emptiness and compassion, called "nonreferential compassion," functions like a thread. "I stitch the rags of all three realms together." "The three realms" refer to the outer desire, form, and formless realms or the inner body, speech, and mind. All three or five poisons are stitched together as the rag garment that exemplifies empty dharmatā. Therefore Kantalipa says, "This ragman yogī is very amazing!" He is amazing because he has made his firm decision by trusting himself.

983. DVS (fol. 105a.4–105b.2) says that the text speaks of "unity awareness," because if something is a unity with something, all phenomena of dualistic appearances—appearance and emptiness, calm abiding and superior insight, saṃsāra and nirvāṇa, happiness and suffering, and being and nonbeing—do not exist separately from the essence of self-awareness. Since

this awareness provides all that is wanted and needed and fulfills all intentions, it is exemplified by a "precious treasury." How is this awareness a unity? It "is not [found] by seeking in nonduality's natural state." That is, it is not different from nondual bliss. That this natural state of nonduality itself is not determined by seeking it is "like the mindset of letting go of your duties." What is this mindset like? It is said that King Ghadrapa once was struck by a disease caused by earth lords and thus had to let go of performing any of his duties for the kingdom. Then nāga kings and so on poured nectar water as siddhi onto the king. Thereafter, even when the king was sitting in the midst of thorns, he was happy. The same goes for nondual unity being free of searching and effort.

984. I follow DVS *ji ltar rnam rtog rjes 'brang 'khrul* against GZ CDNP *ji ltar rnal 'byor rjes 'brang 'khrul* ("The ways in which yogīs chase after anything is delusion").

985. I follow DVS *ma 'breng* against GZ CDNP *ma 'brel* ("don't connect").

986. GZ CDNP *gzhan la btsal ba de yang min* DVS *gzhan las btsal bas de rnyed min* ("It is not found by searching elsewhere"). DVS (fol. 105b.2–8) says that when Udhilipa had no realization, he was deluded by following all kinds of thoughts about geese and clouds, as well as all kinds of thoughts about outer perceived objects and the inner perceiving consciousness. When self-illuminating realization dawned in him, he realized that all phenomena are as unobservable as the sky. By not following his thoughts, he did not discard their latent tendencies but caused them to become exhausted within dharmatā. Therefore he says "seize them!" "Not abiding anywhere" means that once the web of thoughts has been withdrawn into dharmatā, the bliss of dharmatā has no abode either. This very nonabiding without any abode "is not found by searching elsewhere." It is found neither by searching anywhere among subjects or objects nor by meditating.

987. I follow CDNP DVS comments *thod pa* against GZ *thogs pa* ("wearing") DVS *thos pa* ("hearing").

988. DVS (fols. 105b.8–106a.6) says that it was guru Kṛṣṇācarya who showed the basic nature of entities to master Kapālapa. At the time of realization, he attained the vajra-like samādhi of nonduality and thus realized all phenomena's own essence. At that point, he realized that this being free of effort and searching is like fainting on top of a mountain or one's eyes becoming deluded while watching a show. When he realized this, "the ornaments" (pieces of bone from his deceased children) and "the skull" (the head of his deceased wife) were all seen to have arisen from adventitious conditions. "But does true reality exist on the other side of having relinquished delusion?" No, "the delusion of clinging to 'me' is also true reality," that is, the actuality that is the essence of clinging to "me." "How do you know this essence?" "It does not happen by searching for the nature of everything." The nature of everything without exception is the uncontrived essence, but it is not found by searching, that is, if it is taken as an object.

989. I follow DVS *ji srid . . . bar du* against GZ CDNP *ji ltar . . . bar du.*

990. GZ CDNP *rang bzhin* DVS *rang sems* ("your own mind").

991. DVS (fols. 106a.6–107a.2) says that King Kirapāla was fettered by not realizing (text: *ma gtogs phas* emended to *ma rtogs pas*) self and others since beginningless time. In terms of the relationships between a self and forms, feelings, discriminations, formations, and consciousness, each have four permutations: their nature being the self, dwelling in or on the self, they themselves being what is mine (text: *bdag ni* emended to *bdag gi*), and possessing the self. When these twenty mountains of the views about a real personality or the clinging to a self are taken to be "us," this is called "ourselves." Since people over there are different from ourselves, they are called "others." We are fettered in saṃsāra, because thoughts of dualistic clinging arise within the nature of nonduality. How are we fettered? The thoughts about ourselves and others fetter themselves similar to a silkworm weaving its own cocoon. Upon realizing the delusion of dualistic clinging as nonduality or the twenty mountains of clinging to a self as the twenty kinds of lacking a self, both ourselves and others are not established. The twenty kinds of lacking a self consist of form not being the self, form not dwelling in or on the self, form not being what is mine, and form not possessing the self. The same four permutations apply to feelings, discriminations, formations, and consciousness. Form is not the self, because the self has the nature of being permanent (text: *brtags pa* emended to *rtag pa*) and single, while form has the nature of being impermanent. The analogous applies to the remaining permutations and skandhas. That others are not established by virtue of lacking a self is called "the awakened buddha mind free from dualistic clinging." "Hence, what is called 'buddhahood' is our own appellation." This is said in terms of what has just passed or a beginning. As explained above, since there is no type of clinging to a self at all in realization, "buddhahood" is simply imputed as our own appellation but is not something that exists among entities. Since this awakened buddha mind is a mere appellation, it is inexpressible. Therefore, "seize your own mind in uncontrived and nondiscursive true reality's own place." That is, seize your own mind in its natural state free of discursiveness.

992. DVS (fol. 107a.2–107b.5) says that the example of showering down a rain of sense pleasures for sentient beings by squeezing the nāga king Vāsuki illustrates what is taught by "within the inner great abode of suchness . . ." This is the inner knowable object that is seen by looking inside. "The great abode" is the abode of the ālaya. It is called "great" because all phenomena of saṃsāra and nirvāṇa arise from it and there is not a single one that does not fit into it. Thus there is nothing greater than it. What is going on in this great abode? "The nāga king of awareness is squeezed." How? The king of awareness is squeezed like a wish-fulfilling jewel. The qualities of that jewel are that first, it is difficult to hear about it or find it. Second, it is difficult to keep it. Third, it is difficult to venerate it. Fourth, by venerating it, everything that is wanted and needed arises from it. Likewise, first, the nāga king of awareness is difficult to introduce. Second, once it has been introduced, it is difficult to make it a living experience. Third, once

it has been made a living experience, it is difficult for wisdom to arise directly. Fourth, once wisdom has arisen directly, the inexpressible qualities of peaceful nirvāṇa arise. Whose welfare is promoted through these qualities? "The rain of the awareness of secret mantra is brought down upon male and female fortunate awareness holders." "Fortunate" refers to the awakening of the karmic propensities of having trained before: being fortunate to meet the Mahāyāna dharma, being fortunate to possess great devotion and faith, being fortunate to have diligence, and being fortunate to give rise to realization through prajñā. "Awareness holders" refers to the birth places of the ten bhūmis and to the awareness holders who are bodhisattvas. "The secret mantra" has the two qualities of knowledge and protection. "Knowledge" refers to a yogī's knowledge of the path, and "protection" to protecting all beings since beginningless time. "Awareness" refers to the full realization of perfect awareness.

993. Lines a and c correspond closely to lines ab of stanza 41 by Bhusuku.

994. GZ *tha dad med* CDNP DVS *bde ba che* ("are great bliss"). DVS (fols. 107b.5–108a.7) says that "without realization" means not realizing essential reality. What is wrong with that? At the time of not realizing that, by virtue of great abdominal heat, food was neither clean nor filthy, all kinds of flavors greatly differed for Sarvabhakṣa. "At the time of realization, the essence of flavors is without distinction." Accordingly, through the instructions of the guru, Sarvabhakṣa took all possible appearances as food and his mind as the fire at the end of an eon. By eating the three realms as food, his previous distinctions between all kinds of tasty and distasteful foods disappeared. Therefore all flavors became without any difference. "If not realized, saṃsāra and nirvāṇa appear differently," just like different flavors. When Sarvabhakṣa realized the actuality of the nonduality of appearance and emptiness, "saṃsāra and nirvāṇa were great bliss." How so? By virtue of understanding that saṃsāra is without pith, there are neither any adverse factors to be relinquished nor any wisdom that is the remedy of what is dark. Therefore, since nirvāṇa is nothing to be adopted either, saṃsāra and nirvāṇa are great bliss. Implicitly, this means that since saṃsāra itself is the dharmakāya, it is not relinquished. Since nirvāṇa is nothing to be accomplished either, Sarvabhakṣa did not bring it about.

995. Compare this with stanzas 23 in text 179 and I.48 text 183. DVS (fols. 108a.7–109b.4) says that the four examples here teach four points. (1) The example of a kapāla with siddhis is the example of attaining the first bhūmi. Once, a yogī called Kumarūpa dug up a piece of a skull and kept it. Later, he thereby attained supernatural knowledges similar to those of bodhisattvas on the first bhūmi, thus being very fortunate. As in this example, "if you dwell on the ground, all is of excellent fortune"—that is, the irreversible bhūmis are attained. During the paths of accumulation and preparation, bodhisattvas should abide on the bhūmi of the triad of generosity, discipline, and patience. At the time of the path of seeing, they abide on the bhūmi of seeing actual reality through the eye of prajñā. During the path of familiarization, they abide by not being distracted

from dhyāna and samādhi. Therefore, though an affliction and so on may arise in one moment, it is relinquished in the second moment through the wisdom that is its remedy. In the third moment, this abides as wisdom alone. Finally, they abide on the bhūmi of traveling to and maturing the ultimate abode. All those on these bhūmis are of excellent fortune, because they possess the fortune for both the path to be traveled and the fruition to be attained. (2) "If you go to the ocean's depths, you are free of poverty." At a place in the ocean where there are precious gems, the Indian ethnicity called Camri engages in meditation by training in a certain type of prāṇāyāma. Having accomplished it within five years, they can hold the vāyus without the breath moving for half a month and there arises heat like a circling firebrand in their bodies. Through this kind of power, they dive in the ocean like fish, picking up all kinds of gold, silver, pearls, and precious gems. Inviting all their relatives to their possessions, they eliminate poverty. Likewise, the ultimate fruition—the dharmakāya—gives rise to all precious qualities, just like the ocean. By stepping on them, they become free of the afflictions and gem-like dharmatā manifests. Thus there is freedom from the poverty of the afflictions. (3) "If you hold a sword in your hand, this is a great enjoyment." Once, King Gopāla of Śrāvastī encountered a huge army coming from the west and lost all his territory to it. In the south of his lands lived a householder called Samaśrī with seven sons and four grandsons, who all were swordsmen but so poor that they did not even possess swords. The king went there, gave them swords, and then defeated that hostile army together with them, thus regaining his territory. Finally, the king gave them many possessions and thus eliminated their poverty. As in this example, the ultimate fruition—the dharmakāya—cuts through all phenomena that are entities with characteristics. This is a great enjoyment, because the sword of wisdom enjoys dharmatā. (4) "If you amble around without direction, you meet friends." Once, in the east of India, there lived a householder who had a four-year-old son. Since he hated both his parents, the son wandered the directions going for alms. When he came to the temple of Khasarpaṇa, he stayed there, eating food that he stole from the offerings for the deity. Eventually, he made offerings to a statue of Avalokiteśvara there and developed great devotion for it. Through the blessings of that, he remembered his entire life, went back to the home of his parents and relatives in Campaka, and told them this story. All were amazed, and he was reinstated as their son. Hence the text says, "you meet friends." Similarly, since the ultimate fruition—mahāmudrā, the dharmakāya—is free of biased thinking, "it ambles around without direction." "To meet friends" means to meet the dharmakāya that is the friend of all.

996. GZ DVS comments *de bsal* CDNP DVS *bde gsal* ("lucid bliss").

997. Compare this with stanzas 18 in text 179 and I.44 in text 183. DVS (fols. 109b.4–110a.6) says that "bliss" refers to the wisdom of the uncontaminated dharmakāya. It is "great" because there is nothing higher than it. "It lies within us"—that is, without needing to be searched for elsewhere, the

wisdom of the great bliss of the dharmakāya exists in us in an inherent manner. However, "it is not realized and obscured by delusion." At the time of ordinary beings, this relinquishment and realization is obscured by the veiling delusion of thoughts. Through what kind of means should this delusion of thoughts be dispelled? "Those wishing to dispel this should gather the accumulations of merit and wisdom." Since the play of dharmatā is asserted to have the essence of lucidity and nonthought, what veils it should be dispelled through the two accumulations. By cultivating the causal accumulation of merit from the path of familiarization onward, at the time of the ultimate fruition, the fully perfect accumulation of wisdom will be attained. Without gathering the two accumulations, great bliss will not be attained. "When not gathering the two accumulations, even if you strive for a hundred lives . . ." The fruition exists inherently in the two accumulations, a fruition that is not such is not found anywhere at all, even if you strive for a hundred lives. The accumulations are gathered by relying on the gurus. "Without any gurus, great bliss will not be realized." Here, the gurus are those who teach the meaning of gathering the two accumulations. Not having such gurus, the fruition—the accumulation of wisdom, great bliss—is not realized.

998. I follow GZ *dbang rnams lhan cig skyes pa de'i / ro yis kun la khyab bya ste /* against CDNP *dbang rnams lhan cig skyes pa des / ro yis kun la khyab bya ste /* DVS *dbang blang lhan cig skyes pa des / ro yi kun la khyab byas te /*.

999. Compare with stanzas 62 above, as well as stanzas 25 in text 179 and III.15 in text 183. DVS (fol. 110a.6–110b.7) says that first, there is the instruction for the king on meditating without being divided by biased states of mind about deities being good or bad. Since all Buddhists and non-Buddhists have the natural state or nature of a sugata, you cannot say, "My deity is this; it is good" or "Your deity is that; it is bad." To take your own and others' deities to be good or bad, respectively, is established by your own thinking mind that is the wrong path. If you make efforts on the path of pith by relinquishing this wrong path, the fruition of pith is beyond any doubt. Through which means is this fruition attained? The means come "from the true guru"—the one who introduces the actuality of empty bliss. "Those" refer to the persons who entered the path of pith. As for "who took empowerments," based on the causal empowerments, they are freed and matured through the two paths of creation and perfection to be traveled. Thus the fruition is attained as the fruition called "the connate." When is it attained? "When being pervaded by its taste everywhere." "Taste" refers to the taste of great bliss. "Pervaded" means that all six classes of sentient beings are pervaded by it: not needing to be searched for elsewhere, it pervades us in a connate manner. What is the essence of the connate like? "To be sealed by the unborn is Vajradhara." When sealed by the unborn essence, the twelfth bhūmi—the one of Vajradhara—is attained. As mentioned before, these two stanzas have some close parallels in stanza 62 by Dhilipa.

1000. GZ DCNP *rang dgar gnas* DVS *rang gar min* ("not being ordinary").

1001. DVS (fols. 110b.8–111a.6) says that since the essential reality of bodhicitta—the form of the sugata—is uncontrived, it is "native." What happens through contemplating it one-pointedly without distraction? "It is realized in just the way it is contemplated." "Just the way" means that the essence of mind as such is realized just as it is. This is the realization that its own essence that lacks any desire for anything at all, no matter how it may appear through conditions, is without any partiality or bias. "Hence, true reality is not ordinary," because this realization cannot be said to be a certain "this" for certain reasons. What is definitely the case is that the native essence constitutes the awakened buddha mind. Through what is this recognized? Within the precious gem of the awakened buddha mind, inexpressible qualities arise. Therefore "everything desirable comes forth with ease."

1002. GZ CDNP *zhen 'dod* DVS *zhe 'dod*.

1003. Compare stanzas 15 in text 179 and III.11 in text 183. DVS (fol. 111a.6–111b.3) says that letting go of worldly activity with dualistic clinging is twofold. First, you need to evaluate the eight worldly dharmas and eventually also let go of any dharma activities. Kokilipa says that "letting go of doing constitutes the pith instruction," because the unborn essence of the dharmakāya's qualities that is free of any doing and effort will not be realized through any examination or analysis. All activities consist of the mind, and mind consists of clinging, while the dharmakāya is without clinging and not known through examples or the mind. Therefore, "lacking any wanting is realization." By thus being free of wanting, there is no entity established anywhere: "insubstantial bliss is what constitutes the meditation."

1004. According to DVS (fols. 111b.3–112a.5), the first four lines teach that Anaṅgapa's own body is bound by haughty clinging. "Saṃsāra" is that which arises and circles since beginningless time. Assuming the bodies of threefold saṃsāric existence by wandering around in it, is there any happiness in the desired enjoyments of gods and humans or the undesired sufferings of the three lower realms? No, they are without any pith. A partial example for that is a firefly: though its fire appears brightly to the eyes, you cannot find any pith among entities where this fire comes from. Similarly, the nature of saṃsāra is that it has no pith at all, just like a rainbow. "This body that is like a rainbow" refers to Anaṅgapa's body. "Ignorance" refers to not knowing that saṃsāra lacks any pith. By being in the grip of pride (thinking, "There is no one like me or above me") due to clinging or vanity, saṃsāra is fixated on as being real. The last two lines teach that the dharmakāya is identified by the poison of clinging clearing up. "Clinging" refers to fixating on inner and outer phenomena: it is what binds, similar to the poison of hyoscyamus. Once this poison has cleared up, you recover from the poison of delusion under the sway of conditions. Similar to the deluded things that appear for someone with blurred vision, when the clinging to saṃsāra is put to an end, "saṃsāra itself is the dharmakāya." This means the following:

On the other side of having relinquished saṃsāra,
there are no qualities called "buddhahood."

These two lines are found almost identically in the *Sarvadharmamahāśanti-bodhicittakulayarāja* (H792, fol. 66b.6–7), Avadhūtipa's *Dohakoṣa-hṛdayārthagītāṭīkā* (D2268, fol. 103a.2), and the *Sarvayogatattvālokānāmasa kalasiddhavajragīti* (text 182; D2453, fol. 101b.1–2; attributed to an Ahara), with the second line reading "There is nothing called 'nirvāṇa.'"

1005. Compare stanzas 30 in text 179 and III.18 in text 183. According to DVS (fol. 112a.5–112b.2), for ordinary beings who travel the path, the fruition to be attained based on the progressive empowerments by the guru is introduced as connate awareness by way of symbols. Then, the dharmakāya needs to be realized by nonreferential prajñā. Therefore, "first, the intelligent give rise to realization." Since this needs to not be separated from experience, "second, they familiarize undistractedly with the basic nature." Once experiences have become manifest by meditating, "they should gradually engage in the conduct." The way to do so is that, no matter which signs and wisdoms may arrive, they should examine and engage them through their own experience. This is taught by something like noble Nāgārjuna's intention.

1006. Rākṣasīs are female rākṣasas, a class of fierce demons who eat human flesh.

1007. Compare this with stanzas 13 in text 179 and II.3 in text 183. According to DVS (fols. 112b.2–113a.1), the example of there being no benefit without experience even if there is realization is "a child carried in the hands of a rākṣasī." The city of the rākṣasas is in the northwest of India, but once they smell flesh or blood, they come running for thousands of miles to devour humans. If they don't find human flesh or blood, they eat their own children. The point here is that though the rākṣasas are certain that these are indeed their own children, they are not moved by parental love but eat their flesh and blood due to being tormented by their craving for these. Likewise, even if unborn reality is realized, but its actuality is not experienced, the spheres of the eight consciousnesses are no different from the afflictions of ordinary beings. Therefore, this is similar to being carried away by rākṣasas. The example of there being no benefit if there is experience but no recognition of the basic nature is that of an elephant stuck in the mud. Since an elephant's body is very heavy, once he has sunk into the mud, only he can extract himself; others cannot move him. Likewise, the actuality of the unborn basic nature—the wisdom of the buddhabhūmi—is beyond the mind. Without it recognizing and experiencing its own face, you may keep many vows of body and speech, experience many progressive paths that involve a plethora of thoughts (text: *rtogs tshogs* emended to *rtog tshogs*), and attain the happiness of gods and humans, but you will not master the buddhabhūmi. Thus, this "resembles an elephant who is stuck in the mud."

1008. Compare this with stanzas 38 in text 179 and II.7 in text 183. According to DVS (fols. 113a.1–113b.4), there are three gurus: the lineage guru who links symbols and meaning, the guru of the Buddha's words who instills trust, and the actual guru of cutting through doubts. When you have gained trust by virtue of true actuality having been introduced by the first two gurus and then mind cuts through all doubts, "you see the true guru." That is, by seeing the mind or the actual guru, you see the true guru. Why is true reality seen by seeing the true guru who is the mind? Since what is called "true reality" does not exist separately as something that is not the essence of the mind, it is nothing but "seeing mind's essence" that is called "seeing true reality." What are its characteristics like? It has four characteristics, similar to unconditioned space. Though you can express space's mere specific characteristics, it cannot be described as being "exactly that." Space's own essence is empty. Since space itself is not established as any center or fringe, it is free of any directions and parts. Since everything arises within space, it provides room for all kinds of appearances. Likewise, the actual guru has these four characteristics. "If you meditate in the sky's expanse, this is solitude supreme." By virtue of being isolated from afflictions and thoughts, this is the supreme solitude. "If you realize phenomena, there is nothing unfavorable." If all phenomena of saṃsāra and nirvāṇa are realized as mind as such that has the characteristics of space, there is nothing unfavorable, because you cannot say that empty space "is this because of this" or "is not this because of that." Since this nature of empty space is the nectar of true reality, it has the nature of space. Since it is the nectar of the dharmakāya, "drinking this milk will be your livelihood" because it transforms the māra of the afflictions.

1009. PDMT, 27:326–40.
1010. I follow GZ NP *'dug pa* against CD *'dus pa*.
1011. GZ *zla rgyal* CDNP *gza' rgyal* ("king of planets").
1012. I follow GZ CD *gdan* against NP *gnang*.
1013. GZ *mkhan por* CDNP *mkhan po* ("Gold-making alchemist, look!").
1014. I follow NP *snying chung* against GZ CD *snying phyung*.
1015. I follow GZ CD *chu shing* against NP *shing gi* ("of a tree").
1016. GZ CD *rlabs ni* NP *rlangs na* ("if . . . and vapor").
1017. GZ *'khor ba yul na med* CD *'khor ba'i yul na med* NP *'khor ba'i yul sa med* ("there is no place of the object that is saṃsāra").
1018. I follow NP *gsal ba* against GZ CD *bsal ba* ("dispelled").
1019. This is an alias of Carbaripa (mahāsiddha no. 64).
1020. This is an alias of Medhini (mahāsiddha no. 50).
1021. I follow GZ NP *lhug par* against CD *lhag par*.
1022. I follow GZ NP *che* against CD *cha*.
1023. GZ NP *'gyur med* CD *'gyu med* ("immovable").
1024. Durjayacandra was a famous commentator on the *Hevajratantra*, the *Catuṣpīṭhatantra*, and the *Mahāmāyātantra* (Tg contains twelve works attributed to him).
1025. I follow CDNP *rtog pa* against GZ *rtogs pa* ("realization").

1026. I follow GZ NP *'char* against CD *'chang* ("is held").
1027. I follow NP *a ma* against GZ *'o ma* ("milk") CD *'a ma*.
1028. DPR: the first line refers to agitation, the second to dullness, and the last two to the meeting of mother luminosity and child luminosity.
1029. GZ CDNP *snying rjes* emended to *snying rje'i*.
1030. GZ *brjod med* CDNP *rjes med* ("tracelessness").
1031. This stanza is also contained in a song by the ḍākinī Sukhasiddhi, who, together with Niguma, was one of the two principal forebears of the Shangpa Kagyü school (see Zangpo 2003, 49).
1032. I follow GZ *la* against CDNP *lo*.
1033. I follow GZ *gi lam* against CD *gis las*.
1034. GZ CDNP *bye ma lung pa* has no feminine ending, but given that the other persons before and after are women, this is probably a woman too. The same goes for the persons under nos. 70 and 73–77.
1035. GZ *nam mkha'i ngang du* CDNP *nam mkha'i dbyings su* ("in the expanse of the space").
1036. GZ CD *ngor* NP *ror* ("as the taste").
1037. I follow GZ NP *brten pa* against CD *bstan pa* ("teaching").
1038. This collection contains stanzas by only seventy-nine masters. Either the contribution by one of them has been lost in the transmission or "eighty" is just an approximate number (which is not unusual in Indian and Tibetan texts).
1039. Tib. Dam pa rgya gar; better known as Patampa Sangyé (Tib. Pha dam pa sangs rgyas; born eleventh century).
1040. I follow GZ CDNP *ma rtogs* against DVS *ma gtogs* ("except").
1041. Compare stanzas 16 in text 177 and I.9 in text 183. In more or less similar forms, thirty-five out of the forty-five stanzas in text 179 are also found in text 177, and a number of them is also shared with text 183. However, many of these stanzas are attributed to persons with completely different names in these texts. In some cases, it may be that these are (unknown) aliases, but often the stanzas here are attributed to certain well-known siddhas as opposed to other well-known ones in texts 177 and 183.
1042. CDNP omit *bla ma'i* ("of the guru").
1043. I follow GZ *zhal* against CDNP *gzhan* ("other").
1044. Compare stanzas 6 in text 177 and I.10 in text 183.
1045. Compare the second stanza 44 in text 177 and I.38 in text 183.
1046. I follow GZ *mngon du* against CDNP *sngon du* ("previously").
1047. Compare stanzas 3 in text 177 and I.39 in text 183.
1048. Compare stanzas 17 in text 177 and I.40 in text 183.
1049. Compare stanzas 30 in text 177 and I.41 in text 183.
1050. Compare stanzas 1 in text 177 and II.2 in text 183.
1051. Compare stanzas 22 in text 177 and III.2 in text 183.
1052. GZ *dus na* CDNP *yul na* ("in the object/sphere").
1053. Compare stanzas 12 in text 177 and III.4 in text 183.
1054. Compare stanzas 20 in text 177 and III.6 in text 183.

1055. Compare stanzas 4 in text 177 and I.42 in text 183.
1056. Compare stanzas 83 in text 177 and II.3 in text 183.
1057. Compare stanzas 41 and 75 in text 177 and III.10 in text 183 (the difference in the first line results from Tib. *ro* meaning both "flavor" and "corpse"; III.10 explicitly speaks of a "rotten corpse").
1058. Compare stanzas 80 in text 177 and III.11 in text 183.
1059. Compare stanzas 29 in text 177 and I.43 in text 183.
1060. Following the commentary on stanza 60 in text 177, which explains "avajra," GZ CDNP *an dza* is emended to *a ba dzra*.
1061. Compare stanzas 60 in text 177 and III.12 in text 183.
1062. Compare stanzas 77 in text 177 and I.44 in text 183.
1063. Compare stanzas 18 in text 177 and I.45 in text 183.
1064. Compare stanzas 43 in text 177 and I.46 text 183.
1065. Compare stanzas 31 in text 177 and I.47 in text 183.
1066. Compare stanzas 76 in text 177 and I.48 in text 183.
1067. Compare stanza 23 in text 177.
1068. GZ CDNP *la* emended to *las*.
1069. Compare stanzas 62 and 78 in text 177 and III.15 in text 183.
1070. Compare stanza 66 in text 177.
1071. I follow CDNP *myong ba mchog* against GZ *myong bas mchog*.
1072. Compare stanzas 42 in text 177 and II.6 in text 183.
1073. Compare stanzas 59 in text 177 and II.5 in text 183.
1074. As mentioned before, often in tantric texts, instead of the more obvious meaning of the phrases "meditating on the nose tip" and "focusing the mind on the nose tip" (for more instances, see some of the songs below), they refer to the mind being focused on the secret space of a visualized deity couple (the nonduality of prajñā and means) and employing techniques of working with vāyus and bindus (such as caṇḍālī).
1075. Compare stanzas 82 in text 177 and III.18 in text 183.
1076. I follow GZ CD *gze reg* against NP *gze rem*.
1077. Compare the first stanza 35 in text 177.
1078. Compare stanza 57 in text 177.
1079. I follow CDNP *brtags pa* against GZ *brtags pas*.
1080. Compare stanzas 39 in text 177 and III.20 in text 183.
1081. CDNP omit this stanza.
1082. Compare stanzas 52 in text 177 and I.50 in text 183.
1083. I follow GZ *ma yengs pa ni* against CDNP *ma yengs pa yi* ("of nondistraction").
1084. Compare stanzas 34 in text 177 and II.4 in text 183.
1085. Compare stanzas 84 in text 177 and II.7 in text 183.
1086. Compare stanza II.8 of text 183.
1087. In accordance with stanza 67 in text 177, GZ CDNP *la chu* is emended to *kyi gru*.
1088. "Seven-lifer" refers to someone who has been reborn as a brahman for at least seven lifetimes and is thus considered to be very pure.
1089. Compare stanza 67 in text 177 and III.21 in text 183.

1090. GZ *rje btsun dag gi* CDNP *rjes su bdag gi* ("Subsequently, with self-blessing . . .").
1091. Compare stanza III.16 in text 183.
1092. Compare with stanza 19 in text 177. CDNP omit this stanza.
1093. PDMT, 27:382–91.
1094. In P3278 (fol. 108a.4), this text is announced as *Mkha' 'gro ma'i 'byams glu ring mo* ("The Long All-Embracing Song of the Ḍākinīs"), while "the expressions of realization of thirty-five wisdom ḍākinīs" in the colophon (which the catalogues list as its title) appears to be a description of the text but not its actual title.
1095. I follow GZ CD *rnal ma'i* against NP *rnal 'byor* ("yoga").
1096. GZ *rang ghzan* CDNP *rang bzhin* ("nature").
1097. I follow GZ *bsten pa* against CD *brtan pa* NP *rtan pa.*
1098. I follow CDNP *rmong pa* against GZ *rmong pas.*
1099. GZ NP *mtha' dang* CD *tha dad* ("the difference").
1100. I follow GZ *mtha'* against CDNP *mkha'* ("space").
1101. GZ *la* CDNP *na* ("if there").
1102. I follow GZ *dangs pa'i sa* against GZ CD *d(v)angs pa yis.*
1103. I follow CDNP *spros dang bral ba* against GZ *spros dang bral bas.*
1104. I follow CDNP *bsam du med pa* against GZ *bsam du med par.*
1105. NP omit *zad* ("solely").
1106. GZ CDNP *mi pho*; lit. "man."
1107. GZ CD *'di* GZ *'dis* ("with this").
1108. PDMT, 27:392–99.
1109. PDMT, 27:400–407. The Skt. means "little song of the ḍākinīs."
1110. I follow GZ NP *ka ma la shrī* against CD *ka ma la shī la.*
1111. From the text itself, it is not clear whether it consists of individual songs sung by different ḍākinīs or whether it is their entire assembly that sings all stanzas together. Given the similarity of the title of this text (*Mkha' 'gro ma'i 'byams glu*; the colophon adds *chen mo*) to the title of text 180 (*Mkha' 'gro ma'i 'byams glu ring mo*) and the fact that there is no single continuous storyline or theme throughout the stanzas, it seems that it consists of stanzas by individual singers. However, it is not clear whether each of them sang only one or several stanzas.
1112. I follow GZ CD *gsos* against NP *gsol.*
1113. I follow GZ *khong skran* against CDNP *khong sran* ("patience").
1114. GZ *co 'u* CDNP *co lu* emended to *khye'u.*
1115. GZ CDNP read *yengs su 'gro'o.* Given the parallel last lines of the previous and following stanzas, one would rather expect "do not head for distraction!"
1116. I follow GZ NP *mnyan pa* against CD *gnyen pa.*
1117. I follow GZ CD *gtam col* against NP *stom rtsol.*
1118. I follow GZ *sgrug gyin* against CD *bsgugs kyi* NP *bsgrubs kyi.*
1119. GZ *'ching* CDNP *'chi* ("dying").
1120. I follow CD *rming* NP *rmang* against GZ *rmeng.*
1121. GZ CD *sgra* NP *dgra* ("enemies").

1122. Here and in the next stanzas, I follow CDNP *lan* against GZ *len* ("taking").
1123. GZ CDNP *gud nas* ("somewhere else") emended to *rgud nas*.
1124. GZ CDNP *ma che* emended to *ma byed*.
1125. I follow GZ CD *rig pa'i phyi bdar* against NP *phyir ba'i phyir*.
1126. I follow CDNP *da* against GZ *de* ("that").
1127. I follow GZ CD *mnyam nyid* against NP *mnyam med* ("incomparability").
1128. I follow GZ *chas* against CD *bcas* N *dbyas* P *dbyangs*.
1129. GZ *gtod de* CDNP *gtong nge*.
1130. I follow CDNP *da* against GZ *nga* ("I").
1131. NP add *rig* ("awareness").
1132. Garuḍas are mythical birds with eagle wings and lion heads that are the natural enemies of the nāgas (the garuḍa is also the mount of Viṣṇu).
1133. GZ CDNP *rem la thob* emended to *rem la thong*.
1134. CD omit the last sentence, while NP add the following after it: *Through the roots of virtue of writing this down, may the state of omniscience be attained!*
1135. PDMT, 27:416–82. My English rendering of the title is a combination of the Sanskrit and Tibetan, since the Tibetan omits Skt. *sakala* ("complete") but has *rnal 'byor pa thams cad* ("all yogīs") versus Skt. *sarvayoga* ("all yogas"). GZ3 has the mistaken header *Grub thob bzhi bcus rdo rje mgur bzhengs pa rnams* ("Vajra Songs Raised by Forty Siddhas").
1136. There are different lists of the eight great charnel grounds in the Hevajra literature, the Cakrasaṃvara literature, four texts in Tg devoted to this topic, and the Nyingma tradition, while the Kālacakra system describes sixteen charnel grounds (see https://www.himalayanart.org/search/set.cfm?setID=1364). One of the earliest lists is found in *Saṃvarodayatantra* 17.36–37 (D373, fol. 34b.4–5): Caṇḍogra, Gahvara, Vajrajvāla, Karaṅkin, Aṭṭahāsa, Lakṣmīvana, Ghorāndhakāra, and Kilikilārava (for details, see Torricelli 2018, 95–98).
1137. Paper was first introduced in India in the mid-eighth century CE, but it was very little known or used before the eleventh century CE. Instead, in northern and western India birch bark was very common, while palm leaves were predominant in central and southern India. Schaeffer 2007 (15–16) points out that a number of other anthologies by Patampa Sangyé also refer to being written down on "white paper," and one even to a "paper scroll," which was unknown in both India and Tibet. Schaeffer says: "One possible answer to this is that Dam pa sangs rgyas came across these book technologies in China, where he is said to have traveled in between his stays at Ding ri. Alternatively, we might suspect that the terms 'paper' and 'paper scroll' are used figuratively in the notices to the anthologies to evoke a connection between the creative activities of Dam pa sangs rgyas and his translator Zha ma Lo tsa ba and the authoritative past of tantric India."
1138. Except for when there are obvious misspellings or feminine endings required, I render the names in this text as they are given in GZ CDNP.

Obviously, many of these names are not in Sanskrit, but in one or another Prakrit vernacular (as indicated by occasional double "aa" and other features). Though a number of them appear to be in need of emendation (especially *suka* in some should probably be *sukha*), it can usually not be determined if or how exactly that is the case. There is also the ambiguity of the Tibetan letter *ba* rendering both *b* and *v* in Indic languages. Note that some of the names in texts 178, 180, and 182 correspond to some names in the lists of Patampa's fifty-four siddha teachers. See BA (868–69) and Schaeffer 2005, appendix 2.

1139. GZ *birva pa* CD *bīrya pa* ("Vīryapa") NP *birya pa*.

1140. Tib. *'dums* usually means "to agree" or "to be in harmony," but it is also an old term for "becoming shorter," which seems more to the point here.

1141. Originally, the term *śabara* (or *śavara*) referred to a wild mountain tribe in the Deccan (to which the famous mahāsiddha Śavaripa belonged). Later, it generally came to denote any kind of savage or barbarian. As a spiritual epithet, it refers to hermits living in isolated areas in the mountains or in the jungle in order to practice meditation. Sometimes (as in some of the songs in text 90), it can also symbolize luminosity. Both Śavaripa and Saraha are sometimes called "the mighty lord of Śabaras" (Skt. *śabareśvara*, Tib. *ri khrod dbang phyug*) or "the great Śabara" (Skt. *mahāśabara*, Tib. *ri khrod chen po*). Thus sometimes the two can be conflated. Since Saraha was already mentioned as an author two stanzas earlier, it could be that this chapter contains two songs by Saraha or that one of them refers to Śavaripa.

1142. "Aftermath" here renders Skt. *pṛṣṭhalabdha* (Tib. *rje thob*), a technical term that refers to the time between formal meditation sessions (I usually translate it as "subsequent attainment"). Often this term is translated as "postmeditation," which at best seems to be too neutral a word or just has the connotation of taking a break, which is far from the truth. For the term refers to the level of realization that is attained when emerging from meditative equipoise. This realization then informs and is actively applied to seeing the illusion-like nature of all appearances and experiences in one's practice of the six pāramitās or yogic conduct during the time between the sessions of meditative equipoise. Thus, one of the synonyms of "subsequent attainment" is "illusion-like samādhi." However, in order to avoid a too-technical terminology in the context of poetry, I sometimes use "aftermath."

1143. GZ CDNP *las* ("from") emended to *la*.

1144. GZ *mtshon du med la ngos gzung bral* CDNP *mtshon du yod la ngos gzung bral* ("it can be illustrated but is unidentifiable").

1145. GZ *bi na pa* CDNP *bhi na pa*.

1146. I follow CDNP *grol ba* against GZ *phrol ba*.

1147. GZ DCNP *phyin* ("gone") emended to *'byin*.

1148. I follow CD *nyams kyi 'phen len* NP *nyams kyis 'phen len* against GZ *nyams kyis 'phel len* ("increase and adopting through experience"). The last line appears to refer to involuntarily being propelled and adopting certain rebirths based on the meditative experiences of bliss, lucidity, and nonthought when one is attached to them and clings to them as being "me" or "mine." It is said that strong and long-lasting attachment to bliss, lucidity, and nonthought leads to rebirths in the desire realm, form realm, and formless realm, respectively.

1149. CD *u mu ka ri* N *a nu ka ri* P *u nu ka ri.*

1150. I follow GZ *'chos ma* against CDNP *tshos ma* ("dyer" or "dyed cloth").

1151. In general, Tib. *rten 'brel* means "dependent origination," but especially in a Vajrayāna context, it (also) refers to the timely manifesting karmic connection between a worthy student and the guru that makes the full and proper transmission of the teachings possible. In that way, "auspicious connection" is a particular case of dependent origination.

1152. Given the following lines and in accord with NP (*mdongs pa gsal,* "illuminate blindness"), GZ CD *ldongs pa* ("stupidity") *bsal* is emended to *mdongs pa bsal.*

1153. I follow GZ NP *rtogs pa* against CD *rtog pa* ("thought").

1154. The very common stories about seafaring merchants in Buddhist literature reflect the extent and importance of the sea trade between India and West Asia, North Africa, and the Mediterranean world in the early centuries of the Common Era, the popularity of Buddhism among the class of merchants, and the theme of treasure hunts on remote islands. Symbolically, such stories use or imply the common Indian (as well as non-Indian) metaphor of "crossing to the other shore" of an ocean or a river. In a Buddhist context, the ocean represents the vastness of saṃsāric experiences with all their many sufferings on the surface, the jewels to be found in it symbolize the precious qualities of mind's nature in its depths, and "the other shore" refers to nirvāṇa. The captain or "the great caravan leader" (Skt. *mahāsārthavāha*) who skillfully leads others across this ocean and is able to find its treasures is either a buddha, a bodhisattva, or a guru.

1155. I follow GZ *rtogs pa* against CDNP *rtog pa* ("thought").

1156. Tib. *yul* can mean "object" and "place." I choose "sphere" because it also carries these two meanings.

1157. I follow GZ CD *gdod nas* against NP *'dod nas.*

1158. I follow GZ CD *lha* against NP *sa* ("earth").

1159. GZ *'char bar 'byung* CDNP *'char bar 'gyur.*

1160. This is yet another example of the term "ordinary mind" not being used as an equivalent of mahāmudrā but in its literal sense of ordinary discursive states of mind.

1161. GZ *rlung gis ngag la bden pa yis / yid kyi tha mal rtog pa spong /* CDNP *rlung gi ngag la bde ba yis / yid kyi tha mal shes pa spong /* ("The bliss in vāyu speech dispels the ordinary mind of mentation").

1162. I follow GZ *ni* against CDNP *la.*

1163. I follow GZ CD *sa gzhi* against NP *sa bon* ("seed").

1164. I follow GZ *bangs pa'i sa* against CDNP *bdas pa'i ser.*

1165. I follow GZ *kyi* against CDNP *kyis.*

1166. I follow CDNP *so tshis* against GZ *so chis.*

1167. GZ NP *ru pa ta* CD *ru pa ti.*
1168. GZ *g.yang* CDNP *g.ya'* ("blemishes").
1169. I follow NP *gtsang rme* against GZ CD *gtsang sme.*
1170. I follow GZ CD *sems nyid de* against N *sems nyid do* P *sems nyid re.*
1171. Caṇḍālas are a class of people in India considered to be outcastes and untouchables. According to the ancient law code of the *Manusmṛti*, the class originated from the union of a Brahman woman (the highest caste) and a Śūdra man (the lowest class). The term is also used in modern times for a specific caste of agriculturists, fishermen, and boatmen in Bengal, more commonly referred to as Namaśūdra.
1172. GZ *candra lī yis* CD *tsan ta li yi* NP *tsandha li yi.*
1173. I follow GZ *sgrogs ma* against CDNP *sgrog sa ma.*
1174. GZ *pha la bya de wa* CDNP *la bya de ba.*
1175. The Sanskrit word *karaṇa* has a vast range of meanings, such as "doing," "making," "action (especially a religious one)," "means of action," "cause," "spell," "mind," "the posture of an ascetic," and "a posture in sexual intercourse." Given that this term has not been translated here into Tibetan and its specific use in some of the stanzas below, it most likely refers to the last two of these meanings—that is, more specifically, to the practice of karmamudrā.
1176. I follow GZ CD *go cha* against NP *cho ga* ("ritual").
1177. "The two genuine ones" refers to the two kinds of kāyas—the dharmakāya and the form kāyas.
1178. GZ *kampa la* CD *ka ma la* NP *ka pa la.*
1179. I follow GZ *stong* against CD *stod* NP *bstod* ("praise").
1180. I follow GZ CD *rgyal sa* against NP *rgyal ba* ("victor").
1181. I follow CDNP *dar med* against GZ *ngar med* ("without strength").
1182. I follow GZ DP *'phro* against C *'gro* ("going") N *'pho* ("shifting").
1183. I follow GZ CD *rgyal sa* against NP *rgyal ba* ("victor").
1184. GZ *mkha' nas* CDNP *nam mkha'i.*
1185. GZ *rang rig* CDNP *rang nyid.*
1186. I follow GZ *'phrad pa* against CDNP *'phra ba* ("kick").
1187. GZ *bden med* CDNP *bde med* ("without happiness").
1188. GZ *brtan pa* CDNP *bstan pa* ("shown").
1189. GZ CDNP *ko ta ri.*
1190. I follow GZ *rtogs pa* against CDNP *rtog pa* ("thoughts").
1191. CDNP omit *rtog pa* ("thoughts").
1192. This could also be read as "he in whom thoughts dawn as realization in a manner that is beyond momentary time."
1193. I follow GZ *don med spyod pa ma spangs pas* against CDNP *don dam spyod pa ma spangs pa'i* ("of not relinquishing ultimate conduct").
1194. This could also be read as "phenomena lack any essence, base, or root."
1195. I follow GZ *yi* against CDNP *yis.*
1196. I follow GZ3 *'dra min* against GZ1 NP *'dra men* CD *'dra man.*
1197. I follow GZ *rag* against CDNP *ra* ("goat").
1198. GZ *gha ngha ba* CDNP *gha dha pa.*

1199. I follow CDNP *'phro* against GZ *khro* ("wrath").
1200. GZ *an dzu ba* CDNP *a dzu ba.*
1201. GZ CD *yi* NP *yis.*
1202. I follow GZ *rtogs pa* against CDNP *rtog pa* ("thought").
1203. "Indra's bow" is an Indian metaphor for a rainbow.
1204. I follow GZ CD *rang gi* against NP *rang rig* ("self-awareness").
1205. GZ D *snang* CNP *nang* ("in").
1206. Skt. *kumārī* means "young girl" or "virgin."
1207. I follow GZ CD *de yi* against NP *de la* ("in that").
1208. I follow GZ *kyis* against CDNP *kyi* ("of").
1209. GZ *dznyā na bi nu* CDNP *dznyā na bhi nu.*
1210. I follow CDNP *yi* against GZ *yis* ("by").
1211. I follow GZ NP *rtogs pa* against CD *rtog pa* ("thought").
1212. GZ CDNP *lung* ("scripture") is emended to *rlung.*
1213. GZ CD *gsang gi gnad* NP *gsang gi gsang* ("the secret of secrets").
1214. The "ūrṇā hair" is one of the thirty-two major marks of a buddha. It is described as either a single coil of white hair between the eyebrows that radiates light and extends for many miles when uncoiled or a tuft of such hair.
1215. I follow GZ CD *'phen* against N *'phan* P *phan.*
1216. I follow GZ NP *rtogs pa* against CD *rtog pa* ("thought").
1217. Given the context, GZ *brtag pa* CDNP *rtags pa* are emended to *rtogs pa.*
1218. GZ *rtogs pa gru bzo las mkhas pa* CD *rtog pa gru bzo la mkhas pa* N *rtogs pa gru gzo las mkhas pa* P *rtogs pa grub gzo las mkhas pa* emended to *rtogs pa gru bzo la mkhas pa.*
1219. I follow GZ NP *rtog* against CD *rtogs* ("realization").
1220. I follow GZ CD *rtog* against NP *rtogs* ("realization").
1221. GZ CD *rtsol* NP *blo* ("mind").
1222. GZ NP *dengs* CD *dangs* ("are pellucid").
1223. GZ *shrī bi su pa* CDNP *shrī si su pa.*
1224. This stanza is virtually identical to IV.43.
1225. I follow GZ NP *'dzin* against CD *'jan.*
1226. I follow NP *yi* against GZ CD *yis.*
1227. I follow CDNP *blo* against GZ *glo* ("lungs").
1228. GZ *su ka si ta* CD *su kha siddhi* NP *su ka si ti.*
1229. GZ *rang gsang* CDNP *rang gsal* ("self-lucidity").
1230. GZ *'khyil* CDNP *'khyim.*
1231. GZ NP *shrī si ti* CD *shrī siddhi.*
1232. I follow GZ *rab tu 'gengs* against CDNP *rab tu 'ging.*
1233. GZ CDNP *dbang na.* I use a transliteration of the rather obscure Tibetan (lit. "in empowerment"), because *dbang* renders a vast range of Sanskrit words.
1234. GZ *bsten* CD *brten* NP *rten.*
1235. I follow CDNP *yin* against GZ *yi.*
1236. GZ *tsa di la* CDNP *ta di la.*
1237. GZ *la lanta* CDNP *la lanta li.*

1238. I follow GZ CD *'da'* against NP *mnga'* ("possess").
1239. GZ *si ra nu pa* CD *si ra nu sa* NP *si ra nu si*.
1240. This stanza is virtually identical to IV.14.
1241. I follow CDNP *rang rkya* against GZ *rang rkyar* ("will not become self-sufficient").
1242. I follow GZ *rtogs pa phyag rgya ma las shar ba* against CDNP *rtog pa phyag rgya ma la shar ba* ("he whose thoughts dawned in mudrā").
1243. I follow GZ *dbang las rtogs pa shar ba* against CD *dbang la rtog pa shar ba* ("he in whom thoughts dawned in empowerment") NP *dbang la rtogs pa shar ba* ("he whose realization dawned in empowerment").
1244. I follow GZ *las* against CDNP *la*.
1245. GZ *bden pa* CDNP *bde ba* ("bliss").
1246. GZ *na ri ka* CDNP *na ri pa*.
1247. GZ *bden par 'dzin pa 'khrul* CDNP *bden par 'dzin pas 'khrul* ("delusion is due to clinging to reality").
1248. I follow GZ CD *sbubs* against NP *dbugs* ("breath").
1249. GZ *ci ru rung* CD *ci phyir rung* ("why would they be suitable?") NP *ci cir rung*.
1250. GZ CDNP *khro bo* ("angry") emended to *'phro ba*.
1251. I follow GZ *mthong ba las rtogs pa shar ba* against CDNP *mthong ba la rtog pa shar ba* ("he in whom thoughts dawned in seeing").
1252. I follow GZ *yongs btsal* against CDNP *'ongs btsal*.
1253. GZ *kha ngha ga ga ti* CDNP *kha dha ga ga ti*.
1254. I follow GZ CD *dben pa i la pa* against NP *beṃ pa i pa*.
1255. GZ *ba su dha ra* CDNP *ba su dha ri*.
1256. I follow GZ *rtogs pa* against CDNP *rtog pa* ("thought").
1257. I follow GZ *'tshong ba* against CDNP *'tshogs pa* ("gathering").
1258. I follow GZ *rtogs pa* against CDNP *rtog pa* ("thought").
1259. GZ *bha ga dha ra* CDNP *bha ga dha ri*.
1260. GZ *stong pa* CD *stong ngas* NP *stong pas* ("since it is empty of letters").
1261. I follow GZ CD *'dod 'jo ma* against NP *'od 'jo ma*.
1262. GZ *ga na ku nu pa* CD *ka na ku na pa NP ka na pa*.
1263. GZ D *ang tsing pa* C *mang tseng* NP *ong rtsing*.
1264. GZ *bo dhi ni pa* CDNP *bo dhi pi pa*.
1265. I follow GZ CD *khegs* against NP *khebs* ("cover").
1266. GZ CD *bsal ba* NP *gsal ba* ("cleared up").
1267. Tib. *ma mo* can also refer to flesh-eating spirits.
1268. GZ CDNP *snang dang stong pa'i rkyen dang bral* ("free of the conditions of appearing and being empty") emended to *snang dang stong pa rkyen dang bral*.
1269. GZ *brjod du med par tshig tu brjod* CDNP *brjod du med pa'i tshig tu brjod* ("they are expressed as inexpressible words").
1270. GZ CD *mkhar* NP *mthar* ("end").
1271. GZ *bha su ka ma* CD *bha su ka ra* NP *bha su ka ri*.
1272. GZ *dri ma bsags* CD *dra ba btags* ("weave the web") NP *dri ba btags* ("weave the questions").

1273. GZ *su ka dha ra ki* CDNP *su ka ra ki.*
1274. GZ *gha ma li ta* CDNP *gha ma li ti.*
1275. GZ *bzang po* CDNP *bzod pa* ("patience").
1276. GZ *shra rdhā na* CD *shrīddhā na* NP *shraddha na.*
1277. I follow GZ *gnyen pos* against CDNP *gnyen po'i* ("of remedies").
1278. GZ CD *bha ta ra* NP *bha ra.*
1279. I follow CDNP *rtog pa* against GZ *rtogs pa* ("realization").
1280. This line could also be read as "It is the absence of both thought and nonthought."
1281. I follow GZ *gya ba* against CDNP *bya ba.*
1282. GZ *gding* CDNP *gdeng.*
1283. I follow GZ CD *brtags pa* against NP *rtags pa.*
1284. GZ *snang ba* CDNP *sgo nga* ("egg"), probably *sgo lnga* ("while objects and the five [sense] gates meet").
1285. GZ CD *mdangs ldan ma* NP *dangs ma* ("she with the pellucidity").
1286. GZ *bha ba bha dra* CD *bha dra pa* NP *bha tra pa.*
1287. I follow GZ CD *'gyu ba* against NP *'gyur ba* ("change").
1288. I follow GZ CD *rtog pa* against NP *rtogs pa* ("realization").
1289. I follow GZ NP *de snyed* against CD *de nyid.*
1290. I follow GZ CD *srangs* against DNP *srungs* ("protection").
1291. I follow GZ *der* against CDNP *dar.*
1292. GZ *'gal zhing 'khrul pa* CDNP *'gal na 'khrul pa* ("if nonthought . . . is in opposition to the mindstream, this is delusion").
1293. GZ *sa li dza dha ri* CDNP *sa la dza dha ra.*
1294. GZ *longs pa* CD *slong ba* NP *slongs pa* ("raising").
1295. GZ *bu la kha dha* CDNP *su la kha dha.*
1296. GZ *shrī pā ra nā* CD *shrī pa ra nā* NP *shrī pa ra na.* The final -ā of this name suggests that it is feminine. However, the following apposition lacks any feminine ending (*ma* or *mo*) as it is present in all other parallel cases in this text.
1297. GZ *dha nu ro ha* CDNP *bha nu ro ha.*
1298. GZ *bde ba'i mdzod 'dzin* CD *bde ba'i ngos 'dzin* ("identifies bliss") NP *bde ba'i'od 'dzin* ("holds the light of bliss").
1299. GZ *ngar chen* CD *ngar can* ("powerful") NP *rang can.*
1300. GZ *bde ba'i sgrol ma ma dha la* CDNP *bde ba'i sgron ma la dha li* ("Ladhalī, the Lamp of Bliss").
1301. GZ *grung pa* (can also mean "powerful" and "clever") CDNP *drungs pa.*
1302. Tib. *rten 'brel* can also be understood as "dependent origination."
1303. I follow GZ NP *rtogs pa* against CD *rtog pa* ("thoughts").
1304. Again, Tib. *rten 'brel* can also be understood as "dependent origination."
1305. GZ *dvangs pa* CD *dangs pa* NP *dengs pa* ("has vanished").
1306. GZ *bden pa mthong bas* CD *bden par mthong ba* NP *bden par mthong.*
1307. Tib. *rtsa ba phyin pa* might be a misspelling of *rtsa ba 'byin pa* ("eradicating").
1308. I follow GZ *bzung ba'i rjes* against CDNP *bzung bas rjes.*
1309. I follow GZ CD *dran pa* against NP *bral ba* ("being free").

1310. I follow GZ *der 'dzin* against CDNP *deng 'dzin.*
1311. GZ *brtan* CD *rten* ("support") NP *gtan* ("must not lapse from one-pointedness").
1312. GZ *bzung du med par ngos zin* CDNP *bzung du med pa'i don zin* ("the actuality that is ungraspable is seized").
1313. I follow GZ CD *rgyal po* against NP *rgyal ba* ("victor").
1314. GZ *gnyis med shes pa dngos po'i gshis* CDNP *gnyis med shes bya dngos po'i gshis* ("is the basic ground of knowable entities"; "nondual" would then have to go with "wisdom" in the second line).
1315. GZ *ma* CDNP *pa* ("he").
1316. GZ CDNP *kyis* emended to *kyi.*
1317. I follow GZ CD *gzhi med* against N *bzhi med* ("without four") P *zhi med* ("peaceless").
1318. GZ *brdas go ba* CDNP *brda'i go ba* ("an understanding of symbols").
1319. I follow GZ *gzung 'dzin* against CD *gzugs 'dzin* ("clinging to forms") NP *bzang 'dzin* ("clinging to goodness").
1320. GZ NP *bzang mo don* CD *zab mo don* ("she who seizes the glory of profound actuality").
1321. I follow CDNP *rags pa* against GZ *rigs pa* ("appropriateness," "reasoning").
1322. GZ NP *rā dza me tog ha li* CD *rā dzā me tog ha li.*
1323. I follow GZ *dngos po* against CDNP *dad po.*
1324. I follow GZ *ci yi phyir mi gzigs /* against CD *ci phyir mi gzigs zhes /* NP *ci phyir mi gzigs /.*
1325. This could also be read as "that the realization of these entities that appear enters the natural state of being unborn."
1326. I follow GZ P *pha la* against CD *pa la* N *pha pa.*
1327. GZ *rin chen sems* CDNP *rang bzhin sems* ("natural mind").
1328. I follow CDNP *yin* against GZ *yis.*
1329. I follow CDNP *gyi* against GZ *gyis.*
1330. GZ *gang la mngon par zhen pa yis / 'ching ba'i rgyu* CDNP *gang la mngon par zhen pa ni / 'ching ba'i rgyu* ("whatever you may be clinging to, it is the cause of bondage").
1331. GZ NP *ra bhi na da* CD *ri bha na da.*
1332. GZ *gīrti singha* CD *girti bing da* NP *girti sim da.*
1333. I follow GZ *'od gsal* against CDNP *ngo gsal.*
1334. I follow GZ *rtogs pa* against CDNP *rtog pa* ("thoughts").
1335. I follow GZ *mdud grol 'gyur* against CDNP *mdud par grol.*
1336. GZ N *ratna bo dha* CDP *ratna bo dhi.*
1337. I follow GZ CD *bzi ba* against NP *gzi ba.*
1338. I follow GZ CD *mi rtog* against NP *mi rtag* ("impermanent").
1339. I follow GZ *ngang* against CDNP *dang.*
1340. I follow GZ *snang ba rgyud la nges shes skyes* against CD *snang ba rgyud la nges skyes* NP *snang rgyud la nges shes skyes.*
1341. GZ1 illegible GZ3 *ratri ta* CDNP *ratni ta.*
1342. GZ CDNP *yid la ma yin* emended to *yod pa ma yin.*

1343. I follow GZ CD *glod* against NP *slod* ("impair").
1344. Tib. *ma rig (b)sgom gyis* could also mean "through ignorant meditation."
1345. GZ *'chum* CDNP *chud* ("insert yourself").
1346. I follow GZ NP *bsgrims* against CD *bsgribs* ("obscure").
1347. I follow GZ CD *glod* against NP *slod* ("impair").
1348. This could also be read as "seen its root to be baseless."
1349. GZ *rang mtshang* CDNP *rang mtshan* ("specific characteristic").
1350. I follow GZ *til gyis mar gyi don mi nus* against CDNP *til gyi mar gyis don mi nus.*
1351. The first line of stanza IX.13 contains *ji ltar* ("just as"), but the meaning that corresponds to the example in that stanza is only found in IX.14. Thus I connected the two stanzas in this way.
1352. I follow GZ *a bha ra dha* against CDNP *bha a ra dha.*
1353. I follow GZ CD *mdangs* against NP *mda'* ("arrow").
1354. GZ *rtsal las* CNP *rtsa la* ("in the root") P *la.*
1355. I follow GZ CD *bcas* against NP *chas.*
1356. I follow GZ NP *rtogs pa* against CD *rtog pa* ("thought").
1357. GZ *gol sa* CDNP *gol ba* ("going astray").
1358. I follow GZ *'dod 'jo ma* against CDNP *'od 'jo ma.*
1359. GZ *pas zin pa* CDNP *sa zin pa* ("seizing the ground of").
1360. GZ *sho po ri pa* CDNP *sho so ri pa.*
1361. GZ *ma gyur med* CDNP *ma gyur gang* ("which one is not food . . .?"). In Indian mythology, makaras are sea monsters whose frontal part consists of a terrestrial animal (stag, deer, or elephant), while their hind part is an aquatic animal (usually the tail of a fish, a seal, or a snake, but sometimes the tail of a peacock or even a floral tail). Iconographically, makaras are the emblem of Kāmadeva (the god of love) as well as the mounts of the river goddesses Gaṅgā and Narmadā and the sea god Varuṇa. Being the most commonly recurring creature in Hindu and Buddhist temple iconography, makaras are considered as the guardians of doorways and thresholds, protecting throne rooms as well as shrines and temples. They also appear frequently as gargoyles or spouts attached to natural springs.
1362. I follow GZ *rtogs pa* against CDNP *rtog pa* ("thoughts").
1363. I follow GZ *mis* against CDNP *yi.*
1364. GZ *dul ba yi / 'di yis yon tan* CDNP *dul ba ni / 'di yi yon tan* ("those whose own mindstream is tamed through study cast the need for the qualities of these into the wind").
1365. GZ *ra nu tsanda* CDNP *ra nu tsandra* (both *canda* and *candra* mean "moon").
1366. GZ CD *'gyu ba* NP *'gyur ba* ("change").
1367. GZ *tsi ra de va mo* CD *tsi ra de ba* NP *dzi ra de ba.*
1368. GZ *ngo sprod gnad la phog pas phyag rgya chen po thog babs su shar ba* CDNP *ngo sprod gnad la phog pa'i phyag rgya chen po thog babs su shar ba* ("she in whom the mahāmudrā of striking the vital point of introduction dawns in lightning-like suddenness").

1369. Probably the eight worldly dharmas.
1370. This could also be read as "as the ground."
1371. PDMT, 27:483–507 (for an alternative translation and a critical edition of the Tibetan, see Mathes 2015, 273–311 and 511–42).
1372. I follow GZ NP *zhing* against CD *zhi* ("peace").
1373. I follow GZ NP *yang* against CD *pas*.
1374. I follow GZ *'grul* against CDNP *'drul* ("rotten").
1375. GZ CDNP *bla ma sangs rgyas e sangs rgyas* (lit. "the guru is the buddha—isn't he the buddha?").
1376. In the following, G, V, and AS refer to the lists of mahāsiddhas in the Gyantse murals, the tradition of Vajrāsana, and the Aṣṭasāhasrikā Pantheon, respectively (full references in von Schroeder 2006, 20 and 194–95). "Sara" may refer to Saraka (= Sāgarapāda; V33). Furthermore, von Schroeder 2006 refers to an unidentified female siddhā Saragī (G81).
1377. Maybe Kambala (mahāsiddha no. 30) or Kamala as an alias of Catrapa (mahāsiddha no. 23), but both are already listed below.
1378. GZ NP *de ki* CD *lde ki*.
1379. Maybe Upanaha (mahāsiddha no. 79).
1380. Possibly Putalipa (mahāsiddha no. 78).
1381. *Karopa is an alias of Maitrīpa's student Bhitakarma (GZ CDNP *ka ru pa*, for which von Schroeder 2006 has "Kāmarūpa [?]" [V53]).
1382. Maybe Ravigupta; see text 178 (36).
1383. Unidentified.
1384. GZ CD *kondha li* NP *ko bho li*. Koṅkalipa is an alias of Kaṅkāripa (mahāsiddha no. 7).
1385. Von Schroeder 2006, Bhagalana (Bhagha) (V67).
1386. Unidentified (possibly *Vīraprakāśa, the compiler of text 177).
1387. GZ CDNP *ni lo pa'i*; von Schroder 2006, Nīlapāda (Nilipa) (G82).
1388. GZ *tsadha* CD *tsandha* NP *tsandra*; maybe Candragomin (V20).
1389. GZ CDNP *ka na*. This must refer to Kāṇhapa (mahāsiddha no. 17), since the corresponding stanza I.40 is attributed to him in texts 177 and 179.
1390. Mentioned in the **Aśītisiddhābhisamaya* (D4317, no. 25).
1391. Unidentified.
1392. It appears that each line of this stanza contains three names, except for the one that begins with "Ḍombi Heruka." However, the corresponding stanzas I.42 and I.43 are attributed to the lesser master Ḍombipa and Ḍombi Heruka in texts 177 and 179. Thus these lines appear to be a list of the forty-two authors of the following forty-two stanzas in the first chapter. The same goes for the forty-two names and the following forty-two stanzas in the second chapter. The third chapter seems to begin with forty-one names (though many of them are uncertain), but contains many more stanzas. As the colophons of each chapter suggest, the stanzas in them were sung at a gaṇacakra.
1393. Compare this with stanzas 16 in text 177 and 1 in text 179, also attributed to Nāgārjuna.

1394. Compare this with stanzas 6 in text 177 and 2 in text 179; lines I.10abd are also similar to Saraha's *Dohakoṣa* 29cd–30a (text 13, 32cd–33a).
1395. I follow NP *rtog* against GZ CD *rtogs*.
1396. I follow CDNP *kyis* against GZ *kyi*.
1397. I follow CDNP *dug* against GZ *drug* ("six").
1398. I follow GZ *chos skyong* against CDNP *chos kyi*.
1399. I follow GZ *pa'i* against CDNP *kyis*.
1400. I follow CDNP *kyi* against GZ *kyis*.
1401. I follow GZ *ros* against CDNP *rol* ("enjoyment" or "play").
1402. I follow GZ NP *sme sha* (rendering the low castes of Ḍomba or Caṇḍāla) against CD *rme sha*.
1403. Compare this with the second stanza 44 in text 177 and stanza 3 in text 179.
1404. I follow GZ *mngon du* against CDNP *sngon du* ("previously").
1405. Compare stanzas 3 in text 177 and 4 in text 179.
1406. Compare this with stanzas 17 in text 177 and 5 in text 179.
1407. Compare this with stanzas 30 in text 177 and 6 in text 179.
1408. Compare this with stanzas 4 in text 177 and 12 in text 179.
1409. I follow GZ NP *rtogs pa* against CD *rtog pa* ("thoughts").
1410. Compare this with stanzas 29 in text 177 and 16 in text 179.
1411. Compare this with stanzas 77 in text 177 and 18 in text 179.
1412. Compare this with stanzas 18 in text 177 and 19 in text 179.
1413. Compare this with stanzas 43 in text 177 and 20 in text 179.
1414. Following the parallel stanzas in texts 177 and 179, GZ CDNP *dmigs* ("focus" or "object") is emended to *mig*.
1415. Compare this with stanzas 31 in text 177 and 21 in text 179.
1416. Compare this with stanzas 76 in text 177 and 23 in text 179.
1417. Compare this with stanzas 52 in text 177 and 35 in text 179.
1418. Kama may be Kambala (mahāsiddha no. 30) or Kamala as an alias of Catrapa (mahāsiddha no. 23).
1419. Kharabha is probably Kharkapa, as an alias of Khaḍgapa (mahāsiddha no. 15) or Karapa as an alias of Sakara (Saroruha; mahāsiddha no. 74).
1420. Viku is possibly Vikuṇṭhana; unidentified.
1421. Toka is probably Dokhaṅdi, as an alias of Dukhaṅdhi (mahāsiddha no. 25).
1422. Bheni may be V83 *bha yi ni* (unidentified).
1423. Vinasi is possibly Vīṇāpa (mahāsiddha no. 11); V43 *bhi na sa* for Vīṇāpa.
1424. Ghuna[pa] is possibly Guṇḍhari or Guṅḍari (a guru of Medhini, mahāsiddha no. 50).
1425. Tapa may be Tantipa (mahāsiddha no. 13).
1426. Teli is an alias of Dhilipa (mahāsiddha no. 62).
1427. Unidentified; usually, Oḍra (northern Orissa) is one of the twenty-four power places in the *Cakrasaṃvaratantra*.
1428. Saka[ra] is an alias of Saroruha (mahāsiddha no. 74).
1429. CD *ni tra yi* NP *na tri yi*; unidentified.
1430. Sana[ka] is an alias of Upanahapa (mahāsiddha no. 79).

1431. Unidentified.
1432. Capa[ripa] is an alias of Carbaripa (mahāsiddha no. 64).
1433. Suta[pa] is an alias of Putalipa (mahāsiddha no. 78).
1434. Kuruna is possibly Kurmapa.
1435. Kusu[lī] is an alias of Kucipa (mahāsiddha no. 35).
1436. Kumari[pa] is an alias of Kumbharipa (mahāsiddha 63).
1437. Lakha[pa] is possibly Laksmīṃkarā (mahāsiddha no. 82); otherwise, Lākhapuya/Lhākapum is found as the birthplace of Jālandhara.
1438. Dhakha[pa] is probably "Dhaki," as an alias of Ḍeṅgipa (mahāsiddha no. 31); Dhaka is found again two lines below.
1439. Parapusi is found as AS81 and Parasu as V81 (both unidentified).
1440. Viḍa is possibly Vidhyākokilā, a guru of the younger Kuśulu in a Guhyasamāja lineage.
1441. Unidentified.
1442. Oddly, the last name is in Tibetan (Snying po pa), which could be a Tibetan person (as in the list at the beginning of chapter 3), or rendered in Skt. Sāraka, Maṇḍaka, Garbhaka, Karṇika, or Vartika; in any case, this person is unidentified.
1443. Compare this with stanzas 1 in text 177 and 7 in text 179.
1444. Compare this with stanzas 83 in text 177 and 13 in text 179.
1445. Compare this with stanzas 34 in text 177 and 37 in text 179.
1446. Compare this with stanzas 59 in text 177 and 29 in text 179.
1447. CDNP omit *dang mi* ("not . . . with").
1448. Compare this with stanzas 42 in text 177 and 28 in text 179.
1449. Compare this with stanzas 84 in text 177 and 38 in text 179.
1450. GZ D *mnyan* CN *mnyen* ("supple") P *mnyes* ("delighted").
1451. I follow GZ *rkyal ba* against CDNP *rgyal ba* ("being victorious").
1452. Compare this with stanza 39 in text 179.
1453. GZ *gsal stong* CDNP *gsal snang* ("clear illumination").
1454. The sahajakāya as a fourth buddhakāya is described in the *Kālacakratantra* as the basis and source for the dharmakāya, the sambhogakāya, and the nirmāṇakāya. It is the state of awareness that includes and yet transcends time, prajñā and means, as well as male and female, and is perfectly pellucid luminosity. Since it is innate, it is innate to all sexes.
1455. I follow GZ NP *yengs* against CD *yang*.
1456. The last sentence could also be read as "There is no cause of death!"
1457. I follow CDNP *dgra zun* against GZ *dgra zin*.
1458. I follow GZ CD *ye med* against NP *ye shes* ("wisdom").
1459. GZ *ngang* CDNP *dang* ("and").
1460. GZ CDNP *kyis* emended to *kyi*.
1461. I follow CD *snyam* against GZ NP *mnyam* ("equal").
1462. I follow GZ *rang rig* against CDNP *rang gi* ("own").
1463. I take *chos kyi ni/ sku can* as a bahuvrīhi.
1464. Given the parallel line in II.30, I follow CDNP *bde chen sku* against GZ *bden med sku* ("the kāya of nonreality").

1465. Or "the ornament of self-awareness seeing luminosity."
1466. GZ NP *zung 'jug* CD *byang chub* ("awakening").
1467. GZ *bde ba* CDNP *bde'o* ("Bliss! Naturally arising experience without clinging beyond mind . . .").
1468. GZ NP *klong* CD *lam* ("path").
1469. GZ *rang gsal* CDNP *dang gsal* ("pellucid and lucid").
1470. GZ *ngang* CDNP *dang* ("and").
1471. Unidentified. Except for in the fourth line below, the "names" here are determined by following the pattern in the parallel lists at the beginning of the first and second chapters, which have three names per line (with the first two having two syllables each and the third one having three syllables). However, there could be different breakdowns of the nine syllables in each line here.
1472. Unidentified.
1473. Unidentified.
1474. Unidentified (also the name of the Hindu goddess of the night).
1475. Tib. Legs sbyin; unidentified.
1476. Possibly Padmavajra.
1477. Unidentified. Among the three Vajras in this list, one is possibly Vajrapāda, an alias of Mīnapa (mahāsiddha no. 8).
1478. Unidentified.
1479. Probably Mahipa (mahāsiddha no. 37).
1480. I follow NP *ra ri* against GZ CD *ri ri*; Raripa (G77) is an alias of Dārikapa (mahāsiddha no. 77).
1481. Tib. 'Bar ba; probably Jālandhara (Tib. 'Bar 'dzin; mahāsiddha no. 46).
1482. Possibly the yoginī Cintā.
1483. Unidentified.
1484. Possibly Medhini (mahāsiddha no. 50).
1485. Probably Bhadrapa (mahāsiddha no. 24). All following names except Kanapa (mahāsiddha no. 17) and Bhūti (probably Indrabhūti; mahāsiddha no. 42) are unidentified.
1486. Compare this with stanzas 22 in text 177 and 8 in text 179.
1487. GZ CDNP *thos*; one would rather expect *thob* ("attain").
1488. Compare this with stanzas 12 in text 177 and 10 in text 179.
1489. I follow GZ NP *stor* against CD *ston* ("the guru's eyes that show the path of wisdom lead to awakening").
1490. Compare this with stanzas 20 in text 177 and 11 in text 179.
1491. GZ CD *me* NP *che* ("great").
1492. Compare this with stanzas 41 in text 177 and 14 in text 179.
1493. Compare this with stanzas 80 in text 177 and 15 in text 179.
1494. Following the commentary on stanza 60 in text 177, which explains "avajra," GZ CDNP *a dzan* is emended to *a ba dzra*.
1495. Compare this with stanza 60 in text 177 and stanza 17 in text 179.
1496. I follow GZ NP *rtog* against CD *rtogs* ("realization").
1497. Compare with stanzas 62 and 78 in text 177 and 25 in text 179.
1498. Compare with stanza 41 of text 179.

1499. GZ *nyams myong gdams pa dang bral* CDNP *nyams myong gdams pa don bral* ("devoid of the meaning of experiential instructions").
1500. Compare with stanzas 82 in text 177 and 30 in text 179.
1501. Compare with stanzas 35 in text 177 and 31 in text 179.
1502. Compare with stanza 39 in text 177.
1503. Compare with stanzas 67 in text 177 and 40 in text 179.
1504. I follow NP *kyi* against GZ CD *kyis*.
1505. I follow GZ CD *gru gzings kyis* against NP *gru rdzings kyi*.
1506. The last two lines are almost identical to the famous last two lines of *Uttaratantra* I.154 and *Abhisamayālaṃkāra* V.20.
1507. I follow CDNP *yis* against GZ *yi*.
1508. GZ *sgra don 'bral med thos dang ni* CDNP *sgra don 'brel med thos nas ni* are emended to *sgra don 'bral med thos nas ni*.
1509. NP mistakenly insert here *nyams myong smrar med gnyug ma yi*.
1510. I follow GZ NP *yin* against CD *yengs* ("distracted").
1511. I follow GZ NP *gnyug ma* against CD *bla ma* ("guru").
1512. This could also be read as "thoughts of clinging to nonclinging."
1513. GZ *dung* CDNP *dus* ("time").
1514. The end of this line—GZ CD *gyi* NP *gyis*—would connect it to "ocean" in the next line. Thus, *gyi/gyis* is emended to *dang*.
1515. Similar to the wish-fulfilling cow, the wish-fulfilling tree, and the harvest that needs no toil, "the excellent vase" (Skt. *bhadraghaṭa*, Tib. *bum pa bzang po*) is a traditional Indian symbol for effortlessly granting all desires.
1516. I follow GZ CD *rtog pa yis* against NP *rtag pa yi* ("of permanent").
1517. I follow GZ *las* against CDNP *la*.
1518. GZ *'khor ba'i rgyu 'grul gcad* CDNP *'khor ba'i 'khrul bcad de*.
1519. GZ CDNP *rtog pa* emended to *rtogs pa*.
1520. Tib. *rang rgyud* could also mean "anything independent."
1521. I follow GZ *gis* against CDNP *gi*.
1522. *Kusali* (more correctly *kuśalin*) literally means "one with virtue." It is a name for hidden yogīs or yoginīs who practice secretly, while outwardly appearing as ordinary people or even beggars. In the Tibetan tradition, *kusali* is usually equated with *kusulu* ("one who only eats, sleeps, and defecates"), and both terms are often (wrongly) taken as synonyms of *bhusuku*. However, according to Sakya Paṇḍita, *kusulu* is incorrect and should be *kusali* (*kuśalin*). He adds that a paṇḍita is someone well-versed in the inner and outer fields of knowledge, while a *kuśalin* has cut through all outer discursiveness and reference points and is supremely absorbed within (*Snyi mo sgom chen gyi dris lan* in *Sa skya bka' 'bum*, vol. na, fol. 248b2–5).
1523. I follow GZ *yis* against CDNP *yi*.
1524. I follow GZ CD *bung ba* against NP *bum pa* ("vase").
1525. This could also be read as "the nirvāṇa that is the complete purity of phenomena."
1526. I follow GZ CD *chen* against NP *can*.

1527. I follow GZ *'dzin gyis* against CDNP *'dzin gyi.*
1528. I follow GZ CD *myang 'das* against CDNP *ngan 'das.*
1529. GZ *ātma ta kṛta ni* CD *ātma ta kṛ ni* NP *ātma ta kri ni.*
1530. Skt. *dhāraṇī* refers to either the power of total recall (remembering every word of dharma ever heard or read), is used as a synonym for mantra, or indicates a genre of texts. Here it is obviously used metaphorically, since it refers to dharmatā.
1531. GZ *grib mas* CDNP *grib la* ("in your shade").
1532. GZ *'jig rten srid gsum* CDNP *'jig rten gsum na* ("in the three worlds").
1533. In general, yoginīs are classified as three types: connate, field-born, and mantra-born. Karmamudrā consorts are classified as three types as follows: mantra-born (fully qualified consorts with the same realization, attained through the power of Vajrayāna practices), field-born (ḍākinīs who live in external power places), and family-born (consorts with the insignia, colors, and mudrās of the five buddha families). Another fourfold classification of consorts consists of connate (sambhogakāya forms residing in the pure realm Akaniṣṭha who manifest in the form of deities), field-born (practitioners with unsurpassable meditation who manifest as yoginīs in external power places), mantra-born (practitioners trained in the Vajrayāna who are born as ḍākinīs in conducive environments), and karma-born (practitioners who have attained the path of familiarization through Vajrayāna practices in a previous lifetime).
1534. CDNP omit *thams cad* ("all").
1535. I follow NP *gyis* against GZ CD *gyi.*
1536. PDMT, 27:508–19.
1537. I follow NP *de nyid* against GZ CD *de yi.*
1538. GZ *de nyid kyi / dus su* CDNP *de srid kyi / dus gsum* ("it's during the three times").
1539. GZ *mtshungs ltar* CDNP *mtshungs pas.*
1540. I follow GZ *su zhig yid ni rton* against CDNP *su zhig la ni rton.*
1541. The last two lines are also found in Nāgārjuna's *Pañcakrama* (III.36ab; D1802, fol. 49a.7).
1542. I follow GZ *mdza' ba* against CDNP *mdzad pa* ("a deed").
1543. This refers to four especially powerful medicines made from minerals.
1544. GZ *sdong dum* CDNP *ldum dum.*
1545. GZ NP *dgang* CD *dag* ("becomes pure").
1546. I follow CDNP *yi* against GZ *yis.*
1547. GZ *bsten bgyid* CDNP *brtan bgyid* ("stabilize").
1548. GZ *bdag gis tshe 'dir gnas mi byed* CD *bdag gis tshe 'dir gnas mi bya* NP *bdag gi tshe 'di gnas mi byed.*
1549. I follow GZ NP *thag pa* against CD *theg pa* ("yāna").
1550. I follow GZ *'dzem* against CDNP *'jom* ("vanquish").
1551. This stanza uses an above-mentioned (note 618) famous episode in the ancient Indian myth of creation and reinterprets it from a Buddhist perspective. In this episode, the gods and the asuras used the nāga king Vāsuki as a churning rope around the churning rod of Mount Maṃdara.

Pulling Vāsuki's head and tail back and forth, the mountain rotated and thus churned the ocean of milk, which first produced a lethal poison that even the gods could not withstand, and later the nectar of immortality.

1552. I follow CDNP *rnal 'byor pa'i rtog pa'i gegs sel ba* against GZ *rnal 'byor pa'i rtogs pa'i gegs sel ba* ("Dispelling Obstacles to the Realization of Yogīs"). Though both versions make sense, given the general contents of stanzas 19–22 and the phrases "the obstacles of thoughts" and "the thoughts of mind that are hindrances" in the concluding stanza in particular, CDNP's version of the title seems more likely.
1553. I follow CDNP *mang* against GZ *ma* ("not").
1554. Mahoragas are large-bellied serpent demons living on the earth and below.
1555. I follow GZ CD *srung ma (b)sko* against NP *srungs ma sgo*.
1556. GZ CDNP *la* emended to *las*.
1557. Here and in the third line, I follow GZ CD *bsal* against NP *gsal* ("clear").
1558. I follow CDNP *rtog dang rtog* against GZ *rtog dang rtogs* ("thoughts and realizations").
1559. GZ *zhi* CDNP *zhig* ("be undone," "fall apart").
1560. I follow GZ CD *brnyes pa* against NP *mnyes pa* ("delight").
1561. PDMT, 27:520–23.
1562. I follow CDNP *'jig* against GZ *'jigs* ("afraid of").
1563. I follow CDNP *dkyer ba* against GZ *dgyer ba*.
1564. I could not locate this stanza in Kg or Tg.
1565. As the following will show, among the many meanings of Skt. *tantra* (Tib. *rgyud*), here the term refers to the five main types or sets of characteristics of persons who have different predominant afflictions.
1566. I follow GZ CD *brlang ba* against NP *blang ba*.
1567. NP add here *gzhan gyis phrogs* ("are carried away by others").
1568. Skt. *jīva*.
1569. This ubiquitous stanza (our text omits the first line) is generally attributed to the Buddha. However, it is not found in the Pāli canon, the *Udānavarga/Dhammapada*, or Kg; a few Tibetan texts attribute it to the lost *Abhidharmamahāyānasūtra*. The stanza is also incorporated without attribution in the *Jñānasārasamuccaya* (attributed to Āryadeva; stanza 31; D3851, fol. 27b.5) and in Śāntarakṣita's *Tattvasaṃgraha* (D4266, 130b.7–131a.1).
1570. GZ NP *dngos su sgrol ba* CD *yongs su sgrol ba*.
1571. GZ C *don rtags* D *dan rtags* ("clear signs") NP *ngan rtags* ("bad signs").
1572. NP omit *gnyid bsam gyis mi khyab pa dang* ("the inconceivable sleep").
1573. GZ *bla na med pa'i gdams pa* CDNP *bla ma'i gdams pa* ("the highest instructions," or, less likely, "the instructions of the guru").
1574. GZ *dug lngar 'dus mod kyi* CD *dug lnga 'dus mod kyi* ("no doubt include the five poisons") NP *dug lnga 'dus mos kyi*.
1575. These two lines appear in the *Āryamañjuśrīkarmacatuścakraguhyatantra* (H802, fol. 104a.6) but are more well-known as part of Āryadeva's famous *Catuḥśataka* 191 (D3846, fol. 9b.6):

Whoever is the seer of one entity
is declared to be the seer of all
What is the emptiness of one,
that is the emptiness of all

1576. GZ *dug med par bya'o* CDNP *dug med par byas so* ("have been rendered poison-free").
1577. I follow NP *sbyar bar bya la* against GZ CD *sbyar bar byas la.*
1578. I follow CDNP *bdag gi* against GZ *bdag gis.*
1579. I follow GZ CD *bdag gis* against NP *bdag gi.*
1580. I follow GZ CD *zhad* against NP *zhang.*
1581. GZ *gang zag kha cig la mchog tu ma gdams na* CD *gang zag gis gcig la mchog tu ma gdams na* NP *gang zag gi gcig la mchog tu ma gdis na.*
1582. The first three lines are found in the *Śrīcaturpīṭhamahāyoginītantrarāja* (H404, fol. 122a.3–4), while the remainder of this quote is unidentified.
1583. I follow GZ *gsal ba 'das nas* against CDNP *gsal ba'ang sa nas.*
1584. I follow GZ *srab* against CDNP *sa* ("earth").
1585. I could not locate these stanzas in the *Guhyasamājatantra* or anywhere else in Kg or Tg.
1586. This stanza is also unidentified.
1587. Ajātaśatru was the son of King Bimbisara, one of the patrons of the Buddha. He killed his father and was in turn killed by his son, being reborn in the hell Lohakumbhiyā.
1588. GZ NP *'bri* CD *spong* ("relinquish").
1589. I follow GZ *des pa* against CDNP *nges pa* ("certain").
1590. *Svapnanirdeśasūtra* (H48, fol. 365b.2–3; confirms GZ's readings).
1591. PDMT, 27:524–33.
1592. PDMT, 27:534–38.
1593. GZ *phyogs dus kun gyi* CD *phyogs bcu dus kun* ("ten directions and all times") NP *phyogs bcu dus gyi.*
1594. I follow CDNP *tshogs* against GZ *chogs.*
1595. I follow GZ *deng gi nyin zhag* against CD *deng gi nyin zhig* NP *deng gis nyin zhag.*
1596. I follow GZ *gnyen pos* against CDNP *gnyen por.*
1597. According to *Madhyāntavibhāga* V.8cd–10ab, these ten are (1) writing the letters of the dharma, (2) venerating it and those who proclaim it, (3) practicing generosity for both of these, (4) listening to the dharma, (5) reading it, (6) memorizing it, (7) explaining it to others, (8) reciting it, (9) reflecting on it, and (10) meditating on or familiarizing with it.
1598. PDMT, 27:539–41.
1599. I follow GZ NP *dag tu* against CD *rtag tu* ("constantly").
1600. I follow GZ NP *ldon* against CD *'don.*
1601. DPR: this refers to exaggerating the actual value of objects that belong to one in order to impress others.
1602. I follow GZ *sam* against CDNP *bsam* ("thinking").

1603. I follow GZ *bral* against CDNP *'brel*.
1604. I follow GZ *skyes pa* against DNP *skyes ngan* ("bad birth").
1605. GZ NP *brtun te* CD *brtan te* ("firmly").
1606. I follow GZ NP *yun thung* against CD *yun thun*.
1607. I follow GZ CD *dus 'gyur ba yis* against NP *dus su 'gyur ba'i*.
1608. Bhabhiti is a name in Hindi.
1609. GZ *bhe lo sha* CD *bha lo sha* NP *le lo sha*; another name.
1610. PDMT, 27:542–44.
1611. I follow GZ NP *dang po* against CD *dang po'i*.
1612. I follow NP *la* against GZ CD *pa*.
1613. I follow CDNP *de ltar* against GZ *de dag*.
1614. GZ CDNP *mi mthun phyogs* ("what is discordant") is emended to *gyi mthun phyogs*, because the following stanzas speak exclusively about the things that yogīs should do or have as the opposites of what is discordant with samādhi.
1615. GZ *yis* CDNP *yi* ("of").
1616. I follow GZ NP *gang bya ba'i* against CD *bya ba yi*.
1617. PDMT, 27:545–47.
1618. I follow GZ CD *rig* against NP *rigs*.
1619. Tib. Bsam yas lhun gyis grub pa. NP add "*It was translated by this paṇḍita himself and lotsāwa Śākya Lodrö.*"
1620. PDMT, 27:548–55.
1621. I follow GZ CD *rtogs* against NP *rtog*.
1622. Tib. *sbyangs* means both "purification" and "training," and "refinement" also conveys both meanings.
1623. NP omit "what is to be accomplished" (*bsgrub bya*).
1624. In the following, the text discusses each of the four points in each of the first three lines of stanza 2—what is to be contemplated, what is to be accomplished, and the supreme yogas, respectively—through four stanzas. That is, according to the first three lines of this stanza and the summaries in stanzas 19, 36, and 53, respectively, the four points to be contemplated are the precious human body (stanzas 3–6), impermanence (7–10), karma (11–14), and the shortcomings of saṃsāra (15–18); the four points to be accomplished are confidence in the proper objects (stanzas 20–23), loving-kindness and compassion for all beings (24–27), the prajñā of realizing dependent origination and emptiness (28–31), and vigor (32–35); and the four points of what is to be practiced as yoga are to supplicate and rely on the blessings of the deity and the guru (stanzas 37–40), to cultivate the superb ritual of deity, mantra, and samādhi as the display of wisdom (41–44), to cultivate uncontaminated nonthought, luminosity, and great bliss in meditative equipoise (45–48), and to dedicate all virtues (49–52).
1625. I follow CDNP *rtsig* against GZ *rtsis* ("calculation," "astrology").
1626. The traditional examples for the rarity of attaining a precious human body are that it is even more unlikely to obtain such a body than a turtle could stick its neck through a yoke that is tossed about on the vast ocean,

a pile of mustard seeds being balanced on the tip (or the eye) of a needle, and dried peas thrown at a smooth wall sticking to it.

1627. I follow GZ NP *lus can* against CD *las can*.
1628. I follow GZ *'dod pa'i / skyes bus* against CDNP *'dod pas / skyes bu'i*.
1629. I follow CDNP *gru bo* against GZ *gru pa* ("captain").
1630. I follow CD *yang ye* against GZ *yong yer* NP *yong yi*.
1631. Given the parallel line "AHO, what lacks support has become a support" in stanza 14 of text 192, I follow CDNP *rten med* against GZ *rtog med* ("what is without thought").
1632. I follow GZ *sol mal* against CDNP *so mal*.
1633. This mythological flower is said to bloom only every three thousand years.
1634. I follow CDNP *bzhi* against *gzhi* ("ground").
1635. GZ NP *dad pa* CD *dang ba* ("openness").
1636. GZ *dad pa* CDNP *dang ba* ("openness").
1637. I follow CDNP *rigs* against GZ *rig* ("awareness").
1638. The edible fruits of the rattan palm yield an astringent red resin that is used medicinally and as incense (also known as "dragon's blood").
1639. GZ *ngo mtshar che* CDNP *ngo mtshar phyir* ("Hence, since it is . . . and amazing").
1640. I follow CDNP *'di yi* against GZ *'di yis*.
1641. I follow GZ *dal ba* against CDNP *ngal ba* ("fatigued").
1642. I follow CDNP *bzhi* against *gzhi*.
1643. Tib. *rnam par gzhag pa* can render Skt. *vyavasthāpana* or *prakriyā*, among whose many meanings "to perform," "to persevere," "to engage," as well as "procedure," "ceremony," and "observance" appear to apply here.
1644. I follow GZ *bzhin* against CDNP *zhing*.
1645. I follow CDNP *'od gsal* against GZ *'di gsal*.
1646. I follow GZ *de bdag* against CDNP *de dag*.
1647. GZ *byang chub* CDNP *mngon chub*.
1648. I follow GZ NP *chos shes* against CD *chog shes* ("being content").
1649. I follow GZ *bskyod* against CDNP *bskyong* ("protected").
1650. I follow CDNP *bzhi* against *gzhi*.
1651. I follow GZ *rab gnag* against CDNP *rab gnas*.
1652. I follow GZ CD *gdengs* against DNP *gdangs*.
1653. NP add: "*It was translated by the paṇḍitas Jaganmi[tr]ānanda and Buddhaśrījñāna as well as lotsāwa Jampa Bal.*"
1654. PDMT, 27:556–62.
1655. GZ *gzhan mi gnas* CDNP *gzhan min gnas*. "The wrestler's jewel" refers to an ancient Indian story of a wrestling champion who wore a gem on his forehead. Once after a wrestling match, he couldn't see it and went searching for it everywhere and without respite. Finally, someone pointed out that he had a bump on his forehead, and it was discovered that the gem had slid into a cut on his forehead and had lodged itself in there. Thus, this is a metaphor for looking everywhere in vain on the outside while we already have what we search for.

1656. I follow GZ NP *grol ba* against CD *gol ba* ("go astray").
1657. GZ *rmongs pa* CD *phongs pa* NP *'phongs pa* ("the destitute").
1658. Given the parallel line "That which is without support is their support" in stanza 13 of text 191, I follow CDNP *rten gyur pa* against GZ *brten gyur pa.*
1659. I follow GZ *rten bral brten pa rnams kyi mchog* against CDNP *rten 'brel brtan pa rnams kyi mchog* ("Dependent origination is the supreme of what is immobile").
1660. I follow CDNP *rtag la bya ba* against GZ *brtag par bya ba.*
1661. GZ CD *rtags* CD *brtags* ("examinations").
1662. I follow GZ CD *kyi* against NP *kyis.*
1663. Except for the last line, this stanza corresponds to stanza 9 of text 196.
1664. I follow GZ NP *bdag* against CD *dag.*
1665. I follow GZ CD *nus* against N *nas* P *bzung.*
1666. GZ *kun gzhi'i* CDNP *kun gzhi'am* ("or").
1667. Stanzas 34–35 are virtually identical with stanzas 10–11 of text 196.
1668. GZ *gzhan gyi min* (probably should be *gzhan ni min*: "nor other") CDNP *bdag gis min* ("nor by a self"; probably should be *bdag gi min*: "nor mine").
1669. GZ *gang la yang* CDNP *gang la gang.*
1670. I follow GZ *gri* against CDNP *dri* ("smell").
1671. GZ *sgyu mas sgyu ma la / brgyabs ltar* CDNP *sgyu mas sgyu ma yi / rgyal ltar* ("like an illusory victory by an illusion").
1672. GZ *bsnad* CDNP *gnod.*
1673. GZ CD *sgra* NP *dgra* ("foes").
1674. I follow GZ CD *dgra* against NP *sgra.*
1675. I follow GZ CD *smyos pa* against NP *brnyos pa* ("seized").
1676. As mentioned before, it is possible that Niṣkalaṅka is an epithet of Jaganmitrānanda, since text 192 contains two stanzas (34–35) and a number of other lines that are identical to certain ones found in texts 191, 195, and 196.
1677. PDMT, 27:563–64.
1678. CD omit *rje* ("lord").
1679. PDMT, 27:565–66.
1680. Ajita ("the invincible") is an epithet of Maitreya.
1681. The three excellencies consist of the generation of bodhicitta as the preparation, nonreferentiality as the actual practice, and dedication as the conclusion.
1682. Tib. Yam 'gal.
1683. PDMT, 27:567–68.
1684. For the first two lines of this stanza, compare *Hevajratantra* I.9.19ab and stanza 2 of text 196. The first three lines are also found in stanza 2 of text 197. The last two lines correspond to the first two lines of stanza 3 of text 192.
1685. Tib. Gu lang gser khang ("The Golden House of Śiva"). Other sources refer to this place as a hermitage in the jungle.
1686. PDMT, 27:569–71.
1687. The Tibetan rather suggests "The Certain Path to Genuine Accomplishment."

1688. As mentioned before, this a form of Avalokiteśvara.
1689. For the last two lines of this stanza, compare *Hevajratantra* I.9.19ab, stanza 1 of text 195, and stanza 2 of text 197.
1690. I follow GZ CD *sbra* against NP *sgra* ("sound").
1691. Except for the third one, the lines of this stanza are shared with stanza 3 of text 197.
1692. Except for the last one, the lines of this stanza are shared with stanza 24 of text 192.
1693. Stanzas 10–11 are virtually identical with stanzas 34–35 of text 192.
1694. Given the three distinct points in the first three lines of this stanza, I follow CDNP *dran pa yin* against GZ *dran pa yis* ("through the mindfulness of letting . . .").
1695. This text 196 uses some of the exact same phrases and metaphors as texts 191, 192, 195, and 197. Moreover, its structure suggests that it may be a very abridged version of text 191. Hence, text 196 appears to be another work by Jaganmitrānanda.
1696. PDMT, 27:572–74.
1697. This stanza corresponds to stanza 1 of text 201.
1698. The last three lines of this stanza are shared with the first three lines of stanza 1 of text 195; the second and third lines also with the last two lines of stanza 2 of text 196; and the fourth line with the first line of stanza 3 of text 192.
1699. Except for the third one, the lines of this stanza are shared with verse 8 of text 196.
1700. This stanza corresponds to stanza 3 of text 201.
1701. GZ CDNP *de nyid* could also be read as "these very [appearances]."
1702. Tib. *bkra shis kyi tshong 'dus chen po mgur mo rin po che'i gling.*
1703. Tib. *Rgya 'bre lam lo dro gzhen.*
1704. PDMT, 27:578–80.
1705. This could also be read as "by virtue of the samaya of devotion and compassion."
1706. GZ *bzhi pa'o* CDNP *zhi ba'o* ("peace").
1707. Tib. *rol* can also mean "play" or "frolic."
1708. NP adds here *paṇḍi ta de nyid dang* ("this paṇḍita and").
1709. In accordance with the very similar text 136, GZ CNDP *phan pa med* ("no benefit") are emended to *phan pa nyid.*
1710. PDMT, 26:1579–80.
1711. This text is not found in Tg.
1712. This stanza is basically a summary (with a few additions) of the first three stanzas of the *Anāvilatantra*. Many of the following stanzas also contain lines that are identical or very similar to those in this tantra.
1713. In accordance with the parallel line in the *Anāvilatantra*, GZ *khyab byed* is understood as *khyab 'jug*. *Khyab 'jug* also renders Skt. *keśava, hari, govinda, sanātana, śārṅgapāṇi, aja, koka, haṃsa* (all epithets of Viṣṇu, but some are likewise epithets of Kṛṣṇa, Indra, Brahmā, or Śiva); it can also be an abbreviation for Vaiṣṇava (followers of Viṣṇu).

1714. Skt. *homa* refers to the Brahmanical fire offering of clarified butter and other substances to the gods, which is also performed in the Buddhist tantras in a nontheistic manner.
1715. "Consecration" (Skt. *pratiṣṭhā*, Tib. *rab gnas*) refers to consecrating sacred objects such as stūpas, statues, or paintings by invoking buddhas, bodhisattvas, or deities to remain in such objects and thus benefit the beings who come in contact with them.
1716. In the *sandhyābhāṣā* chapter of the *Hevajratantra* (II.3.56–61), *māṃsa* ("flesh" or "meat") is glossed as *bala* ("strength").
1717. It is not clear what "these seven sādhanas" (*sgrub thabs bdun po 'di*), with this text being the seventh, are. Tg and GZ contain only two texts translated by a Ratnaphala.
1718. PDMT, 25:523–26. For a detailed commentary on text 201 by Jamyang Kyentsé Wangpo, based mainly on Tropu Lotsāwa's now lost commentaries (abbreviated ZGND), see appendix.
1719. ZGND *E MA HO/ rang sems gdod nas ma skyes pa/* ("AHO! Your own mind that is primordially unborn").
1720. This stanza corresponds to stanza 1 of text 197.
1721. I follow CDNP and ZGND *bdag* against GZ *dag* ("dual").
1722. This stanza corresponds to stanza 5 of text 197.
1723. I follow ZGND *khrims btson* against GZ *khri btsun* CDNP *khri btson*.
1724. I follow ZGND *gcig pu'i grogs* against GZ CDNP *gcig pur grogs*.
1725. I follow GZ ZGND *na* against CDNP *nas*.
1726. I follow GZ CD ZGND *ma bcos* against N *ma bcod* P *ma gcod*.
1727. I follow CDNP ZGND *brag cha sgra* against GZ *brag cha'i sgra*.
1728. CDNP omit this and the next line.
1729. I follow GZ ZGND *yid kyi* against CDNP *yid kyis* ("by the mind").
1730. I follow CD *nas* NP ZGND *na* against GZ *dang*.
1731. I follow GZ CD ZGND *sbyin sreg* against NP *sbyin sred*.
1732. I follow ZGND *chu rlung* against GZ *chu klung* ("river") CDNP *chu lhung* ("plunging into the water").
1733. Tib. *sgra can 'dzin* usually renders Skt. Rāhula (a proper name). However, given the sequence of the preceding examples in connection with the fact that Rāhu is the demon in ancient Indian mythology who is held to occasionally swallow the sun or the moon, thus being the cause of solar and lunar eclipses, as well as the concordant comments in GZND that the expression here refers to "vāyus and mind uniting," it seems more likely that "being seized (*'dzin*) by Rāhu (*sgra can*)" is what is meant. Besides, it is hard to see how the name Rāhula would illustrate the uniting of vāyus and mind.
1734. I follow GZ CD *myang* against NP *sbyang*.
1735. GZ *aṃ ba ra par ta* CDNP *aṃ pa ra pa ra ta* ZGND *am bha ri . . . parpa ta*.
1736. PDMT, 25:527–31. The translation of the title follows the Tibetan. Usually, as a Buddhist text genre, Skt. *avadāna* refers to stories from the past that demonstrate the principle of karma by linking the actions of a particular person to the results of those actions in a later life.

1737. I follow GZ *brtan pa* against CDNP *bstan pa.*
1738. I follow GZ NP *g.yo ba* against CD *g.yon pa* ("left").
1739. GZ *ye shes sbyangs* CDNP *lnga yis sbyong* ("are purified by the five").
1740. I follow GZ NP *'di na* against CD*'di ni.*
1741. "Essence of the Ocean" is also a particular samādhi of bodhisattvas.
1742. This stanza refers to the practice of caṇḍālī. "Mount Meru's life-pillar" is an expression for the avadhūtī.
1743. GZ *sems mthong ba ni ma mchis* CDNP *sems mthong mthong ba ma mchis* ("seeing the mind is not seeing").
1744. I follow CDNP *'jigs pa* against GZ *'jig pa* ("destruction" or "perishing").
1745. I follow GZ *tsam snyam de la'ang* against CD *tsam de la yang* NP *tsam snyam de'ang.*
1746. I follow CDNP *las ni* against GZ *las kyis.*
1747. I follow GZ *ngang pa* against CD *dang po* NP *dang ba.*
1748. GZ *bdag go rtogs* CDP *bdag gis rtogs* ("I realize") N *dag gis rtogs.*
1749. I follow GZ NP *khong khro* against CD *khro khro.*
1750. I follow GZ CD *gtan bcom* against N *brtan bcos* P *brtan bcom.*
1751. Text 202 concludes vol. 5 of GZ3.
1752. This is a translation of the section of the word-by-word commentary on text 201 in 'Jam dbyangs mkhyen brtse dbang po 1999b.
1753. This part of the text is not translated here, since it basically consists of an abbreviated version of Mitrayogī's hagiography as found in BA (1030–43); for a brief summary, see the final note on text 191 in NG.
1754. The details of all these preliminaries are explained in 'Jam dbyangs mkhyen brtse dbang phyug 1999 (565–74); specifically, "the fifty syllables" refers to a long mantra that is mentioned there (572).
1755. ZGND *rtogs pa* emended to *rtogs pa.*
1756. Following the phrasing of this quote in the collected works of the twenty-seventh Sakya Trizin, Ngawang Kunga Sönam (Tib. Ngag dbang kun dga' bsod nams; 1597–1659/60; https://www.tbrc.org/#!rid=W29307), who attributes it to a text called "Self-Arising Lucidity" (Tib. Rang byung gsal ba), GZND *mnyam par* is emended to *mngon par.*
1757. Numbers in [ ] indicate the numbers of the stanzas of text 201 on which this commentary comments.
1758. ZGND only says "second" but not what the content of this second point here is, so the numbering and the meaning of this heading are not really clear. Thus I inserted what seems to make most sense in the context of the overall outline.
1759. ZGND *phyed las* emended to *byed las.*
1760. Following 'Jam dbyangs mkhyen brtse dbang phyug 1999 (579; see below), ZGND *rdzing* ("pond") is emended to *gzings.*
1761. Tib. *sdang ba* ("hatred") emended to *snang ba.*
1762. Tib. *yi ge* ("letter") emended to *ye shes.*
1763. ZGND *dri na'ang* emended to *dri ma'ang.*
1764. Tib. *rgyu yan* emended to *rgya yan.*
1765. Tib *lta* emended to *lha.*

1766. Tib. *jo bo* can render the Sanskrit terms *ārya, svāmī, prabhu, vibhu, prabhaviṣṇu, bhagavān,* and *vallabha.*
1767. Tib. Spyan ras gzigs for Avalokiteśvara literally means "the one who beholds (*gzigs*) with his eyes (*spyan ras*)."
1768. As confirmed by Bu ston rin chen grub 1999a, this refers to the chapter of Dharmodgata in the *Prajñāpāramitāsūtra in Eight Thousand Lines* (H11, fols. 445b.2–446b.1), which mentions twenty-five samādhis by name (beginning with the samādhi "the equality of all phenomena") and refers to a further six million samādhis (see Conze 1973, 297–98). However, Butön matches Dharmodgata's twenty-five sentences that immediately precede and correspond to the list of samādhis in that chapter with the twenty-five stanzas of text 201: (1) "Since all phenomena are equality, prajñāpāramitā is equality," (2) "Since all phenomena are solitary, prajñāpāramitā is solitary," (3) "Since all phenomena are immovable, prajñāpāramitā is immovable," (4) "Since all phenomena are without conceit, prajñāpāramitā is without conceit," (5) "Since all phenomena are without haughtiness, prajñāpāramitā is without haughtiness," (6) "Since all phenomena are of the same taste, prajñāpāramitā is of the same taste," (7) "Since all phenomena are boundless, prajñāpāramitā is boundless," (8) "Since all phenomena are without arising, prajñāpāramitā is without arising," (9) "Since all phenomena are without ceasing, prajñāpāramitā is without ceasing," (10) "As space is boundless, prajñāpāramitā is boundless," (11) "As the ocean is boundless, prajñāpāramitā is boundless," (12) "As Mount Meru is variegated, prajñāpāramitā is variegated," (13) "Since space is without thoughts, prajñāpāramitā is without thoughts," (14) "Since form is boundless, prajñāpāramitā is boundless," (15) "Likewise, since feelings, discriminations, formations, and consciousness are boundless, prajñāpāramitā is boundless," (16) "Since the element of earth is boundless, prajñāpāramitā is boundless," (17) "Likewise, since the element of water, the element of fire, and the element of wind are boundless, prajñāpāramitā is boundless," (18) "Since the element of consciousness is boundless, prajñāpāramitā is boundless," (19) "Since the element of space is boundless, prajñāpāramitā is boundless," (20) "Since the vajra-like dharma is equality, prajñāpāramitā is equality," (21) "Since all phenomena are unique, prajñāpāramitā is unique," (22) "Since all phenomena are unobservable, prajñāpāramitā is unobservable," (23) "Since all phenomena are indestructible equality, prajñāpāramitā is indestructible equality," (24) "Since all phenomena are without doing, prajñāpāramitā is without doing," and (25) "Since all phenomena are inconceivable, prajñāpāramitā is inconceivable." Note that similar lists are found in the prajñāpāramitāsūtras in one hundred thousand lines (H9, fols. 517b.6–518b.4), twenty-five thousand lines (H10, fols. 532b.7–533b.7), eighteen thousand lines (H12, fols. 313a.6–314a.5), ten thousand lines (H13, fols. 184b.3ff.), and the *Kauśikaprajñāpāramitā* (H23, fols. 253b.3–254b.1). In addition, Bu ston rin chen grub 1999b matches most lines of text 201 with quotes from the tantras.

1769. Tib. Gnubs nam mkha'i snying po (eighth century), one of the twenty-five main disciples of Padmasambhava.
1770. ZGND is corrupt here: *am bha ri zhes grags pa'i sa'i mthong/ mthong / parpa ta'i bsil khang*.
1771. Tib. 'Jam dbyangs bla ma dgyes pa'i 'bangs mkhyen brtse dbang po.
1772. The following is a partial translation of 'Jam dbyangs mkhyen brtse dbang phyug 1999 (565 and 574–84). The five stanzas 12–16 of text 201 are identified summarily in an interlinear gloss in the present text and in full in 'Jam dbyangs mkhyen brtse dbang po 1999c, 595. The present work first explains the above-mentioned common, uncommon, and special preliminaries in detail (not translated here; also explained in 'Jam dbyangs mkhyen brtse dbang po 1999c, 590–94), and then describes the main practice primarily through the five points of letting mind as such take a rest.
1773. II.4.69ab. The third and fourth lines of this stanza, which are referred to below in the text, are:

Due to the removal of these, no doubt,
beings are definitely buddhas.

1774. According to the outline of this text in 'Jam dbyangs mkhyen brtse dbang po 1999c (595–96), everything in this section on the main practice up through here consists of cutting through superimpositions onto the actuality with which to familiarize, doing so through study and reflection by way of the triad of scriptures, reasonings, and pith instructions. What follows consists of making this actuality that has been analyzed a living experience by way of meditation, which has three parts: (1) coming to a resolve through the view with prajñā, (2) making this a living experience through cultivating the means, and (3) eliminating the obstacles to these two.
1775. This part of the outline is discussed below as "second" after point 2.2. However, as just mentioned, 'Jam dbyangs mkhyen brtse dbang po 1999c first lists this part as the third main point after "2.1. Coming to a resolve through the view with prajñā" and "2.2. Practicing through the cultivation of the means," but later, just as this text here, identifies it as "second" after point 2.2. Thus, by following the actual order of the text, I treat "Eliminating the obstacles to that" below as point 2.3., though that does not accord with the outline here.
1776. The distance between the tips of the extended thumb and middle finger.
1777. ZGND *hams len* emended to *nyams len*.
1778. ZGND *yul* emended to *g.yul*.
1779. ZGND *ma rtogs* emended to *ma gtogs*.
1780. ZGND *rgya lan* emended to *rgya lam*.
1781. Tib. Dpal mo dpal thang; also known as "the plain of plains"; the place where Padmasambhava is said to have subdued the twelve Tenma goddesses (local protectresses of Tibet).

1782. ZGND *ngon* emended to *don*.

1783. The Tsarpa (Tib. Tshar pa) school is one of two subschools that branched off from the main Sakya school of the Khön (Tib. 'Khon) lineage, the other one being the Ngorpa (Tib. Ngor pa) school. The author of this text, Jamyang Kyentsé Wangchug (1524–68), the fourteenth grand abbot of Shalu Monastery, refers here to his guru, Tsarchen Losal Gyamtso (Tib. Tshar chen blo gsal rgya mtsho; 1502–66), who was the founder of the Tsarpa lineage.

1784. This is a translation of Mitrayogī 1999.

1785. The inserted outline of this text stems from the practice instructions in 'Jam dbyangs mkhyen brtse dbang po 1999d (abbr. GCST), and the colophon seems to be composed by this author as well.

1786. GCST does not comment on the first stanza per se but explains the second one as follows. One gives rise to intense renunciation and weariness of saṃsāra, takes refuge, and generates bodhicitta in front of Avalokiteśvara and his retinue. Visualizing him and his retinue on the crown of one's head in the function of the guru and in one's heart in the function of the deity, one supplicates them. Thus, nectar flows down from the guru, which purifies all diseases, evil spirits, wrongdoings, and obscurations and bestows all blessings and siddhis. Then, one visualizes oneself as Avalokiteśvara and recites his mantra OṂ MAṆI PADME HŪṂ. Finally, the guru, the deity, their retinues, and the entire world with its inhabitants successively dissolve into light, which dissolves into oneself. Oneself as Avalokiteśvara also dissolves into light and becomes emptiness. Then, without being interrupted by any other thoughts, as much as one can, one rests in meditative equipoise within the state of emptiness free of discursiveness that is the unity of calm abiding and superior insight. When one rises from that, one once again visualizes oneself as Avalokiteśvara, understanding that the entire world and its inhabitants are like illusions. Thus, with great compassion, one dedicates one's practice to all beings who do not realize this. During the periods between one's sessions, one should train in never being separated from the view that all appearances, sounds, and awareness are the display of Avalokiteśvara's three secrets.

1787. GCST instructs to visualize a field of merit as in the case of guru yoga in front, mentally offering one's body to the guru. Through light rays radiating from the guru's heart, one's body becomes youthful and resplendent. Offering goddesses with hooked knifes from the guru's heart chop up one's body, arranging it in a skull cup. By virtue of the guru reciting OM ĀḤ HŪṂ three times, one's body becomes boundless wisdom nectar, which is offered to all gurus, buddhas, bodhisattvas, ḍākas, ḍākinīs, and protectors. Thus, one gathers the two accumulations and purifies the two obscurations. The remainder of the nectar is given to all sentient beings, turning into whatever they desire. Through consuming it, their bodies and minds are satisfied by uncontaminated bliss. While visualizing this, one keeps reciting OṂ ĀḤ HŪṂ. Finally, one rests in the state of not focusing on anything. Then, since it is uncertain who is a friend or a foe and since one's body and possessions lack any pith, one severs all ties to any of them. On top of Mount Meru, one visualizes the realm of Tuṣita with Maitreya in its center. At the level of one's heart cakra in the avadhūtī in the center of one's own empty body, Avalokiteśvara resides as the inseparability of one's vāyus and mind. By supplicating Maitreya to transfer one's consciousness to Tuṣita, a yellow tube of light emerges from his heart and pierces the crown of one's head. Inside it is a hook of light that descends through the avadhūtī and ties one's own mind at the heart cakra to Avalokiteśvara's tuft. With the three notions of the tube of light being the path, one's own mind being the one who travels on it, and one's mind being transferred into Maitreya's heart, one supplicates and pulls up one's mind in its entirety. Once one's mind reaches Maitreya's heart, one thinks briefly that it has become inseparably fused with his awakened mind. Then, one lets it sink down to its own place at the heart. In this way, one trains repeatedly. When ending the session, one visualizes that the tube of light is cut completely and the crown of one's head is closed firmly. When the time comes to practice this for real at the time of dying, one does not visualize that one's mind sinks back down but rests in meditative equipoise in the state of it being fused inseparably with Maitreya's awakened mind.

1788. To practice this, GCST says, at the beginning, one thinks that all daytime appearances are dreams. Having trained well in this, one will recognize dreams to be dreams. Then, one fervently thinks that all daytime appearances are the intermediate state. Once one has become familiar with that, the entire outer world transforms into a pure realm and all beings in it into Avalokiteśvara's body: appearing but lacking any nature of their own, they resemble water-moons or rainbows. Thus, any clinging to ordinary appearances is forcefully relinquished. In particular, in the intermediate state, thoughts of attachment and aversion toward one's parents function as obstacles to obtaining a good rebirth. Therefore, as the remedy for attachment, by cutting through the root of its arising, abiding, and ceasing, it is sealed as bliss-emptiness. As the remedy for hatred, by rousing the great compassion of recollecting that all beings have been our parents, one wishes that, by all means, one will seize a saṃsāric existence as one wishes, attain a precious human body throughout all lifetimes, practice properly by virtue of being cared for by authentic spiritual friends who teach this path, and thus attain the state of unity in a single lifetime. One also aspires that one may be able to actually do this and supplicates the gurus and the three jewels to support one to attain that ability.

1789. Following GCST, *dran pa ro som* is emended to *dran pas ro snyoms*.

1790. According to GCST, identifying whichever thoughts may arise at all times and in all situations means to understand that they are without reality, just like space. This is the essential point of the view. Relinquishing all flaws such as agitation and dullness and resting one-pointedly in meditative equipoise within that state is the essential point of meditation. The equal taste of suffering and happiness through being mindful during the aftermath of meditative equipoise that all appearances are like dreams and illusions is the essential point of conduct. As for needing to make practicing like this the most important thing, this is the profound instruction of the great siddha Mitrayogī—Avalokiteśvara appearing in human form—whose life story is adorned by twenty amazing events. Since it is the complete and unerring path to accomplishing buddhahood, one should extract the essence of the precious human body as much as one can.

1791. According to 'Jam dbyangs mkhyen brtse dbang po 1999d (609), this stanza was transmitted by Mitrayogī but is an experiential instruction spoken by Avalokiteśvara himself.

Selected Bibliography

Indic Works

Abhayadatta. **Dohāvṛttisahitacaturaśītisiddhāvadāna*. (*Grub thob brgyad cu rtsa bzhi'i rtogs brjod do ha 'grel pa dang bcas pa*). P5092. N3874.

Bhitakarma. *Mudrācaturaṭīkāratnahṛdaya*. (*Phyag rgya bzhi'i rgya cher 'grel pa rin po che'i snying po*). P3104. D2259.

Kangyur (*bka' 'gyur dpe bsdur ma*). 2006–2009. Beijing: Krung go'i bod rig pa'i dpe skrun khang [China Tibetology Publishing House].

Maitrīpa. *Advayavajrasaṃgraha*. Sanskrit editions. Edited by H. Shastri. Baroda: Oriental Institute, 1927. Also edited by the Study Group of Sacred Tantric Texts (Mikkyō-seiten kenkyūkai), "The Results of a Joint Study on the Buddhist Tantric Texts: *Advayavajrasaṃgraha*—New Critical Edition with Japanese Translation," *Annual of the Institute for Comprehensive Studies of Buddhism Taisho University*, Institute for Comprehensive Studies of Buddhism Taisho University, Tokyo, 1988–1991: 10: 234–178; 11: 259–200; 12: 316–282; 13: 291–42.

Mitrayogī. 1999. *Grub chen mi tra dzo kis mdzad pa'i snying po don gsum gyi man ngag gi rtsa ba rdo rje'i tshig rkang*. In *Gdams ngag rin po che'i mdzod*, 16: 605–7. Delhi: Shechen Publications.

Śrīsena. **Aśītisiddhābhisamaya*. (*Grub thob brgyad cu'i mngon par rtogs pa*). D4317.

Tengyur (*bstan 'gyur dpe bsdur ma*). 1994–2008. Beijing: Krung go'i bod rig pa'i dpe skrun khang.

Tibetan Works

Bkra shis chos 'phel. 2009. *Gnas lugs phyag rgya chen po'i rgya gzhung glegs bam gsum yi ge'i 'byung gnas su ji ltar bkod pa'i dkar chag bzhugs byang mdor bsdus pa sgrub brgyud grub pa'i rna rgyan*. In *Nges don phyag chen rgya gzhung dang bod gzhung*, 1: 1–98. Chengdu, China: Si khron mi rigs dpe skrun khang.

Bu ston rin chen grub. 1999a. *Phyag rgya chen po sems nyid ngal bso'i rtsa ba mdo'i lung dang sbyar ba*. In *Gdams ngag rin po che'i mdzod*, 16: 553–58. Delhi: Shechen Publications.

———. 1999b. *Phyag rgya chen po sems nyid ngal bso'i rtsa ba rgyud kyi lung dang sbyar ba*. In *Gdams ngag rin po che'i mdzod*, 16: 558–65.

'Gos lo tsā ba gzhon nu dpal. 1996 [1949]. *The Blue Annals*. Translated by G. N. Roerich. Delhi: Motilal Banarsidass.

'Jam dbyangs mkhyen brtse dbang po. 1999a. *Phyag rgya chen po tshig bsdus kyi man ngag rgyud kyi lung dang sbyar ba gtso bor bton pa'i 'grel chung rtogs par sla ba*. In *Gdams ngag rin po che'i mdzod*, 7: 49–62. Delhi: Shechen Publications.

———. 1999b. *'Phags pa spyan ras gzigs kyis grub chen mi tra dzo ki la gsungs pa'i phyag rgya chen po sems nyid ngal gso'i gzhung 'grel snying po bsdus pa*. In *Gdams ngag rin po che'i mdzod*, 16: 525–52.

———. 1999c. *Phyag rgya chen po sems nyid ngal gso'i khrid kyi 'chad thabs bla ma'i zhal lung bdud rtsi'i snang ba*. In *Gdams ngag rin po che'i mdzod*, 16: 585–99.

———. 1999d. *'Phags mchog thugs rje chen po'i dmar khrid snying po don gsum gyi nyams len mdor bsdus pa grub pa mchog gi shing rta*. In *Gdams ngag rin po che'i mdzod*, 16: 609–16.

'Jam dbyangs mkhyen brtse dbang phyug. 1999. *Sems nyid ngal gso'i khrid kyi zin bris*. In *Gdams ngag rin po che'i mdzod*, 16: 565–84. Delhi: Shechen Publications.

Karma phrin las pa phyogs las rnam rgyal. 2009. *Do ha skor gsum gyi tshig don gyi rnam bshad sems kyi rnam thar gsal bar ston pa'i me long / btsun mo do ha'i ṭī ka 'bring po sems kyi rnam thar ston pa'i me long / rgyal po do ha'i ṭī ka 'bring po sems kyi rnam thar ston pa'i me long*. Sarnath, India: Vajra Vidya Institute Library.

Khro ru klu sgrub rgya mtsho, ed. 2009. *Phyag rgya chen po'i rgya gzhung*.

In *Nges don phyag chen rgya gzhung dang bod gzhung*. 6 vols. Chengdu, China: Si khron mi rigs dpe skrun khang. (W1KG12589).

Krang dbyi sun, et al. 1985. *Bod rgya tshig mdzod chen mo*. 2 vols. Beijing: Mi rigs dpe skrun khang.

Kun dga' grol mchog. 1982. *Nag po spyod pa'i rtogs pa brjod pa'i yal 'dab*. In *Kun dga' grol mchog blo gsal rgya mtsho'i gsung 'bum*, 1:49–127. New Delhi. Tibet House Publishers.

La dvags khrid dpon 'khrul zhig padma chos rgyal, ed. 1978–85. *Do ha mdzod brgyad ces bya ba phyag rgya chen po'i man ngag gsal bar ston pa'i gzhung*. In *Dkar snying gi skyes chen du ma'i phyag rdzogs kyi gdams ngag gnad bsdus nyer mkho rin po che'i gter mdzod rtsibs ri'i par ma*, 4: 1–47. Darjeeling: Kargyu sungrab nyamso khang.

Nor brang o rgyan. 2008. *Chos rnam kun btus*. 3 vols. Beijing: Krung go'i bod rig pa dpe skrun khang.

Padma dkar po. 2005. *Phyag rgya chen po man ngag gi bshad sbyar rgyal ba'i gan mdzod*. Sarnath, India: Vajra Vidya Institute Library.

Phun tshogs rgyal mtshan, ed. n.d. *Phyag rgya chen po'i rgya gzhung*. 3 vols. Dpal spungs block print. (W3CN636).

Tāranātha. 2008. *Kahna pa'i do ha thor bu rnams kyi 'grel pa ngo mtshar snang ba. In Jo nang rje btsun tā ra nā tha'i gsung 'bum dpe bsdur ma*, 19:166–219. Beijing: Krung go'i bod rig pa dpe skrun khang.

English Works

Apple, James B. 2018. *Jewels of the Middle Way: The Madhyamaka Legacy of Atiśa and His Early Tibetan Followers*. Somerville, MA: Wisdom Publications.

Bareau, André. 2013. *The Buddhist Schools of the Small Vehicle*. Translated from the French by Sara Boin-Webb. Edited by Andrew Skilton. Honolulu: University of Hawai'i Press.

Basu, Anath Nath. 1927. "Tattvasvabhāvadṛṣṭigītikā Dohā: An Old Bengali Dohā and Its Tibetan Version." *Indian Historical Quarterly* 3.4: 676–82.

Beer, Robert. 1999. *The Encyclopedia of Tibetan Symbols and Motifs*. Boston: Shambhala Publications.

Bharati, Agehananda. 1965. *The Tantric Tradition*. London: Rider & Company.

Bhattacharyya, Narendra Nath. 1991. *The Geographical Dictionary: Ancient and Early Medieval India*. New Delhi: Munshiram Manoharlal Publishers.

Brunnhölzl, Karl. 2004. *The Center of the Sunlight Sky*. Ithaca, NY: Snow Lion Publications.

———. 2007. *Straight from the Heart*. Ithaca, NY: Snow Lion Publications.

———. 2010. *Gone Beyond*, vol. 1, *The Prajnaparamita Sutras, The Ornament of Clear Realization, and Its Commentaries in the Tibetan Kagyu Tradition*. Ithaca, NY: Snow Lion Publications.

———. 2011. *Gone Beyond*, vol. 2, *The Prajnaparamita Sutras, The Ornament of Clear Realization, and Its Commentaries in the Tibetan Kagyu Tradition*. Ithaca, NY: Snow Lion Publications.

Butön Rinchen Drup. 2013. *Butön's History of Buddhism in India and Its Spread to Tibet*. Translated by Lisa Stein and Ngawang Zangpo. Boston: Snow Lion Publications.

Callahan, Elizabeth, trans. 2014. *The Profound Inner Principles*. Ithaca, NY: Snow Lion Publications.

Conze, Edward, trans. 1973. *The Perfection of Wisdom in Eight Thousand Lines & Its Verse Summary*. Bolinas, CA: Four Seasons Foundation.

Dasgupta, Shashibhusan. 1946. *Obscure Religious Cults*. Calcutta: Calcutta University Press.

Davidson, Ronald. 1991. "Reflections on the Maheśvara Subjugation Myth: Indic Materials, Sa-skya-pa Apologetics, and the Birth of Heruka." *Journal of the International Association of Buddhist Studies* 14.2: 197–235.

———. 2002a. "Reframing *Sahaja*: Genre, Representation, Ritual and Lineage." *Journal of Indian Philosophy* 30.1: 45–83.

———. 2002b. *Indian Esoteric Buddhism: A Social History of the Tantric Movement*. New York: Columbia University Press.

Densmore, Frances. 2012. *How Indians Use Wild Plants for Food, Medicine, & Crafts*. Mineola, NY: Dover Publications.

Dowman, Keith. 1985. *Masters of Mahamudra: Songs and Histories of the Eighty-Four Buddhist Siddhas*. Albany: State University of New York Press.

———. 1989. *Masters of Enchantment: The Lives and Legends of the Mahasiddhas*. London: Arkana.

Edgerton, Franklin. 1953. *Buddhist Hybrid Sanskrit Grammar and Dictionary*. 2 vols. New Haven, CT: Yale University Press.

Frauwallner, Erich. 1956. *Geschichte der indischen Philosophie*. 2 vols. Salzburg: Otto Müller Verlag.

Gray, David B. 2001. "On Supreme Bliss. A Study of the History and Interpretation of the *Cakrasaṃvara Tantra*." PhD diss., Columbia University.

———. 2007. *The Cakrasaṃvaratantra (The Discourse of Śrī Heruka): Śrīherukābhidhāna. A Study and Annotated Translation*. Treasury of the Buddhist Sciences Series. New York: American Institute of Buddhist Studies, Columbia University.

———. 2016. "The Purification of Heruka: On the Transmission of a Controversial Buddhist Tradition to Tibet." In *Tantric Tradition in Transmission and Translation*, edited by David B. Gray and Ryan Richard Overbey, 230–56. New York: Oxford University Press.

Gyatso, Desi Sangyé. 2010. *Mirror of Beryl: A Historical Introduction to Tibetan Medicine*. Translated by Gavin Kilty. Boston: Wisdom Publications.

Hiriyanna, Mysore. 1973 [1932]. *Outlines of Indian Philosophy*. Bombay: George Allen & Unwin.

Hopkins, Jeffrey. 1983. *Meditation on Emptiness*. Boston: Wisdom Publications.

Isaacson, Harunaga, and Francesco Sferra, eds. (with contributions by Klaus-Dieter Mathes and Marco Passavanti). 2014. *The "Sekanirdeśa" of Maitreyanātha (Advayavajra) with the "Sekanirdeśapañjikā" of Rāmapāla: Critical Edition of the Sanskrit and Tibetan Texts with English Translation and Reproductions of the MSS*. Manuscripta Buddhica 2. Naples: Università degli Studi di Napoli "L'Orientale" and Asien-Afrika Institut, Universtität Hamburg.

Jackson, Roger R., trans. 2004. *Tantric Treasures: Three Collections of Mystical Verse from Buddhist India*. Oxford, NY: Oxford University Press.

———. 2008. "The Indian Mahāmudrā 'Canon(s)': A Preliminary Sketch." *IIJBS* 9: 151–84.

———. 2009. "Two *Bka' 'gyur* Works in Mahāmudrā Canons: The *Ārya-ātajñāna-nāma-mahāyāna-sūtra* and the *Anāvila-tantra-rāja*." *JIATS* 5. http://www.thlib.org?tid=T5706.

Kapstein, Matthew. 2000. "King Kuñji's Banquet." In *Tantra in Practice*, edited by David G. White, 52–71. Princeton, NJ: Princeton University Press.

Kongtrul Jamgon, comp. 2003. *Timeless Rapture: Inspired Verse of the Shangpa Masters*. Translated and introduced by Ngawang Zangpo. Ithaca, NY: Snow Lion Publications.

Kongtrul Lodrö Tayé, Jamgön. 2005. *The Treasury of Knowledge: Book Six, Part Four: Systems of Buddhist Tantra*. Translated by the Kalu Rinpoché Translation Group (Elio Guarisco and Ingrid McLeod). Ithaca, NY: Snow Lion Publications.

———. 2008. *The Treasury of Knowledge: Book Eight, Part Three: The Elements of Tantric Practice*. Translated by the Kalu Rinpoché Translation Group (Elio Guarisco and Ingrid McLeod). Ithaca, NY: Snow Lion Publications.

———. 2011. *The Treasury of Knowledge: Book Nine and Ten: Journey and Goal*. Translated by the Kalu Rinpoché Translation Group (Richard Barron). Ithaca, NY: Snow Lion Publications.

Kvaerne, Per. 2010 [1977]. *An Anthology of Buddhist Tantric Songs: A Study of the Caryāgīti*. Bangkok: Orchid Press.

Lindtner, Christian, trans. 2003. *A Garland of Light: Kambala's Ālokamālā*. Fremont, CA: Asian Humanities Press.

Lopez, S. Donald Jr. 2109. *Seeing the Sacred in Saṃsāra: An Illustrated Guide to the Eighty-Four Mahāsiddhas*. Boulder, CO: Shambhala Publications.

Loseries, Andrea. 2015. "Virūpa's *Karmacaṇḍalikā Dohākoṣagīti*: A Translation from the Tibetan with an Analysis and Commentary Based on the Hevajra Tantra." In *Sahaja: The Role of Dohā & Caryāgīti in the Cultural Indo-Tibetan Interface*, edited by Andrea Loseries, 53–62. Delhi: Buddhist World Press.

Mallinson, James. 2018. "Yoga and Sex: What Is the Purpose of *Vajrolīmudrā*?" In *Yoga in Transformation: Historical and Contemporary Perspectives*, edited by Karl Baier, Philipp A. Maas, and Karin Preisendanz, 181–222. Vienna: Vienna University Press.

Mathes, Klaus-Dieter. 2008. "The Succession of the Four Seals (*Caturmudrānvaya*)." *Tantric Studies*. Hamburg: Centre for Tantric Studies, University of Hamburg.

———. 2011. "The Collection of 'Indian Mahāmudrā Works' (Tib. *phyag chen rgya gzhung*) Compiled by the Seventh Karma pa Chos grags rgya mtsho." In *Mahāmudrā and the Bka' brgyud Tradition*, edited by Roger R. Jackson and Matthew T. Kapstein, 89–127. *PIATS 2006: Tibetan Studies: Proceedings of the Eleventh Seminar of the International Association for Tibetan Studies, Königswinter 2006*. Germany: International Institute for Tibetan and Buddhist Studies GmbH.

———. 2015. *A Fine Blend of Mahāmudrā and Madhyamaka—Maitrīpa's Collection of Texts on Becoming Mentally Disengaged (Amanasikāra)*. Vienna: Verlag der Österreichischen Akademie der Wissenschaften.

Miller, Roy Andrew. 1966. "Buddhist Hybrid Sanskrit *Āli, Kāli* as Grammatical Terms in Tibet." *Harvard Journal of Asiatic Studies* 26: 125–47.

Robinson, James Burnell. 1979. *Buddha's Lions: The Lives of the Eighty-Four Siddhas*. Berkeley: Dharma Publishing.

Schaeffer, Kurtis Rice. 2005. *Dreaming the Great Brahmin*. Oxford: Oxford University Press.

———. 2007. "Crystal Orbs and Arcane Treasures: Tibetan Anthologies of Buddhist Tantric Songs from the Tradition of Pha Dam pa sangs rgyas." *Acta Orientalia* 68: 5–73.

Schroeder, Ulrich von. 2006. *Empowered Masters: Tibetan Wall Paintings of Mahasiddhas at Gyantse*. Chicago: Serindia Publications.

Shaw, Miranda. 1994. *Passionate Enlightenment: Women in Tantric Buddhism*. Princeton, NJ: Princeton University Press.

Stenzel, Julia. 2015. "The Four Joys in the Teaching of Nāropa and Maitrīpa." *Indian International Journal of Buddhist Studies* 16: 193–214.

Sugiki, Tsunehiko. 2009. "The Structure and Traditions of the Systems of Holy Sites in Buddhist Saṃvara Cycle and Its Related Scriptural Cycles in Early Medieval South Asia—The Geography of Esoteric Buddhism in the Eyes of the Compilers of the Scriptures." In *Genesis and Development of Tantrism*, edited by Shingo Einoo, 515–62. Institute of Oriental Culture Special Series 23. Tokyo: University of Tokyo, Institute of Oriental Culture.

Tanaka, Kimiaki. 2013. *Mitrayogin's 108 Maṇḍalas: An Image Database*. Kathmandu: Vajra Publications.

Templeman, David, trans. 1989. *Tāranātha's Life of Kṛṣṇācārya/Kāṇha*. Dharamsala, India: Library of Tibetan Works and Archives.

Torricelli, Fabrizio. 2018. *Tilopā: A Buddhist Yogin of the Tenth Century*. Dharamsala, India: Library of Tibetan Works and Archives.

Tsongkhapa. 2013. *A Lamp of Illuminating the Five Stages*. Translated by Gavin Kilty. Boston: Wisdom Publications.

Walshe, Maurice, trans. 1987. *The Long Discourses of the Buddha*. Boston: Wisdom Publications.

Wedemeyer, Christian K. 2007. *Āryadeva's Lamp That Integrates the Practices (Caryāmelāpakapradīpa): The Gradual Path of Vajrayāna Buddhism According to the Esoteric Community Noble Tradition*. Treasury of the Buddhist Sciences Series. New York: American Institute of Buddhist Studies, Columbia University.

———. 2011. "Locating Tantric Antinomianism: An Essay toward an Intellectual History of the 'Practices/Practice Observance' (*caryā/caryāvrata*)." *Journal of the International Association of Buddhist Studies* 34.1–2: 349–420.

———. 2013. *Making Sense of Tantric Buddhism: History, Semiology, and Transgression in the Indian Traditions*. New York: Columbia University Press.

White, David Gordon. 1996. *The Alchemical Body: Siddha Traditions in Medieval India*. Chicago: The University of Chicago Press.

———, ed. 2003. *Kiss of the Yogini: "Tantric Sex" in Its South Asian Contexts*. Chicago: The University of Chicago Press.

Willson, Martin, and Martin Brauen, eds. 2000. *Deities of Tibetan Buddhism: The Zürich Paintings of the Icons Worthwhile to See: Bris sku mthoṅ ba don ldan*. Translated by Martin Willson. Boston: Wisdom Publications.

Zangpo, Ngawang, trans., introd., and ed. 2003. *Timeless Rapture*. Ithaca, NY: Snow Lion Publications.

About the Translator

Karl Brunnhölzl, MD, PhD, was originally trained as a physician. He received his systematic training in Tibetan language and Buddhist philosophy and practice at the Marpa Institute for Translators, founded by Khenpo Tsultrim Gyamtso Rinpoche, as well as the Nitartha Institute, founded by Dzogchen Ponlop Rinpoche. Karl also studied Buddhism, Tibetology, and Sanskrit at Hamburg University, Germany. Since 1989 he has been a translator and interpreter from Tibetan and English. Karl is a senior teacher and translator in the Nalandabodhi community of Dzogchen Ponlop Rinpoche, as well as at Nitartha Institute. He is the author and translator of numerous texts, including *The Center of the Sunlit Sky: Madhyamaka in the Kagyü Tradition* (2004), *Straight From the Heart: Buddhist Pith Instructions* (2007), *Luminous Heart: The Third Karmapa on Consciousness, Wisdom, and Buddha Nature* (2009), *Gone Beyond: The Ornament of Clear Realization and Its Commentaries in the Tibetan Kagyü Tradition*, 2 vols. (2010–11), *When the Clouds Part* (2014), *A Lullaby to Awaken the Heart* (2018), and *Luminous Melodies: Essential Dohās of Indian Mahāmudrā* (2019). He lives in Seattle.

Karl has set some of the songs of realization in this and the following volumes to contemporary melodies; recordings can be accessed at the "Doha Hub" (https://soundcloud.com/karl-brunnholzl).

What to Read Next from Wisdom Publications

A Lullaby to Awaken the Heart
Samantabhadra's Aspiration Prayer and Its Tibetan Commentaries
Karl Brunnhölzl

"Among translators, Brunnhölzl is unsurpassed in his knowledge of Tibetan and Sanskrit Buddhist literature. His deep practice experience brings the meaning and intent of texts to life. In *A Lullaby to Awaken the Heart* he brilliantly presents the teachings in *The Aspiration Prayer of Samantabhadra*, a gateway into the profundity of the Dzogchen teachings."—Andy Karr, author of *Contemplating Reality*

Luminous Melodies
Essential Dohās of Indian Mahāmudrā
Karl Brunnhölzl

"These beautiful songs of experience offer glimpses into the awakened minds of the Mahāmudrā masters of India. Karl Brunnhölzl's masterful translations are a joy to read for how they express what is so often inexpressible."—His Eminence the Twelfth Zurmang Gharwang Rinpoche

A Song for the King
Saraha on Mahamudra Meditation
Khenchen Thrangu Rinpoche

"A lively commentary [on] a poetic classic of Buddhist literature. Editor Michele Martin has supplemented Thrangu Rinpoche's lucid commentary with notes and appendices that make the book as accessible for novices as it is rewarding for experienced practitioners and scholars."—*Buddhadharma*

Drinking the Mountain Stream
Songs of Tibet's Beloved Saint, Milarepa
Translated by Lama Kunga Rinpoche and Brian Cutillo

Jetsun Milarepa, Tibet's renowned and beloved saint, is known for his penetrating insights, wry sense of humor, and ability to render any lesson into spontaneous song. His songs and poems exhibit the bold, inspirational leader as he guided followers along the Buddhist path.

Essentials of Mahamudra
Looking Directly at the Mind
Khenchen Thrangu Rinpoche

"Makes the practice of mahamudra, one of the most advanced forms of meditation, easily accessible to Westerners' everyday lives. A wonderful way of bringing us to the path."—*Mandala*

Mahāmudrā
The Moonlight—Quintessence of Mind and Meditation
Dakpo Tashi Namgyal

"This updated edition of an English translation of a great classic for mastering mind and meditation comes recommended by the Dalai Lama. . . . A fundamentally valuable addition to one's Dharma library."—*Mandala*

The Mind of Mahāmudrā
Advice from the Kagyü Masters
Translated by Peter Alan Roberts

"Quite simply, the best anthology of Tibetan Mahāmudrā texts yet to appear."—Roger R. Jackson, author of *Mind Seeing Mind*

About Wisdom Publications

Wisdom Publications is the leading publisher of classic and contemporary Buddhist books and practical works on mindfulness. To learn more about us or to explore our other books, please visit our website at wisdomexperience.org or contact us at the address below.

Wisdom Publications
199 Elm Street
Somerville, MA 02144 USA

We are a 501(c)(3) organization, and donations in support of our mission are tax deductible.

Wisdom Publications is affiliated with the Foundation for the Preservation of the Mahayana Tradition (FPMT).